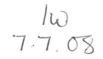

CONSTITUTIONAL HISTORY OF THE UK

Cavendish
Publishing
Limited

London • Sydney • Portland, Oregon

COMPANION WEBSITE

This book is supported by a Companion Website, created to keep *Constitutional History of the UK* up to date and to provide enhanced resources for both students and lecturers.

Key features include:

- ◆ updates and further information on the subject
- ◆ links to useful websites
- ◆ 'ask the author' – your questions answered

Visit

www.cavendishpublishing.com/constihistory

CONSTITUTIONAL HISTORY OF THE UK

Ann Lyon
Lecturer in Law
University of Wales, Swansea

Cavendish
Publishing
Limited

London • Sydney • Portland, Oregon

First published in Great Britain 2003 by
Cavendish Publishing Limited, The Glass House,
Wharton Street, London WC1X 9PX, United Kingdom
Telephone: + 44 (0)20 7278 8000   Facsimile: + 44 (0)20 7278 8080
Email: info@cavendishpublishing.com
Website: www.cavendishpublishing.com

Published in the United States by Cavendish Publishing
c/o International Specialized Book Services,
5824 NE Hassalo Street, Portland,
Oregon 97213-3644, USA

Published in Australia by Cavendish Publishing (Australia) Pty Ltd
3/303 Barrenjoey Road, Newport, NSW 2106, Australia

British Library Cataloguing in Publication Data
Lyon, Ann
Constitutional history of the UK
1 Constitutional history
I Title
342'.009

Library of Congress Cataloguing in Publication Data
Data available

ISBN 1-85941-746-9

1 3 5 7 9 10 8 6 4 2

Printed and bound in Great Britain

ACKNOWLEDGMENTS

As a book approaches publication, the writer feels a combination of emotions, a mixture of relief and regret that the work of writing is at an end, together with gratitude towards those others who have in their different ways made it possible, and whose influence has shaped the work in its final form.

This book was begun while I was working at De Montfort University, Leicester, and completed at the University of Wales, Swansea. I owe a debt of gratitude to colleagues and former colleagues at both institutions, in particular Professor David Hughes, who has in a sense been the godfather of this book. I have also benefited enormously from the wise counsel of Professor Sir James Holt of Fitzwilliam College, Cambridge, who had no idea what he was letting himself in for when he raised the subject of King John over lunch at the British Legal History Association Conference in July 1999.

A book such as this also reflects what is quite literally a lifetime's fascination for history, and there are many whose influence has been indirect but nonetheless vital, including my parents, who first nurtured my interest, teachers and university tutors.

Turning to those directly involved in bringing the book to a publishable state, I must thank in particular Jon Lloyd, my editor at Cavendish Publishing, and Frederick Hogarth, who produced the map and genealogical tables and whose website is an Aladdin's cave for anyone remotely interested in heraldry and related matters (www.baronage.co.uk).

Finally, any text on the history of the British constitution must be to a considerable extent a history of the British monarchy, central as the monarchy is to our constitutional system. This book reached its final form during the Golden Jubilee year of the present Queen and is published as the 50th anniversary approaches of her coronation in 1953. I can therefore do no better than to dedicate it, by gracious permission, to Her Majesty Queen Elizabeth II.

Ann Lyon
Swansea
December 2002

CONTENTS

MAPS AND GENEALOGICAL TABLES

Britain before the Norman Conquest

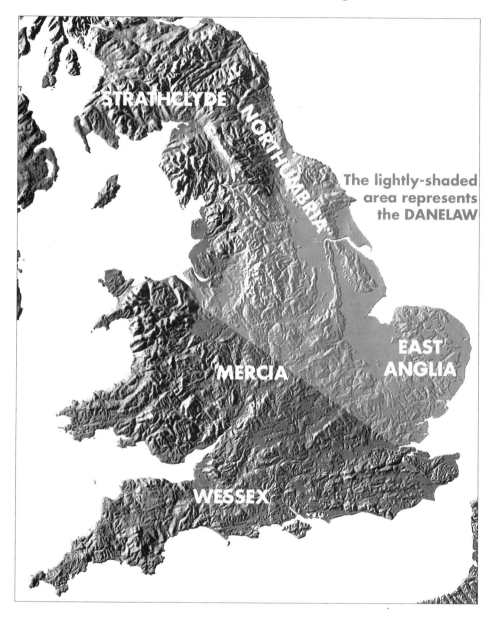

TABLE 1

KINGS OF ENGLAND (1)

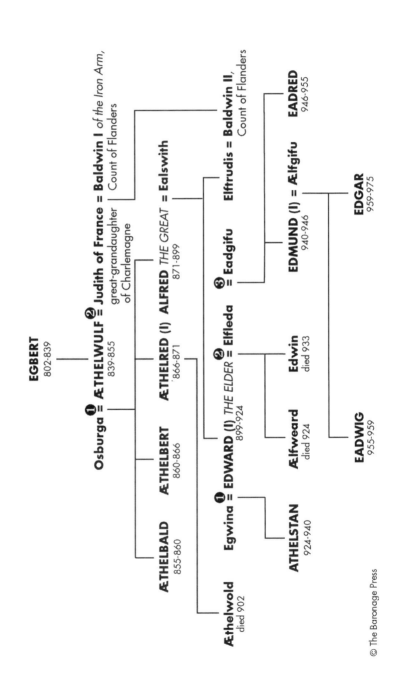

TABLE 2

KINGS OF ENGLAND (2)

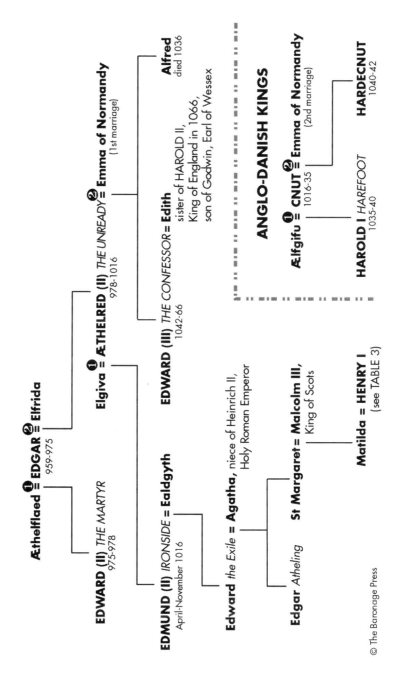

Æthelflaed ❶ ≡ **EDGAR** ❷ ≡ **Elfrida**
959-975

Aethelflaed ❶ ≡ **EDGAR** ❷ ≡ **Elfrida**

EDWARD (II) *THE MARTYR*
975-978

Elgiva ❶ ≡ **ÆTHELRED (II)** *THE UNREADY* ❷ ≡ **Emma of Normandy**
978-1016 (1st marriage)

EDMUND (II) *IRONSIDE* ≡ **Ealdgyth**
April-November 1016

EDWARD (III) *THE CONFESSOR* ≡ **Edith**
1042-66 sister of HAROLD II,
King of England in 1066,
son of Godwin, Earl of Wessex

Alfred
died 1036

Edward *the Exile* ≡ **Agatha,** niece of Heinrich II,
Holy Roman Emperor

Edgar *Atheling*

St Margaret ≡ **Malcolm III,**
King of Scots

Matilda ≡ **HENRY I**
(see TABLE 3)

ANGLO-DANISH KINGS

Ælfgifu ❶ ≡ **CNUT** ❷ ≡ **Emma of Normandy**
1016-35 (2nd marriage)

HAROLD I *HAREFOOT*
1035-40

HARDECNUT
1040-42

TABLE 3

KINGS OF ENGLAND (3)

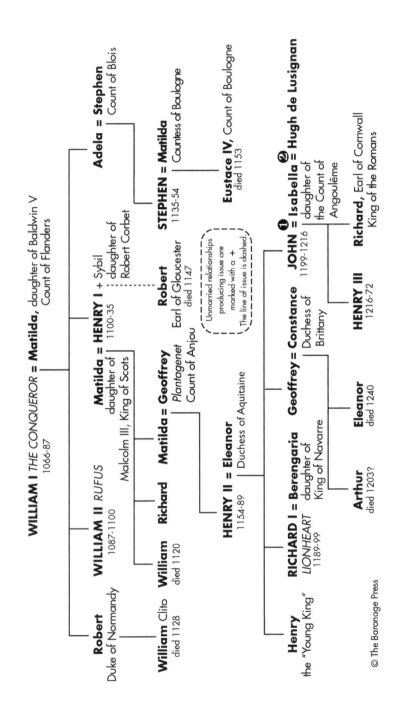

© The Baronage Press

TABLE 4

KINGS OF SCOTLAND (1)

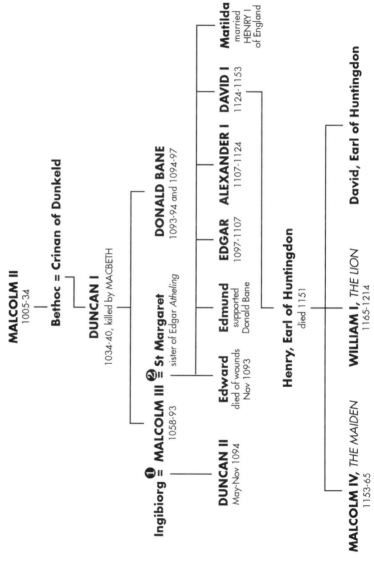

MALCOLM II
1005-34

Bethoc = Crinan of Dunkeld

DUNCAN I
1034-40, killed by MACBETH

Ingibiorg ❶ = MALCOLM III ❷ = St Margaret
            1058-93   sister of Edgar Atheling

DONALD BANE
1093-94 and 1094-97

DUNCAN II
May-Nov 1094

Edward
died of wounds
Nov 1093

Edmund
supported
Donald Bane

EDGAR
1097-1107

ALEXANDER I
1107-1124

DAVID I
1124-1153

Matilda
married
HENRY I
of England

Henry, Earl of Huntingdon
died 1151

MALCOLM IV, *THE MAIDEN*
1153-65

WILLIAM I, *THE LION*
1165-1214

David, Earl of Huntingdon

TABLE 5

KINGS OF ENGLAND (4)

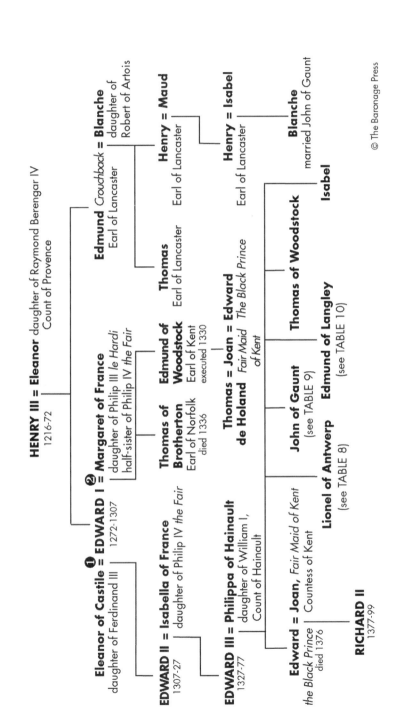

© The Baronage Press

TABLE 6

KINGS OF SCOTLAND (2)

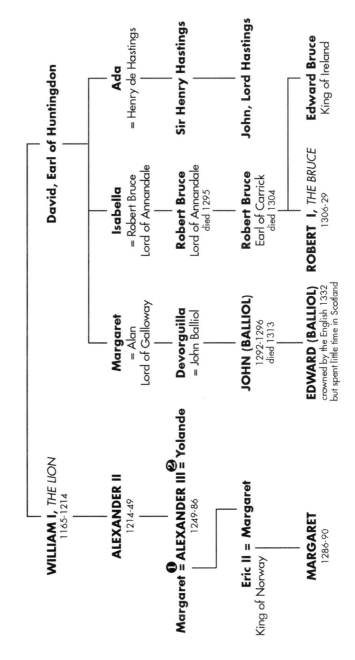

TABLE 7

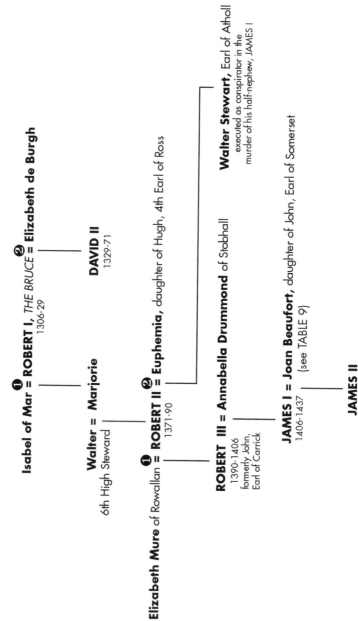

KINGS OF SCOTLAND (3)

Isabel of Mar ❶ = **ROBERT I,** *THE BRUCE* ❷ = **Elizabeth de Burgh**
1306-29

DAVID II
1329-71

Walter = **Marjorie**
6th High Steward

Elizabeth Mure of Rowallan ❶ = **ROBERT II** ❷ = **Euphemia,** daughter of Hugh, 4th Earl of Ross
1371-90

Walter Stewart, Earl of Atholl
executed as conspirator in the
murder of his half-nephew, JAMES I

ROBERT III = **Annabella Drummond** of Stobhall
1390-1406
formerly John,
Earl of Carrick

JAMES I = **Joan Beaufort,** daughter of John, Earl of Somerset
1406-1437   (see TABLE 9)

JAMES II

TABLE 8

KINGS OF ENGLAND (5)

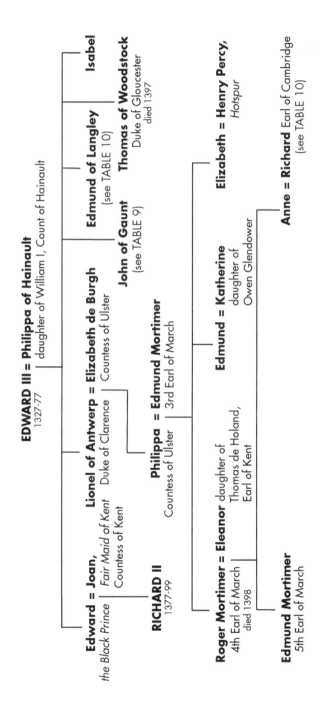

EDWARD III = Philippa of Hainault
1327-77
daughter of William I, Count of Hainault

Edward = Joan, *the Black Prince* | *Fair Maid of Kent* Countess of Kent

Lionel of Antwerp = Elizabeth de Burgh Duke of Clarence | Countess of Ulster

John of Gaunt (see TABLE 9)

Edmund of Langley (see TABLE 10)

Thomas of Woodstock Duke of Gloucester died 1397

Isabel

RICHARD II 1377-99

Philippa = Edmund Mortimer Countess of Ulster | 3rd Earl of March

Roger Mortimer = Eleanor *daughter of* 4th Earl of March | *Thomas de Holand,* died 1398 | *Earl of Kent*

Edmund = Katherine | daughter of Owen Glendower

Elizabeth = Henry Percy, | *Hotspur*

Edmund Mortimer 5th Earl of March

Anne = Richard Earl of Cambridge (see TABLE 10)

TABLE 9

KINGS OF ENGLAND (6)

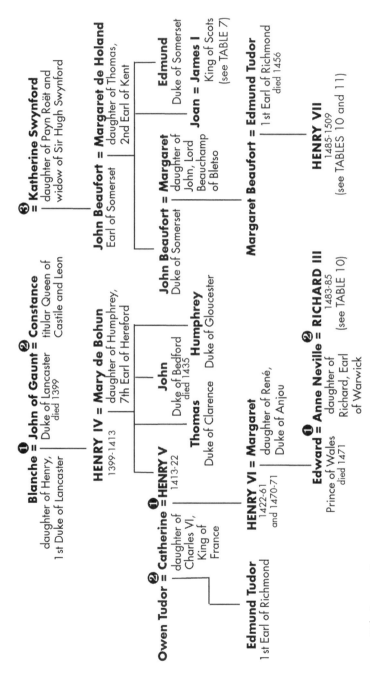

© The Baronage Press

TABLE 10

KINGS OF ENGLAND (7)

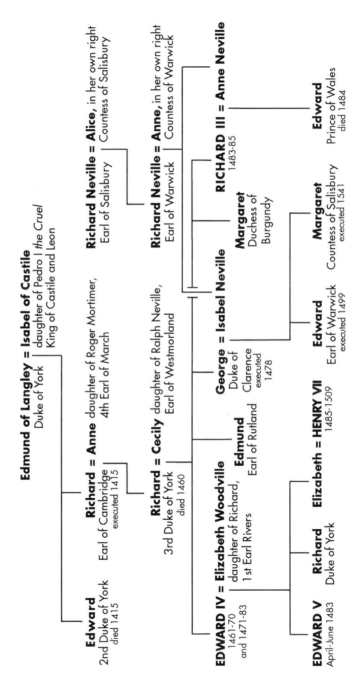

Edmund of Langley = Isabel of Castile
Duke of York   daughter of Pedro I *the Cruel*
                       King of Castile and Leon

Edward
2nd Duke of York
died 1415

Richard = Anne daughter of Roger Mortimer,
Earl of Cambridge   4th Earl of March
executed 1415

Richard = Cecily daughter of Ralph Neville,
3rd Duke of York   Earl of Westmorland
died 1460

Richard Neville = Alice, in her own right
Earl of Salisbury   Countess of Salisbury

Richard Neville = Anne, in her own right
Earl of Warwick   Countess of Warwick

RICHARD III = Anne Neville
1483-85

Edward
Prince of Wales
died 1484

Margaret
Duchess of
Burgundy

George = Isabel Neville
Duke of
Clarence
executed
1478

Edmund
Earl of Rutland

Margaret
Countess of Salisbury
executed 1541

Edward
Earl of Warwick
executed 1499

EDWARD IV = Elizabeth Woodville
1461-70   daughter of Richard,
and 1471-83   1st Earl Rivers

Elizabeth = HENRY VII
1485-1509

EDWARD V
April-June 1483

Richard
Duke of York

© The Baronage Press

TABLE 11

KINGS AND QUEENS OF ENGLAND (8)

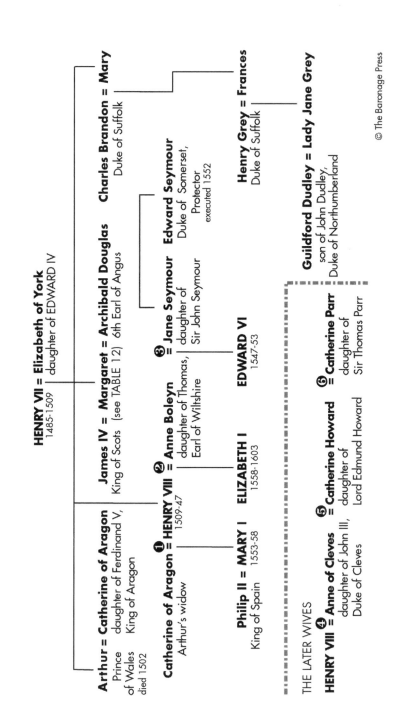

HENRY VII = **Elizabeth of York**
1485-1509   daughter of EDWARD IV

Arthur = **Catherine of Aragon**   **James IV** = **Margaret** = **Archibald Douglas**   **Charles Brandon** = **Mary**
Prince   daughter of Ferdinand V,   King of Scots   (see TABLE 12)   6th Earl of Angus   Duke of Suffolk
of Wales   King of Aragon
died 1502

Catherine of Aragon = ❶ **HENRY VIII**   ❷ **Anne Boleyn**   ❸ **Jane Seymour**   **Edward Seymour**
Arthur's widow   1509-47   = daughter of Thomas,   = daughter of   Duke of Somerset,
                                  Earl of Wiltshire   Sir John Seymour   Protector
                                                                                  executed 1552

Philip II = **MARY I**   1553-58   **ELIZABETH I**   **EDWARD VI**   **Henry Grey** = **Frances**
King of Spain   1558-1603   1547-53   Duke of Suffolk

Guildford Dudley = **Lady Jane Grey**
son of John Dudley,
Duke of Northumberland

THE LATER WIVES

HENRY VIII = ❹ **Anne of Cleves**   ❺ **Catherine Howard**   ❻ **Catherine Parr**
          daughter of John III,   = daughter of   = daughter of
          Duke of Cleves   Lord Edmund Howard   Sir Thomas Parr

TABLE 12

KINGS AND QUEENS OF SCOTLAND (4)

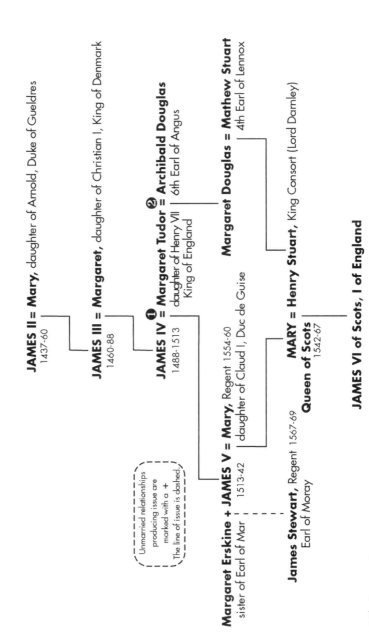

JAMES II = **Mary,** daughter of Arnold, Duke of Gueldres
1437-60

JAMES III = **Margaret,** daughter of Christian I, King of Denmark
1460-88

❶ **JAMES IV** = **Margaret Tudor** = **Archibald Douglas** ❷
1488-1513   daughter of Henry VII   6th Earl of Angus
                 King of England

Margaret Douglas = **Mathew Stuart**
4th Earl of Lennox

Margaret Erskine + JAMES V = **Mary,** Regent 1554-60
sister of Earl of Mar   1513-42   daughter of Claud I, Duc de Guise

MARY = **Henry Stuart,** King Consort (Lord Darnley)
Queen of Scots
1542-67

James Stewart, Regent 1567-69
Earl of Moray

JAMES VI of Scots, I of England

Unmarried relationships
producing issue are
marked with a +
The line of issue is dashed.

© The Baronage Press

TABLE 13

HEIRS TO ENGLAND AND SCOTLAND IN 1565

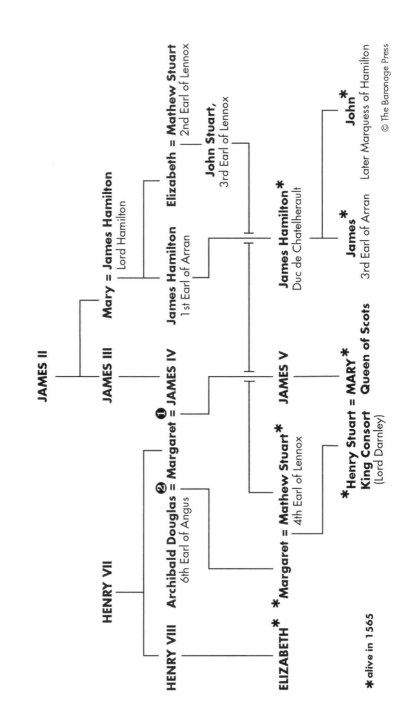

© The Baronage Press

* alive in 1565

TABLE 14

KINGS AND QUEENS OF ENGLAND AND SCOTLAND

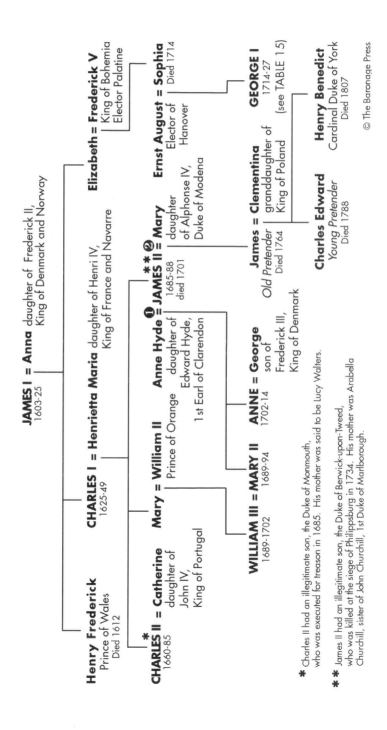

JAMES I = **Anna** daughter of Frederick II,
1603-25   King of Denmark and Norway

Henry Frederick
Prince of Wales
Died 1612

CHARLES I = **Henrietta Maria** daughter of Henri IV,
1625-49   King of France and Navarre

Elizabeth = **Frederick V**
King of Bohemia
Elector Palatine

CHARLES II = **Catherine**
1660-85   daughter of
               John IV,
               King of Portugal

Mary = **William II**
          Prince of Orange

Anne Hyde ❶ = **JAMES II** ❷ = **Mary**
daughter of   1685-88   daughter
Edward Hyde, died 1701 of Alphonse IV,
1st Earl of Clarendon   Duke of Modena

Ernst August = **Sophia**
Elector of   Died 1714
Hanover

WILLIAM III = **MARY II**
1689-1702   1689-94

ANNE = **George**
1702-14   son of
          Frederick III,
          King of Denmark

James = **Clementina**
Old Pretender granddaughter of
Died 1764   King of Poland

GEORGE I
1714-27
(see TABLE 15)

Charles Edward
Young Pretender
Died 1788

Henry Benedict
Cardinal Duke of York
Died 1807

© The Baronage Press

* Charles II had an illegitimate son, the Duke of Monmouth,
who was executed for treason in 1685. His mother was said to be Lucy Walters.

** James II had an illegitimate son, the Duke of Berwick-upon-Tweed,
who was killed at the siege of Philippsburg in 1734. His mother was Arabella
Churchill, sister of John Churchill, 1st Duke of Marlborough.

TABLE 15

KINGS AND QUEENS OF GREAT BRITAIN

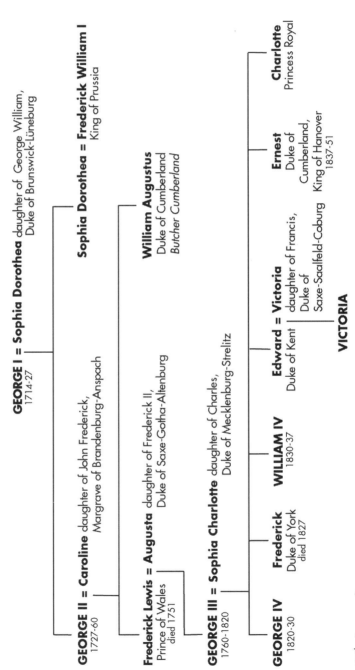

© The Baronage Press

KINGS AND QUEENS OF THE UNITED KINGDOM

TABLE 16

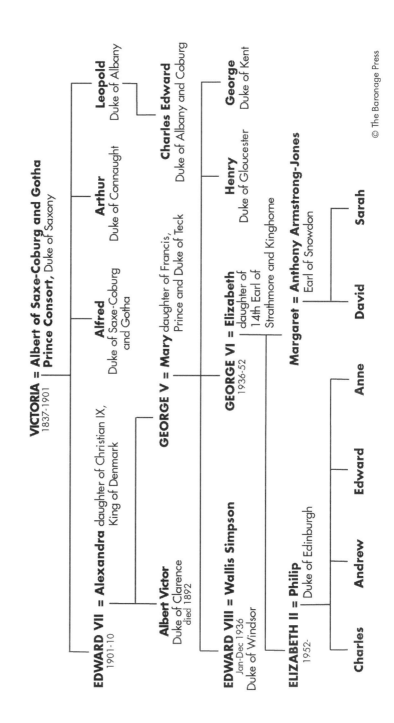

INTRODUCTION

This book has grown out of several years' experience of teaching Constitutional and Administrative Law to LLB students and to graduates in other disciplines taking the Postgraduate Diploma in Law. Britain's unique and unwritten constitution is the product of a process of evolution over many centuries and, unlike most others, is not wholly or even predominantly the child of an identifiable event or period of time. Coming as I did from an academic background as a historian, it became increasingly clear that the overall nature and the specific elements of such a constitution can only be understood against the background of the historical events which shaped that evolutionary process.

Looking at the world at large, most of the written constitutions which have stood the test of time – the classic example is the United States constitution – were produced by constituent assemblies of lawyers and statesmen summoned in the aftermath of the downfall of an earlier system of government through war or revolution. Alternatively, as part of a peaceful transition to independence from a colonial power, a constitution based on that of the colonial power was imposed in a more or less benevolent fashion. All these constitutions represent attempts to create something new from what was to a greater or lesser extent a clean slate, drawing on what was best in the earlier system, in contemporary systems of government elsewhere and on the philosophical ideas of their age.

By contrast, the constitutional systems of the United Kingdom and its constituent nations have developed slowly over many centuries. Each of the major changes which can be identified, at least until very recent times, was essentially a short term response to the crisis of the moment. In between, there was a period of relative stability, with at times a continuation of development by natural evolution, at other times a period of slipping back towards the ways which had led to the earlier crisis.

Traditional textbooks on constitutional and administrative law assume a historical knowledge which the majority of law students no longer possess. Most history texts deal either with specific periods of history, where divisions are made, perhaps arbitrarily, on the basis of major political events and changes in royal dynasty, or with specific themes such as political, social or economic history. Equally, the works of legal historians concentrate, relatively narrowly, on the development of substantive law in areas such as land law, tort and contract, and on the evolution of the system by which justice is administered.

Constitutional history has not, perhaps surprisingly, been the subject of any recent specialist text. As a result, modern works deal with it as one of a large number of themes in a work covering a particular period of history or the reign of a particular ruler, and tend to give it second place to political events. The classic texts on constitutional history are the multi-volume works of Bishop Stubbs and TF Tout, produced in the late 19th and early 20th centuries, which by reason of their sheer size must be daunting to a student seeking a working knowledge of the development of the British constitution over the centuries, and which were in any event produced by historians rather than lawyers.

There have been two comprehensive single-volume histories of the British Isles in recent years, produced by Norman Davies and Simon Schama respectively. Both are extremely valuable to students seeking an introduction to British history, but neither is concerned specifically with constitutional matters. *The Constitutional History of England* of FW Maitland is the only single-volume work of constitutional history produced specifically for an undergraduate audience by a scholar who was both historian and lawyer, and has rightly held its place as a classic since its publication in 1908. However, it is even older than it appears from its publication date, being a posthumously assembled edition of lectures given by Maitland to Cambridge undergraduates in 1887–88. In the century and more since then, much has changed. No longer is Britain a world power, ruling an empire on which the sun never set, and no longer do historians see constitutional history as a smooth progression to the system idealised by AV Dicey and the writers schooled in the Whig tradition, of whom Winston Churchill in his *History of the English-Speaking Peoples* is perhaps the final personification. For present-day writers, history is very much more complicated than that.

This book therefore attempts to introduce students, not only of law, but of other disciplines, particularly history, politics and government, to that historical background in a way which is lively and accessible as well as scholarly, focusing on the events and ideas which most influenced constitutional development in what has been, since 1801, the UK. It can make no claims to original scholarship, drawing as it does very largely on secondary works. Indeed, I must express a particular debt of gratitude to three great series of historical texts: the magisterial *Oxford History of England* in 15 volumes; the *Longman History of England*; and the series of royal biographies first published under the Methuen imprint and now continued under the auspices of Yale University Press.

WHAT IS A CONSTITUTION?

What is a constitution, and at what stage in legal and political evolution may a state be said to have a constitution? The term 'constitution' has two meanings, and it is only in the broad sense, rather than the narrow sense of a single written document setting out the constitutional system, that a British constitution can be said to exist at all. 'Constitution' in its broad sense has been defined as 'the system of laws, customs and conventions which define the composition and powers of organs of the state, and regulate the relations of the various state organs to one another and to the private citizen'.[1] VH Galbraith argued that England did not have a constitution even in this sense before the 14th century, but a developing constitutional framework can be identified very much earlier.

However, it is only in the 13th century that a legislature separate from the person of the king and his close advisors began to emerge, and it was later still and by fits and starts that it developed any degree of independence from the king. Government, until comparatively recent times, was centred on the king. Only in the 17th century, following a civil war, the execution of one king, a period of republican rule, a restoration of the monarchy and the deposition of a second king, did legislative power pass finally from the king alone to the King in Parliament, although the philosophy that the king might only legislate through Parliament is identifiable very much earlier. It was later still, and only gradually, that the practice of government passed wholly from the king to his ministers.

---

1   O Hood Phillips, *Constitutional and Administrative Law*, 7th edn, 1987, Sweet & Maxwell, p 5.

This is not to say that the power of kings was unconstrained. There emerges in pre-Conquest times a philosophy that the king owes his throne to God's grace, that he must rule justly and in ways which foster the good of his people. As early as 757, a king of the West Saxons was deprived of his kingdom because of his 'unlawful actions'. In 1014, the exiled Æthelred the Unready was invited to resume his throne provided he would rule 'more justly than before'. In the early 13th century, Magna Carta, although primarily the product of baronial self-interest, acted as an acknowledgment that the king must rule in accordance with the law which he and his advisors defined in an act of self-limitation, an act of commission by the king which purported to be voluntarily or freely granted. In the following century, two kings were deprived of their thrones and murdered on the pretext that they had ruled unjustly.

METHODOLOGY

In writing a text on constitutional history, there are two very obvious difficulties. The first is that the topic appears at first sight to be the very quintessence of dullness, involving weighty themes, obscure events and ideas, and matters far removed from the experience of life of the 21st century undergraduate. How, then, is a text to be rendered accessible and relevant to that undergraduate who may well have studied little or no British political history previously, while at the same time doing the subject justice?

What has remained firmly lodged in my brain from a compulsory course in historical writing during my degree course is the *dictum* of Leopold von Ranke, considered by some scholars to have been the first great historian of the modern era, that the task of the historian is to present the past *wie es wirklich war* – 'as it really was'. To present British constitutional history as it really was is what I have tried to do in this book, seeking to depict events, changes and the processes and philosophies which shaped them as far as possible as they appeared to those living at the time, and endeavouring to avoid the convenient but distorting lens of hindsight. At the same time, I have sought to identify and analyse long term trends, so that an element of hindsight has inevitably crept in.

The second difficulty is one of method. In dealing with a long process of evolution, any writer is first faced with the question of when to begin and when to end. British history knows few if any cut-off dates. Maitland viewed the period prior to 1066 to a very large extent as a single unit, and dealt only briefly with developments prior to the accession of Edward I in 1272. When one begins to probe around even the major turning points such as the Norman Conquest, there is at least as much of continuity apparent as there is of change and innovation. Did not Henry I in his Coronation Charter of 1100 declare that he would observe and maintain the good old laws as they were in the time of Edward the Confessor? Any choice of a starting point is therefore somewhat arbitrary, although my decision to begin my introductory chapter on law and government prior to the Conquest with the issue of the first Anglo-Saxon law code by Æthelbert of Kent, rather than to go back into the period of Roman occupation, has at least the justification of the separate development of England's common law tradition outside the mainstream of Roman Law found in continental Europe.

At the same time, a flexible and unwritten constitution is in a continuing state of evolution, so that the finishing point of any study must be equally arbitrary, especially as at the time of writing, constitutional change is part of the government's legislative programme, and following the removal of voting rights from hereditary peers in November 1999, the future composition of Parliament is itself undecided. I have therefore chosen to end with a consideration of the major areas of concern and controversy as they exist at the time of writing, and various of the proposals for change which have been made.

THE PLACE OF KINGS

Reviewing the sweep of 14 centuries, the continuity of themes becomes apparent. In relation to kingship, it is noteworthy that the monarchy only finally became strictly hereditary with the passing of the Act of Settlement in 1701, which itself vested the succession in a dynasty only remotely related by blood to its immediate predecessors. From Anglo-Saxon times, we see a hereditary succession developing, but alongside a concept of 'throneworthiness', under which a king must rule justly and in the interests of his people, rather than following his own instincts. Although hereditary succession and male primogeniture became the norm by the 10th century, on several occasions, we see the late king's adult brother being preferred over an infant son, and over and over again, an 'unworthy' king being removed from his throne and replaced by a rival with a lesser claim by blood, though most of these rivals also claimed to be the true king by hereditary right. Even in our own time, Edward VIII's abdication and supplanting by a younger brother was ultimately the consequence of his perceived unworthiness to be king.

We see too ebb and flow in the balance of power between the king and his subjects. Up to the 16th century, if not later, sovereignty and initiative in government lay with the king. However, under weak kings, power shifted to the greatest among their subjects, and it was for their stronger successors to restore the power of the monarch. The over-mighty subject closely connected by blood or marriage to the ruler is a feature of the 11th and 14th centuries as well as the 15th. Godwine, Earl of Wessex, occupied much the same position under Edward the Confessor as Warwick the Kingmaker did in the first years of Edward IV's reign. Each attempted to make the reigning king his puppet, though Godwine never went to the extreme pursued by Warwick, who tried to replace a king who refused to accept his tutelage with another more pliable candidate, and temporarily succeeded. Over and over, however, such over-mighty subjects protested their loyalty to the monarch and, until the final step of deposition, claimed only to be rescuing the king from domination by 'evil counsellors'.

PARLIAMENT

Parliament first emerges in the 13th century as a body under royal control and, from the early 14th century, it became a regular organ of government, being used increasingly as a means not only of giving legitimacy to the actions of the king and his advisors, on the basis that the monarch governed with the assent of his subjects, but as a means of legitimising a change of monarch, the first example of which occurred in

1327, when a parliament of doubtful legality accepted the abdication made by Edward II under duress. This was the beginning of a process which culminated in 1688, when a parliament of similarly doubtful legality invited William of Orange and his wife, Mary, to accept the throne in place of the legitimate king, James II, on terms it dictated, and in 1701, when a lawful parliament passed the Act of Settlement which vested the succession to the throne in persons it deemed suitable on the basis of religion. The period from the 14th century to the end of the 16th century saw kings ruling to a greater or lesser extent through Parliament, albeit a parliament which they largely controlled, and tacitly accepting the philosophy that important legislation should be made through Parliament. The attempts of Charles I and James II to legislate without Parliament or to render ineffective that legislation passed by Parliament resulted in direct conflict between king and Parliament, and in the Revolution Settlement of 1689, which finally and unambiguously vested sovereignty in the King in Parliament. From then on, the balance of power shifted to Parliament, but, increasingly since the development of Cabinet government in the 18th century and particularly since the 1970s, power has shifted again, so that ministers now in practice pay only lip service to the concept that it is Parliament which holds the supreme power.

CONSTITUTIONAL MYTH AND REALITY

Another theme which pervades the British constitution is the 'constitutional myth'. A number of writers from the 17th century onwards developed the idea that the English enjoyed a golden age of bucolic independence and liberty before being forced into subjugation and serfdom by their Norman conquerors, that constitutional development since then marked a slow and partial return to that primeval freedom, and that the same desire for self-rule motivated Englishmen in the 16th century and after as in the 11th:

> We must recognise the spirit which dictated the Petition of Right as the same which gathered all England round the banners of Godwin, and remember that the 'good old cause' was truly that for which Harold died on the field and Waltheof on the scaffold.[2]

Even in the last years of the 20th century, we saw the persistence of the myth of pre-Norman liberty. An advocate of the 'right to roam' writing in *The Times* on 20 February 1999 held forth sourly on the English peasantry's loss of land ownership and descent into bondage as the result of the seizure of land by incoming Normans in 1066 and after. Equally, a resurgence of nationalistic feeling in Scotland in the late 1990s has been linked with the success of the film *Braveheart*, which expresses national myth far more than historical reality.

MAGNA CARTA AND CONSTITUTIONAL MYTH

Nowhere is the importance of constitutional myth more important than in relation to Magna Carta. The document to which King John appended his seal in the summer of

---

2   EA Freeman (WRW Stephens (ed)), *Life and Letters*, vol 1, 1895, Macmillan, p 125.

1215 was the product of the short term grievances of a relatively small group of magnates who had taken up arms against him. It was very largely a re-statement of law and custom as they were believed to exist rather than any new and radical state of principle, and it was annulled by Pope Innocent III at John's behest within weeks. It was re-published in a modified form on a number of occasions in the 13th century as a statement of what should prevail, first to encourage support for the young Henry III on his accession during a civil war, then as a concession by kings, and from the mid-14th century largely disappears from view until the 17th century, when it was hailed by those advancing the rights of Parliament against Charles I as the cornerstone of English liberty. It is still viewed in this guise by lawyers and civil libertarians today, although none of those originally responsible for it would recognise it in this form.

How is one to reduce the developments of 1,400 years and the events which shaped them to manageable proportions? Maitland chose to consider the state of public law at the deaths of four monarchs: Edward I in 1307; Henry VII in 1509; James I in 1625; William III in 1702; and finally at the time he was writing, in 1887–88. I have taken a more chronological approach, focusing in particular on the periodic crises which brought about more rapid constitutional change and shaped the course of the development of that public law. This has meant that the book includes a good deal of political history, for which I can make no apology.

TERMINOLOGY

Over 14 centuries, many figures bear the same names as others, and a single individual might undergo several changes of style during his lifetime. The second husband of Mary Queen of Scots was by birth Henry Stuart (or Stewart); as the elder son of the Earl of Lennox, he was by courtesy Lord Darnley in English usage and Master of Lennox in Scotland. Following betrothal to Mary, he was successively created Earl of Ross and Duke of Albany, and by marriage, he became King Henry. Several persons may bear the same name or, given the existence of rival claimants and the effects of attainders, the same title, at the same time. I have tended to opt for clarity rather than precision, and have used the style by which the person is best known or held for the greatest portion of his or her career. I have also made use of the picturesque by-names which some figures acquired, though, alas, nothing in Western European history quite compares with the 10th century Byzantine who was known in his day as Theophylact 'the Unbearable'. Edward, Prince of Wales and Aquitaine, eldest son of Edward III, is therefore the Black Prince, though the sobriquet was not coined until after his death, and his brother, John, Duke of Lancaster, is John of Gaunt.

In the same way, I have not been consistent with non-English names, and have tended to opt for the version most familiar to me, or which will minimise the possibility of confusion. So, Philip II of Spain, but Carlos II for his descendant, the last of the Spanish Habsburgs, since the anglicised version of the latter's name invites confusion with his British contemporary, Charles II. Old English names which have not survived in use are rendered in their original forms, but those still used are given their modern form – Æthelred the Unready, but Edward the Elder.

National terminology has become a sensitive issue in recent years and, without going to extremes, I feel some embarrassment that fellow English writers, along with many from continental Europe and elsewhere, did until very recent times use

'England' and 'English' indiscriminately to refer to the whole of the British Isles and their various peoples. Before 1603, this is not a major problem, as England and Scotland were separate kingdoms ruled by independent dynasties, and Ireland, a lordship of the English Crown from the 1180s, only became a kingdom in 1540. From 1707, England and Scotland were united politically and governmentally as Great Britain, but between 1603 and 1707, though ruled by a common monarch, they remained politically separate, as did Ireland until 1801. James VI of Scotland and I of England adopted the title 'King of Great Britain', but his descendants up to 1707 did not follow his example, being kings of England, Scotland and Ireland. Increasingly after 1603, I have tended to use the terms 'Britain' and 'British' to refer to matters common to England and Scotland, and, less frequently, Ireland, simply to avoid the Scylla of simplistic use of 'England' and 'English', or the Charybdis of repetition and syntactical clumsiness. As an alternative, I have at times followed Professor Davies in using the term 'the three kingdoms'. I have also used 'Britain' for the post-1801 UK. Nationalists will, I hope, forgive me.

As an English-trained lawyer and historian, although now based in Wales, I must apologise for my relative neglect of legal and constitutional development in Scotland, Wales and Ireland. Perhaps an academic from one or other of these nations will now aspire to redressing the balance?

NOTE ON DATING

Until relatively recent times, there was no consistency in the dating systems used. The solar 'Julian' calendar was ordained in the Roman Empire by Julius Caesar in 45 BC, and in around 52 AD, Dionysius Exiguus proposed that time should be reckoned from the birth of Christ, hence the BC/AD dichotomy. This system was gradually adopted throughout western Europe in the period 500–1000, but the calendar year was taken to begin on different dates at different times in different places, the most frequently used being 25 December, 25 March and 1 January. From the 12th century until 1752, the year was generally taken to begin in England on 25 March.[1]

A discrepancy of approximately one day per century gradually developed between the Julian calendar and solar time, and Pope Gregory XII sought to remedy this in 1582 by an adjustment which created the modern 'Gregorian' calendar. This in turn was adopted at different times in different places, in Great Britain and Ireland not until September 1752, by which time, the Julian calendar had fallen behind the Gregorian by 11 days. Two dating issues emerge therefore emerge, most acutely in the 17th and early 18th centuries. I have taken the year to begin on 1 January at all stages, and reconciled Julian and Gregorian dates where necessary during the period 1582–1752, so that, for example, no one apparently arrives in England before setting out from France.

---

1   Though this appears strange to modern eyes, it was, in fact, entirely logical. The *Anno Domini* dating system originally devised in the sixth century begins with the birth of Christ. Originally, the year began on 25 December, the date ascribed to the Nativity, but at some later date, it was held appropriate to begin the year with the *conception* of Christ. Subtracting the assumed human gestation period of nine months from 25 December gives 25 March, the Annunciation of the Virgin, or Lady Day.

CHAPTER 1

THE DEVELOPMENT OF ENGLISH LAW AND GOVERNMENT PRIOR TO THE NORMAN CONQUEST

1.1   THE EARLIEST KINGDOMS

Before the Viking invasions of the late 9th century, England was a land of several kingdoms. The scanty written evidence, supplemented by archaeology, poetry and analogous material from continental Europe, depicts a warrior society whose rulers functioned principally as war leaders, linked to the men they led by ties of personal loyalty which were reinforced by the giving of gifts in the form of treasure and land. There is little direct evidence about the nature and practice of government. Conclusions must be drawn from the indirect evidence provided by the written records of the activities of kings and royal officials, surviving law codes and charters, being aware always that we are dealing with a period of some 300 years, over which some development by evolution probably took place. One must be cautious in extrapolating backwards from the later 9th century, for which the Anglo-Saxon Chronicle gives a full and relatively contemporaneous account of the political background, and for which charters are reasonably abundant, or indeed forward from Bede, whose *Ecclesiastical History*, completed in 731, provides a detailed picture of the 7th century. Equally, we cannot necessarily assume the existence of identical institutions in the different kingdoms. With these caveats, however, it is possible to set out a reasonably clear picture of government in the English kingdoms as they emerged into recorded history.

1.1.1   Early kingship

A king was the ruler, not primarily of a territorial entity, but of a people, a concept reflected in royal titles for several hundred years after – John (1199–1216) was the first monarch to style himself *Rex Angliae*, 'King of England', not *Rex Anglorum*, 'King of the English' – and his principal role was as the protector and defender of his people, and the leader of a warband in battle. In the poem that bears his name, Beowulf's greatness lay as a warrior, and his main concern in the speech put into his mouth by the poet as he was dying was that the enemies of his people would seize the opportunity to invade, and he lamented his lack of a son to defend his people after him. Though the poem is myth, being concerned with warfare against monsters rather than human enemies, the mores it depicts accord well with what is known of royal and aristocratic life in the early part of the Anglo-Saxon era.

The king's military role is seen in the 'sceptre' which forms part of the Sutton Hoo treasure, deposited with one of the East Anglian kings in the 620s. It takes the form of a huge ceremonial whetstone, symbolising the king as the giver of swords. A king retained his kingship only as long as he retained his strength. In England, unlike contemporary Ireland or in Byzantium, where blinding was the usual means of disposing of dynastic rivals, there seems to have been no explicit requirement that a ruler be physically whole, although in practice he had to be of age and physique to bear arms.[1] After the conversion to Christianity, at least two West Saxon rulers chose to abdicate and went to Rome to live out their days as monks, and several other kings retired into monasteries in England. It is tempting to suggest that they did so when they were no longer capable of leading armies. There are many examples of a king being succeeded by his adult brother rather than an infant son, particularly in times of crisis, and presumably on the basis of the brother's ability to lead an army.

From the 7th century, as the influence of Christianity spread, written evidence places increasing emphasis on the non-military functions of kings. Edwin of Northumbria (616–34) was so successful in bringing peace to his kingdom that, proverbially, a woman could without fear walk the length of Northumbria with her newborn child on her hip.[2] Also, beginning with Æthelbert of Kent (565–613), the first Anglo-Saxon ruler to renounce paganism, a number of kings produced codes of laws. However, the military function remained vastly predominant: of the nine kings who reigned in 7th century Northumbria, four were killed in battle, three were murdered by rivals and only two died natural deaths.

Certainly, it would appear that succession to the throne was to a large extent based on military prowess and, in some cases, the elimination of rival claimants. The remoteness of the alleged blood tie between, for example, Offa of Mercia (757–96) and his predecessor Æthelbald, his cousin twice removed, and between Æthelbald and his own predecessor Ceolred (709–16) strongly suggests that military strength was the deciding factor where succession was disputed. However, then and much later, it was essential that a claimant to the throne was a member of the ruling family of his kingdom in the male line. Harold II (January–October 1066) was unique among Anglo-Saxon kings in not being a blood relation of his predecessors.

1.1.2 Early law codes

From the time of the conversion to Christianity, written codes of law begin to appear, that of Æthelbert being conventionally dated to as early as 602–03,[3] and significant not only as the earliest extant law code, but also as the one least influenced by Christianity. Æthelbert's 'laws' deal entirely with the levels of compensation to be paid in the event of a crime, presumably by the criminal to his victim (although in some circumstances, additional payments are to be made to the king), and the compensation to be paid for the causing of death or bodily injury, whether criminously or accidentally. The levels of compensation vary markedly according to the social status of the victim: the *wergild* or 'man price' payable to the kindred of a dead man was 100 shillings in the case of an ordinary freeman and 300 shillings in the case of a man of noble birth.

---

1   See G Mac Niocaill, *Ireland before the Vikings*, 1972, Gill & Macmillan, p 45. Mac Niocaill remarks that, to judge by the number of kings by-named 'the One-Eyed' in the Celtic world, it was not physical perfection but the ability to bear arms which was essential.

2   Bede (B Colgrave and RAB Mynors (eds)), *Historia Ecclesiastica Gentis Anglorum (Ecclesiastical History of the English People)*, 1969, Clarendon (hereafter HE), II 16. This may, however, be no more than a conventional literary depiction of a powerful king.

3   EHD I No 29n. Statutes are cited as they appear in *Statutes of the Realm*.

Sanctions other than monetary payments do not appear in Æthelbert's laws, and first make their appearance in Kent at the end of the 7th century. They are an alternative to payment of compensation in the Laws of Wihtred, dated to 695,[4] and only in respect of those of servile status. A slave who sacrificed to devils was to pay six shillings compensation or be flogged; similarly, an unfree labourer who rode on his own business between sunset on Saturday and sunset on Sunday should pay six shillings to his lord or be flogged. The contemporaneous Laws of Ine of Wessex provided that a thief caught in the act was to suffer death, or his life could be redeemed by his *wergild*; a penally-enslaved Englishman who ran away was liable to be hanged. That the death penalty was more widely available may be the implication of the provision that anyone liable to the death penalty who reached a church was to retain his life and to pay compensation as the law provided.

All this indicates a violent society in which a major concern of kings was the preservation of the peace and prevention of armed conflict between their followers. The payment of *wergild* was intended as an alternative to the blood feud which, in Germanic tradition, the kindred of a slain man were expected to pursue against the killer and his kindred. Vengeance was expected not only for a kinsman, but for a lord, and it is vengeance for both categories which emerges into the historical record, most famously in the Anglo-Saxon Chronicle's annal for 757, where the deposed West Saxon king Sigeberht was killed by a swineherd in vengeance for an ealdorman whom Sigeberht had earlier killed. Sigeberht had been deposed by Cynewulf 'and the counsellors of the West Saxons … because of his unlawful actions', thus suggesting that a king only reigned while he enjoyed the confidence of his people, not only as a war leader, but in other spheres as well.[5]

The blood feud was a major concern of the church and increasingly of kings. Alfred the Great (871–99) endeavoured to discourage over-hasty recourse to the blood feud. A man who knows the man against whom he has a legitimate blood feud to be dwelling at home 'is not to fight before he asks justice for himself'. If he has sufficient power to besiege his enemy in his house, Alfred prescribes a cooling-off period of seven days, at the end of which, if the enemy is prepared to surrender and give up his weapons, the avenger is to keep him unharmed for 30 days and inform his family and friends of the surrender. However, Alfred does not proscribe the blood feud, and indeed declares that a man may fight on behalf of his lord or kinsman who is being attacked, or a lord on behalf of his man, without incurring the blood feud.[6] His grandson Edmund (940–46) endeavoured to restrict the blood feud to the slayer alone,[7] but also found it impossible to declare it unlawful.

The tenor of the law codes makes it clear that, at least in theory, it was the responsibility of the king to maintain peace and justice among his people and, moreover, that the relationship between the king and his subjects was regarded as a personal one, any free man being entitled to seek justice from his king. However, we have no indications as to the system by which these laws were applied; the institutions of justice only emerge into the historical record much later. Indeed, it is possible that the early law codes were issued as a form of 'image-building' exercise,

---

4   EHD I No 31.
5   ASC 757.
6   EHD I No 33, cl 42.
7   EHD I No 38.

designed to show the king as a defender and preserver of the peace and protector of his subjects, rather than in any anticipation that they would be enforced. Further, in a largely non-literate society, it seems likely that vast areas of law and practices in relation to that law were never committed to writing, because they were matters of common knowledge and there was no necessity for writing.

However, the prominence given to various subjects in the surviving laws gives some idea of areas of concern. Æthelbert's laws are concerned very largely with death, physical injury, abduction of women, invasions of property and theft, indicative of a society in which the king's ability to preserve peace among his people was somewhat limited. In the immediate aftermath of Æthelbert's conversion, laws concerning the church are limited to provisions relating to the theft of the property of the church and its clergy. The Laws of Wihtred, 90 years later, show much stronger Christian influences and include penalties for illicit cohabitation and pagan worship, suggesting that active paganism remained common in Kent almost a century after the initial conversion.

1.1.3   Kings and the church

Kings were closely involved in religious affairs. The conversion of every kingdom took place with, as a minimum, the acquiescence of its king in the appointment of a bishop to minister in his kingdom and, more usually, his active participation. Christianity very much progressed from kingdom to kingdom, a king who had already come under Christian influences being persuaded to accept a bishop, or a king converted elsewhere inviting a bishop into his kingdom. Æthelbert agreed that his Frankish queen should be permitted to practise her faith, although neither she nor her bishop appear to have made any attempt at ministering to the king or his people.[8] The daughter of that marriage, Æthelburh, married Edwin of Northumbria, and again it was a condition of the marriage that she be permitted to practise her faith and be accompanied north by a bishop. Bede's lengthy account of Edwin's conversion makes it very clear that Bishop Paulinus concentrated his early efforts entirely on persuading the king to accept baptism, and that his mission made no real progress until Edwin did so.[9] Moreover, in both Kent and Northumbria, there was a relapse into active paganism on the deaths of Æthelbert and Edwin respectively.

Later kings were closely connected with the synods held to consider matters of doctrine and practice. Oswiu of Northumbria presided over the Synod of Whitby of 664 and summed up in favour of the Roman rather than the Celtic Easter. A century later, the legates sent to England in 786 by Pope Hadrian I to investigate the state of the English church were received by Offa of Mercia and Cynewulf of Wessex, and then journeyed to York, where a council was summoned by Ælfwold, King of Northumbria. On the legates' return to Mercia, a further council was held, presided over by Offa and the Archbishop of Canterbury. Both councils promulgated decrees, to which the kings and their counsellors subscribed as well as the bishops.[10]

---

8   HE I 25.
9   HE II 9–14.
10 Report of the Legates to Pope Hadrian, EHD I No 191.

1.1.4   Royal government

In considering the development of government in England before the 10th century, we are faced with a paucity of information. However, tantalising hints appear in both the Anglo-Saxon Chronicle and in Bede, and can be supplemented by the charters recording land grants to monasteries which begin to appear at the end of the 7th century. Then and later, kings in the larger kingdoms appointed sub-kings to rule parts of their kingdoms, either their sons or younger brothers, or members of formerly independent ruling families.[11] According to the Anglo-Saxon Chronicle,[12] Edwin's campaign against Cwichelm of Wessex in 626 led to the deaths of no fewer than five West Saxon kings; Bede records that on the death of Cenwealh of Wessex in around 674, 'sub-kings [subreguli] took upon themselves the government of the kingdom dividing it up and ruling it for about 10 years'.[13] Unfortunately, he gives no indication of what 'government' then involved.

From the 8th century, the Anglo-Saxon Chronicle refers increasingly to ealdormen, most frequently as the commanders of armies from specific districts or shires. Who were they?

Ealdormen were royal officials, and their office may pre-date the 8th century; the *dux* Berht who led a Northumbrian expedition to Ireland in the reign of Ecgfrith (670–85) is Ealdorman Briht in the Anglo-Saxon Chronicle.[14] In Wessex, the ealdorman's sphere of jurisdiction seems originally to have been the shire. He led the armies of his shire and also had responsibilities in the administration of justice; under the Laws of Ine, he is liable to be deprived of his shire if he allows a thief to escape,[15] and the man who has a legitimate blood feud and lacks the resources to surround his enemy in his house may look to him for assistance.[16] In return for his services, he received a portion of the fines due to the king,[17] he may have had official lands, and the 10th century will of Ealdorman Alfred suggests that he had a *wergild* by virtue of his office in addition to his ordinary *wergild* as a thegn.[18]

At the same time, we see references in the surviving sources to the king's counsellors or wise men. In 757, it was Cynewulf 'and the counsellors of the West Saxons' (*Westseaxna wiotan*) who deposed King Sigeberht because of his unlawful acts; 100 years later, Burgred of Mercia 'and his counsellors' requested West Saxon assistance against the Viking Great Army.[19] *Wiotan* is generally translated as 'councillors'. Such references, then and later in the Anglo-Saxon period, led a number of 19th century historians to postulate the existence of a primitive national parliament, or *witanagemot*, involved in the election of kings, the promulgation of new laws, the

---

11   In around 655, Peada, son of Penda of Mercia, was 'placed by his father on the throne of the Middle Angles' (HE III 21); Oswiu of Northumbria had 'as a partner in the royal dignity' his cousin and dynastic rival, Oswin. Frithuwold, ruler of Surrey, in his charter to Chertsey Abbey (EHD I No 54, cl 672–74) describes himself as 'sub-king of Wulfhere, king of the Mercians', who confirmed the grant.
12   ASC D sa 626.
13   HE IV 12.
14   ASC 684.
15   EHD I No 32, cl 36.1.
16   EHD I No 33, cl 42.3.
17   *Ibid*, cl 37.1.
18   EHD I No 97.
19   HE V 23.

making of treaties and the appointment of bishops, and saw it as a direct precursor of the parliaments which emerged from the 13th century. However, references to the *wiotan* are generally shadowy and tangential, and its relationship with the king is unclear. It is more realistic to think of a group of counsellors, drawn from the leading magnates and ecclesiastics, than of a formal council with defined powers, although the counsellors might assume a leading role in times of crisis, particularly when the succession was disputed and during royal minorities.[20] In the 11th and 12th centuries, the king wore his crown three times a year, and these 'crown-wearings' may have acted as occasions for gatherings of the king's counsellors, but the precise relationship between king and counsellors must remain unknown, although it presumably varied according to the personal stature of individual kings.

1.1.5   The growth of effective overlordship: the 8th and 9th centuries

Bede lists seven kings as having ruled over all the southern English kingdoms (*in regibus gentis Anglorum cunctis australibus eorum provinciis*).[21] Æthelbald of Mercia, although not included in this list, is described by Bede as having all the kingdoms south of the Humber 'together with their kings' subject to him at the time he completed his history in 731.[22] For most of the 8th century, Mercia was much the most powerful of the kingdoms, but it is clear from the surviving sources that this supremacy was very much the product of the reigns of two strong kings and was divided by a period of instability between them. Charter evidence shows Æthelbald to have wielded effective power in Kent, parts of Essex, including London, and parts of Wessex. In the 740s, Æthelbald and Cuthred, King of Wessex, witnessed the sale of land to Glastonbury Abbey; Æthelbald's consent to the sale was required, and the charter makes clear his precedence over Cuthred. Overall, it is in the 8th century that there is evidence for the emergence of an effective overlordship of one ruler over other kings, as distinct from his own sub-kings. However, overlordship was a matter appertaining to the personal stature of a ruler, and was the prerogative of individual rulers rather than of the kings of a particular kingdom. Æthelbald's overlordship seems not to have survived his murder and the battle for the Mercian kingship which followed, and had to be built anew by Offa (757–96), whose greatest influence lay in Kent and the south-east, rather than in Wessex.

By the 820s, Mercia had been superseded as the leading kingdom by Wessex. *Sub anno* 829, the Anglo-Saxon Chronicle states that Egbert, grandfather of Alfred, 'conquered the kingdom of the Mercians and everything south of the Humber' and that in the same year, he received the submission of the Northumbrians, apparently without resort to battle. The following year, Egbert led an army against the Welsh and 'reduced them all to humble submission to him'. However, power continued to be transitory. Within a year of Egbert's conquest, Mercia regained its autonomy.[23] In 853, the Mercian king Burgred obtained support from Egbert's son, Æthelwulf, for a campaign against the Welsh and married Æthelwulf's daughter, an alliance suggestive of equality rather than submission.[24] Burgred again requested West Saxon assistance

---

20   Alfred P Smyth, *King Alfred the Great*, 1995, OUP, pp 422–24.

21   HE II 4.

22   HE V 23.

23   ASC 830.

24   ASC 853.

in 868, this time against the Danish 'Great Army' which had landed in England in 866, and Mercia appears to have remained autonomous at least until 872, when the Mercians made peace with the Danes.[25]

From 823, the formerly independent kingdoms of Kent, Sussex, Essex and Surrey were possessions of the West Saxon house and, until 860, seem to have been held by the *atheling* (throneworthy prince) next in succession, as co-ruler with his father or elder brother.

It was during this initial period of West Saxon paramountcy that Viking attacks, which first developed as isolated raids on coastal areas in the closing years of the 8th century, emerged as a serious menace. The Anglo-Saxon Chronicle records nine attacks between 835 and 851, when for the first time a Viking army wintered in England. Attacks continued through the 850s and early 860s, before the 'Great Army' landed in 865 with the intention of settling. Although the Viking invasions brought Wessex her greatest peril, almost bringing her to her knees, paradoxically, they also served to confirm West Saxon paramountcy and ultimately enabled the West Saxon kings to extend their rule over the whole of England.

1.2   THE VIKING AGE

The period of the Viking invasions, lasting initially until the early years of the 10th century and succeeded by a phase of consolidation and extension of West Saxon power over much of modern England before attacks resumed during the reign of Æthelred 'the Unready', is usually seen as a watershed. However, elements of continuity are clearly apparent. The process of centralisation, and absorption and amalgamation, of smaller kingdoms into larger units is evident in the 8th century if not earlier, although the invasions and the failure of kingdoms other than Wessex to resist the invaders brought about an intensification of the process.

From 900, the West Saxon kings extended their power over areas which had come under Danish rule in the 860s and 870s, a process which involved governmental and religious development in addition to military conquest. That this was no smooth and uninterrupted process is very clear from the surviving records, which show successive West Saxon kings as having to reconquer the same areas and re-establish the same overlordships several times over. In particular, the arrival of Norsemen from Ireland brought about the establishment of a Scandinavian kingdom based on York, at times uniting York and Dublin under the same ruler, which lasted intermittently until 955 and proved a thorn in the flesh of a succession of kings. However, when the Danish Cnut gained the English throne in 1016, he stepped into the shoes of his West Saxon predecessors, the descendants of Alfred, as the ruler of what had evolved into a relatively centralised state, in which power lay with the king and was devolved by him to his magnates, and in which the apparatus of government, with mints under royal control and a developing system of royal justice, was emerging. This contrasts markedly with the position on the continent where, following the break-up of the Carolingian empire in the 9th and 10th centuries, power came to lie with regional magnates.

---

25   ASC 872.

1.2.1　Kingship 865–978

The political history of the Viking era makes it very clear that the king continued to act as his kingdom's leader in war, although the command of individual armies might well be exercised by ealdormen, who led the levies of their own shires. Alfred the Great succeeded in 871 to a kingdom imperilled by the Great Army, and passed the first seven years of his reign in near-continuous warfare against the invaders, spending the 880s, the period of a series of truces, in consolidating and re-ordering the defences of his kingdom, and the 890s in renewed warfare with a second large Danish army. According to the written sources, responsibility both for command in battle and for military organisation rested with the king in person, and this picture continues under his successors for another century, until the reigns of Æthelred and his son Edward the Confessor mark a temporary break with tradition, for reasons which are unclear but which probably relate to their personalities.

What is also very clear is that although the earlier pattern of ebb and flow of territorial power according to the relative strength or weakness of the particular king as against his enemies continued, and the lack of a clear and settled system for determining the royal succession meant that there was a political crisis on the death of almost every king, royal administration had developed by the late 10th century to a level at which it could function relatively independently of the personality of the king, and could continue to operate during the upheaval of the renewed Viking onslaught during the reign of Æthelred.

Alfred died in October 899, leaving Wessex in control of England south of the Thames and at peace with the Danes, whose writ ran north and east of the Fosse Way, the so called Danelaw. The reigns of his son, Edward the Elder (899–924) and grandsons Athelstan (924–40), Edmund the Elder (940–46) and Eadred (946–55) were marked by the gradual and fluctuating extension of West Saxon power over the rest of England. All these kings, except Athelstan, have gone down in history principally as war leaders, although the other traditional responsibilities of kings, as makers of laws and protectors of the church, emerge into the historical record from time to time. Alfred, Edmund and Edgar (959–75) all produced law codes which have survived, and Alfred devoted much time and energy towards promoting the survival of learning and monasticism in his kingdom, a priority which emerged again during the reign of his great-grandson Edgar.

This is not to say that the position of the West Saxon kings in the century after Alfred's death was secure against internal rivals. Edward the Elder's kingship was initially imperilled by a rising by his cousin Æthelwold, son of Alfred's elder brother Æthelred I and who had been passed over for the crown as an infant in 871, who now made common cause with the Danes against him. This was a serious threat to the fragile autonomy of Wessex.[26] The support given to Æthelwold, along with much of the internal political history of Wessex in the 10th century, demonstrates clearly that no settled system of royal succession had developed, although the concept of 'throneworthiness' was becoming confined to the sons of kings, rather than being shared by all the male descendants of a common ancestor. The deaths of Edward the Elder, of two of his sons and of his grandson Edgar were all followed by serious succession disputes within the West Saxon house, resulting in the suspicious deaths of

---

26　See Smyth, *op cit*, pp 401–20.

at least two claimants and the murder of one king allegedly on the orders of a stepmother pressing the claims of her own son.[27]

The political history of the period demonstrates that by the end of the 10th century, succession was narrowly confined within one family, and moreover to those members of the dynasty closest to the late king. In this period, only sons of kings who had actually reigned bore the title *atheling*, signifying throneworthiness.[28] Sons of the late king were preferred over brothers, at least where those sons were old enough to bear arms, or would shortly be old enough to bear arms.[29] In times of crisis, an adult brother would be preferred to an infant son. It seems significant that the four minor and untried rulers, Eadwig, Edgar, Edward the Martyr and Æthelred, all succeeded at times of peace from Viking attack, which was renewed shortly after Æthelred's accession,[30] and apparently had no surviving uncles. The king's counsellors seem to have played some role in the selection of the new ruler on each occasion, but the extent of this role is unclear.

1.2.2   The expansion of West Saxon power 899–978

Edward the Elder's reign was devoted to the extension of West Saxon power into other parts of England, and he also established a shadowy suzerainty over the rulers of what is now Scotland. Athelstan, however, began to involve himself on the continental stage. This was not entirely unprecedented; over a century earlier, Offa had established relations with Charlemagne, and at least two of Athelstan's forebears had taken Carolingian wives. However, the extent of Athelstan's marriage alliances was without parallel. One sister was married to the future emperor Otto the Great, and two others to Conrad, Duke of Burgundy, and Hugh the Great, Duke of the Franks, another sister having earlier married Charles the Simple, King of the West Franks. In addition, Athelstan invaded and ravaged Scotland in 934, and forced its king, Constantine, to give his son as a hostage. If a charter granted by him on 7 June, on his way north, is genuine, the witness list indicates that his army included three Welsh sub-kings and six ealdormen with Scandinavian names who were, presumably, at the head of contingents drawn from the Danelaw.[31]

However, power remained transitory. Athelstan had himself rebuilt the authority asserted by his father over the rulers of northern England, and after his death in 940, his half-brother Edmund had to rebuild his authority in a similar manner. By the time of his murder in 946, Edmund had re-asserted West Saxon authority over

---

27   For detail on these events, see the Companion Website for this book (www. cavendishpublishing.com/constihistory).

28   Smyth postulates that by the late 9th century, only the sons of reigning kings were eligible for the kingship, and Æthelwold's bid for the throne was prompted not only by personal ambition, but also to ensure the future throneworthiness of his own branch of the West Saxon house.

29   Eadwig (955–59) and Edgar succeeded their uncle Eadred (946–55) when in their early teens, having been passed over on the death of their father, Edmund. Eadred seems to have been the last survivor of Edward the Elder's sons. Edward the Martyr (975–78) was about 13 when he succeeded his father, Edgar, and also had no surviving uncles. Contemporary ideas as to what constituted military age can be deduced from the fact that King Edmund took part in the Battle of Brunanburh at the age of 15, in 937.

30   A circumstance blamed by contemporary writers on the unprecedented crime of the murder of Edward the Martyr on 18 March 978.

31   EHD 1 No 104.

Northumbria, and ravaged Cumberland before granting it to his ally, Malcolm I of Scots, perhaps in recognition of his inability to hold an area so far from his power base.[32] West Saxon authority over Northumbria was nominal and exercised through earls, who until 1016 were Northumbrians holding office virtually by hereditary right who enjoyed virtual independence until after 1066.

Other than Athelstan's marriage alliances and the surviving law codes of Edmund, there is relatively little evidence of the non-warlike activities of Alfred's successors until the reign of Edgar, now remembered mainly as a patron of the monastic revival which took place in his reign. Edgar is also the first English king, indeed the only king prior to the Norman Conquest, known to have been consecrated twice; initially at the time of his accession, as was usual, and then a second time in 973.

Consecration, which gradually evolved into coronation, was pre-eminently a demonstration of a king's legitimacy in the eyes of God, making it essential in the event of a disputed succession for the favoured candidate to be crowned as soon as possible after his predecessor's death. Edgar's second consecration is of particular significance as the earliest known example of the coronation rite as it is followed today, beginning with the monarch's acceptance and acclamation by his people; his swearing a threefold oath, to protect the church, to defend his people against enemies, and to administer justice among his people; and climaxing with his anointing and crowning.

1.3   ROYAL GOVERNMENT IN THE 9TH AND 10TH CENTURIES

Taken as a whole, the period from 870 to the 950s is one of fluctuations in kingly power, the building of an overlordship by one king which had to be created afresh by his successor following his death, a demonstration that the ties which bound ruler and ruled were still very largely personal. However, an infrastructure of royal government was developed, which provided Wessex with the means first to resist the Viking invasion and then for its kings to exert their authority over much of England and Wales.

1.3.1   Military organisation

This began to emerge under Alfred, who founded a number of fortified strongpoints known as *burhs* within Wessex and built on existing obligations of military service. The *Burghal Hidage*, a list of 30 such *burhs* together with the number of hides (divisions of land for the purposes of tax assessment) allocated to provide for the maintenance of each, dates in its extant form from 911 or later, but it is clear that many if not the majority of *burhs* listed were built during Alfred's reign.[33] It is in the 9th century that ealdormen begin to be associated with particular shires, suggesting that the division of Wessex into shires instead of the earlier folk-groupings was a development of this period. This hypothesis is strengthened by the frequent correlation of the Domesday Book assessment for a particular shire with the number of hides required under the *Burghal Hidage* formula for the maintenance of its *burhs*. For instance, the assessment

---

32   ASC C 944–45.
33   See Smyth, *op cit*, pp 135–38.

for the Dorset *burhs* of Wareham and Shaftesbury is 2,300 hides, while Dorset is assessed in Domesday at 2,277 hides.[34]

From 840 and with increasing frequency thereafter, the Anglo-Saxon Chronicle speaks of the men of a particular shire fighting against the Danes under the leadership of their ealdorman, demonstrating that the development of the shire system and of compulsory military service began prior to Alfred. In creating *burhs* and providing for their upkeep and garrisoning from a particular shire, Alfred was building on an established framework, as his son and grandsons were to continue doing after him. A distinction was made between the field army and the static garrisons of the *burhs*. When, according to the Anglo-Saxon Chronicle for 893, Alfred famously divided his army into two, 'so that always half his men were at home, half on service', he excepted 'the men who guarded the boroughs', presumably because they were close to home and able to continue to work the land.

1.3.2   The coinage

The *burhs* acted not only as military strongpoints but as foci of royal authority, much as did royal castles in later centuries. The majority of *burhs*, for example, housed mints. Prior to the later 8th century, there was no effective coinage in England. In about 775, two Kentish kings began to issue silver pennies from a mint in Canterbury, which was taken over by Offa of Mercia around 785. Later Mercian kings continued to issue silver pennies of high quality, and their example was followed by East Anglian rulers and by Egbert of Wessex. However, it was the Viking Age which brought about an explosion in the number of mints and the amount of money in circulation – some 70 mints were in operation during the reign of Edward the Confessor.

Numismatic studies show that 10th and 11th century kings exercised close control over the coinage, whose design was changed at frequent intervals, whereupon the bulk of the obsolete coins rapidly went out of circulation. If the practice of the post-Conquest period were followed, such coins were called in, melted down and re-minted according to the new design. Coin dies were issued to moneyers by royal officials and at any one time, the same design was being produced at all mints.[35]

1.3.3   The law

The means by which law was enforced in this period are not clear, no reliable records having survived. However, it would seem that both the royal law codes and the unwritten body of customary law were applied by a number of overlapping bodies. Parties to disputes were able to seek justice from the king; grants of land by the king were frequently accompanied by the privileges of *infangenetheof* and *utfangenetheof* – jurisdiction over persons on that land. Such powers of seignorial justice were to be a feature of the later feudal system. Aside from seignorial justice, it is not clear how law was enforced. The traditional view, followed by Professor JH Baker in his *An Introduction to English Legal History*,[36] sees justice as being administered by 'the community' through primitive 'folk moots' or local assemblies. Professor Frank

---

34   PH Sawyer, *From Roman Britain to Early England*, 1st edn, 1978, Routledge, pp 227–28.

35   III Edgar 8. On the coinage generally, see Sawyer, *ibid*, pp 218–19.

36   JH Baker, *An Introduction to English Legal History*, 3rd edn, 1990, Butterworths, pp 4–11.

Barlow on the other hand[37] sees these as being converted by the mid-10th century into a network of shire and hundred courts, based on the administrative areas into which the country was divided, and presided over by royal officials, principally the sheriff, who had now emerged alongside the ealdorman.

The practices of these early courts are less in dispute, and it is clear that they in no way resembled those of a modern court. There was no judge as such, there were no lawyers and no attempt was made to establish the true facts. Indeed, Baker has said that the procedure obviated any need to make formal inquiry as to the facts of the case.[38] The way in which matters came to the attention of the courts is also unclear, although a jury of accusation, later to become an integral part of the judicial system as the jury of presentment, is mentioned in Cnut's laws of 1020–23.[39] Each of the parties in both criminal and other matters swore by holy oath as to the truth of his case, and might bring 'oath-helpers' or 'compurgators' to support him by similar oath. If these oaths were considered insufficient, either because the case was a serious one or the word of one or other of the parties was not accepted, then appeal was made to God for judgment by means of a physical 'ordeal'.

Several forms of ordeal were recognised by the church, but those most commonly used in England were the ordeals of fire and water. In the first, the party concerned was required to carry a heated iron bar in his unprotected hand for a set number of paces; the hand was then bound up, to be inspected a few days later. If the burn was healing cleanly, God had demonstrated the truth of his case; if his hand festered, that was proof of his lie. In the ordeal by water, the party was bound and lowered into a pond; if he sank, God's holy element had received him, thereby proving his innocence.

There was as yet no firm division between civil and criminal law, disputes being treated as primarily between the parties, and dealt with by orders for compensation rather than specific punishments. However, by this period, the concept of the king's peace, an aspect of the king's role as protector and defender of his people, was firmly established, and under Cnut's laws, the most serious breaches of the king's peace – murder, treason, arson, attacks on houses, open theft, persistent robbery and false coining – were capital offences reserved to the king's courts. To these were added as further 'pleas of the crown', homicide, wounding, mayhem and rape, and certain offences directly touching the crown, such as neglect of a royal order, giving of unrighteous judgment or failure to perform military service due to the king.

1.4   ÆTHELRED THE UNREADY AND AFTER: 978–1065

Æthelred's reign (978–1016) is traditionally portrayed as one of disaster, and Æthelred as a weak and impotent king, although his modern by-name 'the Unready' derives not from a lack of preparedness but from a contemporary pun on his name, meaning 'the ill-advised' (*Æthelraed* – 'noble counsel', *Unraed* – 'no counsel'). In his Sermon of the Wolf to the English of 1014,[40] Wulfstan II, Archbishop of York, speaks in apocalyptic

---

37   F Barlow, *The Feudal Kingdom of England 1042–1216*, 5th edn, 1999, Longman, pp 1–37, 41–42. This work provides a convenient yet scholarly coverage of the period 1042–1216.

38   Baker, *op cit*, p 5.

39   EHD I No 50.

40   EHD I No 240.

tones of the calamities which had befallen the English people and puts the blame squarely on their sins and neglect of God, though he refers to the sinful in general terms and mentions none by name. This is a strange omission if Æthelred were so incompetent a ruler as is sometimes suggested, since he was then in exile in Normandy, having fled overseas after the acclamation of the Danish ruler Swein 'Forkbeard' as king. More strangely still in the light of Æthelred's perceived ineptitude and past tyrannical acts, including the murders of various leading noblemen,[41] after Swein's death on 3 February 1014 and the proclamation of his son Cnut as king by the Danish fleet:

> All the councillors who were England, ecclesiastical and lay, determined to send for King Æthelred, and they said that no lord was dearer to them than their natural lord, if he would govern them more justly than he did before ... Then during the spring King Æthelred came home to his own people and was gladly received by them all ...[42]

It should be noted that the counsellors and people were concerned that Æthelred should rule 'more justly than before', and it seems likely that they regarded him as a better prospect than Cnut, who must have been largely an unknown quantity, though the ruthlessness he was to show towards his enemies in the future may already have been apparent. However, we see an early demonstration of the idea that a king ought to rule within the law, and was only acceptable in the eyes of his people while he did so.

However, under Æthelred, we see the system of royal administration flourishing independently of the person of the king. No fewer than five Danegelds were demanded between 992 and 1018, the sums rising from 10,000 pounds to 72,000 pounds,[43] in addition to large sums for the maintenance of various Danish armies in England and the cost of providing land and sea defences against the Danes. This amply demonstrates the existence of a rich economy and an efficient tax-gathering system, despite the periodic ravaging of the Danish armies and fleets, and the need to raise, equip and feed armies to face them.

1.4.1 Royal government

The way in which this system of royal administration operated is unclear. To judge from early post-Conquest practices and written materials such as the *Constitutio Domus Regis* ('The establishment of the King's Household'), drawn up in Stephen's reign (1135–54), the central institutions of administration formed part of the king's itinerant court, the clerks of the king's chapel acting as a secretariat. By 1100, the treasury had a fixed base at Winchester, at which most of its physical assets were held, but financial officials travelled with the king. Three times a year, at Christmas, Easter and Whitsun, the king wore his crown and seems to have sought the counsel of his bishops and magnates, and exercised his role as a dispenser of royal justice. The collection of royal revenues was the responsibility of the 'shire reeve' or sheriff,

---

41 For example, in 1006, Ælfhelm, Ealdorman of Northumbria, was murdered on Æthelred's orders and his sons were blinded.

42 ASC C 1014.

43 The only coin in circulation until the late 13th century was the silver penny. All other monetary units were units of account, of which the pound, the mark (two-thirds of a pound) and the shilling were the most significant.

appointed by the king in each shire, whose role overlapped that of the ealdorman and eventually replaced it. The sheriffs emerged in the 10th century and seem to have been responsible for the enforcement of royal justice and the collection of royal revenues in their shires, including successive Danegelds, which were a regular tax from the reign of Edward the Confessor and financed the kingdom's military organisation. The sheriff came to command the military levies of his shire and was also responsible for the maintenance of the king's peace.

There were differences between various parts of the country, in particular between the northern and eastern areas known as the Danelaw,[44] where Danish social and legal systems pertained under the treaty between Alfred and Guthrum agreed in the period 886–90. Some of these differences seem to have been mainly semantic; in the 'English' areas, taxation was based on the 'hide' of land, in the Danelaw, on the 'carucate'; shires in English areas were divided into 'hundreds', nominally of 100 hides, in Danish areas, into 'wapentakes'.[45] However, social structure in the Danelaw was also different, as is apparent from Domesday, there being a greater proportion of free men among the peasantry than in the south and west.

It is also in Æthelred's reign that we see initiative in government moving away from the person of the king, and the beginnings of the concentration of political power in the hands of his greater servants that was to be a major feature of the reign of his son Edward the Confessor (1042–66). Remarkably for a king in a period where the first responsibility of a ruler was the command of armies, Æthelred appeared with his army or fleet only on rare occasions, and is portrayed by the Chronicle on these occasions as being with the army rather than in command of it, command being vested in ealdormen.

The increase in the power of the king's greatest servants continued under Cnut (1016–35), who by 1018 had appointed a number of 'earls', successors of the ealdormen in their governmental role, to govern provinces under royal authority. From the mid-10th century, Northumbria was governed by earls, who enjoyed virtual independence and hereditary office. Under Cnut, this system spread to the rest of the country, and developed under Edward the Confessor to the point where a single earl was not only the most powerful man in the country, but became the last of the Anglo-Saxon kings. Most of Cnut's original earls were Danes, much the most important exception being Godwine, the son of a minor Sussex thegn, who became Earl of Wessex in the 1020s and seems to have acted as regent for Cnut during some of the King's absences abroad.

Cnut was king not only of England, but of Denmark and later of Norway and part of Sweden as well, and could not hope to govern the whole of his scattered domains directly. It was inevitable that there would be greater delegation of royal power than in previous reigns. However, he seems to have been able to keep a reasonable degree of control over his earls, unlike Edward the Confessor, who was dominated for most of his reign by them, particularly Godwine, whose daughter he married, and after Godwine's death in 1053 by Godwine's son, Harold. It is significant that all the three leading earls came from families of only minor significance before 1013, Cnut having

---

44 The boundary between the two roughly followed the line of the Roman road known as Watling Street, running from London to Chester.

45 Since both hides and carucates were measures of value for tax purposes rather than units of area, the size of both, and therefore of wapentakes and hundreds, varied very widely according to the agricultural value of the land concerned.

largely destroyed the old Anglo-Saxon aristocracy. The earls were in a very real sense Cnut's creations, owing their power to him and dependent on him in a personal way. This was not the case under Cnut's successors, who were in any event men of much lesser calibre.[46] In this period, as elsewhere in the medieval period, a governmental system created by a strong king required a strong king to operate it, and crisis came under weaker successors.

The key to political power throughout the Anglo-Saxon period was royal favour, which seems largely to have depended on personal qualities rather than birth and blood. However, increasingly from the reign of Æthelred onwards, the greater landowners were able to rely on another source of power, independent of the king. Traditionally, the king rewarded his servants with gifts of land, and that land itself became a source of power, especially as it came to be a hereditary possession. From the 8th century onwards, kings increasingly gave grants of land known as bookland (from *boc*, the charter or diploma recording the grant), not specifically in return for services, but granted in perpetuity and free of all services except the so called *Trinoda Necessitas* – military service and the maintenance of fortifications and bridges. With the land went rights of legal jurisdiction over those dwelling on that land. Bookland was forfeit to the king if the landowner neglected his duties, especially military service, and an heir was obliged to return to the king a substantial *heriot*, often including horses and arms, before he could enter into his inheritance. Such holdings of bookland were supplemented by lands granted for life and also lands held on lease. By the 11th century, most of the leading families held some bookland, and this gave them a degree of independence from the king which had been lacking at a time when their landholding depended entirely on their provision of services. At the same time, a period of some 30 years under three weak kings produced a concentration of power in the hands of the earls, to the near-exclusion of the king.

Events of the reigns of Cnut's two sons, Harold 'Harefoot' (1035–40) and Hardecnut (1040–42) are shadowy in the extreme, but neither was particularly secure on his throne; the early part of Harold's reign was dominated not only by his struggles with Hardecnut, but also by the claims of the surviving sons of Æthelred, Edward and Alfred, who had spent Cnut's reign in exile in Normandy.[47] Harold died in 1040 and was succeeded, apparently without opposition, by Hardecnut, whose own insecurity is suggested by his inviting Edward, his maternal half-brother, to return to England and, according to some sources, to share in its government. Hardecnut dropped dead at a wedding feast in 1042 while still only in his early 20s, and was succeeded by Edward, apparently without opposition.

1.4.2   Edward the Confessor 1042–66

The Confessor is traditionally considered a weak and ineffectual king, under whom power was exercised by his earls, and whose political history was dominated by conflict between those earls, particularly in the later years, when the question of the

---

46   See NJ Higham, *The Death of Anglo-Saxon England*, 1997, Sutton, especially pp 98–106.

47   Harold, the elder, was Cnut's son by an informal marriage, and his legitimacy was doubted by the church. Hardecnut was Cnut's son by Emma of Normandy, widow of Æthelred the Unready and mother of Edward the Confessor. For a recent summary of events, concentrating on the role of Earl Godwine, see IW Walker, *Harold, The Last Anglo-Saxon King*, 1997, Sutton, pp 12–15.

succession assumed increasing importance. This view is not entirely without foundation. Following Godwine's death at Easter 1053, Harold, his eldest surviving son, became the most powerful man in the kingdom, assisted in his rise by the deaths of the two other great earls who had survived from Cnut's reign, and their replacement by younger and less well-tried successors. That Edward surrendered the initiative in relation to his earls is also implied by the fact that two of the three leading earls were succeeded on their deaths by their sons. Harold was a man of high calibre in his own right, but both he and Ælfgar, son of Leofric of Mercia (died 1058), had spent periods in rebellion against the king, and Ælfgar would do so again.

By the 1050s, when the Confessor was in his late 40s and his marriage to Godwine's daughter remained childless, the question of the succession came to the fore. It seems reasonable to conclude that the power struggles between the sons of Godwine and the heirs of Leofric, which dominate the last years of the reign, had their origins at least in part in the desire of both to establish sufficient power to make a bid for the throne on Edward's death. There was no obvious heir. Sources favouring William I, then Duke of Normandy, were later to claim that Edward had chosen William as his heir as early as 1051, but this appears unlikely. Even if Edward accepted that he would never father a child, William was not of English royal blood, being related to him only as the great-nephew of Edward's Norman mother.

In 1054, a mission went to the continent to seek the return of Edward the Exile, the survivor of the two sons of Edmund Ironside, the Confessor's elder half-brother, who had led the English resistance to Cnut until his death in 1016. The Exile and his brother had been taken abroad in infancy for safety, and his whereabouts were eventually traced to Hungary. He seems to have arrived in England in September 1057, but died in London, possibly but not certainly by murder, before he could meet his uncle. However, the Exile left a young son, Edgar, and two daughters, all of whom arrived safely at Edward's court and remained alive. Edgar, the last representative of the male line of the West Saxon house, was accepted as Edward's heir and accorded the style of *atheling*, but was destined never to reign.

By the 1060s, power in England was concentrated to a still greater extent in the hands of Godwine's sons. Harold became Earl of Wessex on Godwine's death; the second surviving son, Tostig, was appointed Earl of Northumbria in 1055. Another son, Gyrth, became Earl of East Anglia and a fourth, Leofwine, Earl of Middlesex and Hertfordshire. This bloc broke up to some extent late in 1065, when the Northumbrians rebelled against Tostig and drove him out, to be replaced by Morcar, the second of the sons of Ælfgar and, like his brother Edwin, Earl of Mercia, an untried teenager. Harold remained much the most powerful man in the country.

Edward the Confessor died on 5 January 1066 at a time of crisis. The peace settlement with the Northumbrians included Tostig's outlawry; the deposed earl took refuge in Flanders and planned to regain his earldom by force. As Edward's health failed in the last months of 1065, there seems to have been an awareness of the likelihood of an invasion by William of Normandy in support of his claims. There were also 'external' claimants: Harald 'Hardrada',[48] King of Norway, the last of the great Viking leaders and an almost legendary figure in the northern world, who had

---

48   Literally 'Stern in Counsel', colloquially 'the Ruthless'.

inherited a thin claim to Cnut's domains from his predecessor, Magnus; and Swein Estrithsson, Cnut's successor as King of Denmark.

In these circumstances, it is unsurprising that the pragmatism which had been a factor in the succession on previous occasions re-asserted itself and the young and untried Edgar was passed over for the kingship.[49] Uniquely, he was passed over in favour of Harold Godwineson, a man not of royal blood, although he was the Confessor's brother-in-law. The mechanism by which Harold was accepted as king is not entirely clear, but it seems crucial that he was finally named by Edward as his heir, or at least that he plausibly claimed to be so named. To what extent this designation was of greater importance than his established power base is not clear, but it is significant that there was no serious internal opposition to his accession. There was no rising in support of Edgar, nor any internal support for either of the invaders of 1066. It may also be significant that in asserting his own claim, William relied on his being named as heir by Edward, suggesting that designation by the late king was a crucial factor where there was no obvious suitable heir.

In the last century before the Norman Conquest, we can see a system of royal administration, including law-giving, collection of revenue on the basis of assessed land values, and moneying, which was able to operate independently of the person of the monarch, though how the system operated is not clear. Sheriffs had also emerged, responsible for the enforcement of royal justice, though the mechanisms by which they did so and the significance of royal justice in comparison with unwritten customary law cannot be known. However, the political sphere remained at the personal level, and the precise interactions and relative strengths of the king, his magnates and advisors, depended very much on the personality of individual rulers. A strong king such as Cnut was able to maintain his position and rule successfully through his earls, but Edward the Confessor seems to have been virtually the tool of his great men rather than their master.

---

49   The date of Edgar's birth is not known, but he was still a young boy in January 1066. He seems not to have been a strong character, appearing as a presence at a number of major events in the latter part of the 11th century, including the First Crusade of 1096–99 and the Battle of Tinchebrai in 1106, but never as an active participant.

CHAPTER 2

THE NORMAN CONQUEST
AND AFTER: 1066–1189

2.1   WILLIAM I 1066–87

William I lacked any claim to the English throne by hereditary right. In reality, he was king by conquest, and by the deaths of his adult rivals. He and his Norman followers were a very small minority in a foreign land.[1] Certainly, in the first years after 1066, the new king attempted to rule not only through established institutions, but through personnel inherited from his predecessors. The Norman Conquest is traditionally seen as one of the greatest watersheds in English history, yet, beneath the surface, much is apparent of continuity from the Anglo-Saxon period.

Until the 12th century, the greatest change was not in the institutions, but in the personnel who staffed those institutions. Indeed, the change of personnel was a gradual one, particularly in the religious sphere, and did not take place on any scale until after 1070. However, under a succession of strong kings in the first two generations after the Conquest, we see a re-development of centralised power in the hands of the king, delegated to his greater servants only insofar as he was prepared to delegate. That such centralisation was only workable in the hands of a strong ruler was made very clear by the succession dispute and so called 'Anarchy' of 1135–53.

2.1.1   England 1066–70

Viewing the events of 1066 with hindsight, it is easy to forget that the Norman Conquest was by no means a foregone conclusion, that William's success was in no small part due to a series of chances. First, that Harold II faced two separate and unrelated invasions over 200 miles apart at one and the same time. Second, that the king was a casualty of Hastings and the last representative of the West Saxon dynasty was an untried boy. Third, that the surviving earls, heavily defeated by the Norwegians, were licking their wounds in the north and unable or perhaps unwilling to campaign against the Normans. William's expeditionary force comprised no more than 7,000 fighting men before the casualties of Hastings, which may well have been heavy – the battle lasted for many hours and was remembered long afterwards as particularly hard-fought. With winter approaching, it would have been difficult to obtain reinforcements from Normandy, particularly of war horses for the knights whose presence at Hastings had been crucial,[2] and there were substantial English garrisons in London and elsewhere which remained hostile. Exeter, for example, held

---

1   'Norman' is here used as a convenient shorthand for those who came to England under William I and his sons, since painstaking research has demonstrated that many individuals had their origins in Flanders and Brittany rather than Normandy.

2   Pre-Conquest English armies fought almost exclusively on foot, using horses only as transport. Horses require considerable training in order to operate in the cavalry role, so that William's knights could not simply requisition local mounts for immediate use. Since horses are physically unable to vomit, they make poor sea travellers, and the transporting of large numbers is a formidable undertaking. For a recent revisionist study of military organisation in England in the post-Conquest period, see Stephen Morillo, *Warfare under the Anglo-Norman Kings 1066–1135*, 1994, Boydell.

out against the Normans until the end of 1067. The Conquest was not so much the result of Norman success, but of English failure.

Although the adherents of Edgar the Atheling crumbled during October and November 1066, and eventually agreed surrender terms at Berkhamsted, William's position remained precarious even after he was crowned as king on Christmas Day. His actions in the early years of his reign were those of a man consolidating his position and moving carefully in an enemy land. William was faced with potential hostility not only from his new subjects, but also from his Norman followers. He had had to battle for his dukedom in his youth against over-mighty relatives, and the political history of his reign in England demonstrates a determination not only to put down existing opposition among the English, but also to prevent any of his own followers from developing a sufficiently strong power base from which to challenge his authority.

This was no easy task, as is clear from the long catalogue of rebellions and succession disputes which represent much of the political history of the ensuing centuries. In order to establish foci of Norman authority in England, it was necessary to build castles. Some, notably the Tower of London, were royal strongholds, but others were held by William's followers, to whom power, in an age without modern communications or standing armies, had perforce to be delegated. At the same time, those of William's Norman vassals who had followed him to England had to be rewarded for their services in bringing him to the throne and to ensure their loyalty in the future. The new king had to strike a delicate balance, in order to subdue English opposition and to prevent any future English threat to his kingship arising, while avoiding the accretion of too much power in the hands of any one individual.

Most of William's initial acts stress continuity rather than change. He claimed to be the lawful successor of Edward the Confessor, Harold's reign being treated for official purposes as though it had never existed. At his coronation, he made oath to obey just law, and if the early 12th century *Leges Henrici Primi* can be trusted, he ordained that all men should have and hold the law of King Edward as to lands and all other things, together with those additions which William had ordained for the good of the English people.

William did not immediately re-distribute English lands among his Norman favourites, but the surviving English nobles were rapidly deprived of real authority, many being required to give hostages for their good faith. He relied extensively on English ecclesiastics, in the temporal as well as the spiritual sphere, notably Ealdred, Archbishop of York, who acted as his viceroy in Northumbria. His precarious position in the first years after Hastings is shown by his using Stigand, the suspended Archbishop of Canterbury, as one of his advisers, even though William had earlier used Stigand's simoniacal appointment and the need to reform the English church as a major pretext for his invasion. William faced not only local opposition in the west and north, where regional concerns led to sporadic risings and the terrain lent itself to guerrilla warfare, but as well the claims of Swein Estrithsson, Harald Hardrada's son, and the sons of Harold.

2.1.2 The feudal system

Popular tradition and, indeed, legal historians speak of a 'feudal system' being imposed on England by William I. As with many national myths, the idea is simple, the reality much more complex.

Under the traditional model, William I took all the land in the realm into his ownership[3] and granted estates, known as fiefs, to his greater followers to hold from him as 'tenants-in-chief'. These owed the king homage and fealty – personal loyalty – together with the military service due in respect of their land. The tenants-in-chief then granted portions of that land to their own followers – their vassals – in return for homage and fealty, reserving that due to the king. Military service was owed only to the king, so that vassals of the tenants-in-chief were not obliged to serve their lords in rebellion. The tenants-in-chief fulfilled their military obligations not only by serving the king personally, but also by making their vassals available to serve in his armies. In practice, feudal landholders led retinues composed of their vassals in the service of the king when called upon. In addition to homage, fealty and military service, a feudal lord was entitled to receive payments known as 'reliefs' from his vassals on occasions such as the knighting of their eldest sons and the marriage of their eldest daughters, and when an heir came into possession of a fief. He was further entitled to payments known as 'aids' on the knighting of his own eldest son and the marriage of his eldest daughter.

The practice of 'subinfeudation', the grant of land by a feudal landholder to his followers, might take place at a number of levels. Not only did a tenant-in-chief grant land to his vassals, those vassals might then grant all or part of that land to their own vassals, in return again for homage and fealty, and performance of the military service owed to the king, and so on. At the lowest end of the feudal scale, a knight held an estate known as a knight's fee – sufficient to provide for one knight, his squire, horses and equipment – in return for 40 days' military service per year.

Various other forms of feudal land tenure existed. The church might hold land (termed its 'spiritualities') from the king and others on the basis of *frankalmoign* – free and perpetual alms, in prayers and masses for the grantor's soul. *Frankalmoign* was unique to the church, but both dioceses and religious houses also held land in return for homage and the military service of their lay vassals – the 'temporalities' of the church. Laymen, often men of less than knightly status, might hold land in *sergeantry*, in return for services which were not purely military. Such services took many forms; Henry II, clearly a poor sailor, gave one retainer land in sergeantry in return for holding the royal head during Channel crossings.

The ties created by the feudal system were personal, based on the oaths taken, and on the services due in person from the vassal to his lord. They were also reciprocal. Just as the vassal owed a duty of faith to his lord, so the lord had a twofold duty to his vassal: to protect him and his holding, and to exercise his feudal rights in a fair and just manner. If the lord did not, the vassal was entitled to withdraw his homage and fealty, an act known as *diffidatio*, as a prelude to armed rebellion, without suffering any penalty other than the loss of the lands he held from that lord. Equally, a feudal lord was entitled to resile from his ties to an unsatisfactory vassal. This principle extended

---

3   Even today, all land in England and Wales is owned by the Crown and an individual may only possess an *estate* or *interest* in land.

as far as the king; rebellion was not treason, as it would be in later centuries, provided the vassal had previously made *diffidatio*. Indeed, the history of the period shows that the great majority of baronial rebels were quickly restored to the king's favour once peace was achieved.

This concept of a Norman-imposed feudal system is, as with many things in history, an over-simplification. In particular, it is erroneous to suppose that feudalism in England was exclusively the creation of the Norman monarchs, and that previously, free Englishmen were now reduced to bondage. Long before 1066, every free man was bound to his lord by ties of personal loyalty, indistinguishable for practical purposes from homage and fealty, and many lords were granted powers of seignorial jurisdiction along with their land. Land other than bookland was granted by the king to his followers only for life, and the king required even holders of bookland to perform the *Trinoda Necessitas* of military service and construction of fortifications and bridges. Social structure before the Conquest was complex, including, at the lowest level, slaves, who were to disappear before 1200. There were *ceorls*, free peasants with their own land, who might rise to the rank of thegn if they acquired sufficient land, but also many categories of semi-free peasants, farming their lord's land and under his jurisdiction and protection. It seems likely that the position of the lower elements in society was little different in practice from that of their post-Conquest descendants.

In any event, 'pure' feudalism soon began to break down, if, indeed, it had ever existed. Land was frequently alienated from its original holder or his heirs by means outside the relationship of lord and vassal: through gifts, particularly to the church, marriage portions, mortgages, sales and leases. A system where land was held in return for military service was well-suited to a country where there were frequent domestic campaigns. However, domestic rebellions were relatively infrequent in England; most royal campaigning took place on the continent, or in Wales and Scotland, and there was considerable reluctance on the part of landholders in England to serve in these campaigns. It was to be a frequent complaint of magnates in conflict with successive kings from John onwards that they and their vassals were expected to serve on campaign outside England, something they argued was not part of the duties which they owed to the king. By 1100, landholders were increasingly commuting their service to payments of scutage ('shield money') or paying fines for their failure to serve. This money was then used by the king to hire mercenaries. Morillo makes a convincing case for the use of mercenary armies being a far more efficient means of servicing medieval warfare than reliance on feudal service, and that feudal service was resorted to on relatively rare occasions.[4] By the same time, fiefs were fast becoming hereditary, passing virtually automatically to the heirs of the original holder on payment of a relief.

2.1.3 Developments in government

Finance was, with the need to maintain the loyalty of the magnates, the greatest preoccupation of medieval kings. Not only did a king have to defend his land and subjects against both internal and external enemies, he was expected to show generosity to his followers and to the church, and to demonstrate his greatness (his 'majesty') by conspicuous display. This last requirement became more pronounced in

---

4   Morillo goes into considerable detail on the arguments of specialists in this field.

later centuries, being brought perhaps to its apogee by Henry VIII, but was never entirely absent.

Under 'normal' conditions, a king might be expected, at least in the early post-Conquest period, to maintain himself and his household and to fulfil the responsibilities of kingship from the profits of the lands he retained in his own hands – the royal *demesne* – together with the profits of royal justice and the incidents to which he was entitled under the feudal system. However, any extraordinary calls on royal resources, most obviously the demands of war, meant that revenue had to be raised by extraordinary means. Much of English constitutional history, as late as the 18th century, demonstrates very clearly that the periodic crises which the monarchy faced and which led to structural change in government came about to a considerable extent because of the financial exactions of kings, particularly before there was a proper separation between the king's government and his household. Over and over again, there is a direct causal link between the various stages in the development of the constitution and the pressure placed on kings to make concessions in return for the grant of extraordinary taxation.

Feudalism provided extensive sources of royal revenue for post-Conquest kings, and much baronial opposition in the period up to Magna Carta and after concerned the kings' excessive exploitation of the profits of the system. Reliefs had to be paid to the king by his tenants-in-chief before an heir could take possession of a fief. Wardships of heirs and heiresses – valuable since they carried control of the ward's land – were bought and sold, as were the marriages of heiresses and widows for the same reason. The lands of tenants-in-chief who died without heirs *escheated* – reverted to the crown.[5] Reliefs were payable for the knighting of sons and the marriage of daughters. Equally, the king, as the pinnacle of the feudal pyramid, was able to demand aids (*auxillia*) from his vassals on occasions such as the knighting of his eldest son and the marriage of his eldest daughter. Until the late 13th century, when other sources of revenue began to become available, the temptation for a king to obtain necessary funds by exploiting the profits of the feudal system and by demanding unprecedentedly high sums in scutages and fines was very strong, and it was this 'squeezing' of the magnates which was at the heart of the baronial grievances and which found expression in Magna Carta.

One source of income which survived from before 1066 was the old Danegeld, now known simply as *geld*, which was payable on the basis of assessed land values – Domesday Book was the official record of the assessment carried out in 1086. Interestingly, Morillo links the compilation of Domesday Book to William's need to raise and equip a large army for a major continental campaign which began in 1085.

2.1.4   The Norman takeover

The greatest change in the early Norman period was in personnel, and in much more vigorous assertion of royal power, through institutions whose origins pre-dated the Conquest but which evolved to meet changed needs. Power, which had devolved to earls under the Confessor, was once again centred on the person of the king, whose tenants-in-chief had no more power than he was prepared to give him. After 1076,

---

5   This concept still survives, in that the property of persons who die without a valid will and without heirs within the statutory rules of intestacy passes to the Crown.

internal threats to William's position came from his sons rather than his subjects, and in Normandy, not England.

By 1086, only two Englishmen held large estates as tenants-in-chief, though a number still held smaller holdings, particularly in Yorkshire. Englishmen had already been removed from political power. By 1070, only two English earls remained in office, and they too disappeared after rebelling in the ensuing years.[6] The great pre-Conquest earldoms were gradually replaced by smaller units, in strategic locations and under the control of the most trusted of William's followers. William's half-brother, Odo, Bishop of Bayeux, became Earl of Kent, with responsibility for defence against attack from across the Straits of Dover. Three new earldoms were created along the Welsh border, at Chester, Shrewsbury and Hereford, each facing one of the three main Welsh principalities. These and the earldom of Northumberland, controlling the Scottish march and much reduced in size from the old earldom of Northumbria, were all held by Normans from 1076. In this same period, William purged the English episcopate, in collusion with three papal legates who reached England in 1070. Archbishop Stigand and five bishops were deposed; continental churchmen closely tied with William were appointed to these vacancies and those arising from deaths. By 1076, only two English bishops remained in office.

English sheriffs were replaced by Normans, mostly drawn from the secondary level among William's followers rather than from the magnates. Their duties seem to have remained unchanged from the pre-Conquest period, apart from their holding authority over the royal castles in their shires. William and his sons sought to control the sheriffs by granting them office for limited periods, but this policy was only partially successful, the office tending to become hereditary.

In considering the impact of the Conquest, we should remember that until 1204, the primary focus of the activities of kings was on their continental domains. Rulers spent the bulk of their time across the Channel, occupying themselves with frequent continental wars and the putting-down of risings among those of their vassals who had remained in Normandy. This was so even though William sought to separate England from Normandy by giving the ancestral duchy to his eldest son, and England to the second. Therefore, apart from the need for change in personnel, the destruction of the pre-Conquest earldoms and the creation of new ones to meet changed circumstances, there was no pressing desire on William's part for institutional change. Provided England was secure from internal and external enemies, and moneys due to the king were properly paid, England could be left to be run by the institutions and in the manner which had developed under the native dynasty, albeit by trusted Normans rather than by Englishmen. However, the lengthy absences of kings from England and the increasing royal need for money to finance their continental operations meant that institutions had to evolve in order to operate more efficiently, to function in the absence of the king and, to some extent, to separate themselves from the person of the king and his itinerant court.

---

6   William's relative weakness in the first years after 1066 is made clear by his appointments to the earldom of Northumbria. Morcar seems to have been dispossessed in 1068, but William, rather than appointing a Norman to this most distant and turbulent of earldoms, allowed its purchase by Gospatric, a descendant of the 10th century earls with close ties to Malcolm III of Scots. Gospatric was involved in the risings of 1069–70, but was not finally ousted until 1072. His replacement, Waltheof, also participated in the risings of 1069–70, but was received back into the king's peace and given William's niece in marriage. He was hanged in 1076 after a further rebellion.

2.2   THE CONQUEROR'S SONS 1087–1135

2.2.1   William Rufus 1087–1100

On the death of William I in 1087, the English kingdom passed to his second son, William 'Rufus'. This choice of successor, passing over the claims of the eldest son, Robert, who became Duke of Normandy, is often interpreted as a demonstration of the Conqueror as treating England as his private estate, acquired by conquest and capable of being passed to whomsoever he chose, rather than as a kingdom whose succession traditions were to be followed. But it has already been noted that pre-Conquest succession practices were not solely based on primogeniture, and that there were precedents in England as well as on the continent for a division of lands between the sons of kings. All the same, the Conqueror's sons were avaricious; the administrative history of their reigns is mainly concerned with the maximising of royal revenues, and in this way, they did treat England as a private estate.

Rufus's reign is marked in the administrative sphere by extremes of avarice. The king was in constant need of revenue in order first to secure his throne in the face of rebellion from the supporters of Duke Robert, and then to prosecute his struggle against Robert for Normandy. This occupied most of the period 1089–96, when a settlement was reached in order to enable Robert to leave his duchy and go on crusade. Rufus exploited the profits of the feudal system to the fullest extent. During episcopal vacancies, the revenues of the lands of the bishopric were due to the crown. Rufus therefore allowed bishoprics to remain vacant for lengthy periods and, unprecedentedly, demanded feudal reliefs when new bishops were eventually appointed. Sheriffdoms were also bought and sold, and those families which already regarded a particular sheriffdom as their hereditary due were willing to pay large sums for the office.

All this was a logical extension of previous practice. However, Rufus did make one key innovation in government, foreshadowing the developments of the next reign. Ranulf Flambard acted as the king's agent in legal and financial affairs while Rufus was abroad or occupied with hunting. His office cannot be exactly defined, but it was similar to that of the justiciar, which emerged under Henry I, and involved the administration of vacant fiefs and ecclesiastical estates on behalf of the king, investigation of the rights and revenues of the king, and the supervision of sheriffs. Flambard, rewarded by Rufus with the rich bishopric of Durham (after a three-year vacancy), was a gifted administrator, and his efficiency in financial exactions led to his vilification by contemporary chroniclers.

This is not to say that Rufus's government involved a complete break with the past. Seriously ill in 1093 and believing himself to be dying, Rufus issued a charter pledging himself, if he recovered, to rule according to the good old laws of Edward the Confessor. When Flambard began work on the building of a wall around the White Tower in London, on Westminster Hall, and on the first stone bridge in London, he required the men of the area to carry out the traditional duties of 'bridge-work' 'wall-work' and 'fortress-work', part of the *Trinoda Necessitas* due to the king before 1066.

2.2.2   Henry I 1100–35

It was under Henry I, the youngest of the Conqueror's sons, that new institutions of royal administration emerged: the Exchequer and Chancery. Henry was as much in need of money as Rufus; the struggle with Duke Robert resumed on the latter's return from crusade in 1100, and continued until Robert's defeat and capture at the Battle of Tinchebrai in 1106.[7] Henry also spent much of his reign in strengthening his continental domains.

Henry gained his throne by a coup d'etat, following his brother's mysterious death while hunting in the New Forest on 2 August 1100.[8] Immediately upon the king's death, he forced its custodian to hand over the treasury, including the royal regalia, and rode hard for Westminster, where, having gained the support of the leading magnates in the vicinity, he was crowned on 5 August, with such haste that neither Archbishop was present.

Then, as in 1066, coronation made the king, but Henry remained anxious to secure the loyalty of the magnates at large and also of the English. He issued a coronation charter in which he undertook to re-establish the good old laws of the Confessor, as amended by William I, renounced the 'unjust oppressions' of his brother and vowed also to remedy a range of abuses of feudal custom which had been practised by Rufus. Concessions were made both to Normans and English. Knights, like barons, were exempted from geld on their own *demesne* – the land farmed by them directly rather then let to their peasants – and from wall-work, bridge-work and fortress-works. Freemen at large were granted a pardon for certain classes of debt owed to Rufus and an indemnity for unlawful acts committed during the interregnum between the two reigns. Here, although Henry was no more committed to observing the terms of his charter than Rufus had been to observing the pledges made from his sickbed in 1093, there is a formal acknowledgment that a king ought to rule justly and in accordance with existing law and practice, and that he should not exploit his realm and its people for his own purposes. Henry's charter retained its importance for a considerable period, forming the basis for the terms of Magna Carta. In a further harking back to the mythic golden age of Edward the Confessor, Henry took steps to strengthen his legitimacy in the eyes of his subjects by marrying the Confessor's nearest living female relation, Eadgyth, the daughter of Edgar the Atheling's sister, Margaret, who had married Malcolm III of Scotland.

For much of his reign, Henry followed a policy reminiscent of that of Cnut, promoting men of lesser rank within the nobility on the basis of their loyalty to him. The new administrative offices were largely in the hands of the clergy, not only because of their literacy, but because the offices were unlikely to become hereditary.[9]

---

7   Robert remained Henry's prisoner for the remainder of his life, dying only in 1134.

8   No contemporary writer accuses Henry of complicity in Rufus's death, which is attributed to an accident of a type then commonplace; indeed, another son of the Conqueror and an illegitimate son of Duke Robert had earlier been killed hunting in separate incidents in the same area. However, Rufus's death happened at a most fortuitous time for Henry, since Robert, recently married, was known to be on his way home from crusade. Fringe writers have identified Rufus as a member of a pagan cult which had survived underground from the pre-Christian era, and his death the sacrifice demanded of a king under that cult.

9   Clerical celibacy in this period was far from fully established, having only been decreed by Pope Gregory VII in the later years of the 11th century. Certain bishops were notorious for their neglect of their vows and promotion of their relations into high ecclesiastical and secular office. The very term 'nepotism' comes from the practices of bishops in seeking preferment for their 'nephews' – their illegitimate sons.

However, the bishops who held offices of state should not be thought of primarily as ecclesiastics, but as professional royal servants who received their sees and the associated revenues as rewards for their services.[10]

Like Cnut's earls, Henry's 'new men' were his creations. As under Cnut, such a system of patronage was successful provided there was a strong king to whom those creations felt a personal loyalty, but became a real threat to royal power and to the stability of the kingdom under a weaker successor. Indeed, some of the blame for the 'Anarchy' of the next reign can be laid squarely at Henry's door. By his favour to his nephew, Stephen, Count of Boulogne, he gave Stephen the power base from which he could seize the throne, and by his favour to Robert of Gloucester, the eldest and most able of his numerous bastards, the power base from which Gloucester could back Henry's legitimate daughter, Matilda, in the war for the crown.

2.2.3   Government under Henry I

In about 1109, Henry sought to deal with the practical problems of ruling an empire divided by the English Channel by creating a permanent royal administration in each of his domains under a resident 'justiciar', or chief minister, royal officials in England and Normandy being responsible to the appropriate justiciar as well as to the king. The justiciar's main spheres of activity were royal finance and royal justice, although his power in these spheres did not exist independently, but was delegated by the king; a justiciar was the king's viceroy rather than a minister in the modern sense.

Finance lay at the centre of royal government – indeed, the chief financial office was in the king's bedchamber. Day-to-day financial administration was in the hands of the Exchequer, which from 1116 seems to have functioned under the system described in the *Dialogus de Scaccario* ('Dialogue of the Exchequer'),[11] written under Henry II. Twice a year, at Easter and at Michaelmas, the Exchequer sat to audit the accounts of the sheriffs and certain other royal officials, and to settle disputes arising between those officials. A final reckoning took place at Michaelmas, when a summary account for each shire was recorded on a 'pipe' – two sheepskins sewn together – and the pipes for the entire country rolled up to form the Great Roll of the Exchequer – the Pipe Roll. A single pipe roll survives from Henry I's reign, and a virtually unbroken series from 1155 to 1837. In the same period, the royal secretariat operating from the king's chapel emerges into a recognisable chancery, though that chancery did not begin to emerge as a court of equity until the 14th century.

Royal administration in the shires, including the gathering of revenues and the preservation of the king's peace, remained the responsibility of the sheriffs. In most shires, there was a royal castle, in the charge of a royally-appointed castellan (often the sheriff) and this acted as a centre for royal administration as well as military strongpoint. As in pre-Conquest times, a number of mints existed in various parts of the country, often within the physical confines of royal castles, and always under strict royal control. Coin dies were issued centrally and replaced at regular intervals by new patterns. It is no accident that false coining was among those offences most severely

---

10   When more than 200 years later, Edward III appointed a layman to the chancellorship for the first time, he had to allow him an additional £500 per year to replace the episcopal revenues which previous chancellors had enjoyed.

11   EHD II No 70.

punished in the medieval period, with blinding and castration as the only alternative to execution, since the coinage bore the image of the king and was deeply symbolic of his royal authority.

2.2.4   Law and justice

The administration of justice and finance was closely linked. There was then no formal system of appeals from the decisions of non-royal courts applying feudal and customary law, whose full competence is unclear as no records survive. From 1109 to 1111, under the Ordinance of the Hundred, disputes concerning land held from different feudal lords were automatically referred to the shire courts rather than the seignorial courts, but it became increasingly usual for those who could afford it to seek justice from the king in other types of case. Since the king was frequently absent from England, and was anyway continuously on the move, it became convenient to seek justice in matters involving finance from the Exchequer, which was relatively static and soon became permanently based at Westminster, and whose officers had the necessary expertise in matters of feudal law. An Exchequer court thus emerged, presided over by the justiciar and consisting of about six bishops and barons who were not professional lawyers, but developed a competence in the areas of law with which they dealt, so that the Exchequer gradually acquired the authority of a regular court of justice.

The justiciar also sent parties of his colleagues into the shires on periodic 'general eyres'. Their duties were to investigate royal rights and the pleas of the crown that had been reserved to the royal courts since Cnut's reign: to hear common pleas – all other matters – at the request of the parties, and to levy fines for derelictions of royal duty. Here we see the origin of the system which still pertains today, under which High Court judges go into the provinces 'on circuit' to hear serious civil and criminal matters. That this delegation of judicial power to royal justices was popular is clear from the events of John's reign, when among the magnates' complaints was the difficulty in obtaining access to royal justices, who were few in number and virtually as itinerant as the king.

How laws were made remains unclear. At his crown-wearings, the king apparently consulted with his bishops and magnates, and seems to have gained their assent to new policies, but to what extent there was real discussion and consideration cannot be known. It is therefore unwise to see the Great Council, or colloquium, as these assemblies came to be known, as Parliament in embryo. The Great Council, to be sure, evolved gradually into a parliament, but this development came very much later. It is clear from future events, however, that the greater magnates regarded themselves, along with the bishops, as the companions and natural counsellors of the king, hence the intensity of opposition to the relatively low-born and foreign favourites who acquired the confidence of Henry III, Edward II and Richard II.[12]

---

12   See M McKisack, *The Fourteenth Century*, Oxford History of England, 1st edn, 1959, OUP, pp 19–20.

2.3   THE ANARCHY

Although some degree of separation of royal administration from the person of the king begins to appear under Henry I, the successful operation of royal government was heavily dependent on the individual king and on his ability to prevent excessive power from accruing to his magnates. Henry I proved an astute diplomatist in foreign affairs, and was very largely successful at keeping control of his baronage. However, events following his death demonstrate the essential weakness of a system so dependent on the strength and personality of the king.

Henry's only legitimate son drowned in the sinking of the White Ship in November 1120. Despite a second marriage in 1121, Henry was unsuccessful in his attempts to beget another male heir, eventually taking the unprecedented step of naming his daughter, Matilda, as his heir. At New Year 1127, he required his tenants-in-chief to swear that if no other son was born to him, they would on his death recognise her as ruler (*domina*) of England.

In the climate of 900 years later, it is difficult fully to appreciate the momentousness of Henry's decision. No woman had ever reigned in western Europe unchallenged, and none was to do so for another three centuries.[13] Moreover, Matilda, widow of the Holy Roman Emperor Heinrich V, was unpopular with the Anglo-Norman baronage and childless after 11 years of marriage, casting doubt on her ability to bear further heirs. She was married in 1128 to Geoffrey, Count of Anjou, and eventually had three sons, but the first, the future Henry II, was not born until 1133. This makes it unlikely that Henry intended in 1127 to allow the English crown to pass to Matilda's husband and thence to her sons, in accordance with ordinary feudal law. However, there was a distinct absence of viable alternatives. None of Henry's numerous bastards seems to have been considered. Henry's elder brother, Duke Robert, was now in his 70s and had been Henry's prisoner since 1106; his son, William 'Clito', was making war on Henry in Normandy.[14] There remained only Henry's two other nephews, the sons of his sister Adela. One appears to have had no interest whatever in England, but the other, Stephen, Count of Boulogne, lavishly endowed with lands and honours in England, seems to have regarded himself as Henry's natural successor.

On Henry's death in Normandy on 1 December 1135, Stephen crossed rapidly to England, and pre-empted any assertion of power by Matilda by, in a manner similar to that of his uncle a generation earlier, seizing the royal treasury and having himself crowned as king. Like Harold II, Stephen claimed that the old king had on his deathbed chosen him to be his successor. For a period, he was able to establish himself on the throne, gaining the support of the bulk of the magnates and even satisfying Pope Innocent II that he was Henry I's legitimate successor. However, a series of disputes culminating in his attempt to deprive the justiciar, Roger, Bishop of Salisbury,

---

13 A number of women were named as heirs by their fathers during the medieval period, but in practice as a temporary measure pending the birth of male heirs. In the few cases where a woman attempted to gain possession of the throne, civil war was the norm. A contemporaneous example was Urraca of Castile (1109–26), most of whose reign was taken up with war against the supporters of her second husband, Alfonso I of Aragon, and of her son. The first woman to establish herself as a ruler was Isabella of Castile (1474–1504), in circumstances where there were no male heirs, and then only after a civil war.

14 He died in 1128 from wounds received in rebellion against Henry.

of his lands and honours in 1139 led a significant portion of the magnates, including Robert of Gloucester, Henry's eldest bastard, to support Matilda in a bid for the throne.

The triggers for the rising against Stephen seem largely to have involved self-seeking on behalf of the magnates, and the threat to their position and privileges manifested by Stephen's attack on Bishop Roger. If Matilda gained the throne, those who supported her could expect to be richly rewarded. Further, a woman ruler might be expected to be more pliable than a man, although Matilda's known character militates against this. Alternatively, the throne might have passed to Matilda's son, Henry, then six years old, and a long minority would give further opportunities for baronial aggrandisement.

Yet, ultimately, can we see a concern over Stephen's 'throneworthiness'? Stephen was a brave and chivalrous man, and had in full measure the generosity so admired of kings at that time, as well as great personal charm, but he was unable to maintain the loyalty of his followers, to inspire the awe necessary to bend them to his will and to discourage them from taking arms against him, and he was entirely lacking in the ruthlessness and lack of scruple required of a successful medieval king.

The political history of the period from 1139 to 1153 is of the ebb and flow of power between Stephen and Matilda, and little evidence survives of the pattern of royal government in this period. For a period in 1141, Stephen was Matilda's prisoner; she occupied London and made preparation for her coronation, which would transform her from *Domina Anglorum*, the uncrowned Lady of the English, to Queen ordained by God. However, Matilda's own arrogance led the people of London to drive her out, she never again regained such a strong position, and intermittent war dragged on for another 12 years. Stephen's brother, Theobald of Blois, who had assumed power in Normandy without opposition on Henry I's death, was gradually overcome by Matilda's husband, Geoffrey of Anjou. After the death of his heir in August 1153, the fight seems to have gone out of Stephen, and a peace settlement was finally brokered between the two sides. Stephen would remain king for his lifetime, but on his death, the crown would pass to Matilda's son, Henry, now emerging as a considerable figure in his own right.

2.4   HENRY II 1154–89

Royal government under Stephen was to a considerable extent a nullity, though the description of '19 long winters' when 'Christ and His saints slept'[15] reflects only the situation in East Anglia. Magnates took advantage of the weakness at the centre to settle old scores against neighbours, to build 'adulterine' castles and to sell their loyalties to the highest bidder, but royal administration remained intact in the areas which Stephen controlled. The Exchequer system and issue of coinage continued; sheriffs and royal justices carried out their duties. However, large areas were, intermittently at least, quite outside royal control, and after 1138, Stephen never regained any firm authority over the magnates. The centralised system of coinage,

---

15   ASC E 1154. This manuscript of the Anglo-Saxon Chronicle, which was last written up for this year, was produced at Peterborough, which lay in the area most affected by the depredations of such magnates as Geoffrey de Mandeville, Earl of Essex.

with the issue of standard official dies from London, broke down after 1140; some mints issued coins in the name of Stephen, others in the name of Matilda, and still others in the names of Rufus and Henry I. Following his accession, Henry II had therefore to rebuild royal power and to re-establish a firm structure of government, but not only did he restore the systems which had emerged under his grandfather; he developed and extended them.

Stephen died on 25 October 1154. Henry, unlike his immediate predecessors, seems not to have been in any particular hurry to claim his inheritance, not landing in England until 8 December. This in itself indicates that the strife of Stephen's reign was now over, and the peace reached a year earlier not under threat. Henry was fortunate that most of the main protagonists of the civil war had now died, and that he was the first king since 1066 to succeed without a dynastic rival. As a descendant of the native dynasty through his maternal grandmother, he could claim the loyalties of the English as well as the Normans. But England was in disorder, the adulterine castles which had sprung up in many parts of the country could be held against the king for lengthy periods, a number of royal castles were held by magnates with no particular loyalty to any king, and he himself was a virtual stranger in this country.

However, Henry was a man peculiarly well-equipped to develop as well as restore royal power. Along with intelligence, he possessed enormous physical energy, as is attested by many chroniclers' anecdotes. He was well educated for a layman of his time, an experienced soldier and had profited from observing the events of Stephen's reign. With these good qualities, he had many faults. He was rash, he was devoid of patience, he was subject to ungovernable outbursts of temper; his actions towards his wife and sons led to their repeated rebellions against him. These characteristics recurred repeatedly in his descendants and were attributed by contemporaries to the alleged descent of the Counts of Anjou from the Devil. Nevertheless, Henry can fairly be considered a great king in his day, extending his personal power from Ireland to the Auvergne, from the Cheviots to the Pyrenees, and placing royal government on so firm a footing that it could flourish not only during his own absences abroad, but also under his successor, Richard I, an absentee for all but seven months of his 10 year reign.

However, Henry's assertion of royal power, continued and extended under his sons, particularly John, brought about a collision between the king on the one hand and elements in the church and the magnates on the other. This led to the first cogent attempt to define and limit the king's power, and to subject the king both to existing law – or his opponents' conception of existing law – and to an enforcement mechanism for that law. The threat to Henry II's throne came from his sons and their allies in attempts to gain power. In the 13th century, we see attempts to curb royal power, to subject the king's actions to external scrutiny and even control, and the beginnings of a re-emergence of the pre-Conquest idea that an unworthy king might be deposed.

2.4.1   Henry II and government

Henry was initially concerned with gaining military control over his English and continental possessions, and neutralising possible foci of opposition. Not for some years did he turn his attention to changes in government and administration. In his coronation charter, he promised to uphold the liberties and customs which his grandfather had approved and to avoid those bad customs which his grandfather had condemned. Like Henry I, he appointed justiciars in both England and Normandy, and had his tenants-in-chief do homage to his heir.

It was not until the early 1160s, after he had secured his dominions, that Henry's programme of administrative change began in earnest. However, he did not make any revolutionary changes. Like his grandfather, he recreated and improved the system developed earlier. In particular, he strengthened the administration of royal justice and left as his legacy a governmental system which was able to function in the absence of an effective ruler. Never again would royal government cease to function as it had under Stephen; after 1154, the issue in times of weak rule was who controlled that government.

Henry, like his predecessors, sought to maximise royal revenue, seeking new sources of money as well as exploiting existing ones. Geld, levied only on land, was largely superseded by *dona* (gifts) and *auxilia* (aids) demanded from specific groups within Anglo-Norman society: from the shires, cities and boroughs, the sheriffs and the Jews.[16] These sums could be very substantial; in 1159, aids were demanded from bishops and abbots, five being assessed at 500 marks apiece. Tax was still levied on the basis of land assessments – scutage typically at one or two marks per knight's fee – but the Saladin Tithe of 1188 was levied in addition on 'moveables', assets other than land. This precedent was increasingly followed by later kings.

By the Inquest of Sheriffs of 1170, the king attempted to tighten royal control over local administration by removing virtually all the sheriffs from office, appointing commissioners to enquire into their conduct by seeking information from local freemen on oath. Those sheriffs permitted to remain in office were required to renew their oaths of allegiance to Henry and his heir, and to pay large sums into the Exchequer.

2.4.2 Developments in the law

As well as seeking to maximise the profits of royal justice, Henry was anxious to make the system more efficient, particularly the criminal law. Under Cnut's laws, all males over the age of 10 were organised into *tithings*, each responsible for the good behaviour of its members, a system known as *frankpledge*. However, the social pressures exerted by the tithing and by the church did not prevent serious criminal offences from occurring, and those who committed offences could be dealt with by one of several courts. There were manorial and other seignorial courts, under the control of the feudal lord; church courts, dealing mainly with offences against morality or committed by the clergy; and the king's courts, those shire and hundred courts which had survived from the pre-Conquest period. Further, offences committed in the large areas of the country under the special forest law created by William I were dealt with in specific forest courts. All this multiplicity of jurisdictions, and the differences in the law they applied, created inconsistency both in procedure

---

16 Jews at this time were under the king's protection. Since they were forbidden to hold land or to participate in conventional trades, the only occupation open to them was money lending, forbidden to Christians. They were required to pay dearly for the king's protection and, given that the king was every Jew's heir, and could therefore profit from the debts owed after that Jew's death, they formed an extremely lucrative source of revenue.

and punishment. This was particularly so in the case of the church courts, which extracted spiritual penalties only, mainly penances.

The changes introduced in the reign of Henry II reflect his desire for speed, efficiency and consistency in the administration of justice, and represent a movement away from the traditional practices of proof by oath and ordeal towards proof by investigation. The jury became a more significant body in England in his reign, but it should be made clear that the 12th century jury bore little resemblance to that of today. It was an evidentiary and investigative rather than a decision-making body, not required to give a verdict on the basis solely of the evidence put before it. It gave its verdict on the basis either of the prior knowledge of its members or evidence uncovered by its investigations. It did so in both criminal and civil matters, being particularly prominent in investigations ordered by Henry II and successive kings into matters of concern, such as corruption among royal officials. However, unlike the traditional oath-helpers, the jurors were not summoned by the parties, but by royal officials with, in theory at least, no personal interest in the case, and therein lay its main advantage.

The role of royal justice in relation to the criminal law was strengthened after 1166 with the establishment of regular assize circuits in the shires. Royal justices henceforth travelled from place to place by defined routes. Increasingly, royal justice was exercised by the king's servants rather than by the king in person. Not only was royal justice therefore more available, but royal authority in the shires was strengthened, and a separation was beginning to develop between the person of the king and his power and authority.

The role of royal justice was also considerably increased in civil matters, particularly in disputes over land. Again, we see emphasis on speed and efficiency, though quite possibly at the expense of ascertaining the truth. Land disputes, by their nature, tended to be lengthy, and slowness was further encouraged by the procedures used, which were derived from French models and designed to persuade the parties to settle. Final judgment was in the hands of God, through the ordeal by battle, a judicial duel introduced by the Normans, though by the Grand Assize of 1179, Henry gave the defendant in such actions the option of having the matter determined conclusively by a jury of 12 knights.

The major innovation in this sphere was the introduction of the 'Petty Assizes', a summary procedure by which a recently-dispossessed plaintiff could be restored to his land (*novel disseisin*), an heir could gain possession of lands seized by another on his father's death (*mort d'ancestor*) and a landholder could establish that he had last appointed a priest to a particular benefice, and was therefore entitled to do so again (*darrein presentment*). The Petty Assizes differed from the established system in two significant ways. First, they were concerned with possession rather than ownership as such. Under *novel disseisin*, for example, the plaintiff merely had to prove that he had been in possession of the disputed land and had been unlawfully ejected, not that he was the person lawfully entitled to that land. Second, the procedure was designed to avoid delay; the parties were required to appear before the king's justices at the Exchequer or the justices in eyre on the appointed day, and a verdict was given by a jury of 12 neighbours on the basis of knowledge and investigation.[17]

---

17 It is perhaps not going too far to see an early precursor of the Woolf Reforms in civil justice introduced in 1999 and designed to streamline and speed up the processes of civil litigation by, *inter alia*, giving the courts greater control over the conduct of the proceedings.

These and other changes introduced under Henry II mark a significant stage in the gradual process by which the administering of justice became a prerogative of the king alone, and the real origin of the common law. From this time, the matters within the ambit of the non-royal courts gradually diminished in importance, because certain matters became reserved to the king's courts, and the increasing availability of royal justice, both in terms of its scope and its practical availability, meant litigants increasingly chose to seek justice from the king's courts. At the same time, law became increasingly defined. Henry II's various assizes represent the first official legislative documents since the Norman Conquest, and cover both substantive and procedural matters, with particular emphasis on procedure.

2.5   MONARCHS AND THE CHURCH

The close association between kings and the church continued in the last years of the Anglo-Saxon period and beyond. The protection of the church was among the most important of the king's duties and continued to be included in his coronation oath. Many monasteries were royal foundations and all were the objects of rich gifts from successive kings and their magnates. Bishops were to a considerable extent royal appointees, and even when appointed by other means, their appointment was in practice approved by the king. The position was similar in continental Europe.

However, from the mid-11th century, the papacy, long sunk in internal corruption, re-asserted itself, sought to reform the church from within and, in particular, to separate the church from secular control. The church should be subject only to God and His Pope. This movement, spearheaded by popes such as Gregory VII, came into direct conflict with the ambition of successive rulers, both in England and on the continent, who sought to increase their own power and made extensive use of the senior clergy in royal administration. This came to a head in England in the lengthy dispute between Henry II and Thomas Becket.

The strengthening of royal authority was at the heart of the changes wrought by Henry II, and nowhere is this more apparent than in his dispute with Becket, whom he appointed as Archbishop of Canterbury in 1162. Becket was one of the rising class of professional royal servants and already held office as Henry's chancellor, responsible for the king's chancery, which had by this period grown from the secretariat of earlier years into a major office of royal administration. By appointing his trusted servant and personal friend who, scandalously, was not even an ordained priest, as Archbishop, Henry sought to increase his authority over the church. In particular, he sought to end the abuse by which the clergy and, indeed, anyone who could claim 'benefit of clergy' – which might mean no more than being able to recite the Lord's Prayer – were outside the scope of royal justice. However, this policy was a complete failure. Becket resigned the chancellorship on his appointment as Archbishop. He refused to accept the Constitutions of Clarendon of 1164, drawn up by Henry as a purported statement of the traditional relationship between church and state in England, and went into exile. Henry petitioned the Pope for his deposition, but Pope Alexander III threw his weight behind Becket.

A precarious peace was achieved in the summer of 1170, mainly because Henry required a compliant Archbishop and the approval of the Pope in order to crown his eldest son in his own lifetime to ensure the succession. But Becket's continued high-handed behaviour following his restoration to Canterbury brought about his death. At Henry's Christmas crown-wearing in Normandy, the king was moved by fury to denounce any of his followers who refused to silence Becket: 'Will no man rid me of this turbulent priest!' Henry had in full measure the famous Angevin temper, and many similar utterances had doubtless passed without reaction, but four knights took him at his word, crossed to England, forced their way into Canterbury Cathedral as Becket was celebrating Vespers on 29 December 1170 and murdered him at the foot of the high altar.

2.6   ENGLAND AND HER NEIGHBOURS

The relationship between England, Scotland and Wales was uncertain and fluctuating. English kings as far back as Edward the Elder had periodically gained the 'submission' of Welsh and Scottish rulers, but what this entailed is unclear. By the 11th century, English influence in both territories was growing, and the process continued in the Norman period.

2.6.1   Scotland

Scotland was not a single entity, although its mainland was nominally under the rule of one king from 1034, when Duncan I, previously ruler of Strathclyde, succeeded Malcolm II, who had held sway over the Lothians, Dalriada (roughly Argyllshire), Fife and Pictland. Orkney and Shetland were held by the Norwegian crown until the 14th and 15th centuries respectively. The Hebrides, Caithness and Sutherland had been settled in the 10th century by Norsemen and also did not accept the authority of the King of Scots until much later. In addition, Galloway, theoretically part of the Scottish kingdom, enjoyed virtual independence until well into the 12th century.

Until the time of Malcolm II (1005–34), the Scottish throne had passed not from father to son, but alternately between different branches of the royal dynasty. Malcolm II named Duncan I (1034–40), his grandson, as his heir, but Macbeth, heir according to traditional usage, later seized the crown. The position of Duncan's son, Malcolm III, who gained his throne in 1057 by dispossessing Macbeth with English aid, was initially insecure. Later, with the main focus of their power in Fife and the Lothians, Malcolm and his successors sought to extend their possessions as far south as the Tyne, leading to recurrent war in the frontier area. William I was unable to deal with Malcolm until 1072, when he mounted an expedition as far north as Abernethy on the Tay, where Malcolm submitted, did homage and gave William his eldest son, Duncan, as a hostage. This submission formed the basis of later English claims that Scotland was held by successive kings as a fief of the English Crown.

Malcolm did homage during William's reign to Robert Curthose as William's heir, but did not do homage to William Rufus until 1091, following a second punitive expedition. By this date, Malcolm held lands in England and it was to be argued in the future that the homage of successive Scottish kings was in respect only of those lands, not their kingdom.[18] Rufus also expelled Dolfin, who had been ruling Cumbria as the Scottish king's vassal, so re-asserting English claims in the north. Two years later, Malcolm complained that Rufus had broken their treaty. Negotiations for a peaceful settlement fizzled out, and on 13 November 1093, in the course of another raid into Northumbria, Malcolm was ambushed and killed near Alnwick, along with his eldest son by his second marriage, whom he had earlier named as his heir.

Malcolm's death prompted a succession crisis. His younger brother, Donald Bane, seized the throne, only to be ousted the following year by Duncan, Malcolm's eldest son, with Norman aid. Confusion followed. Duncan was killed; Donald Bane temporarily regained power with the support of another of his nephews, and it was not until 1097 that Edgar, the fourth of Malcolm's sons by St Margaret, was able to establish himself as the Scottish king. He and the two brothers who succeeded him, Alexander I (1100–25) and David I (1125–53), had both spent periods at the English court and held lands in England as feudal vassals of the English king.

Norman influence, which had had its tentative beginnings under Malcolm, then spread increasingly into the southern half of Scotland as David I in particular made extensive grants of land to members of families such as that of Bruce; Robert de Brus I, lord of Skelton in Cleveland, was granted the lordship of Annandale in 1124. Thereafter, the same man frequently held land in both Scotland and England, and it was not until the Scottish wars of Edward I that families split into English and Scottish branches. This was an important factor in the emergence of royal administration in Scotland on the model developing in England. However, David's death in 1153 was followed by another Celtic reaction and disputed succession, and the new king, David's 12 year old grandson, Malcolm IV, 'the Maiden'[19] (1153–66) was still insecure on his throne when, in 1157, Henry II sought his submission. Henry was able to extract a high price for friendship and required Malcolm to do homage.

Events in 1173–74 allowed Henry to strengthen his claims of overlordship over Scotland. William 'the Lion', who succeeded Malcolm IV, was captured at Alnwick whilst a party to the rebellion of Henry's three eldest sons against their father. By the Treaty of Falaise of December 1174, William gained his freedom at the price of doing public homage for Scotland and all his other lands, and surrendering five castles in Scotland to Henry's nominees. Here was the unequivocal homage for the Scottish kingdom itself which Henry's great-grandson, Edward I, was able to rely on 120 years later when he intervened in Scotland's search for a king after the death of Alexander III.

2.6.2 Wales

Wales was not even nominally a single entity, but a land of several principalities, which fluctuated in extent and importance under individual rulers. Under Edward the Confessor, the growing power of Gruffydd ap Llywelyn, ruler of Gwynedd and Powys, who came to dominate most of Wales, led to war in the marches. Hereford

---

18 In feudal law, there is no difficulty about this concept. A man might hold land of several lords, owing homage and fealty to each of them. There was nothing to prevent one king from holding lands of another; successive Kings of England did homage to Kings of France for their continental lands, including Normandy. A kingdom might be held as a fief; the Norman Kings of Sicily held the island and parts of the Italian mainland as a fief of the papacy.

19 So called because he was young and unmarried, not because of any lack of masculinity.

was sacked in 1055 and Worcestershire ravaged in 1062, but a brilliantly executed campaign by Earls Harold and Tostig in 1063 brought about Gruffydd's death. His head was sent to the Confessor, his ancestral lands divided between two kinsmen, and the rest of the Welsh principalities restored to their former rulers.

After 1066, Norman magnates, the 'Marcher lords', carved out territories for themselves along the Welsh border and in much of South Wales with the approval of successive kings, who accepted that a complete conquest of Wales was not a realistic possibility. However, care had to be taken to avoid the accretion of too much power in the hands either of a single Welsh prince, or of the Marcher lords themselves, whose territories enjoyed a high degree of legal and practical independence until the 16th century. The power of the Welsh princes remained weak until Owain of Gwynedd came to prominence in the mid-12th century, and affairs in Wales were largely left in the hands of the Marcher lords. But, early in Henry's reign, Owain was at the height of his power and a punitive expedition was required before he was persuaded to submit and give hostages.

2.6.3 Ireland

Ireland was another land of petty principalities, its kings sometimes acknowledging, sometimes not, the precarious High Kingship of the King of Connacht. Little outside attention was paid to Ireland, except by the Norsemen, who established Dublin and other coastal towns, until 1155, when Adrian IV, the only English Pope, issued Henry II with the Bull *Laudabiliter*, authorising him to conquer Ireland in order to bring reform to its church. Henry was preoccupied with other matters and the powers granted by the Bull remained unexercised until 1171, by which time, a number of Henry's vassals, principally among the Marcher lords, had established new lordships in Ireland, following a request for aid by the King of Leinster, Dermot MacMorrough, who had earlier been driven out by his own people. Anxious to prevent these magnates from gaining too much power and to restore himself to the Pope's favour after Becket's murder by appearing to deal with the abuses in the Irish church, Henry landed in Ireland in 1171, extracted homage and fealty from the Anglo-Norman magnates, and persuaded the native chieftains to become his vassals in return for his protection. He then returned to England and left Ireland, with its unruly and quarrelsome combination of native chiefs and feudal magnates of Anglo-Norman origin, to its own devices, setting the pattern of English involvement in Ireland for the next 400 years.

In 1185, Henry gave the title Lord of Ireland (*Dominus Hiberniae*) to his youngest son, John, and sent him to Ireland to be crowned. John, by his foolish behaviour and that of his followers, attracted the opposition of the Irish to such an extent that he was forced into ignominious retreat before any coronation could take place. Future English kings all claimed dominion over Ireland, and Lord of Ireland as one of their titles. However, they intervened in Irish affairs only at occasional intervals – after John's expedition in 1210, no English king set foot in the country until Richard II in 1394 – and exercising their influence through their appointed lieutenants, who were either absentees or Norman-Irish magnates themselves.

CHAPTER 3

MAGNA CARTA AND ITS GENESIS 1189–1216

3.1   THE SIGNIFICANCE OF MAGNA CARTA

> … There is no mention in Magna Carta of Parliament or representation of any but the
> baronial class. The great watchwords of the future here find no place. The actual charter
> is a redress of feudal grievances extorted from an unwilling king by a discontented
> ruling class insisting on its privileges …
>
> Magna Carta must not, however, be dismissed lightly … If the 13th century magnates
> understood little and cared less for popular liberties or parliamentary democracy, they
> had, all the same, laid hold of a principle which was to be of prime importance for the
> future development of English society and English institutions. Throughout the
> document it is implied that here is a law which is above the king and which he must not
> break.[1]

Winston Churchill's words embody many truths about Magna Carta, but ignore its
central paradox: that although the king was subject to the law, only the king had
power to make law, so that King John could subordinate himself to the law which he
and his predecessors had made, but he could amend that law.[2] Indeed, he sought to
do so in order to nullify Magna Carta in the 16 months that remained of his reign after
he set his seal to the charter. Not for many years after 1215 did a power to make laws
independently of the king develop. Magna Carta marked the beginning of this
development, but legislative power remained firmly in the king's hands, so that it
represents terms conceded by John, not a democratic structure which circumscribed
his powers and those of his heirs.

Nonetheless, Magna Carta is a seminal document in the constitutional history of
the English-speaking world. Its importance, however, lies not in its written terms,
since it is a product of its times, of the forces which led to its production and of the
specific feudal milieu of the day. It can in no sense be seen as an early European
Convention on Human Rights, nor as the product of any idealism, save to the small
degree inserted into it by Archbishop Langton. Neither is it anything other than an
essentially conservative document, harking back to a semi-mythic era when kings did
not abuse their feudal privileges, and seeking to compel John to act within the law as
it was believed to be. The bulk of its clauses deal with the narrow grievances of John's
baronial and clerical opponents in 1215. Only two are general statements of principle,
and even these were narrower in scope than is assumed today. The council of 'twenty-
five overkings' predicated by Magna Carta lasted only briefly, the charter as a whole
was annulled by Pope Innocent III within weeks of its granting, and the full-scale civil
war which it was intended to prevent erupted shortly after.

The importance of Magna Carta lies in its symbolic significance, its philosophy
that the king's power is not unrestrained, but is circumscribed by the law, and that the
law can be enforced over the wishes of a king who seeks to evade it. It was re-issued
on several occasions in the 13th century as a statement of the limits of the king's

---

1   WS Churchill, *A History of the English-Speaking Peoples*, vol I, 1956, Cassell, pp 200–01.
2   Professor JC Holt in discussion with the author.

power, most frequently at the behest of kings themselves, much as their 12th century predecessors had issued coronation charters, but on occasion at the demand of the magnates. It came to be relied on by the landed opponents of successive kings as a statement of the basic liberties of those landholders and of the limits of the king's power over them.

From around the end of the 14th century, Magna Carta largely disappears from political view, having been overtaken by later developments and the slow growth of a representative parliament. It was studied by students of the Inns of Court in the 15th century, the first translations into English dating from this period, but had by then ceased to be of interest to non-lawyers. Shakespeare's *King John*, conventionally dated to 1595–96, deals with the strife between John and his nephew, Arthur, and Arthur's disappearance and death. Magna Carta, now regarded as the climax of John's reign, is wholly absent. However, commentators seeking to condemn the actions of James I and Charles I, who placed their own construction on its statements of general principle, elevated this essentially feudal document to the position of cornerstone of English liberty that it has never lost in national consciousness.

The genesis of Magna Carta has both long term and short term elements. Its short term background lies in the political events of John's reign: his alienation of his tenants-in-chief, quarrel with the papacy and ultimate capitulation to Innocent III, harsh treatment of his foes, unceasing financial exactions, and repeated military failures, which meant that not only had the money he forced out of his vassals been frittered away in useless campaigning, but that John was unable to inspire the trust and confidence of his magnates. The long term causes involve the increasing restlessness and hostility of the magnates in the face of increasingly efficient royal government from 1154 onwards. Under Henry II and Richard I, both strong and militarily successful kings, this hostility was prevented from developing into full-scale rebellion, but under John, hostility developed into civil war with the aim of replacing him as king with the son of his lifelong enemy, Philip Augustus of France.

3.2   THE REIGN OF RICHARD I

Henry II died on 6 July 1189, broken-hearted at the treachery of John, his youngest and favourite son, who had joined with his elder brother, Richard, in the last of a succession of filial rebellions. Born in 1157, Richard I (1189–99)[3] was from the age of 14 Duke of Aquitaine, the ancestral possession of his mother's family. This sprawling southern French duchy was his spiritual home and, with his other continental possessions, the major focus of his activities. In a reign of a little less than 10 years, he spent a total of seven months in England. His concerns then were to secure the government of the realm and to raise revenues for his campaigns.

Richard's reputation, in his own time and posthumously, is based on his military prowess, in particular as a crusader. In no sense was he an innovator in the constitutional sphere, except in creating the office of coroner, though even this development probably reflected his desire for money rather than any great concern for the administration of justice. However, he cast a long shadow over his successor. The

---

3   The fullest account of Richard's life and reign is to be found in J Gillingham, *Richard I*, Yale English Monarchs Series, 1999, Yale UP.

crisis which came to a head in Magna Carta 16 years after his death was in no small part the result of his actions, and the opprobrium in which John was held in his own time and later is due in considerable measure to his poor performance in the military sphere in comparison with Richard. Whether Richard would have been able to hold the continental domains which John lost is a question which cannot be answered, but it is perhaps fortunate for Richard's reputation that he died at the height of his powers.

What is not in doubt is that royal administration had developed sufficiently by his accession to allow it to function in the absence of the king, though events were to show that suitable appointments to the greater offices were of crucial importance in ensuring that this delegation of power was successful. Power remained closely linked to personality. Richard's initial appointee as viceroy rapidly aroused the enmity of the magnates and had to be removed from office, though the actions of the cabal which acted against William Longchamp went no further than replacing him with a more acceptable successor; they did not strike at the structure of royal government, but only against its officers as individuals.

3.2.1 Government under an absent king

Henry II had spent 21 of the 35 years he reigned outside England, so lengthy absences on the part of the king were hardly unprecedented. What was unique about Richard's absence on crusade was the distance he put between himself and his kingdom. Both Henry I and Henry II appointed justiciars to act as their viceroys in England and Normandy, but the comparatively short distances involved made it possible for them to keep in regular contact with their ministers. A journey between England and the Holy Land occupied many months and considerable dangers; Richard's ministers were in practice free agents, constrained by their own consciences rather than by the king's power and force of personality.

Richard was unmarried at his accession, and he was to remain without legitimate children. Moreover, he and all his legitimate brothers had at various times been in rebellion against their father, even at precociously early ages,[4] and had campaigned against one another in addition, so that the loyalty of the last survivor and of other relations could not be relied upon during his absence. An attempt by one of them on his throne and continental domains was a real possibility, the more so since succession law was not in any way settled. There were three potential heirs who, in Richard's absence, were potential usurpers: John, the youngest of Henry II's legitimate sons; Arthur, the posthumous son of Henry's third son, Geoffrey, Duke of Brittany, killed in a tournament in 1186; and another Geoffrey, a bastard son of Henry II who, with John, seems to have posed the most obvious threat, notwithstanding his irregular birth.

Richard attempted to neutralise both John and Geoffrey, providing John with a source of independent wealth in the form of the revenues of five English counties and marriage to the country's richest heiress, and forcing Geoffrey to accept the archbishopric of York. A priest could not be a king, and so forcible tonsure was used on occasions in the Middle Ages as a convenient and merciful means of thwarting the ambitions of dynastic rivals. Both were required to abjure the realm for three years,

---

4   Richard had taken a leading role in the rebellion of 1173–74 at the age of 15, and his brother Geoffrey at 14.

the expected length of Richard's absence. Arthur, an infant, was left in the wardship of his Breton relations. In administration, Richard attempted to divide and rule. Justiciars were appointed in each of his dominions and England was sub-divided into two justiciarships; William Longchamp, already Richard's chancellor and now consecrated Bishop of Ely, was given authority south of the Trent, and Hugh du Puiset, Bishop of Durham, in the north.

Richard's crusade was largely financed by the sale of public offices. All sheriffdoms were declared vacant and offered to the highest bidder – not infrequently, the most recent office-holder. It is no coincidence that a number of historic English towns received their charters from Richard, since town charters were also available at a price. Richard, like his father, also made full use of his feudal prerogatives in the raising of revenue, and those of his vassals who had earlier taken crusaders' vows but now had second thoughts were given the opportunity to buy off their obligations for appropriately large sums.

3.2.2   Crisis

These arrangements rapidly broke down, and power became concentrated into too few hands. The two justiciars soon came into conflict, and from June 1190, Longchamp was simultaneously sole justiciar, chancellor, papal legate and bishop of one of the country's richest sees, thereby holding every office necessary for supreme power. He seems in fact to have remained loyal to Richard, but his rapid rise to a position of unprecedented power from relatively humble beginnings, his efficiency in extorting money on behalf of the King, his favouritism towards his relations and a certain heavy-handedness in dealing with the magnates aroused intense hostility among those English barons – the great majority – who had remained in England. Longchamp was also a Norman of Normandy, and in the hostility towards him, we see an early flickering of the dislike of prominent foreigners which was to become a significant factor in the opposition to later kings.

In defiance of his oath to abjure the realm, Richard's brother John returned to England before April 1191 and rapidly established himself at the head of the opposition to Longchamp. The justiciar lasted a further six months before being deposed on 7 October 1191 by a cabal of bishops and barons led by Richard's envoy, Walter of Coutances, Archbishop of Rouen.[5] However, the cabal went beyond the king's instructions to Coutances, and their actions show some features which were to emerge with more force in Magna Carta. At a meeting on 8 October, they took an oath of fealty to Richard and ordained 'by the common deliberation of the king's vassals' that John should be regent and Coutances justiciar. Further, John was to be Richard's heir should he die childless.

Here we see for the first time the king's magnates acting semi-independently of the king to remove a servant of the king whose loyalty was not in doubt, to replace him with another not chosen personally by the king, and to name an heir who was not of the king's choice – Richard had recently named Arthur as his heir while in Sicily. The case against Longchamp was not that he had acted out of disloyalty to the king, but that he had acted in an autocratic fashion and abused the powers entrusted to

---

5   The immediate trigger for the deposition was Longchamp's actions in opposing Archbishop Geoffrey's arrival in England and imprisoning him in Dover Castle.

him. Twenty-four years later, the basis of Magna Carta was to be that the king had acted in a similar autocratic fashion and in defiance of established law. It is to be noted that there was no attempt to alter the existing mechanisms of government, still less to limit the power of the king or his greater servants. Rather, the events of October 1191 involved the replacement of an unacceptable royal servant by another, more acceptable figure.

The naming of John as heir presumptive seems to militate against this, but was probably no more than a temporary expedient, designed to mollify John and to lessen the danger to the throne from his ambition. John, having the revenues of five counties and the support of many of the barons, was now an over-mighty subject. He had already demonstrated a propensity for disloyalty by rebelling against his father and returning to England in defiance of his oath, and was clearly in a position to make a bid for the throne. It should not be assumed that it was recognised at the time that Richard would have no son. He was betrothed to Berengaria of Navarre when Walter of Coutances set out for England; by the time of Longchamp's fall, he was married, and it is unlikely that anyone in 1191 could have predicted that the marriage would be childless.[6] Against that, the danger of Richard dying whilst on crusade and before fathering a son was high.[7]

Until Richard's return, power was then exercised by the justiciars of the various dominions acting together, with Walter of Coutances at their head. John was increasingly sidelined and moved into rebellion in the spring of 1193 on hearing of Richard's imprisonment. However, neither then nor later was there any open baronial opposition to Richard's rule. Support for John in 1193–94 was very limited and did not re-surface after his submission to Richard. Given that John was faced for the bulk of his reign with baronial opposition, which developed into full-scale rebellion in 1215–16, and Richard's financial exactions were as great as John's, this is remarkable, and must be attributed to the personal awe which Richard inspired in his subjects and to the campaigns for which the exactions were made being largely successful.

3.2.3   Coroners

In the constitutional sphere, the one lasting development of Richard's reign was the creation of the office of coroner. Following his return from imprisonment in 1194, Richard ordered that a knight should be appointed in each shire as Keeper of the Pleas of the Crown (*custos placitorum coronae*). The counties thus acquired a permanent royal officer with responsibilities in the administration of justice in addition to the sheriff. The role of the present-day coroner is concerned almost exclusively with deaths within the area over which he has jurisdiction, but the responsibilities of his 12th

---

6   Richard acknowledged an illegitimate son born before his accession (who is sufficiently well recorded to be a major figure in Shakespeare's *King John*). Although he is often assumed today to have been homosexual, there is no contemporary evidence to substantiate this view, first suggested as recently as 1948 (Gillingham, *op cit*, pp 263–66).

7   Richard was seriously ill while on crusade and was reduced to conducting siege operations at Acre from a litter, quite apart from the normal hazards of battle and medieval travel. After sailing from Sicily, his fleet was scattered by a storm and many ships were sunk. His capture during his return journey from Palestine occurred after the ship in which he was travelling was driven ashore on the Adriatic coast. He was to die at 41 as a result of a wound which would probably not have been fatal had he not attempted to pull the crossbow bolt out himself in order to avoid alarming his followers, breaking off the shaft and leaving the head embedded, leading to unsuccessful surgery and gangrene.

century counterpart were very much broader, covering all those crimes triable by the king's justices and all matters involving the king's feudal prerogatives.

Before a charge of murder – the most significant of the pleas of the crown – could be brought, it was necessary to establish whether or not any death resulted from a criminal act. A major part of the coroner's role was therefore the investigation of any death not clearly due to natural causes. He was required to hold an inquest into such a death, at which a finding as to the cause of death would be made by a jury on the basis of knowledge of the matter and the evidence of witnesses. In cases of murder and manslaughter, the coroner was further responsible for apprehending the suspect and ensuring that he appeared before the king's justices when they next visited the county. Whether or not death resulted from a criminal act, the coroner was under a duty to secure for the king the *deodand* – the physical instrument of death, for example, the horse which had knocked down a person killed crossing a road. The *deodand* would then be sold and the proceeds passed to the Exchequer.[8]

More generally, the coroner's duty of investigation and apprehending of suspects extended to other pleas of the crown. He was required to ensure that the profits of royal justice were collected and delivered to the crown, including the property of convicted felons, and that the king received that which was his due under his feudal prerogatives in relation to items of treasure trove (objects of gold and silver buried in the ground with the intention of retrieval, but whose original owner or his heirs could not be identified) and wreckage washed up on the English coast, together with whales and sturgeons found in English waters. This jurisdiction survives today in the coroner's responsibilities in respect of archaeological remains.

3.3   THE REIGN OF JOHN: 1199–1216

By the reign of Henry II, the Great Seal, used in the execution of royal documents, had assumed a standard form. Its obverse depicted the king crowned and seated on his throne, bearing the orb and sceptre as symbols of his dominion and majesty. On the reverse, the king, armoured and bearing sword and shield, rode a charging warhorse against unseen enemies. The obverse represented the king as ruler, governor and law-giver, the reverse the king as warrior and commander. John was a failure in both roles, but it is as a war leader that his failure is more obvious, leading finally to the alienation of his magnates and the attempt by his enemies to depose and replace him. Yet, on his premature death, far from his dynasty being superseded and his monarchy swept away, he was succeeded by his nine year old son, the first child ruler since Æthelred the Unready, and internal peace was rapidly secured, showing that the opposition to him was to him as an individual, rather than to his dynasty or to the institution of kingship.

---

8   The concept of the deodand survived until 1840, when it was finally abolished by statute. One of the last was the locomotive which knocked down the casualties of an early railway accident.

3.3.1   A disputed throne

John was Richard's acknowledged heir in 1199, having been designated by Richard on his deathbed,[9] but his rights of succession were not undisputed. The issue was the old one of whether an adult heir should have priority over a minor, but with the novel feature, at least in relation to the succession to a crown, that there was real doubt as to whether a childless ruler should be succeeded by a surviving brother, or by the son of a nearer brother, now dead. Was the true heir John, fourth son of Henry II, or Arthur, son of Henry II's third son, Geoffrey, Duke of Brittany? The position was complicated further as neither candidate could argue for priority over the other on the basis of personal suitability. Arthur was a boy of 12 with no military or governmental experience, and John's excursions into the political sphere had largely ended in ignominy. Furthermore, Philip Augustus of France, who had been at war with Richard since 1194, saw an obvious opportunity to profit from the situation.

Such an issue had not arisen in relation to the throne since the Conquest, but painstaking work by Professor Holt has revealed several near-contemporaneous instances in relation to fiefs, both in England and on the continent. Certainly, it was to the advantage of Philip Augustus to protest Arthur's priority, but was the state of the law on Arthur's side?

Holt has shown that the only two contemporary law books were commentaries on the succession issue of 1199 and did not pre-date it.[10] In any event, the two do not come to a single conclusion. Holt reminds us that the situation was essentially the same as that already seen prior to the Conquest. Should the son of the deceased elder son of the common ancestor succeed as the *representative* of his father's title, or the younger son, the *cadet*, as being closer to the common ancestor? Holt finds that 12th century precedents in England were firmly on the side of the representative, and sees sound reasons for this, since it avoided the danger of conflict when the representative reached adulthood, as between Edward the Elder and his cousin Æthelwold;[11] 12th century literary works also favour the representative.

From this, it might be presumed that Arthur was the rightful ruler, John a usurper and, in due course, the murderer of the rightful ruler. However, the position was not so simple. There was no dispute over Brittany, to which Arthur was heir via his mother. Arthur seems never to have laid claim to either England or Normandy, where there was at this stage no open opposition to John, although there was some unease among the leading counsellors as to the legitimacy of John's claims. Aquitaine was not disputed either, since John's mother was still legally its Duchess. However, although John was initially able to establish himself as Duke of Normandy without opposition, this honeymoon was not to last. A more immediate difficulty in 1199 was that the magnates of the Angevin patrimony of Anjou, Maine and Touraine were divided between John and Arthur, and the wily French king sought to draw full advantage from this. Further, these three counties lay between Normandy and Aquitaine, making it more difficult yet for John to exercise control over his mother's turbulent duchy, a

---

9   For once, the fact of a deathbed designation is not in dispute.

10   JC Holt, 'The *casus regis*: the law and politics of succession in the Plantagenet dominions 1185–1247', reprinted in JC Holt, *Colonial England 1066–1215*, 1997, Hambledon Press, pp 308–12; and JC Holt, 'King John and Arthur of Brittany', Nottingham Medieval Studies, forthcoming.

11   It is not clear whether this example was known in John's reign.

task which had occupied virtually all the Lionheart's energies and very considerable military skill prior to his accession to England.

Most of the political history of the next five years is concerned with events on the continent, as John first forced Arthur and his mother Constance to capitulate and agreed terms with Philip Augustus (May 1200), and then as war broke out again in 1202 and led to the loss of all John's continental lands. The question of rights of succession between John and Arthur has been dealt with in some detail because it was the strife between them which led to this failure, to his low reputation as a military commander, the contempt in which he was held by men of his day, and to his financial extortions, which were designed to put him into the position to wage war against Philip Augustus in order to win back those lands.

3.3.2   The road to Runnymede

Of the six kings who reigned between 1066 and 1199, only two both died and were buried in England (William Rufus and Stephen). The remaining four met their deaths in their continental domains, and of them only Henry I ordained that his body should be buried in his kingdom. From John's loss of his continental lands, the position changes entirely. Except for Henry V, who died on campaign in France but was buried at Westminster, James II, who died in exile following his deposition, and the German-in-sentiment George I, every subsequent monarch died and was buried within his kingdom. Although continental interventions on the part of English kings were to remain a significant part of their activities, England, and more widely, the British Isles, was now the main focus of their actions. No longer were kings to remain absentees for the greater part of their reigns; indeed, it has been plausibly suggested that the main reason why John attracted so much opprobrium was that he was in England and seen by his enemies as personally responsible for his unpopular policies, rather than a distant absentee who left government to his servants.

Following the loss of his continental lands, John's overriding concern was to regain them. For this, he needed money and he made the fullest use possible of the feudal incidents to which he was entitled. Scutages, levied only occasionally by his predecessors, became almost annual. Fines and amercements – the sums charged in respect of failure to perform public duties such as bringing criminals to justice, and for procedural errors made by litigants in the royal courts – became much heavier, as did aids, gifts and the sums charged for wardships and the marriages of widows. In particular, royal justice was no longer exercised in a relatively disinterested fashion, as it had begun to be under Henry II, but inconsistently, depending to some degree on the favour or disfavour in which the litigants were held by the king.

Perhaps what alienated the magnates more than any other single factor was John's pathological suspicion. Believing, with some justification, that a major factor in the loss of his continental lands had been the disloyalty of the magnates of Normandy and Poitou,[12] he did not hesitate to 'break' a number of barons who had aroused his suspicions, and their families with them. He demanded hostages from them or

---

12 Though this was in part due to his high-handed behaviour towards them, particularly in relation to his second marriage, to Isabella of Angouleme, a great Poitevin heiress, who was at the time betrothed to Hugh IX de Lusignan. John's action led to a Lusignan revolt and, ultimately, since Philip Augustus weighed in against him, to John's ignominious defeat. See WL Warren, *King John*, Yale English Monarchs Series, 2nd edn, 1997, Yale UP, pp 68–99.

required them to pay large sums to regain royal goodwill, and went so far as to declare the lands of those who had incurred the greatest enmity forfeit, even though they had previously been his trusted servants.[13]

Although the suspicion that John had had Arthur murdered, or even killed him with his own hands in a fit of the famous Angevin temper, never developed into the opprobrium with which Richard III, the other 'wicked uncle' of English history, was viewed in some quarters, it seems to have led many magnates to the conclusion that John, unlike his father and brother, could not be trusted even by those loyal to him, and indirectly to John's paranoia towards those same magnates.[14]

At the same time, John's suspicion of his English vassals led to his placing increasing reliance on men from outside the Anglo-Norman magnate class, particularly a small clique headed by Peter des Roches, Bishop of Winchester, John's justiciar from the end of 1213. They have frequently been referred to as Poitevins, though most actually came from Touraine, but, whatever their birthplaces, they were outsiders of relatively low birth. It would be premature and over-simplistic to see the hostility of the Anglo-Norman baronage as the beginnings of a conception of Englishness; it was much more the instinctive distrust of the traditional ruling class in the face of change which they did not understand and which threatened their position. This hostility, first seen in embryo in the downfall of Longchamp, was, however, an important feature in the successive crises which befell the English monarchy in the medieval period.

The antipathy towards John which led to the extorting of Magna Carta from him was converted into organised opposition as a result of two events: first, his surrender to the Pope in 1213; and, second, the final failure of his attempts to recover his continental lands in the summer of 1214.

It was not John's original breach with the church in 1206 which led to the formation of the baronial bloc against him, but, paradoxically, his making of peace with Innocent III in 1213. The crisis was essentially another manifestation of the 'investiture contest' which had been simmering between Pope and temporal ruler for 150 years. The see of Canterbury fell vacant in 1205, the power to elect a successor lying with the monks of Christ Church, Canterbury. They elected their prior, Reginald, as Archbishop, and he duly set out for Rome to secure the ratification of his election by the Pope. John then descended upon Canterbury and pressured the monks into a second election in favour of his own candidate, John de Grey, Bishop of Norwich and a trusted royal servant. When the two Archbishops-elect arrived in Rome, Innocent III, of all the medieval Popes one of the most determined to establish the primacy of the papacy over earthly rulers, accepted neither candidate, but persuaded the monks of

---

13 The best known victim of John's enmity was William de Braose, a leading Marcher lord with extensive estates in Ireland, who was also, it is hinted by the chroniclers, one of the very few with knowledge of the true fate of Arthur of Brittany. See Warren, *ibid*, pp 81–84, 184–87.

14 Arthur, then 16, was taken prisoner by John while in arms against him in the summer of 1202 and was not seen, alive or dead, after Easter 1203. Despite his youth, Arthur was in no sense an innocent young boy, and no contemporary writer attempts to portray him thus, or even as a brave and noble youth foully done to death. In fact, he seems to have had in full measure the precocious bellicosity which his father and uncles had manifested in rebellion against Henry II as adolescents, and was apparently unwilling to reach any settlement with John which would involve his doing homage for Brittany. He made a dangerous enemy for John, the more so as he had the support of Philip Augustus, always ready to exploit John's difficulties. For a detailed discussion on Arthur's fate, see Holt, 'King John and Arthur of Brittany', *op cit*.

Canterbury to declare both elections void and to elect his own man. Stephen Langton was an Englishman, but had spent most of his life on the continent as a distinguished theologian and academic. Pope Innocent had recently made him a cardinal and considered him the ideal man to carry forward his plans for reform. To King John, however, Langton was quite unacceptable, not for reasons of his personality or doctrinal views, but for the manner of his appointment and his being an outsider in the sense of having come to prominence outside the Anglo-Norman milieu.

John could not prevent Langton's consecration as Archbishop, but he refused to allow him to land in England and take possession of the see of Canterbury. In August 1207, having given John a cooling-off period in which to accept the Archbishop, Pope Innocent placed England under an interdict and shortly afterwards declared John excommunicate. An interdict was essentially a mass excommunication. Just as an excommunicate was outside the church, forbidden Christian burial and doomed to eternal damnation if he died unreconciled to the church, in a kingdom under interdict, there were no church services other than the baptism of infants and the confession of the dying. In a world where death, famine and pestilence were never far away, ghouls and hobgoblins were believed to walk abroad at night, and the sacraments of the church were all that stood between man and the Devil and his works, it might be expected that an interdict, acting on the innocent as much as the guilty, would rouse the populace against the king.

However, this did not happen. Rather, it would seem that John's stance against the Pope was largely accepted, even by the bulk of the clergy. To men of the time, other than hard-line ecclesiastics, it was entirely proper that the primate of a church which benefited from the king's especial protection, who in relation to the temporalities of his see was one of the greatest of the king's tenants-in-chief and one of the king's chief counsellors by virtue of his office, ought to be a man acceptable to the king, not one forced upon him by a distant pontiff. John de Grey, from what is known of him, was entirely acceptable to the English church. All that counted against him, in the eyes of Pope Innocent, was that he was John's man. Further, if Pope Innocent's policy of freeing the English church from temporal control was successful, the magnates would no longer be able to count upon their brothers and younger sons receiving rich sees and monasteries as rewards for loyal service to the king. To the leading Englishmen of the day, both ecclesiastical and lay, Innocent's actions over the archbishopric of Canterbury must have appeared not only high-handed, but a threat to their position.

It was for his own reasons, not on grounds of any hardening of opposition to him, that John sought an accommodation with the Pope from the summer of 1212. A planned campaign to recover his continental lands was forestalled by a serious rebellion in Wales and a smaller baronial rising which, according to rumour, involved a conspiracy to drive John from the kingdom and install another king in his place. These events seem to have led John to take stock and persuaded him that it was time to make peace with his enemies, both internal and external, in order to be in a better position to mount a fresh continental campaign.

John's reconciliation with Rome seems to have inspired his opponents into imposing restraints upon him. Perhaps his abject surrender to the papacy suggested that 'John Softsword', who had already lost his continental lands, would also crumble in the face of baronial obduracy? Not only did John finally accept Langton as Archbishop of Canterbury, return the church property he had seized during the interdict and pledge himself to pay compensation for the seizure in the sum of 100,000 marks, he surrendered the kingdom of England to the Pope, to hold it thenceforth as a papal fief. Also, the oath sworn by John at the time of the formal lifting of his excommunication pointed up the gulf between the theory of kingship and John's practices. John swore on the Gospels that he would love and defend the church, revive the good laws of his ancestors, especially those of Edward the Confessor, abolish bad laws, judge all men in accordance with the just judgments of his court and render every man his rights. However, every time John acted by decree or at his will, he denied his barons the rights which they considered theirs under feudal law.

At the same time, John's attempts to recover his continental lands met with final failure. The expeditions planned for 1205 and 1212 did not sail; another planned for 1213 had to be postponed when a majority of English barons refused to accompany the king to Poitou, claiming that the terms of their feudal tenure did not require them to serve outside the British Isles. Secure in the new-found support of the Pope, John then planned a campaign on two fronts against Philip Augustus for the summer of 1214. His nephew, the Emperor Otto IV,[15] was to strike in the north from Flanders, and John with a mercenary army from Poitou, but, once again, the campaign ended in failure. As on previous occasions, John had difficulty in gaining the support of his English vassals for a campaign which had little to do with them,[16] his actions in Poitou were inconclusive and he was forced to withdraw altogether when the Emperor was catastrophically defeated at Bouvines in Flanders. Deprived of external allies and lacking the support of his English vassals, John was forced to agree to a truce on terms favourable to the French king.

The military failures of 1214 seem to have brought the opposition to John to final coalescence, but the process which led to Magna Carta had begun somewhat earlier, and was not to be completed for almost another year. Two barons, Eustace de Vesci and Robert FitzWalter, both involved in the abortive conspiracy of 1212, had fled the country and were now rousing opposition to John among English exiles in Scotland and elsewhere. When, in the summer of 1213, the English barons refused to accompany John on his planned expedition to Poitou, the king, with typical Angevin fury, set off with a mercenary army to punish the malcontents. Archbishop Langton, newly installed at Canterbury, managed to persuade both parties to accept his judgment in the matter. At the same time, a papal legate was sent by Innocent III to aid John in abating 'all conspiracies and factions'. The three strands in the genesis of Magna Carta, the barons' opposition to John, the king's desire to crush his baronial enemies, and the role of Archbishop and legate in securing a settlement acceptable to both sides, were beginning to come together.

3.3.3   The creation of the Charter

The precise chronology of the creation of Magna Carta is unclear, as is the stage at which John became prepared to treat with his enemies. A document known as the Unknown Charter of Liberties seems to mark an intermediate stage in the negotiations, and may date from the winter of 1213–14 (Warren) or 1214–15 (Holt).

---

15   Son of Henry II's daughter, Matilda, and Henry the Lion, Duke of Saxony and Bavaria.

16   Although many Norman families had held lands on both sides of the Channel in the immediate post-Conquest period, these families had since tended to split into English and continental branches, the lands being partitioned accordingly, a process largely completed as a result of the loss of Normandy in 1204.

Certainly, it was not until after the defeat of John's continental allies at Bouvines that the baronial clique was in a sufficiently strong position to force its terms, moderated to some extent by the church's mediation, on the reluctant king, and for this reason, the later date appears more plausible, unless the Unknown Charter – apparently very much a rough draft – ought to be seen simply as a statement of baronial aims, agreed by John's opponents among themselves before any negotiations.

Unfortunately, the domestic events of 1213–15 were thinly recorded by chroniclers, and so it is not clear what finally brought matters to a head after John's return from Poitou in October 1214. Peter des Roches had ruled the country with severity in John's absence; there had been a widespread failure to pay scutage by those who had not taken part in the Poitevin expedition, but neither of these elements was anything new. Perhaps, as Warren suggests, John's enemies believed that the king, having come to less than favourable terms with both the Pope and Philip Augustus, should now come to terms with them.[17] It would, however, be quite wrong to depict John as a cowed and defeated ruler, desperate to reach an accommodation with his barons. The events of the last 15 months of his life and reign show that this was very far from the truth.

John may well have been anxious for a breathing space, however, and so prepared to make a gesture which would restore the confidence of his vassals in a similar way to that of Henry I in issuing his coronation charter. His more moderate opponents, perhaps prompted by Archbishop Langton, were coming round to the idea of a charter of liberties, setting out the good old laws as they had been before they were abused by John, his father and brother. Indeed, the idea of the importance of the law seems to have come to prominence in John's reign. Chivalry was no more, lamented the biographer of William the Marshal. 'Nowadays the great have put chivalry and largesse in bondage, so that the life of errantry and tourneys is deserted for law suits.'[18]

Matters finally came to a head when, in the spring of 1215, a group of barons headed by de Vesci and FitzWalter rose in rebellion. These were by no means a majority of the barons, being no more than 40 holders of baronies, together with their sons and vassals. It would seem that it was the 'silent majority' of barons, 100 or more who, together with Archbishop Langton and Gualo, the new papal legate, persuaded both the king and the militants to accept the idea of a charter of liberties and the ultimate form in which it was produced.

Magna Carta, then, is a compromise designed to bring about the settlement of the rebellion of a minority of the baronage, not themselves men of principle, but rather the reverse. For his part, the king had no intention of honouring the terms of the Charter and immediately sent emissaries to Rome to obtain the annulment of the Charter and the Pope's support against the rebels. Magna Carta is, too, a conservative document, an expression of feudal law as it was believed to have been in a semi-mythic past, rather than looking forward to a 'better' future. Its terms are practical and specific, dealing with the individual grievances of the baronial class – this is exemplified by clause 50, which names nine of John's 'Poitevin' followers and requires their immediate removal from England – rather than abstract statements of principle. Few of its terms are relevant to any but the feudal landholding class, and none to the unfree serfs who formed the majority of the population. The only wholly innovatory

17 Warren, *op cit*, p 225.
18 Cited by Warren, *op cit*, p 180.

element was clause 61, which provided for the appointment by the magnates of a council of 25 barons with a supervisory role over the actions of the king, and giving them power to take action against him if he breached the provisions of the Charter and proved intransigent in his refusal to remedy that breach. As a means of settling the rebellion, it was an abject failure, since civil war broke out as soon as John's breach of faith in securing the papal annulment of the Charter became known.

The last 15 months of John's reign was spent in a campaign of sieges against his baronial opponents and against Louis of France, son and heir of Philip Augustus and John's nephew by marriage,[19] whom they had invited to England with the intention that he should become king when John was defeated. In this campaign, John gradually gained the upper hand and had gone on to the offensive before he died at Newark in the early hours of 18 October 1216, from dysentery aggravated by injudicious consumption of peaches and rough cider. He bequeathed his body to Worcester Cathedral and named the papal legate, William the Marshal, Peter des Roches and eight others as executors of his will and, by implication, as guardians of his nine year old heir, who now inherited a divided realm in the grip of foreign invasion.

John's reign was a failure, though in the matter of royal administration, it can be termed a success, since the process of development in royal finance and justice was continued, he brought effective royal control to the northern parts of England for the first time and exerted a greater measure of English control over the Celtic parts of the British Isles. Yet it was John's very successes in this sphere, the ferocity of his financial exactions without the justification of military success against external enemies, his inability, unlike his father and brother, to be generous in victory or magnanimous in defeat, which brought about his failure:

> Even in his achievements there was always something missing. He subdued nations to his will, but brought only the peace of fear; he was an ingenious administrator, but expedients came before policy; he was a notable judge, but chicanery went along with justice; he was an able ruler, but did not know when he was squeezing too hard; he was a clever strategist, but his military operations lacked that vital element of success – boldness. He had the mental abilities of a great king, but the inclinations of a petty tyrant.[20]

---

19 He was married to Blanche of Castile, daughter of John's sister, Eleanor, and Alfonso VIII, King of Castile. Had the baronial plan succeeded, England would have presumably been held by Louis in right of his wife.

20 Warren, *op cit*, p 259.

CHAPTER 4

THE BIRTH OF PARLIAMENT: THE REIGN OF HENRY III 1216–72

4.1   THE MINORITY

Few in 1216 could have predicted that Henry III's reign, chiefly remembered for the Barons' War of 1264–65 and the 'Model Parliament' summoned by his opponents, would occupy 56 largely peaceful years. Henry ascended the throne in a time of crisis. A substantial part of the country, including all the Channel ports except Dover, was in rebel hands. Royal administration had largely collapsed. To forestall any attempt by Louis of France to seize the throne, Henry was hastily crowned at Gloucester in the absence of both Archbishops, with a circlet provided by his mother, since the regalia had been lost when his father's baggage train was overwhelmed by the tide crossing the Wash a few days before his death. It is a tribute to the wisdom and capability of the executors of John's will, acting effectively as a council of regency, and a reflection of the opprobrium in which John had been held, that the civil war was brought to an end within a year.

The success of the regents was in no small measure due to their decision to re-issue Magna Carta in a modified form on 12 November. This re-issue omitted clause 61, providing for the creation of the Council of 25, and clauses specific to the conditions of 1215 that had now been overtaken by events. It is important to remember that it was the re-issued form of 1216, and the further re-issue of 1217, which divided the original charter into the Great Charter (Magna Carta) and the Forest Charter dealing specifically with forest law, that is the Magna Carta remembered by posterity and which was to be so significant in the events of the rest of the 13th century, not the original charter of 1215. This later form was both more moderate and less context-specific, so was more capable of acting as a statement of standards to which all monarchs should adhere.

The regents, too, demonstrated their wisdom by the merciful terms imposed on the rebels following the successful conclusion of the civil war, whereby they were entitled to the restoration of their pre-civil war lands via a procedure under which the sheriffs summoned juries to adjudicate on claims on the basis of their local knowledge and of enquiry. Here we see the re-emergence of settled royal administration after the long period of turmoil, and application of the methods introduced by Henry II.

In 1225, a re-issue of Magna Carta was used for the first time as a negotiating tool, it being recorded that the grant of a tax of a Fifteenth on moveables had been made specifically 'in return for the concession and gift of these liberties'.

Who 'made' this grant? Henry III's long reign was the period when not only was it accepted that the king was subject to the law, but a recognisable parliament began to emerge from earlier institutions. It has already been noted that early medieval kings wore the crown three times a year and on these occasions received the counsel of their magnates and prelates. Previously, the Latin term *colloquia* had been used of these meetings, termed by historians the Great Council and distinguished from the King's Council, composed of the monarch's closest advisors, that controlled royal government on a day-to-day basis. Now, in the first half of the 13th century, the term *parliamentum* came into use.

It would be unwise to assume debate and agreement on the model of the later English Parliament, still less that these early parliaments were able to exert any control over an unwilling monarch, but under Henry III and later kings, we see a shift in the relationship between kings and their counsellors. Previously, the king had the upper hand and was able to dictate to the Great Council when he chose. Under Henry III, a relatively weak king, we see the counsellors, at times counsellors imposed on the king rather than chosen by him, adopting a more decisive role, on occasions dictating to the monarch and extracting concessions from him in return for their agreement on taxation. This was a pattern which continued in subsequent reigns, intermittently at first, but gradually becoming a regular feature of the English constitutional system.

We also see the composition of these early parliaments moving beyond the magnate class, with the introduction of representation of the freemen of the shires by knights, and of the boroughs by burgesses, although this did not become the rule until much later – of the 52 parliaments held in the reign of Edward I, only 13 included knights of the shire. It is not clear how these representatives were chosen; it should not be assumed that they were chosen by the people they represented, still less that there was any form of election as we know it.

However, we see the beginnings of the transition from the king as an absolute, and in a sense dictatorial ruler to the concept of the king ruling through institutions, and of his ruling only while he retained the trust and confidence of his people. Edward I, a strong and decisive ruler, was able for the most part to exert his will over his parliaments, making concessions only to the extent he was prepared to make them. By contrast, under Edward II, parliaments were summoned by persons other than the king and eventually, an assembly of doubtful legality, acting without precedent, declared the king deposed.

4.2   THE CRISIS OF 1258–65

Having attained his majority, Henry III proved considerably less adept a ruler than his regents. Success in kingship depended much upon wise leadership and the maintenance of the respect and goodwill of the ruler's subjects. Henry III, like his father but for different reasons, failed on both counts, and his personal rule was marked by confrontations with his magnates, the last of them much the most serious, but all involving the question of how and through whom a king should actually rule.

4.2.1   Henry the man

Unlike the first three Angevin kings, Henry III comes across as an insubstantial, almost shadowy figure, lacking their ruthlessness and titanic energy, which re-emerged in his descendants.[1] Dante, writing in the early 14th century, consigned him to the corner of Purgatory reserved for simpletons. Dante must be seen as an intelligent continental observer, and his portrait as embodying the views of European contemporaries, but 'simpleton' Henry III was not, although for much of his reign, he

---

1   There is has been no scholarly biography of Henry III since FM Powicke, *Henry III and the Lord Edward*, 2 vols, 1947, OUP. I have relied on FM Powicke, *The Thirteenth Century*, Oxford History of England, 2nd edn, 1962, OUP; and MC Prestwich, *Edward I*, Yale English Monarchs Series, 2nd edn, 1997, Yale UP.

showed a quite childlike naivety. His greatest interests were religious: he was a devotee of the growing cult of Edward the Confessor, after whom he named his elder son, and was responsible for the rebuilding of Westminster Abbey. In secular politics, he lacked circumspection; his ambitions were always greater than his ability to fulfil them, most notably in foreign policy, where he severely over-stretched the resources of his kingdom and achieved little of lasting substance.

Henry was also a devoted father, brother, and husband. His favouritism towards his Lusignan half-brothers and his queen's numerous relations led to the crises of 1237 and 1244, which had at their root the question of whether the king alone had power to choose his ministers. Both these crises fizzled out, but the barons' tentative plan of 1244 for the creation of a council chosen by the common assent of the realm to be part of the King's Council and to act as the conservators of liberties re-emerged in the great crisis of 1258–65, in which the magnates attempted to impose government via a council chosen by them, and came very near to succeeding.

4.2.2 Origins of the crisis

Henry's policies all required considerable amounts of money and, following the precedent of 1225 and the confirmations of the Charters in return for further tax concessions in 1237 and 1245, the initial confrontation in 1258 involved an attempt to impose a system of control over the king's actions, that the Great Council would grant authority for taxation only in return for royal concessions. This involved the imposition of conciliar supervision over the king, and so a limitation of his power to act independently, not the mere assertion by the king that he would abide by the terms of the Charters. For the first time, indeed perhaps uniquely in the medieval period, the reform programme of 1258–65 was based not only upon baronial self-interest, but on the interests of the ordinary freeman, though not on the interests of the unfree majority. Also, when the attempts to achieve their aims by peaceful means met with stalemate, an attempt was made to impose conciliar government on the king by force; for a period, this attempt succeeded.

It was Henry III's bungling attempts to provide for his younger son, Edmund, and his support for his brother, Richard, Earl of Cornwall, in his attempts to establish himself as Holy Roman Emperor in succession to Frederick II of Hohenstaufen, which ignited opposition to him in 1258. Emperor through his father and King of Sicily through his mother, Frederick succeeded his parents in 1196 at the age of two. He was deposed by a General Council of the Church in 1245 and successive Popes were anxious to install suitably orthodox rulers on his thrones. When the imperial crown was offered to Richard of Cornwall, he had no illusions as to his chances of success, observing that the Pope might as well have asked him to climb into the skies and capture the moon, but nevertheless attempted to install himself in Germany. In 1254, after Frederick's death, the Pope offered, and Henry III accepted, the crown of Sicily on behalf of the young Edmund.

Sicily was, however, in the hands of Frederick's illegitimate son. Henry rashly vowed himself to the Pope to campaign in Sicily on pain of excommunication and made himself responsible for a vast papal debt of 135,541 marks, to be met by Michaelmas 1256, under pain not only of excommunication but also of interdict. Baronial discontent was already simmering as a result of the king's previous financial exactions and the favouritism he showed to his four Lusignan half-brothers, the sons of his mother by her second marriage.[2] Here we see again the jealousy of foreign upstarts which had been a feature of the crisis of 1213–15. The Lusignans might have been members of a distinguished Poitevin and crusading family, but they were aliens in England and were rewarded by Henry to an extent out of all proportion to their abilities.

Through 1256 and 1257, the magnates remained obdurate, refusing to grant Henry the taxes he required to rescue himself from his increasingly desperate financial position. At the same time, the Pope required Henry to make peace with France, where a dispute over the lands of the old Angevin Empire had been simmering for years, and to reach Sicily with 8,500 armed men by 1 March 1259. Finally, a rebellion by the ruler of Gwynedd, Llywelyn ap Gruffydd who, like his grandfather, Llywelyn ap Iorwerth, had ambitions to be the ruler of a united Wales, resulted in a series of English defeats.

The king's precarious position gave the magnates their opportunity. The Great Council of April 1258 was summoned to discuss Henry's demands for money for the Sicilian expedition, the problem of Wales and other urgent business. Just before the Council met, there occurred one of those dramatic set-piece confrontations which pepper the chronicles of the Middle Ages. A sworn confederacy of seven magnates, headed by Richard de Clare, Earl of Gloucester, Hugh Bigod, Earl of Norfolk, and Simon de Montfort, Earl of Leicester, went fully armed to Westminster Hall and, leaving only their swords outside the king's chamber, demanded that Henry accept their terms. Henry and his heir, Edward, swore on the Gospels to accept their counsel and to consent to what they proposed.

At the Great Council, the bishops withdrew from the discussions and the magnates, threatening the use of force, demanded the expulsion of the king's favourites and thorough reform of royal administration. They made a solemn oath to grant financial aid for the 'Sicilian adventure' only under conditions. The state of the realm was to be reformed and the Pope induced to moderate the terms of Henry's oath, in return for which, the barons would seek a general aid from the 'community of the realm'. The detailed programme of reform was to be worked out by a council of 24, 12 members of the King's Council and 12 chosen from the magnates, which would begin its work at Oxford on 12 June. The result of their deliberations would be issued before Christmas. On 30 April, the king and Edward swore, reluctantly, to accept whatever the Council of 24 decided.

4.2.3   The Provisions of Oxford

The results of these deliberations are known as the Provisions of Oxford.[3] They required change at both local and national level, designed to make the king's servants accountable to persons other than the monarch, to limit their ability to abuse their positions, and to shift the control of government from the king alone to the king acting with his baronage. A Council of 15 was to be appointed by four members of the existing Council of 24, and royal castles were to be distributed to new castellans, who were to be sworn not to surrender them except by command of the 15, a requirement

---

2   To Hugh X de Lusignan, to whose father she had been betrothed before her marriage to John.
3   EHD III No 37.

which would make it difficult for the king to mount armed resistance to the magnates in future.

The office of justiciar, which had lapsed earlier in the reign, would be revived, and the justiciar, treasurer and chancellor appointed annually instead of indefinitely. The justiciar would have the central role in the prevention and punishment of wrongdoing by royal officials and others; he would have power to amend all wrongs committed by all other justices, bailiffs, barons, earls and all other men 'in accordance with the law and right of the land'. Hugh Bigod, who seems to have been acceptable to all parties, was appointed as justiciar. Likewise, sheriffs were to be appointed for one year only; they should be local men of knightly class rather than outsiders, and were to be paid for their work so that they were not under an incentive to take bribes. Four knights were to be chosen in each shire to hear complaints against the sheriffs and other officials, and to pass records of these complaints on to the justiciar. Three Great Councils were to be held each year and, to secure fulfilment of this provision, a standing legislative Commission of 12, elected by the baronage, was to act with the Council of 15 at these times.

However, the Provisions had serious weaknesses. In particular, they neither defined the powers of the Council of 15, nor did they set out the role of the king in the future. They have the feel, as with many of the first fumblings towards constitutional change which occur in the medieval period, and indeed much later, of being incompletely thought through.

As with Magna Carta, the terms of the Provisions reflect the concerns of the milieu in which they were produced. These were, in particular, the financial exactions of the king and the corruption of royal officials at both local and national level. None of these was entirely novel, nor were any the actions of the Council of 24 during the next 18 months. However, during this period, it was this Council, not the king or a justiciar acting as his viceroy, who held the initiative in government, a situation which *was* unprecedented. By this time, the idea that the king was subject to the law had gained a firm foothold: 'The king ought to be subject to God and the law,' said Bracton, 'for the law makes him king.' But no one had previously dealt with the issue of how a reluctant king could be forced to comply with that law against his will, nor had it been considered whether, and by what mechanism, a king who refused to act within the law might be removed. The question of deposition never seems to have arisen in relation to Henry III, although it came to a head in the next reign but one.

Not only were the reformers anxious to obtain the commitment of the king, magnates and bishops to the Provisions, they wished to extend this to the free populace generally. A royal proclamation issued during the Great Council of October 1258 declared, first, that the king's will that the things done or to be done for the good of the realm by the Council 'should be steadfast and lasting in all things without end' and, second, required all freemen to take the oath to abide by the Provisions which had previously been sworn by the barons and royal officials. A second proclamation was to be read frequently each year in the shire courts, and attempted to re-assure the ordinary freeman that amendment of the existing administrative wrongs would soon begin.

4.2.4   Descent into civil war 1259–64

The political history of the next few years involves the swinging of the pendulum between the supporters of the Provisions and the king, until the differences between them became irreconcilable and all-out civil war ensued. At first, the king seems to have been prepared to acquiesce in the changes; his heir, Edward, was initially a supporter of the reform movement.

A unique aspect of the Provisions of Oxford, and the actions taken under them, was that they were not solely the product of self-interest, but reflected the interests of the broader free populace. A resolution by the Council of 24 in February 1259, confirmed by a royal proclamation on 28 March, represented an unequivocal assertion by the barons of their duty to the free populace. Existing liberties, embodied in Magna Carta, were to be maintained and existing procedures were to be followed in law suits, but the barons themselves were required to submit to the new processes created by the Provisions. The Provisions of Westminster issued on 13 October 1259 extended the existing common law to cover abuses by the servants of the magnates as well as royal servants,[4] and limited the powers of the seignorial courts that still dealt with the majority of civil cases. This marked a further step in the gradual replacement of the various overlapping systems of law by a unified system of royal justice.[5]

As well as dealing with past abuse by royal officials, the Council sought to prevent future abuses. In late 1259, it created a financial committee, composed of the justiciar, treasurer, a royal clerk and two judges, to enquire into royal resources with a view to the establishment of a permanent fund for the maintenance of the royal household. This change was never carried through. Had it been, it would have remedied one of the greatest causes of friction between the king and his magnates. As it was, the financing of the royal household and its activities, some governmental in nature, others not, was to be a cause of strife and source of difficulty for many centuries to come. The committee selected the sheriffs for the coming year, and the barons of the Exchequer and the royal justices were given assessors appointed by the Council. Sworn men in each hundred were given responsibility into investigation of official abuses, and every man who had been a royal or baronial bailiff in the previous seven years was commanded to appear before the royal justices.

From early in 1260, however, the reform programme fizzled out and began to meet open opposition from the king and his heir. At this stage, the reformers lacked a decisive leader and external events induced the king to intervene. Henry III was in France negotiating a final settlement of the dispute over the lands of the old Angevin Empire[6] when in January 1260, Llywelyn ap Gruffydd renewed the war in Wales. Henry wrote to the justiciar, ordering the Great Council due on 2 February to be postponed until after his return, and the Council of 24 to take measures for the protection of the Welsh Marches. Simon de Montfort, previously absent in France,

---

4   EHD III No 40.

5   Powicke, *op cit, The Thirteenth Century*, p 149.

6   The agreement concluded at the end of 1259 involved the English Crown's surrender of claims to Normandy Anjou, Maine and Touraine, and provided that a reduced duchy of Aquitaine, today referred to as Guyenne or Gascony, would be a possession of the English Crown in return for the homage and fealty of each King of England to each King of France. Henry thus conceded most of the French claims, but gained the support of Louis IX against his own subjects.

now returned to England and questioned the right of the king to suspend the clause in the Provisions of Oxford requiring a Great Council to be held three times a year. This was the first in a series of disputes over the Provisions which ended ultimately in civil war and the military defeat of the reformers. Each of these confrontations followed a similar pattern. First, the king re-asserted his independence and regained the initiative in government, then the reformers, gradually shifting from moderation to extremism, snatched control once more.

4.2.5   Simon de Montfort

Simon de Montfort, born in 1208, was an unlikely champion of representative government and the rights of the common man. As Earl of Leicester, he was among the greatest magnates in England, in addition to vast French holdings. Although one of the seven who had burst into the King's chamber in 1258, he played only a minor role in subsequent events. He was also an unlikely leader of a baronial movement partly based on opposition to the king's foreign favourites, since he was a Frenchman, and, intermittently at least, a royal favourite. Moreover, he was Henry III's brother-in-law, having in 1238 married Henry's youngest sister in secret and against his express wishes. Having been forgiven, Montfort was sent by Henry in 1248 to take control of Gascony, then in rebellion. His actions there aroused the hostility of the local baronage and after a commission of enquiry in 1251, he was recalled and effectively impeached. Montfort thus had his own grievances against the king, as did his wife, who was engaged in a lengthy land dispute with the family of her first husband. The hostility of both Montforts towards the king was reciprocated and formed a major element in the future escalation of the crisis.

Montfort, though idealised by some writers,[7] was a man of his times: arrogant, with the medieval man's absolute conviction in the righteousness of his own cause, possessed of high ideals and the sense of purpose lacking in the original reformers, but also obstinate and litigious, and prone to sulk on his French estates. What motivated the concern for the common man which was apparent from his actions is not clear, though the teachings of his contemporary, St Francis of Assisi, may have had some influence. But events were to show that his actions, leading to the Barons' War of 1264–65, were motivated not only by ideals, but by his personal quarrel with the king.

By the beginning of 1261, the king was regaining the initiative in government. The judicial enquiries into abuses were allowed to lapse, the new procedure for appointing sheriffs was circumvented by re-appointing the existing sheriffs. On 13 March, Henry presented the barons with a detailed statement of his objections to the Provisions of Oxford and permitted his dispute with them to be submitted to arbitration by the agents of the King of France. At the end of May, a papal bull arrived absolving Henry from his oath to observe the Provisions on the basis that it had been obtained from him by duress, and annulling the Provisions and instruments made under them. Having established that he had the support of his son and of the more conservative magnates, the king installed himself in the Tower of London and hired a substantial

---

7   An article by Conrad Russell in *The Sunday Telegraph*, 23 January 2000, emphasises the importance of the Model Parliament of 1265 and Montfort's view of himself as his king's loyal subject, but avoids the uncomfortable fact that Montfort had recently been in armed rebellion against the king, and was to be again, and that the king summoned this parliament under duress, when his son and nephew were hostages in Montfort's hands.

force of mercenaries. Outright conflict, however, was avoided by agreement that matters should be submitted to Louis IX for arbitration.

On 2 May 1262, Henry sent letters to all sheriffs confirming that both Magna Carta and the Forest Charter were to be observed, but ordering the sheriffs publicly to denounce the ordinances and statutes earlier annulled by the Pope, stating that his appeal to the Pope was justified by the barons' failure to observe the conditions under which he had accepted the Provisions. Every opponent of his royal rights was to be arrested. Believing his position to be restored, Henry decided to make another visit to Paris to seek a solution to the continuing problem of Gascony and to deal with the grievances of Simon de Montfort, who also returned to France and sought redress from King Louis.

Montfort was not concerned solely with his personal grievances against the king, but was also anxious to obtain a restoration of the Provisions of Oxford. However, Henry unwittingly hardened Montfort's attitude to him by his desire to reach a settlement of the Gascon problem, since this involved the resurrection of the complaints arising from Montfort's governorship. In a manner all too typical of the medieval magnate, Montfort took umbrage, believing that his honour was in question and that hidden forces behind the king were seeking to bring him down.

A fresh crisis then developed at home, when Llywelyn once again broke the truce in Wales, and a confederacy of Marcher lords was created to oppose him. This confederacy included younger barons who had not acquiesced in the submission to the arbitration of King Louis, and attracted those who, under the baronial oath to maintain the Provisions of Oxford, were sworn to treat all opponents of the Provisions as public enemies outside the law. The confederacy called upon Simon de Montfort to come from France to lead them and in April 1263, he came.

Montfort's return from France is a pivotal point in the process by which a reform movement operating through peaceful means and seeking to work with the co-operation of the king and his household became an armed rebellion and brought about civil war. Events now showed that Henry III as a medieval king, even one weak in personal authority, was not ready to have his power circumscribed by conciliar government, and would fight to restore the integrity of his throne.

In March 1263, the magnates, the Londoners and freemen of the shires were ordered to take oaths to the king and to Lord Edward as his heir. On 25 May, the king issued writs for a gathering of the feudal host – all persons from whom military service was due on the basis of their landholdings – to march against Llywelyn. At the same time, the leading reformers, headed by Simon de Montfort, issued written demands to the king for a restoration of the Provisions of Oxford and the treatment of all those opposed to the Provisions, other than the king, the queen and their children, as public enemies.

Henry III refused these demands and the rebels seized Gloucester and the Cinque Ports on the coast of Kent and Sussex. The Londoners rose against the king, forcing him to agree reluctantly to abide by the Provisions. Initiative in government again passed from the king, but this time into the hands of men who had gained that initiative not even by reluctant royal acquiescence, but by rebellion. Montfort and his adherents took control of the Tower and from there appointed a new justiciar, chancellor and castellans to hold the royal castles. Each shire was given a 'warden of the peace' to carry out the functions of the sheriff. Lord Edward initially held out in

Windsor Castle, but was persuaded to surrender on hearing of .. capitulation. In the face of all this, the opponents of the Provisions gradually crumbled and were induced to take oath to uphold the Provisions as the condition of retaining their lands. Commissions of *oyer et terminer* – special commissions of enquiry – were sent out into the shires to hear complaints against opponents of the Provisions who had taken advantage of the disorder to attack their local enemies. An uneasy peace was concluded on 9 September, when the king accepted his enemies' terms.

Powicke makes it clear that, far from simply turning the clock back to 1258–59, by resorting to armed force, Montfort and his supporters had divided the country and created a political impasse which could only be ended by the military defeat of one or other party.[8] At the same time, there was no general acquiescence to the restoration of the Provisions. Reform by the consent of the king was one thing; forcing reform by armed might was quite another. In particular, Edward, once Montfort's sworn ally, was now quite irreconcilable.

Deadlock ensued at the October Great Council over the king's right to appoint members of his household. Once again, the King of France offered himself as mediator. Representatives of both sides met at Amiens on 12 January 1264, King Henry complaining that the barons had unlawfully deprived him of his prerogative rights to appoint his own ministers, judges and local officials, and sought to regulate the royal household and castles. King Louis gave judgment for his brother monarch on every point. Civil war was now inevitable.

4.2.6   The Barons' War

While Montfort was laid up with a broken leg, Edward struck at the king's enemies in the Marches, including Llywelyn, to whom Montfort had promised his daughter in marriage. There was a wave of popular unrest in the major towns, including a vicious outbreak of anti-semitism. In April, Edward carried the war into England. Both sides made *diffidatio* on 4 April. Having gained control of London, Montfort moved towards the Cinque Ports, which were held by the king.

The two armies met at Lewes, a few miles from Brighton, on 14 May. The battle ended in a rebel victory and the capture of both King Henry and Richard of Cornwall. Montfort, still portraying himself as Henry's faithful vassal, imposed stringent terms on him in order to create a suitable climate for the fulfilment of his aims. Edward and his cousin, Henry of Almain, son of Richard of Cornwall, were given over as hostages to ensure the king's observance of the Provisions of Oxford.

Montfort and his followers lost no time in putting their plans into effect. In June, the shires were once again put under the authority of wardens of peace. A parliament was summoned for 22 June and, for the first time, writs of summons were not simply sent out to named magnates and prelates, but each shire court was instructed to select four knights to act as representatives of the shire.

This parliament gave the task of establishing a provisional form of government to Montfort, the Bishop of Chichester and Gilbert de Clare, Earl of Gloucester. Once more, the king's authority would be constrained by a council, with three of its members in constant attendance on the king. However, the Montfortians by no means

---

8   Powicke, *op cit, The Thirteenth Century*, p 177.

had everything their own way. War continued in the Marches throughout the summer. Louis of France, previously a mediator, now threatened invasion in support of the royalists. The Pope too was hostile. In August, the papal legate, having forced the rebels to admit him to England, fixed a date for the renunciation of the Provisions of Oxford on pain of excommunication.

The rebels briefly regained the upper hand, forcing the Marchers to agree to terms in December, under which the whole of western England from the Severn to the Mersey was to come under Montfort's control. Edward, still a hostage, agreed to exchange his lands in this area for others of equal value elsewhere, and the leading Marchers were sent into exile in Ireland for a year and a day. Believing Edward to be a spent force, Montfort was now prepared to agree terms for his release, and in the interim summoned a parliament to meet on 20 January 1265 to agree final peace terms. This summons again broke new ground, since not only were two knights summoned from each shire, but also two burgesses each from York, Lincoln and other selected boroughs. This parliament was thus the 'Model Parliament' for which Montfort is now remembered, but it was to be a considerable period before the representation of the shires and then of the boroughs was to become the norm.

Under the terms which parliament finally agreed, Edward was required to adhere under oath to the provisional government and to remain in England for three years from Easter 1265 on pain of disinheritance. His household was to be purged of 'suspect' elements and placed under the supervision of the new Council. The majority of strategic castles were to remain in Montfort's hands. On 10 March, Edward and Henry of Almain were given into the custody of the king, though they remained under Montfort's supervision, and the king and his heir swore to maintain the terms of the settlement and to observe the Charters. On the following day, every freeman in the land was ordered to renew his homage and fealty to the king, saving, uniquely, the terms of the peace settlement.

This peace was a hollow one. Before long, the Earl of Gloucester put himself at the head of a rebellion inspired by jealousy of Montfort. Then, on 28 May, Edward escaped from custody and rejoined Gloucester and his Marcher allies. War was renewed. The two armies met at Evesham on 2 August, as Montfort attempted to cross the Severn, and the battle ended in Montfort's defeat and death.

4.2.7   Aftermath of civil war

After the Battle of Evesham, the rebels crumbled, except for Montfort's sons, who held out for a period in their castles. The king and Edward were quick to restore royal authority, seizing the lands of the rebels and distributing them among royalists by the Ordinance of Windsor of 16 September. In the longer term, the settlement imposed by the king was mild. The Dictum of Kenilworth, promulgated in its final form on 31 October 1266, allowed the majority of rebels to regain their lands on payment of a fee based on the annual value of those lands and the extent of the individual landholder's involvement in the events of the war. Like the settlement of 1217, the scheme made use of legal procedures which had begun to be developed under Henry II. Twelve justices were appointed to traverse the country in four separate circuits in order to hear claims for the restoration of land, and their decisions were made on the basis of the sworn evidence of local juries. However, the Dictum also stressed that the king was to 'exercise his dominion, authority and royal power without impediment or contradiction' and that the king's subjects were henceforth to seek justice in the king's courts, no longer by violence or rebellion.

This was the last occasion on which armed rebellion against a lawful king was treated in the traditional fashion of the feudal system. Henceforth, under ideas culled from Roman Law which were beginning to influence the contemporary legal mind, a distinction was made between the king as personification of the crown, and the king as the summit of the feudal pyramid. No longer would rebellion against the king be treated merely as a breach in the relationship of lord and vassal, for which the vassal would simply forfeit his lands. Instead, such rebellion was high treason, a crime against the crown and, through the crown, against the state, attracting the most savage of penalties. This can be seen 17 years later, when in 1283, Dafydd ap Gruffydd, brother of Llywelyn and the last native Prince of Wales, who had fought at Lewes as Edward's ally, was condemned as a traitor after breaking his homage to Edward and was hanged, drawn and quartered.

However, in 1266–67, the emphasis was on peace and reconciliation. The king and his heir accepted that the grievances relied on by the rebels were to a degree well founded, and took steps to remedy the most urgent. Indeed, the Statute of Marlborough of November 1267 not only restated the bulk of the earlier Provisions of Westminster, but went further. Henceforth, writs alleging breach of any provision of the Charters were to be issued without fee, so that any freeman, whatever his means, could seek a remedy before the king or his justices. This meant that the detailed provisions of the Charters became enforceable in the same way as the statutes promulgated more recently. This provision was of little effect in practice, but by the *Articuli super Cartas* of 1300, it was ordered that three knights or other suitable persons were to be elected in each shire and appointed by royal letters patent as local justices to hear and determine complaints alleging breach of the Charters, if such breaches had no available remedy at common law. This marked a stage in the development of the office of Justice of the Peace, which was to be formalised by Edward III in 1361. Again, this was a stage in the replacement of a multiplicity of systems of law and justice by a single system of common law and royal justice.

Ultimately, the events of 1258–65 are more important in hindsight in relation to constitutional development than they must have appeared to contemporaries, since in the next reign, Edward I was able to a large extent to preserve his paramountcy over his magnates. However, there is under Henry III a very clear demonstration that the king and his servants are subject to the law, and the first gropings towards a system by which that subjection may be enforced.

CHAPTER 5

THE REIGN OF EDWARD I

5.1   MAN AND KING

Edward I may be bracketed with Henry II as among the greatest of England's medieval kings. Indeed, there are many similarities between them. Both restored firm royal authority after a period in which it had been lacking, both presided over major developments in the law. Both ended their reigns in relative failure and disappointment. In Henry's case, this was due to the rebellions of his sons, in Edward's, his over-stretching the resources of his kingdom and the goodwill of his subjects in his wars in France and Scotland. Henry died before there was serious discord at home, but after 25 years on the throne, Edward faced a major domestic political crisis, which might well have threatened the security of a less formidable and less awe-inspiring monarch.

In Edward's reign, Wales was conquered and largely absorbed into the English system of royal government. Scotland might well have gone the same way were it not for the determination of a few among the Scots to maintain their ancient independence. At the same time, considerable developments took place in law and in the administration of justice, and Edward's financial insecurity in the last years of his reign led to his making concessions which mark a further step in the slow evolution of representative government.

Aged 33 at his accession, Edward was quite unlike the ineffectual Anglo-Saxon king whose name he bore. He had served a long apprenticeship for ruling, spending a period of relative autonomy as suzerain of Gascony and gaining a stature on the national and international stages through his military activity during the Barons' War and participation in a crusade. His crusading endeavours achieved little, since his allies never reached the Holy Land and his own force was too small to campaign on any significant scale, but Edward nevertheless returned home in 1274 a hero. Many had taken the cross, but few actually fulfilled their crusading vows, and Edward's fame was heightened by his surviving a serious assassination attempt.

A fine figure of a man (when his tomb was opened in 1774, he was found to be six feet two inches tall), Edward I would also prove a very different ruler from his father. As well as much greater physical and intellectual abilities, he had a streak of unscrupulousness which, like Henry II, he used at times for his advantage, and a full measure of the famed Angevin temper. The household accounts dispassionately record the repairs required to a coronet belonging to one of the king's daughters after Edward had thrown it into the fire during an argument.

Edward I's reign falls into two halves. The first, up to the early 1290s, was one of success: the consolidation of royal power through the strengthening of royal justice, the conquest of Wales, and extension of English authority to Scotland following the death of Alexander III. In the second period, Edward's earlier successes to a large extent fell apart. There was war with France, the long war for control over Scotland from 1296, and an outbreak of domestic opposition roused by the king's financial exactions. To some historians, the death in 1290 of his beloved queen, Eleanor of

Castile,[1] marked the beginning of the decline of his fortunes, and in his last years he may well have grown increasingly concerned over the character of his heir and his capacity to rule.

5.2 THE YEARS OF TRIUMPH

In domestic affairs, the first years of the reign are remembered chiefly for the great series of legal reforms which began with the Statute of Westminster, promulgated in 1275 by Edward's first parliament. The earliest measures termed 'statutes' pre-date the reign, but it was in Edward's time that the first true statutes, made in assemblies which can legitimately be described as parliaments and specifically designed to amend the common law, were passed. However, such statutes were not made by the king in parliament as they are today. Rather, it seems that they were simply announced by the king or his ministers in a parliament. Much of the business of early parliaments seems to have been judicial rather than legislative, or dealt with matters raised by individuals via petitions. Further, in this early period, a 'statute' was the sum of the legislation approved in a particular parliament, and might therefore cover a very wide range of areas of law, although some dealt with specific topics, such as the Statute of Merchants of 1285 and the Statute *Quia Emptores* of 1290.[2] It must also be recalled that until much later, a king could make legislation independently of parliament in the form known as ordinances, and that writs issued by the king giving instructions to his courts might in practice have the same status.

5.2.1 Developments in law and justice

Immediately after his coronation on 19 August 1274, Edward instituted a major enquiry into royal administration in the shires, and abuses by sheriffs, and royal and baronial bailiffs, on the pattern of that of 1258–59, and preceded by a wholesale dismissal of the existing sheriffs. Pairs of commissioners were appointed for each shire, to put a series of 40 questions or 'Articles', based on previous enquiries, to juries summoned for this purpose in each hundred and borough. The findings, recorded in Hundred Rolls which have survived on a considerable scale, demonstrate that official wrongdoing was universal and took many forms. Some of these were dealt with in the Statute of Westminster 1275, which, *inter alia*, made provision for the bailing of prisoners, so that fewer would now languish in the sheriff's prison for lengthy periods before coming to trial, and made changes in the law relating to wardship, where the Hundred Rolls revealed large-scale abuses. Similar enquiries into specific matters of concern went on throughout the reign.

Like Henry II, Edward I was not attempting to create a new legal system, but to refine and improve that which already existed, and had developed very considerably by internal evolution since Henry's death in 1189. Permanent courts of the King's Bench, dealing with matters touching and concerning the king, and Common Pleas,

---

1   She died at Harby, Nottinghamshire, and the desolated king caused 12 'Eleanor Crosses', three of which survive, to be erected at the places her cortege halted overnight on the journey to Westminster Abbey.
2   EHD III No 64.

dealing with matters between the king's subjects, had now come into existence, and the system of judicial eyres, where the king's justices progressed through the shires to hear cases, was well established. A specialist legal profession had emerged, operating its own system of training on the apprenticeship model.[3]

Official records show that the maintenance of law and order was a major concern throughout Edward's reign, though it is not clear whether the period was any more lawless than hitherto; this may simply be the impression created by the greater volume of records. Under Edward, the general eyres were supplemented by commissions sent out at intervals to deal with specific types of case, in practice, when the volume of cases was beyond the capacity of the eyre to deal with. A commission of gaol delivery heard cases involving prisoners held in gaols, and a commission of *oyer et terminer* heard all cases in a particular shire. A commission of *trailbaston* was empowered to punish all types of criminals.

The common law, however, was an unwieldy instrument. A wide variety of forms of action had developed – the result of piecemeal change to meet the pressing problems of the moment. Each was begun by its own specific writ, and much of lawyers' expertise in this period involved the ability to choose the appropriate form of action. The changes which occurred in Edward's reign were also piecemeal; they attempted to deal with specific difficulties which emerged in cases heard by the king's courts, or were revealed by the various enquiries or by petitions sent to the king by his subjects. Few statutes dealt solely with one area of law, and changes in particular areas were incorporated in several statutes produced at different dates, as new points of difficulty emerged. For example, changes in the law governing the action of *novel disseisin*, first introduced by Henry II, were included in the Statute of Westminster 1275,[4] the Statute of Gloucester 1278[5] and the Statute of Westminster 1285.[6] Changes to the criminal law were included in both Statutes of Westminster and in the Statute of Winchester 1285. The changes had, however, three overall purposes: first, to deal with the ever-present problems of maintaining order and of abuse by royal officials; second, to enable the law to operate more effectively and more consistently; third, to increase royal authority.

Some of the problems with which Edward I and his advisors grappled have a familiar ring. The Statute of Westminster 1275 imposed for the first time a sentence of imprisonment for rape, but this was something of a two-edged sword, since records show that convictions for rape fell markedly in comparison with the period when rape was punished by a modest fine. The situation did not improve when the penalty of loss of an arm or leg was added by the Statute of Westminster II. It appears from surviving court records that juries became markedly more reluctant to convict, even in cases where the evidence was apparently conclusive. Heavier penalties also seem to have led to a fall in convictions for other offences. By 1285, the compilers of the Statute of Winchester were complaining that not only was crime more frequent than in the past, but it was more difficult to persuade juries to convict offenders.

---

3 See Chapter 10.
4 EHD III No 47. This Statute introduced the concept of 'time immemorial', fixed at 1189 by cl 39, which provides that no man may claim that his ancestor had seisin of any land further back than the time of Richard I.
5 EHD III No 52.
6 EHD III No 57.

There was also a suspicion that much crime was not being reported. In 1285, each hundred was therefore required to take responsibility for loss and damage caused by robbery in that hundred, and watch patrols were to take place in cities and boroughs at night. Trees, undergrowth and bushes within 200 yards of roads were to be cut back, so that robbers could no longer hide there, and the items of military equipment which all free men had been required to keep since the 12th century were increased, so that such law-worthy men were better equipped to deter and apprehend criminals.

At the same time, the king was anxious to ensure that non-royal justice and other powers normally exercisable only by the Crown, such as the charging of customs duties, were exercised only by those entitled to this privilege. The writ *Circumspecte Agatis* of 1286[7] limited the jurisdiction of ecclesiastical courts to matrimonial, testamentary and moral questions, and cases involving attacks on the clergy that did not attract financial penalties. The Gloucester Parliament of 1278 instituted the *Quo Warranto* inquisitions, on the now-standard pattern of enquiries by royal commissioners of local juries of sworn men, into various rights claimed by landholders, what these rights were, and by what warrant they were held, since the king wished to ensure that only those which were properly held by royal grant would continue. This was not popular with some of the magnates, who claimed that their rights had been acquired by conquest and could not be removed by any king. When challenged by the commissioners to prove his rights, John de Warenne, Earl of Surrey, is said to have brandished a venerable sword and told them, 'My lords, here is my warrant'. In practice, the king was prepared to allow such magnates to continue to hold their 'franchises' and did not investigate the more extensive rights claimed by the Marcher lords in their Welsh territories, a demonstration once again that royal power was circumscribed by the need to maintain the support of the greatest subjects.

Other changes, particularly in the field of land law, were of advantage to the magnates as well as the king. It is instructive to remember that the provisions made by Edward I formed the basis of English land law right up to the great reform made in 1925, and some elements still pertain today. Provisions in the Statute of Westminster II form the basis of the doctrine of conditional gifts, which allows a gift of land to take effect only if a condition specified by the donor is satisfied. An interpretation of this provision in a case in 1311 allowed the creation of the entail, under which landed estates could remain intact in the possession of one family, rather than be divided among co-heiresses on the failure of male issue, as under the common law. This allowed land to remain in one family for many generations, facilitating the creation of regional power bases by the magnates.

5.2.2   Finance and administration

Edward returned from crusade heavily in debt to Italian bankers, loans from whom now provided an important element in royal finance. The parliament of 1275 granted him a new and reliable source of income, in the form of a levy of half a mark (6s 8d) on each sack of wool (364lb) exported from England. As wool was now emerging as England's major export trade, to become a source of vast wealth in the centuries to come, and this revenue was simple and cheap to collect, producing a steady £8,800 or more per year, this was a most important development, even if, as at this time, this

7   EHD III No 60.

magna et antiqua custuma had to be assigned immediately to the king's creditors. Later in the reign, the king's pressing need for money to prosecute his wars with France and Scotland led to his making, unwillingly, concessions which quickened the slow pace of development of representative government, and it became the norm for taxation only to be levied with the agreement of a parliament.

During the reign, there were further developments in royal administration. During the 12th century, the Exchequer had become permanently based at Westminster. Now the Chancery also acquired a permanent home and became a separate body from the royal household. This meant that the king was more often than not separated from the main departments of state through which he exercised his rule, and from the Great Seal kept by the chancellor, which was used to authenticate all royal documents. How, then, was the king to give instructions to the departments of state, and how were the heads of those departments to be certain that such instructions came genuinely from the king? This difficulty was dealt with by the creation of a 'Privy' Seal, used for written instructions from the king to his ministers. Both Henry III and Edward I also used those elements of the household which remained with the king as a means of circumventing unwelcome supervision by the magnates, particularly in financial matters. Henry III relied on his chamber as a financial body during the periods of conciliar rule, and the financial aspects of Edward I's Scottish wars were conducted largely through the royal wardrobe.

5.2.3   The conquest of Wales

Llywelyn ap Gruffydd profited considerably from his support for Simon de Montfort in the Barons' War. In 1267, Henry III formally recognised him as Prince of Wales and accepted most of his territorial gains during the war. Llywelyn agreed to do homage and fealty to the king, but events proved that he was not prepared to be treated simply as one magnate among many. Llywelyn's continuing support for the surviving Montforts, along with his ambitions to unite all Wales under his rule, to the detriment of the Marcher lords who included Edward himself, were an obvious basis for Edward's determination to subdue Wales.

Convenient pretexts for an invasion came when in 1275, Llywelyn refused to attend parliament to do homage. Edward was able to attack Wales at an opportune moment, since Llywelyn was distracted and Wales was divided as a result of attempts by Llywelyn's brother Dafydd to establish himself in lands he believed to be his by right, under the Welsh tradition of equal division between sons. The campaign of 1276–77 was highly successful. Wales under Llywelyn's rule was limited to Snowdonia and Anglesey, although Welsh law and custom were permitted to run within his domains under the terms of the Treaty of Conway of November 1277.

There matters might have rested, had not Dafydd risen against Edward in 1282. He was joined by an apparently reluctant Llywelyn, and for a period, most of Wales was in arms against the English. The Welsh were initially successful, but when Llywelyn was killed in November during a minor skirmish near Builth Wells, their resistance collapsed. Though Dafydd tried to hold out in Mid Wales with a small band of followers, he was betrayed to the English and, after a show trial before a specially-summoned parliament at Shrewsbury, hanged, drawn and quartered as a traitor to the English king.

5.2.4   Aftermath of conquest

The terms of the Statute of Wales of 1284 and the actions of Edward I after Dafydd's death have been seen in very different lights by English and Welsh commentators. To the English, the terms were merciful, and the acts of the English administration no more than were appropriate to ensure peace and good order among a hostile people. To the Welsh, 1284 brought the end of their independence, the destruction of their traditions and the imposition of an alien and harsh system of rule. Throughout his reign, Edward showed a ruthless absence of clemency towards defeated enemies, and he now took care that no member of Llywelyn's family was in a position to act as a focus for the rebellious tendencies of the Welsh. Llywelyn's head was set up on a pike in London. Dafydd's two small sons were kept in captivity at Bristol, one dying in 1287, the other still living in 1325. Dafydd's daughters and Llywelyn's only child, a daughter by his marriage to Eleanor de Montfort, all spent the remainder of their lives in separate convents in eastern England.

English security in Wales was assured by the building of the great castles, Conway, Carnarvon, Harlech and Beaumaris, all designed to be supplied by sea so that their garrisons could not be starved into submission, which ring Snowdonia and are the most enduring physical memorial to Edward I.[8] Welsh lands were shared out among the most trusted of Edward's followers, and Englishmen were settled in planned fortified boroughs such as Conway and Flint. A number of existing castles were rebuilt and given English garrisons, while the remainder were dismantled. Llywelyn's own lands – much of the western half of Wales – were retained in the hands of the English Crown, greatly increasing royal power in relation to the Marcher lords.

The Statute of Wales,[9] promulgated at Rhuddlan on 19 March 1284, set out the new framework of administration for Wales, creating shires on the English model in the north, and a justiciar of North Wales, with sheriffs, bailiffs and coroners under him. Though Welsh law was permitted to operate in some spheres, the criminal law was to be that of England. Senior appointments, down to the level of the sheriffs, were, in practice, all held by Englishmen, though local offices remained in Welsh hands. No attempt was made at this stage to define the relationship between Wales and the English Crown.

5.2.5   Edward I and Scotland 1286–92

With Wales effectively subdued, Edward's attentions within the British Isles then turned to Scotland. Relations between the two kingdoms had been good for most of the century. William the Lion did homage to John in 1212, and his successors both married into the English royal dynasty. However, events were to take a succession of tragic turns.

On 18 March 1286, Alexander III, newly remarried, decided to return from Edinburgh to his bride, who was at the manor of Kinghorn on the Fife coast, although a storm was brewing. In the dark, Alexander became separated from his squires,

---

8   The strength of these castles was amply demonstrated during the rebellion of Owain Glyn Dwr in the early 1400s. To take only one example, Harlech held out against Glyn Dwr for several years with a garrison of fewer than 20 men.

9   EHD III No 55.

wandered off the road and was killed riding over a cliff. His children had predeceased him. The sole heir to Alexander's throne was his granddaughter, Margaret, the child of his daughter's marriage to Eric II of Norway, and whom he had named as heir should he die without further issue.[10]

Perhaps surprisingly, considering that Margaret was not only female, but three years old and sickly, she was accepted as the rightful ruler without significant dissent, and six 'Guardians of the Realm' were appointed to govern on her behalf until she was of riper years. These Guardians looked towards Edward as in some rather vague way the proper overlord of Scotland and external guarantor of the interests of the infant, a role which Edward was happy to fulfil. He and Alexander III had maintained friendly, indeed affectionate relations, and in the period 1286–90, there seemed no reason why such amity should not continue.

However, the Guardians were cautious about compromising Scottish independence by too close a tie to the English Crown, and therefore the agreement by which Margaret should marry Edward's heir, Edward of Carnarvon, and their issue should rule over both kingdoms, contained in the Treaty of Birgham of March 1290, included provisions ensuring that Scotland's administration should remain separate and that Scottish customs and traditions would be respected. It was further agreed that Margaret should come to England or Scotland by 1 November 1290, that she should not be married without the consent of the Kings of England and Norway, that any new Guardians should be appointed by agreement between the Scots and the Norwegians, and that disputes between the Scots and Norwegians should be settled by the English.

But the projected union of crowns three centuries before the accession of James VI of Scotland as King of England was not to be. Margaret died before she ever reached Scotland, in Orkney, which was still Norwegian territory, apparently from seasickness on 26 September 1290. A major crisis ensued. Not only was Margaret the last descendant of Alexander III, she was also the last living issue of Alexander's grandfather, William the Lion. Not only was there thus no obvious heir, but there were no fewer than 13 prospective candidates.

Some means had to be found for adjudicating on the various claims. It is not clear whether the Guardians actually invited Edward to arbitrate on the question, or whether he simply imposed his will over them in order to give practical effect to his claims to be Scotland's feudal overlord. An assembly was summoned at his behest in May 1291 to determine both the mechanism by which the Scottish succession might be decided, and the question which underlay it, the extent of the English king's power to intervene in a Scottish legal matter. The solution eventually reached was that the various claimants would accept Edward's right to lordship and jurisdiction, and that he might take the realm of Scotland into his hands for the purpose of granting it to the successful 'competitor'. A court was then set up of 104 auditors, 40 chosen by each of the two leading competitors, Robert Bruce of Annandale and John Balliol, and 24 by Edward, its hearings to be held at Berwick, then in Scottish hands but the nearest Scottish town to England.

The situation with which the 104 auditors had to grapple was unprecedented. All the leading competitors traced their claims to the kingship through the female line,

10   EHD III No 57.

from one or other of the three daughters of David, Earl of Huntingdon, younger brother of Malcolm IV and William the Lion. If the normal principles of feudal law were followed, Scotland ought to be divided between the heirs of these three co-heiresses. If Scotland were to be regarded as a single entity, it must pass to a single heir, but which one? The final decision lay between John Balliol, grandson of the eldest daughter, and Robert Bruce, who argued that as the son of the second daughter, he was closest to the common ancestor.

After extensive searches for legal precedents, the court held in favour of Balliol. In this period, Edward seems to have acted with complete propriety. On 12 June 1291, he had formally promised to maintain the laws and customs of Scotland, and to hand the kingdom over to the rightful claimant within two months of the court's decision, on pain of a penalty of £100,000 in aid of the Holy Land. Now he abided by the rulings of the auditors. He gave Scotland into Balliol's hands, in return for Balliol's homage and fealty. If the position was less ideal than it would have been had Margaret lived and married his son, the events of 1290–92 still left Edward in a commanding position. He had secured practical recognition of his claims to be feudal overlord of Scotland in Balliol's homage and in the means by which Balliol had been accorded the crown. No longer could Scottish kings claim that their homage only related to lands held by them in England. However, yet again, events soon took an unexpected turn.

5.3   EDWARD I: THE YEARS OF DIFFICULTY 1293–1307

The last years of Edward I's long reign are entirely different both in tenor and detail from those before 1290, when he established himself, with Philip IV (the Fair) of France, as the dominant secular ruler of his age. In these years came war with France, the first stages of the long and far from glorious war over Scotland, conflict with the Pope over the taxation of the church, and conflict at home over secular taxation, which never reached the armed strife of his father's and grandfather's reigns, but might well have done had Edward not been prepared to make the concessions demanded, at least as a matter of form.

5.3.1   Scotland

John Balliol has gone down in Scottish national myth as Edward's puppet king, as *Toom Tabard* or 'Empty Surcoat'. However, in 1292, when he was awarded the Scottish crown, there was little to suggest it. True, Balliol held lands in England of the English crown, but so did the Bruces. Moreover, it might be presumed that the latter would be more malleable than Balliol. The senior Robert Bruce, 'the Competitor', was over 80 years old; his son had served under Edward at Evesham; his grandson, the future king, was still adolescent and an unknown quantity. In fact, it was Balliol's attempts to assert his independence from Edward which brought about a fresh crisis and his own downfall.

Friction rapidly developed over Edward's claim to be entitled, as superior feudal lord, to hear appeals from Balliol's legal judgments, and even to summon the Scottish king to answer for his actions in Edward's courts. Balliol argued that he could not answer in any matter concerning his kingdom without the counsel of the good men of his realm. This argument was rejected by Edward's parliament, at which Balliol appeared, but Balliol continued to assert his independence, to the point of entering into a treaty of alliance with Edward's enemy, Philip the Fair.

Meanwhile, relations between England and France had sharply deteriorated, mainly over Gascony once again. Philip made no secret of his desire to rejoin this valuable duchy to the French Crown, and a minor engagement between English and French ships off the coast of Brittany provided a pretext which led ultimately to Philip's confiscation of Gascony on 19 May 1294. Edward was then under pressure as a result of serious rebellion in Wales, which continued well into 1295, and the deteriorating situation in Scotland, so was unable initially to send large forces to Gascony. Philip then entered into an alliance with Norway, under which King Eric agreed, in return for a payment of £50,000, to provide 100 ships for four months each year as long as there was war between England and France.[11] This French problem, combined with circumstances in Scotland which led to a campaign of conquest and then a long-drawn out war against the rebellion led by William Wallace, brought a domestic crisis over the king's need for money, which lasted intermittently for the rest of Edward's reign and which also dogged his successor.

In March 1296, after Balliol refused to appear before him in parliament, Edward crossed the Tweed, captured Berwick and, having received Balliol's *diffidatio*, carried on northwards. From this point, Balliol seems to have become a broken reed. Most of the Scottish leaders surrendered after a defeat of the Scottish feudal host at Dunbar; Edward 'perambulated' the east coast as far north as Elgin until August and received Balliol's submission. At Brechin, Balliol surrendered his kingdom to Edward and was ceremonially stripped of the trappings of monarchy – the ripping of the royal arms from his surcoat gave rise to his nickname. He was imprisoned in England for three years and was then handed over to the custody of the papacy. He spent the remainder of his life in exile, dying in France in 1313.[12] The Scottish regalia, including the Stone of Scone on which Scottish kings sat during their inaugurations, was carried off to Westminster, and a new coronation chair was built which accommodated the Stone beneath its seat.[13]

It seems clear from Edward's actions that he was becoming increasingly autocratic, even tyrannical, as he grew older, and he would no longer be satisfied by mere feudal overlordship. The throne of Scotland was declared vacant. A parliament was summoned and the magnates did homage to Edward. John de Warenne, Earl of Surrey, was appointed to govern Scotland with the title of Keeper, and an English treasurer was also appointed.

---

11 Given that Norway still held Orkney, Eric's 100 ships posed a greater threat to English security than might appear to be the case today.

12 Balliol's stock in Scottish myth had fallen so low by the end of the 14th century that when John, Earl of Carrick, succeeded Robert II in 1390, he deemed it appropriate to abandon his baptismal name and reign as Robert III.

13 There are persistent tales that the true Stone was hidden away and that taken by Edward I was a substitute. Legend has it that the Stone was originally Jacob's pillow when he had the vision described in the Book of Exodus, and that it was brought to Scotland by incomers from Ireland around the 6th century AD. However, the present Stone, substitute or not, has been identified by geologists as a piece of Perthshire sandstone.

5.3.2   The crisis of 1297

In 1297, Edward faced a major crisis. Scotland, apparently subdued, burst into rebellion under the hitherto quite obscure figure of William Wallace, who was rapidly joined by the youngest Robert Bruce and a number of other Scottish magnates, and was appointed as sole Guardian of the Realm during the vacancy of the throne. At the same time, Edward wished to deal once and for all with the French incursion into Gascony by an ambitious campaign on two fronts. He himself would invade Flanders and link up with his continental allies, who had been wooed into supporting him by lengthy and expensive diplomatic manoeuvrings, while a second force under Roger Bigod, Earl of Norfolk, and Humphrey de Bohun, Earl of Hereford, landed in Gascony.

At this point, opposition at home came to a head. Edward's finances had become increasingly strained in the past few years. His policies were expensive; the cost of constructing the four great Welsh castles alone was £80,000, and there had been further heavy expenditure on military campaigns. The revenues of Gascony, the king's most prosperous province, were currently out of Edward's reach, and a calculation carried out by the Exchequer after the Statute of Wales had established that the revenues of the Crown available from normal sources amounted to no more than £26,828 3s 9d, far below what was needed even to service the king's current debts. Indeed, Prestwich has estimated the cost of the French war as some £450,000 and total military expenditure in the period 1294–98 at £750,000.[14]

Before 1290, Edward was able to finance his activities without frequent recourse to extraordinary taxation. There had been a Fifteenth on moveables in 1275, a Thirteenth in 1283, but there would be no fewer than seven such 'lay subsidies' in the years 1290–1307, suggesting that the king now considered these a normal rather than exceptional means of raising revenue. Lay subsidies grew increasingly unpopular, with widespread evasion.

The first coherent opposition came from the clergy. A tax on them in 1294 had been much criticised, as was Edward's earlier extension of royal justice as against ecclesiastical courts. Complaints from English and French clergy that their respective kings were plundering their livings to pay for the war led to the issue by Pope Boniface VIII in 1296 of the Bull *Clericis Laicos*, forbidding the taxation of the clergy for secular purposes without authority from the Holy See. On the strength of this, the Archbishop of Canterbury, Robert Winchelsey, refused the king's demand for a Fifth from the clergy in the parliament of November 1296. Edward retaliated by placing the clergy outside the king's peace and so, effectively, outlaws, and ordered the seizure of all the temporalities of the church, redeemable by payments equal to a Fifth. Had Winchelsey been a Becket or a Stephen Langton, this stand-off might have continued indefinitely. However, he opted not to stand on principle, but to allow the clergy to follow their individual consciences. The majority submitted and a peace of a sort was gradually cobbled together, assisted by a useful precedent in France, where the bishops chose to petition Pope Boniface to allow them to grant a subsidy to their king.

But by then, secular opposition had emerged into the open. In the February parliament of 1297, the co-leaders of the Gascon expedition, Roger Bigod, Earl of Norfolk, and Humphrey de Bohun, Earl of Hereford, flatly refused to go overseas

---

14   MC Prestwich, *Edward I*, Yale English Monarchs Series, 2nd edn, 1997, Yale UP, pp 398–400.

except in the personal company of the king. They claimed that they had only been 'affectionately requested', not commanded, to go to Gascony, and were therefore entitled to refuse; further, that their hereditary offices of Marshal and Constable required them to be in constant attendance on the king. By July, they had deepened their opposition and challenged not only the Fifth, but an earlier demand that all men with lands worth more than £20 per year should accompany the king to Flanders. They held a large assembly in the Forest of Wyre on the Welsh border, which must have revived memories of the actions of Montfort and his cohorts a generation earlier. In the same month, the two appeared armed at Westminster to protest against the levy of an Eighth, which had been granted, according to one account, by a group of *plebs* assembled in the King's chamber. At the same time, a levy, or *maltolte* of £2 on each sack of wool exported and a *prise* of wool ordered at Easter aroused further anger, as did the calling-in of debts owed to the crown. Prises – the requisitioning of goods without payment or later compensation – were a common and widely disliked means of providing for the physical needs of armies.

At the core of the secular opposition to Edward in 1297 seems to have been a sense among those who bore the brunt of campaigning – the household knights, the tenants-in-chief and their retainers – that they were increasingly taken for granted by the king. 1297 marked the second occasion on which Edward summoned all £20 landowners to serve outside England, and it was service outside the British Isles which had been one of the chief concerns of the rebels of 1213–14. Edward's reign in fact marks a watershed between the raising of armies via the feudal system and the paid national levies, which were to form the mainstay of Edward III's armies. Under Edward I, his household knights formed the core of armies, 'national' manpower supplementing the feudal when large forces were required. To Wilkinson, this transition created further insecurity in the minds of the magnates as to their position in society. Not only were they in danger of being displaced from their role as the king's counsellors, but also from their traditional position at the forefront of his armies.[15] At any rate, by the time the magnates were summoned to assemble for military service on 7 July, a considerable number were openly refusing to serve abroad.

By 14 July, the king decided that a reconciliation with Winchelsey was necessary and, recognising a need for royal 'spin', organised an elaborate ceremony at the time the leading men of the country did homage to Edward of Carnarvon as keeper of the realm during his father's absence. The king joined Winchelsey on a platform specially built outside Westminster Hall, asked his pardon for any wrongs he and his ministers might have committed, and sought the loyalty of his subjects when he left the country to deal with his enemies.

However, even this eloquent plea from a royal warrior already approaching 60, who almost immediately had another of those narrow escapes from death to which he was rather prone,[16] when his horse shied at a windmill and fell down a rampart on the way to embarkation, had limited effect. Edward's Flemish expedition numbered

---

15 B Wilkinson, *The Later Middle Ages in England*, 1969, Longman, pp 110–11.

16 There was the assassination attempt on crusade and an accident in Gascony in 1287, when the floor of an upper room collapsed beneath him. There would be two more during the Scottish wars: in 1298, when Edward was kicked in the chest by a horse when spending the night in an open field, and fought the Battle of Falkirk the following day with two broken ribs; and at the siege of Stirling in 1304, when a crossbow bolt passed through his clothes and embedded itself in his saddle.

only some 100 bannerets[17] and knights and 570 squires, instead of the 2,000 knights he had hoped for. A clerical council summoned by Winchelsey rejected the king's request for taxation of the clergy, despite his promise to confirm the Charters and to redress their grievances on his return from Flanders, insisting that no tax would be granted unless the Pope consented. The king ordered the Exchequer to collect an Eighth from the laity, regardless of the lack of parliamentary consent.

Before the king sailed, his opponents drew up a statement of grievances, the *Monstraunces*,[18] and delivered them to him, though he was later to deny that he had received them. The authors of the statement complained that they had not been informed where they were expected to serve. No service, they claimed, was required in Flanders and in any event, the king's subjects were too impoverished by his exactions to perform military service anywhere. Further, the campaign in Flanders was unwise, given the rebellion in Scotland. There were protests about the arbitrary deprivation of baronial franchises, the king's failure to abide by the terms of Magna Carta, the burden of taxation and the harsh application of the Forest Law.

The king attempted to soothe the opposition in a series of letters produced, but to no avail. As he was embarking at Winchelsea, Bigod, Bohun and a group of bannerets and knights arrived at the Exchequer at Westminster and, claiming to speak on behalf of the community of the realm, set out the main heads of grievance against the king. All present declared their opposition to the Eighth and to the prise of wool. Edward attempted to mollify his opponents. He ordered proclamations to be issued that the Eighth would not be used as a precedent in favour of taxation without consent, that there was no intention to reduce anybody to serfdom, as Bohun had claimed, and reminding his subjects of their fealty and homage. However, civil war was a real possibility, and King Edward therefore took a very calculated risk in leaving the country.

Affairs in England were left during the king's absence in the nominal charge of Edward of Carnarvon, then aged 13. A parliament was summoned to meet in London from 30 September, probably to obtain retrospective consent to the Eighth. Chronicle accounts of events at this time are scanty, but they do suggest an atmosphere of tension and that military preparations were made on both sides.

What took place in the October parliament seems to have been dictated in part by the news of the quite unexpected defeat of the Earl of Surrey and his army by William Wallace at Stirling Bridge, which had reached London by 24 September. The king's opponents could bask in the satisfaction of knowing that their advice that Edward should not campaign on the continent when the situation in Scotland was so serious had been correct, but they recognised an obligation to reach a settlement, so that steps could be taken to restore the English position there. They were therefore prepared to moderate their demands, which were set out in a document known as *De Tallagio non Concedendo*,[19] put to the King's Council. Many demands were culled directly from the *Monstraunces*, but there was a clear statement that no aid or 'tallage' was to be taken without the consent of all, from archbishops to freemen. Further, prises should only be taken with the consent of those whose goods were seized, and all those who had refused to take part in the expeditions to Flanders and Gascony were pardoned.

---

17 A banneret was a knight who commanded other knights on campaign.
18 EHD III No 69.
19 EHD III No 75.

The King's Council acted cautiously in the king's absence. They were not prepared to make additions to Magna Carta, nor to issue a general pardon, but promised in letters patent to do all in their power to persuade the king to release the 'rancour and indignation' in which he held them, and to confirm the Charters once more. In return for these, and the further concessions set out in the document known as the *Confirmatio Cartarum*, parliament was prepared on 14 October to grant a Fourteenth. The *Confirmatio* represents a partial acceptance of some of the major provisions of *De Tallagio*, but couched in vague terms. In future, 'aids, mises and prises' would not be taken without the 'common consent of the realm, and for the common profit of the same realm', though there was no indication as to what constituted 'common assent'. The 40 shilling tax on wool exports imposed earlier in the year was abolished, but, unlike *De Tallagio*, the *Confirmatio* provided for its re-imposition with the common assent of 'the greater part of the community', another very vague formula.

All this had been agreed without the king's consent; indeed, it appears that the king had agreed in advance to nothing more than a confirmation of the Charters themselves, and that the levying of the Eighth would not be taken as a precedent. However, the king accepted the *fait accompli*, in the letter if not in the spirit. Shortly afterwards, the Pope modified the stance he had expressed in the Bull *Clericis Laicos*, and in a further Bull, *Etsi de Statu*, accepted that secular rulers might tax the clergy without papal consent in emergencies, making the considerable concession that those secular rulers were the proper judges of what constituted emergencies.

What can be made of this episode in relation to the evolution of parliament? First, that formal recognition had been given to the principle that taxation, as distinct from normal royal revenues, could only take place with the assent of representatives of the realm, though it was not yet clear what the composition of a parliament should be in order to be representative. It would seem that a mere summons of *plebs* or a limited group of nobles and prelates to the king's chamber was insufficient, and also, though this is less certain, that a parliament composed only of magnates and prelates summoned by name was also insufficient. Second, that a parliament could sit in the absence of the king, although no precedent was established as to whether it could sit in the absence of the king's representative, or be summoned other than by the king. These were issues which were to emerge in the next reign. Further, since the king's councillors made concessions on his behalf which satisfied the opposition, and the king acquiesced in those concessions, the question of whether a king who flouted the law could be lawfully deprived of his throne remained unasked.

5.3.3   The final years

The last years of Edward I's reign were troubled. Though peace had been made with France, with Philip the Fair conceding English rule over Gascony and Edward contracting to marry Philip's half-sister and Edward of Carnarvon his daughter, the king's desire to subdue the rebellious Scots grew to an obsession and led to long, costly and indecisive warfare for the rest of the reign and beyond.

Before long, the king was ignoring the agreement of 1297 and the atmosphere between the magnates and himself grew more suspicious as financial exactions resumed their former scale and form. In January 1298, the magnates refused to serve on the punitive expedition against Wallace until the Charters were publicly proclaimed. In 1300, a further confrontation led to another solemn re-issue of the

Charters and the issue of a further 20 articles as the *Articuli super Cartas*,[20] which made further concessions, though as each article ended with the phrase 'saving the right and prerogative of the Crown', these concessions were limited in effect. The main provisions of importance were that three knights were to be appointed in each shire to deal with infringements of the Charters, and that in future, prises were to be taken only by authorised purveyors, and only for the purposes of the king's *military* household. Sheriffs should in future be elected by the county concerned, not appointed by the king. Although these concessions could be revoked by a king determined to override them, they still represent a movement towards the restriction of the arbitrary power of the king, and towards greater democracy at local level.

In fact, after 1301, the opposition to Edward grew less determined, for reasons which are unclear, though it is possible that his enemies now recognised that he could not live much longer, and that his heir was a mediocrity. However, the king grew steadily more autocratic and more unscrupulous in his determination to gain the necessary revenues for the Scottish war. Further, in the autumn of 1305, when the Scottish problem appeared at last to have been settled and his domestic opponents were quiescent, putting him in a position of renewed strength, he persuaded Pope Clement V to annul the new legislation made in the period 1297–1300, on the basis that it had been forced from him, and was entirely different in nature from those laws which had been made by him freely and with the common assent of the realm, in the same way as John had secured the annulment of the original Charter by Innocent III. This action was to provide an unfortunate precedent. Future reformers were faced with the possibility that a king might grant the changes they sought and then renege on his promises by gaining papal absolution from them. Something which had been granted by the king when in a position of weakness could thus be put aside when the king had gained strength. What were reformers to do when faced with such an impasse? That question was to be answered in the next reign.

Very gradually, the Scots were subdued. Most of their leaders surrendered in 1304, after the English captured the great castle of Stirling, but it was not until William Wallace was betrayed and captured in August 1305, as he lay with his mistress, according to one account, that Edward could declare in parliament that Scotland was conquered. Wallace was subjected to a show trial at Westminster, on the basis of treason to his feudal lord, and was hanged, drawn and quartered.

Having seen his greatest enemy executed in the most brutal fashion even a brutal age could devise, Edward's actions towards Scotland moderated, with a recognition that English forms could not simply be imposed on the Scots, and some compromise was necessary. Ten Scots named by Edward as representatives of Scotland met with 20 of the king's councillors to draw up an ordinance. John of Brittany, Edward's nephew, was appointed as royal lieutenant in Scotland, and Guardian of the Land, no longer the Realm, of Scotland. The Scottish chancellor and chamberlain remained in office. Royal justice in Scotland would be administered by four pairs of justices, each pair composed of an Englishman and a Scot. Castles and sheriffdoms were divided between Englishmen and Scots, the most important passing into English hands. An enquiry was to be made into Scottish law, and 'the laws and customs which are clearly displeasing to God and to reason' would be corrected by John of Brittany and his council, which included 22 Scots. Matters which required the King's assent would be

20   EHD III No 85.

put before parliament at Easter 1306. The oath to be sworn by councillors and officials in Scotland carefully avoided any suggestion that Scotland was a kingdom. Triumph seemed to have arrived at last.

Yet again, events took an unexpected turn. Less than six months later, on 10 February 1306, the youngest Robert Bruce, who had made peace with Edward as far back as 1302, murdered a former confederate and rival for the vacant throne, John Comyn the Red, Lord of Badenoch, in a church at Dumfries. It is unclear what led to the killing, which ranked not only as murder, but as sacrilege, and brought about Bruce's excommunication and condemnation by the entire Christian world. Immediately after, perhaps because he no longer had anything to lose by a bid for the throne, Bruce declared himself king and had himself crowned and installed at Scone on 25 March. The English were taken completely by surprise, and the work of conquering Scotland had to begin all over again, with extremes of savagery on both sides. By the murder of Comyn, following on the actions of Wallace and his rebels since 1297, it was considered by the English that the Scots had put themselves outside the bounds of chivalry which bound honourable enemies, and they exacted terrible revenge on any of the Scottish leaders who fell into their hands. Three of Bruce's brothers were executed; his sister and the Countess of Buchan, who had exercised her family's hereditary right of crowning the Scottish kings in favour of Bruce, were both imprisoned in iron cages until 1310. This desire for vengeance, already seen in his treatment of Dafydd ap Gruffydd and his children after 1282, is one of the less pleasant features of Edward's character, and undoubtedly grew more pronounced in his final years. Bruce himself took refuge either in the Hebrides or on Rathlin Island, off the North Irish coast, and it is to this period when his fortunes were at their lowest ebb that the famous but apocryphal story of the spider is attributed.

Edward led another expedition north, but was now so weakened by age and illness that he spent much of the winter of 1306–07 bedridden at the monastery of Lanercost. He recovered enough in the spring to sit a horse and set out on campaign again, but on 7 July 1307, he died at Burgh by Sands just south of the Scottish border, commanding his heir, according to one chronicler, to boil his body until the flesh was stripped from his bones and then to bear the bones at the head of his army until the Scots were finally defeated. Edward II, however, broke off the campaign at once and took his father home for a magnificent burial in Westminster Abbey.

CHAPTER 6

A KING DETHRONED: EDWARD II 1307–27

6.1   INTRODUCTION

Edward I was the last medieval English king who was completely secure on his throne. Of his nine descendants who reigned between 1307 and 1485, no fewer than four lost their crowns and died by violent means at the hands of supplanters. A fifth was temporarily deposed and forced into exile. The rot set in with Edward II.

Every second or third generation, the Plantagenet dynasty threw up an exception to its normal run of able, dynamic, ruthless men of war.[1] These, simplistically, may be placed in the famous category created by the authors of *1066 and All That*: the Weak King. The first was Henry III, the second his grandson, Edward II.

6.2   THE MAN AND HIS TRAGEDY

Nearly seven centuries after his dreadful death, Edward II remains an enigma. As heir apparent, he made no mark. As king, he appears a largely passive figure, the tool of his favourites and enemies, only on the rarest of occasions displaying the energy of his ancestors. To his contemporaries, he was a puzzle. Although he was cast in the physical mould of his father, he had the conventional aristocratic military education, and held nominal command of expeditions against the Scots from the age of 16, he seems to have had little enthusiasm for war. Though he had four children by his marriage and acknowledged an illegitimate son, it is likely that his relationships with his male favourites were homosexual. In character, he was so unlike his father that it was rumoured that he was a changeling. Edward I's recreations were conventionally aristocratic – jousting, hunting, falconry and chess. His son preferred the distinctly unkingly pursuits of farriery, hedging and ditching, and delighted in the company of minstrels, jugglers and other 'simple people'.[2]

Like John, Edward II's difficulties were to a considerable extent inherited. Edward I bequeathed a burden of debt estimated by Prestwich at £200,000, plus the continuing Scottish war. His policies and financial demands had given rise to considerable baronial and clerical opposition, which reached a height in the crisis of 1297. Although domestic discord became less open afterwards, it continued to fester and emerged again on the new king's accession. Edward I was also an extremely hard act for an inexperienced young man of 23 to follow. However, Edward II's tragedy was to an equal extent of his own making. He seems to have been quite unable to recognise the strength of the opposition to him, the hatred engendered by his devotion first to Piers Gaveston, later to the Despensers, or to take any constructive steps to

---

1   The term 'Plantagenet dynasty' is anachronistic, but convenient. Although Henry II's father, Geoffrey of Anjou, received the by-name Plantagenet as a result of his association with a sprig of broom (*planta genista*), it was first used as a surname by Richard, Duke of York, father of Edward IV, as late as 1460.

2   They, at least, seem to have nurtured an affection for him; the earliest version of the Robin Hood legend, dating from later in the 14th century, refers to him as 'Edward, our comely king'.

deal with it. In times of crisis, he became completely passive and acted entirely at the dictate of his enemies.

For 16 years or more, Edward's enemies were content to impose restraints upon him and to try to ensure that he operated only within them. This followed the precedent set by Montfort under Henry III, if in a more brutal and less principled fashion. It also demonstrates the essential conservatism of medieval movements for reform; they were attempts to turn back the clock to a semi-mythical age where the king did not 'abuse' his powers and acted in co-operation with his magnates. But after this policy of restraint proved a failure several times over, Edward's enemies, led by his queen and her lover, took the unprecedented step of dethroning him, and so set a pattern for the future. This deposition, and those which followed, were palace revolutions rather than popular revolutions, but, nevertheless, elements of the philosophies of 1258–64 emerged again, and were used to create a conceptual framework for the separation of an anointed king from his crown and kingly power.

6.3   THE ORDINANCES

6.3.1   The beginning of the reign

A desire that the actions of Edward I in ignoring the concessions made by him in 1297–1300 would not be repeated was probably behind the additional clause added to the coronation oath at the time Edward II was crowned on 25 February 1308. Not only did the new king swear to maintain the laws and customs allowed by earlier kings, particularly those of Edward the Confessor, to maintain peace and do justice, and to protect the church, he also swore to 'maintain and preserve the laws and rightful customs which the community of your realm shall have chosen'. This therefore was an oath not simply to maintain existing law, but to maintain the law as it might develop during the reign.

6.3.2   Piers Gaveston

Edward's relationship with Piers (or Peter) Gaveston was a cause of concern even before his accession. Gaveston was a handsome young Gascon whose father had been one of Edward I's household knights, and had grown up alongside the heir. However, as an adult, he was considered unsuitable for a place in his household, and when early in 1307, Edward proposed that Gaveston should be given the county of Ponthieu, which had come into Plantagenet possession through Eleanor of Castile, the king not only physically attacked his son, but banished Gaveston from the realm for good measure.[3]

---

3   It is unclear whether the thoroughly heterosexual Edward I was aware of the apparent nature of his son's affection for Gaveston, but the relationship between the two was certainly uneasy in Edward I's final years. Quite apart from the events of early 1307, there was a period between June and October 1305 when the heir was forbidden his father's presence and deprived of financial support after disputing possession of land with the Archbishop of Canterbury.

It was only after Edward II's death that any writer stated unequivocally that he 'delighted inordinately in the vice of sodomy',[4] but the manner by which both Edward and the younger Despenser were put to death strongly implies that the king was considered in his lifetime to be homosexual, a matter of repugnance in the 14th century, when even heterosexual relations within marriage were regarded by the omnipotent church at best as a regrettable necessity for the procreation of children. In the secular world, the fashionable cult of courtly love was based on the premise that the object of devotion was unattainable, and so was by definition unsullied by physical lusts. Close male friendships were a common feature of what was essentially a warrior society, but, again, acceptable only where there was no physical relationship.[5] If, as seems likely, Edward II was believed to adopt the passive role in homosexual acts, then in the eyes of contemporaries, this also demonstrated a contemptible want of masculinity.

As soon as his admirer became king, Gaveston was recalled and granted the earldom of Cornwall, previously a royal possession, together with marriage to Edward's niece. When early in 1308, Edward went to France to be married to Isabella, to whom he had been betrothed in 1299, Gaveston was appointed keeper of the realm. This was a position of great power, normally held by a close male relation of the king, since its holder not only acted on behalf of the king in government, but exercised his powers of patronage in relation to grants and restorations of land, marriages, wardships and other matters of immediate concern to the magnates. Edward II had acted as keeper of the realm in 1297, and the post was held on other occasions by Edward I's brother, Edmund, Earl of Lancaster, and paternal cousin, Edmund, Earl of Cornwall.[6] The noses of the great nobles were therefore put considerably out of joint when Gaveston was appointed. Very shortly, the new queen's kinsmen were complaining that the king loved Gaveston more than he did his wife.

Had Gaveston been a man of ability, who had in some degree earned his rewards by service to the monarch, or a senior member of the English magnate class, then the hostility engendered by Edward's generosity might have been less extreme and might not have had the consequences it finally did. As it was, it was not long before the first of many storms broke over the hapless king.

At the April parliament of 1308, the disaffected barons appeared in arms and demanded that the king banish Gaveston, on the basis that he had disinherited the crown by being given the earldom of Cornwall, alienated the king from the magnates and bound confederates to himself by oath. Not only did they claim that the fourth clause of his coronation oath bound the king to order Gaveston's banishment at the will of the community of the realm, if the account of events given by an anonymous canon of Bridlington Priory is accurate (this is uncertain), they identified a distinction between the crown and the person of the king, and claimed that their homage and fealty was due only to the former.[7]

This seems almost too convenient for the small cabal who finally deposed Edward II at early in 1327. Not only is the person of the king separate from the

---

4   *Chronica Monasterii de Melsa* (EA Bond (ed)), Rolls Series, London, 1867, vol II, p 355.

5   VHH Green, *The Madness of Kings*, 1993, Sutton, p 49.

6   Admittedly, Edward II's half-brothers – the sons of Edward I's second marriage – were infants, and the Earls of Cornwall and Lancaster now dead, but Lancaster's two sons were adult, and there were also non-royal persons of stature who could have been given the post.

7   MH Keen, *England in the Later Middle Ages*, 1st edn, 1973, Methuen, pp 78–79.

institution, so that the allegiance of those who owe homage is owed to the institution and not the man, but if the king acts outside the law, his vassals are under a duty to compel his observance of it, by violence if necessary.

The king was compelled to issue letters patent promising to suffer no impediment to Gaveston's departure from England, and the Archbishop of Canterbury declared the favourite excommunicate should he fail to depart on or before 25 June. However, the form of Gaveston's exile was hardly redolent of disgrace, and certainly not what his enemies were prepared to accept, since Edward appointed him lieutenant in Ireland, responsible for exercising royal authority there as, effectively, the king's viceroy, and granted him extensive lands in both England and Gascony.

6.3.3   The making of the Ordinances

By April 1309, the king had recalled Gaveston and there was again an atmosphere of confrontation between king and magnates. This set the pattern for the rest of the reign. Edward would be forced into concessions and to divest himself of his favourites; he would then renege on his promises; there would be a further confrontation and more concessions. In the July parliament, Edward was forced to re-issue the *Articuli Super Cartas* as the price of acquiescence in Gaveston's return, but it soon became apparent that the passion between king and favourite was, if anything, more intense than ever and that both were quite blind to the worsening hostility of the baronage. According to the chroniclers, although Gaveston had promised to behave well and live in peace, he once more treated the magnates as his servants and encouraged discord between them and the king. He affronted baronial dignity further by inventing scurrilous nicknames for some of the leading magnates – the Earl of Warwick was 'the Black Dog of Arden', the Earl of Pembroke 'Joseph the Jew' – but the final straw was his ability to defeat the greatest among them in the joust. Five earls refused to attend the October parliament 'because of Peter'. In December, the king attempted to arrest scandalmongers. Given the tense atmosphere which now prevailed, he formally prohibited unauthorised gatherings of armed men and instructed the Earls of Gloucester, Richmond and Surrey to ensure that none appeared armed at the February parliament.

It was therefore an act of open defiance when the same three earls went armed into the February parliament and laid before the king a statement of their grievances and a demand for a commission of inquiry. The thrust of these was that the king had been led by 'evil counsellors' into living on extortion, that grants made to him by earlier parliaments had been wasted on extravagance and on favour to those evil counsellors, and that by discontinuing the campaign to hold Scotland after his father's death, the king had dismembered the crown.

At this stage, the opposition to the king was principled in nature, and followed the precedents set in earlier reigns, particularly of the period 1258–59. By letters patent of 16 March 1310, Edward agreed to the appointment of 21 'Ordainers' with full powers to reform his realm and household, who would draw up ordinances setting out the programme of reform. However, the magnates themselves accepted that the appointment of Ordainers was not to be taken as a precedent in the future.

By the summer of 1311, the king was in such financial difficulty that he was forced to use the crown jewels as security for an Italian loan. Debts inherited from his father remained unpaid and a renewal of the Scottish war brought further expense. Not only that, the new king was personally extravagant to a much greater extent than his father. He was thus in a weak position when parliament assembled in August to hear the demands of the Ordainers.

6.3.4   Terms of the Ordinances

The Ordinances of 1311[8] comprise some 44 clauses, which can be grouped under two heads. First, there is the inevitable condemnation of Gaveston and a fresh demand that he should be exiled. Three other named individuals are also condemned, though in less extravagant terms. Much of the remainder of the text comprises an attempt to curb the king's extravagances, to establish baronial and parliamentary control of royal finances and to place those finances on more secure lines. Previous alienations of royal lands were to be annulled and none made in the future, until the king's debts were paid. Revenues were to be paid into the Exchequer, not to the household; the Exchequer was thus to have first call on income, and a portion of available moneys would be paid to the king for the maintenance of himself and his household. No prises were to be made without the agreement of the owner of the goods, and all new customs and *maltoltes* levied since 1274 were abolished.

This financial programme, though it dealt with all the grievances inherited from Edward I's time, would have put Edward II in an even worse position had it been put fully into effect, since only by giving him permanent access to the domestic sources of revenue of which they wished to deprive him could the Ordainers lessen his heavy reliance on foreign credit with its high interest payments. They wished the king to 'live off his own', but failed to recognise that, such was the increase in the demands on royal revenues since any king had last been able to live off his own, and the inextricable entanglement of royal and national finances, this was now impossible. They sought to rid the country of the king's financial abuses, but failed to put into place a system of regular grants, agreed by parliament, which would have made such abuses unnecessary.

The remaining provisions of the Ordinances sought to restrict the king's independent freedom of action in ways which acted as a severe affront to royal dignity. Edward II was neither to leave the realm, nor to engage in foreign war, nor to appoint a keeper of the realm without the consent of the baronage in parliament. If he engaged in war without such consent, the military service due from the barons would be denied him. His power to choose his servants was severely restricted, since the appointment of all the chief officers of state and household required the consent of the baronage in parliament. Sheriffs were to be appointed either by the chancellor, treasurer and Council, or by the Barons of the Exchequer, the treasurer and the chief justices. All officials would take an oath on appointment to maintain the Ordinances. Restraints were placed on the king's use of the Privy Seal, restricting the extent to which he could act independently of his chief officers. Parliaments were to be held once or twice each year. All statutes would be maintained, provided they were not contrary to the Charters or the Ordinances. Finally, the Ordainers claimed sole right to determine points of doubt in the Charters, and a committee of magnates was to be appointed to hear complaints against the king's ministers.

---

8   EHD III No 100.

The Ordinances are a mixture of old and new. Some clauses are re-statements of matters which had been at issue in 1297, indeed, as far back as 1258. Others related specifically to recent concerns, but many of these involved Edward I's later years and were not simply concerns about his son. They are conservative rather than radical, and are to some degree a backward step, since they reflect exclusively the concerns of the aristocracy.

6.3.5 Crisis

Ultimately, the discord which came to a head in 1311 arose through aristocratic envy and loathing of Gaveston, but though the king acceded reluctantly to the Ordinances, he was still not prepared to renounce Gaveston. In November, a parliament composed entirely of magnates produced a second set of Ordinances, demanding the removal of named office-holders. This was deeply repugnant to the king, who set about the building up of a party to contest the Ordinances. Gaveston was back in England by January, more favoured than ever.

The ensuing conflict proved disastrous for the king. This marks a distinct departure from the pattern of 1258–65, when civil war only came much later, and 1297, when there was no fighting, but is similar to that of 1215. Gaveston, having escaped from Newcastle by sea with the king, took refuge in the royal castle at Scarborough. He surrendered to Aymer de Valence, Earl of Pembroke, and Earl Warenne, two moderate Ordainers, on a promise of surety, but was 'sprung' by the Earl of Warwick as he travelled south in their custody. Nine days later, on 19 June 1312, Gaveston was summarily beheaded on Warwick's orders and in the presence of Thomas of Lancaster, the king's first cousin and future chief enemy.

It could be argued that Warwick had acted in accordance with the law, since the Ordinances had declared Gaveston an outlaw should he ever set foot in any of the king's domains, and thus he was outside the king's peace and liable to death without trial. Edward II, acting independently of parliament and baronage, had specifically repealed the relevant clause of the Ordinances, though it remains unclear whether he was acting within his legal powers by doing so. Edward henceforth harboured a bitter hatred of Lancaster, whom he considered the main instigator of Gaveston's 'execution'.

The events of 1312 and disputes among the baronial Ordainers led what had hitherto been a united body to split up. Pembroke and Warenne, both believing that their personal honour had been slighted by the failure of Warwick and Lancaster to respect the surety they had given to Gaveston, went over to the king's side, putting Edward in a strong enough position to return to London, but not to resume the fight. The relative weakness of both sides created a suitable atmosphere for peace negotiations, which were carried out under the auspices of a cardinal and bishop sent for this purpose by the Pope. At length, in October 1313, the king's leading opponents made a public apology in Westminster Hall, in return for which they and 500 lesser malcontents were pardoned and restored to the king's peace. Implicitly, the Ordinances were set aside. The king therefore emerged from the crisis of 1311–12 in a position of strength, but he was about to suffer a blow to his prestige from which he never recovered.

6.3.6 Bannockburn

Robert Bruce spent the period 1307–14 in retrenchment and the consolidation of what had been an extremely precarious position, by gaining possession of the large areas of land held by his domestic enemies, augmenting the Scottish treasury by raids into England and taking steps to recover the major Scottish castles, which had come into English possession in the period 1303–06. By the spring of 1313, he was in a vastly stronger possession than he had been on the death of Edward I.

In the summer of 1313, the English garrison of Stirling Castle, the strongest in Scotland, came to an agreement with their besiegers that they would surrender if an English army failed to appear within three leagues of the castle by Midsummer Day 1314. Even Edward II's unwarlike soul was stirred into action. He announced his intention to invade Scotland after Easter. The magnates reminded him that, under the Ordinances, which they considered to be still in force, he should not engage in war without the consent of parliament, but the king ignored this protest and marched on Scotland in May.

The English army, an enormous one for the day, did indeed reach Stirling before Midsummer Day 1314, and the Scots accepted without argument that the castle had been relieved, but the king, encouraged by his magnates, insisted on fighting. The Battle of Bannockburn was a complete disaster for the English, due in no small measure to their commanders making the fundamental military error of underestimating their enemy. Edward II fled from the field, leaving many knights dead or in Scottish hands. From then on, the Scottish situation grew steadily worse, the Scots raiding deep into England and capturing Berwick in 1318. In March 1315, Robert Bruce's brother Edward invaded Ireland and, after a series of spectacular victories, was crowned King of Ireland in May 1316. His success was, however, short-lived, since he rapidly lost the support of the leading Irish chiefs and was killed near Dundalk in 1318.

By these military failures, Edward II lost any respect which he might still have held. The success or failure of a medieval king was based principally on two things: his personal prestige, itself based largely on his military achievements and the trust he engendered in his subjects; and on his maintaining the support of his greatest magnates. Edward II was an abject failure in both respects and, most dangerously for him, his enemies could produce a potential monarch to replace him, for the first time since Louis of France a century earlier. More dangerously still, that potential monarch was no foreign invader, but a Plantagenet. It is not clear whether Thomas of Lancaster, Edward paternal cousin, saw himself as a future ruler, but after Queen Isabella became estranged from her husband around 1324 and threw in her lot with the king's enemies, the baronial opposition had an appropriate alternative king in the person of the young heir, born in 1312. Simon de Montfort and his confederates seem never to have considered deposing Henry III, but the point at which that might have become a real possibility, had they an alternative candidate of their own,[9] was never reached. Under Edward II, this Rubicon would be crossed.

---

9   Henry III's two sons, his brother and nephews were all irreconcilable enemies of Simon de Montfort by the time civil war broke out, even if deposition had been considered.

6.4   THOMAS OF LANCASTER

Following Gaveston's murder, Edward relied mainly on Pembroke for support, but after Bannockburn, Pembroke's reputation and influence were much diminished for a period. Gilbert de Clare, Earl of Gloucester, was killed at Bannockburn leaving no male heir, and the Earl of Warwick died in the following year. This left Thomas of Lancaster without a serious rival among the magnates, and he lost no time in turning this to advantage in his dealings with the king.

Lancaster seems to have been a man with little in the way of principles or moral scruples, whose actions from 1315 onwards were dictated by personal ambition rather than a sincere desire for reform. In this he was unlike Simon de Montfort, though, ironically, he was also to be seen by the common people as their great champion. Lancaster was the first of the semi-royal magnates, the paternal cousins of kings, who were to threaten the throne from 1399 onwards. He was Edward II's first cousin through their fathers; his mother had been Queen of Navarre by her first marriage; his half-sister married Philip the Fair of France, making him uncle to Queen Isabella. However, neither Edward I nor his son had given Lancaster the position and prominence which he believed were his by right of his illustrious pedigree.

To McKisack, Lancaster's aim was to reduce Edward II to a puppet king, by using the powers he believed to be inherent in his hereditary office of Steward of England. The king would be guided and controlled by a small baronial council under Lancaster's presidency, with a household whose officers were appointed by Lancaster. Events were to show, however, that Lancaster was not a man able to win or to hold the loyalty of either his fellow magnates or his own retainers.

In 1315–16, the king put up little or no resistance to Lancaster's ambitions; for most of 1315, the Earl was effectively in control of royal administration and at the parliament of February 1316, the king appointed him to be chief of the King's Council and to take charge of his affairs. At the same time, the king declared that he now wished to observe the Ordinances.[10] Though power very much lay with Lancaster, he could not always command the support of Council or parliament and, like Montfort at times of difficulty, retired to his estates to sulk. This resulted in paralysis in government, at a time when external events made this particularly dangerous. The period 1315–18 was marked by particularly severe weather, which caused repeated bad harvests, famine and pestilence, leading to social unrest and increased incidence of crime in many parts of the country. At the same time, the Scots raids became more frequent and more serious, and it must have appeared to many in the north that the king's government was incapable of protecting them.

6.4.1   The Middle Party

Lancaster's position was not unchallenged. A 'Middle Party' gradually emerged under the leadership of the Earl of Pembroke, supporting the Ordinances but opposed to Lancaster. It comprised a number of leading magnates, including the king's half-brother, Thomas of Brotherton, Earl of Norfolk, a confederation of Marcher lords and a group of officers of the royal household. Although the Middle Party's objectives are not entirely clear, its members seem to have wished to persuade the king to act

---

10   M McKisack, *The Fourteenth Century*, Oxford History of England, 1963, OUP, p 48.

according to the Ordinances and to improve royal government and defence against the Scots. Their attitude to Lancaster is also unclear. Pembroke was opposed to him for personal reasons, following Lancaster's slight on his honour in seizing Gaveston. McKisack considers, however, that the baronial and episcopal element within the Middle Party recognised, pragmatically, that Lancaster could not be ousted from his position without violence, and therefore hoped to persuade him into at least a semblance of co-operation.

Co-operation and moderation were concepts fundamentally alien to Lancaster's character but, following a series of parleys from April 1318, he agreed that the Ordinances should be maintained, the king's evil counsellors should be removed and that he and his allies should be pardoned for all their trespasses against the king. Edward then made a solemn declaration at St Paul's that he would confirm the Ordinances, make peace with Lancaster and rely in future on the advice and counsel of his barons.

Lancaster, however, refused to consent to these terms unless two conditions were satisfied. First, that lands alienated and gifts made in contravention of the Ordinances should be resumed by the Crown. Second, that the evil counsellors were removed, as only then could he approach the king in safety. Whether Lancaster's apparent fear of the king's vengeance was justified is uncertain. Events proved that by 1322, Edward was determined to gain revenge for Gaveston's death, for which he had come to blame Lancaster entirely. Further, Lancaster was Edward's cousin and older contemporary; presumably he knew him well and may have recognised in Edward the seeds of his father's lust for vengeance upon his enemies.

Further negotiations followed, and agreement was finally reached at Leake, Nottinghamshire, between Lancaster and the remaining Ordainers on the one hand, and the Middle Party on the other, that the Ordinances should be maintained, a parliament should be summoned and a standing council appointed, whose consent would be required before the king could perform any of the normal acts of sovereignty. This 'Treaty of Leake' seemed to have placed the king in a position of subjugation never before seen in England, but in fact brought little substantive change. The October parliament removed most of the sheriffs from office, hardly an unprecedented act, but little was done to deal with the question of the king's counsellors. Lancaster seems by then to have been mainly concerned to secure recognition of his position as hereditary Steward of England, which brought effective control of the king's household. The Middle Party too had other concerns besides that of the identity of the king's counsellors, since they now considered that the Scottish situation demanded urgent attention.

6.4.2   The rise of the Despensers

In January 1320, Lancaster refused to attend parliament, probably on the pretext that this parliament would be dominated by his enemies at court. In the summer, the king went to France, leaving Pembroke as keeper of the realm. However, the power of the Middle Party was now being challenged as the king's new favourites, the Despensers, father and son, both named Hugh, began to rise to prominence and wrest the initiative from Pembroke and his adherents.

The elder Despenser was an experienced royal official who had been close to the king throughout his reign. The younger was the king's contemporary and, unlike

Gaveston, of sufficiently noble birth to be a member of his household as Prince of Wales. He was appointed as the king's chamberlain in 1318 and at about the same time came into possession of a substantial portion of the Welsh estates of the Clare Earls of Gloucester through his marriage. The situation of some 10 years earlier was beginning to repeat itself. Though Despenser was a member of the English baronage by birth, unlike Gaveston, he was not a member of a leading magnate family, and so was considered by the greater magnates to be another upstart. Like his predecessor as favourite, he now rose to a position of great power, but was greedy for further gains, wishing to acquire all the Gloucester lands and earldom. Inevitably, this brought him into conflict with the husbands of his wife's sisters, both leading Marcher lords, and their fellows, determined, as ever, to prevent an outsider from gaining a position of pre-eminence amongst them.

Before long, the younger Despenser's acquisitiveness led to the formation of a confederacy of Marchers, who ignored the king's explicit instructions not to hold armed assemblies in the Marches and began a seizure of the favourite's lands in Glamorgan. Although Thomas of Lancaster was lord of Kidwelly, he remained aloof from the Marcher confederacy, being on bad terms with certain of the Marchers, and preferred to assemble his own confederacy among the magnates of northern England. They met at his castle at Pontefract in May 1321 and took oath to defend their lands and one another should any of them be attacked. There is no specific mention of the Despensers in this oath, and it is possible that the threat which they were concerned with came from the Scots, since the truce made in 1318, which had been extended, was now about to expire.

However, Lancaster's concern with events at the centre became apparent on 28 June, when a much larger assembly was held at Sherburn in Elmet, between York and Leeds, to discuss matters which included the bad character of the king's ministers, various forfeitures and banishments which had occurred without the judgment of peers, the inequities of the taxation system and the making of treaties with foreign powers, including Scotland and France. In addition, some 60 magnates, who included the leading Marchers, sealed a document pledging themselves to the destruction of the Despensers. However, the group which bound themselves by these 'indentures' did not include either the major northern magnates, who suspected Lancaster, with good reason, of being too friendly towards the Scots, or the northern prelates.

The opposition to the king was thus far from united. Further, moderate magnates such as the Earls of Pembroke and Arundel had not yet committed themselves, and might therefore act as mediators between the opposition and the king. In fact, it seems to have been Pembroke who persuaded the king to agree to the principal demand of the opposition and to get rid of the Despensers, threatening, along with others, to make *diffidatio*. Unfortunately, no official record survives of the parliament of July 1321, but it appears that the opposition withdrew their original demands for a statute against the Despensers and formal recognition of the doctrine distinguishing between the Crown and the person of the king. On 19 August, the parliament sentenced both Despensers to total forfeiture of property and lifelong banishment from the domains of the Crown, as 'evil and false counsellors, seducers and conspirators, and disinheritors of the Crown, and as enemies of the king and kingdom'.[11]

Once again, events repeated themselves. The elder Despenser did leave the country, but the younger went no further than the Cinque Ports, and allegedly

---

11   N Denholm-Young (trans), *Vita Edwardi Secundi*, 1957, Nelson, p 113.

embarked on a career of piracy in the Channel with the connivance of the king. At the same time, the Middle Party, having apparently achieved its aims, began to break up.

6.4.3   The crisis of 1321–22

The crisis which followed derived from one of those apparently minor slights which roused disproportionate ire among medieval royalty and magnates. While travelling through Kent, Queen Isabella sought a night's accommodation at Leeds Castle, which was held by Bartholomew Badlesmere, a leading member of the Middle Party. He was away, and in his absence, his wife was not prepared to accede to the queen's request. To Edward, this made a convenient pretext for dealing with his enemies once and for all. He raised an army and laid siege to Leeds Castle. Badlesmere's Marcher allies moved to support him, but at this stage, Lancaster remained aloof. Initially, the king enjoyed a rare military success, moving into the Marches in January 1322 and forcing some of his Marcher enemies to surrender to him and others to retreat northwards. The king's army followed and Edward apparently decided that this was an opportune moment to deal finally with Lancaster. The Earl was formally proclaimed a rebel on 12 March and support for him seems to have melted away. Castles such as Pontefract surrendered without a fight, many of his retainers deserted him, and he and his remaining allies apparently decided to seek refuge in Scotland. Earl Warenne and the king's half-brother, Edmund, Earl of Kent, pursued him northwards from Pontefract, but it was in fact Sir Andrew Harclay, sheriff of Cumberland, and an army drawn from the northern counties who reached Lancaster first, barring his way at Boroughbridge, north of York, on 17 March.

The Battle of Boroughbridge ended in defeat for Lancaster and his surviving allies, who surrendered to Harclay and were turned over to the king. Edward II now saw the opportunity to gain a fit vengeance for the death of Gaveston. Lancaster and the other leading rebels were brought before him at Pontefract, and in a summary trial on 22 March were found guilty of high treason by a small group of magnates, condemned to death and executed.

The king seemed now to have triumphed and could look forward to a peaceful reign at last. His leading opponents were either dead, his prisoners or otherwise out of the way. Pembroke had lost his former influence and did not recover this before he died in 1324. But the king by his own actions again destroyed the advantage he had gained.

6.5   DEPOSITION

6.5.1   1322–24

At first, things seemed to go well. Parliament, which assembled at York on 2 May and included, along with the established magnates, prelates, knights and burgesses, proctors representing the lower clergy, representatives of the Cinque Ports and 24 representatives of the *communitas* of Wales, condemned and repealed the Ordinances, condemned the manner of their making and outwardly restored the king to full dignity.[12] Like his father, Edward II was here ruling, both for the past and for the future, that changes forced on an unwilling king were null and void. Only those changes which were agreed in parliament could be enforced and, since only the king could summon a parliament and could still, at this stage, control the composition of the parliament by varying the terms of the summons, no binding change could be forced on an unwilling king.

This doctrine was dangerous, since it produced an impasse which could only be broken by violent means and then, potentially, only temporarily. It might not have mattered to any great extent at that time had Edward not recalled the Despensers from exile and restored them to their former positions. Interestingly, cl 39/29 of Magna Carta was used as the pretext for the revocation of the process against them, as the Despensers had not received the judgment of their peers. The king shrank from awarding the earldom of Gloucester to the younger Despenser, but the earldom of Winchester was created for his father, and both were well rewarded with lands declared to have been forfeited by the king's enemies. In practice, they now had no serious rivals and were in almost complete control of South Wales. Edward II, by the destruction of his enemies, and the making of a 13 year truce with the Scots,[13] seemed to be in an almost unassailable position.

However, once again, weaknesses began to show themselves. Less than a year after his victory at Boroughbridge and before the Scottish truce, Andrew Harclay, raised to the earldom of Carlisle in recognition of his loyal service to the king, was revealed as having entered into secret negotiations with Robert Bruce. Harclay was arrested, brought to London, summarily tried and executed as a traitor. Trouble then began to brew over Gascony. In 1324, the French king, Charles IV, declared the duchy to be confiscated. Although there was no fighting, this was yet another humiliation for Edward II.

By this period, the king's new favourites had earned themselves as much hatred and jealousy as had Gaveston. The Despensers, although avaricious, seem not to have been merely greedy and irresponsible as Gaveston had been. The elder Despenser in particular sought to develop the strength of the royal household so as to give the king greater independence from the great officers of state, who tended to be magnates or be subject to control by magnates. Some elements of the Ordinances were allowed to continue in effect, perhaps as a result of the moderating influence of the former Middle Party. 'Establishments', confirmed by statute later in the reign, confirmed the rights of the church as set out in Magna Carta and other statutes, the amendments to the Forest Law set out in the Ordinances, and the Statute of Kenilworth of 1316, which was concerned with the powers of the sheriffs.

However, neither the Despensers nor the king had learnt anything from experience. The younger Despenser in particular became notorious for his greed and unscrupulous pursuit of personal advantage. By 1326, he was the Italian bankers' most significant client in England and had more money on deposit with them than the Pope. His methods of gaining such wealth were dubious. It was complained that in order to approach the king, it was first necessary to bribe Despenser, who as his

---

12 Statute of York, 1322, EHD III No 103.
13 A permanent peace could not be reached, since the English refused to recognise Bruce as a lawful king.

chamberlain controlled access to him, and the favourite had at least one heiress kidnapped and held her for over a year to induce her to make over her lands to him.

Discontent was growing once again. Lawlessness was a particular problem, with armed gangs roaming the countryside and making a profession of highway robbery. In 1326, a gang led by one Eustace de Folville was able to ambush and kill no less a personage than the Chief Baron of the Exchequer near Melton Mowbray as he travelled on official business.

6.5.2   The emergence of a Queen's Party

By 1324, another opposition party was emerging, this time within the king's immediate family and centred on his queen, Isabella of France. It included his half-brothers, Thomas of Norfolk and Edmund of Kent, and cousin, Henry of Lancaster, younger brother of Thomas. It is uncertain what led to the queen's final estrangement from her husband. Their marriage is not known to have been particularly unhappy previously. They had four children, born from 1312 onwards, suggesting that Edward's apparent homosexuality had not previously driven them apart, though it is always possible that a physical relationship with the younger Despenser, following on that alleged between the king and Gaveston, was the final straw for Isabella, a much stronger character than her husband. The queen's party also included the Bishops of Hereford, Lincoln and Bath and Wells, and Roger Mortimer of Wigmore, a Marcher lord who soon became her lover.

The spark which ignited the queen's active opposition seems to have been the seizure of her estates in September 1324, ordered by the king on the advice of the Despensers in the light of a possible French invasion. When in 1325 she went to France to negotiate with her brother, Charles IV, over Gascony, she refused point-blank to return unless the Despensers were removed from office and favour. A truce was agreed with the French, under which Edward's heir, Edward of Windsor, aged 12, would be invested with the duchy of Gascony and do homage to the French king, subject to a relief of £60,000 and the payment of compensation for the damage to the rights of the French Crown and French subjects during the quarrel. These payments, and the explicit requirement for homage, must have seemed to the increasingly restive English to represent one more humiliating climbdown by their king.

6.5.3   Invasion

Young Edward then went to Paris to do homage for Gascony. Once there, his mother refused to allow him to return, so giving her possession of her husband's heir. Both sides made military preparations during the summer of 1326, Isabella negotiating an agreement with William II, Count of Hainault, for aid in return for the marriage of her son to his daughter. On 23 September, she sailed from the Hainault port of Dordrecht with a force of some 700, landing near Ipswich the following day.

The strength of hostility to Edward is demonstrated by the fact that Isabella's small force was rapidly augmented by many of the East Anglian gentry and their retainers, and that the king was unable to rouse any significant support. At the end of September, he and both Despensers fled from London towards Bristol. London declared for the queen and a wave of violence followed, order not being finally restored until 15 November. At Bristol, the townsfolk opened the town to the queen, and the elder Despenser, who had remained there while his son fled with the king into

Wales, surrendered without any show of resistance. In Bristol, on 26 October, the magnates assembled there proclaimed young Edward as keeper of the realm which his father was held to have deserted. The next day, the elder Despenser was sentenced to death by a council of magnates and hanged.

While Isabella and Mortimer established themselves in Hereford, Henry of Lancaster went on into Wales to hunt for the king and the younger Despenser. Finding them at Neath Abbey in Glamorgan, Lancaster conducted the king to his own castle at Kenilworth. Despenser was brought before a council of magnates on 24 November. The charges against him were numerous and went right back to 1314. *Inter alia*, in the course of the flight from Bannockburn, Despenser had induced the king to abandon the queen at Tynemouth, leaving her to the mercy of the Scots. He had despoiled the Bishops of Lincoln, Ely and Norwich of their plate, induced the king to confer the earldom of Winchester on his father and that of Carlisle on the notorious traitor Andrew Harclay, while he himself had acquired extensive lands and wealth belonging to the crown. He had been the means of depriving the queen of her estates in 1324, and when she and her son were abroad, he had tried by means of bribery to prevent their return. After a mockery of a trial, Despenser was taken out, crowned with a wreath of nettles and hanged. His genitals were sliced off while he was still living and burnt before his eyes to symbolise his alleged intimacy with the king. After he was dead, his head and quarters were distributed among the main towns of England.[14]

6.5.4   The process of deposition

By this time, and even before his father's capture, the young Edward had on 28 October issued writs in his father's name and was using his own Privy Seal as Earl of Chester and Duke of Gascony[15] for the summoning of a parliament to assemble at Westminster on 15 December. These writs stated that the king would then be absent from the realm and the business would therefore be heard before the queen and young Edward himself. What the heir's own feelings were about all this cannot be known but, since he was not yet 14 years old and did not rouse himself into action on his own initiative for another four years, it may be presumed that the driving force came from his mother. Neither is it known when Isabella and her allies decided to take the ultimate step of dethroning the anointed king, but it seems likely that this was their intention by the time the writs of summons went out, if not at the time of their departure from Dordrecht.

To appreciate the enormity of the actions which the conspirators were taking, it must be borne in mind that no English king had been deposed by his own subjects since Sigeferth of Wessex in 757, a precedent of which the plotters of 1326–27 were unlikely to be aware. There was no legal mechanism for deposing a king and doubt existed as to whether a lawful deposition was even possible. Further, if the king's death was already contemplated, then this was an act still more awesome in its nature. In the medieval mind, a king was a semi-sacred person by virtue of his anointing, and his killing, other than in the heat of battle, was not only murder but sacrilege. The awesome nature of their acts was the reason why the queen, Mortimer and their

---

14   Though a handsome tomb and memorial effigy can be seen in Tewkesbury Abbey.

15   Edward had not been created Prince of Wales, a title which he revived for his eldest son, Edward the Black Prince, in 1331, inaugurating a practice which continues to this day.

cohorts were so concerned to give the actions by which Edward II's deposition was effected the aura of legality, why also there was a reluctance actually to kill the dethroned king rather than merely to procure his death from 'natural' causes.

By 30 November, the rebels had obtained the great seal from the king's custody and issued further writs postponing the parliament to 7 January. It was no longer possible to maintain the fiction that young Edward was merely acting in his father's absence, so the rebels now declared that the king had resumed the government of the realm. The parliament of January 1327 was summoned so as to appear fully representative, with representatives of Wales and the Cinque Ports and the people of London. In order to maintain the fiction that this was a true parliament, the king was requested to attend, but he refused, or was said in a proclamation of 12 January to have refused.

The first days of the parliament were spent by the queen and her allies in efforts to overcome the reluctance of certain of the bishops and others to agree to a deposition. On 12 January, the mayor, aldermen and commonalty of London sent a letter to the magnates now assembled in parliament asking whether they were willing to be in accord with the Londoners, to maintain the cause of the queen and her son, to crown young Edward as king and to depose Edward II for his frequent offences against his oath and his crown. On the following day, the Bishop of Hereford, a partisan of Isabella, stirred up still more popular clamour against the king by preaching a public sermon on the text 'A foolish king shall ruin his people'. That day too, representatives of all estates of the realm – a number of bishops and magnates, together with representatives of the clergy and the boroughs – took an oath at the Guildhall to maintain the queen's cause, 'to uphold all that has been ordained or shall be ordained for the common profit' and to maintain the liberties of the city of London.

On 15 January, the Archbishop of Canterbury announced at Westminster Hall that, by the unanimous consent of the magnates, the clergy and the people, Edward II was deposed from his royal dignity, never more to reign and govern the people of England, and that the magnates, the clergy and the people had unanimously agreed that young Edward should be king. The formal Articles of Deposition drafted by the Bishop of Winchester charged Edward II with being incompetent to govern, unwilling to listen to wise counsel, destroying the church and many noble men, losing Scotland, Ireland and Gascony, breaching his coronation oath to do justice to all, stripping his realm and, by his cruelty and wickedness, showing himself incorrigible and without hope of amendment.

This was an attempt by what was a relatively small group of enemies of Edward II, most of its leaders motivated by personal grudges against him, to give an aura of legality to acts which were unprecedented and on that basis illegal. The fiction was that Edward II was deposed by the will of the English people, but now a precedent had been set, and the same fiction could be used again.

On the same day (15 January), a deputation composed of representatives of all estates of the realm set off to Kenilworth to inform Edward II of his deposition. Two other bishops had earlier gone ahead, charged with persuading him to abdicate, promising that if he laid aside the crown, his elder son would succeed him and that he himself would be maintained in a state of royal dignity for the remainder of his life. If, however, he refused to abdicate voluntarily, the people would repudiate both him and his two sons and take a person not of the royal blood as the new king. Edward, by this time a broken man, immediately capitulated to this threat, with many tears and lamentations. William Trussell, a knight of the shire, renounced homage and fealty on behalf of the whole realm, and the reign of the new king was held to begin on 25 January.

The fiction was maintained that Edward II had abdicated voluntarily, but the deposition raised a number of problems. First, can the assembly of 7 January 1327 properly be called a parliament? The parliament of 1297 had been summoned and presided over by a keeper of the realm in the absence of Edward I, but the king was kept fully informed of developments and appears to have approved them. Further, even if the assembly of 1327, summoned first by the young Edward as keeper of the realm and then postponed and re-summoned under the fiction that Edward II was still the ruler, was a lawfully summoned parliament, it rapidly became a revolutionary body, acting in a manner which was quite unprecedented.

Second, there was no rule or precedent in English law permitting or providing any procedure for the deposition of a king on the grounds of unworthiness. McKisack believes it unlikely that the revolutionaries truly appreciated the significance of their action or had a coherent idea of what was to be done with a dethroned king who, since he was only 42 and physically robust, despite his pitiful weaknesses of character, might live for many more years.[16] The revolutionaries were reluctant to bring the king before any sort of assembly to answer the charges laid against him, and seemed determined to secure some agreement, whatever the degree of coercion, to abdication. This fiction was maintained into the following reign. Two days before he was crowned, Edward III issued a proclamation stating that his father 'of his own goodwill and the common consent of the earls, prelates, barons and other nobles and the community of the realm had removed himself from the government and willed that it should devolve on his heir, who had therefore undertaken the task of ruling the kingdom'. Even so, some of those who assembled in the pseudo-parliament were clearly troubled; the Bishop of Rochester took the oath of 15 January under protest, saving his order and everything contained in Magna Carta.

Third, why was the revolution so quickly and completely successful, despite the personal unpopularity of Queen Isabella and Roger Mortimer, whose affair was a major scandal? It seems that the success was based more on Edward II's failure than any attraction they might have. Before the end of his reign, contemporaries were writing of Edward II with undisguised contempt. Ever since 1307, he had shown himself a besotted fool in dealing with his favourites and a weakling in relation to his enemies. His liking for rustic pursuits might now be seen as a pleasant unpretentiousness, but in his own time was regarded as quite foreign to the dignity necessary in a monarch. Militarily and diplomatically, he was an abject failure. He seems never to have learned from his mistakes, but merely repeated earlier errors. His unfittedness to rule must have been particularly apparent when he was compared with his father, whose character and achievements must by 1327 have been passing into legend. The rebels too pursued an effective propaganda campaign, claiming that the Pope had absolved the people from allegiance to Edward II, that the queen was a wronged wife and the unfortunate king a degenerate, idiot or changeling.

---

16 Edward I had lived to 68, Henry III to 65. Robert, Duke of Normandy survived 28 years of imprisonment to die aged 82.

6.5.5　Aftermath

Following Edward II's deposition, little actually changed in the short term. The corps of professional royal officials had largely held aloof from events, so that administration continued in uninterrupted fashion. Edward III's first parliament reversed the judgment against Thomas of Lancaster, conferred his titles and estates on his brother Henry, and re-affirmed the judgment of 1321 against the Despensers. However, Mortimer proceeded to use his new-found power in exactly the same way as the Despensers, acquiring vast estates from the forfeitures of their estates, gifts from the queen and grants from the royal demesne. In 1328, he was created Earl of March. The policy of Mortimer and Isabella towards Scotland was as unsuccessful as Edward's had been, leading to the Treaty of Northampton of 1328, in which the English agreed to all the Scots' demands by formally recognising Robert Bruce as the lawful ruler of an independent kingdom with no feudal ties to England. Disgust at this retreat seems to have been the trigger for a rising led by Henry of Lancaster and Edward II's two half-brothers. This fizzled out early in 1329 and its leaders were treated leniently, but clear proof of the arbitrariness and vindictiveness of Mortimer's regime was to follow. Early in 1330, the Earl of Kent was arrested and executed on trumped-up charges of conspiring to restore his half-brother to the throne.

Although even in 1330 there were rumours that Edward II was still alive, the new regime, faced with a difficulty which was to burden all future usurpers, had already set a pattern for the future. Though Edward II's personal prestige must have been non-existent, he was an anointed king who had been deprived of his throne by proceedings of extremely doubtful legality. While he lived, he was a danger to Isabella and Mortimer as the potential focus of plots, and might remain so for many years. It would seem, however, that his enemies at first shrank from outright murder. After a period in relative comfort at Kenilworth, the former king was moved to Berkeley Castle in Gloucestershire and was subjected to steadily worsening physical conditions in the hope of bringing about his death from disease. However, Edward's physique withstood all the worst that medieval dungeons could provide. Moreover, at least two attempts were made to free him.

Some time in September 1327, appalling screams of agony are said to have been heard issuing from Berkeley by night. A few days later, the former king's death was announced and his body was taken to the Abbey of St Peter at Gloucester, now Gloucester Cathedral, for burial. No marks of violence were visible and it was announced that Edward had died from natural causes. However, it was generally believed that a red-hot iron had been inserted into his bowels through a drenching horn, a particularly grim reflection on his supposed sexual proclivities.

CHAPTER 7

EDWARD III 1327–77

Despite the unpropitious circumstances of his accession, during Edward III's long reign, the English enjoyed unprecedented success and the king established himself in the eyes of contemporaries as the archetype of a medieval monarch and the greatest patron of the cult of chivalry. However, he lived too long. In 1360, he was the ruler of more than half of France; the Kings of both France and Scotland were his prisoners,[1] but in the late 1360s, his glory began to fade; as he slid into senility, he became increasingly the pawn of an avaricious and calculating mistress. In the last year of his life, he witnessed the loss of his heir, Edward, the Black Prince, and the impeachment of his mistress and her confrères by the Good Parliament of 1376.[2]

7.1 THE EARLY YEARS

All this was far in the future when, on the night of 19 October 1330, Edward III, then just short of his 18th birthday, entered Nottingham Castle by an underground passage at the head of a body of young noblemen, seized Roger Mortimer, who for the past four years had been king in all but name, and bore him to London, where he was tried before his peers as a traitor and hanged on 29 November. Thus, Edward threw off the tutelage of his mother and her paramour but, even more than his grandfather, he faced the task of restoring a monarchy whose stock had fallen very low.

The deposition of Edward II and the military failures of the past 20 years had brought humiliation on a scale never before seen. It was to be a number of years before the monarchy and its supporting infrastructure were sufficiently strengthened for the military campaigns on which Edward III's reputation rests to become successful. Edward's early expeditions, though often successful in the short term, brought little long term gain. They caused a serious drain on royal finances and discontent among the populace over high levels of taxation. This led to a confrontation during the parliament of 1341, where the king was forced to agree to demands that his ministers should be appointed by the king in parliament and sworn therein to obey the law. It was after this crisis that Edward III, now aged 28 and 14 years a king, came into his political maturity and adopted the practice of ruling by co-operation with his parliaments and those represented therein, which is the hallmark of the rest of his reign until his senility gave the initiative in government to his favourites.

---

1 David II of Scotland, taken prisoner at the Battle of Neville's Cross in 1346, and John II of France, captured at Poitiers 10 years later.

2 Readers seeking detail of Edward III's French campaigns, as well as a splendid, scholarly and eminently readable depiction of the period as a whole, need look no further than BW Tuchman, *A Distant Mirror: The Calamitous Fourteenth Century*, 1980, Penguin.

7.2   EDWARD III AND GOVERNMENT

In the constitutional sphere, the reign can too easily be dismissed as a peaceful interlude between the two great crises of 1327 and 1399. The period from 1341 until the early 1370s was free from threat to the monarchy not simply as the result of chance, but rather because Edward III was before all else a pragmatist in the governmental sphere. He accepted that he must gain and maintain the co-operation of his subjects if he was to carry through his policies successfully and was prepared, at least when it suited him, to work through parliament for this purpose. This was not itself a new development, but the crucial differences between Edward III and his grandfather were that Edward I allowed parliament to become on a regular basis the body which authorised the raising of revenues by the king, and that Edward III was prepared to make concessions to parliament in return for revenue-raising powers. For this reason, parliament, managed by the king and summoned by him when additional revenues were needed, increasingly became a normal element in royal government, rather than a body which had its greatest importance in times of crisis.

But a dangerous precedent had already been set, by which an 'unworthy' king could be deposed by his subjects. More dangerous still, it was for those subjects to define unworthiness. Edward III's reign was a period in which, literally, the seeds of future crisis were sewn, by the fertility of the king and his queen, the king's favour to his younger sons and the failure of the direct line of the dynasty by the successive deaths of the Black Prince and Richard II. After Edward's death, the long war for the Crown of France which he began,[3] the decline of royal power in relation to that of the greatest subjects and uncertainty over the right to the succession created a vicious circle of instability in government, with intermittent warfare between the great magnates for control of king and government, if not for the throne itself. This caused further instability, and greater accretion of power to the magnates, the circle tightening until it was finally broken by the deaths by battle, execution and murder of virtually all the leading protagonists.

7.2.1   Law and justice

The reign saw the emergence of permanent Justices of the Peace to enforce royal justice in the shires under the supervision of the justices of assize, by hearing cases involving minor infringements of the king's peace. The procedure by which a person may, with his consent, be bound over to keep the peace and be of good behaviour, under financial surety, without having to be convicted of any offence, is first recognised by a statute of the parliament of 1361–62 and, though its ambit may have

---

3   From 987 to 1314, the French Crown passed directly from father to son. However, John I, posthumous son of Louis X (1314–16), died at a few days old, and it was then declared that only a male could occupy the French throne. John's sister was therefore passed over in favour of her uncle as Philip V (1316–22). Philip and his younger brother, Charles IV (1322–28), also left only daughters, and on the latter's death, the throne was seized by Philip, Count of Valois, son of Philip the Fair's younger brother, as Philip VI (1328–50). Edward III's mother was Philip the Fair's daughter, and Edward claimed the French throne on the basis that although no woman could herself reign, she could pass a right of succession to her son.

been reduced by the recent decision of the European Court of Human Rights in *Steel v UK*,[4] it forms a useful means of discouraging minor disorder even today.

Among these long lasting developments was the Statute of Treasons made by the parliament of 1351–52, which remains in force after 650 years, to form the basis of the law of treason for the United Kingdom. No narrative of the proceedings of the parliament survives, but circumstantial evidence suggests that the Statute represents a concession made by the king in return for a grant by parliament of fresh revenues, in a session which the king's most recent biographer, WM Ormrod, characterises as a resolution of matters left over from the 1330s, in both the financial and the political and judicial spheres.[5] Edward III was constantly seeking revenue to finance his wars. His conscious projection of an image of majesty, his building projects, which included St George's Chapel, Windsor, built as the chapel of his great Order of the Garter,[6] and his generosity to his greater subjects all necessitated considerable additional expenditure. Though in the early 1350s he was at the zenith of his power, nevertheless, he had a definite need to consolidate his international position and to gain the support of his subjects for further campaigning which might bring a final end to the war. Ormrod notes that by 1352, there had been eight years of near-continuous direct taxation, although fighting had died away to a sporadic level since 1346–47, partly as a result of the Black Death. Parliament must have expected concessions from the king in return for their grant of a three year lay subsidy in order that the king could mount a further campaign to bring the war with France to a final and successful conclusion. Indeed, the knights and burgesses summoned to the parliament presented the King's Council with a long list of grievances, principally to do with the king's methods of raising revenues.

At the same time, the traditional concerns about lawlessness and the proper administration of justice remained, at least as a hangover from the reign of Edward II and Edward III's own early years on the throne. The 1330s, when the king's attentions were largely directed towards war with France and his attempts to secure the Scottish throne for a puppet king in the person of Edward Balliol, son of the unlamented John, were years of renewed disorder and crime, particularly in rural areas.

The Statute of Treasons, therefore, was one element in a number of legislative changes which took place in the 1340s and early 1350s, and seems to have been motivated in part by a need to persuade parliament to agree further revenue-raising measures, in part to enable the king to employ newer and more efficient methods of raising and supplying his armies, and in part by the need to improve the administration of justice; overall, by the need to secure the long term support of Edward III's subjects for his rule. However, the Statute of Treasons also represents a very early example of the translation of a vague concept of the common law into a more precise statutory form.

---

4   Where two hunt saboteurs established that a binding-over breached Art 6 of the European Convention on Human Rights on the basis that they had not been made aware of the forms of behaviour they were required to desist from, but the European Court of Human Rights accepted that a binding-over did not *prima facie* constitute a breach of that Article. That the applicants were fully aware of the form of behaviour which had led to their binding-over was not considered sufficient explanation.

5   WM Ormrod, *The Reign of Edward III*, 2nd edn, 2000, Tempus, p 30.

6   The present Chapel was begun by Edward IV and completed in the reign of Henry VIII.

It has already been noted that the concept of treason emerged in the course of the 13th century, appearing first in legal and philosophical texts, and was given a concrete form in an English context in the proceedings against Dafydd ap Gruffydd in 1283. In 1322, 1326–27 and again in 1330, a number of individuals had been condemned and executed as traitors in makeshift proceedings characterised by their haste. As precedents, these left the scope of high treason – treason against the king, as distinct from petty treason by a wife towards her husband, or a servant towards his master – both broad and very vague.

All cases of high treason at common law involved rebellion against the king by a person who was, or could be construed as, a feudal vassal of the king, but it was by no means clear which acts of rebellion were regarded as treasonous and which might be dealt with along traditional feudal lines only. Indeed, it would be fair to say that the distinction between the two was distinctly arbitrary. In 1328–29, Henry of Lancaster and Edward III's two uncles of the half-blood, Thomas, Earl of Norfolk, and Edmund, Earl of Kent, launched a brief rebellion against the Mortimer regime. They were quickly forgiven and restored to favour, but when, a year later, Kent was accused, implausibly, of plotting to restore Edward II to the throne, he was condemned and executed for treason. The Statute of Treasons was passed in order to bring an end to the broad ambit and the potential abuses of the common law. Henceforth, high treason would constitute only:

(a) making war against the king 'in his realm';

(b) being 'adherent to the king's enemies';

(c) 'compassing the death' of the king, his queen or his eldest son;[7]

(d) violating the chastity of the queen, the wife of the king's eldest son, and the king's eldest daughter unmarried.[8]

7.2.2   Military organisation

It has already been noted that Edward I's reign was a time of transition between the raising of armies in the feudal manner and a new practice of raising armies by indenture, which became overwhelmingly dominant under his grandson. From 1341, it became increasingly the practice for military commanders, often but by no means always from the magnate class, to enter into contracts ('indentures') with the king, under which they agreed to provide a specified number of men for a set period, all their expenses in doing so being defrayed by the Exchequer. Under this system, every soldier from the commander down was paid a daily rate for his services, ranging from 13s 4d for a duke to 2d for an ordinary soldier. Pay tended to be long in arrears, but a further source of income came from important prisoners of war. These could be ransomed direct, or the right to the prisoner and the ransom due for him sold to the highest bidder. The most valuable prisoners were the prerogative of the king, but the

---

7   Though the terms of the Statute assume a male sovereign and male heir apparent, as can be expected of legislation of this date, Gunn and Lyon have established that this provision creates liability for compassing the death of a female sovereign or heir, or male consort. See MJ Gunn and AE Lyon, 'Compassing the death of the Queen's consort; would it be high treason?' (1998) Nottingham Law Journal 34.

8   No prosecution has ever been brought under these provisions, although it has been suggested that James Hewitt, as the lover of Diana, Princess of Wales during her marriage, could be regarded as guilty of treason under this head.

original captor was usually rewarded handsomely for surrendering his prize. Ransoms had long been a significant source of income among the magnate class, but now ransoms and booty became major routes to wealth and gave the aristocracy a commitment to the king's overseas wars for the first time since the Conquest.[9]

However, effective though the system was in the short term, while the king and later his sons were militarily successful, in the long term, it was to prove another source of danger to the monarchy, since it not only brought great wealth to the magnate class and its adherents, but also fostered the acquisition by its members of large retinues of trained and experienced soldiers, wearing the livery of their leader and owing loyalty only to him. Over the next century, such magnates were to become increasingly closely related to the royal family, a process beginning with the marriages of Edward III's younger sons to the heiresses of leading families. This was a convenient means of providing those sons with vast lands and wealth, but one which was to have serious consequences for the future, when magnates not only supported their cousins and brothers-in-law in their bids for the throne, but challenged for the crown in their own right.

7.3   ECONOMIC AND SOCIAL CHANGE

Although the slow decline of feudalism was much accelerated by the first major outbreak of plague in 1348–49, it may be strongly argued that this change could not have been identified as early as 1351–52. Indeed, there were determined efforts to forestall it. Ormrod notes that a death rate of at least 30%, which seems to have borne most heavily on the rural peasantry and the poorer inhabitants of the towns, coupled with panic movements of survivors away from the worst affected areas, created a serious shortage of tenants and manpower on estates all over the country. These estates had traditionally been farmed by unfree villeins who performed labour services on their lords' demesne land in return for sufficient land to support themselves. Now, the movement towards wage labour and money rents which had already begun before the Black Death became widespread. Wages rose markedly and attempts to curb them by legislation, beginning with the Ordinance of Labourers of 1349 and culminating in the Statute of Labourers of 1351, were in the long term a failure, but in the short term represented attempts by the king and magnates, through parliament, to preserve their feudal prerogatives. The legislation may have been prompted mainly by the king's desire to keep down costs on his own demesne land and to retain the support of his tenants-in-chief, but this demonstrates that in the early 1350s, the feudal system was not yet dead, still less buried.[10]

---

9   See Ormrod, *op cit*, pp 99–101.

10   Ormrod, *op cit*, pp 29–30.

7.4   THE LATER YEARS

7.4.1   War renewed

Intermittent war between England and France had occupied much of the 1340s and 1350s, England gaining the advantage in the longer term through the victories of Crecy and Poitiers and the campaigning of the Black Prince from his base in Gascony. The Treaty of Bretigny of 1360 was intended to bring about a permanent peace between England and France, on the basis that the French recognised English sovereignty over an enlarged duchy of Aquitaine, together with Calais, taken in 1347, in return for Edward's renunciation of his claims to the French throne. However, following the death of John II of France in 1364, it rapidly became clear that neither side had any intention of respecting the Treaty. Indeed, though the English had not campaigned against France itself in the interim, Edward intervened in Brittany in support of its Duke against the French Crown, and in 1362 concluded a treaty with Pedro the Cruel, King of Castile, by which he agreed to support Pedro against his bastard half-brother, Enrique of Trastamara, who had French backing in his bid for the Castilian throne. Furthermore, the attempts of the Black Prince, Prince of Aquitaine from 1363, to impose government on the English model on his principality led to a large proportion of the rebellious local lords, until then valuable allies of the English, throwing in their lot with the French.

War with France was renewed in 1369, conducted initially by the Black Prince and John of Gaunt, and then by Gaunt alone, and English arms met with a series of reverses. Despite the Black Prince's great victory at Najera in 1367, Pedro the Cruel was murdered in 1369 by his half-brother's own hand. More ominously still in the long term, while in Spain, the Black Prince contracted the disease, possibly amoebic dysentery, which from 1370 left him incapable of active participation in government and killed him a year before his father's death. Meanwhile, the French, who now had a wily and diplomatically astute king, Charles V, to replace the chivalrous but inept John II,[11] had found an inspired and inspiring commander in the rough-hewn person of the new constable, Bertrand du Guesclin.

7.4.2   Financial pressures

A feature of the medieval period is that although the king's subjects were prepared, if reluctantly, to accept heavy taxation as the price of military success, nothing brought about discontent and monarchical crisis as surely as heavy taxation to finance unsuccessful campaigns. Between 1369 and 1375, Ormrod calculates,[12] the crown spent in excess of £670,000 on the war with France, raised by means of a wool subsidy in 1369, a triennial Tenth from the clergy in 1370, £50,000 each from the clergy and laity in 1371, three Fifteenths and Tenths authorised by the parliament of 1372–73, and a further Tenth from the clergy in 1373.

---

11   John was captured at the Battle of Poitiers in 1356 and released in 1359 on payment of the first instalment of a £700,000 ransom and the giving of high-born hostages against the balance, but insisted on returning to the Tower of London when the balance was not forthcoming.

12   Ormrod, *op cit*, p 41.

7.4.3 The king's favourites

In addition, the death of Edward III's queen, Philippa of Hainault, in 1369 mar.   , the beginning of the process by which he withdrew from direct participation in government, which was increasingly left to his unscrupulous favourites – his mistress, Alice Perrers, the steward, Lord Neville, and chamberlain, William Latimer – who took advantage of the increasingly senile king to enter into dubious deals with Richard Lyons, a London financier. Whereas earlier in his reign, the king had made full use of his powers of patronage to reward his trusted servants and allies and those who had performed acts of bravery on the battlefield, from the early 1370s, such patronage passed under the control of the favourites, who also controlled access to the king.

Inevitably, there were rumblings of discontent even before the crisis fully emerged in the Good Parliament of 1376. The 1371 parliament insisted on the dismissal of both the chancellor and the treasurer and their replacement by men of whom they approved, a serious blow to royal authority. Although a truce with France was concluded in 1375, bringing an end to further financial demands on the populace, this was unpopular, as it gave the French a breathing space and the opportunity to regroup before resuming their campaign to win Gascony. Indeed, Ormrod suggests that it was fear of the tide of popular discontent which led to decisions not to summon parliament in 1374 and 1375.[13]

7.5   THE GOOD PARLIAMENT

The decisions and procedures of the parliament of 1376, traditionally known as the Good Parliament, are of importance, as it is then that parliament first took upon itself the power to impeach the king's ministers, and for the first time, a major political and parliamentary initiative was taken by the commons rather than by a relatively small group of magnates. However, its significance is magnified because it was far better recorded than most of its predecessors and, like that of Magna Carta, it is more apparent through the distorting lens of hindsight than it could have been in the immediate short term, since all its decisions were overruled little more than six months later by the next parliament. It should also be remembered that in 1376 and for a long time to come, parliament could only be summoned at the will of the king and did not enjoy any real independence of the Crown.

Parliament was summoned in 1376 for the traditional reason that extraordinary revenue-raising powers were required but, unprecedentedly, it was then parliament, and in particular the commons, which took the initiative and held it throughout the session. Throughout the previous history of parliament, much of its business had involved dealing with commons petitions to the king, and general unhappiness with the government of the realm was manifested in no less than 146 such petitions, the largest number so far recorded. After the formal opening of parliament, the commons met to debate the issue of taxation. They concluded that there would have been no need for further taxation had the king been properly advised and decided to deliver that message to the government by the hand of the representative they chose. This

13   Ormrod, *op cit*, p 42.

was Sir Peter de la Mare, a knight of the shire for Herefordshire and steward of the Earl of March, and it is with his appointment that the office of Speaker of the House of Commons is considered to have been created. Though the Speaker's best known role is in presiding over sittings of the Commons, preserving order among the members and maintaining the independence of the House from government, he retains the original function of representing the House as a whole in its dealings with the monarch and with the government.

Since the king and the Black Prince were incapacitated, it was John of Gaunt, soon to be Edward III's eldest surviving son, with whom de la Mare treated on behalf of the commons. The latter secured the appointment of a small committee of lords and bishops to join in discussions with the knights and burgesses. In the course of these negotiations, Gaunt, by then effectively regent, was persuaded to accept the commons' proposal for a new royal council, which included several members of the committee, plus others with personal grievances against the court and thus sympathetic to the commons.

De la Mare appeared before Gaunt on 12 May 1376 and informed him of the commons' concern that the king had 'with him certain councillors and servants who are not loyal or profitable to him or the kingdom', making it clear that he was acting on behalf of the commons as a whole. A process by which a charge could be brought jointly by a group of accusers acting in the name of the king had already developed at common law, and here it was being used for the first time by parliament as a means of dealing with the traditional problem of the king's 'evil counsellors'.

The charges against Alice Perrers, Neville, Latimer and Lyons, having been brought by the commons, were tried by the lords, presided over by Gaunt. The specific allegations were that Latimer and Lyons had sold licences exempting merchants from the Calais Staple[14] and had organised loans to the crown at extortionate rates of interest. In addition, Latimer was blamed for the loss of two fortresses while acting as the king's lieutenant in Brittany. The charges against Perrers and Neville were less serious. The lords having found all four guilty, Latimer and Neville were dismissed from their offices and stripped of their emoluments, Lyons was imprisoned for life, and Perrers was banished from the royal household.

7.6   THE ROYAL SUCCESSION

However, the concerns of the Good Parliament were not fully allayed by the success of the impeachment proceedings. A particular concern was the increasingly powerful position of John of Gaunt, now much more a force in domestic affairs than he had been in the first half of the decade, when he had devoted his energies to pursuing the claim to the Castilian throne he had acquired by marriage to the elder daughter of Pedro the Cruel. Following the Black Prince's death on 8 June, the Archbishop of Canterbury brought his son Richard before the commons, who loudly demanded that he be created Prince of Wales in order to guarantee the succession. Although the plea met with failure, since the lords refused to put the matter to the king, it is here for the first time that the commons sought to influence an uncertain royal succession. Further,

---

14   All traffic in wool to and from England was channelled through Calais under the scrutiny of royally-appointed officials, who ensured that the proper duties were paid. Exemption from this was therefore a valuable privilege.

the commons, although prepared to grant the crown a wool subsidy for three years, refused, again unprecedentedly, to grant a lay subsidy.

We are informed that the king's youngest sons, Edmund of Langley, Earl of York, and Thomas of Woodstock, Earl of Buckingham, joined the celebrations hosted by de la Mare following the dissolution of the Good Parliament. This was clear evidence, if any more were needed, of the serious rift which had by now developed within the royal family in the context of the incapacity of the king, and the incapacity and death of the Black Prince. The old question, last seen in relation to John and Arthur of Brittany in 1189, emerged once more. Was the rightful heir the nine year old Richard or John of Gaunt, his eldest surviving uncle and now the wealthiest and most powerful man in the kingdom? The king was 63 and frail. In all likelihood, he would die while Richard was still a child. True, Henry III had succeeded without an internal rival at the age of nine, but he had not had three powerful uncles. Certainly, the Black Prince was concerned that Richard might not be permitted to succeed when the time came; on his deathbed, he called the king and Gaunt to him and in the presence of a number of magnates, commended his wife and son to their protection, and then required all present to 'support his child and maintain him in his right'.[15]

Edward III, in what was effectively his last act as king, chose to deal with the matter in a way in which he presumably hoped would satisfy both factions and leave the succession following his death beyond doubt. In a charter which seems from internal evidence to date from the autumn of 1376, most probably around 7 October, when the king, now seriously ill, made his last will, he designated the young Richard as his heir, followed, if Richard predeceased him or had no male issue, by his three surviving sons in order of birth, followed by their male issue. Thus, Edward III effectively entailed the crown in tail male.[16]

The discovery of this charter, by Professor Michael Bennett of the University of Tasmania in the early summer of 1997, led to a great deal of uninformed media speculation, most of it based on the mistaken premise that there had been nothing hitherto which prevented a female from succeeding to the English throne, and that Edward III, in passing over the claims of Philippa, his granddaughter by his late second son, Lionel, Duke of Clarence, and Isabella, his eldest daughter, had for the first time barred women from succeeding. In fact, he did no such thing, since it is clear from previous practice that a woman would only be considered as a potential ruler if there were literally no male heirs. In 1376, Edward III had a grandson by his deceased eldest son and three living sons, and it must have appeared unlikely that the succession rights of females, or of males claiming through the female line, would become a live issue.

Rather, Edward III's charter is interesting for other reasons. First, it deals finally with the representative-cadet issue. Second, it seems that it is here for the first time that a king went beyond the immediate future in designating his heirs, provision being made not only for the succession on his own death, but also for the death of his immediate successor without male issue. Pragmatism may well have dictated this action, since Richard would not be of an age to beget heirs of his body for some years.

---

15 MK Pope and EC Lodge (eds), *Life of the Black Prince by the Herald of Sir John Chandos*, 1910, OUP, pp 129, 170.

16 See MJ Bennett, 'Edward III's entail and the succession to the crown, 1376–1471' (1998) English Historical Review.

Though the entail of the throne in tail male is entirely explicable for the reasons discussed above, there remain difficulties. Bennett is in no doubt about the genuineness of the 1376 charter, but it seems curious, to say the least, that its terms were not used by the House of Lancaster in 1460 and after as a weapon against the Yorkist claim to the throne, which was derived through Philippa of Clarence by her marriage to Edmund Mortimer, 3rd Earl of March. Further, when Richard II reached the age of 18 in January 1385, he named Philippa's son as his heir. Bennett suggests that the neglect of the charter in the 1460s may be derived from the fact that in 1406, Henry IV entailed the crown on his own four sons and their issue. It also seems possible that Richard II who, as he emerged from childhood and the dominance of Gaunt, developed a high consciousness of his own majesty, considered that he was as much entitled as his grandfather to designate a successor.

The triumph of the Good Parliament was to be short-lived. In October 1376, perhaps at the same time as Edward III was settling the succession, Perrers, Latimer and Neville were pardoned and restored to their former positions, whilst de la Mare was arrested and imprisoned in Nottingham Castle. Though distrust of Gaunt had led to an angry mob storming his Savoy Palace in the summer of 1376, the parliament which assembled at Westminster in January 1377 meekly accepted his demands for the reversing of the impeachments, and granted revenues in the unprecedented form of a poll tax. The stage was now set for the troubled reign of Richard II.

CHAPTER 8

SAD STORIES OF THE DEATH OF KINGS: RICHARD II

8.1   INTRODUCTION

There are several parallels between the fates of Edward II and Richard II. Both were successors to powerful kings who had enjoyed the confidence and respect of their subjects, but nevertheless ended their reigns in difficulties. Both inherited messy political situations from their predecessors and aroused the anger of their greater subjects by their devotion to favourites. Both ended their reigns by deposition and their lives by murder. Yet Richard emerges from the pages of history as a much more positive and commanding individual than his great-grandfather. Where it was ultimately Edward's incompetence which brought him down, the coup against Richard arose directly from his tyranny towards his greatest subject, in the last of a series of confrontations with the magnate class stemming from Richard's conception of his unique position as a king ordained by God and his determination to subdue all his subjects to his will.

Although the deposition of Edward II broke any pre-existing taboo on the violent removal of an anointed king from his throne, that of Richard II cast the longer shadow, being regarded by Tudor historians and many more recent scholars as the major long term cause of the dynastic strife of the 15th century, when the king ceased to be truly set apart from other men, and the crown and the power it brought were a prize to be fought over by magnates in whose veins flowed the blood of Edward III and his four younger sons.

8.2   THE BOY KING

Edward III's 1376 charter confirmed Richard's position as his heir and resolved any doubts which might have existed as to his right to the throne. On 20 November, he was formally invested as Prince of Wales, Duke of Cornwall and Earl of Chester, and his uncles and all other magnates were required to 'swear to uphold and maintain him, as their only lord and undoubted sovereign'.[1] The following June, Richard was crowned in all the magnificent ceremony of the traditional rite, with its emphasis on the unique position of the King of England as the chosen and anointed of God. This must have been heady stuff for a pre-adolescent boy who had been thrust suddenly into the limelight, and it seems not unreasonable to see in the adulation of this period the seeds of the exaggerated sense of majesty that was ultimately the source of his downfall.

8.2.1   Government 1377–80

The constitution as it had developed made no specific provision for a royal minority, and there was no consistency in the apparatus assembled to govern the kingdom until

---

1   MJ Bennett, *Richard II and the Revolution of 1399*, 1999, Sutton, p 16. This is the most recent study of Richard's reign and deposition.

a boy king was of age. The age of royal majority was itself a vague concept. On Richard II's accession, arrangements were made 'on the hoof' and on the basis of the power and influence of a small cabal close to the throne. Formal power was vested in a 'continual council' of magnates elected in the immediate aftermath of the coronation, but lay in practice with John of Gaunt.

8.2.2   The Peasants' Revolt

As the king entered his 14th year in January 1380, the period of continual councils came to an end, but Richard remained under Gaunt's domination, from which he did not fully emerge until 1385. This was a particularly difficult period for the government, most critically in the summer of 1381 when the mass uprising remembered as the Peasants' Revolt occurred. This had a number of causes, its long term roots lying in the upheaval, both social and economic and emotional, caused by the Black Death of 1348–49 and more recent visitations of plague, most seriously in 1362. The initial epidemic killed some 30% of the population of England. It killed indiscriminately, sparing no level of society, although it seems to have struck most heavily at the peasantry and the urban poor.[2] The bonds of serfdom were already weakening before the epidemic, with increasing numbers of the peasantry working for wages and paying money rents for the land which provided themselves and their families with food. An acute shortage of labour followed, leading to wage inflation which in turn created more general inflation in the economy and the legislation, mentioned in the previous chapter, which attempted to peg wages to their pre-plague levels.

At the same time, the horror of the Black Death, coupled with disgust at the state of the traditional church, in which the papacy had reached its lowest moral point since the 10th century, with the 70 years of exile at Avignon, followed immediately by the Great Schism of 1378–1415,[3] led to the emergence of a radical religious movement, known in England as Lollardy and regarded by the established church as heresy, which preached an unprecedented doctrine of social equality:

> When Adam delved and Eve span
>
> Who was then the gentle man?

To this potent brew was added that traditional source of discontent, heavy taxation for foreign wars. The eruption followed the imposition of a poll tax at the unprecedented level of one shilling for every person in the realm except beggars and those under the age of 15. The burden of this tax can only be appreciated in the context of the monetary values of the time, when the wages of a ploughman averaged no more than 13s 4d per year. Initially, the peasants resisted the poll tax by the traditional passive

---

2   The most accessible amount of the plague and its consequences can be found in P Ziegler, *The Black Death*, 1998, Penguin.

3   Pope Gregory XI returned the papacy to Rome in 1377. On his death the following year, the cardinals first elected Bartolemeo Prignani his successor as Urban VI, but a faction rapidly assembled in a fresh conclave to pronounce him deposed and elected a second Pope, Clement VII, with the support of the French king. The rival Popes took up residence in Rome and Avignon respectively, each with a college of cardinals that elected its own Pope as the original rivals died off. The Council of Pisa of 1406 declared both Popes deposed and elected another, but this only created a third line of rival Popes. The Schism was only finally resolved when the Council of Constance, which convened in 1415, gained the support of all the major secular rulers for the deposition of all three and the election of yet another as Martin V.

method of understating the number of adults in their households. When the commissioners' returns to the Exchequer in January 1381 showed an absurdly small number of people in the realm over the age of 15, the King's Council appointed new commissioners and ordered them to return to the villages to seek out and punish those who had earlier lied.

The Peasants' Revolt began in localised opposition to the activities of these commissioners in Kent and Essex, but escalated rapidly, and what seems to have started spontaneously soon became a relatively organised uprising led by extremists, most notably the Lollard priest, John Ball. A mob occupied Canterbury, murdered a number of their enemies and indulged in an orgy of destruction among the records in the lawyers' offices. However, at all stages, all but the most extreme rebels protested their loyalty to King Richard, whom they considered, in time-honoured fashion, had been led astray by his evil counsellors, notably Gaunt, Simon Sudbury, the Chancellor and Archbishop of Canterbury, and the Treasurer, Sir Robert Hales.

Given the suddenness of the descent into extreme violence, it is not surprising that the government failed to organise any coherent resistance to the rebels. To make matters worse, two military expeditions had just left the country, one bound for Spain under the command of Edmund of Langley, in another attempt to place Gaunt on the Castilian throne, the other marching on Scotland under Gaunt himself. Southern England was thus denuded of experienced troops and of Gaunt, who, for all the arrogance and avarice which made him the main focus of the rebels' hatred, was at least capable of firm action in a crisis.

The main events of the Peasants' Revolt are well known. The king and his leading counsellors retreated to the Tower of London as the mob burned the Savoy Palace, opened the gates of the prisons, sacked the premises of the Knights Hospitaller at Clerkenwell (the Treasurer was Prior of the Order) and murdered both Chancellor and Treasurer. The great confrontation occurred at Smithfield, where the Mayor of London struck down Wat Tyler, now the leading figure among the rebels, and the 14 year old king pre-empted an immediate return to bloodshed by spurring his horse forward and shouting to the mob: 'I am your king. I am your captain and your leader; follow me into the field and you shall have anything it pleases you to ask for.'

Richard's personal intervention, demonstrating the almost mystical authority of a king who ruled by divine grace, marked the beginning of the end of the great revolt. Never again would the government of the realm be threatened by a popular uprising on anything like that scale, and it was not long before the full authority of the king's ministers and counsellors was restored. In the longer term, the Peasants' Revolt is most significant in relation to the development of Richard's sense of his kingly power and destiny. In those days of crisis, it had been the boy king's assertion of the power and mystique of monarchy, and the sense that there was a direct tie between him and the lowliest of his subjects which was the most important single factor in preventing the uprising from escalating any further. At the critical moment, it was Richard, not his ministers nor his absent uncles, who had held a violent mob in the palm of his hand and persuaded them to draw back from a further orgy of murder and violence – rich meat for an adolescent who was now beginning to emerge as a ruler in his own right.

8.2.3 The adolescent Richard

Not surprisingly, all this seems to have gone to Richard's head, and over the next few years, chroniclers consistently wrote of his arrogance, petulance, laziness and fondness for dissolute living. For a further four years, the leading figures in the government retained their hold on power, while the young king turned increasingly to a small group of noble favourites, notably Robert de Vere, Earl of Oxford.

In January 1385, Richard celebrated his 18th birthday and wasted no time in seeking to prove himself on the battlefield, leading a military expedition to Scotland. Although this achieved nothing, Richard returned with an enhanced sense of his own position and took the opportunity not only to create the new dukedoms of York and Gloucester for his younger uncles, but made de Vere Marquess of Dublin, and thus the first man in England not of royal blood to be granted a title more senior than that of earl. Earlier, de Vere had married the king's cousin, Philippa de Coucy, daughter of Edward III's eldest daughter. Now he aroused further anger by petitioning the Urbanist Pope for an annulment of this marriage so that he could marry his mistress. The parallels with Piers Gaveston are only too clear.

8.2.4 Countdown to the Merciless Parliament

Gaunt's departure at the beginning of 1386 on another expedition to win Castile marked the beginning of a new crisis. With the bulk of England's military resources out of the way, the French king, Charles VI, decided that the time was opportune for an invasion of England, and mustered a large army along the Channel coast. Though the invasion force never actually sailed, due to bad weather and division among its commanders, the crisis exposed the weakness of Richard's ministers, and the presence of a large, hastily-raised and ill-led army in the southern counties brought a serious outbreak of disorder and crime even after the fear of invasion receded. In October 1386, the commons assembled in parliament petitioned for the removal of Richard's chancellor, treasurer and other ministers.

The power of appointment and dismissal of ministers, the question of whether this was solely a royal prerogative or whether it could be exercised only with the approval or at the direction of parliament, or even lay with parliament alone, was to be a bone of contention for centuries to come. The Good Parliament had been successful in impeaching the favourites of Edward III, if only temporarily, and presumably the 1386 parliament wished to emulate its predecessor. Richard, like his forebears, considered the power of appointment and dismissal to lie with the king alone. He retired to his palace at Eltham, declaring that he would not dismiss even a scullery boy at parliament's behest, and that he would rather submit to the King of France than to his subjects. However, Thomas Arundel, Bishop of Ely, reminded him forcefully of the fate of Edward II, and Richard backed down.[4] On 23 November, he dismissed his chancellor, Michael de la Pole, Earl of Suffolk, appointing Bishop Arundel in his place. The commons then impeached Suffolk and committed him to prison in Windsor Castle. Next, a 'great and continual council' was given power to govern in the king's name for the next 12 months. This council was composed mainly

---

4 *Knighton's Chronicle*, pp 354–61, cited in Bennett, *op cit*, p 27.

of the king's baronial opponents, who included his uncle, Thomas, Duke of Gloucester.

As on previous occasions when conciliar government was imposed on a reluctant king, this status quo did not last long. Following the example of Edward II with Gaveston and the younger Despenser, the king secured Suffolk's release before Christmas 1386, and from February 1387 sought to frustrate the activities of the council and ministers by making himself inaccessible when official business required his assent. In the same period, and particularly in his own earldom of Chester,[5] he sought to build up an armed following, anticipating that his dispute with parliament and the council could slide into war. Having created this base of support, Richard embarked on an ideological counter-offensive.

In late August 1387, Richard summoned the Chief Justice of the King's Bench, Sir Robert Tresilian, and six of his fellow judges, and put to them 10 questions concerning his regality and prerogative in the light of recent events. In particular, the judges were asked to rule on whether the acts of the last parliament were derogatory to the king's regality, whether the king had control over the business of parliament and power of dissolution at his pleasure, and whether parliament could impeach and remove the king's ministers against his will. On every issue, the judges found in favour of the king, who further asked of them how his opponents in parliament, who were now shown to have acted outside the law, should be punished.

Here, the judges showed themselves willing to be all things to all men.[6] Though not prepared to define any of the alleged offences against the king's authority as treasonous, they nevertheless found that the persons who had acted against the king, by various means, including the reference to Edward II's deposition, should suffer death as traitors, unless the king wished to remit such punishment as an act of grace. According to MV Clarke,[7] the judges here created new forms of treason, the most important of which, impeding the king in the exercise of his prerogative, took a form quite outside the terms of the Statute of Treasons and was capable of being extended to cover the entire policy of the king's opponents.

Richard did not move immediately on receipt of these convenient opinions, but waited until the council's term was about to expire before making for London with a large armed retinue. His three leading opponents, the Duke of Gloucester, the Earl of Warwick and Bishop Arundel's elder brother, Richard, Earl of Arundel, all traitors under the new definition, had nothing to lose by rebellion in order to force the king to retract. They mustered their forces and once again, confrontation ensued. The three named the king's leading supporters, Alexander Neville, Archbishop of York, de Vere, Suffolk, Tresilian and Sir Nicholas Brembre, a former Mayor of London, as traitors in having carried off the king to distant parts of the kingdom, advised him to perform

---

5   The earldom of Chester passes with the title of Prince of Wales, each heir apparent from the Black Prince onward being created Prince of Wales and Earl of Chester (the dukedom of Cornwall, created for the Black Prince in 1331, passes to each heir apparent automatically at his birth or at the accession of his father or mother if later). Since Richard was childless, there was no heir apparent during his reign, so that the earldom remained in his hands.

6   Chrimes, however, considers that the judges' answers accorded with the law as it had developed to that date: SB Chrimes, 'Richard II's questions to the judges, 1387' (1956) LQR 365–90.

7   MV Clarke, 'Forfeitures and treasons in 1388', in LS Sutherland and M McKisack (eds), *Fourteenth Century Studies*, 1937, OUP, pp 126–32.

acts 'to the disinheritance and dismemberment of his crown' and turned him against his magnates and natural counsellors.

The king was sufficiently concerned at the military strength of his enemies to agree to a meeting. On 17 November 1387, Gloucester, Arundel and Warwick rode to Westminster Hall with 300 armed men and, with the 300 stationed menacingly in the courtyard, approached the king, who was seated on his throne, in full armour, just as Simon de Montfort and his confrères had once confronted Henry III and the Earls of Hereford and Norfolk Edward I. Having already announced their intention to accuse the king's supporters, they now challenged them to prove their innocence by judicial duel, an ancient Norman practice which had become almost forgotten.

Richard again backed down, agreeing that the accusations would be tried before a parliament to be summoned for 3 February 1388. Though the fires had been drawn for the moment, both sides made military preparations. Gloucester, Arundel and Warwick were now joined by Henry of Bolingbroke, Gaunt's heir and now emerging as a major figure in his own right, and Thomas Mowbray, Earl of Nottingham. De Vere raised a substantial army in Cheshire and the northern Welsh Marches, but as he moved south, he encountered his enemies at Radcot Bridge in Oxfordshire on 20 December and his force was cut to pieces. He himself escaped by swimming the river, but fled overseas and had no direct role in future events.

Richard, having lost any military initiative he might have had, as well as the bulk of his army, retired into the Tower and, according to some chroniclers, was now threatened with deposition by the five 'Lords Appellant', who made the thinly veiled threat that his heir was now of full age and prepared to rule according to their advice for the good of the kingdom. Who this heir was is not clear, but Bennett considers that the Lords Appellant were referring to Henry of Bolingbroke or one of the king's uncles, rather than Roger Mortimer, whom Richard had named as his heir in 1385. He considers Bolingbroke the most likely candidate, given that he had just turned 21 at this time.[8] One chronicler goes so far as to claim that Richard was actually deposed for three days, but was reinstated after Bolingbroke and Gloucester disputed the succession. Bennett feels that the true version of events, which fell just short of actual deposition, can be found in the confession allegedly made by Gloucester in 1398, in which he stated that he and his fellows sought advice about renouncing their allegiance to Richard and for two or three days were resolved in favour of deposition.[9]

8.2.5   The Merciless Parliament

Richard, now 21, was at the nadir of his early fortunes. However, he was still in possession of life and throne, and the Lords Appellant humbly protested their allegiance to him when the Merciless Parliament opened on 3 February. For the time being, he assured Gloucester that as he was of royal stock, he could not be suspected of plotting the death of his nephew, and acquiesced in the proceedings against his supporters.

The Lords Appellant presented a formal indictment, or appeal, of treason in 39 articles, claiming that their five enemies had taken advantage of Richard's youth to

---

8   Bennett, *op cit*, p 30 and n 6.
9   If this is correct, then it demonstrates that the opposition of Bolingbroke and Gloucester to the king was not wholly principled, but also involved motives of personal gain.

turn him against his loyal lords and had themselves taken royal power and stripped their ruler of his sovereignty. Specific clauses included proposing to create de Vere king of Ireland, and de Vere's accroaching royal power by raising an army in Cheshire and displaying the king's banner in the king's absence. Four knights of Richard's household, including his former tutor, Sir Simon Burley, were accused of seeking French military assistance against the council in return for the cession of Calais.

Asked to rule on the future conduct of the proceedings, a panel of judges and doctors of civil law advised that the appeal of treason was not in conformity with the processes of either common law or continental civil law. This was far from being the end of the matter, for the lords, allegedly with the king's assent, declared that by ancient custom, it was for parliament to be judges in cases of treason. Here, again, new ground was being broken. Not only had the crime of treason, uniquely at this time, been defined in parliament by statute, but parliament was taking upon itself the power to try charges of treason, so removing the highest crime against the crown and sovereign from the ambit of the royal justices.[10]

By now, de Vere, Suffolk and Archbishop Neville had fled abroad and Tresilian was in hiding, so that Sir Nicholas Brembre was left to face trial alone. Parliament refused his request for a judicial duel, though no fewer than 300 lords, knights and squires threw down their gauntlets in protest. Tresilian was then discovered in sanctuary at Westminster Abbey, disguised as a beggar. Against all custom he was dragged out from the Abbey precincts by Gloucester and an armed body of lords, and informed that his failure to appear before parliament constituted an admission of guilt. Both he and Brembre were then hanged.

The Merciless Parliament was not satisfied with this bloodletting and their proceedings against Richard's adherents continued. The six judges who had, with Tresilian, ruled in Richard's favour the previous summer were all adjudged guilty of treason, although their death sentences were commuted to exile in Ireland. Before parliament adjourned for Easter, it was resolved that all the lords and commons should swear an oath to keep the king's peace, and to live and die with the Lords Appellant against every man, saving their allegiance to the crown, and that the same oath should be taken by the sheriffs and leading gentry in the shires, and all the magistrates of the towns.

A pause for thought over Easter brought no immediate lessening of the blood lust. In the proceedings against the four household knights, the Duke of York, who had hitherto kept aloof from events, offered to prove Burley's innocence in personal combat, although neither this intervention, nor that of the queen, Anne of Bohemia, who went down on her knees for three hours before the Earl of Arundel and implored him to show mercy towards her husband's old tutor, saved Burley from the axe.

Burley's execution and those of his fellows marked the end of the bloodletting. As the session ended, parliament sought to defend the decisions it had taken and the powers it had taken upon itself against any future re-assertion of royal power, but took care to proclaim that its pronouncements and judgments should not be taken as precedents for the future, and that the legal definition of treason was to remain as embodied in the Statute of Treasons. The oath taken before Easter was repeated and, in a solemn ceremony in Westminster Abbey, Richard renewed his coronation oath

---

10   A parliament had been summoned in 1283 specifically to try Dafydd ap Gruffydd on charges of treason, but it was given this power by the king.

and the lords their homage. There too, the bishops solemnly warned that excommunication would follow for anyone who broke his oath or sought to rouse the king's anger against the lords.

The Merciless Parliament marked the beginning of the practice of obtaining condemnation for treason through parliament and outside the courts, mainly via Bills of Attainder introduced into parliament at the behest of the king and passed by parliament at his direction. These allowed a range of actions which did not properly fall within the purview of the Statute of Treasons to be considered treason in the case of the individual specified, and the full penalties to be exacted. As to penalty, an Act of Attainder not only deprived the offender of his titles and property, but 'corrupted' his blood, so that his issue could not inherit from or through him. Thus, entire families could be deprived of property, which then passed to the crown, though in practice a proportion of attainted traitors managed to obtain pardon, which suspended the death sentence on sureties for good behaviour, and the majority of attainders were lifted once the family of the condemned traitor had proved their loyalty to the crown afresh.

8.3   THE ADULT RICHARD

8.3.1   A charm offensive

The end of the Merciless Parliament was not the end of Richard's difficulties, but was the point at which the tensions between king and subjects were temporarily obscured and the cracks papered over. Richard, having lost his closest friends and allies, seems to have resolved to wait until he was strong enough to crush his enemies once and for all. Future events would show that he had not forgotten the period of ignominy when he was forced to acquiesce in the proceedings against his adherents as the only means of saving his throne. For the time being, however, he accepted the necessity of ruling by consent and allowed the sense of majesty central to his personality to find expression in patronage of the arts and the magnificence of his court.

At the same time, the Lords Appellant were less than fully successful in dealing with the issues which most concerned the political nation. Northern England was invaded by two Scottish armies and Henry 'Hotspur', eldest son of the Earl of Northumberland, was defeated at Otterburn in August 1388. The crisis in public order continued. Now, the principal concern was the problem of the armed retainers of royalty and magnates who, wearing their masters' badges and swaggering around the country in large bodies, did not hesitate, it was claimed, to rob, extort and make it impossible for ordinary people to carry out their lawful business or to find justice. In an astute move, Richard promised in the parliament of September 1388 to give up his own badges, a clear means of embarrassing those of his enemies who had failed to keep control of their followers.

Richard now put aside his dislike of John of Gaunt and a bond emerged between uncle and nephew which lasted for the remainder of Gaunt's life. Gaunt, returning to England in the autumn of 1388 after relinquishing his claims to the Castilian throne in return for the marriage of his daughter by Constance of Castile to the heir of Enrique of Trastamara, soon showed himself to be out of sympathy with the Lords Appellant.

By spring 1389, Richard, supported by Gaunt, was in a sufficiently strong position to declare himself formally of age before a great council in Westminster Hall, drawing attention to the great burden of taxation the people of England had laboured under during the 12 years in which the country had been ruled by others in his name, and pledging himself to work tirelessly for the prosperity of his realm and the well being of his people. He now assumed personal control of government, appointing new ministers and seeking to improve the administration of justice by appointing new commissions of the peace to restore order in the most lawless areas. Along with Gaunt, he assumed personal direction of the negotiations for a permanent peace with France, with whom a truce had held since 1372. Gaunt also removed a potential source of friction by encouraging his son, Henry of Bolingbroke, to spend most of the years from 1390 to 1394 out of the country, first joining the Teutonic Knights in Lithuania and then making a pilgrimage to Jerusalem.

The next five years were the most stable of the reign, during which Richard created a magnificent court which provided a vehicle for some of the greatest artistic achievements of the day. These include the remodelling of Westminster Hall, originally built under William Rufus, and the creation of its great hammerbeam roof, which survives today.

8.3.2   New dissensions

The succession emerged again as an issue in 1394. Richard and Anne of Bohemia remained childless and Roger Mortimer was now approaching manhood. According to one chronicler, Gaunt petitioned in parliament to have Bolingbroke named as heir in place of Mortimer. Gaunt and Mortimer, according to another account, quarrelled publicly on the floor of parliament, until they were silenced by the king himself.

At the same time, the situation in England's two overseas possessions had reached crisis point. Although all kings since John had borne the title 'Lord of Ireland', only John himself had actually set foot on Irish soil, most of the lieutenants appointed to exercise royal power in Ireland were absentees and the country and its turbulent people left very largely to their own devices. Now, large areas acknowledged the authority of neither king nor Pope, the island, once a modest source of revenue for the crown, was now a drain on its resources and for some years, the royal administrators in Dublin had been begging the king to come in person to re-establish English authority. Expeditions planned for 1385–86 and 1391–92 had been postponed indefinitely, and now one Art MacMorrough, a descendant of the last native King of Leinster, had styled himself king and established a power base dangerously close to Dublin.

In the spring of 1394, revolt broke out in Gascony, after Richard conferred the dukedom of Aquitaine on Gaunt and his heirs in perpetuity. The city of Bordeaux, its prosperity based on the wine trade with England, and a number of Gascon lords feared the separation of the duchy from the English crown. On 6 April, the Archbishop of Bordeaux and others took a solemn oath to be ruled thenceforth by none but the king of England and to stand together in a union against any who denied them this. Before the end of the year, the seriousness of the revolt necessitated Gaunt's departing for Gascony with an army.

Meanwhile, on 7 June 1394, Anne of Bohemia, still under 30, died suddenly, possibly from plague. Richard had been devoted to her and in the immediate aftermath of her death, some of the less throneworthy elements in his character re-asserted themselves. Histrionically, he vowed that for a year, he would not enter any building, other than a church, in which she had set foot, and ordered the destruction of the palace of Sheen where she died. When the Earl of Arundel arrived late for the Queen's funeral in Westminster Abbey, Richard seized a staff from an attendant and struck him across the face with it.

With Anne of Bohemia, Richard lost the last of the companions whose loyalty he had never doubted. Both Robert de Vere and Archbishop Neville had died in exile. Henry of Bolingbroke and Thomas Mowbray, both companions of his youth, were among the Lords Appellant. Soon the paranoia and suspicion which ultimately brought about Richard's fatal confrontation with Bolingbroke was to emerge.

His queen's death brought one benefit to Richard: he could now seek an advantageous marriage to cement the peace with France. It seems that it was only a genuine desire for permanent peace which induced him to accept the hand of Charles VI's eldest daughter, Isabella of Valois, who, although a bride of suitably exalted status, was only seven years old when the marriage took place in 1396. This meant that uncertainty over the succession must continue for at least another decade.

The crisis which brought about Richard's deposition began in the traditional fashion of a dispute over taxation. Although Isabella brought with her a substantial dowry, the cost of the marriage was high – one chronicler estimates it at £200,000 – and to this was added the expense of her coronation. At the same time, there was disquiet over the terms agreed with the French, support for which declined still further when the basis on which the treaty had been made largely disappeared with the defeat at Nicopolis in Anatolia of the mainly French army which had set out in the spring to recover the Holy Land.

8.3.3   Crisis renewed

When parliament opened on 22 January 1397, the Chancellor, in the name of the king, sought financial aid for an expedition to assist the French in Italy. The commons expressed misgivings and evaded any decision making by referring the matter to the lords. The king, affronted, demanded to know what conspiracy led him to oppose his 'honourable purpose', at which the commons denied any conspiracy and declared that they should not be obliged to pay for an enterprise which was a matter for the king alone, not his kingdom. The immediate dispute was smoothed over when the French cancelled their own expedition, but this was only the beginning of Richard's attempt to deal finally with his enemies which led inexorably to his deposition.

On 1 February, the commons presented a petition to the lords, detailing four points of grievance against the king. Richard responded to three,[11] but was roused to a indignation by complaints about the high cost and size of the king's household, angrily claiming that such criticism was a breach of his regality. Issues of 'regality', albeit different in nature, had brought about the crisis of 1386–88, and Richard was soon to show that he had lost any wisdom he had learned from his earlier mistakes.

---

11   (a) That some sheriffs and escheators were kept in office beyond their terms.
     (b) The government's failure to provide adequately for the defence of the Scottish marches.
     (c) The widespread distribution of badges contrary to the statute of 1389.

Richard concluded that one or other of the magnates was fomenting opposition to him. At the same time, according to the chronicler Jean Froissart, the Duke of Gloucester disputed with Richard over foreign policy, proposing that the war with France be resumed in order to take advantage of Nicopolis. There is no record of this dispute reaching parliament, but it was not long before the king's suspicion of his youngest uncle was brought out into the open. Richard seems to have taken steps to confirm Gaunt in his support of him, announcing in parliament the legitimation of Gaunt's four Beaufort issue,[12] and creating the earldom of Somerset for the eldest. At the same time, he approved the translation of Thomas Arundel, Archbishop of York since 1388, to Canterbury. Although originally an opponent of Richard, he had since become his close ally, not least because of Richard's opposition to Lollardy.

For some years, Gloucester, Arundel and Warwick had been little involved in the life of the court. Now Richard summoned the three to a feast on 10 July 1397. The others sensing a trap, Warwick alone attended and was promptly despatched to the Tower. Archbishop Arundel was persuaded to induce his brother to surrender and Richard himself arrested Gloucester at his manor of Pleshy, Essex. Arundel was imprisoned on the Isle of Wight, Gloucester at Calais. On 13 July, the king sent letters across the realm announcing the arrests of the three and detailing their alleged extortions and oppressions, and prohibiting, under pain of treason, all assemblies and congregations.

Further proclamations were issued two days later, stating that the three had not been arrested in respect of their actions 10 years earlier, but for 'other offences against the king's majesty', to be detailed in parliament. Orders were sent to the sheriffs of 12 counties to arrest all their retainers whom they found in arms, and writs were issued in respect of a parliament to be held at Westminster on 17 September. On 28 July, the keepers of the peace in four counties nearest London were commanded to arrest and imprison 'all who by word, deed, or craft were stirring against the imprisonment of the disgraced lords, or behaving towards the king otherwise than as a true liege should'.

What brought about Richard's sudden descent on his enemies? French sources allege that Richard acted to pre-empt a new conspiracy against him, English chroniclers that his true motive was a lust for vengeance against those who had humiliated him 10 years earlier. Evidence favours the latter. Thomas of Walsingham adds the interesting twist that the timing of Richard's action was dictated by the arrival of an embassy from Cologne with the news that he was being considered for election as Holy Roman Emperor in succession to his late queen's brother, the drunkard Wenceslas IV. Richard sent emissaries to Germany, who reported that the majority of the seven electors were supportive, but some asked how the English king could hope to govern the Empire when he could not even discipline his own subjects. Humiliated, Richard then set about demonstrating to the Germans that he was indeed master in his own house.[13]

Resolution of the charges against the three lords was postponed to the September parliament. Meanwhile, Richard made preparations, delivering various castles held by the three to persons who had not yet lost his trust, raising an army and amassing

---

12 By Katharine Swynford, long Gaunt's mistress, whom he married after their births.
13 In the event, Wenceslas hung onto the imperial crown until 1410, when the electors chose his brother, Sigismund, to replace him.

funds. The events of 1386–88 then repeated themselves. On 5 August, eight peers came into Richard's presence at Nottingham Castle to make an appeal of treason against Gloucester, Arundel and Warwick. All of the six who survived Richard's deposition later protested that they had acted under duress out of fear of the king. If this is correct, it would seem that Richard sought to avenge himself upon his enemies in the same way as they had brought about the deaths of his allies during the Merciless Parliament.

8.3.4   The Great Parliament

Tension mounted yet further by the time parliament opened on 17 September. According to one chronicler, Richard entered London with a retinue of 5,000 armed men. As parliament opened, Cheshire archers stood guard over the king from the scaffolding which was still in place around Westminster Hall.

The Chancellor, Bishop Stafford, opened the proceedings of what became known as the Great Parliament, preaching a lengthy sermon on the blessings of monarchy and delineating three elements of good government. First, a king must be powerful enough to govern, and for this purpose, a king was given regalities, prerogatives and other rights annexed to the crown, which at his coronation he pledged to maintain. Second, laws should be kept and executed justly. Third, the realm should be obedient to the king and his laws. It was the duty of parliament to punish all those who had attempted to restrain the king's authority, and parliament must provide safeguards against any repetition of previous such attempts. Clearly, the sermon referred to the events of 1386–88, and this became yet more apparent when the chancellor concluded with the news that the king was disposed to be merciful towards those who had sought to usurp his powers. Fifty unnamed persons would be impeached in the course of the parliament, but otherwise, the king would be so gracious as to pardon all other guilty persons, provided they sued for their pardons before St Hilary's Day (13 January) 1398.

Clearly, the king saw the role of the Great Parliament as the confirmation of the treasonous nature of the assaults on his regalities and prerogatives, and the condemnation of his chief enemies, much as the Merciless Parliament had condemned his closest allies 10 years earlier. Bennett considers that the king had instructed the sheriffs charged with summoning knights of the shire to parliament to ensure that those summoned were as far as possible favourable to his cause. Certainly, the commons included a far larger proportion of knights belonging to the king's household than had ever previously sat, and a trusted follower was appointed Speaker. Richard's desire to control the proceedings was made clear when it was announced at the end of the first day that the king's retainers might bear weapons in parliament, but no others.

Initially, the main foci of the king's fury were the Arundel brothers. First, parliament revoked the pardon earlier granted to the Earl, then adjudged that it had been 'traitorously obtained', which condemned the Archbishop, who had as Chancellor issued the pardon. It closed the day's business by ordaining 'that anyone who should be convicted in the future of violating, usurping or undermining the king's regality should be adjudged a false traitor' and sentenced to the appropriate penalties. It was further ordained that as parliament was deliberating on capital crimes, the presence of the bishops and abbots was not required during the impeachment proceedings.

The king and his adherents subsequently revoked the exclusion of the bishops and abbots, on the basis that the involvement of men of principle in the impeachments could only add credence to the proceedings. But, perhaps anticipating difficulties in the case of Archbishop Arundel, Richard was not prepared to give the prelates a direct role, but instead commanded them, on pain of the loss of their temporalities, to appoint a proctor who would consent on their behalf to all that which was done in parliament. The bishops and abbots demonstrated an abject surrender to the threat by appointing as their proctor Sir Thomas Percy, steward of the king's household.

Though the identities of the remainder of the 50 who were to be impeached remained concealed, charges of treason were preferred on Archbishop Arundel, as well as an appeal of treason by the eight new Lords Appellant against Gloucester, Arundel and Warwick. Arundel was found guilty, but not without making a spirited defence of his actions in 1387. Condemned, he continued to protest his innocence of any treasonable act and confirmed the citizens of London in their support for him by his courage and dignity on the scaffold.

When Gloucester was called to stand trial, Mowbray, who had earlier been instructed to escort him from Calais, announced that the Duke was dead, confirming rumours which had begun to circulate around the end of August. By omission, he allowed the assembly to assume that Gloucester had died a natural death, having earlier confessed to his treason before God and so died in a state of grace. According to evidence given to parliament two years later, Mowbray was commanded by the king to put Gloucester to death, but procrastinated for a time, perhaps hoping that the Duke, who had been ill at the time of his arrest and continued to sicken, would succumb to natural causes. Although there remains doubt, it seems that Gloucester was smothered between two pillows as he lay in bed. Gloucester was condemned posthumously. Shortly afterwards, Archbishop Arundel was deprived of his temporalities and was banished from the realm.

Of Richard's principal opponents in 1386–88, there remained but Warwick, Bolingbroke and Mowbray. Warwick, having pleaded abjectly for mercy at the king's feet and blamed others, principally Gloucester, for his earlier acts against the king, was allowed his life. His imprisonment was less than spartan, as Richard granted him an annuity of 500 marks for the maintenance of his household. Bolingbroke and Mowbray were among those richly rewarded for their recent adherence to the king, and were granted the new dukedoms of Hereford and Norfolk respectively. Three of the king's close relations were also raised to dukedoms, and four new earldoms created for Richard's less exalted allies. The lands of those condemned by the Great Parliament were distributed among these men and others.

The Great Parliament ended on 30 September 1397 with, as in 1388, a splendid ceremony in Westminster Abbey, where the lay lords, the knights of the shire and Sir Thomas Percy (now Earl of Worcester) as proctor for the clergy swore to observe the laws and judgments passed by the parliament, saving only the king's regality, and to hold as traitors anyone seeking to annul those laws and judgments.

It must have seemed that Richard had finally triumphed. Gloucester and Arundel were dead, Warwick imprisoned and Archbishop Arundel required to abjure the realm within six weeks. Bolingbroke and Mowbray were among his most loyal supporters and were bound to him by lavish gifts. Parliament, cowed and compliant, had done his will, and there was no reason to suppose that it would not in the future. Finally, all members of that parliament were bound by their personal oaths not to question its judgments. All that was now necessary was to tie up a few loose ends.

8.3.5   The breach with Bolingbroke

However, tension remained and seems to have heightened Richard's increasingly pathological suspicion. A short-lived cult developed around the Earl of Arundel's tomb, when it was reported that his severed head had miraculously reunited with his body. The king instructed a commission led by Gaunt to disinter the body and establish the truth. Indeed, the head and body had been rejoined, but by the hand of man with needle and thread. Thomas Mowbray, now Duke of Norfolk, was popularly regarded as the Duke of Gloucester's murderer; according to the chroniclers, he swore to his innocence with mighty oaths, claiming that all he had done had been by command of the king and that he had acted only through fear of his sovereign.

Trouble, when it came, arose from an unexpected quarter, in the form of the personal quarrel between Bolingbroke and Mowbray which broke out in December 1397. According to Froissart, Mowbray came upon Bolingbroke near Brentford in Essex when both were riding towards London. He informed him that the king was plotting against the House of Lancaster and planned to reinstate the judgment against Thomas of Lancaster, reversed during the minority of Edward III. This, Mowbray informed Bolingbroke, would disinherit them both, as descendants of Lancaster's brother. Bolingbroke allegedly protested his faith in the king, who had sworn by the Confessor, his favourite saint, to be a good lord to him. Bennett notes that Mowbray was becoming dangerously exposed, since he was widely regarded as the murderer of Gloucester and had been implicated in the coup against Gloucester, Arundel and Warwick; perhaps his fear of Richard was genuine and he believed it necessary to gain Bolingbroke's support and pre-empt any action by the king. It is also possible that Mowbray was acting as Richard's *agent provocateur*, to flush Bolingbroke from cover, although later events militate against this. Be that as it may, Bolingbroke reported the conversation to the king, first in private and then, at his command, in public, on around 22 January 1398, claiming that Mowbray had effectively accused him of treasonable acts.

Parliament opened at Shrewsbury on 28 January 1398. Mowbray was a conspicuous absentee and was formally stripped of his hereditary office as earl marshal. Bolingbroke, however, knelt before the king and begged his forgiveness, which the king readily granted. Parliament, for the moment, continued its business, granting the king one and a half subsidies of a Fifteenth and a Tenth, an unprecedented level of taxation in peacetime, together with a wool subsidy for life. In return, Richard granted a general pardon. It was announced on 31 January that the dispute between Bolingbroke and Mowbray would be determined by the king on the guidance of a committee of named persons. Given the composition of the committee, it is clear that the king wished to control it, but its deliberations were overtaken by events.

At this time, it seems that Richard's attitude towards Bolingbroke and Gaunt remained entirely favourable. In February, he made a formal release of all rights and claims in the lands once held by Thomas of Lancaster which might fall to the crown by reason of Lancaster's treason, so allaying their fears that, as Lancaster's heirs, they might be deprived of the bulk of their property. Yet Richard remained insecure. On 15 March, he commissioned the new Dukes of Albemarle and Surrey to 'follow and arrest all traitors found in the realm of England, and after they have informed themselves of their treasons and convicted them by their acknowledgment or otherwise, chastise them at discretion according to their deserts'.[14] A day later, the king issued a proclamation prohibiting persons from taking unauthorised letters out of the country, and royal officials were instructed to intercept letters going in or out of the country.

By this time, Richard's general unpopularity was emerging. The anonymous author of the narrative poem *Richard the Redeless*, written after Richard's deposition, wrote in critical terms of Richard's visit in 1398 to Bristol, despairing of his vast army of retainers who despoiled the country and terrorised the populace, and speaking of the king's evil counsel in scathing terms. The king lost 10 loyal hearts, he claimed in an appalling pun, for every badge of the white hart which he issued.

At the end of March, there was a popular uprising in the upper Thames valley. Though brief, it demonstrates the strength of feeling against Richard, or at best indifference to his fate which, as in the case of Edward II, is an important element in the ease by which he was supplanted. Richard continued to seek a role on a larger European stage, tasking the Archbishop of Cologne to go to Rome to push his candidacy for the Holy Roman Empire with the Pope, but he clearly believed that the disobedience of his own people was a threat to his ambitions.

On 28 April, Bolingbroke and Mowbray came before the king at Windsor, demanding justice in the form of a judicial duel. Richard assented, the date being set for 16 September. Meanwhile, the king continued to seek to bolster his position by the raising of revenues and repeated assertions of royal power, and to place his closest adherents in the most powerful offices. By a remarkable coincidence, within days of his appointing his nephew, the Duke of Surrey, as lieutenant in Ireland in succession to Roger Mortimer, the news came that Mortimer had been killed in a skirmish with the Irish. Mortimer's son was an infant, and circumstances suggest that Richard had already ceased to see Mortimer as his heir for some time. This left Henry of Bolingbroke, Richard's first cousin and heir to the ailing John of Gaunt, a step nearer to the throne.

One may speculate on the consequences for Richard II had he not intervened to stop the judicial duel moments before Bolingbroke and Mowbray first charged one another with pointed lances, a combat which would have continued to the death. Had either killed the other, the quarrel between them would have been ended, the victor able to proclaim his innocence before the world, perhaps to continue indefinitely as the king's loyal supporter. Had Mowbray killed Bolingbroke, Gaunt's death might have occurred rather earlier than it did, so removing the main prop of Richard's throne, but Gaunt was to die in February 1399 in any event. Beyond that, it is impossible to speculate. But by intervening, even if his motive was, as the official record informs us, avoidance of 'the great dishonour which would befall one or other of them', and sending both men into exile, Bolingbroke for 10 years and Mowbray for life, the king made implacable enemies of them. Once Gaunt was dead, there was no longer anything to restrain Bolingbroke from bidding for the crown itself.

---

14 *Calendar of Patent Rolls, Richard II, 1377–99*, 1895–1909, HMSO, p 365.

Having disposed of his two remaining enemies of 1386–88, Richard II embarked on the last phase of his rule. The term 'tyranny', used of his rule in the articles of his deposition, is rather too strong a word in respect of his reign as a whole, but from Christmas 1396, he behaved in a quite arbitrary fashion towards his principal subjects. One cannot know whether the plots he suspected were realities or merely the product of a mind which, like that of his ancestor, King John, had become increasingly paranoid.

Following Gaunt's death, Richard finally over-reached himself with regard to Bolingbroke, extending his comparatively comfortable 10 year exile in France and Spain to life,[15] and denying him the titles and lands which were his as Gaunt's heir. At this point, unaware of the plans being put into effect by Bolingbroke from France, Richard sailed for Ireland, where the gains made by an expedition in 1394–95 had now been dissipated and the situation again required his urgent attention, leaving his last surviving uncle, Edmund, Duke of York, as keeper of the realm. It was a singularly inopportune time to leave England.

8.4   THE FINAL MONTHS

8.4.1   Bolingbroke's invasion

After the deprivation of his inheritance in March 1399, Bolingbroke quietly built a base of support among those who had little cause to love Richard, most obviously Archbishop Arundel, in exile since September 1397, and Thomas FitzAlan, son of the executed Earl of Arundel. Even after his landing, Bolingbroke proclaimed that his intention was only to secure his rightful inheritance, but details recorded by the chronicler of the French Abbey of St Denis suggest that his real target was always his cousin's crown. Perhaps he believed that he had nothing to lose in seeking the throne; his eldest son, the future Henry V, aged 11, had accompanied Richard to Ireland, a hostage in all but name, and his fate lay in Richard's hands whether Bolingbroke sought the dukedom of Lancaster or the throne.[16]

Bolingbroke's landing in Yorkshire on 4 July took the government completely by surprise. His expeditionary force was tiny, perhaps only 100 men, but he mounted an active propaganda campaign, encouraging individuals and corporations to see him as the popular champion against Richard's tyranny. The Duke of York and the legitimate government seem to have been content to wait upon events, pulling back in the face of Bolingbroke's advance through the Midlands. It is not clear when York – uncle to Bolingbroke as well as Richard – decided to throw in his lot with the latter, but he never seems to have contemplated a decisive move against him. As in the case of Edward II 70 years before, support for the legitimate king appears never to have emerged, except to a limited degree among the Welsh.

Richard II's knowledge of events was inevitably delayed by the slowness of medieval communications, but he seems to have known of Bolingbroke's landing by

---

15 Mowbray's exile, much less pleasantly, was to take place in Germany, Hungary and the lands of the Saracens. He died in Venice in 1400 while en route to Jerusalem.

16 In fact, Richard seems to have taken a liking to young Henry, knighting him and showing him much favour.

the second week in July, by which time, order had been restored in Ireland. However, his own forces were scattered and it was not until 24 July that he and his expeditionary force landed at Milford Haven. Richard remained for some days in South Wales with his troops, but then, learning of York's capitulation, decided that there was no purpose to be served in remaining there and resolved to link up with the Earl of Salisbury, whom he had sent to secure Cheshire. Desperate haste meant that Richard left his army behind, riding across Wales with only a few companions, disguised, according to one chronicler, as a Franciscan friar for fear of capture.[17] Salisbury had been able to muster an army, but his ranks were being steadily thinned by desertion by the time Richard joined him at Conway. Having separated from one army in order to join another, Richard now found himself with neither.

By now, Bolingbroke had begun his vengeance on the king's closest adherents, summarily condemning and hanging three as traitors immediately after Bristol fell to him. If his ambitions had ever been limited to the regaining of his inheritance, he had now crossed the Rubicon. He moved rapidly northward through the Welsh Marches, meeting armed opposition only from the Welsh. The hitherto faithful Cheshire archers deserted, fearing for their own lives and property if captured in the field. When Chester capitulated without a fight, Richard, still at Conway, lost any will to resist and concluded that his only hope lay in persuading Bolingbroke to seek his pardon in return for the grant of his father's honours. By this time, however, the situation had gone far beyond redemption.

A few days later, Henry Percy, Earl of Northumberland, came to Richard with Bolingbroke's terms, which were that Richard would henceforth be governed by the advice of a parliament convened by Bolingbroke, acting as 'chief judge' of England, and that five named individuals, including Exeter, Surrey and Salisbury, would be tried for treason. At this, Richard seems briefly to have put aside his passivity. He agreed to meet Bolingbroke to accept the terms, but with the intention of slipping away to put himself at the head of an army once more.

But Bolingbroke and Northumberland outwitted Richard. That Bolingbroke had no intention of losing the inestimable advantage of having the king in his hands was rapidly made clear by the size of the armed escort which accompanied Northumberland, most of which had been kept hidden from sight during the negotiations in Conway Castle. Richard demanded that he be permitted to return to Conway, but that he was Northumberland's prisoner in all but name was clear.

On meeting Bolingbroke at Flint, Richard seems finally to have appreciated that his position was hopeless and formally surrendered. The course and timing of events over the next few days is unclear, but it would seem that negotiations took place in private between Richard, Bolingbroke and Archbishop Arundel. There is no evidence to support the official statement that Richard agreed to renounce the crown, and on around 16 August, he was taken to Chester under heavy guard. On his arrival there, Richard's household was formally disbanded and Bolingbroke began to rule in his name, issuing writs for a parliament to be held at Westminster on 30 September.

Richard's unpopularity was made clear by events in London. On 11 August, rumour swept the streets that he had entered the city in secret and taken refuge in

---

17 Given that his companions included the Dukes of Exeter and Surrey, three bishops, various knights and clerks, and the usual Cheshire archers, the disguise could not have been particularly convincing.

Westminster Abbey, and the citizens went in arms to the Abbey. As Richard was escorted south, a deputation of Londoners came to Bolingbroke at Lichfield and petitioned him to behead Richard and his companions. Bolingbroke, however, declared that the proper course was to leave matters to the judgment of the parliament which was shortly to meet.

8.4.2 Deposition

By 10 September at the latest, Bolingbroke had decided that Richard could no longer remain king, the Chancery clerks quietly dropping the use of Richard's regnal year on official documents. Past events showed only too clearly that he was not to be trusted to abide by oaths he had sworn. As in 1326–27, the problem was in finding a satisfactory mechanism for his dethronement, and it was to the precedents of that time that Bolingbroke and his confederates now returned. Then, Edward II's collapse into complete passivity allowed his enemies to present his subjects with the fiction that he had renounced the crown of his own free will. Richard was a tougher individual altogether and one who may well have believed that as a priest could not resign his orders, so a king could not abdicate his sacred position. Deposition was essential to the security of the new regime. It may well also have been recognised that total security could only be gained by Richard's death.

Distancing themselves from the issue, Bolingbroke and Archbishop Arundel set up a panel of senior clergy and canon lawyers who, conveniently for future scholars, included the chronicler Adam of Usk, to consider precedents for deposition. The panel found a suitable example of a deposition of a monarch for 'major crimes' in that of Frederick II in 1245, and ruled that Richard's 'perjuries, sacrileges, sodomitical acts, dispossession of his subjects, the reduction of his people to servitude, lack of reason and incapacity to rule' provided the necessary grounds in canon law. However, there was the obvious difficulty that Frederick II had been deposed by a Pope and a General Council of the church, neither of which was available to Bolingbroke. The panel decided that, as in 1327, it was necessary to secure a voluntary abdication by the king and then, to prevent any reneging on that abdication, a deposition.[18] The question of whether a parliament summoned in the name of a king could depose that king remained open, for Richard was finally deposed only 'if anything of his dignity shall remain in him'.

The other pressing issue was the way in which Bolingbroke was to prove his right to the crown. He might be the obvious successor to Richard, but was he the lawful heir? In 1327, the right of Edward III to succeed his father was not in question, but in 1399, there remained the claim of the young Edmund Mortimer, son of the man Richard had named as his heir in 1385. This seems not to have been treated as a thing of much consequence – Mortimer was only seven years old and did not have any strong following – but it remained essential for Bolingbroke to present himself as a lawful king rather than a usurper.

Consideration was given to impugning Richard's paternity or legitimacy, and then to utilising an old story that Edmund 'Crouchback', Earl of Lancaster, Bolingbroke's direct ancestor through his mother, had in truth been the elder son of Henry III and

---

18 Of course, in 1327, a parliament had first deposed Edward II, then its emissaries induced him to abdicate.

not the younger, but no evidence could be produced to support either claim. By the time parliament met on 30 September, Bolingbroke had settled for a title with several elements: first, that the throne was vacant through Richard's voluntary abdication and his deposition by parliament; second, that Henry, by his descent from both Edward III and Edmund of Lancaster, was a member of the royal house through both parents.[19] He was also, though much less stress was laid on this, a lawful king by conquest and by the will of the people.

However, Richard had not yet agreed to forsake the throne, and Bolingbroke and his allies now sought to break his resistance, confining him in the Tower and subjecting him to interrogation. Predictably, the official 'Record and Process' of Richard's departure from the throne and royal state claims that on being visited by a deputation of notables on 29 September, he renounced his crown voluntarily and even placed his coronation ring on Bolingbroke's finger. Other, less partial, sources indicate that the process of securing his submission was lengthy and that he was by no means resigned to his fate. He declared that he could not renounce his anointing or the characters it imprinted on his soul, and laid his crown on the ground and resigned his right to God.

The following day, 30 September, parliament assembled in Westminster Hall, although, as in 1327, it could not be considered a true parliament in the absence of the king or his appointed representative, and the throne was left empty. Richard Scrope, Archbishop of York, read Richard's statement renouncing the throne and absolving his subjects from their allegiance. Archbishop Arundel then asked those present whether they wished, for the good of the realm, to accept the cession. Richard still merited some loyalty, or perhaps there was a more basic concern as to the validity of the proceedings; the Bishop of Carlisle demanded that Richard be brought into the chamber to confirm or deny his willingness to abdicate. However, this protest was brushed over, and lords and commons gave their consent. It was then declared that, for the avoidance of doubt, a statement of Richard's crimes and specific instances of misgovernment, meriting his deposition, had been prepared by Bolingbroke's panel of canon lawyers, and this was read to the assembly.

The Articles of Deposition are, if one-sided, relatively sober in tone, confining themselves to matters within public knowledge. They demonstrate a concept of kingship and good government, going back to Magna Carta and embodied in the coronation oath, that the king would rule according to law, with the counsel of his magnates and judges, and in the interests of all his people. They focus specifically on Richard's alleged breaches of individual laws, but leave open the question of whether they believed Richard to consider himself above the law as an entity.

The assembly was then asked, both together and singly, whether the accusations contained in the Articles of Deposition and Richard's own 'confession of inadequacy' in the statement of abdication were sufficient grounds for him to be deposed and, according to the 'Record and Process', assented unanimously. Commissioners representing the three estates were then appointed to depose Richard from 'all his royal dignity, majesty and honour, on behalf of, in the name of and by authority of, all the estates, as has been observed in similar cases by the ancient custom of the realm'. The only similar case in which this 'ancient custom' had been observed was a mere 70

---

19   The same was true of Richard, since Joan of Kent was the daughter of Edmund, Earl of Kent, younger son of Edward I by his second marriage.

years old, but the fiction that ancient custom legitimised unprecedented acts has been seen on a number of earlier occasions.

Richard II having been disposed of, in regality though not yet in body, parliament now turned to the enthronement of his usurper. Henry of Bolingbroke spoke first, claiming the throne on the basis of his descent from Henry III twice over, and God's grace in sending him to save the kingdom from 'default of government and undoing of good laws'. Where the process against Edward II had been conducted in French, Bolingbroke spoke in English, now becoming the language of court and government after three centuries of submergence. Again, the lords and commons were asked for their assent and, this being given, Bolingbroke was raised to the empty throne by the two Archbishops.

Archbishop Arundel preached a sermon, stressing Bolingbroke's manliness and Richard's shortcomings as a ruler, before Bolingbroke spoke again to re-state his claim to the throne. Once more, he stressed his hereditary right, but now stated his intention of ruling in accordance with established law and insisted that neither that law nor the rights of his subjects would be compromised by the manner of his succession. The coronation would take place on 13 October – there was no intention of allowing the popular enthusiasm for Bolingbroke to die down before he was safely anointed and crowned.

On 1 October, the commissioners of the three estates went to Richard II in the Tower, led by the Chief Justice, informed him of all the stages of the deposition process and then renounced their homage and fealty. According to Adam of Usk, the commissioners ended the encounter and thus the legal process by informing Richard that he was henceforth to be regarded simply as Richard of Bordeaux, a knight. A Spanish chronicler alleges, however, that he was subjected to a process of degradation reminiscent of that of John Balliol, being first seated in majesty and then stripped successively of crown, sceptre, orb, sword and finally the throne itself.

Bolingbroke was duly crowned as Henry IV on 13 October, the feast of Edward the Confessor. The choice of the day dedicated to Richard's patron saint can only have been deliberate, an attempt to obtain in the eyes of the people the support of the royal saint for the new dynasty. In order to strengthen the new king's claims to legitimacy, the legend was given out that the holy oil used for the first time at this coronation dated from the time of Christ Himself, and had been discovered by Thomas Becket during his exile in France. Why this holiest of oils had been left at Canterbury unused for more than 200 years was left unrevealed. However, the symbolism of the coronation was marred by inauspicious events. The head on which Archbishop Arundel placed the crown swarmed with lice and the coin used for the king's offertory rolled off its platter and disappeared.

As Henry IV got down to the normal business of government, the problem of what should be done with his predecessor remained. Henry was at first disposed to be merciful to Richard's adherents, but before long, plots began to emerge. Richard was first moved out of London for greater security and was confined in the northern Lancastrian stronghold of Pontefract. However, this was not sufficient. On 17 December, a group of noble conspirators met at Westminster, determining on a plot to capture the new king and his sons at Windsor as they celebrated the Epiphany, and then to liberate Richard and restore him to the throne, with concurrent risings in various parts of the country.

The plot was betrayed and subdued before it could escalate into a serious threat. That Henry was the people's hero was made clear in brutish fashion when the Earls of Kent and Salisbury were captured and summarily beheaded by the townsfolk of Cirencester, and another conspirator was lynched by the people of Bristol. As in the case of Edward II, Richard's fate was sealed by this failed attempt at rescue. The manner of his death is unclear, but by 17 February 1400, he was dead. His corpse was conveyed to London with his body blanketed in lead, but with his face exposed. He may have died by violence or as a result of ill-treatment, or even, as has been suggested, from self-induced starvation after the failure of the plot finally broke his resistance.

CHAPTER 9

THE 15TH CENTURY

'Are you Edmund Mortimer? If not, have you got him?'

1066 And All That

9.1 INTRODUCTION

The 15th century is not a time of innovation in constitutional matters, but rather one of consolidation of previous practice, particularly the manipulation of parliaments by usurping monarchs in order to legitimate their positions. This manipulation reflected the importance of parliament in constitutional thinking, the idea that the king was subject to the law and that, in Bracton's words, it was the law that made him king.

9.2 AN INSECURE DYNASTY – THE HOUSE OF LANCASTER 1399–1461

9.2.1 Henry IV 1399–1413

The reign of Henry IV began in a blaze of popular enthusiasm, but soon degenerated into a holding operation. Within a year of the usurpation, Wales, quiescent for more than a century, erupted into rebellion under the leadership of Owain Glyn Dwr of Glyndyfrdwy ('Owen Glendower'), the greatest of the remaining Welsh landowners, and a descendant of earlier princes of South and Mid Wales. Glyn Dwr's rising had its roots in a dispute with a neighbouring Marcher lord, but became a national uprising after he proclaimed himself Prince of Wales on 16 September 1400 and associated himself with Welsh tradition of a heroic past before the coming of the English. Glyn Dwr's rising was a very serious threat to the Lancastrian throne, the more so because of its support for the claims of Edmund Mortimer, whose uncle and namesake was Glyn Dwr's leading English ally, and alliances with the French and Scots, and through Mortimer with the Percies of Northumberland. Glyn Dwr was a well-educated man, having studied law at the Inns of Court in London. His plans for an independent Wales included the creation of two universities, one each in the north and south. In addition, he summoned a parliament at Macynlleth in November 1403, at which laws were passed in imitation of established English practice.

The rebellion of the Percies – Henry, Earl of Northumberland, his son, Henry 'Hotspur', and the Earl's brother, Thomas Percy, Earl of Worcester and steward of the king's household – seems to have been motivated by a sense of the king's ingratitude. In their eyes, he had failed properly to reward them for their crucial role in the coup and showed undue favour to Ralph Neville, Earl of Westmorland, their rival for dominance in the north. To compound this, he failed to repay the vast sum of £10,000 which he owed them and demanded that they surrender to him the five Scottish earls they had captured in repelling a Scottish invasion in August 1402, so depriving them of lucrative ransoms. At the same time, not only did the king fail to ransom Sir

Edmund Mortimer, Hotspur's brother-in-law and recently captured by Glyn Dwr, but forbade anyone else to ransom him – no doubt Mortimer, not only uncle to young Edmund Mortimer but with a claim to the throne in his own right, was better kept safely out of the way.

By the summer of 1403, all Henry IV's actual and potential enemies had united against him; Glyn Dwr, who now controlled much of Wales, the former adherents of Richard II in Cheshire and Shropshire, the Percies and Sir Edmund Mortimer. Their plan was simple and realistic. The Percies and their English allies would march on Shrewsbury, from which Henry of Monmouth, the king's eldest son, was conducting operations against Glyn Dwr, capture him and then join forces with Glyn Dwr and Mortimer. Once Henry IV was defeated, they would place young Mortimer on the throne, although they publicly proclaimed that Richard II was still alive and that they were seeking to restore him.

However, Henry IV's military skill, which had deserted him since his usurpation, re-asserted itself in this most critical moment of his entire reign. He and his army made a forced march to Shrewsbury which enabled him to link up with his son before the Percies could reach the town. The Battle of Shrewsbury, fought on 21 July 1403, ended, narrowly, in defeat for the Percies. Hotspur was killed on the field and Worcester was beheaded two days later. However, Northumberland escaped and Owain Glyn Dwr remained at large and in control of much of Wales. In May 1404, his ambassadors concluded a treaty of alliance against Henry IV with Charles VI of France. This led to a French landing at Milford Haven in August 1405, planned to coincide with a renewed rising by the remaining Percies with their northern allies, and by Sir Edmund Mortimer in alliance with Glyn Dwr. Again, the threat to Henry IV's kingship was serious, the French and their Welsh allies penetrating England to within eight miles of Worcester, though they retreated without doing battle.

The tide was beginning to turn. The Welsh, though numerous and afire with passion for their country's independence, were poorly armed, and in Henry of Monmouth – not yet 20 – they faced an adversary of remarkable military skill. From the spring of 1406, the English held the upper hand, first capturing the island of Anglesey, the principal source of grain for Wales, and cutting off food supplies from Glyn Dwr's stronghold in Snowdonia. In February 1408, the Percies were finally defeated and Northumberland was killed at Bramham Moor near Tadcaster.

Two other external enemies of the House of Lancaster were neutralised at the same time. The heir to the Scottish throne, the future James I, was captured at sea while being taken to France for safety from his father's enemies at the end of 1406, his father, Robert III, dying after hearing the news. James was to be held captive for the next 18 years. Charles VI, intermittently mad since the summer of 1392, was now distracted by civil war between his most powerful magnates, the Dukes of Orleans and Burgundy, and their adherents (the Armagnacs and the Burgundians respectively), who each sought to rule him and so rule the country.

In the summer of 1408, Aberystwyth, one of Glyn Dwr's main strongholds, finally surrendered after a lengthy siege, followed early in 1409 by Harlech. Sir Edmund Mortimer, Glyn Dwr's last effective ally, died from plague during the siege of Harlech. After a final campaign in 1410 ended in defeat, Glyn Dwr held out in Snowdonia as a hunted fugitive for another three years, before disappearing from recorded history. The date, place and manner of his death remain unknown.

9.2.2 The succession

By 1408, Henry IV, still only 41, was afflicted with a mysterious illness which incapacitated him. His eldest son increasingly ruled on his behalf. Following the king's death on 20 March 1413, the insecurity of the Lancastrian monarchy was again demonstrated by plotting in support of Edmund Mortimer's claims. The planned rising was betrayed and most of its leaders rounded up, but a second, apparently betrayed by Mortimer himself, followed in 1415. For all that Edmund Mortimer seems to have preferred a quiet life to seeking the throne, the Mortimer claim was not going to die quietly. Indeed, the dynastic strife that emerged in the Wars of the Roses, which occupied the years 1455–71 and re-emerged in 1483–85, can be traced all the way back to 1399 and was only placed in abeyance by Henry V's military successes in France.

The parliament summoned to depose Richard II and legitimise Henry of Bolingbroke as king also recognised Henry of Monmouth as heir apparent. In 1404, against the background of Glyn Dwr's rebellion and the Percy defeat at Shrewsbury, Henry IV settled the succession on his four sons and their issue, both in order of seniority, making no express distinction between his male and female issue after the first generation. In June 1406, with the Percy rebellion renewed and a French invasion force within his domains, the king issued a charter entailing the crown on his sons and their heirs male, which was sealed by the lords and by the Speaker of the commons when parliament met. This entail was repealed only three months later, for reasons which are obscure, restoring the more liberal succession settlement of 1404.

This use of parliament to give legitimacy to a usurper or conqueror and to vest the succession in his issue was confirmed over the rest of the 15th century and demonstrates that parliament had by now acquired a central position in the governmental system. In 1376, Edward III had dealt with the succession by royal charter without reference to parliament. In 1399 and after, parliament was not only involved in the change of monarch, but was used to secure the succession for the usurper's dynasty after him. Admittedly, this had not been necessary in 1327, since Edward III was his father's lawful heir, but Henry IV's repeated recourse to parliament in order to establish the position of his heirs of the body strongly merits emphasis. During the 15th century, although the king – or those who wished to seize the crown – continued to dictate when and whether parliaments sat, and to a very large extent their composition and programme, parliament was at the same time no simple tool of the king, important only as a means of securing extraordinary powers of raising revenue. Its development as a legislature independent of the king was beginning, albeit slowly, uncertainly and in ways dictated by the issues of the moment.

Parliament made the House of Lancaster *de jure* kings, but it was Henry V's victories which persuaded actual or potential enemies of the dynasty to accept the status quo. On Edmund Mortimer's death in 1425, his claim passed to his sister's son, Richard, Duke of York, but was not to be pressed by him or his allies for more than 30 years, and only after the third Lancastrian king had demonstrated an incapability to rule more complete even than that of Edward II.

9.2.3   Henry VI 1422–61

Henry V was perhaps the greatest soldier of the Plantagenet dynasty. His sense of his own destiny led him to renew the war with France and, following his extraordinary victory at Agincourt on 25 October 1415, he was able after a long campaign of attrition to reduce the French to a position where he could give effect to Edward III's claim to the French throne. By the Treaty of Troyes of 1420, Henry not only became Charles VI's son-in-law but also his heir, the claims of Charles's surviving son being set aside. However, he died on 31 August 1422, 16 days before his 35th birthday and six weeks before Charles's death, with his grand strategy incomplete and ultimately doomed to failure.

Henry V's heir in both England and France was an eight month old infant, the most extreme of the 'atypical' Plantagenets. Both Henry III and Edward II were capable on occasions of rousing themselves from their habitual passivity and dependence on favourites, but in Henry VI, these active interludes seem to have been entirely absent. Even his madness was of a passive kind. Where that of Charles VI, probably schizophrenia, was characterised by florid delusions and frenzied violence, his grandson's, which seems first to have emerged in the summer of 1453, involved stupor and complete absence of reaction to stimuli. Even during his lucid intervals, his ineffectual and over-trusting nature led him into dependence on those close to him, originally the Dukes of Suffolk and Somerset, and later his queen, Margaret of Anjou. Otherwise, Henry VI had no interest in military matters, was conventionally religious and was an enthusiastic patron of learning, being the founder of both Eton (originally a college for poor scholars) and King's College, Cambridge. Good man he may well have been, but as a king he was an abject failure.[1]

The unpromising situation on Henry's accession was handled relatively well. On his deathbed, Henry V appointed as his son's regents his two surviving brothers, Humphrey, Duke of Gloucester, in England and John, Duke of Bedford, in France, the latter having paramountcy. Bedford was a highly capable man and governed the Lancastrian domains in France in a conscientious fashion until his death in 1435. However, the task facing him was too great for there to be any chance of ultimate success in enforcing a permanent English sovereignty over the whole of France, and it was the debacle in France, along with Henry VI's mental illness, which finally and fatally undermined the Lancastrian regime.[2] In England, a power struggle quickly developed between the Duke of Gloucester and the Beauforts, issue of John of Gaunt by Katharine Swynford. In confirming Richard II's legitimation of the Beauforts in 1407, Henry IV had specifically excluded them from the succession, but they appear to have inherited many of the most valuable characteristics of their Plantagenet forebears: the intelligence, the restless energy and the streak of ruthlessness and unscrupulousness which characterised the dynasty's most successful rulers. If they could not themselves sit upon the throne, they would be the power behind it.

The political history of the reign is complex, but can be summarised as a power struggle between the Beauforts, particularly John Beaufort, 1st Duke of Somerset

---

1   Since Henry VI was so utterly unlike Henry V, it seems remarkable that even at the time of his deposition, his paternity was apparently never questioned.

2   The success and failure of the Lancastrian war for France is well dealt with in D Seward, *Henry V as Warlord*, 1987, Sidgwick & Jackson, which also provides much useful detail on his earlier campaigns against Owain Glyn Dwr as Prince of Wales.

(1403–44), and the Duke of Gloucester until the latter's mysterious and highly suspicious death in 1447, then subsequently between the next two Dukes of Somerset and Richard, Duke of York, now the nearest adult male of the legitimate blood royal to the king and much the greatest magnate in the realm. By his marriage to Cecily Neville, daughter of Ralph Neville, 1st Earl of Westmorland, York also gained the support of the ruthless, energetic and politically astute members of the vast Neville clan, who were, with the Percies, the most powerful family in the north.[3] From 1447 until the birth of Henry VI's son on 13 October 1453, York was heir presumptive to the throne as the grandson in the male line of Edmund, Duke of York. By the time the king succumbed to his first attack of madness in August 1453, York had precious little cause to love his Beaufort cousins or Margaret of Anjou, whom Henry VI had married in 1445.

Failure in France

Henry V's military successes had been to no small degree made possible by disunity among the French – the struggle between the Armagnacs and the Burgundians for control of Charles VI which amounted almost to civil war. Once the French gained a precarious unity under the mad king's son, Charles VII, and war against the occupying English had been given an impetus by the example of Joan of Arc in the late 1420s, the loss of Henry's conquests was inevitable. For two periods, in 1436–37 and again in 1440–45, the Duke of York was Henry VI's lieutenant in France, effectively commander-in-chief. However, at the end of 1445, he was removed to the comparative backwater of Ireland and was replaced by Edmund Beaufort, 2nd Duke of Somerset. His antipathy to the Beauforts seems to date from this period and derived from jealousy of Somerset's prominence at court and anger at his military failures, which cost York his own estates in Normandy. This antipathy was only exacerbated by the failure of a government dominated by the Beauforts and their adherents to provide adequate finance for York's official activities in France and Ireland, so that his forces had to be raised, provisioned and paid from his own resources.

Henry VI's marriage was attended by the cession of Anjou and Maine as part of the marriage settlement, and this paved the way for the loss of Normandy itself in 1449, following an unnecessary assault by Somerset on the Breton port of Fougeres which provided a greatly strengthened French government with a convenient pretext to renew the war. All that was now left of the English possessions in France were Calais and a strip of the Gascon coast.

The drift towards civil war

An already tense and uncertain political situation came to a head from 1450, the following decade being one of almost continuous governmental crisis, popular

---

3   Ralph Neville married twice and had a total of 23 children. The 14 children of his second marriage largely gave their allegiance to the Yorkist cause, initially by reason of family disputes with the descendants of the first marriage. Several of the 14 and their issue made brilliant marriages and so gained enormous wealth and influence, most notably Richard Neville, who became Earl of Salisbury by his marriage, and his eldest son, another Richard, Earl of Warwick and known to history as 'the Kingmaker'.

discontent and disorder giving way to civil war between the leading magnate factions. In January of that year, the Keeper of the Privy Seal was murdered in Portsmouth by a mob of soldiers and sailors enraged at the government's failure to pay them. Shortly afterwards, there was a minor rising in Kent, whose leaders demanded the heads of those around the king, particularly Somerset. In February, the commons of parliament impeached the king's chancellor, William de la Pole, Duke of Suffolk, whom they blamed for the loss of Normandy, the high burden of taxation and the government's failure to secure law and order. Although the evidence against Suffolk as the author of the government's policies was slim, he was duly condemned and was only saved from a death sentence by the king's hasty decree that he should be banished for five years. However, while Suffolk was in the very act of sailing into exile, the ship in which he took passage was intercepted and his head was summarily struck off with a rusty sword on a block improvised from a tree trunk.

Shortly afterwards, a much more serious rebellion broke out, again in Kent, under the leadership of one Jack Cade, who adopted the pseudonym of John Mortimer and claimed to be a cousin of the Duke of York. There is no evidence that the Duke, then in Ireland, was involved in the rising in any way, but Cade and his confederates raised him to the position of popular saviour. The rebels, who were not primarily a band of disorganised peasants, unlike those of 1381, seem initially to have been motivated by local concerns, but as the rising spread out from Kent to the rest of south-east England, national issues took precedence. The proclamation of June 1450 refers to all too traditional concerns, going back to 1215 and earlier: that 'certain false and unsuitable persons who are around [the king's] highness' asserted that the king was above the laws 'and that he may make them and break them as he pleases', and that the same 'false traitors' prevented loyal subjects from approaching the king. In order to remedy this, the king should give the Duke of York the place in his counsels which his position warranted. This proclamation, clearly prepared by educated men, was sealed by two former sheriffs of Kent and a member of parliament.[4]

By early June, the rebels were encamped on Blackheath and seeking a meeting with the king, in the same way as their forebears of 70 years earlier. Henry VI and his ministers retreated to Kenilworth. At around the beginning of July, Cade and his followers entered London, where they were initially greeted with enthusiasm by the populace. However, before long, an outbreak of violence and looting cost the rebels their popular support, and a large scale skirmish took place between the Londoners and the rebels on the night of 4 July. When offered a general pardon, the majority of the rebels dispersed and returned to their homes. Cade, however, fled into Sussex, pursued by the sheriff of Kent, and was fatally wounded.

From the second half of 1450 onwards, the mutual hatred between York and two successive Dukes of Somerset was out in the open. This meant there could be no consistent or disinterested royal government while the protagonists retained their power bases. In November, violence erupted in London between the rivals' retainers. Somerset continued, however, to enjoy the king's complete confidence. According to one chronicle, he remained 'most familiar with the king' and 'controlled everything, both within the royal household and outside it'. One of York's retainers petitioned in parliament in May for his master to be formally recognised as heir presumptive, but

---

4   The proclamation is edited and translated in K Dockray, *Henry VI, Margaret of Anjou and the Wars of the Roses: A Source Book*, 2000, Sutton.

was swiftly despatched to the Tower. York remained excluded from the king's inner circle of advisors by Somerset and his intimates.

Although it was to be a further eight years before York openly sought the throne for himself, it was now that he resorted to armed force for the first time, marching to London with a force drawn from his Welsh estates early in 1452. Shut out from the capital by the king's orders, York moved to his lands in Kent and drew up his army at Brent Heath, near Dartford. However, facing a much larger and better-equipped royal army, York backed down and announced his willingness to negotiate. In the course of negotiations, apparently believing that Somerset would now be arrested and required to answer charges in relation to his incompetent administration in both France and England, York went to Henry's tent and surrendered himself. As on a number of occasions in his career, he seems to have misjudged the situation; instead of gaining a legal triumph over his enemy, he now found himself a virtual prisoner and, in order to secure his liberty, had to make a solemn and public oath of allegiance to the king in St Paul's on 10 March. By the spring of 1453, when the queen was found to be pregnant, York's eclipse must have seemed permanent. The position, however, would shortly change irrevocably.

The Lancastrians' French venture was finally ended in July 1453, when the army commanded by John Talbot, Earl of Shrewsbury, was overtaken and destroyed at Castillon as it sought to cross the River Dordogne and escape towards the Pyrenees. This cost the English their last foothold on French soil other than Calais, and the news of this calamity may have acted as the final trigger for Henry VI's mental collapse some time in August. For more than a year, the king remained in a state of withdrawal from the world, completely incapable of exercising the functions of monarch. Even the birth of his son elicited no response – indeed, Henry was to declare after his recovery that the new Prince of Wales must have been fathered by the Holy Ghost, for he himself had no recollection of doing so. Had Henry's mental incapacity been permanent, the consequences might have been less disastrous, since the spells of total torpor alternating with periods of lucidity provided the perfect context for the consolidation of factional politics.

The main protagonists were the Duke of York, no longer heir presumptive, and ranged against him, the queen, Margaret of Anjou, and Edmund, Duke of Somerset, whom many suspected of being the true father of the new Prince of Wales. Political power oscillated between the two according to the king's mental condition until the spring of 1455, when the rivals retired to their lands and proceeded to arm. The first Battle of St Albans followed, ending in York's victory and the death of Somerset. At this, the queen's loathing of York became yet more intense and she allied herself firmly with the new Duke of Somerset, soon rumoured to have succeeded his father in her bed.

By 1459, the situation had deteriorated into open war. Margaret of Anjou was very much the leader of the Lancastrian faction and was apparently less concerned to maintain the position of her hapless husband than to preserve her son's inheritance. York was firmly isolated from court and concentrated on building up support among his fellow magnates, particularly his wife's Neville relations. At an assembly held at Coventry in June, the Yorkist leaders were proclaimed traitors at the queen's urging; this marked the final severing of any prospect of civilised relations between duke and queen.

The war was initially inconclusive. The Yorkists under Salisbury gained a victory at Blore Heath, near Newcastle-under-Lyme, in September, but twice in the following month, Yorkist troops refused battle with armies under the nominal command of King Henry. Even at this stage, it would seem, there was a reluctance to take up arms against an anointed king directly. Deciding to regroup, York and his second son, Edmund, Earl of Rutland, made for the family lands in Ireland. Salisbury, his eldest son, Richard Neville, Earl of Warwick, and York's eldest son, Edward, Earl of March, escaped to Calais. Meanwhile, a parliament meeting at Coventry in October was persuaded to proclaim a lengthy list of York's crimes against the crown since 1450 and the failure of all previous attempts to restrain him, as a preliminary to his attainder for treason.

As with Henry of Bolingbroke 60 years earlier, the period in exile seems to have hardened York's resolve and committed him to seeking the throne in his own right. Like Bolingbroke, he now had nothing to lose. His eldest son and the Nevilles made good use of their time in Calais, using the port as a base for raids on English coastal towns and Lancastrian shipping assembled against them, and conducting a vigorous propaganda campaign. Yet York failed now to act with the ruthlessness or instinct for seizing the day shown by Bolingbroke or earlier by Isabella of France and Roger Mortimer, and few if any deserted from Henry VI or the queen to join him. Unlike Bolingbroke and Queen Isabella, York came to England not as a future ruler who would restore good government and defend the weak, but merely as the leader of a narrow faction.

9.3   WAR FOR THE CROWN 1460–61

For those students of history who believe in the innate nobility of man or at least that political action should be motivated by high ideals, most of the 15th century constitutes a singularly dismal period, when the main motivation for activity at the highest political level was self-interest. That the leading magnates of the day and their close kin were able to challenge successfully for a disputed throne represents the culmination of a series of developments which had occurred gradually over the previous 70 or so years.

Thanks to the philoprogenitive abilities of Edward III and his queen, several of the greatest among the king's subjects were themselves of royal blood. These men now held enormous wealth and power through Edward III's initial generosity, several generations of advantageous marriages, their close ties with great non-royal magnates such as the Nevilles, and the power vacuum that resulted from the decline in strong central government. For many generations, lawlessness had been a major political and social problem. The efforts of strong kings such as Edward I and Edward III had temporarily reduced its incidence, but failed to eliminate it, and since the death of Edward III in 1377, little had been done in this sphere. What has become known to historians as 'bastard feudalism' had gradually taken root, partly in response to the failure of royal government in the 'police' and judicial spheres, partly through the growth of magnate power blocs. Increasingly, magnates gave protection to their own retainers and followers in return for their absolute loyalty and for military service in return for wages. The reciprocal nature of true feudalism entirely disappeared. The violence and other criminal acts of aristocratic retainers wearing their lords' badges had been a regular feature of political life since the reign of Richard II, but nothing effective had yet been done by the government to remedy this.

At the same time, the deposition of Richard II and usurpation of the throne by Henry of Bolingbroke, a man with close blood ties to the king who was also the greatest magnate in the realm, created the most dangerous of precedents for a time when the power and prestige of the reigning monarch had declined more sharply than ever before. If a usurpation had happened once, it could happen again.

That self-interest was the main motive for the actions of the major protagonists of the Wars of the Roses may not be the full story, although higher motives appear to have occupied a secondary position. Official propaganda emerged from both sides and an active ideological war was fought between York and Lancaster. Each side naturally claimed to be acting in the common interest of the kingdom and its people, but the perception of that common interest varied. The Lancastrians, ironically perhaps, argued that the common good could only be served by maintaining obedience to the king and to his laws, and that the final arbiter on all legal and constitutional issues could only be the king, with whom ultimate sovereignty lay.[5] By contrast, the Yorkists took on the mantle of earlier campaigners for constitutional reform, protesting their loyalty to the occupant of the throne but at the same time the need to separate the king from his evil counsellors, to restore law and order and the proper administration of justice, to protect the people from oppressive financial burdens and to return the magnates of ancient lineage to their proper place in the king's counsels.[6]

Why did York seek the throne at this time? Once attainted as a traitor, he had nothing to lose, but that seems not to be the whole story. Earlier in the 1450s, he appears to have been content with being the power behind Henry VI's throne and having his 'proper' place in the king's confidence as the greatest magnate of the realm and the adult male nearest to the king in blood; however, the rivalry with the 2nd Duke of Somerset and also with the queen prevented him from establishing a firm hold on this position. By the autumn of 1459, York's patience was exhausted, but, unlike Bolingbroke, he did not make his bid for the crown from a position of military strength. True, Bolingbroke had landed at Ravenspur with a bare 100 men, but he had moved cautiously, not committing himself fully until his advantage in manpower was overwhelming, and he had in the eyes of both aristocracy and people assumed the mantle of popular hero and deliverer. Bolingbroke carefully avoided pitched battle; York had sought to do battle, but had seen his armies desert, unwilling to make war directly on an anointed king. Most telling of all, York's base of support among the aristocracy was narrow, being mainly among the Nevilles who, as northerners, were regarded with great suspicion by the southern English.[7] Crucially perhaps, York at this stage did not display the courage of his convictions by leading his expeditionary force himself. His actions show a want of political judgment, even a rashness,

---

5   See, for example, *Somnium Vigilantes: A Contemporary Defence of the Proscription of the Yorkists at the Coventry Parliament, 1459*, edited and translated in Dockray, *op cit*, pp 33–34.

6   Cf *Yorkist Manifesto Promulgated by the Earl of Warwick, on his Way from Ludlow, 1459*, edited and translated in Dockray, *op cit*, pp 34–35.

7   There was a much greater north-south divide in the 15th century than that which is spoken of today. The English spoken in the north was unintelligible to southerners, and vice versa, and northerners were regarded in the south as rough, lawless, brutal, violent and uncouth.

alongside an inability to pursue his cause with sufficient ruthlessness, coupled with indecisiveness at critical moments.

The Earls of Salisbury, Warwick and March landed at Sandwich on 26 June 1460 and garnered much support from the disaffected populace of south-east England. London, support from which was a vital element in the Yorkist success of the next few years, opened its gates. Leaving Salisbury in charge in the capital, Warwick and March continued north, hoping to run the king to earth. They defeated a royalist army near Northampton and, finding Henry VI in his tent, paid him all due honour. Having escorted him back to London, they began to govern in his name. Had York accompanied the three earls to England, he might have come to the throne on a tide of popular enthusiasm, but missing his opportunity, he did not return until September, and when he did seek the crown, it was not by force of arms but, in a fashion unprecedented in England, by appeal to law. Even now, self-interest or no, he shrank from violent usurpation.

9.3.1 An appeal to parliament

In October 1460, York rode to London for the new sitting of parliament at the head of his retainers, preceded by trumpeters displaying the royal arms and with his sword borne upright before him, the sole prerogatives of a reigning king. On arrival at Westminster Hall, he strode up to the empty throne and laid his hand upon it, an act which horrified even his brother-in-law and leading supporter, the Earl of Salisbury. When parliament opened on 16 October, counsel acting on his behalf laid a claim to the crown not simply as Henry VI's heir, but immediate and in his own right. Whereas York had hitherto traced his descent (and his claim to the throne) from Edmund of York, he now revived the Mortimer claim, giving precedence to his descent from Lionel of Clarence through his mother, claiming that this gave him priority in the succession over Henry VI, the heir male of John of Gaunt.

Attempts were made to settle the matter peaceably. York laid his claim before the lords in parliament, who referred it to the king. Henry VI, apparently rational at this time, returned the claim to the lords, requiring them to refute it. The lords passed the matter to the judges, who declared it beyond their competence, and passed it once again to the lords.

The lords, faced with this unprecedented recourse to their authority, itself a very clear demonstration of the standing parliament had by now acquired, found themselves in difficulties. Had the 1376 charter been widely known and its authority accepted, the matter might have ended there, since it vested the succession in the male issue of Edward III. However, collective memory seems to have extended back no further than Henry IV's short-lived entail of 1406. This had been repealed and normal feudal principle allowed inheritance through heirs female. If the throne was merely a species of private property, York was clearly the rightful king.

However, there were obvious practical difficulties, not least that the Lancastrians had now reigned since 1399. Three monarchs had been anointed, crowned and fully accepted as lawful rulers, and the lords could not simply declare the legislation of 61 years to be void. In any event, the English lawyers who had ruled on the Scottish succession after 1290 had specifically rejected the argument that a throne was no more than a species of feudal holding, though no such ruling had ever explicitly been made in relation to the English throne. The same argument had been rejected by the French in the period 1316–28.

After lengthy deliberations in secret session, the lords formally put a solution to the king. In a manner reminiscent of the agreements between Stephen and Matilda in 1153 and between Henry V and Charles VI in 1420, it was proposed that Henry VI should remain king until he died or willingly abdicated, but that York should be his heir rather than the seven year old Prince of Wales. Initially, the compromise was accepted with relief by both parties. York and his sons swore fresh oaths of loyalty to Henry VI. A statute granted York immunity from charges of treason and gave him all the lands and revenues of the heir to the throne, though he was not created Prince of Wales or Earl of Chester, nor did he succeed to the dukedom of Cornwall. Parliament repealed the entail of 1406 a second time.

9.3.2   War renewed

But where such a compromise had brought peace between rival claimants on previous occasions, it did not in 1460. Any political initiative had long passed from Henry VI, and his queen and her supporters were not prepared to accept this solution. York's triumph was short-lived in the extreme as all-out war followed. Two months after being declared heir apparent, he was dead. After marching north with Salisbury in order to muster troops to deal with Margaret of Anjou and Somerset, York celebrated Christmas at his castle of Sandal, just outside Wakefield. On 30 December 1460, he made a sortie when a small enemy force was sighted nearby, and took his army straight into the position occupied by a concealed Lancastrian army. York was killed; his second son, Edmund, Earl of Rutland, and Salisbury were put to death after surrendering. The heads of all three were displayed on the walls of York, the Duke's mockingly adorned with a crown of paper.

However, the fact that fortunes could change in the 15th century with bewildering speed was amply demonstrated in succeeding months. The war resolved into campaigns on two fronts, one in the Welsh Marches prosecuted by York's eldest son, Edward of March, and the other in the eastern counties, between the armies of the queen and the Earl of Warwick. Early in February, March was successful at Mortimer's Cross, not far from Ludlow, where the appearance of a parhelion, an optical illusion giving the appearance of three suns, was eagerly seized on by the Yorkists as proof that York's three surviving sons had the support of the three members of the Holy Trinity. However, Warwick was defeated in an encounter at St Albans and Henry VI was removed from Yorkist hands.

The Londoners' role now proved critical. Margaret of Anjou, needing to regroup and unwilling to risk her husband being captured again, retreated to Yorkshire, which was largely Lancastrian in sympathy. Had she made for London and taken advantage of the strong defences of the Tower and its arsenal of weapons, events might have turned out very differently. As it was, March, coming from the Welsh border, was able to link up with Warwick unmolested. The citizens opened the gates of London and March entered the city to wild enthusiasm.

Unlike the hapless Henry VI, March was young, handsome and virile, very clearly capable of ruling in his own right rather than being the tool of queen and favourites. Unlike previous usurpers, however, he did not have the anointed king in his hands, nor did he enjoy overwhelming support. Most critically of all, a large Lancastrian army, which had defeated his leading ally once already, was still in the field. There was no time to waste in putting forward a claim to the crown and summoning a parliament to give it effect. March instead seized the day. On 4 March 1461, he had himself proclaimed king as Edward IV by the small cabal of Yorkist lords headed by Warwick. The logical next step would have been a quick coronation, to secure recognition before God of his right to the crown. But even before this, the queen and her army had to be dealt with.

Young though he was – he did not celebrate his 19th birthday until 28 April – this self-proclaimed king was already a considerable soldier. Marching north with Warwick, he encountered the queen's army at Towton, near Tadcaster in the Vale of York, on 29 March, where, in a snowstorm which lasted all day, the bloodiest battle ever fought on English soil ended in the defeat of the Lancastrian army, though its leader escaped, along with Henry VI and the Prince of Wales, for whose inheritance the queen would fight on in great bitterness for another 10 years.

Henry, unlike the two earlier deposed monarchs, held on to his life for the time being. It was not until 1465 that he was finally taken by the Yorkists again, after desertion by his queen who, with her son, took refuge first in Scotland and then in France. By then, his supplanter was prepared to be merciful, either because Henry posed no threat, even as a focus for plots or, more cynically, because there was no point in putting him to death while his son, now adolescent, remained at large. In his final years, the former king seems to have withdrawn permanently into a twilight world, apparently entirely content with his confinement in the Tower and evincing little interest or concern when he was restored to the throne by the improbable alliance of Warwick and Margaret of Anjou in 1470–71. His son's death at the Battle of Tewkesbury sealed his fate. His restoration demonstrated that while he lived – and he was not yet 50 – he was a danger to any Yorkist king. On the night of 21 May 1471, Henry died in the Tower, officially from 'pure displeasure and melancholy', but almost certainly by murder on Edward IV's orders.

Edward IV, having defeated his leading enemies in the field, departed from previous precedent by having himself crowned without first having a parliament legitimise his position. Indeed, it was not until the following November that this step was taken. According to the argument put before parliament and accepted, there was no need for Henry VI to be deposed or for Edward's place as his successor to be ratified, since the parliament of October 1460 had already accepted the Duke of York's claim to be the rightful king. Then, under the solution accepted by parliament, York had agreed to postpone his claim for the balance of Henry VI's lifetime, but the compact between Henry and York was immediately broken by Henry's conspiring with his queen and others to destroy York. Therefore, in March 1461, Henry was not the lawful king and, since York's death, his eldest son was the lawful heir. The proclamation of 4 March and Edward's coronation on 28 June merely gave effect to what was already the position in law.

9.4 THE YORKIST KINGS 1461–85

9.4.1 Edward IV 1461–83

The reign of Edward IV falls into two halves; indeed, it is now often seen, uniquely in English history, as two reigns, broken by the 'Readeption' of September 1470 to April 1471, when Henry VI was nominally restored to the throne.

In the first period, the young king's hold on the throne was uncertain, at first because of the substantial rump of Lancastrian opposition which remained after Towton and was only gradually worn down, and later on because of much more dangerous opposition from his cousin Warwick and from his own brother, George, Duke of Clarence, an unstable youth who fully deserved Shakespeare's epithet 'false, fleeting, perjur'd Clarence'. The Nevilles, led by Warwick, had played a pivotal role in Edward's gaining of the throne, but were gradually sidelined, particularly after the king's marriage to Elizabeth Woodville in 1464, as her large and avaricious family came to dominate the court. Warwick seems unable to accept the king's detaching himself from his tutelage and made common cause with Clarence, who was also becoming increasingly discontented.

Following an abortive rising in 1469, which left them more isolated than ever, Warwick and Clarence rebelled in 1470 and, taking temporary refuge in France, Warwick threw in his lot with Margaret of Anjou and agreed to marry his younger daughter, Anne Neville, to Margaret's son, Edward of Lancaster. His elder daughter was already married to Clarence, who was Edward IV's heir pending the birth of a Prince of Wales; whether it was York or Lancaster which eventually triumphed, Warwick's grandson would one day sit on the throne. Warwick invaded England in September 1470, forcing Edward to flee to Burgundy, brought Henry VI out of the Tower and ruled in his name. However, when Edward landed in England in March 1471, Clarence, ever a fair weather friend, rapidly joined him, along with those of the nobility who were opposed to the Nevilles. Supported by his youngest brother, the future Richard III, who came to prominence at this time, Edward defeated and killed Warwick at Barnet on 14 April, and three weeks later, defeated an army commanded by the Duke of Somerset at Tewkesbury, where Edward of Lancaster was killed and Margaret of Anjou was captured.

The events of 1470–71 demonstrate the fundamental instability of the crown in the 15th century. Even a strong king was dependent on the continuing support of his greatest subjects, themselves virtual 'mini kings'. Were he to lose that, at a time when no one had a unique and unambiguous title to the throne, his position was in peril.

The second period of Edward IV's reign, with his domestic enemies destroyed and the last males of the House of Lancaster dead, along with all those in the male line of the Beauforts, was a time of peace, prosperity and prestige. Edward's close links with Burgundy, where his sister was Duchess, benefited English trade with the continent, particularly in wool and cloth; he concluded a permanent peace with France in 1475 and was a leading patron of William Caxton, the first English printer. Such success might have endured for an indefinite period had not Edward died at 19 days short of 41, leaving a 12 year old heir and an ambitious brother, Richard, Duke of Gloucester, who had emerged in the 1470s as an over-mighty subject in the traditional mould, particularly after Clarence's execution in 1478.

9.4.2 Edward V and Richard III

Along with John, Richard III is the most notorious of England's monarchs, and views of him remain polarised to a degree quite unique in relation to a historical personage. Henry IV and Edward IV could claim to be avenging wrongs done to themselves and their fathers, as well as taking the place of a predecessor unworthy of the crown. Richard III seized the throne from a boy very clearly innocent of any personal wrongdoing. The murders of Edward II, Richard II and Henry VI are regarded with hindsight as demonstrating the twisted values of a brutal age. The disappearance and probable murder of Edward V and his brother inspire a unique popular revulsion.

Seen from a constitutional standpoint, Richard III's seizure of the throne followed earlier precedents, though a number of issues, particularly the point at which he resolved to seek the crown in his own right rather than establish himself as effective regent for his nephew, are matters of debate.

Edward IV's death on 9 April 1483 was unexpected and seems to have taken all those close to the throne by surprise. One contemporary writer records that the king designated the Duke of Gloucester as Protector and defender of the realm, and intended that Gloucester should not only be responsible for government during his son's minority, but should have care and control of all his children. However, Gloucester's assumption of power was resisted by the new king's mother, Elizabeth Woodville.

Edward V, born on 2 November 1470, was at the time of his father's death at Ludlow, undergoing his knightly education under the tutelage of a maternal uncle, Anthony Woodville, Earl Rivers. As was then the norm for an heir apparent, he had from an early age been given his own household and lived apart from his parents, his five sisters and younger brother, Richard, Duke of York. Following a practice inaugurated for Henry V, the most recent Prince of Wales to attain adolescence in his father's reign, he had earlier been made titular ruler of Wales, but government of the principality was conducted on his behalf by a council headed by Rivers. After a lapse of 500 years, it is difficult to scrape away the conventional portrait painted by contemporaries of a handsome, charming, and virtuous young prince of great promise, and the sentimentalities of later generations, but the balance of the surviving chronicle accounts suggests that he was intelligent and well-educated – Rivers was one of the most erudite laymen of his time and Edward IV had set out a detailed syllabus for his instruction.

Given that Gloucester was the most powerful man in the land and had an unrivalled record of loyal service to his brother's crown, he was the obvious person to take control of the government, whether or not any designation was made by Edward IV. However, at the time of Edward's death, Gloucester was more than 200 miles from Westminster and did not receive the news for a week. This delay allowed the Woodville faction time to act. They gained control of the royal treasure and persuaded the majority of the King's Council to schedule the coronation of Edward V for as early as 4 May, so, it could be argued, causing Gloucester's appointment as Protector to lapse. Whether their argument had any basis in precedent is unclear, since there had been no consistency of practice during previous minorities.

Whatever the precise legal position, Gloucester gained the initiative on 30 April. Travelling south from Yorkshire and joined by the Duke of Buckingham with a large following, he took Edward V into his custody as Rivers brought him to London from Ludlow. Rivers was arrested and the coronation was postponed.

From then on, we see a period of uncertainty, which may be viewed in a number of ways. Was it a time of procrastination, while Richard of Gloucester consolidated his position before making his own bid for the throne? Or did Gloucester govern on behalf of his nephew, only seeking the throne when there was a fresh alliance against him? Certainly, the seizure of the king appears to have been more in the nature of a pre-emptive strike than a retaliation following the Woodvilles' efforts to exclude him from power, but it is not necessarily the case that Gloucester was already seeking the crown for himself, as opposed to trying to establish himself as the power behind the throne.

Before Gloucester's arrival in London with the king in his custody, the queen retreated into sanctuary with her younger son and daughters. Clearly, Gloucester was in a commanding position: he had possession of the king and a large body of troops. Force would have been required to counter this. It seems that the King's Council were unwilling to take this step and the Woodvilles did not command sufficiently large a following. On this basis, the Council seems to have accepted Gloucester's leading role. According to the Crowland Chronicler, Gloucester was formally installed as Protector on 10 May, by which time, Edward V was resident in the Tower. This does not of itself imply any nefarious purpose on Gloucester's part; the Tower was then an important royal residence where, *inter alia*, a king spent the period immediately prior to his coronation. The coronation itself was now rescheduled for 22 June.

Gloucester consolidated his position by dismantling the Woodville power base. His attempts to have Rivers attainted and executed on the basis that he had sought to murder him failed, as the Council held that any such conspiracy was not treasonable since Gloucester had not been Protector at the material time.[8] However, he was able, from mid-May, to secure the forfeiture and seizure of Woodville lands and the lands of their allies, as well as removing various Woodvilles from influential offices.

Examining the actions of Richard and the Council during the period from early May until mid-June, Rosemary Horrox concludes that the political position was relatively stable and the Council able to act effectively.[9] The Woodvilles appear to have been neutralised for the time being, though the queen's remaining in sanctuary with her brood must have been a source of embarrassment to Gloucester and his allies. However, the position apparently changed entirely on 13 June with the summary execution of William, Lord Hastings, in the course of a Council meeting.

Hastings had been Edward IV's Lord Chamberlain and was also his close friend and confidant over many years; the two went so far as to share a mistress. Before 13 June, Hastings had enjoyed Gloucester's confidence, being confirmed in his office and place on the Council, but on that day, things changed utterly. According to the later and dramatic account of Sir Thomas More, as the Council met in the White Tower to finalise arrangements for the coronation, Gloucester, without warning, accused Hastings and three other members of the Council of plotting with the queen against his authority and life. Several sources state that Gloucester had placed armed men outside the council chamber and that they now burst in and arrested the four accused in the course of a violent scuffle. Having been hastily shriven, Hastings was taken

8   This difficulty could, however, have been circumvented by an Act of Attainder.
9   Rosemary Horrox, *Richard III: A Study in Service*, Cambridge Studies in Medieval Life and Thought, 1989, CUP.

outside and beheaded on an improvised block. No form of legal process took place, although parliament, where by now peers were customarily attainted for treason, was due to meet on 25 June immediately after the coronation, so that proceedings could have been instituted without significant delay.[10]

Whether Hastings, hitherto a loyal Yorkist of long standing and no friend of the Woodvilles, was actually plotting against Gloucester can now never be known; the same uncertainties exist over whether Gloucester's actions in the second half of June 1483 derived from a genuine belief that his nephew was the product of a bigamous marriage, from a perceived need for pre-emptive action against Woodville plotting or from lust for power combined with paranoia. Whatever Gloucester's motivation, the pattern of events is clear.

Though circumstantial evidence suggests that Gloucester may by now have made up his mind to seek the throne, it was not for several more days that he acted unambiguously on his own behalf. Later, on 16 June, the parliament was cancelled and the coronation was postponed to 9 November. Horrox notes that business in the various departments of state began to wind down, a far smaller volume of documents being produced than usual, suggesting expectation of a change of regime, but it was not until 22 June that Gloucester's claim to the throne emerged into the public eye.

Precedent had by now established that a usurper must demonstrate, first, his predecessor's unworthiness for the throne and, second, his own superior title, the two strands involving both blood-right and suitability. Richard of Gloucester's claim to the throne was first preached in a sermon by Dr Ralph Shaw at St Paul's on 22 June. Its basis was originally confused, several versions emerging over the next few days, and was only finalised in the parliament roll for 1484.

Initially, it seems the basis of the claim was that Edward IV was not the son of the Duke of York, but this was soon replaced by the allegation that his children by Elizabeth Woodville were illegitimate, since at the time of the marriage, the late king had been betrothed to another woman. Under the canon law of the day, a formal betrothal – a plight-troth or pre-contract – prevented either party from making a valid marriage to another person, unless it was dissolved by agreement between the parties or a dispensation was obtained. No issue of Edward V's character was raised, presumably because of his youth.

Whether the 'betrothal story' is true is yet again something that can never be known. There is circumstantial evidence in both directions.[11] Whether the tale was true or not, it certainly emerged at a most convenient time for Gloucester and his supporters. Horrox considers that by the last days of June, the usurpation was regarded by contemporaries as a *fait accompli*, based on Gloucester's military strength and the absence of effective opposition, noting that strictly contemporary chroniclers have almost nothing to say on the constitutional issues involved, a sharp contrast to the full accounts of the earlier depositions of Edward II and Richard II. At any rate,

---

10   Strictly speaking, any conspiracy in which Hastings was involved was not treasonable, since the Statute of Treasons did not proscribe actions against a Protector, but, again, this difficulty could have been circumvented by an Act of Attainder.

11   Edward IV's womanising was notorious, and according to chronicle accounts, he married Elizabeth Woodville in 1464 after she refused to sleep with him without marriage. The marriage took place in secret and was not made public until five months later. It is certainly not impossible that Edward earlier entered into a pre-contract with a lady, usually named as Eleanor Butler, who resisted his advances in a similar fashion.

those peers and commoners who had come to London for the coronation were summoned to Westminster on 25 June in order to hear the reasons for Hastings's execution. The Duke of Buckingham then presented a petition to the assembly.

This petition does not itself survive, although it was apparently incorporated into *Titulus Regis*, the statute passed by the 1484 parliament legitimising Richard III's position, and its gist was set out by several chroniclers. The petition first condemned Edward IV, who had let himself be ruled by the Woodvilles, then went on to state that his sons were bastards, his marriage to Elizabeth Woodville being invalid. Having disposed of Edward IV's sons, it then disposed of the claims of the young Earl of Warwick, son of the Duke of Clarence and indisputably legitimate, on the basis of his father's attainder, which, on the normal principles of the law of attainder, had 'corrupted' Clarence's blood, so that his issue could not inherit any title from or through him.[12] On that basis, the petition continued:

> ... at the present time no certain and incorrupt blood of the lineage of Richard, Duke of York was to be found, except in the person of Richard, Duke of Gloucester.

Having disposed of the blood-right of Edward V and demonstrated that of Gloucester, the petition went on to demonstrate his personal throneworthiness. It praised his past career in royal service, his blameless morals and high qualities which, along with 'the great noblesse and excellence of his birth and blood', fitted him for the crown, though, according to Buckingham, he was properly reluctant to accept it. The assembly, having been given time to consider the petition, was unanimous in requesting Gloucester to accept the crown, although, according to one writer, they were swayed by fears for their own safety were they not to acclaim him.

On the following day, 26 June, a deputation assembled from the lords, commons, knights, mayor, aldermen and chief citizens of London attended on Gloucester. Buckingham presented the petition, calling on Gloucester to accept the crown so that the country could escape the dangers of a minority and a disputed succession and benefit from the firm and stable government which he was capable of providing. Gloucester accepted the petition and rode to Westminster Hall, where he placed himself on the throne and took the sovereign's oath. The same evening he was proclaimed king by the heralds and on 6 July, he was crowned as Richard III.

Therefore, although the assembly of 25 June was not a properly constituted parliament, not having been summoned by the king or by his representative with specific authorisation, the steps taken follow those taken in 1399. Once more, a close male relative of the rightful king, having that king in his custody, placed himself on the throne apparently at the will of the estates of the realm and on the basis of his greater suitability and better blood-right, but in reality by means of his military strength and the power he derived from his position as the greatest magnate in the land. As with Richard II, and earlier with Edward II, the deposed king appears to have been done away with within a matter of months. The unusual feature was that while the deaths of his predecessors were made public within days, if spuriously attributed to natural causes, those of Edward V and his brother were concealed, making them a subject of fascination to future generations and leaving a controversy which continues to smoulder 500 years later.

---

12   Strictly speaking, Clarence's attainder dealt only with his peerages, not with his place in the succession, although this may have been considered unnecessary, as in 1478, Edward IV had three living sons.

Suffice it to say that Edward V and his brother, who had joined him in the royal apartments in the Tower on 16 June, were not seen alive after September 1483. Rumours that they were dead soon emerged, and reached the French court before January 1484. Perhaps their fate was sealed by Richard's III's memory of the restoration by Warwick of Henry VI; the gentle Lancastrian king, enfeebled by his mental illness, posed no direct danger to his supplanter, but as a focus of plots, he remained dangerous as long as he lived. So it was with the 'Princes in the Tower'. In addition, within five years Edward V, an intelligent and well-educated boy, whose father had fought his way to the throne at 18, would be a young man eminently qualified to plot on his own behalf.

Richard III's reign was short, lasting a little more than two years, and the strong and stable government which his earlier rule over the north suggested that he was capable of providing never really emerged, due to a succession of plots, the first headed by his former ally, Buckingham, as early as October 1483, although Richard's only parliament made legislation for the traditional purposes of enhancing law and order and dealing with official corruption.[13]

One Lancastrian pretender remained. This was Henry Tudor, whose mother, Margaret Beaufort, was the only child of the 1st Duke of Somerset. His father, Edmund Tudor, Earl of Richmond, was one of three sons born to Henry V's widow by a liaison with Owen Tudor, a Welsh squire.[14] Strong circumstantial evidence that the sons of Edward IV were dead, or at any rate were believed dead, is seen in the fact that all conspiracies against Richard III occurred in the name of Henry Tudor;[15] indeed, before the end of 1483, Elizabeth Woodville pledged her eldest daughter to this last heir of Lancaster in marriage. On 1 August 1485, Tudor sailed from Harfleur with a French fleet, landing at Milford Haven a week later. Having gathered support during his journey through Wales and the English midlands, he met King Richard and his army at Bosworth, some 12 miles west of Leicester, on 22 August. The outcome of the battle was in doubt until its final phase, when the Earl of Northumberland, commanding Richard's reserve, did not intervene when the king's army was hard pressed, and Sir William Stanley, summoned with his own retinue and that of his brother, Thomas, Lord Stanley, opted to fight on behalf of the invader.

Seeing his forces being repulsed, Richard III staked all on a desperate gamble and, with his closest adherents, attempted to cut his way through the Lancastrians to Tudor himself. Amidst the melee, and instantly recognisable by the crown he had insisted on wearing, he became separated from his companions and was unhorsed and cut down within feet of Tudor, who was then proclaimed king by Sir William Stanley. Even hostile chroniclers praised the manner of Richard's death. Nevertheless, Tudor, in a fashion far removed from the chivalric tradition that held a brave enemy worthy of all honour, had his body stripped naked and carried to Leicester flung over the back of a horse, with a halter round the neck, as was the custom with condemned felons, before it was exposed for three days in the conventual church of the Franciscan friars.

---

13 It was also the first parliament to record its proceedings in English.

14 There is no firm evidence that the pair ever married, a detail discreetly glossed over by the Tudor monarchs.

15 Nobody seems to have taken the young Earl of Warwick seriously as a possible pretender, perhaps because of memories of his father, though there have been suggestions that he was feeble-minded. The Duke of Buckingham, a descendant of Edward III's youngest son, may have sought the throne in his own right, but he certainly allied himself with Tudor.

CHAPTER 10

GOVERNMENT AND ROYAL JUSTICE
IN THE LATER MIDDLE AGES

10.1 INTRODUCTION

Despite political instability, the machinery of royal government and justice continued to develop during the 15th century. Government remained capable of functioning despite the changes of regime, though the apparent breakdown of law and order was both a cause of political instability and a reaction to it. It has been estimated that active warfare during the Wars of the Roses occupied only some 13 weeks of 30 years and, since battle was largely the preserve of the nobility and their professional fighting men and campaigning took place only in limited areas of the country, the population at large felt the effects of domestic war comparatively little.

10.2 KINGSHIP

> When Richard the Third was slain at Bosworth and with him John Howard Duke of Norfolk, King Henry the Seventh demanded of Thomas Howard, Earl of Surrey, the Duke's son and heir, then taken Prisoner, how he durst bear Arms in the behalf of that Tyrant Richard. He answered: 'He was my crowned King, and if the Parliamentary authority of England set the Crown upon a stock, I will fight for that stock; And as I fought then for him, I will fight for you, when you are established by the said authority.'
>
> William Camden, *Remains Concerning Britain*[1]

This story may represent a projection backwards of the ideas of the Tudor period, but political events of the 15th century make clear the contemporary view that the proper means of legitimising a doubtful title to the throne lay with parliament. What of the role and concept of monarchy?

The concept of the monarch and his position which had developed over previous centuries was not fundamentally altered by continuing uncertainty over the rights of the various claimants to occupy the throne, but seems to have given greater emphasis to certain elements within that concept. The rituals of coronation and the increasing elaboration of royal ceremonial, seen in particular under Edward IV, stressed the unique position of the king as the ruler ordained by God with dominion over his realm and subjects. Changes introduced into the coronation *ordo* when Henry VI was crowned in 1429 gave priority to the king's presentation to God by the clergy over his acclamation and 'election' by representatives of the people.

However, there was at the same time a dichotomy in the concept of monarchy. Political events, as well as the political treatises produced at this time, the most important of which were *In Praise of the Laws of England* and *The Governance of England* of Sir John Fortescue, emphasised the subject's duty of obedience to the monarch, but at the same time made clear the importance of the king ruling wisely, justly, in

---

1   William Camden, *Remains Concerning Britain*, 1870 edn, p 294, cited in JD Mackie, *The Earlier Tudors*, 1952, OUP, p 12.

accordance with the law and with the consent of his greater subjects. Fortescue (c 1395–1477) was a leading member of the corps of professional lawyers which had developed over the two preceding centuries,[2] and a distinguished public servant, being appointed Chief Justice of the King's Bench in 1442 and serving as a member of eight parliaments. In 1461, he fled with Henry VI and Margaret of Anjou to Scotland, and thence became a member of Margaret's court in exile in France. Having been taken prisoner after the Battle of Tewkesbury, he seems rapidly to have accommodated his principles to the restored Yorkist regime, producing a revised version of *The Governance* which he presented to King Edward, as well as acting as a member of the Council.[3]

Fortescue drew on the general intellectual and philosophical background of his day, in particular the writings of Aristotle as interpreted by Thomas Aquinas, and of Cicero via St Augustine of Hippo. A specifically English gloss was added by reference to government as it had developed in England by his day, the English systems being, Fortescue considered, naturally superior to those of other countries, rather as Dicey and others of his intellectual milieu in later centuries idealised English parliamentary democracy as the supreme form of government. Even in the 1460s, the national myth of the continuous development of English law over many centuries and its superiority over all other forms of law was emerging:

> The kingdom of England was first inhabited by the Britons, then ruled by the Romans, then again by Britons and then it was possessed by Saxons, who changed its name from Britain to England. Then for a short time the kingdom was dominated by Danes, and then again by Saxons, but finally by Normans, whose posterity hold the realm at the present time. And throughout the period of those nations and their kings, the realm has been continuously ruled by the same customs as it is now, customs which, if they had not been the best, some of those kings would have changed for the sake of justice or by the impulse of caprice, and totally abolished them, especially the Romans, who judged almost the whole of the rest of the world by their laws ...[4]

These various strands of thought came together in Fortescue's concept of the king as a hereditary monarch who ruled by his will, but in the interests of his subjects and after proper consultation with them, and who was subject to the laws of his realm and could not tax his people without their consent. Among the king's primary duties was to ensure that justice was done; *In Praise of the Laws of England* is couched in the form of a dialogue between Fortescue as master and Henry VI's son as pupil, and begins by exhorting the young man to be devoted to the study of the laws with as much zeal as to that of arms.[5] Unlike kings of other nations, where 'what pleases the prince has the force of law', the powers of English kings derived from law, which the kings were themselves bound to observe by their coronation oath.[6]

Of all the 15th century kings, only Henry V was largely secure on his throne, and then only as a result of his military successes abroad and the prestige and awe which they inspired. The armed opponents of other kings, though motivated to a great extent by self-interest, justified their actions by the inability or refusal of the reigning king to

---

2   See below, pp 157–59.

3   S Lockwood (ed), *On the Laws and Governance of England*, Cambridge Texts in the History of Modern Thought, 1997, CUP, pp xviii–xix.

4   *Ibid, In Praise of the Laws of England*, Ch XVIII, pp 26–27.

5   *Ibid*, pp 3–4.

6   *Ibid*, pp xxi, xxx–xxxi.

rule according to the current perceptions of justice and wisdom in kingship, in addition to his lack of dynastic legitimacy. On a practical level, a king was still expected to lead armies in battle, and some at least of the contemporary view of Henry VI as being quite unfitted for kingship rested on his total absence of martial virtue and enthusiasm.

10.3   THE MACHINERY OF GOVERNMENT

Though important institutions of government, including parliament and the great departments of state, had now been established, government in the modern sense of the word did not emerge until very much later. In the 15th century, there was no standing army other than the small garrisons of Calais, Berwick and Carlisle, no police force and no civil service except for the clerks employed within the departments of state. In order to raise armies and to preserve law and order in the provinces, kings relied to a very great extent on the nobility, whose large retinues provided military manpower that could also be used, where necessary, in a policing role, and who held the reins of power in civil matters in the areas in which their lands were concentrated. It was under the Tudors that this dependence on the great magnate families began to decline, as much as the result of attrition within the ranks of the old nobility during the Wars of the Roses and the failure of many families to produce male heirs as through deliberate policy.

Kings still ruled directly, though the apparatus of government had continued to evolve, so that day-to-day administrative practices were separated from the person of the king, and the major departments of state – principally the Exchequer and Chancery – no longer followed the king in his peripatetic lifestyle, but occupied permanent homes at Westminster. Indeed, the office of the Privy Seal and the Wardrobe, once parts of the royal household, were now themselves departments of state, the latter acting as a war office. All had developed as elaborate bureaucracies, and means to circumvent these were continually developing.

There remained many matters which could only be dealt with by the king, or after communication with the king, so that suitable channels had to be developed. In particular, the Great Seal was now permanently in the possession of the Chancellor, who was himself permanently at Westminster, and the Privy Seal and its associated office had developed earlier in the medieval period as a means by which the king and/or his council could authorise the issue of documents under the Great Seal. The Privy Seal Office was itself supplemented from about the beginning of the 15th century by the Signet Office; the Signet was an additional seal used by the king for the issue of his personal commands.

With kings constantly on the move, often at a considerable distance from Westminster, and political crisis frequent and requiring quick action, the royal household continued to occupy an important role in government, and there was at times a tension between the household and the departments of state. In addition to the use of the Signet Office as a means of direct communication with subjects, the Chamber, the household financial office, was often used to collect and expend revenues due to the crown, thereby circumventing the cumbersome procedures of the Exchequer.

Reference has already been made to the Council. Given that the king was expected to govern with the consent of his greater subjects and that those greater subjects, along with the chief officers of state and the senior clergy, expected to hold some role in government, a vehicle had to exist by which this could be achieved. By the middle of the 15th century, a regular royal Council had emerged, the precursor of the Privy Council created by of Henry VIII, whose role was to advise the king and to co-ordinate the government of the kingdom on the king's behalf. In council, the king might make legislation in the form of ordinances, also known as proclamations, the latter term later superseding the former. Enforcement of legislation made in this manner appears to have been a matter for the council itself, under its judicial function, and the Star Chamber from the early 16th century.

The Council, which met normally at Westminster, consisted of the Chancellor, Treasurer and Keeper of the Privy Seal, senior clergy, including the two Archbishops, and a more *ad hoc* group of great noblemen and close associates of the king, who often held senior posts in the royal household. It was chaired by the Chancellor in the absence of the king, and in practice was the main forum of government during a royal minority or incapacity. Inevitably, its powers of action were lessened when an adult and capable king ruled, but even so, the Council might be given delegated powers in certain areas.

Three regional councils also emerged during the 15th century, each with judicial and executive functions. These were the Council of the Marches; the Council for Wales, which came into being in the 1470s to administer Wales on behalf of its Prince;[7] and the Council of the North, created at about the same time, when Richard, Duke of Gloucester, was given authority in England north of the Trent as an effective viceroy for Edward IV.

10.4   PARLIAMENT

It was by now well-established that extraordinary taxation required the assent of a parliament, whose basic composition was now clear. The lords comprised some 60 'lords temporal' – peers summoned by name[8] – together with the bishops and the heads of the greater religious houses – the 'mitred abbots' – making a total of about 45 'lords spiritual'. In the commons sat two knights from each shire and about 180 representatives of the boroughs (the 'burgesses').

The knights of the shire were, in theory, directly elected in a session of the shire court, the qualification for the county franchise being set in 1429 at an annual income from freehold land of 40 shillings. Given that the threshold qualification for knighthood had been set at £20 per year since the days of Henry III, the '40 shilling freehold' encompassed a fairly broad segment of the population and extended well below gentry level. However, knights of the shire tended to be nominated by the nobility and gentry of the shire concerned, and rarely was there more than one candidate for each of the two positions. In any event, the fact that the 'election' was by show of hands meant that pressure could easily be brought to bear on electors.

---

7   The Council of the Marches became subsumed into the Council for Wales following the legal and political union of England and Wales in 1539.

8   Indeed, a definition of nobility had now emerged, in that 'nobility' meant that the head of a family was entitled to sit in the lords, and new peerages were created by writ of summons to the lords from the middle of the 15th century.

The borough representatives, generally two per borough, were also, theoretically, elected, but not directly by the residents, rather by a variety of indirect means, most frequently by the corporation – mayor, alderman and common council – of the borough.[9] In contrast to the upper house, the commons had no representatives of the clergy who, by the end of the 14th century, had been separated from parliament to form two convocations, one each for the provinces of Canterbury and York. They, like parliament, had powers to vote taxation to the crown. Both convocations were represented in parliament by proctors. The practice initiated in 1376 of the commons choosing a Speaker to represent them in dealings with the king continued, but in the 15th century, the Speaker of the commons was frequently the king's nominee.

The length and frequency of parliaments, and the type and quantity of business transacted, depended very much on the prevailing political situation, and in particular on the needs of the crown. The demands of war increased the need for revenue and so parliaments were summoned more frequently in times of strife. Theoretically, a king was still expected to live off his own, and taxation granted by parliament was intended to be used only for the defence of the realm by land and sea against internal and external enemies. Therefore, as in previous centuries, the crown was in a permanent state of financial crisis, the extent of which depended on the circumstances, and new means of raising money had on occasions to be sought. One such was the 'benevolence', a forced gift to the crown. Richard III's only parliament outlawed these, but this prohibition was quickly circumvented by his Tudor supplanters, Henry VII requiring from his subjects a 'loving contribution' and Henry VIII an 'amicable grant'.

Parliament continued to deal with a variety of business, including the petitions put to it by individuals and miscellaneous bodies. Statutes were considered to be declaratory of existing law, rather than sources of new law. Increasingly, it was accepted that certain legal matters, mainly those touching and concerning the monarchy, could only be properly dealt with by a parliament, but as yet the limits of parliament's power were unclear and much of that power rested on consensus or, as when the supplanters of kings sought to give legitimacy to their positions, political expediency. There was also no clear conception of the limits of the monarch's ability to legislate in council by means of ordinance or proclamation, nor any clear view of the extent of the king's prerogatives in relation to the formulation and execution of policy without reference to parliament. These issues were to be at the centre of the 17th century conflict between the Crown and Parliament.

Parliament's role as a court in relation to treason and related matters had also developed. In 1376, parliament, specifically the commons, had taken upon itself the power of impeachment of the king's servants. The events of Richard II's reign gave the lords the power to hear appeals of treason, where the lords themselves were the accusers, and Bills of Attainder, where the accuser was the king. In the course of the 15th century, attainder became the normal means of dealing with accusations of treason, not least because it made possible the circumventing of the limitations imposed by the Statute of Treasons on the nature of actions constituting treason. The frequency of the use of attainder also reflects the nature of treason in this period. Those accused of the offence tended to be noblemen in armed rebellion against the

---

9   The Corporation of the City of London survives as the last relic of the medieval common councils, those elsewhere having been abolished in the various 19th and 20th century changes to local government.

king for the time being, and the principle was by now well-established that a man was entitled to be tried by his peers, making the lords the appropriate forum for the trial of any person of noble birth. Further, where, under the Statute of Treasons, the property of a condemned traitor was forfeited to the crown, the additional principle was developed under the law of attainder that the blood of an attainted traitor was 'corrupted', and his titles reverted to the crown. Such forfeited titles and lands provided a useful source of patronage for the crown, since they could be re-granted to other persons, either because the latter were more faithful or because the king wished to encourage – 'bribe' may not be too strong a word – them into greater faith.[10]

10.5   LAW AND ADMINISTRATION OF JUSTICE

Having spent some time persuading his pupil of the benefits of the study of law, Fortescue then moved in *In Praise of the Laws of England* to a description of some aspects of the English legal system and its advantages over the civil law prevailing in continental Europe. The process of slow and haphazard evolution of the legal system continued during the later 14th and 15th centuries, the paramountcy of royal justice and the common law becoming ever more established.[11] The King's Bench continued to deal with pleas of the crown, and Common Pleas with disputes between the king's free subjects, particularly over land and debt, but both now had permanent homes in Westminster Hall. Judges of the King's Bench travelled on six regular circuits to sit at twice-yearly assizes where the most serious cases were dealt with. Lesser matters were dealt with by local Justices of the Peace at quarter sessions held four times a year.

10.5.1 Justices of the Peace

The office of Justice of the Peace, first formally recognised in a statute of the parliament of 1361–62, had its origins some 150 years earlier, when the practice began of appointing a number of knights in each shire as 'keepers of the peace'. Their function seems originally to have been one of policing rather than administering justice, but holders of this office were before long called upon to take part in the commissions of oyer and terminer and gaol delivery, which supplemented the assizes. Gradually, their judicial function, originally informal, came to predominate. A judicial commission of any kind, and its members, held authority only on the basis granted to them by the written commission issued by the king, which could be revoked or superseded at any time, and this provided the crown with a means of control and supervision over these local justices.

The powers of the medieval Justice of the Peace, who continued to be a knight or other gentleman, were a good deal wider than those of his 21st century successor. A commission charged the justices named to keep the peace and 'to enquire into, hear and determine' a list of specific offences. Each justice had an individual responsibility for policing the area covered by the commission and could arrest and detain suspects,

---

10   For this reason, those noblemen killed in the course of rebellion were often attainted posthumously.

11   The development of the system of justice in the 14th century is dealt with in detail in A Musson and WM Ormrod, *The Evolution of English Justice: Law, Politics and Society in the Fourteenth Century*, British Studies Series, 1999, Macmillan.

and require any person to give surety for keeping the peace – the origin of the power of binding over which is still in use. Two justices, together with a *quorum* of named lawyers, had what was effectively the power to act as a commission of oyer and terminer in the area for which they were responsible, and the justices collectively had power to hear pleas of the crown in the quarter sessions, although, in practice, the more serious cases were reserved to the king's justices in the assizes. Gradually, the practice developed of individual justices hearing minor matters in 'petty sessions' held in the intervals between the regular quarter sessions, the origin of the present day magistrates' courts.

Further, the Justice of the Peace had powers and responsibility in administrative matters which he retained until the 19th century re-organisation of local government. In particular, he was responsible for the maintenance of highways and bridges, and had powers in relation to the poor and orphans, the latter a delegation of the king's traditional responsibility to protect and succour his weaker subjects. In the course of the 15th century, the powers and prestige of the office of Justice of the Peace increased, as the powers formerly held by sheriffs were transferred to them and the latter post became largely honorific.

10.5.2 Civil justice

Those civil matters not heard by the professional judges of the Common Pleas were dealt with by a broad and overlapping array of local courts, such as the manorial courts, which continued to exercise seigneurial powers of justice, and borough courts, which had jurisdiction over the residents of the boroughs concerned. In addition, these courts and a variety of other bodies, such as trade guilds, had powers to deal with what would now be described as 'anti-social behaviour', that is, activity which is not criminal as such but is at odds with contemporary moral standards and causes a nuisance to neighbours. In the 14th and 15th centuries, according to the interesting study conducted by MK McIntosh,[12] areas of concern included unruly alehouses, persons feeding and sheltering vagabonds, 'eavesdropping', which in its medieval sense meant concealing oneself beneath the eaves of another person's house in order to overhear conversations within, verbal abuse and malicious gossip ('scolding') and going out at night without legitimate purpose ('nightwalking').

A development of the 15th century was the gradual emergence of further 'central' courts in response to the shortcomings of the regular common law courts. All the regular royal courts had by now developed elaborate and bureaucratic procedures of their own, and the obtaining of justice by these means was dependent very much on: first, issuing proceedings in the correct court; second, selecting the appropriate form of writ, of which there were many; and, third, the lawyers concerned – for a professional class of lawyers had now emerged – applying the procedure concerned in the optimal fashion.

The Court of Star Chamber (the name comes from the decorated ceiling of the chamber at Westminster in which it met) did not acquire the rather sinister reputation it now has until Tudor times, when it became the usual forum for the enforcement of legislation made by proclamation. Originally, it developed under the aegis of the Council to hear cases of minor violence and gradually extended its jurisdiction by

---

12 MK McIntosh, *Controlling Misbehaviour in England 1370–1600*, 1998, CUP.

evolution to cover civil matters involving violence. It seems to have emerged as a popular court for private litigants, not least because its procedures were simple and conducted in English, rather than in Latin or the evolved form of Norman-French known as 'Law French' which were used by the traditional common law courts.

The Court of Chancery also began to evolve in this period and came to operate a jurisdiction separate from the common law, known as equity. The only remedy available to civil litigants in the common law courts was an award of damages representing the loss to a plaintiff caused by the action or inaction of the defendant. However, all too frequently, what was desired was an order requiring an opponent to do a particular act or to desist from that act, to carry out the terms of a contract or to deliver up property, including land. There was an obvious gap in the system, and this was filled by the emergence of equity.

Among the traditional duties of a king was that of doing justice to his subjects. Even after the exercise of common law justice passed into the hands of a separate judiciary, the king retained a residual power to administer justice, and a free subject remained able to petition the king for justice in a particular matter as an act of grace. Such petitions, or 'bills', were common by the end of the 13th century and, in suitable cases, were dealt with by passing the bill to the justices of the general eyre or to a commission of trailbaston, so that the petitioner could have a remedy via an action at common law.

However, there remained matters where the common law did not provide an appropriate remedy. In particular, under the ancient prerogative principles that the king could do no wrong towards his subjects and that it was the king's responsibility to do justice, it was impossible to sue the king by writ in his own courts, so that a remedy against the king or a king's officer could only be obtained as an act of grace. Bills on matters not amenable to a common law remedy, if of sufficient general importance, usually where permanent change in the law was sought, might be passed to parliament, leading to the possibility of a statute.[13] More private matters were usually dealt with by the Council on the king's behalf, either as a body or by delegation to individual councillors, in particular the Chancellor, head of the official writing office who, by the latter half of the 14th century, was usually a layman and often a professional lawyer. Inevitably, it became the practice to address petitions directly to the Chancellor, so leading to the development of a Court of Chancery, over which the Chancellor presided.

Given that the Chancellor exercised the prerogative power of the king to grant remedy to a subject as an act of grace, independently of the highly formalised and bureaucratic common law, his jurisdiction was a flexible one, capable of adapting to the specific facts contained in a petition. In the 13th century, one form of remedy had been the creation of new forms of writ for use in the common law courts, allowing novel types of action; a little later, a solution might be found via parliament by legislation. However, by the end of the 14th century, the practice had developed of issuing 'decrees' which did not set general precedents, as was the case with decisions

---

13 An example was the statute *De natis ultra mare* of 1351–52, whose general provisions exempted issue born overseas of fathers out of the realm in the king's service from having to prove their right to inheritance of any land by the customary means, which involved a jury of 12 men with personal knowledge of the claimant summoned in the place of his birth. Since the king's writ did not run overseas, a person born outside the realm was effectively disinherited, an issue put to the king by a petition of 1343. See K Kim, *Aliens in Medieval Law: The Origins of Modern Citizenship*, 2000, CUP, pp 103–25.

of the common law courts, but bound only the parties to the specific case. In the 15th century, such decrees came to be issued by the Chancellor in his own name, rather than by the king in Council as previously. Gradually, the seeking of a decree from the Chancellor became the preferred form of action in disputes relating to contracts, trusts and land.

However, the emergence of the Chancellor's jurisdiction should not be seen as an alternative to the common law courts, since it was only available where common law could not provide an adequate or appropriate remedy and, as such, was supplemental to the common law rather than entirely separate from it. Further, it was, like the common law, a jurisdiction derived from the very ancient kingly responsibility to do justice to and on behalf of his subjects.

In addition to the various 'central' royal courts, each of the three regional Councils exercised a jurisdiction in legal matters, and the Duchy of Lancaster, although in the hands of the crown from 1399, had its own system of courts analogous to those of Westminster.

10.6   THE LEGAL PROFESSION

Alongside the development of the legal system through the medieval period came the development of a legal profession. Professional judges first emerged in the 12th century, though they were not trained in the law itself. Indeed, there was a complete dichotomy between the law taught in the universities that emerged in England during the 13th century, which was Roman law and canon law, and the common law, whose practitioners at all levels learned by practical experience. The justices required clerks to assist them in administrative matters at least, and by 1200, justices were in practice appointed from those who were already serving or had served as clerks.

At about the same time, a corps of professional advocates or pleaders began to emerge, as certain individuals acquired knowledge of the increasingly complex forms of procedure which were developing in the king's courts, and were engaged by litigants. The evidence for this comes from the recurrence of certain names in the surviving records of the king's courts. At this time, legal proceedings were exclusively oral, but they were conducted in Norman-French, so that the advocates were presumably drawn from the French-speaking upper echelons of society.

The professional lawyer had emerged sufficiently by 1275 for a provision to be included in the Statute of Westminster that lawyers found guilty of deceit should be punished. In 1280, the City of London made regulations for the administration of an oath to newly-admitted practitioners, and for keeping separate three types of function: the pleader, who was analogous to an advocate in the modern sense; the attorney, who represented his client and acted on behalf of the client, a function closer to that of the solicitor; and the *essoiner*, who made formal excuses for the non-appearance of a party in court.[14]

Before 1300, the distinct function had emerged of attorney in the royal courts, which involved the representation of clients in the formal elements of litigation, managing suits for clients, issuing writs and instructing the pleaders who would act as advocates in the courts. These came to be selected by the judges and put under oath

14   This function was subsumed into that of attorney during the 14th century.

to act as officers of the court. In the same period, the pleaders of the Court of Common Pleas also became a distinct group, again selected by the judges and put upon oath. Indeed, they may have emerged by 1230, when they were referred to by the chronicler Matthew Paris. Gradually too, it became the practice to appoint the judges for each of the royal courts from the relevant group of pleaders only, so beginning the link between the Bar and the judiciary which continues today.

In the Court of Common Pleas, the role of the pleaders was to set out the plaintiff's case and to engage in argument on his behalf. These pleaders seem early to have emerged as an elite group, whose arguments were noted by the early law reporters for the benefit of future advocates. Early in the 14th century, they formed themselves into a professional fraternity known as the order of serjeants at law, which lasted until the end of the 19th century. By 1329, admission to this fraternity involved an elaborate ceremony conducted by the judges of the Common Pleas, complete with the taking of an oath and the leading of the new serjeant to the Bar by two senior serjeants. According to Baker, 'the estate and degree of a serjeant at law' was an honour of comparable status to knighthood.[15] For the balance of the medieval period, the serjeants enjoyed a pre-eminence among lawyers, arising from their monopoly of advocacy and judicial appointments in Common Pleas. However, they did not enjoy the same monopoly in the other royal courts and from the 16th century, even their special position in the Common Pleas was lost.

Necessarily, professional advocates required training and, again, this developed on an *ad hoc* basis from the 13th century. A system emerged by the 1280s under which 'apprentices of the Bench', apparently attached to the court itself, learned by observation in the courts, attending lectures and disputations, and by conducting cases themselves, since it appears that they could act on behalf of clients in any sphere other than those restricted to the serjeants at law. The Inns of Court began to emerge at about the same time, originally simply as shared accommodation for the apprentices at the Bench, but some also assuming some responsibility for the legal education of apprentices residing in those inns, and by the 1420s, these had become known as the Inns of Court.

The origins of the four Inns of Court are not entirely clear and, again, they seem to have emerged by evolution. The Temple was originally the English headquarters of the Knights Templar and, after the dissolution of the Order in 1308, the premises began to be let to lawyers who, by 1388, had formed themselves into the two societies of the Middle Temple and the Inner Temple. Gray's Inn was originally the London house of the family of Lord Gray of Wilton, and began to be let to lawyers at about the same time as the Temple, its residents again forming themselves into a society. Lincoln's Inn is not mentioned in surviving records before 1417, but tradition holds that it was originally the town house of Henry de Lacy, Earl of Lincoln, who died in 1311.

In addition, there evolved a group of so called Inns of Chancery, nine in number by 1500, which in fact had no direct link with the Chancery; rather, some of them were probably used for the accommodation and training of Chancery clerks. By the later 15th century, a fairly settled system of training had developed, under which the aspiring pleader entered an Inn of Chancery for his initial grounding in the law, via observation of proceedings and attendance at lectures and disputations, though cases

15   JH Baker, *An Introduction to English Legal History*, 3rd edn, 1990, Butterworths, p 180.

were now being recorded in order to provide teaching materials. By this time, the term 'barrister' had come into use to denote pleaders and it had become customary for the student to spend seven years in one of the four Inns of Court as an 'inner barrister', during which time, he attended proceedings, performed moots, attended lectures and dined with his fellows and seniors. By doing so, he not only received direct professional training, but absorbed the ethos of his profession – it is for this reason that aspiring barristers are still required to eat dinners in their respective Inns. On completion of this *de facto* apprenticeship, he could expect to be called to the Bar of his Inn and thereafter to practise on his own account. Some barristers eventually became serjeants, but the majority did not progress to this dignity, and barristers came to practise in all the fields not restricted to serjeants.

The solicitor's profession also began to emerge in the 15th century, through the function which developed of 'soliciting causes' – piloting clients into the appropriate jurisdiction, giving advice and instructing attorneys and pleaders. This function was not initially separate from the Bar, since it was customary for young barristers to gain experience by soliciting causes. The division between barristers and solicitors emerged in the 17th century and, at about the same time, the profession of attorney, originally much more directly involved with litigation, became subsumed into that of solicitor, though not without a number of demarcation disputes which appear in the court records. This left two groups within the legal profession: the barristers, with the serjeants as a distinctive sub-stratum, and the much larger body of solicitors.

CHAPTER 11

THE EARLY TUDORS 1485–1547

11.1 INTRODUCTION

The year 1485, inaugurating a new dynasty after 331 years of Plantagenet rule, is the second of the great traditional watersheds of English history. The period is best known for its two larger-than-life rulers, Henry VIII (1509–47) and Elizabeth I (1558–1603), but it also saw the re-establishment of royal authority and effective government after the long period of instability, although that authority was not entirely secure. The success or otherwise of the individual ruler continued to depend on his political abilities and capacity to command the respect and loyalty of his leading subjects. That much did not change, nor did it change until much later the practice of government became separated from the person of the monarch.

However, the focus of government began to change and England began for the first time to emerge as a leading maritime power, while at the same time significant developments took place in the progress towards political unity of the various nations of the British Isles. Wales, a possession of the English Crown since 1282, was administratively united with England in the 1530s. In the same period, the lordship of Ireland became a kingdom and gained an increasing significance in political affairs. Finally, the failure of Henry VIII's children to produce issue led to a union between the crowns of England and Scotland on the death of Elizabeth I.

This is also the period in which the monarch's greatest servants became significant political figures in their own right, no longer merely giving effect to their master's policies, but themselves developing those policies. Prior to the reign of Henry VIII, the identities and roles of the king's ministers are matters known only to specialists, but from then on, they emerge fully into the light of history.

Perhaps most significantly, England and Wales underwent a religious revolution under the aegis of successive monarchs, in which the traditional authority of the Pope was put aside and a species of the reformed Protestant faith was imposed by legislative means as the national religion. This development was not only important in itself, it also gave England an ideological separation from the mainstream of continental politics and encouraged her development as a maritime power and the acquisition of her first major overseas possessions. Further, the authority of Parliament moved into new spheres, and this formed part of the impetus for the conflict between the Crown and Parliament which followed in the 17th century. In the same period, Scotland underwent a process of religious change not dissimilar in form but different in result, while Ireland for the time being remained resolutely Catholic. However, under James I (and VI of Scotland), official policy began to encourage the settlement of Protestants in the north Irish province of Ulster, so inaugurating a new division within Ireland in addition to the existing divisions and fostering internal conflict to add to the traditional animosity of the native Irish towards the English who ruled them.

11.2   HENRY VII 1485–1509

11.2.1 The path to the throne

Henry Tudor, who by his victory at Bosworth and the death of Richard III assumed the throne as Henry VII, was the sole living male of the House of Lancaster, but his claim to the throne by hereditary right was doubtful in the extreme. That he was a usurper and there was much initial opposition to his rule tends to be glossed over, since, unlike Richard, he maintained his hold on power and inaugurated a dynasty. Henry, born in January 1457, spent his early years at Pembroke with his mother and paternal uncle, Jasper Tudor. After Jasper fled abroad in 1461, Henry's wardship was sold to the new Yorkist Earl of Pembroke, and he seems to have been separated from his mother before she remarried in 1464. During Henry VI's brief restoration, Jasper Tudor returned from exile and he and his nephew spent time at the revived Lancastrian court, but on Edward IV's return, both fled to Brittany, where they were given refuge by Duke Francis II. Henry seems not to have been taken seriously as a pretender until after Richard III's accession and the presumed deaths of Edward V and his brother. For their own purposes, Duke Francis and the French king, Charles VIII, were prepared to render assistance to him in his aspirations towards the English throne. However, he only emerged as a significant figure when Edward IV's widow made common cause with him in the autumn of 1483, and especially after she promised him her daughter in marriage.

Following previous precedent, Henry's first actions after Bosworth were directed towards consolidating and legitimising his position as king. His biographer SB Chrimes[1] sets out his immediate priorities as coronation, for still coronation demonstrated a king's legitimacy in the sight of God; the summoning of a parliament, not least because it was necessary to attaint his surviving enemies and to reverse the existing attainders on himself and most of his chief adherents; marriage to Elizabeth of York; the rewarding of those who had followed him and whose services he must continue to enjoy if he were to reign with any degree of security; and the appointment of suitable ministers and administrators so that government in his name could begin. The last was especially important, given that Henry had no governmental, military or diplomatic experience.

Establishing his title to the crown raised several difficulties, not least because Henry and his mother were themselves attainted. Not only was he thereby disabled from inheriting any title, but also, since he could not claim the crown by inheritance, from summoning a parliament to lift that attainder. There was no other person with jurisdiction to summon parliament on his behalf.[2] His position would be considerably strengthened by marriage to Elizabeth of York, but they had a common great-great-grandfather in John of Gaunt, and no valid marriage could take place without a papal dispensation. Inevitably, this would mean delay, but there must be no room for doubt as to the validity of the marriage and the legitimacy of its issue. Then there was the uncertain position of Elizabeth's two brothers. Though both were presumably dead,

---

1   SB Chrimes, *Henry VII*, Yale English Monarchs Series, 1999, Yale UP.
2   This difficulty was unique to Henry VII, since the earlier attainder affecting Richard, Duke of York and his sons was lifted in October 1460.

they had been bastardised by the Act *Titulus Regis* of 1484. If they were bastards, so was Elizabeth, much reducing her value for Henry's purposes.

Henry VII departed from previous precedent and did not seek the approval of a parliament or a quasi-parliamentary assembly for his kingship; rather, he presented the country with a *fait accompli*. He was crowned on 30 October, the judges of the Exchequer having earlier come to a convenient conclusion that the attainder was discharged by Henry taking the crown upon himself.[3] When parliament opened on 7 November, no attempt was made to demonstrate Henry VII's title to the crown; it was simply declared that title now vested in him and his issue. Previously, a former king was said to have departed the throne, either of his own volition by abdication, by deposition or because of his ineligibility (Edward V), and his supplanter assumed the throne by a combination of greater hereditary right, the desire of the estates of the realm and the will of the people. Henry VII did not even seek explicitly to rely on his victory at Bosworth and the death in battle against him of his predecessor, proofs, in the eyes of medieval man, of the righteousness of his cause.

Next, parliament revoked the Acts of Attainder passed under the Yorkists against various leading Lancastrians and restored their possessions. Then, without precedent, parliament was induced to pass an Act of Attainder naming 28 persons who had fought for Richard III at Bosworth, who, by assembling at Leicester under Richard 'late Duke of Gloucester', by usurpation calling himself King Richard III, on 21 August 1485 on the first day of the reign of the new king, traitorously intending, imagining and compassing the death of their sovereign lord Henry VII, levied war against him. Thus, whereas previously, adherence to a king for the time being was no crime, Henry VII retrospectively imposed liability for high treason upon his enemies, so ensuring the forfeiture of their property to the crown, and thus was not only a valuable injection of resources into the depleted treasury, but also a convenient source of reward for his own supporters. Further, he sent a clear and harsh message to any who might seek to oppose his rule in the future. However, Henry seems later to have thought better of this dangerous principle and it was reversed in 1496.[4]

11.2.2 The reign

Like his recent predecessors, Henry VII was not entirely secure on his throne, his position being threatened by Yorkist plots for a number of years, one impostor, Lambert Simnel, being proclaimed as the imprisoned Earl of Warwick, and a second, Perkin Warbeck, as Edward IV's younger son, Richard, Duke of York.

Although the world did not suddenly change in a few hours on 22 August 1485, the reign of Henry VII was nonetheless a bridge between the late medieval world and that of the high Renaissance. It was in his time that Columbus sailed to the New World, England took its first steps to establishing colonies across the Atlantic, with the voyages of John and Sebastian Cabot to Newfoundland, and when the Tudors developed the dynastic ties with Spain which were to be of huge importance over the rest of the century, being, in particular, the cause of Henry VIII's break with papal authority.

---

3   Chrimes, *op cit*, p 61.
4   11 Hen VIII c 1 Statutes of the Realm.

Henry VII began negotiations for the marriage of his elder son, Arthur, to Catherine, youngest daughter of Ferdinand and Isabella, rulers of Aragon and Castile, as early as 1488, when both were infants, but it was not until the end of 1501 that the pair were wed. Arthur died only five months later, probably of tuberculosis. 'Last night I was in Spain', the 15 year old Prince of Wales is said to have boasted on the morning after the wedding, but whether the marriage was ever consummated was to become a pressing issue in later years. A marriage alliance with Scotland, by the union in 1503 of Henry VII's elder daughter, Margaret Tudor and King James IV (1488–1513) was more successful, at least in the long term, being the route by which the crowns of England and Scotland were united 100 years later.

11.3   HENRY VIII 1509–47

Henry VII was a shrewd and calculating monarch, prepared to work slowly to build his authority and a chain of foreign alliances to protect it. Henry VIII, his second son, was a very different man, much more like his maternal grandfather, Edward IV, in his love of conspicuous display, exemplified by the magnificence of his meeting with the French king on the Field of the Cloth of Gold in 1520, and of the pleasures of the flesh. Though his prowess as a seducer seems to have been much exaggerated, he was an enthusiastic jouster and dancer, and addicted to hunting. Like Edward IV, his health suffered from his gargantuan appetite after he ceased to sustain the physical exertions of his youth. An alarming increase in his girth is evidenced from his surviving suits of armour, and he was an invalid from his early 50s, this decline being exactly contemporaneous with the increasing tyranny of his rule and his final desperate attempts to secure the continuance of his dynasty.

11.3.1 The break with Rome

Dissolution of a marriage

One of Henry VIII's first acts as king was to marry Catherine of Aragon, about whose fate Henry VII had procrastinated since 1502, being unwilling to incur the expenditure which would result from her remarriage to his second son, but unwilling to sacrifice her dowry by allowing her to return to Spain. The marriage produced only one living child, Mary, born in 1516. By the mid-1520s, it was clear that Catherine would bear no more children. Henry VIII was a Catholic of a kind conventional in his time and was hitherto a firm supporter of Rome.[5] He seems to have become convinced that the failure to produce healthy male issue was God's judgment for the sin of marrying Catherine, his brother's widow; they came well within the prohibited degrees of consanguinity and Henry now argued that the Pope had no power to issue an effective dispensation in this case. His desire to put an end to the marriage set in motion a sequence of events of enormous religious and constitutional significance. Most significantly for the purposes of this book, the powers of parliament were for the first time used to impose the king's will on the church, so formally extending those

---

5   The title Defender of the Faith, borne by every monarch since, was granted to Henry by Pope Adrian VI as a gesture of thanks for his *Treatise on the Seven Sacraments*, produced in 1521 as a riposte to Martin Luther.

powers beyond the traditional legal fiction that a statute did not create new law, but was simply declaratory of existing law.

Some time between 1525 and 1527, Henry appears to have fallen in love with Anne Boleyn, a lady of his court considerably younger than Catherine, and sought an annulment of his marriage on the basis of consanguinity. This was nothing unusual. The prohibited degrees of consanguinity were so broad that most royal marriages were made within them, and consanguinity had often provided a pretext for the annulment of a barren union, or one which failed to produce sons.[6] However, Henry VIII's attempts in 1527 to obtain an annulment by normal means foundered on the rock of the implacable opposition of Catherine's nephew, Charles V, who was at one and the same time Holy Roman Emperor, King of Spain and ruler of the Low Countries as Duke of Burgundy.

Henry's Chancellor, Cardinal Wolsey, was papal legate in England; after some collusion, he summoned Henry to appear before his legatine court to explain why he was living in sin with his brother's widow. This would allow Henry to establish a *prima facie* case for the invalidity of the marriage, which could then be confirmed by the Pope. However, Clement VII, with the Emperor and a large army at the gates of Rome, not unnaturally wished to have nothing to do with the matter, suggesting that Henry should divorce in England in any way he liked, so long as he did not involve the Papacy. This was of no use to Henry, since it was vital that there was no doubt as to the validity of a second marriage.

The Pope then procrastinated, and attempts to persuade Catherine to end the marriage by retiring to a convent foundered on her own determination to have right done to her. Wolsey found himself between a rock and a hard place. His diplomacy had failed to persuade the Pope to support Henry. For reasons of his own, the Emperor was prepared to have the matter remitted to Rome, but Pope Clement was most unlikely to find in Henry's favour, with disastrous consequences for Wolsey. The proceedings before Wolsey dragged out, and no decision had been reached when, in the summer of 1527, Clement bowed to imperial pressure and ordered that the matter be remitted to Rome. At this point, Henry VIII abandoned his hopes of gaining what he sought by co-operation with Rome. For the next three years, he tried to undermine the Pope by threats, having first disposed of Wolsey.

Assault on the church

In their endeavours to rebuild and then to extend the authority of the monarchy, the two Tudor kings had already acted to curb the enormous powers of the church of Rome and the scope it gave Englishmen for the evasion of kingly power. Despite Henry II's struggle with Thomas Becket more than 300 years earlier, those in holy orders could still rely on benefit of clergy to escape the jurisdiction of the king's courts, at least for a first offence.[7] A statute of 1491 required clerics convicted before the ecclesiastical courts to be branded on the hand, so that they could not seek to

---

6   Under canon law, the legitimacy of any children of a consanguinous union was not affected, provided that at the time of the marriage, the parents were ignorant of the link between them. The church seems prepared to stretch a point in such cases, since members of royal families were unlikely to be ignorant of their genealogies.

7   The ecclesiastical courts could deprive clerics of their holy orders, rendering them subject to the jurisdiction of the king's courts in respect of further offences.

evade secular trial for a second offence, and an Act of 1512 restricted benefit of clergy
to those in major orders, so removing this effective immunity from a large swathe of
the population. The other area of difficulty was the privilege of sanctuary, which
applied to any person who took refuge within church precincts. *Prima facie*, he was
entitled to remain there for 40 days and remained immune from punishment
thereafter, provided that he abjured the realm promptly. The king's writ did not run
over large areas where this privilege had been granted. Most of these areas lay in the
north, which kings had for centuries encountered difficulty in controlling, and where
Yorkist sentiment continued to exist, and were frequently in the hands of the church.

The fortunes of the church were at an increasingly low ebb, not necessarily
because it was in any worse state than it had been during the medieval period, but
because there was a belief that it was more corrupt, more worldly, more afflicted with
simony and nepotism, that a greater proportion of supposedly celibate churchmen
had mistresses and illegitimate children, and that the ignorance of the parish clergy
was greater than ever before. Challenge to religious orthodoxy was in the air.

From 1529 onwards, Henry VIII, first seeking to put pressure on Pope Clement
and then for more direct ends, took action against the church in relation to its secular
powers and wealth rather than its theology. In the summer of 1530, a number of senior
clerics were accused in the Court of the King's Bench of breaching the Statute of
Praemunire, passed in 1393 to protect the king's prerogatives from encroachment by
the papacy, by their obedience to Wolsey in his capacity as papal legate. Within a few
months, this accusation was extended to all the English clergy who, in their two
convocations, agreed to purchase a royal pardon for the alleged offence for a total sum
of £118,000. The penalties of the Statute included forfeiture of property, so that if
Henry VIII had pursued the matter to its conclusion, the church in England would
have been deprived of all its vast wealth and property by a single process.

Henry then, in February 1531, demanded that the clergy recognise him as supreme
head of the church in England, so seeking to destroy the historic 'dual allegiance'
which the clergy had hitherto owed to Pope and king. Not surprisingly, there was
much opposition in both convocations, but Archbishop Warham of Canterbury then
proposed the formula 'singular protector, only and supreme lord, and as far as the
Law of Christ allows even supreme head', to which the clergy were deemed to assent
by their silence. What this distinctly woolly phrase meant was even then far from
clear, and it was not for another two years that Henry VIII acted upon his own
interpretation.[8]

The next phase

All attempts to have the king's marriage declared void continued to come to naught.
Catherine insisted that her first marriage had not been consummated, so that she had
gone into her marriage to Henry a single woman. Pope Clement formally forbade
Henry to remarry in 1531, but refused to declare his marriage to Catherine fully valid.
Stalemate appeared to have arrived, but was broken in the course of the next two
years by the radical actions of Henry and his new advisor, Thomas Cromwell.

Cromwell was a man of distinct anti-clerical tendencies and had spent periods as a
soldier of fortune in Italy and as a merchant before taking up business as a lawyer. In

---

8   See GR Elton, *England Under the Tudors*, 3rd edn, 1991, Methuen, p 125.

November 1529, he became a member of parliament and it may have been his appearance among the anti-clerical faction during debates which brought him into the king's service, where he quickly demonstrated the administrative abilities which gained him Henry's confidence. From early in 1532, with the full support of the king, Cromwell set about dismantling the secular power of the church.

First, a 'Commons Supplication against the Ordinaries', demanding action against the ecclesiastical courts, was put by parliament to the king, who then put a series of demands arising from it before convocation. Henceforth, the clergy were to enact no legislation without the king's licence, and the existing canon law would be examined by a commission of 32, half the members laymen appointed by the king. Next, Henry summoned a commons deputation and demanded to know the steps he should take to prevent the clergy from being but half his subjects by their oath of obedience to Rome. The threat to destroy canon law and, via parliament, to end the link with Rome caused the clergy to accept Henry's demands, in a document known as the Submission of the Clergy. This was only the beginning; effectively, the church was emasculated as an opponent as Henry and Cromwell pushed ahead to widen the breach with Rome.

At the same time, a Bill was introduced in the lords to abolish the payments made to the Pope by bishops on succession to their sees. Rated at one-third of annual diocesan income, these 'annates' represented a considerable gain to the papacy and, according to the Bill, a significant loss to the nation. The Bill further provided for the consecration of bishops-elect by English authority alone. Had this Bill taken effect, it may well have become an effective two-edged sword against Rome by depriving the papacy not only of a major source of revenue, but also of a significant means of spiritual control. However, the Bill was held up by the opposition of the bishops and abbots in the lords, as well as in the commons.

The lasting point of importance about the Bill is that it incorporated the first example of what has become known to constitutional lawyers as a 'Henry VIII clause'. The term is now used to denote legislation which allows Acts of Parliament to be repealed or amended by members of the executive via statutory instrument with only limited scrutiny by Parliament. That contained in the 1532 Bill was more limited, giving the king power to bring its provisions into effect at his discretion by means of letters patent.

At this point, Sir Thomas More, Wolsey's successor as Chancellor, retired into private life, before long to be condemned and executed for refusing to accept Henry's superiority over the Pope, and leaving Cromwell in an unassailable position vis à vis the king. Non-political events then brought matters to a head. Suspicion that Anne Boleyn was pregnant – the future Elizabeth I was born on 7 September 1533 – may well have been behind the secret ceremony of marriage which took place between Henry and Anne on 25 January 1533. However, no annulment of Henry's first marriage had been granted and Henry had acted in defiance of the Pope's prohibition of 1529 on a second marriage while Catherine lived. Thus, the marriage was bigamous at its outset. However, with Anne Boleyn pregnant, some means had to be found of validating the new marriage.

In March 1533, parliament, with a surprising lack of opposition, passed an Act restraining appeals to papal authority, so allowing the matter of the king's marriage to be dealt with conclusively in England. On 23 May, Thomas Cranmer, the newly-appointed Archbishop of Canterbury, declared the king's marriage to Catherine of Aragon void and the marriage to Anne Boleyn valid.[9]

The Act of Appeals not only declared in its preamble that the king was supreme head of the church in England, but also gave practical effect to this boast by the abolition of appeals to Rome. But Henry's new position, although he was to die believing himself still a Catholic, led to a further and more wide-ranging series of changes, and was the beginning of the development of the Church of England as a body neither fully Catholic nor wholly Protestant, still, 470 years later, acknowledging the monarch as its Supreme Governor and uniquely entwined with secular government.

The position was consolidated in the following year, through measures introduced into the two parliamentary sessions of 1534. Initially, the prohibition on payment of annates was given full statutory effect and formal effect was given to the now-normal practice by which the king chose bishops and abbots, rather than their being elected by the relevant cathedral chapters and monasteries, as had been the theoretical position. A further Act cut off another source of papal revenue by ending the traditional tax known as Peter's Pence, which had been paid intermittently since the conversion of the English. The vacuum concerning appeals from ecclesiastical courts was now filled by a provision granting jurisdiction to the king in Chancery.

The final provision of the parliament of January 1534 was an Act confirming the invalidity of the king's first marriage and the validity of the second, so that Henry's elder daughter, Mary, was removed from the succession and replaced by the infant Elizabeth, and any further children the king might have by Anne Boleyn. The king was highly sensitive about his second marriage and felt himself to be politically exposed, so that this Act added to the categories of treason contained in the Statute of Treasons by making it high treason maliciously to deny or attack the validity of the second marriage 'in writing, print, deed or act' and requiring the entire population to take an oath accepting the second marriage and the new rules of succession.

The parliament of November 1534 was responsible for the Act of Supremacy, which acknowledged the king's position as the Supreme Head of the Church and conferred authority on the king to carry out the visitations of religious institutions which had previously been the responsibility of persons appointed by the Pope or the superior of the relevant religious order. Other payments previously made to Rome also passed to the king, and a Treason Act created a second new form of treason, that of calling the king or queen heretic or schismatic. Perhaps more sinister, while the Statute of 1351 had confined treason to particular deeds, that of 1534 extended it to particular words, where uttered 'maliciously'. Admittedly, such a formulation had already been developed by the common law during the 15th century, when many had been tried or attainted for 'treasons' outside the scope of the Statute, but this extension

---

9   There must be genuine doubt as to the validity of the marriage to Anne Boleyn and the legitimacy of the issue of that marriage. Although the declaration of 23 May removed the impediment to the validity of the marriage, no further ceremony of marriage took place, which the law holds to be required where a marriage is originally bigamous, and which does not even then confer retrospective validity. Catherine of Aragon died in January 1536, while Anne Boleyn was executed 11 days before Henry entered into his marriage with Jane Seymour, so the only one of Henry's children whose legitimacy is unquestionable was Edward VI.

of treason law provided the king's government with a further weapon to stamp on opposition to its increasingly radical policies.

The Dissolution of the Monasteries

Having appropriated to the crown the revenues passing from England to the papacy, Henry and Cromwell's next major move was the seizure of the largest body of religious property in England by dissolving all the religious orders. It seems probable that the grant to the king in 1534 of power to make visitations was a preliminary move, and the process got underway in January 1535, when commissions were issued for the valuation of all ecclesiastical property in England.

The motivation for this action was mixed, but had two main elements: a desire to obtain the great wealth of the religious orders, which between them owned between one-fifth and one-third of the land of England, and a wish to stifle opposition. Regular royal revenues had fallen during the 1530s. At the same time, there was a need to put England's defences in order against a possible attack from Spain following the insult to Catherine of Aragon, together with problems in Ireland and the loss of a pension paid to the crown by France as part of the peace settlement of 1514. As did his predecessors, Henry VIII sought to foster his subjects' loyalty by generous provision of land, offices and money. Not only did the bulk of the still-limited opposition to the religious policy come from the religious orders, but the sequestration of their property would provide a convenient source of rewards.

The monasteries had long fallen from the esteem in which they had once been held. Over and over again, since monasticism had begun in the Near East during the Roman era, the initial strict adherence to the standards laid down in texts such as the Rule of St Benedict had gradually given way to slackness, so that institutions which had originally been citadels of truth and purity had become places where the comforts of the world could be enjoyed without its cares. The religious life, once the only source of education and also a means of acquiring secular power through the accumulation of offices, had now been largely sidelined by the development of a professional corps of royal administrators, the growth of the merchant class and the availability of education outside religious houses. During the 15th century, the tradition of gifts to monasteries had largely given way to the creation by the wealthy of private chantries, staffed by 'colleges' of priests, whose duty it was to say masses for the souls of the founder and his family. Of some 800 religious houses in England, few had more than 25 professed members, and about 600 had only four or five.

A pretext had to be found for dissolution and this was easily obtained by a visitation under the new powers introduced by the Act of Supremacy. In January 1535, as the valuation of ecclesiastical property began, Thomas Cromwell appointed visitors to gather evidence as to the corruption and decay of the religious orders, and to seek to enforce the rules of poverty, chastity and obedience with all possible rigour, with the intention, theoretically, of righting abuses. However, the new stringency, it was anticipated, would also have the effect of encouraging a proportion of monks to seek dispensation from their vows.

The pretext obtained, Cromwell first moved to dissolve the smaller houses, claiming in the Bill introduced in February 1536 that only they were so corrupt as to be beyond redemption; Elton remarks that 'the line between virtue and depravity followed with curious fidelity the line which divided £200 a year from incomes larger than this'.[10] A further statute put into place the administrative measures necessary to deal with the sudden influx of property into the hands of the crown. Members of the dissolved houses who wished to continue in the religious life were allowed to move to the remaining houses of their orders, others were provided with benefices as secular clergy or pensions to enable them to live in the world. Seemingly, a number of former monks became masters in the grammar schools which were being established at this time.

The Pilgrimage of Grace

Both the king and Cromwell accepted that they could not complete the dissolution of all the religious orders at once – there was too much opposition from conservative secular interests. This made itself felt in the northern rising known as the Pilgrimage of Grace, which broke out in the last three months of 1536, and was the most significant internal threat yet to Tudor authority. The north had always been an area dominated by fiercely independent magnates and the feuds between them, where royal authority was limited and little loyalty to the Tudors had developed. The grievances of the rebels arose from a combination of factors, including resentment of the centralising tendencies of Henry and Cromwell, attacks on the traditional liberties of the great feudal families and taxation of the Yorkshire wool industry. Three developments of 1535–36 seem to have acted as the final straw.

The first was the Statute of Uses of 1535. The use, an early form of trust, was devised during the 13th century as a means of allowing gifts of property to be made to the mendicant orders, which under their rules could have no institutional property. Property was put in the hands of trustees for the 'use' of the order concerned, and those trustees, not the order, held the legal title and managed the property. Gradually, the use was developed as a convenient means of avoiding payment of many of the feudal dues owed to the king and, in the event of property passing to a minor, of preventing that property from passing into the hands of another via wardship, since legal title remained with the trustees and there was no transfer on the death of a beneficiary. The Statute of Uses essentially vested the property concerned in the person otherwise liable for reliefs. Within a few years, lawyers had developed new forms of trust which evaded the terms of the Statute, but for a period, this avenue of tax avoidance was closed off.

A further attack on the northern feudal families came through an Act of 1536 which removed all those jurisdictional franchises and liberties which remained. Although the largest concentration of these was in the Welsh Marches, there were also numbers in the north. The traditional independence of England north of the Trent from the full weight of royal authority was being eroded. The other immediate trigger for the Pilgrimage of Grace was the king's religious policy, which impacted particularly heavily on Lancashire and Yorkshire, where there were large numbers of wealthy monastic houses. It was the prominence given to this issue by the disaffected northerners which gave the rising its name.

Though Robert Aske, the leader of the rising in Yorkshire, may have incited up to 30,000 men to take up arms and follow him, the Pilgrimage of Grace never became a serious threat to the king's position. The pilgrims showed a decided reluctance to

10   Elton, *op cit*, p 144.

move south of the Trent and were persuaded to disperse on promises – later ignored – of pardon. The Pilgrimage only accelerated the dissolution. A number of abbots and priors of northern houses were executed for their part in the rising, something unprecedented, since clerics involved in treasonable activities, such as Archbishop Arundel under Richard II, had previously escaped the block by virtue of their holy orders, though they could be subjected to imprisonment, exile and forfeiture of property.[11] Some of the great northern houses bowed to the inevitable and surrendered themselves and their property into the king's hands. Others waited for a further round of Cromwellian visitations which began in 1538, and due condemnation for corruption and worldliness where abbots did not accept a prepared form of surrender. More pressure followed as four more abbots were executed in 1539 for breaches of the Treason Act 1534, and there was a first outbreak of the destruction of the relics and images which occupied a vital place in traditional religiosity. By the beginning of 1540, all the monasteries and friaries were gone.

A small proportion of the sequestered lands remained in the king's hands; more were granted to the king's leading servants. Most were made available for purchase or lease on the open market, and this accelerated the process by which the late medieval nobility were largely replaced in positions of local importance by 'new men' who rose to prominence under the Tudors, often through service to the crown. The Cecils, who rose from minor gentry to the earldom of Exeter, later a marquessate, under Elizabeth I and added the earldom of Salisbury under James I, are the most prominent example. This assisted the security of the dynasty, since the great magnate power blocs which were an important feature in the genesis and history of the Wars of the Roses largely disappeared.

A Protestant church

Theological change then followed, promoted by Cromwell and his ally, Archbishop Cranmer. The 'Protestant' teachings which had first emerged on the continent and were now gaining ground in England had a number of variants, but the basic difference between Protestant and Catholic doctrines, from which most others flowed, was in the concept of the way to salvation. Catholicism preached that the priesthood acted as the link between God and man, and that eternal life in the hereafter could be earned by such mechanisms as the intercession of the saints, the making of pilgrimages and the prayers of others. By contrast, Protestant teachings emphasised a direct link between God and man, and that salvation came by faith alone. John Calvin and his followers took this theology a stage further, by preaching that all were predestined to eternal life or damnation entirely according to the will of God, and an individual's beliefs and actions had no bearing on his fate. Such teachings rendered many of the most important manifestations of traditional religiosity redundant. Protestantism also demanded a return to the purity of the Early Church through greater simplicity of practise, emphasised the word of God as set down in the Bible and considered that worshippers should be able to study the Bible themselves in their vernacular languages.

---

11   The sole exception was Richard Scrope, Archbishop of York (1398–1405), beheaded after rebelling against Henry IV.

Although English opinion remained moderate, still attitudes to 'popish superstition' were hardening by the late 1530s, not least because a papal plan emerged to recover England for the Roman faith. During 1538, Cromwell issued 'Injunctions' attacking popish practices such as pilgrimages, ordering the reading of the English Bible produced by William Tyndale and the keeping of parish registers.[12] Conservative opinion, however, remained influential in parliament, and therefore the Act of the Six Articles, which emerged from the 1539 session, re-stated much of traditional doctrine: transubstantiation,[13] confession to priests, the sanctity of monastic vows for those still subject to them, communion in one kind only for the laity, the propriety of private masses and the prohibition of clerical marriage. However, the precedent was set under which matters of doctrine and purely religious practice could be the subject of legislation by a parliament dominated by the laity.

11.3.2 Henry VIII's later years

The search for an heir

Historians who seek medical explanations for political developments tend to emphasise the mishap which befell Henry VIII during a joust on 17 January 1536, when he fell with his horse and remained unconscious for two hours, as a major factor in the increasingly authoritarian character of his government. Certainly, it had disastrous consequences for Anne Boleyn, who 12 days later miscarried of a son. By now, Henry had lost enthusiasm for Anne's charms and conceived an interest in another young lady of his court, Jane Seymour. With the loss of a male infant, he concluded that Anne was no longer of any use to him.

Whether or not the 'medical' view of Henry VIII's later actions is accurate, it is very obvious that he showed far greater impatience to be rid of Anne Boleyn than to end his first marriage. Evidence suggests that he ceased to sleep with Catherine of Aragon by 1523, but it was not until 1527 that he sought an annulment of their marriage, and 1533 before the marriage was finally ended. Although Anne's position was becoming insecure before the miscarriage, it was only in February 1536 that any process began against her; she went to the block on 19 May. After the events surrounding the end of his marriage to Catherine, Henry could not have a second union declared void in any similar manner. Anne Boleyn had to die. A means was found in a Bill of Attainder which declared her alleged adultery during the marriage to be treasonous, a means to be used a second time in disposing of Henry's fifth wife, Catherine Howard.

A Succession Act then bastardised the young Elizabeth, so that both Henry's daughters were now barred from the succession, and provided mechanisms for the government of the realm in the event of the accession of a minor. As Henry was now in his mid-40s, well past his prime by contemporary standards, this was becoming a real possibility. The longed-for male heir, Edward Prince of Wales, was born on 12 October 1537, but his mother, Jane Seymour, succumbed to the dangerous after-effects of childbirth and died within a fortnight.

---

12 This was the first attempt to create a coherent system of registration of births, marriages and deaths, pre-dating by 300 years the adoption of civil registration in 1837.

13 The doctrine which provides that at the moment of consecration, the bread and wine of communion become the Body and Blood of Christ.

Governmental change

With Thomas Cromwell at the helm, the 1530s were a time of important developments in the machinery of government, though most historians would now deny that they constituted the 'revolution in government' identified by GR Elton. Most significantly, steps were taken to separate governmental institutions from the king's household. During the 1530s, Cromwell reconstituted the royal financial institutions into six self-contained departments. The Exchequer continued to deal with the traditional profits of justice, together with customs and parliamentary taxation, and the Duchy of Lancaster with the revenues from its lands. The Court of General Surveyors dealt with the lands of the crown, the Court of Augmentations with the former monastic lands. Finally, the Court of First Fruits and Tenths was responsible for the income due from the secular church,[14] and the Court of Wards and Liberties for the feudal revenues of the crown. The new system was not foolproof; clearly, there was scope for duplication and its corollary, difficulties over demarcation of responsibility, but it was an important step in the process of developing an efficient system of financial administration for the benefit of royal government.

At about the same time, Cromwell greatly lessened the role of the Chancellor and elevated the king's secretary into a *de jure* as well as *de facto* officer of state. From Cromwell's time as secretary, beginning in 1534, the secretary was effectively a chief executive. There was also a rationalisation and simplification under which the dichotomy between Great Seal and Privy Seal was ended, Cromwell having effective control of both. In addition, Cromwell's methods brought about the development of an institutionalised Privy Council, initially as an inner ring of the King's Council, to supersede the fluctuating role, composition and size of the King's Council. After the accession of Elizabeth I, and building on foundations largely laid by Cromwell, the pattern of government practice was set until the 18th century, where the Secretary or Secretaries of State – latterly there were two – was the monarch's chief minister, and other major responsibilities lay with the Privy Councillors, some of whom also had specific offices, such as that of Treasurer.

It has already been noted that powers to make legislation independently of parliament existed through the power of the king and council to issue ordinances and proclamations. As yet, the limits of this power, as the limits on parliament's power, remained undefined. However, by the Statute of Proclamations of 1539, parliament gave Henry VIII wide powers – powers without express limitation – to legislate by proclamation, such a proclamation having the same force as a statute. Breaches of proclamation were made triable by specified members of the Council sitting together. An important safeguard was provided, in that the Statute prohibited the imposition of the death penalty for breach of proclamation. This Statute was repealed by Edward VI's first parliament in 1547, the powers it granted having been used only to a limited extent, though both Mary I and Elizabeth I continued to legislate in this manner.[15] It was under James I that the limits of this power became an issue.

---

14 First fruits were the sums of a year's income due from the clergy on succession to benefices. Tenths were a 10% annual tax due from each parish.

15 See W Holdsworth (AL Goodhart and HG Hanbury (eds)), *A History of English Law*, vol 14, 1964, Sweet & Maxwell, pp 100–05.

Wales

The consolidation of Tudor authority within the domains of the crown had been begun by Henry VII and was pushed through with much greater urgency by his son during the 1530s. For many centuries, English kings had intermittently claimed dominion over the whole island of Britain and had taken steps to convert that boast into reality. That reality was brought several steps closer under Henry VIII.

Since 1485, there had been a policy of piecemeal destruction of the jurisdictional franchises and liberties which had developed or endured during the medieval period, and which provided local magnates with a major source of power. As well as those in the north, there was a particular block in the Welsh Marches, then covering the border area and most of South Wales. Like the north, the Marches had never been fully under royal authority and, with the north, had been the major power base of the protagonists of the Wars of the Roses.

Henry VIII moved against a number of Marcher lords during the 1520s, in particular, Edward Stafford, 3rd Duke of Buckingham, attainted and executed in 1521. In 1536, Cromwell introduced into parliament an Act for the Union of England and Wales, which removed much of the legal and governmental dichotomy between England and its neighbour which had endured since the Statute of Wales of 1284,[16] though for the time being, royal authority in the former Marches was exercised by a reconstituted Council for the Marches. The Act dissolved the Marcher lordships, annexed some to existing counties and divided the remainder into five new counties. The border between England and Wales was precisely defined for the first time, and thenceforth, the Kingdom of England was properly termed the Kingdom of England and Wales. The full operation of English law was extended to Wales, although this did not have full effect until after a further Act of 1543. Henceforth also, the shires and boroughs of Wales were to send 24 members to parliament. In 1543, English was declared to be the language of government and administration.

English law replaced Welsh not only in the criminal field, but also in civil matters. In particular, the Welsh tradition of partible inheritance between all a man's sons was replaced with primogeniture in the English fashion. Following the Dissolution of the Monasteries, large tracts of land in Wales were available for distribution to Tudor loyalists, so instituting the rise to prominence of a number of families of Welsh blood who took the place of the old Marcher families as the leading landowners of Wales.

Ireland

Since the 1490s, Ireland had returned to its old pattern of domination by great local families descended from the freebooting Norman barons of the 12th century, notably the Butlers and Fitzgeralds. Though Poynings' Law of 1495 prevented the Dublin Parliament from legislating without reference to the English Crown, parliamentary legislation was of relatively little importance in this period, since royal control over Ireland was exercised very largely on the basis of prerogative powers.

Ireland remained papist in sentiment, and therefore the break with Rome made governmental action necessary if Ireland were not to form a stepping stone to an invasion of England by Henry's continental enemies. During the 1520s, Cardinal

---

16   27 Hen VIII c 26.

Wolsey attempted to pre-empt trouble by keeping the Fitzgerald Earl of Kildare in the Tower as a surety for the good faith of his numerous influential kinsmen. However, when, in 1534, it was rumoured that Kildare had been executed, his son, Thomas Fitzgerald, renounced his allegiance to the English Crown and called upon both the Pope and Emperor to come to his aid. Fortunately for Henry, only the Fitzgerald faction rose in rebellion, no help came from the continent and the rising was put down. Kildare was executed, along with Thomas Fitzgerald and five of his uncles. Thus, Fitzgerald was largely destroyed, and in December 1540, Henry conferred upon himself the title of King of Ireland, though he continued to rule through lieutenants and their deputies.

Scotland

In the British Isles, Scotland alone remained independent of England, but had undergone a long period of severely weakened royal authority, which was to continue until the 1580s, as an ugly catalogue of murder, battle and accident removed a succession of kings while their heirs were still infants, so providing a perfect opportunity for magnates and disaffected royal relations to accrue power for themselves at the expense of the monarchy. Although more than one king managed to break the power of successive over-mighty subjects, repeated premature deaths caused the problem to recur. No king succeeded in adulthood between Robert III (1390–1406) and Charles I (1625–49).

James I (1406–37) was a boy of 11 and a captive in English hands when he succeeded Robert III, having been taken prisoner at sea while being conveyed to France for safety, and was not ransomed until 1424. James II (1437–60) came to the throne as a six year old following his father's murder, and was killed when the faulty barrel of an early cannon exploded while he was besieging Roxburgh Castle. James III (1460–88), a particularly weak ruler, was threatened by the intrigues of his younger brother, Alexander, Duke of Albany, who gained English aid for an invasion of Scotland in 1482 which resulted in the permanent loss of the strategic fortress of Berwick.

James IV (1488–1513), who succeeded at the comparatively mature age of 15 after his father's murder, was a successful ruler, but his marriage to Margaret Tudor did not discourage him from invading northern England in the summer of 1513, where he was killed at the Battle of Flodden, along with nine of the 21 Scottish earls and 11 of the 29 Lords of Parliament (equivalent to viscounts or barons). James V thereupon succeeded aged 13 months, but though he proved a strong ruler when he attained his majority, he died in 1542 when barely 30, leaving yet another infant heir.

11.4   THE LAST YEARS OF HENRY VIII

Following Jane Seymour's death on 24 October 1537, the king, still with only one legitimate son and he an infant, continued with ever-increasing desperation to seek to secure the succession, contracting three more marriages, all childless, in the last nine years of his life. It was in around 1540 that the king, increasingly an invalid, entered into the last and most autocratic phase of his reign, his actions towards those he deemed to be his enemies growing ever more arbitrary. Several who had rendered him good service became victims of his paranoia as well as the machinations of their political enemies in a court dominated increasingly by factions in the absence of a firm hand on the reins of government.

Thomas Cromwell's execution in the summer of 1540 removed the last of the great governmental figures of Henry VIII's reign from the scene, and no consistent policy was pursued for the rest of the reign. For a time, Henry attempted to steer a middle course in religious matters, perhaps exemplified by his having three radicals burnt as heretics and three conservatives executed as traitors on the same day, but there was a further lurch towards conservatism in 1543, prompted at least in part by an anti-France alliance concluded with the Emperor. A new Act restricted the reading of the Bible, whether in Latin or English, to those considered capable of understanding its message, that is, clerics, noblemen, the gentry and substantial merchants. Women below gentle rank, servants, apprentices and baser sorts were now forbidden direct access to the word of God, signifying, at least in part, a return to the old tradition where the priest acted as intermediary between God and the laity. A new definition of doctrine, known as the 'King's Book', re-stated traditional Catholic orthodoxies, though it replaced papal supremacy with that of the king. Persecution of radicals for such heresies as denial of transubstantiation was, however, sporadic, and the conservatives were unable to deflect Henry from his support of their chief enemy, Archbishop Cranmer, who occupied the period in composing what became the Prayer Book of 1549.

In foreign policy, Henry returned to former practices, making war on his old enemy, France, and seeking to conquer Scotland. Attempts were first made, unsuccessfully, to seduce James V from his France alliance and, in October 1542, an army under Norfolk invaded Scotland. James counter-attacked in November, but his army was utterly defeated at the Battle of Solway Moss, and James himself died in the first days of December, leaving the crown to his daughter Mary, then barely a week old. Battle casualties on both sides were low, but many hundreds of Scots surrendered and were used by Henry to form the nucleus of an English party in Scotland to counter the French faction which held power in Scotland on behalf of Mary. Initially, Henry's policy was highly successful; the English party overthrew the pro-French regent, Cardinal Beaton, and Henry was able to conclude the Treaty of Greenwich (July 1543), by which a permanent peace was to be secured by a marriage between Mary and the five year old Prince of Wales. But this attempt to bring about a future union of the English and Scottish Crowns was another failure. An anti-English reaction occurred in Scotland, Beaton was restored to power and, within a few years, the young Mary was out of English reach at the French court and betrothed to the Dauphin, leaving Scotland to be governed by her French mother, Mary of Guise.

Also in 1543, Henry VIII embarked on another war with France, in alliance with Charles V after patching up their differences, and insisted on accompanying his army to the continent, though the splendid young prince of the Field of the Cloth of Gold had grown so obese and sick that he had to be carried in a litter. The campaign achieved nothing and its only lasting consequence was that it saw the sinking of the Mary Rose, raised in the 1980s and now on display in Portsmouth.

These two unsuccessful wars had to be paid for, and it was in order to balance the books in the short term that Henry pursued a policy of alienating crown lands and the recently acquired monastic lands, gaining loans from the Antwerp money market at high interest and debasing the coinage. This last measure produced an immediate increase in the income of the crown, but, by destroying confidence in the coinage, had serious consequences for the economy, not least in relation to overseas trade.

Despite a sixth marriage in 1543, Henry's concern about the succession remained. The Succession Act of 1543/44 settled the crowns of England and Wales, and Ireland first on the young Prince of Wales, and then on his half-sisters, Mary and Elizabeth, in that order, and reserved the right to the king of altering the succession by will. In a will executed on 30 December 1546 and taking effect on his death on 28 January 1547, he provided that in default of issue to the heirs of his body, the succession should pass to the issue of his second sister, Mary, Duchess of Suffolk, so excluding Margaret Tudor and the issue of her two marriages from the succession.[17]

---

17 Mary had died in 1533, Margaret in 1541. Margaret's second husband was Archibald Douglas, 6th Earl of Angus.

CHAPTER 12

THE CHILDREN OF HENRY VIII

12.1 EDWARD VI 1547–53

Edward VI was nine years old at his father's death, and government was carried out by others throughout his reign. Since he died at 15, it is often assumed that he was sickly and politically a cipher, but the late Jennifer Loach has convincingly demonstrated that he was robust enough until he contracted his fatal illness[1] and, given his precocious intellect, excellent education, devotion to the new Protestantism and early signs of his father's self-will, he was already developing a degree of authority over those who governed in his name before his death.

By now, religious opinion among the politically influential had become polarised. Broadly speaking, the older generation were conservative and leant towards Roman doctrine, though not necessarily papal supremacy, while the younger were Protestant. The reigns of Henry's three children saw each hold sway in turn and then, under Elizabeth I, a policy of steering a middle course, but ensuring that royal authority was maintained.

12.1.1 A minority

The Succession Act 1536 had given Henry VIII the power to provide for the future government of the realm by will, should his successor be a minor. By his will, Henry named 16 executors who were to form his son's Privy Council, with responsibility for the government and his son's upbringing until Edward reached the age of 18, and authority to 'devise and ordain' whatever they thought best for the fulfilment of their role. Thus, an age of royal majority was specified for the first time. The will then appointed a further 12 non-executor councillors. Most of the Privy Councillors were already members of Henry's Privy Council and held important positions in government, royal administration, the church or the judiciary.

The ideological and religious composition of the Council has been much debated by specialists in the period, particularly as to whether and to what extent Henry attempted to balance the various elements. However, fully conciliar government lasted only four days, after which the Councillors elected the new king's maternal uncle, Edward Seymour, soon to be created Duke of Somerset, as Protector of the realm, giving him sovereign authority until Edward reached his majority. To Loach, this seems a realistic move, conciliar government having on past occasions proven to be unwieldy and prone to factional breakdown. Contemporary practice tended to place a regency, *de jure* or *de facto*, in the hands of either the mother or paternal uncle of a minor ruler. Since Edward had neither mother nor paternal uncles, the choice of a maternal uncle with some experience of high politics was a sensible one.

Government during Edward's reign was dominated first by Somerset and, after his fall in 1550, by John Dudley, Duke of Northumberland, who was never granted the title of Protector, but came to exercise almost untrammelled authority over his fellow

---

1   See J Loach, *Edward VI*, Yale English Monarchs Series, 1999, Yale UP, pp 159–62.

councillors, and a degree of influence over the king which is the subject of much scholarly debate.

Somerset has been portrayed in flattering tones by many historians as a man of liberal ideas and policies in religion, education and government. However, Loach has made it clear that much of this laudatory view is not based on contemporary evidence and that the bulk of Somerset's policy, in religion as elsewhere, was predicated on a desire to maintain royal authority, though he was prepared to set aside some of the extremes of Henry VIII's reign. In particular, most of the new treason laws were repealed in the 1547 parliament. A new climate of religious toleration there was not; all preaching was forbidden in September 1548, having been strictly regulated since May, and a new commission against heresy was created in April 1549. Dissolution of traditional religious institutions continued with an Act of 1547 which gave chantries, colleges and religious guilds to the king, giving the crown access to further sources of funds.

At the same time, Protestant sentiments continued to harden, so that attacks on images, stained glass and candles were frequent, and legal effect was given to certain elements of Protestant doctrine, in particular the communion in both kinds, sanctioned by a royal proclamation of 8 March 1548, and clerical marriage, permitted by a statute of 1548–49. The first English Prayer Book, prepared by a committee headed by Cranmer and given statutory authority by the Act of Uniformity of 1549, greatly reduced the number of ceremonies permitted and simplified those which remained, while practices such as kneeling were left to the individual conscience of worshippers. Again, as under Henry VIII, we see change in matters of religious belief and practice being given effect by secular mechanisms.

12.1.2 Edward VI's Devise for the Succession

Under Henry VIII's will, Edward's heirs, should he die without issue, were his two half-sisters, Mary and Elizabeth, and their respective issue, in that order. Mary was firmly Catholic. Elizabeth was Protestant, but less committed. Both were adult and so had no need of any regent, a factor which concerned the Duke of Northumberland, who could not hope for continued power under either. Some time in the spring or early summer of 1553, by which time he was seriously ill, Edward executed his 'Devise for the Succession'.

This document has engendered much controversy, concerning, first, its legality and, second, the extent to which it reflected the king's own desires rather than those of Northumberland. Then, as now, and with very limited exceptions, only a person of full age was capable of making a valid will. Edward was then 15 and even if it could otherwise be argued that as a king he was in a special position, the 1544 Act had in any case set the age of royal majority at 18. Though the extent of Northumberland's influence over the terms of the devise cannot be known, he clearly benefited greatly from it. The Devise excluded both the king's half-sisters from the succession and vested the crown in the issue of Henry VIII's second sister, Mary Tudor, by her marriage to Charles Brandon, Duke of Suffolk.

Initially, these were defined as the heirs male of Frances Brandon, the eldest surviving child of that marriage, then the heirs male of her three daughters by Henry Grey, Marquess of Dorset. Failing such heirs male, the crown was then to pass to the heirs male of those daughters. The Grey daughters themselves were bypassed entirely.

However, the document was then amended, presumably during May 1553 when it became clear that the king's illness was mortal, so that in the event of the failure of Frances Brandon to produce heirs male, the succession would vest in Jane, the eldest Grey daughter, and her heirs male. It was no coincidence that on 21 May, Jane Grey married Northumberland's third son, Guildford Dudley.[2]

Aware that the royal succession had been settled by Act of Parliament which, strictly speaking, had given only Henry VIII power to amend the succession by will and could only be unambiguously amended by a further Act, at the beginning of June, Edward VI and his closest advisers had writs issued summoning a parliament for September. However, the continuing deterioration in Edward's health meant that the sanctioning of a change to the succession by legislation might not be possible. On 12 June, the Privy Councillors met with the judges of the King's Bench to discuss the planned changes, and the request of the Lord Chief Justice, Sir Edward Montagu, for a few days in which to consult on so momentous an issue met with violent hostility from Northumberland who, according to Montagu:

> … fell into a great anger and rage, and called me traitor before all the Council, and said that in a quarrel of that matter he would fight in his shirt with any man living.[3]

Apparently, the view of the judges was that letters patent could not overrule a statute and that their involvement in an attempt to change the succession without the authority of parliament would constitute treason on their part, showing that by this time, the supreme role of parliament in constitutional matters was accepted by jurists.

It was then suggested that Mary should be permitted to succeed on her undertaking not to make any religious changes and to retain existing ministers. This did not win much support, and both the king and Northumberland remained determined that Jane Grey would succeed. Three days later, on 15 June, the king summoned the judges to attend him on his sickbed and demanded that they assist him in drawing up his will, explaining that he wished to disinherit Mary in order to safeguard the Protestant faith and Elizabeth as the daughter of the adulterous Anne Boleyn. This explanation, and his praise for the virtuous characters of Jane Grey and Guildford Dudley, won over the judges. Letters patent giving effect to the Devise were drawn up with their advice and executed by most of the leading figures in Edward VI's government and household, all but two of the judges, 22 peers and various prominent citizens of London, apparently willingly, although later, under Mary I, they were to plead that they had been bullied by Northumberland into executing both the letters patent and a separate document by which they undertook to uphold the amended succession.

Whether this allegation is true or not, during the second half of June, Northumberland certainly garnered support by grants of lands and titles to those whose support he considered crucial to the success of his cause, and made military preparations. At the same time, he sought support from the French, going so far as to make a secret visit to the French ambassador at the latter's house. On the evening of 6 July, Edward VI was dead.

---

2   The issue of Margaret Tudor by her two marriages were ignored entirely, and no cognisance was taken of Frances Brandon's probable illegitimacy. Mary Tudor was a widow at the time of her second marriage, but Suffolk had two wives living, and there is no evidence that either of these marriages had been validly annulled.

3   *Historic Manuscripts Commission, Report on the MSS of Lord Montagu of Beaulieu*, 1900, HMSO, p 4. Noblemen customarily fought in full armour at this time.

12.1.3 The nine days' queen

Edward's death was not announced for several days. The changes to the succession had not been made public and it appears that Northumberland waited to be sure of his position, and to lodge Jane Grey in the Tower for safety, before having her proclaimed queen regnant on 10 July. However, Northumberland made the error, ultimately fatal to his cause, of under-estimating Mary and so failing to take any steps to confine her. Mary herself, having presumably been made aware of developments, left her main residence, Hunsdon in Hertfordshire, on 4 July and travelled in haste to East Anglia, where she held most of her lands, by tradition leaving one house just before it was burned to the ground by pursuers. Once there, she set about rallying her supporters to her banner.

From the Duke of Norfolk's fortified residence at Framlingham, Suffolk, Mary wrote to the Privy Council on 9 July claiming the throne, and sent further letters to the leading conservative figures. A period of confusion followed, with the rivals being proclaimed queen in different towns, in some cases by rival groups in the same town. Northumberland sent his son Robert Dudley in pursuit of Mary, but Dudley failed to find her and Northumberland then followed on 14 July with an army. This was the second of his fatal errors, since he deprived himself of direct influence over the remaining councillors and those others who had signed the letters patent in favour of Jane Grey.

After the Duke left the capital, the remaining councillors, seeing the strength of the support for Mary among the nobility and gentry of East Anglia and the Thames valley, had second thoughts, and support for Jane Grey rapidly dwindled. Loach considers that the main reason for the support for Mary from these areas was religious, her leading supporters all having strongly Catholic sympathies, and their Protestant neighbours tending to remain uncommitted. On 19 July, Mary was proclaimed queen in London, and on 21 July, Northumberland, no doubt hoping to retain his head, himself proclaimed Mary in Cambridge, where he and his army had taken refuge.

12.2   THE FIRST ENGLISH QUEEN REGNANT

The reign of Mary I, frequently viewed as a period of unbridled bigotry and misery, plus a heavy toll of Protestant deaths for heresy as 'Bloody Mary' sought to return England to the old faith, began in a wave of enthusiasm, based both on her religion and on more general sentiment for her as her father's daughter, which she played upon by stressing that her title to the throne rested on statute and her father's will. Given Mary's merciless reputation, it is only proper to mention that initially, only the leading figures in the attempt to place Jane Grey on the throne were condemned and executed (Northumberland himself and his two major acolytes). The 16 year old pretender was recognised by Mary as the tool of her father-in-law, and she and Guildford Dudley were for the time being confined in the Tower in far from oppressive conditions.

Even in religious matters, the new queen was conciliatory, issuing a proclamation on 18 August in which she stated her wish that her people would return to the Catholic fold, but that there would be no compulsion; meanwhile, she exhorted everyone to live in peace with his neighbour and, in a fashion anticipating the political correctness of a much later age, beseeched them to avoid prejudiced labels such as 'papist' and 'heretic'.

However, this honeymoon did not last. Before long, the queen's stance in matters religious and political became markedly more doctrinaire for three reasons: the rebellion of Sir Thomas Wyatt in the spring of 1554, which sought to place Elizabeth on the throne, and led Mary to order Jane Grey's execution; Mary's marriage to Philip II of Spain; and her realisation that there was little enthusiasm for a return to the Catholic fold.

12.2.1 Constitutional issues

Mary was the first queen regnant in England, so that her accession raised a number of unprecedented issues. At this stage, there seems to have been no doubt as to her title to rule. That all other potential heirs were female no doubt favoured her and in any case, her accession followed the terms of her father's will, Edward VI having died without issue. Unlike Mary Queen of Scots or Juana 'la Loca', who had nominally succeeded Isabella of Castile in 1504, Mary was an adult in full possession of her faculties and so had no need of a regent. However, she was also unmarried and, in an era when government was not considered to be women's work, could not act in partnership with her husband as had Isabella. Mary seems to have been a conventional woman of her times and believed it essential that she marry in order to provide herself with support in meeting her new responsibilities. Further, she needed to produce an heir.

Potential suitors were in short supply. There seems to have been a sense that marriage to an Englishman – one of the new queen's subjects – would lack propriety and would be conducive to factional strife, while the French royal family, normally a fruitful source of marriage partners, could at this time offer no adult prince of the blood. Most German princes who were both adult and unmarried were Protestant, so were unacceptable to Mary on religious grounds. There remained only Philip of Spain, son of Charles V, who was 11 years younger than Mary, but newly widowed and Catholic. Negotiations for the match began shortly after Mary's accession.[4]

There were obvious difficulties. Philip was ruler of a foreign state, acting as Charles's regent in Spain, and was Charles's heir in most of his lands and dignities, though not as Emperor. Steps were therefore taken to limit the possibility of his acquiring power in England and, in particular, to prevent him from drawing on English resources for his own purposes.[5] English opinion was hostile to the match, as is made clear by the tenor of the negotiations between the English court and the Emperor's ambassadors, and the concessions made by Charles V and incorporated into the final text of the marriage treaty agreed in December 1553. Although Philip was to bear the title of king, he would not be accorded the crown matrimonial and so would have no claim to the English throne should Mary predecease him, nor would his son, Don Carlos. Philip was to observe all the laws and customs of England and was neither to intrude his own servants into English offices, nor to seek to involve

---

4   See D Loades, *The Reign of Mary Tudor*, 2nd edn, 1991, Blackwell, pp 64–65.
5   Loades, *ibid*, pp 62–63. Loades postulates that the Emperor favoured the marriage because he had decided that Philip was to be his heir in the Netherlands and wished him to have the advantage of England's resources in putting down opposition there.

England in the continuing Habsburg struggle with France. His role was to be limited to assisting his consort in the task of government, a point emphasised when the marriage treaty was ratified by parliament, and a short Act was passed declaring that 'the regal power of this Realm is in the Queen's Majesty as fully and absolutely as ever it was in any of her most noble progenitors Kings of this Realm'.[6] Had there been doubt as to Mary's right to the throne, it would have been more appropriate to pass this Act in the first parliament of the new reign. It therefore seems that it was enacted in response to an entirely new thesis, not backed by any precedent and propounded by the imperial ambassador, that 'by English law, if His Highness [Philip] marries the Queen, she loses her title to the Crown and His Highness becomes King'.[7]

The constitutional implications of Mary's unprecedented position emerged again when in September 1554, two months after her marriage, she declared herself to be pregnant. Mary was then 38 years old, a very late age for a first pregnancy in the 16th century, and in fragile health. Death in childbirth was commonplace, and queens were no more immune to this danger than their subjects.[8] It was therefore vital that parliament, now accepted as the final arbiter in constitutional matters, made appropriate provision for a regency in the event of Mary's death, leaving an infant as monarch. This was all the more necessary since the father of this putative heir was a foreign ruler and, should both Mary and the child die, there was no obvious heir. Mary had declared at the time of her accession that she did not wish Elizabeth to succeed her, though no formal steps had been taken, and her attitude had only hardened since.[9]

The Treason Act 1555, which would more appositely be titled the Regency Act, therefore dealt with Philip's constitutional position both in Mary's lifetime and in the event of her death with or without issue. It sought to remove any vestige of doubt as to Mary's title to rule, Philip's position as king consort or the position of any child of the marriage. It declared that any person who 'by preaching, express words or sayings, shall maliciously, advisedly and directly say, publish, declare, maintain or hold opinion' to the contrary was to be deprived of his goods and lands for a first offence and deemed guilty of high treason for a second. Further, to compass or imagine the death of Philip was now also to constitute high treason.[10]

---

6 Statutes of the Realm 1 Mary, st 3, c 1. For a detailed study of the political background, see Loades, *ibid*, pp 72–85. In addition, and also in order to keep Philip in check, he was never granted any lands or revenues in England, and so remained financially dependent on his wife.

7 *Calendar of Letters, Despatches and State Papers Relating to the Negotiations between England and Spain 1485–1558*, Vol XII, 1900, HMSO, p 15.

8 Close kinship with Philip II was particularly hazardous, since his mother and first wife had already died in childbirth, and his third wife was to follow them.

9 Elizabeth spent a period in the Tower after the failure of Wyatt's Rebellion and was currently under house arrest. Loades suggests that Mary herself was inclined to favour Margaret Douglas, Countess of Lennox, the only child of Margaret Tudor by her second marriage, despite Henry VIII's exclusion of Margaret's issue from the succession. See Loades, *op cit*, p 78.

10 On this provision of the 1555 Act turned the view of Sir Matthew Hale, accepted by legal scholars almost to the present day, that the provisions of the Statute of Treasons dealing with 'compassing or imagining' the death of a queen consort did not extend to the husband of a queen regnant. This assumption is of doubtful validity. See MJ Gunn and AE Lyon, 'Compassing the death of the Queen's consort; would it be high treason?' (1998) Nottingham Law Journal 34.

In the event, Mary's pregnancy proved to be false, as became clear by July 1555. Already she had drifted away from her earlier conciliatory approach to religion, which may have been based on an assumption that as there had been much opposition to the break with Rome, the Dissolution of the Monasteries and the more directly Protestant changes enacted under Edward VI, even to the extent of armed rebellion, a populace freed from coercion would naturally turn again to Rome. Before the end of 1553, Mary abandoned the title of Supreme Head of the Church, and an Act of the 1555 parliament repealed the religious legislation enacted under Edward VI. However, the repeal was passed only in the teeth of stiff opposition in parliament.[11] At the same time, under the auspices of the new Archbishop of Canterbury and papal legate, Reginald, Cardinal Pole, Catholic religious practices were largely restored, the episcopate was purged of Protestants and there was piecemeal re-establishment of monastic houses.

However, just as religious conservatives had resisted the changes imposed under Mary's father and half-brother, so the radicals resisted Mary's attempts to turn England back to Rome. Underground Protestant groups emerged in London, the south-east and Suffolk, and governmental attitudes became more hard-line. Where only two persons had burned for heresy under Edward VI, 287 went to the stake between February 1555 and November 1558.

Religious intransigence was not the only problem faced by Mary's government from 1555. Except in religious matters, the government lacked cohesion, particularly after Philip of Spain departed from England in August 1555. No one emerged as a dominant figure on the Privy Council, as had happened under Mary's father and brother. A considerable debt was left over from their reigns and this increased steadily, not least because of the restoration to the church of its former revenues. To make matters worse, the harvests of 1555 and 1556 failed, the economic crisis consequent on the decline of the cloth trade continued, and there was an epidemic of influenza in 1557–58 which, it has been suggested, was severe enough to reduce the population by up to 5%.[12]

Under the influence of Philip II, England was drawn into the long-running imperial war with France. This resulted not only in still greater imbalance between governmental income and expenditure, but, in January 1558, in the loss of Calais, England's last possession on the European mainland, largely as a consequence of the running down of its garrison as an economy measure. This defeat was a severe blow in the military sphere and to English prestige abroad, but within a few months, it must have become apparent that the reign was approaching its end. Philip returned to England for four months in March 1557 and, once again, Mary believed herself to be pregnant. By the spring of 1558, as three years earlier, it was clear that this was not the case. Indeed, it has been suggested that what the queen believed were signs of pregnancy were the consequences of advanced ovarian cancer. It was now clear that not only would there be no issue of her marriage, but that Mary could not be expected to live much longer. It appears from Mary's failure to nominate another heir if nothing else that even she now accepted that Elizabeth must succeed her, which she did, without opposition, when Mary died on 17 November 1558, aged 42.

---

11 J Guy, *Tudor England*, 1990, OUP, pp 234–35.
12 See P Williams, *The Later Tudors: England 1547–1603*, New Oxford History of England, 1995, Clarendon, p 132.

12.3   ELIZABETH I 1558–1603

The reign of England's second queen regnant has its own place in national myth, that of England's golden age of prosperity, learning and military success, the deeds of national heroes and the earlier plays of William Shakespeare. England's overseas power developed further, partly through the peaceful activities of such bodies as the Muscovy Company, whose ships had reached the port of Archangel on the White Sea in 1554, and later through the more bellicose exploits of Francis Drake, John Hawkins and others, who made England a serious maritime rival to Spain. Such was the pervasive power of this myth that the accession of the present Queen in February 1952 was hailed as the dawn of a 'new Elizabethan age'.

In part, this myth developed because Elizabeth was, like her father, a larger-than-life figure, and was also well able to use her formidable intellect, the autocratic element in her nature and her particular brand of charm to keep a large number of highly capable men competing to give effect to her will. In particular, she was an expert procrastinator, not least in relation to the attempts of her ministers to secure her a suitable marriage and, when it became clear that she would never marry and would have no issue, to name an heir.[13] Her reign coincided with the greatest years of several distinguished royal servants, who became central figures in her government and were able to a very considerable extent to deal with the problems the new queen had inherited from her predecessors. The most notable was William Cecil, Lord Burghley, Secretary from the immediate aftermath of Elizabeth's accession until his death in 1598. Cecil rose to prominence under Edward VI as a member of Somerset's entourage and spent a period as Secretary during Northumberland's domination of government, but, as a Protestant, retired from royal service following Mary's accession. It is no coincidence that the difficult years of Elizabeth's reign in the 1590s matched the decline in Cecil's health and powers. To Elizabeth, however, must go credit for identifying such men and, from the outset of her reign, fostering a system in which they could flourish to their full potential.

12.3.1 Religion

Elizabeth was Protestant in sentiment, but at this early stage of her reign, she professed to be more concerned with issues of belief than with forms of worship. The changes enacted by Elizabeth's first parliament showed some spirit of compromise in religious matters, but this should not be pushed too far. The Act of Supremacy 1559 rejected papal authority, but since in Protestant doctrine only Christ could be Head of the Church, the monarch was henceforth Supreme Governor of the Church rather than Supreme Head, and so obtained power from Christ and exercised that power in the name of Christ.

The Act of Uniformity 1559 imposed the 1552 Prayer Book, more radical than that of 1549, though the 1549 formula was restored for the administration of the bread and wine of communion, which allowed an implication that Christ was present in the elements in some spiritual sense, rather than communion being commemorative only,

---

13   To an even greater extent than Mary, Elizabeth, as the last surviving child of Henry VIII, had no obvious heir and the need to secure the succession was the principal reason why her advisors were so concerned to see her marry.

as had been the case in the 1552 service.[14] The use of any other rite was forbidden, and absence from services conducted under the new liturgy was made punishable by a fine of 1s per week.

First Fruits and Tenths, which had been re-granted to the papacy in 1555, were restored to the crown, and new provisions increased crown control over episcopal lands during the vacancy of sees. Since all the bishops but one refused to accept royal supremacy over the church, the episcopate was purged in the course of 1559 and the consequent vacancies were gradually filled over the next two years, mostly by men originally appointed under Edward VI who had spent Mary's reign in exile or in retirement. Though Elizabeth was personally hostile to clerical marriage, the clergy were once more permitted to marry.

The major elements of this 'Elizabethan settlement' have remained in place to the present day, in particular the role of the monarch as Supreme Governor and a doctrinal tradition which is neither fully Catholic nor wholly Protestant. However, religious strife was to continue for many more years. Catholicism became a focus for persecution later in the reign, though largely for political rather than doctrinal reasons, and it was not until 1829 that the disabilities imposed on Catholics from this time on grounds of their supposed division of loyalties between monarch and Pope were finally removed.

12.3.2 Government

In the practice of government, the reign was not one of innovation, but rather one of success in refining and operating a system which was already established.[15] It has already been noted that the Privy Council was a development of the final years of Henry VIII; this became a more cohesive and effective body under Elizabeth, though this was as much due to the personalities and abilities of its members as to deliberate policy. The Secretary continued to be the senior minister. He organised the Council and acted as the link between Council and monarch in his role of presenting the advice of the Council to the queen, who attended its meetings only rarely. The role of the Lord Chancellor was now confined to the legal sphere.

The two main functions of the Council were to discuss matters of state and to present advice to the queen on the basis of those discussions. Matters of state at this time extended to a very wide range of business, from the obvious and weighty, such as foreign policy and military strategy, to apparently trivial concerns of individuals, brought to the attention of the Council by the traditional practice of petitioning the monarch. What gave the Council much of its power was its control of finance, the monarch having ceased to exercise personal supervision in this sphere. It also had a quasi-judicial role, since parties to litigation frequently petitioned it for justice against their opponents. As stated in Chapter 10, such petitions were generally passed to other bodies, such as the emerging Court of Chancery, but this 'clearing house'

14 The 1549 formula, used again in the Book of Common Prayer of 1662, was 'The body of our Lord Jesus Christ which was given for thee, preserve thy body and soul unto everlasting life', that of 1552, 'Take and eat this, in remembrance that Christ died for thee, and feed on Him in thy heart by faith, with thanksgiving'. The recent Alternative Service Book attempted to be all things to all worshippers by using both, albeit at different points in the service.
15 For a convenient summary of the governmental apparatus of the period, see Williams, *op cit*, pp 133–52.

function remained a significant one, since it determined not only the forum of the proceedings, but the extent to which justice could be obtained.

12.3.3 Parliament

By the 1560s, it was accepted that matters of high constitutional importance could only properly be dealt with through the mechanism of a parliamentary statute. Such matters included the raising of revenue by the crown and title to the throne itself. Further, it was also accepted that one statute could only be validly repealed or amended by another.

However, parliament was still in no sense a separate entity from the monarch. Rather, as is still formally the case today, the monarch, lords and commons formed for this purpose a single entity, but the monarch was very much the senior member of the triarchy. The monarch had the sole power to summon, prorogue or dissolve parliament, so that it met only when the monarch required legislation of a type only available through parliament. Further, legislation could only become law by the assent of the monarch, so that although parliament might seek to oppose the monarch's will, it could not pass legislation over implacable royal opposition. In the first seven of the 13 parliaments of her reign, Elizabeth I refused assent to no fewer than 34 Bills. When conflict occurred between the monarch and the two houses, it was normally resolved by some form of compromise, as has been seen in relation to some of the crucial legislation on religious matters.

A major recent development was the extension in the scope of parliament's authority in the 1530s. Previously, a fiction was maintained that statutes were merely declaratory and confirmatory of existing law, but the religious changes imposed by Henry VIII could in no sense be passed off in this fashion, so that from then on, there was no effective limitation on the scope of parliamentary legislation.[16]

Parliament's procedures

Though in medieval times, parliaments had met most frequently at Westminster, from time to time sessions took place elsewhere. After 1485, however, parliaments almost always sat at Westminster, within the vast and sprawling royal palace itself. Although the composition of the commons remained unaltered, that of the lords was reduced after 1536 by the removal of the mitred abbots, who were not replaced by any other group.

Evidence of parliament's procedures is more available during the Tudor period than earlier, and the roots can be seen of many of the practices still found today. Then, as now and earlier, parliament dealt with public and private Bills. The former, introduced by the crown or by ministers, broadly concerned matters of national importance, the latter matters concerning specific individuals and localities. The dividing line between the two was by no means clear. A Bill could be introduced in either house and, contrary to the modern position, there was then no particular principle that Bills on certain matters could only properly be introduced in one house rather than the other.

---

16 Guy, *op cit*, p 369.

Then as now, Bills usually had three readings. The first simply informed the house of the purpose of the Bill, by a reading of what is now the long title. The second involved debate on the issue itself and might be followed by a committee stage, in which the terms of the Bill were considered in detail and amendments made. The Bill was then presented to the house at a third reading before being passed to the other house, where the stages were repeated. At the end of the session, the Bill, along with others passed in that session, was presented to the monarch, who might or might not assent to it.

The roots of the historic privileges of parliament and its individual members can also be seen in this period, although they were to emerge more clearly and to be of greater effect in the following century, when there was open conflict between crown and parliament. Members had immunity from arrest in civil matters; this was a much more valuable privilege then than now, since it covered arrest for debt, which was commonplace and could be used as a means of putting pressure on an individual. There was no definite protection as against the crown, although members claimed that their freedom of speech, granted explicitly by Henry VIII in 1523, extended to immunity from arrest by the crown in relation to words uttered in parliament. However, the crown itself interpreted this freedom much more strictly, claiming that it extended only to debate on matters introduced into parliament by the crown, or where debate was explicitly permitted, proclaiming that there was a boundary between liberty and licence. However, any such boundary had yet to be defined.

12.3.4 Mary Queen of Scots

Elizabeth established her personal authority and developed her skills in operating the governmental system of her day within a short time of her accession. The same cannot be said of her cousin and contemporary, Mary Queen of Scots.

Mary is another monarch whose reputation has been gravely distorted. She is portrayed in historical myth as a high-minded, noble, devout and romantic figure, feloniously sent to a martyr's death by a jealous Elizabeth who, with her advisors, deliberately engineered the conspiracy for which Mary was condemned and executed. Inevitably, there are certain truths in this myth, but for all that, Mary was quite unfitted to rule so turbulent a kingdom as Scotland.

Such was the instability of Mary's throne in her early years that she was sent to France at the age of five for safety as well as education, her mother, Mary of Guise, remaining in Scotland to act as her regent. Under Mary of Guise, a member of a great French family with close ties to the Valois monarchy, the traditional pro-French stamp of Scottish government became more marked. At the same time, religious discord emerged. Mary of Guise stood for traditional Catholicism, whilst Calvinist Protestantism gained considerable ground among the nobility. The religious conflict had an important political aspect, since the accession of Elizabeth in England at the end of 1558 raised the possibility of the Scottish Protestants entering into an alliance with England against the French.

In July 1559, Henry II of France died from injuries received in a tournament. His 15 year old heir, Francis II, now married Mary, to whom he had been betrothed in childhood. Francis, always in poor health, died in December 1560, but his brief reign further increased French influence in Scotland, since the powers behind his throne were two brothers of Mary of Guise. As early as August 1559, they began sending French troops to Scotland.

Even at this early stage in Elizabeth's reign, Mary's claim to the English throne was seen as a danger to her security. Margaret Tudor was Henry VIII's elder daughter and Mary was the daughter of Margaret's son by her first marriage; there was no doubt as to Mary's legitimacy or her father's. An English invasion of Scotland early in 1560 ended in the Treaty of Edinburgh of 6 July, under which both the French and English agreed to withdraw their forces, and assurances were given by the Protestant party, now without internal rivals since Mary of Guise's death a month earlier, that Mary would recognise Elizabeth's title to the English throne and allow freedom of worship to Scottish Protestants. The Protestant church was established by an Act of the Scottish parliament in August, although the great bulk of the population remained Catholic.

Mary returned to Scotland in August 1561, evading English attempts to take her captive at sea, and until 1565 was largely content to rule by the advice of her bastard half-brother, James Stewart, created Earl of Moray in 1562. However, and contrary to the terms of the Treaty of Edinburgh, Mary continued to protest a claim to the English crown, so remaining a thorn in Elizabeth's side. In particular, Elizabeth was concerned to prevent her from marrying a mutual cousin, Henry Stuart, Lord Darnley, son of Matthew Stuart, Earl of Lennox, and Margaret Douglas, granddaughter of Henry VII (via Margaret Tudor's second marriage).

Like Elizabeth, Mary had no close legitimate relations on her father's side. Her heirs were distant cousins descended from a daughter of James II. It was therefore important that she remarry and produce issue, though once more, there were difficulties in identifying a suitable bridegroom for a queen regnant. Darnley was a descendant of James II and so among Mary's heirs, so that there were dynastic advantages to the marriage, but the match was bound to arouse jealousies among the proud and turbulent Scottish nobility. He was, nominally, a Catholic. To Mary, this was an advantage, but in fact, it only exacerbated the religious divisions in Scotland. Mary seems to have been blind to the disadvantages. She was infatuated with Darnley, although they had never met.[17]

Crucially, Darnley had his own claim to the English throne and, as an English subject, born in Yorkshire, was arguably not disbarred from the succession by the terms of Henry VIII's will. Elizabeth therefore expended considerable energy in attempting to neutralise the danger by keeping Darnley under house arrest in England and by brokering a marriage for Mary with her own favourite, Robert Dudley, Earl of Leicester.

Such intriguing came to naught and, by marrying Darnley on 29 July 1565, Mary succeeded in alienating not only Elizabeth, but also the Protestant lords with whom she had previously co-existed in reasonable amity. She broke off relations with Moray, attempted to rule alone and, from then, her decline was rapid. Moray rebelled and, following military failure, fled to England. At the same time, and literally after a brief honeymoon period, Mary and Darnley became irredeemably alienated. By his marriage, Darnley become king consort, but he pressed Mary to grant him the crown

---

17 This infatuation seems to have been based on reports of Darnley's rather effeminate good looks and, in particular, his height. Mary was six feet tall at a time when the average height of adults of both sexes was less than that of today. Darnley stood several inches taller.

matrimonial, and so title to the crown in his own right in the event of Mary's death. Mary was not prepared to agree. Melodrama followed.

Mary came increasingly to rely on certain members of her household in her uncertain attempts to govern, notably her Italian favourite, David Rizzio. This enraged the increasingly unstable Darnley who, believing the pair to be lovers, entered into an alliance with the remaining Protestant lords, also violently opposed to Rizzio, which led to Rizzio's savage murder in Mary's presence on 9 March 1566. The Protestants under Moray, now returned from exile, regained control. Temporarily, matters appeared to calm down, but Mary's position, strengthened in the short term by the birth of her son on 19 June, was soon irredeemably compromised.

Mary and Darnley were now hopelessly estranged and it seems likely that Mary wished to have revenge for Darnley's role in the murder of Rizzio. Though responsibility for Darnley's death has never been established, all contemporaries blamed the queen and her new paramour, James Hepburn, 4th Earl of Bothwell. He was a far more masculine and decisive figure than the petulant Darnley and his obvious virility seems to have been a major attraction in Mary's eyes. Primarily, however, Bothwell was an unscrupulous and violent ruffian, who sought to marry Mary as a means to power.

By the beginning of 1567, Darnley, not yet 21, was in poor health, possibly as a result of syphilis, and Mary arranged for him to spend a period of recuperation in a small house called Kirk o' Field, just outside the city walls of Edinburgh. For a brief period, they appear to have been on friendly terms, but in the early hours of 10 February 1567, the house was reduced to rubble by a huge explosion. The bodies of Darnley and his valet were found in the garden, strangled. Mary was immediately suspected, along with Bothwell, who was tried for the murder on 12 April and acquitted, the proceedings having all too clearly been rigged.

Suspicion of the lovers was only increased by their marriage, which took place by Protestant rites on 3 June. The customary view among recent historians, at least those sympathetic to Mary, is that Bothwell abducted Mary and then raped her, so making it impossible for her to refuse to marry him, but contemporary opinion condemned her to a far greater extent than it did her new husband.

The marriage was in any case destined to be short-lived. Bothwell was hated by both Protestant and Catholic lords, and an alliance emerged of 'confederate lords', who bound themselves to 'rescue' Mary from him and to govern on her behalf. An armed confrontation took place on 15 June, at which Mary's army, commanded by Bothwell, refused to fight. Mary was captured and forced to abdicate in favour of her son. She was then consigned to the island fortress of Loch Leven, and on 22 August, Moray, once more holding the reins of power, was formally created regent for the infant James VI.

On 2 May 1568, Mary escaped from Loch Leven, assisted by a 16 year old page who had fallen under her spell, but any hopes she had of regaining the throne were dashed 11 days later when the army raised on her behalf was crushingly defeated by Moray's forces at Langside. The former queen then fled to England, hoping for military aid, but in doing so, threw herself out of the frying pan and into the fire. After a period of uncertainty, she moved from being a person in protective custody to a prisoner, following an abortive conspiracy in her favour in 1569, headed by the Percy Earl of Northumberland and the Neville Earl of Westmorland and remembered as the

Northern Rising, effectively the last expression of the traditional distrust of the old northern nobility for a southern-dominated monarchy.

The rising began in November, the Earls claiming to support true religion and the removal of the queen's false councillors. Having had the Latin mass celebrated in Durham Cathedral, they marched south with a force of some 1,800 cavalry and 4,000 infantry, intending to release Mary, then held at Tutbury, Staffordshire, and to obtain her marriage to a Catholic and her recognition as Elizabeth's heir. The rising was potentially serious, not least because the government had only some 400 cavalry in the whole of northern England, but it soon fizzled out, largely because the Earls were unable to pay their troops. As soon as the rising started, Mary was removed to Coventry, in a staunchly Protestant area, where she was strongly guarded and there was no real hope of releasing her. Having marched as far as Selby, which they reached on 23 November, the Earls withdrew northwards, pursued by a government army of 28,000, and finally fled into Scotland.

The rising, and a further short-lived rebellion by Lord Dacre, head of another of the leading northern families, ended the traditional independence of the north from royal control. Though the subsequent attainder against Northumberland, who was handed over to the English by the Scots in August 1570 and was beheaded at York, was soon reversed, his successor was forbidden to live in the north, and the power of the Percies was never restored. Westmorland and Dacre were similarly attainted and the power of their respective families was broken permanently. Though a Council of the North remained as an instrument of royal authority, its functions dwindled and became confined solely to the judicial sphere.

Elizabeth's security improved only temporarily. On 25 January 1570, the Earl of Moray, whose policy had been relatively favourable towards England, if only because he had no desire for Mary's return, was murdered, and a pro-Mary faction briefly gained power. On 25 February, Pope Pius V published the Bull *Regnans in Excelsis*, which excommunicated Elizabeth, deposed her as queen, absolved Catholics from allegiance to her and anathematised all those persons who continued to support her. This was a most serious development, since it licensed both the Catholic powers and Elizabeth's own subjects to pursue a 'holy' war against her, encouraged Mary's supporters in any attempt to place her on the English throne and sought to subvert the loyalty of Elizabeth's numerous Catholic subjects. It was this, rather than any doctrinal issue, that led to the active persecution of Catholics which is a feature of Elizabeth's reign after this date.

A further immediate result was a new Treason Act, which restored the position created by the 1534 Act by making the mere utterance of words against Elizabeth and her title to the crown treasonous. By this Act, it became high treason, punishable by the traditional gruesome penalties, to publish, write or say that she was not the lawful Queen of England or that she was a heretic, infidel, schismatic, tyrant or usurper. Further, it was now treasonable to bring a papal bull into the kingdom.

In the event, the danger of Mary's restoration in Scotland soon subsided. With the assistance of an English army, the Protestant lords returned to power, though the new regent, Matthew Stuart, Earl of Lennox, father of the unlamented Darnley and so grandfather of the young James VI, lasted only a year before he was murdered in his turn. From the end of 1572, the Catholic magnates in Scotland gradually withdrew their support for Mary, and in February 1573, the majority accepted the so called Pacification of Perth, by which they recognised James as king and the Protestant Earl of Morton as regent. However, plotting on Mary's behalf by Englishmen with support from continental Europe had only just begun.

Roberto Ridolfi, a Florentine banker who acted as a papal agent, made contact first with John Leslie, Bishop of Ross, Mary's representative in London, early in 1571, outlining a plot for an invasion of England by Spanish troops under the Duke of Alba, which would place Mary on the English throne, along with the 4th Duke of Norfolk as her husband. Norfolk allowed himself to be persuaded to join the plot. Philip of Spain promised to provide both Alba and the necessary troops, who would invade from the Netherlands while Norfolk incited a rising by English Catholics against Elizabeth. However, before long, word of the conspiracy reached Elizabeth's Secretary, William Cecil. The Bishop of Ross was arrested on 24 October, despite having diplomatic immunity. He broke under interrogation and his evidence condemned both Mary and Norfolk.

Norfolk, who had already been degraded from the Order of the Garter for his relatively peripheral role in the events of 1569, was duly attainted and beheaded. What was to be done with Mary posed a more difficult problem, not only for the obvious political reasons – those holding power in Scotland might not have desired Mary's return, but would certainly not welcome her trial for treason against the English Crown, and condemnation would swiftly follow from the Catholic powers – but also because of the legal difficulty that Mary was a foreign monarch and so was not a subject of Elizabeth I in any event.

By this time, the common law had interpolated into the original Statute of Treasons of 1351–52 a requirement that a person must owe 'allegiance' to the English monarch before he could be guilty of high treason. Allegiance was not defined, but it was accepted without argument that it was owed by an English subject as a necessary corollary of the protection he was entitled to from the English Crown. In addition, under Henry VIII, it was held by the courts that an 'alien' resident in England owed such allegiance during his residence, since he was also entitled to such protection.

It might be argued that as Elizabeth's guest in England (theoretically at least, she was not a prisoner), Mary was a resident alien and so owed allegiance, but this course seems not to have been suggested. The 1572 parliament, having formally been informed of Mary's misdeeds – the murder of Darnley as well as her involvement in plots against Elizabeth – demanded her execution along with Norfolk. A joint committee of lords and commons was set up and reported on 19 May with two alternative proposals. The majority favoured Mary's condemnation via a Bill of Attainder. Alternatively, an Act could be passed barring her from the English succession. Conflict between the queen and parliament now ensued. Two draft Bills were produced, but Elizabeth allowed only that concerning the succession to be considered. Both houses then petitioned for Mary to be brought to trial, a petition which was refused. Eventually, a divided parliament passed the succession Bill, but Elizabeth then refused her assent. Presumably, she hoped that the problem of Mary would go away. For a time, indeed, it did.

Relations between England and Scotland remained relatively peaceful for the remainder of the 1570s, those who governed on behalf of James VI concentrating attention on domestic affairs. This position changed temporarily in late 1579, inaugurating yet another period of instability before in November 1585, James, now 19 and beginning to rule in his own right, accepted a compact with England and a pension from Elizabeth. For her part, up to around 1582, Mary was involved only to a limited degree in plotting, which was itself limited to attempts to secure her freedom.

However, in 1582, Sir Francis Walsingham, a leading figure in government and who may be regarded as head of the first effective English secret service, began to uncover a new and serious plot orchestrated by the Spanish ambassador, Don Bernardino de Mendoza, by which Mary's cousin, the Duke of Guise, would invade England with a French army and the backing of Philip II and the Pope, in order to place Mary on the throne. The go-between from Mendoza to Mary was an English Catholic gentleman, Francis Throckmorton, whose name is usually given to the conspiracy. The Throckmorton Plot broke down rapidly after Throckmorton's arrest in November 1583, but from then on, the noose began to tighten around Mary, as concern grew about the possibility of a foreign invasion on her behalf. The terms of the Bull *Regnans in Excelsis* had not been forgotten.

Mary's confinement, hitherto comparatively lenient, became much closer. At the same time, Cecil, now Lord Burghley, and Walsingham sought to make provision for the government of England in the event of Elizabeth's murder by persons acting on behalf of Mary. Early in 1585, Burghley drafted proposals to cover this eventuality, under which all officers of state would continue in post, a Great Council would be created to assume the powers of the crown during the interregnum, and a parliament would be summoned to choose Elizabeth's successor. These proposals are extremely interesting, not least because it was assumed that parliament was the appropriate organ for the selection of a new monarch – the succession in 1585 was no clearer than it had been in 1558 – but due to opposition from the queen herself, they were not proceeded with.

In October 1584, a 'Bond of Association' had been circulated by Burghley and Walsingham, which bound its signatories to pursue to the death anyone seeking to gain the English throne by harming the queen, and specifically debarred from the succession any person who sought to gain the throne by attempts on the life of the queen, or on whose behalf such attempts were made. Though Mary was not named, she was clearly the target. When the prorogued parliament, most of whose members were signatories to the Bond of Association, re-assembled in February 1585, a Bill based on the Bond was introduced, although it specifically exempted James VI from the effect of any penalties that might be imposed on his mother. In addition, a separate measure, seemingly prompted by the presence of Jesuit priests among the members of the Throckmorton Plot, provided that any Jesuit or Catholic priest who failed to leave England within 40 days of the statute taking effect should be guilty of high treason, and any person who aided such persons guilty of felony.

In this period, relations between England and Spain also deteriorated sharply, mainly due to the long-drawn-out war pursued by Spain against the Dutch, who, as Protestants, had English support and an intermittent degree of military aid. This was the era of the privateering activities of Drake, Hawkins and others, particularly on the 'Spanish Main', the Caribbean and the area of the Pacific Ocean adjacent to the Spanish possessions in Central America. At the same time, there was considerable instability in France following the death in 1584 of the Duke of Anjou, heir to his childless brother, Henry III. The French king's degeneracy ensured that he had not long to live[18] and the new heir to this last of the Valois was a distant cousin, Henry de

---

18   Though when he did die, in 1589, it was by assassination.

Bourbon, King of Navarre and by religion a Huguenot. The Catholic faction at the French court formed an alliance with Philip of Spain, and in July 1585 persuaded Henry III to withdraw all legal protection from the Huguenots and exclude Henry of Navarre from the succession. Navarre appealed for help and the English responded with financial aid in order to stave off the danger of Spanish domination of France.

It was against this background that the final episodes in the melodrama of Mary Queen of Scots were played out. By the beginning of 1586, Walsingham's intelligence service had discovered an embryonic conspiracy involving Mary and the French ambassador. Using methods often employed since, Walsingham's men acted as *agents provocateurs* in relation to the scheming of a young Catholic, Anthony Babington, who was drawn into the plot. They arranged for letters between Mary and the conspirators to be smuggled in and out of the house at Chartley, Staffordshire, where Mary was then held, in a beer barrel, the brewer acting as a double agent. When Babington wrote to Mary offering to assassinate Elizabeth, and Mary replied approving the plan, the trap was sprung.

It is not entirely clear how much of the evidence used to bring about Mary's condemnation for treason under the terms of the 1585 Act, itself passed to deal with her alone, was genuine in the sense of coming unforced from Mary, her household and their co-conspirators, and how much arose from the scheming of Walsingham and his intelligence agents, together with the confession extracted from Babington under torture. In September, her trial was begun by a commission of 40, which included all Privy Councillors.

Mary denied having written the crucial letter approving the assassination plan, but among the letters intercepted by Walsingham's agents were two to Mendoza, the former Spanish ambassador involved in the Throckmorton Plot. One set out Mary's intention to cede her rights of succession to the English throne to Philip II, the other promised her support for an expected Spanish invasion of England. A further letter asked an English plotter to impress upon Philip II the need for urgency in his invasion plans. Faced with this evidence, Mary's condemnation was inevitable.

Parliament opened on 29 October, the Lord Chancellor emphasising that the main purpose of summoning this parliament was in order that the queen could receive the advice of both houses concerning Mary. Having been formally informed of the extent and nature of the Babington Plot, both houses petitioned Elizabeth for Mary's execution in accordance with the commission's verdict. Once more, Elizabeth procrastinated, though whether she was moved by any personal affection for Mary is a very moot point. Although they were second cousins, she had taken care throughout Mary's captivity that they should never meet. In any case, as in 1571–72, there were good political reasons for her to shrink from the execution of her fellow monarch. Initially, Elizabeth rejected the petition, along with a second from the commons, though she allowed the sentence against Mary to be proclaimed in public on 4 December.

Elizabeth then procrastinated again over the issuing of the death warrant, which she finally signed on 1 February 1587. Machinations then followed which allowed Elizabeth to claim that she had not in fact authorised the despatch of the warrant to Fotheringay, and to blame Burghley, Walsingham and, in particular, Sir William Davison, the junior of the two Secretaries of State, for the execution when it took place a week later. Mary died with exemplary dignity and in a fashion which ensured that she was regarded by many as a martyr. The condemnation of the Catholic powers inevitably followed, together with, in the following year, the long-expected attempt at a Spanish invasion – the Spanish Armada.

What can be said in summary about the process against Mary Queen of Scots from the constitutional standpoint? Here, as in the well-established law of attainder, an Act of Parliament was passed in order to secure the condemnation of a specific individual in respect of actions which would not be treasonable under ordinary law, in Mary's case because in all probability she did not owe allegiance to the English Crown. However, where Acts of Attainder were passed in respect of a named individual and actions which had already taken place, the Act of 1585, under which Mary was condemned, did not refer to her by name, and created a sword of Damocles over her in respect of any future conspiracies in which she might be involved.

Relations with Scotland were, inevitably, strained for a time, though James VI and his government did no more than rail against Elizabeth and her ministers in writing. Though Elizabeth still shrank from naming a successor, more and more it was tacitly accepted that James would be the next monarch. Though he was the only realistic candidate,[19] and a Protestant who had established stable rule in Scotland for the first time in many years, there were arguments that he, as a descendant of Margaret Tudor, was debarred from the English succession by Henry VIII's will. Robert Cecil, Burghley's second son, who had now taken over the reins of government, made his preparations, sending James a draft of the proclamation to be read by the heralds on his accession. As Elizabeth entered into her final illness in March 1603, her godson, Robert Carey, had fast horses placed at intervals on the road from London to Edinburgh. Immediately after Elizabeth's death in the early hours of 24 March 1603, and bearing a ring from her finger, Carey set out for Scotland without waiting for the Privy Council formally to approve James as the new monarch.

In the event, there was no effective opposition to the union of the Crowns of England and Scotland, prefigured over many centuries, which now took place. James's accession to the English throne as James I was duly proclaimed before noon on 24 March, and the new king was welcomed with enthusiasm as he travelled south in a leisurely fashion to take possession of his kingdom.

---

19 The alternative candidates were the Infanta Isabella of Spain, a descendant of John of Gaunt, who as a daughter of Philip II was unacceptable to the English, and Arbella Stewart, daughter of Lord Darnley's younger brother.

CHAPTER 13

THE GENESIS OF CIVIL WAR 1603–42

13.1   INTRODUCTION

The 17th century is unique in British history. Not only was there war for control of the government, but over the very nature of the constitution. Though it was not until the late 1630s that armed conflict broke out, the seeds of war were sown very much earlier. The causes of the civil wars, which began in Scotland in 1638 and encompassed the three kingdoms from 1642 to 1648, the experiment with republican government from 1649 to 1660 and the second revolution of 1688–89, were both long and short term, structural and personal. The 17th century is the period in which the constitutional system, which had developed haphazardly over the centuries, was tested to destruction. However, it was not superseded in its entirety, but modified to a relatively limited extent, then allowed to continue its development by the traditional processes of evolution.

Monarchs continued to be active rulers, so that the political and constitutional history of the period is intimately bound up with the personalities and capabilities of the six monarchs of the Stuart dynasty who occupied the thrones of the three kingdoms from 1603 to 1714.[1] Their abilities formed a major influence over events and at times proved crucial in determining whether the constitutional system endured or collapsed. Ultimately, it was the peculiar obduracy of Charles I and James II in the face of opposition which dictated the form taken by the constitutional crises of the time.

Monarchs in the later medieval and Tudor periods, though accorded and according themselves semi-sacred status – the peculiar mystique of an anointed king – had largely recognised the realities of their position. To a greater or lesser extent, they were prepared to rule in co-operation with Parliament, by accepting that certain legislation could only be obtained through Parliament and being prepared to compromise with Parliament where expedient. Charles I and James II followed James I in the philosophy of the Divine Right of Kings, but without his recognition of its essential corollary that a king must rule justly and in accordance with the law. They were not prepared to cede any role to Parliament other than to give effect to the king's will. Conflict with Parliament in their reigns, coinciding with inflammatory political and philosophical concepts which took hold among various segments of the populace, and a particular social and religious context, led to the civil wars of 1640–49, the Commonwealth of 1649–60 and the Revolution of 1688.

In this period, the crucial issues of which areas of government and policy were the prerogatives of the king alone and which were properly dealt with only by the King in Parliament were, quite literally, fought over, and for the only time in English history, a republican form of government temporarily replaced monarchy. Finally, the Revolution Settlement of 1689 vested sovereignty not in the king alone, but in the King in Parliament, the balance of power lying not with the king, but with the two Houses. This established the concept of parliamentary sovereignty which,

---

1   Though Mary II was joint sovereign with William III, she never took any active role in government.

theoretically at least, remains the keystone of the unwritten British constitution more than 300 years later.

13.2   JAMES VI AND I

James I suffers in reputation from following the larger-than-life Elizabeth I. His reign frequently appears as a lacklustre interlude between the triumphs of her reign and the dramatic events of his son's. Yet the constitutional issues at the centre of the later conflicts first emerged in precise forms under James I and were the subject of a number of landmark cases in the law courts, as well as celebrated disputes between Crown and Parliament.[2] Further, his accession created a union of crowns between England and Scotland, leading to the first moves towards political union; the 'plantation' of Ulster, which began under James, added a further element to the volatile brew of the populace and politics of Ireland.

James was perhaps the most intellectually gifted monarch ever to sit on a British throne and, from the middle of the 1580s, had imposed stable government on the turbulent realm of Scotland, whose political institutions were much less developed than those of England and where success largely depended on a monarch's ability to handle the greater nobles. He was prepared to accept that the absolute power of kings applied only in uncivilised societies and that power in an advanced society such as England was regulated by law. He had also learned caution and an ability to evade outright confrontation. However, certain facets of James's personality and political philosophy did not win him the acclaim of his new subjects. In particular, though his own beliefs were Calvinist, as were those of most of his subjects,[3] he was, in a deeply intolerant age, inclined temperamentally and intellectually towards religious toleration. This engendered enormous suspicion among Protestants, while failing to satisfy Catholics, who hoped for much more from him than he was prepared to give.[4]

13.2.1 Tensions in government

James inherited the political generation of the last years of Elizabeth I, in particular, Robert Cecil, who remained the senior Secretary of State until his death in 1612. However, he also inherited the problems of Elizabeth's last years. Though the Spanish war was concluded in 1604, relations with Spain, the leading Catholic power in Europe, were a major issue in foreign policy. More serious yet was the Crown's financial position. By 1603, Crown debt had reached £400,000 and continued to rise,

---

2   It is at this time that the Crown emerges as an institution separate from the person of the sovereign, hence my use of 'Crown' rather than 'crown' to denote this.

3   Calvinism is characterised by belief in predestination, that after death an individual's fate is pre-ordained. Salvation owes nothing to personal piety or works, but is dependent entirely on the Grace of Jesus Christ, though the 'Elect' manifest themselves on earth by their godly lives. Calvinism also postulates a perpetual struggle between Christ and Antichrist, and in the 17th century, the Pope in particular and the Catholic Church in general were regarded as manifestations of Antichrist, which goes far to explain the anti-Catholic vehemence characteristic of the time.

4   Disappointment among Catholics at James's failure to deliver what they believed to be their due led to the Gunpowder Plot, one of the two or three best-remembered episodes of English history, in which a small group of extremist Catholics planned to blow up Parliament during the State Opening scheduled for 5 November 1605.

reaching £726,000 in 1617. This problem was exacerbated by James's extravagance and generosity towards his favourites, but had a number of long term causes.

Traditionally, a considerable proportion of Crown income came from the land which remained directly in the hands of the Crown (the Crown Estates). However, large amounts of land had been sold off for short term gain since the 1530s. Not only was there a sharp reduction in revenue, but the real value of these revenues was much eroded by inflation. A second major source of revenues was customs, but from the later 16th century, the Crown, seeking to save the costs of the bureaucracy required to collect customs efficiently, franchised collection to syndicates of merchants, who paid an annual sum to the Crown and retained the revenues they collected. Exploitation of feudal incidents raised political opposition, as the Pilgrimage of Grace had shown. All this meant, yet again, that parliamentary taxation, still theoretically available only for extraordinary purposes, had to become a normal source of revenue, supplemented under James by loans from the City of London, and forced loans from subjects. Such methods inevitably engendered political opposition.

Another source of tension was the further extension of royal authority in the provinces. During Elizabeth's reign, the county commissions of the peace and Justices of the Peace were supplemented in each county by a lord-lieutenant appointed, with deputy lieutenants, to organise local defence in times of crisis such as the Spanish Armada. Under James I, the lord-lieutenant became a permanent feature of county organisation, with responsibility for the organisation of the county militia, a very vital function since there was still no standing army. This 'centralising' tendency was viewed with much suspicion in a nation where regional loyalties remained very strong.

Finally, there was the essential weakness of an unwritten and largely undefined constitution. By the early 1600s, the constitutional concepts which had emerged since the Norman Conquest were being referred to by the umbrella terms of 'the ancient constitution' and 'the fundamental law'. However, there was no accepted view of what either of these terms actually meant in any precise sense. It was accepted that the king ought to rule justly and in accordance with the law, and to rule with Parliament, but there was no certainty as to the nature of the relationship between the Crown and Parliament, nor what 'the law' really was. Hitherto, the relationship of king and legislature had involved a large measure of co-operation and the precise bounds of the authority of each had not been tested. The limits of the royal prerogative were also undefined, since Parliament, although expressing concern from time to time, had not in any aggressive manner sought a role in areas such as foreign policy and defence of the realm, leaving such matters to monarch, ministers and council.

Why did the limits of power begin to be tested under James I? The reasons are not entirely clear, but it may be noted that governmental financial demands remained very high without obvious gains to show for them, a classic source of discontent, and that society had grown increasingly litigious through the 16th century, so that the courts emerged as a natural forum for disputes. In addition, the accession of a new monarch after the 45 year reign of a ruler who had known full well how to play the political system may have produced a desire to see how far James could be pushed. Finally, in Sir Edward Coke, Chief Justice of the Common Pleas from 1606 and of the King's Bench from 1613 until he was dismissed in 1616 for seeking to defend judicial independence against the Crown, the judges of the common law courts had a leader who was determined to stand firm against apparent attempts to extend royal power.[5] His views on the importance of a judiciary independent from the Crown were in advance of his time and were not shared by the majority of his fellow judges, though they were to be of enormous influence on later generations, through his posthumously published *Institutes of Law*. However, Coke was in no sense a protagonist of the power of the legislature over the Crown and in many ways, he was an intriguer of a kind typical of his time.

At the same time, the members of the various parliaments had not yet adopted ideological positions which led them to move into direct opposition to the king and his ministers in so extreme a fashion as occurred in the 1640s. Nevertheless, ideological issues relating to restraint of monarchical power became more significant as government in continental Europe, where representative institutions were less developed than in England, moved towards absolutism. Finally, under James I, parliaments ceased to be summoned for single sessions, but remained in being for a number of years, though sessions still took place at the will of the king. This meant that there were much greater opportunities than hitherto for members to act together, though the development of political parties was many years in the future.

Perhaps inevitably, the first of the landmark cases of the reign concerned the revenue-raising powers of the Crown. That direct taxation required authorisation by Parliament was long established, but the position in relation to indirect taxes such as customs duties was unclear. In the *Case of Impositions (Bate's Case)*[6] in 1606, John Bate, a member of the Levant Company which traded with the eastern Mediterranean, refused to pay an additional duty on imported currants imposed by proclamation, though he paid the sums due under a statute of 1603. Bate was committed to prison and claimed, in a Grievance placed before the king by the Commons in Parliament, that the levying of such 'impositions' was contrary to the terms of a statute of 1372, which prohibited indirect taxation without the consent of Parliament.[7] However, when the Attorney General laid an information against Bate in the Exchequer Court, the king prorogued Parliament so that the matter could be dealt with by the courts alone.

Counsel argued on Bate's behalf that the common law required any change in established impositions to be endorsed by Parliament, and that even if at common law, the king had power to levy impositions without grant of Parliament, that power had expressly been removed by various statutes, beginning with Magna Carta. The Exchequer Court rejected this argument entirely, holding that the king could impose what duties he pleased for the purpose of regulating trade and was the sole judge of whether the purpose was the regulation of trade rather than the raising of revenue. In any event, Robert Cecil considered that the king had power to impose indirect taxation solely as a means of raising revenue, and proceeded with a review of Crown finances on this basis, leading in 1610–11 to a direct clash between king and Parliament.[8]

---

5   See JP Kenyon, *Stuart England*, 1985, Penguin, pp 82–83.
6   (1606) 2 St Tr 371. See AW Bradley and KD Ewing, *Constitutional and Administrative Law*, 12th edn, 1997, Longman, pp 55–56; and GDG Hall, 'Impositions and the Courts, 1554–1606' [1953] 69 LQR 200.
7   Statutes of the Realm 45 Edw 3 c 4.
8   See below, pp 202–03.

We see here Magna Carta re-emerging into the political consciousness after a gap of three centuries, not as the redress of specific grievances under feudal law that it was in reality, but as a piece of constitutional mythology, the cornerstone of the liberties of the subject as against the monarch. It was in this time that Magna Carta assumed its place in national myth.

In the following year, 1607, the question arose as to the extent of the king's prerogative to administer justice, specifically, whether he had the power to determine a dispute between the common law courts and the ecclesiastical courts.[9] The common law judges, headed by Coke, held that the king no longer had the power to dispense justice; power now lay with his courts and their professional judges. Further, the king could not claim power to create new courts via the prerogative, though no issue was raised as to the legitimacy of the existing prerogative courts, such as Star Chamber.

Next, in the *Case of Proclamations* of 1611,[10] came the question of the status of a proclamation made by the King in Council which forbade the erection of new buildings in London, and the making of starch from wheat.[11] The king sought an opinion from Coke and three of his fellow judges on the validity of proclamations. The most important element in this opinion is that the royal prerogative, that is, the powers of the monarch which exist and are exercisable independently of Parliament, exists only to the extent that the law allows, and that new prerogatives cannot be created nor can existing prerogatives be extended simply by claims to that effect. Tacitly, it is opined that the courts have the jurisdiction to adjudicate on the existence, nature and extent of prerogatives, and this is the position adopted by the courts ever since. More specifically, it was stated unambiguously that the monarch could not by proclamation create new offences under the criminal law, nor render an existing offence triable in Star Chamber, though the extent of the power to legislate by proclamation in other spheres was not examined. However, where a particular offence already existed at law, failure to comply with a proclamation exhorting subjects not to commit that offence rendered the offender liable to more severe punishment.

A little earlier, perhaps prefiguring the later disputes between Crown and Parliament, was the controversy which emerged in the 1604 Parliament over the election of Francis Goodwin as a member for Buckinghamshire. This election was annulled by the Court of Chancery on the grounds that Goodwin was an outlaw, and a second election returned a man with close ties to the Crown. The House of Commons then voted to reinstate Goodwin as an MP and refused to discuss the matter with the Lords or to seek legal advice, as the king requested. The king argued that all disputed elections ought to be dealt with by the Court of Chancery rather than by the House of Commons themselves, as was claimed, but in the end gave way. Although the affair was settled by a declaration that both elections were invalid and a fresh election would take place, in fact, the next two disputed elections were dealt with by the Commons alone. This marks the emergence of one of the most important elements of parliamentary privilege: that Parliament has the right to determine its own composition. Even if a person is elected to the House of Commons, he may be

---

9   *Case of Prohibitions del Rey* (1607) 12 Co Rep 63.
10 (1611) 12 Co Rep 74.
11 See BA Bicknell, *Cases on Constitutional Law*, 1925, OUP, pp 6–7.

prevented from taking his seat, and no court may interfere with that exercise of privilege.[12]

13.2.2 England and Scotland

The accession of King James to the English throne gave rise to a union of the crowns of England and Scotland, but in no sense was there a legal and political union between the two countries. Each retained its own institutions in government, law and religion. Perhaps one area in which the House of Commons was flexing its muscles in this period was in its opposition to the king's proposals for such a union. At the king's request, Parliament in June 1604 passed an Act appointing commissioners to discuss a detailed scheme for union with Scottish delegates, but when the commissioners reported in the November 1606 session, the opposition of the Commons was clear. The main English concerns were economic, a fear that free trade between the two countries would flood English markets with cheap Scottish goods, and social, that granting naturalisation to Scots born before 1603 would bring Scots flooding into England in the wake of the king's Scottish favourites, who were already viewed with hostility. The unicameral Scottish Parliament was also opposed to union, fearing that it would result in English domination, both politically and economically.

The lasting consequences of this early move towards union were relatively small. The most important was a lessening of the lawlessness of the border counties. Some conflicting laws were repealed and an extradition treaty was concluded. All Scots born after 24 March 1603 were declared in a case brought in the Scottish Court of Session in 1608 to be 'natural-born subjects within the allegiance of the King of England'.[13]

Other movements towards union were symbolic. By a proclamation of 20 October 1604, James declared his royal title to be 'King of Great Britain, France and Ireland, Defender of the Faith etc'. A new currency was issued, to be legal tender in both realms, and on 12 April 1606, all British ships were ordered to fly a new union flag designed by the College of Arms. However, Scotland continued to be governed as a separate kingdom. Royal authority was exercised by a commissioner chosen from the Scottish peerage and through a Privy Council, again composed mainly of peers.

13.2.3 Conflict with Parliament

Finance remained the major source of concern for James I and his ministers throughout the reign, and here the king came into direct conflict with Parliament. Despite attempts to pay off the Crown debt by the usual short term means of selling Crown lands, when Parliament met in 1610, the debt amounted to £280,000, with annual expenditure running at £511,000. Cecil's plea for an immediate subsidy of £600,000 was roundly rejected by Parliament, which proceeded to consider alternatives, in particular, the abolition of the king's feudal prerogatives relating to wardships and their replacement by payment of a fixed annual sum to the Crown.

---

12 See B Coward, *The Stuart Age*, 1980, Longman, pp 115–16. *Bradlaugh v Gossett* (1884) 12 QBD 271.

13 See M Lynch, *Scotland: A New History*, 1992, Pimlico, pp 240–41; and Coward, *ibid*, pp 117–18. *Calvin's Case* (1608) 7 Co Rep La.

Initially, James forbade debate on the issue, declaring that his feudal revenues were no concern of Parliament. Though later he relented and negotiation followed, further conflict ensued over impositions. Parliament considered that all types of indirect as well as direct taxation were properly a matter for Parliament, and challenged the king's pronouncement that impositions were a matter for the Crown alone.

For a time, a successful resolution of the dispute seemed possible. James was prepared to accept an Act which would prevent his levying further impositions in the future without parliamentary approval, though this did not affect those already in place. A limited subsidy was granted and an annual sum of £200,000 was agreed as proper compensation for the abolition of wardships.

However, when Parliament, prorogued on 23 July, re-assembled in October, the 'Great Contract' and co-operation between king and Parliament quickly collapsed. One of Parliament's objections to the proposed settlement was purely practical – how was the necessary £200,000 per year to be raised? More fundamentally, providing the king with a permanent source of revenue independent of parliamentary control was considered highly dangerous. Both sides attempted to re-negotiate and, when the negotiations reached stalemate, James dissolved Parliament and obtained a loan from the City of London to provide for immediate needs. Except for a brief period in 1614, he proceeded to rule without Parliament for the next 11 years.

As had been the case for centuries, it was quite impossible for the Crown to function with only its traditional sources of revenue. The usual extra-parliamentary expedients, the sale of land and monopolies, increasing the cost of wardships and levying forced loans, were by now insufficient to make up the shortfall. Before long, the bodies from whom James and his ministers sought loans on commercial terms found the Crown a poor credit risk. For the first time, though not the last, a monarch was reduced to the sale of honours. The new hereditary dignity of baronet was introduced in 1611, available to anyone prepared to pay a fee of £1,095. Peerages became available for purchase in 1615, at £10,000 for an earldom. Inevitably, the dignity of the Crown was compromised and these expedients could neither provide a permanent solution nor prevent a continuing increase in the debt. By 1619, the Crown's financial position was so parlous that the funeral of James's queen had to be delayed for 10 weeks while the Treasury assembled sufficient funds.[14] Sooner or later, Parliament would have to be recalled, and when this occurred, it was inevitable that there would be conflict between Crown and legislature.

On the death of the Emperor Matthias in 1619, Protestant rebels in Bohemia offered the Bohemian crown, theoretically elective but virtually hereditary among the Catholic Habsburgs, to James I's son-in-law, Frederick, the Elector Palatine, rather than the new Emperor, Ferdinand II. Ferdinand sought aid from his fellow Habsburg Philip III of Spain, who invaded the Palatinate from Flanders. In September 1620, the Elector of Bavaria, offered the Bohemian Crown by Ferdinand, inflicted a crushing defeat on Frederick at the Battle of the White Mountain. James had hitherto followed a pacific foreign policy, seeking, *inter alia*, a Spanish marriage for his heir, Charles, as a counter-balance to the Protestant influences of his daughter's marriage to Frederick. Now he was cajoled into pledging war against Spain unless Frederick was restored to

14   Kenyon, *op cit*, p 77.

the Palatinate by the spring of 1621. The cost of military preparations led James to summon a new parliament in order to raise the necessary funds.

Parliament opened in February 1621 and conflict followed over patents under the prerogative, issued in return for payments which provided short term revenues for the Crown. These gave specified persons a monopoly in the manufacture or trade in a particular item, or power to private individuals to carry out administrative functions such as licensing inns. Acting of its own volition, the Commons set up a sub-committee to investigate all patents referred to it by members. More seriously yet for the Crown, the House of Lords brought impeachment proceedings against the Lord Chancellor, Francis Bacon, Viscount St Albans, alleging that he had accepted bribes when acting as a judge. Bacon pleaded guilty and was fined, imprisoned and excluded from office.

The proceedings against Bacon were largely the product of intriguing by enemies at court, notably Sir Edward Coke. They should not be taken as the result of principled concern on the part of Parliament as a body. However, the king's actions in this period, particularly in order to protect the position of his new favourite, George Villiers, Duke of Buckingham, a leading recipient of patents, struck at the privileges claimed by Parliament. Buckingham's leading enemies, Sir Edward Sandys in the Commons and the Earls of Southampton and Oxford in the Lords, were arrested, though released shortly afterwards. James then followed Elizabeth I in prohibiting the Commons from debating foreign policy, declaring that this was a matter of prerogative alone. He raised further ire with a statement that Parliament's privileges came from royal grant and had not been held by Parliament forever, though he denied seeking to restrict those privileges. On 18 December 1621, the Commons passed a Protestation that their privileges were 'the ancient and undoubted birthright and inheritance of the subjects of England'.[15] The next day, the king adjourned Parliament, shortly to be dissolved, and personally tore out the Protestation from the official Commons Journal. Coke was imprisoned and John Pym, later to be a key figure in the events leading to the Civil War, was placed under house arrest.

For a period, James and his ministers managed to survive on the limited financial resources obtained in the 1621 Parliament, but the continuing likelihood of war with Spain meant that Parliament had to be summoned again in 1624. There was less overt conflict than in 1621, but the king made a number of concessions. In particular, he accepted the Commons' right to consider foreign policy, and a subsidy granted only for specific purposes laid down by Parliament, to be handled by treasurers appointed by Parliament. As in 1621, a leading minister, this time the Lord Treasurer, Lionel Cranfield, Earl of Middlesex, was impeached and dismissed from office, again largely by the machinations of his enemies at court, but suggesting that the precedent set by the Good Parliament of 1376 was now restored to life.

13.3   IRELAND 1547–1625

Although Ireland had been elevated from lordship to kingdom by Henry VIII, the pattern of its rule did not change. Ireland was governed on behalf of the Crown by administrative institutions based in Dublin and modelled on those of England,

---

15 Quoted in Coward, *op cit*, p 135.

headed by a Lord Deputy, in practice, an Anglo-Irish nobleman with limited allegiance to the Crown. In any event, his authority extended only over the Pale around Dublin. Much of what is now the Irish Republic was controlled by the great Anglo-Irish families, the remainder of the island by the indigenous Gaelic chieftains. These groups owed no more than nominal allegiance to the Crown.

Although the power of the Fitzgerald Earls of Kildare was broken after the rebellion of 1534, there was little in the way of lasting change. Under Edward VI, attempts, reversed under Mary I, were made to impose Protestantism on Ireland, but most of the country remained firmly Catholic. In the same period (1547–58), a policy of protecting the Pale through fortification and colonisation led to plantations of English soldiers in the counties of Leix and Offaly, just outside the Pale, but the settlers seem soon to have been absorbed into the indigenous population.

Under Elizabeth, the possibility that the French might use Ireland as a stepping stone for an invasion of England led to a much more aggressive Irish policy, which had the unwanted, though hardly unexpected effect of alienating both the Anglo-Irish nobility and the Gaelic chieftains. In 1558, Shane O'Neill, an anglicised chieftain, rebelled against a governmental decision to award the earldom of Tyrconnell to his bastard half-brother and established himself in such strength that the peace agreed with him in 1563 left him in effective control of Ulster. Later in the 1560s, much of the rest of Ireland was affected by successive feuds between the Fitzgerald Earls of Desmond and the Butler Earls of Ormonde.

Sir Henry Sidney, appointed Lord Deputy in 1565, attempted to strengthen the English position and provide stability in Ireland by the absorption of the south-eastern province of Leinster into the Pale, an expedition against Shane O'Neill, the expulsion of the Scots who had begun to settle in Ulster and the establishment of regional presidencies in the western provinces of Connacht and Munster. This policy met with only limited success, in part because Elizabeth expected it to be financed from local taxation. The consequent exactions had little effect other than to increase the alienation from the English already felt by the bulk of the Irish population. Sidney was able to put down a Fitzgerald rebellion in 1571, but from this time on, English policy towards the Irish became increasingly repressive.

Following the revolt of the Earl of Desmond in 1579–83, Munster was largely 'planted' by English settlers on the lands of Desmond and his adherents. The focus of anti-English activity then shifted to Ulster, where in 1595, Hugh O'Neill, Earl of Tyrone, went into rebellion, supported by his O'Donnell neighbours. Tyrone posed a considerable danger to the English, having a well-trained force of 1,000 cavalry, 1,000 pikemen and 4,000 musketeers, against which the English could muster only about 3,000 men, mainly raw recruits. A truce was concluded in May 1596, but following its expiry in June 1598, Tyrone took up arms again, inflicting a humiliating defeat on the English while, at the same time, the O'Donnells overran much of Connacht and rebels in Munster drove out many of the English settlers.

In January 1599, following much court infighting after the death of Burghley the previous year, Elizabeth's young favourite, Robert Devereux, Earl of Essex, secured his own appointment as Lord-Lieutenant[16] and, in March, set off for Ireland with 16,000 men. Essex was a man of considerable self-belief but limited military experience, and his intervention in Ireland seems largely to have been motivated by

---

16   This title temporarily superseded that of Lord Deputy.

desire for fame and glory, coupled with a determination to establish his ascendancy over his rivals at court. The expedition achieved nothing. Confronted by a much larger army on the northern boundary of the Pale, Essex swiftly agreed to a truce which allowed Tyrone and his allies to remain in possession of the lands they now held. He then returned to England, against Elizabeth's express orders, bursting into the queen's bedchamber as she was dressing on the morning of 24 September 1599.

This was the beginning of the end for Essex, who became increasingly petulant and out of touch with reality as he was outmanoeuvred at court by Burghley's sons. At the beginning of 1601, he and a small group of discontented young noblemen conceived a wild plan to take over the court by a surprise assault and restore Essex to direct communication with the queen. Not surprisingly, the plot was a complete failure and Essex and six others duly went to the block. Meanwhile, the new Lord Deputy, Lord Mountjoy, landed in Ireland in February 1600, along with Sir George Carew, an experienced soldier and former Lord President of Munster. They made a much more formidable combination than the lightweight Essex, and gradually wore down Tyrone's allies and then Tyrone himself, who finally submitted in the spring of 1603.

This was the situation inherited by James I and, from 1607, when Tyrone and the Earl of Tyrconnell fled to the continent, he sought to bring about a permanent solution to the problem of Ulster by a new plantation. Looking back with the hindsight of 400 years, this represents an example of 'ethnic cleansing', under which the indigenous Irish inhabitants were forcibly removed from the province and re-settled in the west of Ireland to make way for settlers from Scotland and England. The plantation was dictated by strategic considerations and the framework of the scheme set stringent conditions for grants of land. The newcomers were to build fortifications on their estates and were forbidden to allow land to fall into Irish hands. 23 towns were to be created, the most important being the modern Londonderry, Belfast and Enniskillen. The process of colonisation was left to private enterprise, via joint stock companies which received the initial allocations of land and parcelled it out to individual proprietors. In the period 1610–40, some 40,000 Scots are estimated to have settled in Ulster, to become the ancestors of the Presbyterian population of Northern Ireland. At the same time, other settlements took place elsewhere in Ireland, less specifically for military reasons. Though there was no immediate opposition to the settlements from the native Irish, there would be a major backlash in later years, the reverberations of which are still felt today.

13.4   CHARLES I 1625–49

James I died on 27 March 1625 and was succeeded by his surviving son as Charles I. One issue which has perplexed historians is why the conflicts over constitutional issues which emerged under the father, but were contained within the courts and Parliament, led to all-out war under the son and, finally, in the trial and execution of an anointed king and the temporary destruction of the monarchy itself. Many writers have seen the personality and limitations of the new king as a major factor. James was crafty, with considerable personal eloquence and skill in negotiation, and had learned much from his rule in Scotland before 1603. Charles was a young man of 25 without significant political experience, lacking what are now termed communication skills.

He also had all the stubbornness and reluctance to compromise of the man who is deeply unsure of himself and his own position.[17] Over the course of his reign, his repeated refusal to countenance compromise and his failure to abide by concessions which he considered to have been forced upon him proved, literally, fatal.

Like his father, Charles was extravagant, which did nothing to improve the Crown's financial position. He assembled a magnificent art collection and acted as the patron of both Anthony van Dyck and Peter Paul Rubens. Further, in a country where the tenor of religion was now largely Calvinist, Charles's personal faith tended towards Arminianism, a creed formulated by the Dutch theologian Jacobus Arminius which rejected predestination, now the official doctrine of the English church, in favour of salvation via free will, and emphasised outward display to a degree regarded by the bulk of the English population as 'papist'. Suspicion of the new king's religious views was only increased by his marriage to Henrietta Maria of France, a pious daughter of Rome.

13.4.1 The Petition of Right

Charles I was soon in need of money. He inherited the war with Spain and was anxious to assist his sister and brother-in-law to recover the Palatinate. His marriage treaty required the English to assist the French against Huguenot rebels who held the important port of La Rochelle. To make matters worse, the money voted by the 1624 Parliament was expended to little apparent effect and the foreign policy pursued by Buckingham, who retained his position as royal favourite despite the change of monarch, led to a succession of embarrassing failures.

Before long, relations between king and Parliament reached confrontation. The 1626 Parliament began impeachment proceedings against Buckingham for high treason. Charles, having first despatched Buckingham's two principal opponents in the Commons to the Tower, dissolved Parliament in order to protect his favourite. The charges against Buckingham were referred to Star Chamber, which acquitted him. As had his father, Charles resorted to extra-parliamentary measures to obtain the funds necessary to finance foreign policy. These included a forced loan collected in the face of widespread opposition and the refusal of the judges to declare it valid.

Shortly afterwards, in *Darnell's Case (Case of the Five Knights)*,[18] the King's Bench refused to issue a writ of habeas corpus for the release of persons committed to prison by the king for refusing to pay the forced loan. This writ had earlier emerged as a creature of common law, allowing examination of the validity of a person's imprisonment by requiring persons having custody of a prisoner to produce him in court and show cause for his imprisonment. Hyde CJ, giving judgment, concluded that the king did have power to imprison a subject without due process of law for reasons of national security, and was the sole judge of the needs of national security.[19]

---

17   Charles was a puny child who suffered from rickets and stood under five feet tall even as an adult. Prior to his elder brother's death in 1612, he was also in the shadow of that handsome, popular and much-admired young prince.

18   (1627) 3 St Tr 1.

19   This remains the legal position today, although the *GCHQ Case (Council of Civil Service Unions v Minister for the Civil Service)* [1985] AC 374 establishes that the courts are entitled to reject a governmental assertion that issues of national security form the context for a particular decision.

By March 1628, it had become necessary to summon another Parliament. This time, the emphasis shifted from attacks on Buckingham to matters of fundamental principle, a determination that the king should accept the illegality of extra-parliamentary taxation, compulsory billeting of troops without compensation, martial law and imprisonment without trial. More radical MPs, including Sir Edward Coke, proposed a Bill of Rights which would set clear limits on the extra-parliamentary powers of the monarch. Moderates on both sides brokered a compromise, by which the king was persuaded to agree to accept what has become known as the Petition of Right, in return for a grant of five subsidies.

The Petition of Right required the king to endorse the propositions that he could not by the prerogative alone levy taxation, imprison without trial, billet troops or impose martial law. Like Magna Carta, it purported to be a declaration of existing law and did not represent any imposition of unprecedented restrictions on the use of the prerogative. Though it has gone down as a key element in constitutional mythology, its immediate significance was small, and tension between king and Parliament continued at a high level. The Petition made no reference to the collection of customs duties (tunnage and poundage) which by tradition were granted by Parliament on the accession of each monarch for the duration of the reign, but had not been granted by the 1625 Parliament because of opposition to Buckingham's foreign policy. Following acceptance by Charles of the Petition of Right, the 1628 Parliament prepared a Bill which retrospectively validated the collection of these duties for the past three years. The king declared that no such validation was required – after all, they had not been mentioned in the Petition of Right. He therefore prorogued Parliament and ordered the arrest of merchants who had refused to pay tunnage and poundage.

Tension was heightened by Charles's continued favour to Arminian clergy, but one source of conflict was removed when on 23 August, Buckingham was murdered by a former soldier with a private grudge. For a brief period, Charles met Parliament with moderation, seeking to persuade the members that he had continued to levy tunnage and poundage not as a matter of right, but from necessity alone, and the validation Bill was introduced early in 1629. Deadlock ensued, however, when Sir Charles Eliot, one of the king's leading opponents, seems deliberately to have engineered a confrontation by raising an issue of privilege, to wit, whether a merchant who was also an MP could speak on this issue. Charles considered that matters of privilege were to be decided by him and exacerbated the tension by continuing to insist that his own interpretation of the Petition of Right was the only correct one.

On 2 March 1629, rumours circulated that the king was about to dissolve Parliament. The Commons refused to acknowledge Black Rod's summons to the House of Lords to hear the king speak. Two MPs held the Speaker down in his chair to prevent him from reading the order for the House to adjourn. Whilst the Speaker was thus rendered impotent, Eliot persuaded the House to pass three resolutions. The first two declared that those advising Arminian innovations in religion or involved in the collection of tunnage and poundage were 'capital enemies to this kingdom and commonwealth'. The third declared those who paid the dues to be 'betrayers of the liberty of England, and enemies to the same'. However, there was no serious opposition to the dissolution, which took place two days later. The king then had nine of his leading opponents arrested; six were soon released, but three, including Eliot, remained in custody. They were tried before the King's Bench in January 1630 and, after being found guilty of conspiring in Parliament to overthrow the king's government, were sentenced to be imprisoned in the Tower until they acknowledged their fault.

13.4.2 Government without Parliament

Parliament was not summoned again for 11 years. Some historians have argued that Charles was able to govern in an effective fashion until the late 1630s and that the recourse to extra-parliamentary government engendered little opposition outside specific interest groups. They note that Eliot, who died in the Tower in 1632, was considered by many MPs to have gone too far and that several of Charles's more moderate opponents were reconciled to him following his acceptance of the Petition of Right, serving him loyally in the 1630s. Other writers consider that opposition to Charles's rule rumbled below an apparently tranquil surface throughout the period before bursting out in 1640–41.

Without access to sources of revenue which required parliamentary approval, it might be expected that the Crown's financial situation deteriorated yet further, but this seems not to have been the case. Peace treaties were concluded in 1629 and 1630 with France and Spain after the king and his ministers concluded that continued participation in the continental war was impossible without parliamentary subsidies. The Lord Treasurer, Sir Richard Weston, instituted a programme of economies in government departments and increased royal revenues by means which included making more efficient use of customs, opposition to which died after 1629.

These attracted relatively little controversy, but other revenue-raising measures aroused considerable resentment, especially after 1635 and among the lesser gentry, on whom they bore most heavily. Forest Law, dating from the Norman period, had been a dead letter for many years, but from 1634, the Crown garnered considerable revenues by fining landowners for encroachments on royal forests such as the New Forest, some of them dating from the reign of Richard I. The circumference of the Forest of Rockingham in Northamptonshire was extended in 1637 from six miles to 60, and fines totalling £51,000 were imposed for encroachments within that circumference.[20] Commissioners were appointed in 1630 to fine any person with annual income over £40 who had not received knighthood, and others to fine landowners for enclosing common land. Although legislation against trading monopolies now existed, the Crown declared that only the grant of monopolies to individuals was prohibited, and proceeded to grant or to restore the monopolies of the great chartered companies such as the East India Company.

The most controversial means of raising revenue was Ship Money, a levy based on land values which had been made on the coastal counties over many years, to provide for the defence of the realm by sea. However, in 1635 and in the four following years, Ship Money was levied on the inland counties in addition, for the purposes of putting down privateering in the Channel, and with an unprecedented degree of efficiency. This provoked the well-known case of *R v Hampden*,[21] in which a Buckinghamshire gentleman pleaded that the demand that he pay Ship Money was unlawful.

Before issuing the writ of 1635 for the collection of Ship Money, the king had, following previous practice, privately consulted the judges, who confirmed that he

---

20   Kenyon, *op cit*, p 110.
21   (1637) 3 St Tr 825. See also Bicknell, *op cit*, pp 22–25.

had power to levy Ship Money by writ under the Great Seal and that he was the sole judge of when the defence of the realm made such a levy necessary. The Sheriff of Buckinghamshire assessed Hampden as liable to pay Ship Money in the sum of 20s. Hampden refused to pay and proceedings were brought against him in the Court of the Exchequer. Oliver St John, soon to be one of the leading opponents of Charles I in Parliament, appeared for Hampden and argued that, although every man was by his allegiance required to contribute to the defence of the realm in time of danger and that the king was the sole judge of danger to the realm and the means by which it should be prevented, nevertheless, the king could not impose taxes without the assistance of Parliament, just as he could not apply the law without the assistance of his judges. The specific issue was whether the writ issued against Hampden, allowing his goods to be seized and sold to defray the tax due, had been properly issued. St John submitted that it had not, since it did not issue from the King in Parliament.

According to St John, the law provided three means for the defence of the realm by sea, that is:

(a) the service due by tenure of land, that is, under the feudal system;

(b) prerogatives settled on the Crown for the defence of the kingdom; and

(c) supplies of money for the defence of the sea in times of danger.

If the ordinary sources of revenue, including Ship Money as due from the coastal counties, were for this purpose insufficient, then the king could properly have recourse to Parliament as the means of supply upon extraordinary occasions. Precedent, together with the charters of William I, Magna Carta, *De Tallagio non Concedendo* and the Petition of Right established that extraordinary taxation could not be imposed by the king alone. The Barons of the Exchequer, by a majority of seven to five, gave judgment in favour of the king

Again, we see Magna Carta as an element in constitutional myth, though it did not sway the judges themselves, whose decision was only questionably based on precedent and was deeply unpopular. From 1638 onwards, the revenue raised via Ship Money dropped markedly as the populace resorted to traditional means of resistance to financial impositions, including violent assaults on tax collectors. After Parliament was summoned again in 1640, a statute reversed the judgment in Hampden and declared Ship Money illegal.

13.5   GROWING TENSIONS

As well as the opposition to Ship Money and other revenue-raising expedients, the late 1630s saw other tensions beginning to come to a head. From the beginning of the decade, the king and his ministers sought to increase efficiency in local government by ensuring, via the local apparatus of lords-lieutenant and Justices of the Peace, that legislation, in the form of both statute and proclamation, was fully enforced, principally for fiscal reasons. This had the effect of further increasing resentment at the heavy-handedness of the king and his ministers. Neither had religious conflict gone away, though there was some change in its direction. Whereas at the beginning of the century, the main division had still been between Protestant and Catholic, this was now being superseded by conflict between the Protestants of the Established Church, increasingly influenced by Arminianism, and the various extreme Protestant, or Puritan, groups who believed that England was being led back towards Rome.

Indeed, the beliefs of William Laud, Archbishop of Canterbury from 1633, and those he influenced did involve a clear movement away from the austerities of Calvinism. Laudians placed greater emphasis on the sacraments than on preaching and favoured more elaborate ritual and ceremonial. Over 350 years later, their beliefs and practices seem insufficiently radical to arouse the hatred than they actually did. Rather, the hatred and the role of religion in the drift towards civil war came from the attempt of Laud and his confederates to impose their doctrines and practices on the kingdom by force, and the growing belief among a deeply anti-Catholic population that the country was being returned to 'Popery'. Suspicion was only heightened by the king's admiration and support for Laud, and his happy marriage to Queen Henrietta Maria, who was doubly unpopular as both a foreigner and a Catholic.

At the same time, there was increasing hostility to the tradition of church government by bishops, the more radical wishing the episcopate they considered irredeemably corrupt to be replaced with the non-hierarchical presbyterian form of government where power was vested in elders elected by the individual congregations meeting in General Assembly. The attacks on bishops were seen, indirectly, as an attack on the monarchy itself, for the idea that bishops and their clergy were divinely appointed via the Apostolic Succession was closely linked with the concept of the Divine Right of Kings.[22] It was at this time that Star Chamber acquired its sinister reputation, being used by Laud as a means of silencing rebellious clerics and writers of anti-Laudian tracts through their trial and punishment for seditious libel.

13.6   IRELAND AND SCOTLAND

A second leading servant of the king who aroused enormous personal hatred through his attempts to impose order on hostile subjects was Thomas Wentworth, numbered among the king's more moderate opponents in the 1620s, but perhaps his most loyal servant in the 1630s. Wentworth had demonstrated his administrative abilities as President of the Council of the North from 1629, and in 1633 was appointed Lord Deputy of Ireland. Refusing to align himself with any of the factions there, Wentworth gradually succeeded in alienating them all. The 'New English' settled under Elizabeth had prospered both in financial terms and in their domination of the Dublin bureaucracy. Wentworth's administrative changes represented a threat to their power, exacerbated by his support for Laud's religious changes and his policy of relative toleration towards Catholicism. Wentworth's plans for a new plantation in Connacht involved confiscation of lands from some of the leading 'Old English' peers in order to provide for the new settlers.[23] Finally, he rode roughshod over the Presbyterians of Ulster. As a money-raising measure, he fined them heavily for breaching the terms of their land grants, then proposed to expel all Scots who were not landowners from

---

22 The doctrine of the Apostolic Succession holds that there is a direct and unbroken link, through ordination by bishops, between the clergy and the Twelve Apostles.
23 See G Davies, *The Early Stuarts*, 2nd edn, 1959, OUP, p 115.

Ulster by proclamation, and imposed governmental control over Londonderry after its citizens asserted their independence of him.

In Scotland, the first flashpoint of the civil wars of 1639–49, conflict again centred on the activities of Archbishop Laud. Though he held no episcopal authority in Scotland, it was at his behest that Charles I sought to impose the new English Prayer Book, heavily influenced by Laud's views, on the Scots. There were violent scenes in St Giles's Cathedral, Edinburgh, on 23 July 1637, when the new Prayer Book was first used, set off by an unidentified woman who hurled a stool at the bishop, shouting 'The mass is entered among us'. The opinions of both sides only hardened thereafter.

Subscribers to the National Covenant of February 1638, who represented a considerable proportion of the Scottish population outside the Highlands, bound themselves to resist to the death the Prayer Book and other Laudian innovations, which were declared to be contrary to the Reformation and to Acts of Parliament, and tending to the re-establishment not only of Popery but of tyranny. As with opponents of royal government in England over many centuries, the Covenanters proclaimed their loyalty to the king, disclaiming any intention of attempting anything to the dishonour of God or tending to the diminution of the king's greatness.

The existing system of church government in Scotland represented a hybrid of presbyterianism and episcopal rule. Each diocese was governed by an assembly, with a bishop as president of that assembly. An overall General Assembly met periodically on the king's summons, but did not include the bishops, who instead sat in Parliament.

Initially, the king was prepared to deal with opposition to the Prayer Book in constructive fashion by summoning a General Assembly for November 1638 and a Parliament for the following May. However, irreconcilable conflict soon ensued between the Assembly and the Scottish bishops. The royal commissioner who exercised the king's authority in Scotland, the Marquess of Hamilton, declared the Assembly dissolved, but it continued to sit, abolishing the Prayer Book, the canons governing the church, the Articles of Perth imposed on the church by James VI, and the episcopate, instituting a wholly presbyterian system of government. Charles I was not prepared to accept this threat to his authority.

After both sides had made their military preparations, the conflict known as the First Bishops' War broke out in May 1639 between the Covenanters and the royal government in Scotland. However, there was still no standing army, so that the king had to rely for troops on the militia, or 'trained bands', and the nobility serving at their own expense. The nobility showed a distinct lack of enthusiasm for the war, several entering into secret communications with the Covenanters, and there was widespread opposition on financial grounds to the calling-up and deployment of the trained bands. Indeed, the king's financial position made the planned three-pronged campaign against the Covenanters impossible, and on 18 June 1639, Charles concluded a truce at Berwick, agreeing to a further meeting of the General Assembly, the summoning of a Scottish Parliament and the disbanding of both armies.

Relations between Charles and his Scottish subjects then deteriorated still further. Neither army was disbanded. The Assembly confirmed the abolition of the Prayer Book and the episcopate, and further enacted that every Scottish subject should subscribe to the Covenant. The great bulk of the population did. The Scottish Parliament then sought to repudiate royal control over government in Scotland by providing that henceforth the Lords of the Articles, a committee of peers and officials that initiated legislation and, along with the royal commissioner, held the reins of power now that the king was an absentee, should be chosen by Parliament, not the king. By the end of 1639, Charles was seeking a means of renewing the war.

It being impossible to raise the £300,000 required for a Scottish campaign without parliamentary subsidies, Charles summoned an English Parliament in April 1640. This Short Parliament manifested considerable opposition to royal policy and members refused to grant the 12 subsidies now demanded unless grievances dating from the 1630s and specified in a large volume of petitions were rectified. At this stage, the opposition was yet to become organised or united, though John Pym, a Devonian member now emerging as an effective leader of the king's opponents in the Commons, made a vigorous speech summing up the abuses of the past 11 years. Stalemate reached, Parliament was dissolved on 5 May after sitting for only three weeks.

Civil war was not then inevitable and could still have been averted if the king and his advisors had adopted a more realistic and conciliatory attitude towards Parliament and the Scots. Instead, the actions of Charles and his close advisors over the following two years only exacerbated a worsening situation and led finally to the opposition concluding that the king could not be persuaded by any peaceful means to govern through Parliament, and that, like his ancestors Edward II and Richard II, he was not to be trusted to abide by any settlement to which he had agreed. The seeds of revolution having been sown when war broke out in 1642, over the remainder of the 1640s and through the 1650s, the three kingdoms of England, Scotland and Ireland reaped a whirlwind.

The Scottish truce did not last long. The Second Bishops' War broke out as early as August 1640, when a large army of Covenanters crossed the Tweed, dispersed the inadequate English force sent against it and occupied Newcastle-upon-Tyne. The terms of the Treaty of Ripon represented a clear English surrender; the Scots were to remain in possession of Northumberland and Durham, and were to receive a subsidy of £25,000 per month until outstanding matters were settled. The king gave way to calls for a new parliament, and what became known later as the Long Parliament assembled at Westminster on 3 November.

13.6.1 The birth of the Long Parliament

The Long Parliament met at a time when differences between Crown and people could still have been settled peacefully. That Charles I and his ministers continued to refuse to work through Parliament and to accept the role which even the principled and moderate element demanded made war inevitable. Though this Parliament was far from being a united body, there was a clear sense among its members that they were there to deal with the abuses which had taken place over the past 11 years and to dismantle the apparatus which had made those abuses possible.

In the great tradition extending back at least to the reign of John, the main targets of the Long Parliament were the king's evil counsellors, who had kept King Charles from acting in the interests of his realm and subjects, and would continue to do so unless they were removed from their positions of power and influence. Like the leaders of the Good Parliament, the first intention of the leaders was to impeach the king's ministers. Their particular targets were Archbishop Laud and Wentworth, now Earl of Strafford, who had aroused the hatred and fear of the Commons to a degree which has no real parallel in modern English history. Not the least part of this hatred was fired by Strafford having once been of the reforming party himself. Whether justifiably or not, John Pym and his confederates feared that Strafford planned to pre-empt the planned impeachment of the leading ministers by bringing to England an army he had recently raised among the much-feared Catholic Gaels of Ireland for use against Parliament and to accuse its leaders of treasonable relations with the Scots at the time of the invasion in August.

On 7 November, in the first sitting of the Long Parliament, Pym called upon the members to seek out and punish the authors of a design to alter both the religion and government of the kingdom, which he described as both a breach of fundamental law and the highest treason, and to land an Irish army to subdue opposition to them.[24] The Commons forthwith resolved to impeach Strafford, who was arrested as he arrived in the Lords and was removed to the Tower, where, on 22 March 1641, he was put on trial before his peers for high treason. Archbishop Laud was also despatched to the Tower and impeachment proceedings began against other ministers.

The impeachments of the Long Parliament have all the hallmarks of vendetta. However, it was equally clear that there was considerable doubt as to whether Strafford could properly be held guilty of high treason. In particular, it was doubted whether 'coming between the king and his people', the principal accusation, could be considered treasonable. It was further doubted that he could be guilty under an improvised concept of 'cumulative' treason (that a series of actions which were not individually treasonable could amount overall to an act of high treason). Strafford defended himself with considerable skill, and the Lords, reluctant anyway to condemn one of their own number, of whose loyalty to the Crown they had no doubt, failed to reach a verdict before they adjourned the proceedings on 10 April as a protest at mob violence around Westminster.

Pym was left in an awkward position. Opinion against Strafford had, if anything, hardened in recent months, but there was the distinct possibility that the impeachment proceedings, if the Lords chose to resume the trial at all, would end in acquittal. The obvious solution was a Bill of Attainder, but aside from the difficulty of principle – that attainder was all too redolent of the arbitrary rule of kings which Pym set himself against – there was the practical difficulty that a Bill of Attainder could not become law without royal assent.

At this point, the initiative in the Commons moved to a 'Merciless Party' led by Sir Arthur Hazelrigg, who introduced a Bill of Attainder which passed its third reading by a majority of 204 to 59. The atmosphere deteriorated yet further as rumours emerged of plotting at court and among troops loyal to the king to dissolve Parliament by force, and a concrete plan emerged to rescue Strafford from the Tower. Pym, by no means always principled in his methods, skilfully orchestrated revelations to the Commons of a 'Popish Plot', led by Queen Henrietta Maria, and was not above encouraging the London mob to continue rioting around Westminster in order to stoke up the tension still further. The Lords, whatever their misgivings on the legal issues, accepted the Bill, so that all now depended on the king. Charles, who had earlier assured Strafford that he should not suffer in life, honour or property, hesitated. Given the stubborn streak in his character, it is entirely possible that he would have refused assent and that the final breakdown of his relations with the Long Parliament

---

24   His speech is printed in JP Kenyon, *The Stuart Constitution*, 2nd edn, 1986, CUP, No 64.

would have been precipitated a good deal earlier than it actually was, but the potential deadlock was resolved by Strafford himself. A brave man, whatever his faults, he wrote to the king from the Tower, offering himself as a sacrifice to appease Parliament. Charles gave his assent to the Bill of Attainder on 10 May and Strafford went to the block, dying before a crowd estimated at 200,000 with the same courage and dignity as his king was later to do.

13.6.2 Calm before the storm

At the same time, the Commons took the first steps which Kenyon considers to have been truly revolutionary,[25] though the Protestation published on 3 May declared that their concern remained the king's evil counsellors and the malign influence of Rome. There was no attack on the king himself, and many of those who were later to take up arms against him were prepared to accept offices in the royal household and administration as a means of giving reliable counsel and preventing him from being led astray again. Much as had the Scottish Covenanters, those who took the Protestation Oath pledged themselves to defend 'the true reformed religion, expressed in the doctrine of the Church of England', along with the power and privileges of Parliament, and the lawful rights and liberties of the subject. The subscribers declared their loyalty to the monarch, desiring to defend 'His Majesty's royal person, honour and estate'.

More specifically, and without precedent, a Commons Bill sought to make it illegal to adjourn, prorogue or dissolve Parliament without its own consent, a clear assault on the royal prerogative as well as an attempt to deal with what the members considered a principal abuse of royal power. This received the royal assent as the Triennial Act, which created a machinery for summoning Parliament independently of the king where three years had elapsed without a summons after the dissolution of the previous Parliament.[26] Kenyon comments that it is highly likely that Charles I only assented to the Act without protest because it was submitted to him at the same time as the attainder against Strafford, for whose death he felt both a personal responsibility and a lasting resentment against Parliament.[27]

For the present, Charles bided his time, assenting between June and August to a series of statutes which dealt with other major areas of grievance. Ship Money was declared unlawful, knighthood fines were prohibited and the limits of the royal forests were defined. Various bodies which existed and functioned as instruments of the prerogative were abolished, notably Star Chamber and the Council of the North.[28] The vexed issue of customs duties was resolved for the time being by a grant of tunnage and poundage, but only for two months at a time, the relevant statute declaring that previous exactions of these duties and impositions had been against the law of the land and could not in the future be levied without the consent of Parliament.[29]

25   Kenyon, *op cit, Stuart England*, p 127.
26   Statutes of the Realm 16 Car I, c 1.
27   Kenyon, *op cit, Stuart England*, p 129. The king's last speech on the scaffold included a clear reference to Strafford.
28   17 Car I, c 10.
29   SR Gardiner, *History of England 1603–42*, 1883–84, Longman, p 404.

13.6.3 The storm gathers

Pym and his allies were now faced with a difficulty common to many reformers. Parliament had been largely united over the necessity to deal with the *lacunae* which had made 'the 11 years' tyranny' possible, but there was no consensus as to what should be put in their place. There was concern as to whether the king could be trusted to abide by the provisions to which he had assented, only encouraged by the remarks of the queen to a papal agent that, according to English law, that which was granted by the king under compulsion was null and void. Predictably, there was strong disagreement in matters of religion. The radicals called for the abolition of the episcopate, but the majority in the Commons were opposed to this through fear that religious freedom would lead to social disorder, a fear only encouraged by numerous outbreaks of rioting in this period.

In the Commons, the compromise solution of an Exclusion Bill to remove the secular powers of bishops and end their presence in the Lords was accepted, but the Lords rejected the Bill outright, together with a Bill providing that all holders of office in church or state must take the Protestation Oath or be regarded as unfit to hold such office. Relations between the two Houses had not yet broken down entirely. On 24 June, the Ten Propositions set out Parliament's position in any future negotiations with the king, representing a programme of reform on which moderate opinion in both Houses was agreed.[30] Had these Propositions ever been put to the king, it is likely that there would have been much difficulty in securing his agreement, since they required him to control his queen and her Catholic connections, to accept restraints on his choice of advisors and control of the army, including the disbandment of a number of regiments at the will of Parliament, and to give Parliament a role in ecclesiastical changes. Catholics were to be barred from the court and in particular from the presence of the Prince of Wales, the future Charles II.

Charles now announced his intention to visit Scotland in August in order to ratify the Treaty of Ripon, but with an ancillary motive of garnering support among Scots opposed to the Covenant. Fear that the king might attempt to raise an army in Scotland led to the appointment of a parliamentary committee of defence and commissioners to accompany the king and to monitor his activities. In the event, Charles gained little support. However, a crisis exploded at the same time in Ireland, its political repercussions constituting the death knell of attempts to secure a peaceful settlement.

Following Strafford's death, the disparate groups which had been briefly united in hatred for him fell into disunity once more. With plans afoot for new measures against Catholicism in Ireland, a Catholic rebellion broke out in Ulster in October. This was the subject of propaganda to a degree hysterical even for the time. The latent anti-Catholicism of England emerged with full force, with claims that the country was now threatened with the Antichrist in the form of an invasion of Irish savages, and panic in places as far from Ireland as Bradford and Halifax. Charles, still in Scotland, proposed to raise an army to deal with the rebellion, but in the prevailing atmosphere, it was widely feared that he would use it against Parliament. On 8 November, Parliament agreed to the raising of this army, but on the condition of an 'additional instruction' sent to the parliamentary commissioners with the king, stating that Charles must

---

30   Kenyon, *op cit*, *The Stuart Constitution*, No 61.

employ 'only such councillors as should be approved of by Parliament', under threat that Parliament 'should take such a course for the securing of Ireland as might likewise secure ourselves'. Two implications are clear: first, and most obviously, that Pym and his confederates did not trust the king; second, that Parliament was prepared to make a further assault on the king's traditional prerogatives by taking control of the defence of the realm. At the same time, Parliament appointed the Earl of Essex to command the trained bands south of the Trent, and an Impressment Bill was introduced to remove the king's power to require men to serve outside their own counties. On 7 December, Sir Arthur Hazelrigg introduced a Militia Bill which was more radical yet, calling for command of the trained bands to be taken out of the king's hands together, commanders in the future to be appointed by Parliament. Both Bills were rejected by the Lords.

Opinion in Parliament was becoming more polarised, the moderates objecting strongly to both the tone and the contents of the Grand Remonstrance, produced during November as a statement of Parliament's grievances.[31] This set out the wrongs which had been done since the king's accession in 1625, most attributed to 'Popish' influences, together with the remedies already granted and proposals for further, more radical change, though, yet again, the framers of the Remonstrance protested their loyalty to the Crown and to Charles I.

Some of the moderates seem now to have concluded that reform had gone far enough and was in danger of turning into revolution. Significantly, the Grand Remonstrance achieved a Commons majority of only 11, and on returning from Scotland at the end of November, the king found that where hitherto he had been almost entirely lacking in parliamentary support, 'champions of the prerogative' could now be found. He seems to have concluded that the time was ripe for dealing with the parliamentary leaders by making use of Parliament's own main weapon of impeachment, but he and his supporters gravely misjudged the situation. Any temporary backlash within Parliament spent its force by the end of December, when the bishops, who had for a period been prevented from attending the Lords by rioting, returned and moved that all business transacted in their absence be declared void. A majority in the Lords held this to be a breach of their privileges and accepted a Commons motion to impeach the bishops.

On 3 January 1642, the king announced the impeachment at his own behest of five of the Commons leaders: John Pym, John Hampden, Denzil Holles, Sir Arthur Hazelrigg and William Strode, together with Lord Kimbolton from the Lords, on charges of treason. The following day, he went in person to the House of Commons to arrest them in the chamber, accompanied by officers with drawn swords. Forewarned, the five had gone into hiding, so that the king's gesture rebounded on him. A Commons committee forthwith declared a grave breach of parliamentary privilege, and Parliament took physical action to prevent a repetition by appointing one of their number, Philip Skippon, to command the London trained bands as a defensive measure against the king. A week later, the king retreated to Hampton Court and the Five Members returned to the House in triumph. Charles I never returned to London or Westminster as a free man. No monarch has attempted to enter the Commons since.

The attempted arrest of the Five Members brought a further hardening of parliamentary attitudes towards the king and increased support for the radical

---

31   Kenyon, *op cit*, *The Stuart Constitution*, No 64.

proposals included in the Grand Remonstrance. On 5 February, the Lords accepted the Exclusion Bill and also the Impressment and Militia Bills. Charles was prepared to assent to the Impressment Bill and so surrendered control of the army raised for Ireland, but refused to approve the Militia Bill, which was then, in a move of dubious legality, given effect by Parliament as the Militia Ordinance. From this point on, Parliament acted independently of the king, and the slide into civil war gathered pace.

With Parliament forcing through legislation without the king and claiming powers to choose the king's advisors and control the army, along with increasing and justified fear of widespread civil disorder, a backlash did develop within Parliament and elsewhere, with the emergence of 'constitutional royalists', who were prepared, as time proved, to support the king by force of arms. On 27 May, the king issued a proclamation forbidding his subjects to obey the Militia Ordinance. In the reply to this, declaring the proclamation to be void, Parliament, though still protesting its loyalty to the king and its belief that he was merely seduced by evil counsellors, moved a little closer to the possibility of direct action against him by making a distinction between the person and office of a king, and implicitly envisaging the possibility of transfer of the latter elsewhere.[32] The authors of this Declaration claimed that 'the fundamental laws of this kingdom' did not proscribe the making of the Militia Ordinance and that instruments made by Parliament against the king's will were made nevertheless by the king's authority. There is also, arguably, the hint of a threat to use the militia against the king, should 'the protection and defence of the kingdom', the ostensible reason for the Militia Ordinance, require it.

A factor in the increasing of support for the king was the issue by Parliament on 1 June 1642 of the *Nineteen Propositions*,[33] which would have amounted to unconditional surrender on his part had he accepted them, since they demanded that he give up all powers of appointment, command and policy-making, to the extent of forbidding him a role in the education, upbringing and marriage of his children. At this point, Charles, whether sincerely or as a matter of expediency, adopted a vastly more liberal stance than hitherto. In his Answer, composed by the leading constitutional royalists, Viscount Falkland and Sir John Culpeper, it was argued that the English constitution was a mixed government, balanced between monarchy, aristocracy and democracy, that the king ruled not by arbitrary power but under the law, though he retained prerogative powers which were properly exercisable independently of Parliament in foreign affairs, control over the militia, power to choose his own advisors and to summon and dismiss Parliament. To transfer those and other powers to Parliament would tip the balance fatally. Not only would this involve 'a total subversion of the fundamental laws', but it raised the spectre of mob rule, since such changes would encourage the common people:

> ... to set up for themselves, call parity and independence liberty, devour that estate which had devour the rest, destroy all rights and properties, all distinctions of families and merit, and by this means splendid and excellently distinguished form of government end in a dark, equal chaos of confusion and the long line of our many noble ancestors in a Jack Cade or Wat Tyler.[34]

---

32 Kenyon, *op cit*, *The Stuart Constitution*, No 69.
33 Kenyon, *op cit*, *The Stuart Constitution*, No 68.
34 Quoted in Coward, *op cit*, p 203.

In the 1640s, the age of popular democracy had not yet come. Society remained rigidly stratified and its higher levels valued order and the security of their property above all things, so that a 'slippery slope' argument of this kind had considerable appeal even to those who felt disquiet at the king's earlier actions. The next few years were to demonstrate over and over again the strength of fear of disorder and the importance of this in the politics of the period.

CHAPTER 14

CIVIL WAR AND COMMONWEALTH 1642–60

14.1 INTRODUCTION

The military course of what can most accurately be termed the Wars of the Three Kingdoms involved several phases:

(a) the two Bishops' Wars between England and the Scottish Covenanters in 1639 and 1640;

(b) the Irish Rebellion from 1641;

(c) the First Civil War between king and Parliament (1642–46);

(d) the Second Civil War between king and Parliament (1648).

The division between the king's forces, soon dubbed the 'Cavaliers' (from the Spanish *caballeros*) by opponents wishing to give the impression that all royalists were gentry who supported Spanish-style absolutism and Popery, and those of Parliament – the 'Roundheads', supposedly militant Puritans favouring close-cropped haircuts – did not follow simple religious, social or regional lines, nor in the initial stages was the Parliamentary party dominated by extremists, whether political or religious. Broadly speaking, support for the king was strongest in northern and western England and in Wales, especially among Catholics, and that for Parliament in the south and east, particularly in the urban areas and among those most influenced by Puritanism. However, as Norman Davies notes, a civil war in miniature took place in many counties. In Lancashire, the nobility and gentry, many of them Catholic, were largely royalist, while the people of the manufacturing towns supported Parliament.[1] Equally, although many combatants were motivated by political or religious ideologies, many others simply followed the allegiance of the owner of the land on which they lived. Though the feudal system had long disappeared, informal ties based on it remained strong.

As the wars progressed, the extremists obtained a dominant role within Parliament and in its military forces, to the point where, as a narrow clique at the centre of power, they were able to bring about the execution of a king and the abolition of the monarchy. How and why this came about is the subject of enormous academic debate. The course of events was complex and the different strands of opinion had varying degrees of influence at different times. War tends to produce polarisation between the opposing sides, especially where, as in 1642–43 and again in 1646–47, attempts to broker a peaceful settlement end in failure. A leading voice of moderation was silenced when John Pym died in December 1643, but divisions had already begun to show themselves within the Commons. Except for conservatives such as Denzil Holles who were prepared to accept peace at almost any price in order to avoid social disorder, Parliament accepted that the military defeat of the king was the essential preliminary to a constitutional settlement, but there was disagreement as to how this victory could be achieved, and the form which that settlement would take.

---

1   N Davies, *The Isles*, 1999, Macmillan, p 495.

14.2   THE GROWTH OF EXTREMISM

The most important single elements in the development of extremism in the party of Parliament were the growing radicalism of Parliament's army from 1647 onwards and of one of its leading figures, Oliver Cromwell, and the king's own actions, which finally led a majority in a Parliament purged of moderates by the army and reduced to an extremist 'rump' to conclude that no settlement with him was possible and that the monarchy itself must be destroyed.

The first year of the war saw Parliament come perilously close to total defeat on the battlefield, but its most effective generals, notably Cromwell and Sir Thomas Fairfax, then took the bold stroke of creating England's first professional army, free from local ties and whose commanders, headed by Fairfax, were responsible to a centralised high command known as the Derby House Committee. At the same time, a Self-Denying Ordinance separated civilian and military leadership by forbidding individuals from being both MPs and military officers, so encouraging military commanders to concentrate on the war effort, but also removing the army's direct channel of influence in Parliament.

The emergence of this New Model Army, along with support from the Scots Army of the Covenant, with which Parliament concluded an alliance known as the Solemn League and Covenant, was a major factor in the turning of the military tide in favour of Parliament from the middle of 1644 onwards. The king's own Scottish allies, led by a former Covenanter, James Graham, 1st Marquis of Montrose, were defeated in Scotland in September 1645 following a series of Parliamentary victories in England, and Charles and his depleted forces then fell back on their headquarters at Oxford. On 27 April 1646, recognising final defeat as inevitable, Charles I surrendered to the Covenanter Army, which handed him over to Parliament in February 1647 in return for a substantial payment.

Following the end of the fighting, Parliament's armies were left in being and became fertile breeding grounds for extremist views at a time when there was increasing general disillusionment with the Long Parliament. Soldiers with too little to do are all too prone to slide into indiscipline. The aftermath of a long war can be a particularly dangerous time, when large numbers of men remain in arms, often poorly led and under conditions which give rise to a justified sense of grievance. The Parliamentary soldiers of 1647 and after had real and serious grievances against their high command, since their pay was hugely in arrears. It has been calculated that the New Model Army, whose pay was less in arrears than the rest, were owed some £601,000 in pay.[2] This averages some £27 per man, a very considerable sum for an ordinary infantryman paid no more than 1s (5p) per day. Further, Parliament, engaged in negotiations with the royalists and the Scots, was not prepared to grant its troops any form of indemnity for potentially treasonable acts committed during the war.

Throughout the war, London had been a hothouse of radical ideas, in a context of heavy fiscal demands to pay for the war effort and a 'selling-out' by the Long Parliament. Among the many groups which emerged were the Levellers, who considered that the populace at large remained oppressed by the failure of Parliament

---

2   I Gentles, 'The arrears of pay of the parliamentary army at the end of the 1st Civil War' (1975) XLVIII Bulletin of the Institute of Historical Research, p 35.

to bring about a 'godly reformation'. The leading Leveller ideologist, John Lilburne, preached that all men were born equal, with equal political rights, and favoured abolition of the monarchy and the House of Lords. For the Levellers, the Long Parliament's legislative changes had not gone nearly far enough. According to the *Large Petition* of March 1647, arbitrary judicial power, once vested in Star Chamber, now lay with Parliament itself, and religious non-conformists such as the Levellers were oppressed by the dominant Presbyterian clergy even if no longer by the bishops. There was particular resentment over tithes, since they were due from all for the upkeep of a church to which by no means all subscribed, and a call for a measure of religious toleration, though not in favour of groups of which the Levellers themselves disapproved. Parliament had failed to reform the law and penal system, and abuses such as monopolies continued to abound. It is not clear when and to what extent the Levellers began to infiltrate the New Model Army, but their playing on the soldiers' grievances rapidly strained relations between army and Parliament and led to the politicisation of the army.

On 25 May 1647, the Commons, currently dominated by conservatives led by Denzil Holles, voted to disband the New Model Army with only eight weeks' arrears of pay. On 2 June, with the possible connivance of Cromwell, Cornet Joyce seized the king from his Parliamentary guards and took him to Newmarket,[3] where Sir Thomas Fairfax, now Lord General of all the Parliamentary forces, had ordered the army to rendezvous. Two days later, the army issued a *Humble Remonstrance* agreeing not to disband until its grievances were met. In the meantime, an Army Council would sit, consisting of two non-commissioned officers and two soldiers from each regiment, the latter known as 'agitators'. No longer under the control of Parliament but a political force in its own right, the army assumed an overt and decisive role in future events.

A Representation of the Army, drafted by Oliver Cromwell, his son-in-law Henry Ireton and Colonel John Lambert, and published on 14 June, declared that the army was not simply a 'mercenary army', but had its own political programme. It demanded a purge of the existing Parliament, future parliaments of fixed duration, a guaranteed right for all persons to petition Parliament and the liberty 'of tender consciences'. This was followed on 2 August by the *Heads of the Proposals*, intended as the army's terms for a settlement with the king, and largely the work of Ireton. This was surprisingly generous to the king, as well as having some basis in idealism, and was in a number of ways ahead of its time. There were to be biennial parliaments, with consequent two-yearly elections; reform of representation in Parliament so that it was linked more accurately to regional variations in wealth and population; parliamentary control of the army and navy; and parliamentary appointment of the great officers of state for terms limited to 10 years. The religious settlement should retain a national church, with bishops, but powers for enforcing attendance at Church of England services were to be abolished, leaving individuals free to worship according to their own consciences.

However, events then made a peaceful resolution impossible. The aftermath of war had brought a conservative reaction among sections of the civil populace, disillusioned at the 'arbitrary' methods used by Parliament to raise revenue,

---

3   A Cornet was a junior cavalry officer. Joyce's baptismal name seems to have gone unrecorded.

concerned about civil disorder and desirous of a return to normality. The conservative element in Parliament, in a position of much greater influence than they had been during the war, was prepared to reach a settlement with the king substantially on the terms of 1641. In the summer of 1647, fearing retaliation from the army, now moving towards London, Denzil Holles orchestrated a series of popular demonstrations in London, which culminated in a mob invading the Commons on 26 July and forcing the House to pass a resolution inviting the king to come to London. Early in August, the army occupied Westminster and the City of London.

For the time being, the army leaders, headed by Fairfax, a man of integrity with moderate political views, endeavoured with their allies within Parliament to achieve a permanent settlement based on the *Heads of the Proposals*. However, the army's presence in London allowed Lilburne and other Levellers to influence the mass of the soldiery, claiming that Fairfax and his fellow generals intended to allow the king to return to power unconditionally. Divisions developed within the army. In October, most of the regiments dismissed their original 'agitators' and elected others to represent them on the Army Council. These drew up the *Case of the Army Truly Stated*, a much more radical document than its predecessor and, in its philosophy that 'all power is originally and essentially in the whole body of the people ... [and] their free choice or consent by representers is the only original or foundation of all just government', heavily influenced by Leveller ideas.[4] The idea of universal male suffrage appears in concrete form for the first time, as well as a call for the power to make or repeal laws to reside in the House of Commons.

This was followed on 28 October by the *Agreement of the People*, largely an expression of Leveller views.[5] This called for the Long Parliament to be dissolved on the last day of September 1648 and for biennial parliaments thereafter. Sovereign power should vest in Parliament, but the people had inalienable 'native rights' to:

(a) freedom of religion;

(b) freedom from impressment for military service;

(c) freedom from punishment for participation in 'the late public differences', except in execution of judgments of the House of Commons;

(d) equality under the law.

This went considerably further than a Parliament currently dominated by conservatism was prepared to go, but a serious split between Parliament and its army was for the time being prevented by the escape of the king from confinement at Hampton Court on 11 November 1647, and a closing of ranks against the threat of counter-revolution.

Charles I, temporarily a free man, allied himself with the Scots, promising to impose Scottish Presbyterianism on England for three years in return for military assistance. It is open to considerable doubt whether he was ever sincere in this accommodation with his former enemies, but before long, he was once more a prisoner, being confined by the Governor of Carisbrooke Castle when he went to the Isle of Wight to rally further support.

4   See Davies, *op cit*, p 149.
5   Printed in JP Kenyon, *The Stuart Constitution*, 2nd edn, 1986, CUP, No 85.

14.3   TRIAL AND EXECUTION OF A KING

Though the king had no direct involvement in the Second Civil War, his escape and alliance with the Scots caused the ranks of the army to lose all patience with him. Either he would never agree to a settlement which forced him to accept limits on his independent exercise of power or, if such a settlement could be reached, he would take the first opportunity to break it. Some elements in the army, heavily influenced by fundamentalist theology of the wrath of God, appear to have become convinced that the renewal of war had come about because of the leniency they had earlier shown to their enemies, a view encouraged by Cromwell.

For Charles, the renewed war proved a fiasco. The New Model Army, now reunited in the face of a common enemy, was far more efficient than its ill-organised opponents. By October 1648, it had defeated a Scottish invasion and a series of conservative risings, an anti-royalist regime had resumed control in Edinburgh, and radicals in the army and elsewhere were calling for Charles's trial for treason.

Relations between Parliament and its army now reached breaking point. Despite having earlier resolved not to negotiate with the king, Parliament began discussions, even accepting the king's request that he be permitted to come to London. This incensed the militants. On 18 November, Henry Ireton, the most influential political figure in the army in the temporary absence of Cromwell (who was in Scotland), persuaded the Army Council to accept his *Remonstrance of the Army*, which called for Parliament to be purged of its ideologically unsound elements and for the king to be put on trial. At about this time, Ireton began negotiations with the civilian Leveller leaders, securing their support for a march on London, which the army reached on 2 December. On the same day, the king finally rejected the proposals put to him, but on 5 December, Parliament voted to continue the negotiations.

At this point, the army acted. Coward considers that its extremism and distrust of Parliament was now so entrenched that retaliation in some form was inevitable, the only concrete issue being whether there should be a purge of Parliament or a dissolution and new elections. The radical MP Edmund Ludlow advised Ireton against dissolution, since new elections would return an anti-army majority to Parliament. On the morning of 6 December, on Ireton's orders, Colonel Thomas Pride and Lord Grey of Groby, standing outside the Commons' chamber along with soldiers of Pride's regiment, forcibly excluded some 110 MPs from the House. A further 260 voluntarily absented themselves, leaving a 'Rump' of about 150 members which sat until the end of the session, augmented after the king's execution by some 100 of the members who had voluntarily absented themselves.

The remainder of December was largely occupied in Parliament in debating whether and on what charges the extreme and unprecedented step should be taken of putting Charles I on trial, though Cromwell remained opposed to the trial until the end of the month. Following his conversion, however, events moved rapidly. On 4 January 1649, the Commons passed the following resolutions:

That the people are, under God, the origin of all just power ...

That the Commons of England, in Parliament assembled, being chosen by, and representing the people, have the supreme power in this nation ...

That whatever is enacted, or declared for law, by the Commons, in Parliament assembled, hath the force of law; and all the people of this nation are concluded thereby; although the consent and concurrence of king, or House of Peers, be not had thereunto.

Again, this was revolutionary; a declaration by an extremist remnant of the Commons elected eight years before that power vested not in the King in Parliament, nor in the two Houses together, but in the Commons alone.

The Rump then passed an ordinance creating a court of 135 commissioners to try the king. The Lords had been reduced by desertions to about a dozen, but this remnant nevertheless refused to pass the ordinance. In a further move of doubtful legal validity, the Commons proceeded with the trial, even though only about half the chosen commissioners could be persuaded to act. The trial opened on 20 January and its outcome was rendered a foregone conclusion by the king's refusal to accept the authority of the court, and so to plead or to defend himself. In a written submission which the commissioners would not allow to be read, he argued that the liberties of his people were bound up with his own and for him to acknowledge the authority of a usurping power would be to deny those liberties. Kenyon remarks that if the king had chosen to defend himself, the trial would have been prolonged, giving time for reaction to build up in the courts of foreign monarchs as well as at home.[6] As it was, the trial concluded on 27 January in the sentence that for levying war against Parliament and the people therein represented, the king should be executed by beheading as a tyrant, traitor, murderer and public enemy. At this point, he attempted to address the court, but was forthwith escorted out by armed soldiers.

After persuasion which may have included threats of physical harm, 59 of the commissioners signed the king's death warrant, and Charles I died on a scaffold erected outside the Banqueting House of Whitehall Palace on the afternoon of 30 January 1649. As was the case with his grandmother, Mary Queen of Scots, the manner of his condemnation and death did much to create a myth of a martyr, who would have been a moderate and successful ruler if only his subjects had allowed him to be, and who was finally subjected to a show trial without legal validity in order to secure the end desired by his enemies. There are many parallels between Charles and Mary. Both came to power inadequately prepared for rule; both lacked the common sense and pragmatism, the willingness to compromise their own beliefs on occasion, which was necessary in a ruler of their times. Charles only became more intransigent as time went on, and in the end amply justified the views of his political enemies that he would neither agree to any settlement which lessened his powers nor adhere to any such settlement if it should be forced upon him.

There is also a parallel in the absence of legality of the process against Mary and against Charles I. The latter is a supreme example of victor's justice, carried into effect by a narrow group determined on retribution and convinced of the absolute and unambiguous rightness of their cause. The trial of a king had no precedent, nor had the charges against him any basis in existing law. Precedent, in the *Case of Proclamations*, established that only Parliament had power to legislate to change existing law; Parliament consisted, by that stage, of King, Lords and Commons, in Parliament assembled. Yet the process against Charles I was authorised by a resolution of a remnant of the House of Commons alone, after the House had been purged of the majority of its membership for ideological reasons. Moreover, when the trial had ended in a guilty verdict, Oliver Cromwell and his hard-line cabal resorted to physical threats to gain the necessary endorsements on the death warrant. It was a far cry from the principled behaviour of 1641.

---

6   JP Kenyon, *Stuart England*, 1985, Penguin, p 164.

14.4   CREATION OF A COMMONWEALTH

With the king dead, the army and its political allies wasted no time in pushing through further unprecedented legislation in order to give effect to the revolution. On 6 February, the Rump voted to abolish the House of Lords and, on the following day, the monarchy, having first ordered the seclusion of all MPs who had voted on 5 December 1648 in favour of continued negotiations with the king. On 13 February, the executive functions of the monarchy were vested for a period of one year in a 40-member Council of State. A process of removing references to the monarchy from institutions and official documents was set in train and, finally, on 19 May 1649, an Act of the new unicameral Parliament declared England to be 'a Commonwealth or Free State'.

14.5   THE REPUBLICAN INTERLUDE

14.5.1 The early years

Benefiting from hindsight, the student is aware that the Interregnum, which saw the first and so far the only republican regime in British history, lasted a mere 11 years, and for much of that period, Oliver Cromwell occupied a position analogous to that of monarch. There is therefore much temptation to pass over these 11 years as a brief aberration, a time of gloom when the country was ruled by Major-Generals and extreme Puritanism brought about the abolition of Christmas. But this brief aberration is nevertheless of interest, if only because it represented something to be avoided in the future.

The junta which now held power was not in any sense a representative body and soon found itself between the rock of conservative demands for a return to normality and stability, and the hard place of radical desires for further sweeping changes in the legal, social and religious spheres. This was a period when further extremist groups came to the fore, notably the 'True Levellers', or 'Diggers', who denounced property as a Norman invention, and the Fifth Monarchists, who believed that the execution of Charles I signified that the Second Coming of Christ was imminent, and that Christ would now reign with His saints for 1,000 years.[7]

The general uncertainty and social discontent of much of the 1640s was only heightened by the continuation of the series of bad harvests, which had occurred from 1646 onwards, and consequent rising food prices. In addition, the threat to the new political order from elsewhere in the British Isles – the Irish rebellion had yet to be suppressed and the Scots government had not accepted the abolition of the monarchy – and from France and Holland, now emerging from the Thirty Years War, meant that a large standing army had to be maintained, and taxation kept at levels which had proved deeply unpopular during the wars. For much of the Commonwealth, the political leadership, themselves revolutionaries, were forced to take repressive measures against public opinion which considered them insufficiently revolutionary.

---

7   The name came from their belief that Christ's kingdom – the Fifth Monarchy – would follow the destruction of the empires of Babylon, Persia, Greece and Rome.

Within months of the king's execution, relations between the military and civilian leadership and the Levellers became irretrievably soured. As early as March 1649, the principal Leveller leaders were arrested, and in May, following mutinies in two regiments, Fairfax had the ringleaders shot and purged other known Levellers from the ranks. John Lilburne was imprisoned and, in October, brought to trial on charges of treason, though his trial ended in acquittal. In September, the Rump passed an Act imposing strict censorship of the press, of some wider interest since the official inspector of all printed matter was the poet John Milton.

In this period, however, the Commonwealth achieved very considerable military success. Cromwell spent the latter half of 1649 in Ireland, where he crushed the rebellion with such efficiency and ruthlessness that his name has been a byword there ever since. He left his deputies with orders to confiscate all Catholic land, to convert the Irish to the Protestant faith and to deport all rebels to the English colonies in the Caribbean. By the Restoration, the proportion of land in Protestant ownership had doubled; the bardic schools which preserved the traditional Gaelic culture were destroyed. 12,000 rebels were transported to penal servitude in the West Indies and another 34,000 were sent to the continent as mercenaries.

Cromwell also dealt with military opposition from Scotland and the royalist remnant in England. The Prince of Wales, who had proclaimed himself king from exile following his father's death, was crowned in Edinburgh after accepting the Covenant and sought to use Scotland as a springboard for recovery of England and Ireland. However, Cromwell invaded Scotland in 1650 and defeated the Army of the Covenant at Dunbar and a second time a year later at Worcester. English garrisons occupied the Scottish lowlands, and the Scottish Parliament and monarchy were abolished. Scotland was henceforth under direct rule from England. In the same period, a navy commanded by former Parliamentary soldiers, notably Robert Blake and George Monck, ended the privateering activities of the French and Dutch in the Channel and was active against piracy as far away as the Mediterranean.

These events left Cromwell without a rival in government. Fairfax, originally the senior military commander, had opposed the king's execution and gradually withdrew into private life as his personal honour prevented him from giving unqualified support to the regime, finally resigning his command rather than lead the invasion of Scotland. Henry Ireton, Cromwell's son-in-law and close ally, but also a potential opponent, died in 1651.

Oliver Cromwell is yet another enigmatic figure, his actions during his years of power not only inconsistent with any particular philosophy, but frequently inconsistent with one another. A minor squire from Huntingdon, he came to prominence as commander of the troops raised by the Eastern Association, demonstrating the capacity to inspire the men under him which is the hallmark of the greatest military leaders. Coward gives an interesting summary of the varying views of the man which attempt to reconcile the inconsistencies manifested by his actions,[8] but what can be said is that Cromwell was a man ruthlessly determined to achieve the goals he set, who was not deterred from action by moral scruples and who believed strongly in his own destiny.

8   B Coward, *The Stuart Age*, 1980, Longman, pp 253–59.

14.5.2 Signs of strain

1650–52 was the high summer of the Commonwealth. From then on, the regime became increasingly repressive, increasingly intolerant of dissent, and dependent on Cromwell to such an extent that within two years of his death, the whole unstable edifice fell apart and the only solution appeared to be to restore the monarchy, without the constitutional restrictions on the king's power that could have prevented a renewal of authoritarian government under James II and a second revolutionary upheaval.

One focus for dissent was the Rump Parliament itself which, however shaky its legitimacy following the events of the 1640s and the loss of the majority of its elected membership through Pride's Purge, was the only institution of the Commonwealth with any real claim to legitimacy. It adopted a moderate, even conservative approach to the great issues of the day, particularly in religion, and so failed to satisfy the radical aspirations of the army or give effect to Cromwell's own policies. Though the Act of 1649 abolishing the monarchy promised a dissolution of Parliament and new elections 'as soon as possible', the Rump showed no sign of dissolving itself and, indeed, entered into a bargain with the army in 1651 to prolong its life to 3 November 1654, the 14th anniversary of its opening, in return for a reduction in the army establishment following the Battle of Worcester.

The army was growing discontented again. Although war with Holland broke out in 1652 over the Navigation Acts passed by the Rump in 1650–51, which provided that goods could only be transported to or from England in English ships and lasted until 1654, it was entirely a naval war, so that the army continued in idleness after Worcester, with the same consequences as in 1646–47. On 13 August 1652, the Council of Officers, the successor to the now-disbanded Army Council, and the effective supplanter of the Council of State, issued a petition to the Rump calling for the implementation of the terms of the *Agreement of the People* of 1647, including an immediate dissolution of Parliament.

For a period, Cromwell temporised, persuading the army to drop its demands for an immediate dissolution. However, on 20 April 1653, after the Rump introduced a Bill of Elections, Cromwell went to Westminster with armed troops and expelled the members by force. There was now no barrier to change initiated by Cromwell, the judges persuading themselves that Parliament was only temporarily suspended. From April to July 1653, Cromwell ruled England in his capacity as military commander-in-chief. On 4 July, an assembly of 140 members nominated by him assembled at Westminster 'that the peace, safety and good government of the Commonwealth should be provided for'.

Though not officially a parliament, the assembly described itself as such and later became known as the 'Barebones Parliament' after one of its members, the otherwise obscure Praise God Barebones.[9] It did not last long. By the end of the year, conflict between a radical minority and moderate majority had reached such a pitch that on 12 December, the latter voted to surrender their authority to Lord General Cromwell, whence it had come. Cromwell expected such a move and had already had the Council of Officers prepare an *Instrument of Government* which vested executive authority in him as Lord Protector of the Commonwealth.[10]

---

9   Some writers refer to it as the 'Nominated Parliament'.
10   Printed in Kenyon, *op cit*, *The Stuart Constitution*, No 91.

14.5.3 *The Instrument of Government*

This *Instrument*, the first written constitution in the British Isles, was in part an attempt to give effect to the *Heads of the Proposals* of 1647. It defined the powers of the head of state, the Lord Protector, and provided that he was to be advised and assisted in carrying out his executive functions by a Council of 15 named persons. Legislative power was vested in the Protector and a unicameral and triennial Parliament, which was to sit for at least five months in each of its sessions. However, this constitution was very much built around Oliver Cromwell, who was specifically named as the first Protector, and its provisions contained a number of *lacunae* where his authority was not subject to scrutiny by Parliament. Provision was made for succession to the Protectorship, but none for the removal of a Protector from office, so that he was head of state for life, much as was a monarch. Although the Protector had no veto on legislation, unless it contravened or sought to amend the *Instrument*, he could, prior to the opening of the first of the new Parliaments in September 1654, issue ordinances which would have the force of law unless rejected by that parliament. He was also granted £200,000 per year for the expenses of civil administration and maintenance for a standing army of 20,000 foot and 10,000 horse, neither subject to amendment by Parliament, together with the remaining Crown Lands and other perquisites of the Crown. Control of the armed forces would vest in the Protector and Parliament when Parliament was sitting, between sittings in the Protector and Council, which was dominated by Cromwell's allies.

Membership of Parliament was set at 400 from England and 30 each from Scotland and Ireland. Attempts were made along Leveller lines to make Parliament more representative of the actual distribution of population by suppressing 'decayed' boroughs and reducing a number of others to one member each, the surplus seats being redistributed among the shires. This produced a balance of representation in favour of the counties, which held 66% of seats, as against 34% in the original Long Parliament. Other provisions seem to have been left deliberately vague, in particular, the power of appointment of officers of state and judges.

The new system was uneasy from its inception. Along with a balance of seats in favour of the counties, the restriction of the county franchise to persons holding real or personal property worth £200 meant that the new Parliament, intended by its composition to give effect to Leveller views on representation, was dominated to a greater extent than its predecessors by country gentry, who tended towards conservatism and the desire for order and stability. Furthermore, in the first half of 1654, Cromwell used his temporary powers to promulgate a series of ordinances which were highly controversial in their content, including a Treason Ordinance which made it treasonable to deny the authority of the Protector and Parliament. Deadlock duly ensued after Parliament opened on 3 September, and it did not augur well for future stability and co-operation that Cromwell, following the example of his executed predecessor, dissolved Parliament on 16 January 1655.

14.5.4 The regime under pressure

From then on, government became more repressive. Following an abortive royalist rising, the Council of Officers, with Cromwell's concurrence, divided England and Wales into 10 military districts, each under the governance of a senior officer. The powers of the 'Major-Generals', set out in Instructions from Cromwell in October 1655,[11] were not restricted to the military sphere. Their primary authority was in the suppression of rebellion and insurrection, but for this purpose, they were given very substantial powers in policing highways and the maintenance of public order, dealing with 'idle and loose people' and suppressing gaming houses and houses of evil fame in London and Westminster. They were also given powers of enforcement of the prohibition now imposed on race meetings, cock fighting, bear baiting and stage plays 'forasmuch as treason and rebellion is usually hatched and contrived against the state upon such occasions, and much evil and wickedness committed' and a general duty to monitor 'disaffected persons'. For these purposes, the Major-Generals were financed by a 10% tax on the estates of the royalists, who were their main targets.

At the same time, there was serious opposition to Cromwell's policies from the judiciary. The abolition of the monarchy and its replacement by a revolutionary regime had little previous impact on the day-to-day administration of justice, except for the formal replacement of Law French by English, still less had the judiciary as a body questioned the legitimacy of government since 1649. Individual judges had on occasion retired into private life, but the government had no difficulty in replacing them. In 1654, however, with their own position under threat from projected changes to the Court of Chancery, the judiciary closed ranks and several declared that they had previously accepted an illegal constitution for the sake of good and stable government, but were not prepared to allow the executive to override that constitution. Though Cromwell had not issued any further ordinances since the dissolution of Parliament, the legality of the original ordinances, never confirmed by Parliament, was now being questioned in court. This was particularly the case in respect of the Treason Ordinance, and the Protector now sought to suppress stirrings of judicial independence.

In *Cony's Case*, a merchant who was imprisoned in November 1654 for refusing to pay customs duty on imported silk, forcibly preventing customs officers from seizing his property and refusing to pay the consequent fine argued that the customs duties concerned were illegal because they had been levied by virtue of an ordinance which had not been endorsed by Parliament.[12] When the matter reached the Court of the Upper Bench, formerly the King's Bench, in May 1655, the Protector and Council ordered that Cony's lawyers be imprisoned for challenging the Protector's prerogative. When Rolle LCJ allowed Cony's action to proceed, he was brought before the Council and chose to resign.

The drift towards repression was only encouraged by events outside the British Isles. Earlier in 1655, an expedition known as the Western Design sailed for the West Indies with the intention of making gains from the Spanish empire in the Caribbean. On 24 July, news reached the Protector of the heavy defeat of this expedition at San Domingo (now Haiti). Coward demonstrates convincingly that this defeat, following the long period of military and naval success since the mid-1640s, left Cromwell's belief that he and his purposes enjoyed God's blessing severely shaken. Coward goes on to link this to the use of the Major-Generals to promote the godly reformation which would lead to the renewal of God's blessing on the Commonwealth.[13]

---

11 Kenyon, *op cit, The Stuart Constitution*, No 94.
12 Coward, *op cit*, pp 271–72.
13 WC Abbott (ed), *The Writings and Speeches of Oliver Cromwell*, 4 vols, 1937–47, Harvard UP, vol IV, pp 377–78.

The Major-Generals varied in the enthusiasm and vigour with which they exercised their power – an extreme case was Major-General Worsley of Lancashire, Cheshire and Staffordshire, who closed down over 200 ale houses in the Blackburn Hundred – but their role aroused hatred in the provinces for the very traditional reason that they represented the imposition of central authority. Further, operating the 10% tax on former royalists meant investigation into the activities of individuals during the 1640s, at a time when old divisions were beginning to heal.

Faced with the possibility that the judges might declare the 1654 Ordinances illegal, so legitimising the all-too-evident opposition to the continuing high levels of taxation and customs duties, Cromwell summoned a further Parliament for 17 September 1656 with the intention of gaining endorsement for the Ordinances. Hostility to the Major-Generals resulted in the election of over 100 MPs who were prevented by the Protector and Council from taking their seats on the grounds that they were likely to be critics of the regime. Initially, there was a reasonable degree of co-operation between government and Parliament, though whether this was because the remaining members were now too cowed to oppose the Protector's will is unclear. However, the confrontation which then followed brought an end to the system created by the *Instrument of Government* and the introduction of a second new constitution, the *Humble Petition and Advice*.

The trigger for this crisis was a legal *cause célèbre* involving a soldier turned Quaker evangelist, James Nayler, who, in the course of a preaching tour of the West Country, rode into Bristol on an ass in a re-enactment of Christ's entry into Jerusalem. Parliament found him guilty of 'horrid blasphemy' on 8 December 1656 and sentenced him to be branded, bored through the tongue and flogged twice before being imprisoned for life. It should be borne in mind that the Quakers, now very much a mainstream religious body, were in the mid-17th century regarded as dangerous and subversive. Quakers argued that actions and thoughts were 'right' if their individual consciences told them this was the case, regardless of the views of any around them. Suspicion of them was only heightened by their pacifism and their refusal to take off their hats in the presence of their social superiors, to take oaths and to pay tithes, and by their close links with radical politics.

Cromwell was not in much sympathy with Nayler's views. 'If this be liberty, God deliver me from such liberty', he wrote to the Speaker of Parliament on Christmas Day 1656,[14] and he did not include Quakers among the groups to whom he was prepared to concede toleration. However, he was concerned that similar repressive measures might be used by a conservative Parliament against more moderate sects such as Baptists. On 27 February 1657, he informed the Council of Officers that the existing unicameral Parliament was in need of 'a check or balancing power [meaning the House of Lords or a House so constituted]'.[15] This might be expected to have led to concerted opposition from Parliament. The opposite was in fact the case, apparently for two reasons. One was the desire of a Parliament dominated by conservatives for stability; the other was Cromwell's own adroit manoeuvring behind the scenes, which included dissociating himself from the army and increasing his support among civilian interests.

---

14 Quoted in Coward, *op cit*, p 273.
15 Abbott, *op cit*, vol IV, p 417.

Already, on 28 October the previous year, a backbencher had suggested that the Protectorship be made hereditary. Now the *Humble Petition and Advice* of Parliament called on Cromwell to assume the crown. This he refused, for reasons which may well include fear of the army's reaction and concern that such a step would see the end of God's blessing on him and his purpose.[16] However, on 25 May 1657, he accepted an amended *Humble Petition and Advice*, together with a further petition on 26 June. Together, these gave him power to nominate his successor as Protector and created an upper House of 40 members nominated by him. He was also granted a greatly increased annual income of £1,300,000, of which £1 million was specifically appropriated to military purposes.

Though Cromwell was apparently in an unassailable position, the change backfired rapidly and only exacerbated the fundamental instability of the Protectorate and its over-dependence on one man. Nomination of the members of the new 'Other House' removed a number of Cromwell's leading supporters from the Commons, and radical opinion was anyway hostile to the existence of the Other House. Cromwell's death from malaria on 3 September 1658 brought matters to a head. His son, Richard Cromwell, followed him as Protector on the nomination of the Council of State, since he failed to choose a successor. The younger Cromwell was an ineffectual figure who earned before long the derisory nickname of 'Tumbledown Dick', and failed either to mobilise support around him or to play the competing factions off against one another.

In any case, there were serious doubts over the legitimacy of the regime, since the *Instrument of Government* had not been approved by a Parliament and the *Humble Petition* had never been passed by a full Parliament. Though the Council of State was itself a creation of the *Instrument of Government*, it nevertheless summoned a Parliament for January 1659 on the pre-1654 system of representation, together with the Other House as nominated by Cromwell. In contrast to the last two Parliaments, with their inbuilt conservative majority, this Parliament proved to be dominated by radicals and republicans. They refused to recognise Richard Cromwell as lawful Protector, while the attempts of conservatives to restrict religious toleration and the freedom of the army to indulge in political activity led the army, once more discontented and under radical influences, to force a dissolution of Parliament on 21 April 1659. Ironically, the army, which had opposed the Rump from 1649 to its expulsion in 1653, now recalled the Rump, which, having failed to satisfy the army's demands and then called for the army to be purged of radicals, was expelled for the second time on 13 October. Richard Cromwell retired into private life, living on in obscurity until 1712.

The Commonwealth now slid into inexorable decline. The army grandees set up an interim government, termed the Committee of Safety, headed by John Fleetwood, on 27 October, but this failed to gain any serious support. The army in Scotland, headed by General George Monck, declared for the Rump. Their example was followed by troops in Yorkshire and Ireland, and the navy. Political turmoil coincided with an acute economic depression, fears that the government could not guarantee law and order, and organised threats to withhold taxes. On 24 December, Fleetwood resigned and handed over his powers to the Rump.

16   Abbott, *op cit*, vol IV, p 473.

On 1 January 1660, Monck, newly-appointed by the Rump as military commander-in-chief, began the last of the army marches on London. He had managed to keep the Army of Scotland outside political influences and under proper discipline[17] and, on arrival in London, was able to take effective control of government, dealing with the problem of unrest among English troops by dispersing them in remote garrisons. Before long, he concluded that the only means of securing stable government was the restoration of the Stuarts in the person of Charles I's eldest son, nominally Charles II since 1649 and currently in exile in Holland. On 21 February, summoned by Monck, the MPs expelled in Pride's Purge 11 years earlier returned to Westminster. The Long Parliament, as reconstituted, declared itself on 16 March dissolved and ordered a general election. Monck had already been in secret communication with Charles II who, on 4 April, issued the Declaration of Breda, in which he offered, subject to the approval of a free Parliament, an amnesty for all offences committed during the Interregnum, full payment of arrears of army pay, confirmation of all land sales concluded since 1642 and so of all titles to land, and the possibility of general religious toleration.

This Declaration was presented to the new Parliament – strictly a Convention, as there was no one available with authority to summon a Parliament – which included a restored House of Lords when it assembled on 25 April. There was near unanimity in both Houses in declaring that government ought to be in the hands of King, Lords and Commons, proclaiming Charles II as king and resolving that a fleet should be sent to bring him home. He wasted no time, landing at Dover on 26 May and entering London in triumph on 29 May.

---

17 Monck's own regiment survives as the Coldstream Guards, taking their name from the town of Coldstream where they crossed the Tweed into England. When the rest of the army of the Commonwealth period was disbanded, Monck's Regiment ceremonially laid down their arms as soldiers of the Commonwealth and took them up again as soldiers of King Charles II.

CHAPTER 15

RESTORATION AND REVOLUTION 1660–89

15.1 CHARLES II 1660–85

15.1.1 Introduction

There is a national myth of the reign of Charles II, the joyous period when the people threw off the shackles of Puritanism after 11 years of misery and the country was united behind its 'Merry Monarch' who, between dalliances with Nell Gwynne and other mistresses, founded the Royal Society and Chelsea Hospital and revitalised the Royal Navy. Then the accession of Charles's doctrinaire Catholic brother, James II, and his attempt to resurrect authoritarian rule based on Divine Right led to revolution and the final triumph of Parliament under a settlement which created the constitutional system which represented perfection in the eyes of writers such as Dicey and Macaulay.

The reality, it need hardly be said, was more complicated and far more ambiguous. Crucially, although most of the 1641 legislation was confirmed at the Restoration, the deep political and religious divisions which brought about the Civil Wars and suppression of the monarchy remained unresolved, and in the euphoria of 1660, no attempt was made to deal constructively with the constitutional issues which had emerged over the previous half-century. To exacerbate matters, there was deep mutual distrust between those who had remained royalists during the Interregnum and those who had served the republican regime. Instead of the myth, the reign of Charles II can more accurately be seen as a period where existing wounds were bandaged over, and a capable and adroit monarch and his ministers succeeded in pre-empting further fundamental crisis. However, major problems were carried over to the next reign and the whirlwind was reaped a second time.

15.1.2 The Restoration Settlement

The principal bones of contention in 1660 remained government finance and religion. In other spheres, the Convention Parliament was relatively successful in settling immediate problems, though deeper wounds remained unhealed. Judicial decisions made during the Interregnum were confirmed and an Act of Indemnity granted a general pardon to all but the few closely associated with the condemnation of Charles I. A settlement in relation to confiscated estates and land sales was worked out which sought to be just and equitable as between those who had been deprived of their lands and those who had then purchased them in good faith. Confiscated lands of Crown and church were restored, as were those of some royalists. However, a loophole was left where an estate had not been confiscated but had been sold in order to raise money to pay fines, and it was suspected that the new king rewarded his former enemies more readily than those who had loyally supported his father. Hatred festered, which found expression in the exhumation, trial and condemnation of Cromwell's decaying corpse.

The Convention Parliament was concerned, like its predecessors, that generous financial provision would make the Crown independent of Parliament, and Coward considers that the members also failed to recognise the true extent of necessary expenditure, in particular that the wider political situation meant that a standing army had to be retained and a substantial garrison provided for Tangier, part of the dowry of Catherine of Braganza, whom Charles married in 1662.[1] Further, the high taxation of the Civil Wars and Commonwealth had been a major source of popular discontent, so that in the short term, it appeared to Charles II and his ministers easier to borrow than to risk further discontent. The Convention Parliament was dissolved at the end of 1660 when Crown debt stood at £925,000 and ordinary revenues were no more than £900,000, well short of the £1,200,000 that the Convention calculated as the sum necessary for ordinary royal expenditure, and itself an under-estimate.

In religion, the toleration hoped for by many and prefigured in the Declaration of Breda failed to materialise. Although the remaining English Catholics had largely supported the royalist cause, there was no real prospect of toleration towards them. However, if only for political reasons, the king was keen to bring at least the less extreme of the Protestant groups together with the Anglicans – the successors to the Laudians – into the umbrella of a single national church. Once again, the issues lay between the different Protestant groupings, in particular between those who favoured restoration of the episcopacy and the Presbyterians. An intensive period of negotiations culminated in the issue by the king of the Worcester House Declaration, which proposed a church settlement that attempted to satisfy both persuasions. In the event, nothing concrete was achieved and the religious issue was left to fester.

Though the settlement of 1660, such as it was, represented the position of 1641, there was some turning back of the clock. The early years of the Cavalier Parliament, which sat from 1661 to 1679, saw the Crown regaining sole control of the militia (the Militia Acts 1661 and 1662) and, implicitly, sole power of appointment of Privy Councillors and officers of state, since Parliament made no attempt to challenge appointments or to seek a role in them. As a check on future assertions of parliamentary authority, an Act of 1661 imposed the penalties of praemunire on any who claimed that Parliament had legislative powers independent of the king. Acts followed against 'tumultuous petitioning' in 1661 and imposing press censorship in 1662. The Corporation Act of 1661 required all office holders to swear a threefold oath, giving allegiance to the Crown, accepting the religious supremacy of the monarch and non-resistance to the monarchy, and effectively restricting membership of municipal corporations to Anglican communicants. In 1664, a new Triennial Act, though it re-stated the maximum period between Parliaments to be three years, removed the mechanism created by the 1641 Act to bypass a failure to summon Parliament.

At the same time, religious toleration was severely restricted, at a time of reaction against extremist sects and their association with anti-monarchism. The Act of Uniformity of 1662 reinstated the Book of Common Prayer, in the revision regarded by many as the greatest strength of the Anglican Church. All clergy who failed to subscribe to the Thirty-Nine Articles of belief by 24 August 1661 were deprived of their livings. Additionally, all clergy were required to renounce the Solemn League and Covenant and to be ordained by a bishop. The Five Mile Act forbade dissenting ministers from preaching within five miles of a town or city unless licenced. These changes set formally in place the division between Anglicans and dissenters, which

---

1   B Coward, *The Stuart Age*, 1980, Longman, pp 286–87. The dowry also included Bombay and £350,000 in cash.

still operates today. Purged of about one-tenth of their numbers, the Restoration church became aggressively monarchist and went to the extreme of establishing a cult of Charles I as a martyr.

On the other hand, Charles II, under the influence of his Catholic queen and Catholic mother, and possibly preferring Catholicism as the faith which supported the absolute monarchies of France, Spain and Austria, sought toleration for Catholics, though opposition remained so entrenched that his efforts made little progress. Suspicion that Catholicism was re-asserting itself as a powerful influence at court gradually worsened, particularly as it became clear the king's marriage would remain barren, so that his successor would be his brother, James, Duke of York, who converted to Rome in around 1668.

15.1.3 Early difficulties

The perennial problem of finance was exacerbated by two factors. One was the Anglo-Dutch War of 1665–67, which arose from trade rivalries. The other was the king's extravagance and self-indulgence. His enthusiasm for horse racing, sailing and the theatres of Covent Garden all had to be paid for, as had his generosity to his mistresses and 14 acknowledged bastards. Initially, Parliament proved tractable over voting finance for the war effort, but their attitudes hardened after the first year did not bring the expected quick victory and handsome gains from captured Dutch vessels and their cargoes. The outcome of the Four Days' Battle in the Channel, in which the English lost 8,000 men and 20 ships, was a precipitating factor in what became a major crisis. At the same time, the Crown's ordinary revenues were drastically reduced by the toll on persons and property in London, much the largest and richest city in the realm, caused by the Plague of 1665 and the Great Fire the following year. The Plague is estimated to have killed some 70,000 people. The Fire destroyed goods valued at £3.5 million as well as 13,200 houses, on which the Hearth Tax introduced in 1662 was levied. It has been calculated that ordinary Crown revenues averaged £824,000 in 1662–65, but dropped to £647,000 in the following two years. Towards the end of 1666, Parliament began to seek scapegoats, attacking the maladministration of royal officials and ordering those responsible for the Navy, ordnance and stores to present their accounts for inspection.

In January 1667, negotiations began for peace with Holland, but assumptions of a speedy end to the war led to the premature paying-off of some warships and the failure to keep others in good repair, so that the Navy was in no position to prevent the Dutch from sailing unmolested up the Thames Estuary in June 1667 and into the Medway to attack the naval base at Chatham. This resulted in an army mobilisation, which had, of course, to be paid for, and thus in the recall of Parliament in July. This gave the two Houses the opportunity to find scapegoats among the king's ministers themselves, especially as the final peace treaty brought England nothing save the former Dutch colony of New Amsterdam, now re-named New York but considered a poor substitute for captured treasure fleets. For some time, the Lord Chancellor, Lord Clarendon, had been increasingly estranged from the king, who objected to Clarendon's criticism of his private life. On 30 August, Charles dismissed Clarendon and, after articles of impeachment were brought against him, the former Lord Chancellor fled to France.

For a time, Parliament's desire for vengeance was appeased and there was a period of co-operation between monarch and legislature, but after 1671, there came a rupture between the two which lasted until the end of the reign, heightened anti-Catholicism among the political classes and set the scene for the crisis which constituted the reign of James II.

15.1.4 The 1670s

From around 1670, Charles II and his ministers adopted a pro-French policy in foreign affairs, if only to gain the support of Louis XIV against the Dutch. This resulted in the secret Treaty of Dover of 22 May 1670, concluded in cloak-and-dagger fashion under the cover of a visit to England by Charles's sister, Henrietta, wife of Louis's brother, the Duke of Orleans. This created an anti-Dutch alliance and provided that Louis was to pay Charles the sum of £225,000 per year during the ensuing war. In a clause whose contents were not revealed even to his ministers, the king agreed 'to reconcile himself with the Church of Rome as soon as his country's affairs permit' and Louis agreed to grant him £150,000 and to provide and pay 6,000 troops.

All this necessarily involved some relaxation of the official line against Catholics; a Declaration of Indulgence of 1672 suspended the penal laws, so allowing both Catholics and Protestant dissenters to worship in private, just as the king declared war in what became the Third Dutch War of 1672–74. The Crown's financial situation remained parlous, the more so as Charles was not prepared to restrain his personal spending. Things reached such a pitch at the beginning of 1672 that on 7 January, the king and his ministers issued the 'Stop on the Exchequer', which suspended repayments to government creditors for a period of one year.

The policies, however, backfired badly. What successes there were against the Dutch were largely achieved by the French, causing the English to recognise the potential threat posed by French expansion in the Low Countries. When Parliament met in February 1673 for the first time in nearly two years, fury at the Declaration of Indulgence caused the Commons to vote unanimously that 'penal statutes in matters ecclesiastical cannot be suspended but by an Act of Parliament'. The controversy over the 'suspending power' – the prerogative power claimed by the monarch to suspend the application of an Act of Parliament – which became central to the conflicts of James II's reign, along with the 'dispensing power' (to dispense with the application of statute to a particular person or category of persons) was beginning to emerge.

Parliament then forced the king to climb down by refusing to vote further subsidies for the war unless he rescinded the Declaration of Indulgence. Charles accepted the first of two Test Acts, which required all persons holding office under the Crown to take the oaths of allegiance, supremacy and non-resistance, and to renounce the doctrine of transubstantiation. This struck directly at Catholics, since no Catholic would give up a central element of his religious faith. Overall, the Act further institutionalised anti-Catholicism and represented a general hardening of attitudes, since MPs who were Protestant dissenters now joined with Anglicans in speaking and voting in favour of the Act. Early in 1674, parliamentary opposition to the Dutch war – unpopular on ideological grounds because the young Dutch *stadtholder*, William of Orange, was seen as the main Protestant bulwark against Catholic France – persuaded the government to seek a peace settlement. No longer was the principal religious division between different Protestant groups, it was once again between Protestant and Catholic.

Why anti-Catholicism persisted, indeed hardened, in the latter half of the 17th century to the point where it became the trigger for revolution is far from clear. Catholics formed only a small proportion of the population – less than 5% in 1676 on the most reliable estimate – and there were no more than 500 of the allegedly dangerous and subversive Catholic clergy operating in England. The papacy also showed no sign of giving clear direction either to its clergy or to Catholic rulers.[2] Rather, the main cause of the hardening of attitudes seems to have been the strong feelings aroused by Louis XIV of France, whose military successes against the Protestant Dutch gave him a status equivalent to that of Philip II of Spain a century earlier, and who also pursued a strongly repressive policy towards his Huguenot subjects. The revocation of the Edict of Nantes, removing the limited toleration there had been in France, did not occur until October 1685, but already there was a trickle of Huguenot refugees into Great Britain, who brought with them proof in English eyes of the cruelty and despotism of unrestrained Catholicism.

The 1673 Act caused the Duke of York to resign his office as Lord High Admiral. Later in 1673, he married the devoutly Catholic Mary of Modena as his second wife and the question of whether he should be permitted to succeed became the leading political issue of the balance of his brother's reign. With Catherine of Braganza still childless after 11 years of marriage, it was accepted that Charles II would have no issue by her and, when Parliament re-assembled in January 1674, a number of Bills were drafted with the intention of reducing the freedom of action of a future Catholic sovereign, in particular requiring his children to be raised as Protestants.

Even before his conversion to Catholicism became public knowledge, James, Duke of York, born in 1633 and Charles II's only surviving brother, was extremely unpopular. The reasons for this are unclear, especially as James had in his earlier years shown quite as much dash and resourcefulness as his elder brother and had shared with him the dangers and hardships of exile. After falling into Parliamentary hands when Oxford surrendered in May 1646, James recognised the danger that he might be put up as a puppet monarch, and in 1648, not yet 15 years old, he escaped from confinement at St James's Palace and managed to make his way to France, pre-figuring his brother's later escape from Worcester.

The Duke's physical courage and high level of competence in public affairs were not in doubt. As Lord High Admiral, he served at sea during the Second Dutch War, commanding the fleet which defeated the Dutch at the Battle of Lowestoft of 1665. His flagship sank the leading Dutch vessel and he was so much in the forefront of the fighting that the king afterwards required him to go ashore out of fears for his safety. Nevertheless, the Duke again commanded an English fleet at the exceptionally hard-fought Battle of Sole Bay on 28 May 1682. Like his brother, James seems to have been quite incapable of marital fidelity and his promiscuity was notorious. More ominously for the future, he lacked his brother's charm, charisma and gift for the common touch. He was haughty in manner and, unlike Charles, who was always prepared to swim with the tide where necessary, he had inherited in full measure their father's obstinacy. Like his father, when thwarted, he only became more obstinate. In particular, he saw all opposition and shades of political opinion in black and white,

2   Coward, *ibid*, p 315.

and tarred all opponents with the same brush as the extremists who had killed his father.[3]

In September 1660, James had married Anne Hyde, daughter of the Lord Chancellor, Lord Clarendon, after seducing her and making her pregnant. The child having died soon after birth, he then lost any reputation as a man of honour by claiming that he was not after all the father and seeking an annulment. Anne Hyde died in 1671, after she as well as James had converted to Rome, but at Clarendon's insistence, the two surviving children of the marriage, Mary and Anne, were brought up as Protestants. However, James's second marriage and the possibility of its producing a son who would displace his half-sisters in the royal succession raised the spectre of a line of Catholic monarchs who would follow Charles II on the throne. The succession thus became the principal issue of the balance of the reign, at a time when MPs, in the aftermath of the passing of the Test Act and the abandoning of the Dutch War, had been made aware for the first time since 1641 that a monarch could be persuaded to climb down by determined and united opposition.

The political climate

This is not to say that political parties began to emerge in this period. It has often been argued that the 1670s were a time when a 'country' party developed to oppose the 'court' party in Parliament, but more recent work has shown this to be an over-simplification. As earlier in the 17th century, members of both Houses believed strongly in their personal independence, and such groupings as there were came together over particular issues. From 1673, there was a clear coalescence of MPs opposing the accession of the Duke of York. We also see Parliament not merely giving effect to the king's will in matters concerning the succession to the throne, as it had done since 1399 if not earlier, but actively opposing the king's will, since Charles II never ceased to support his brother and resisted calls from Parliament and elsewhere that he should divorce Catherine and marry again in the hope of producing legitimate issue.

The crisis of 1673 also brought change in personnel and for the next few years, the king's leading minister was Sir Thomas Osborne, created Earl of Danby in July 1674. As Lord Treasurer from 1673, Danby inherited a parlous situation, so serious that the Stop on the Exchequer, originally intended to last for one year only, had to be extended. However, he had already acquired considerable financial experience as a treasurer of the Navy from 1668 and was able to stabilise the Crown's ordinary revenue at a figure of a little over £1 million per year by the end of the 1670s. At this time, the main sources of revenue were the Hearth Tax levied on dwellings, the excise and the customs, the last becoming the most significant as the result of a commercial boom which began in the late 1660s and continued for the rest of the century. However, Crown debt continued to run at a high level. The most important single cause after the peace with Holland was the king's extravagance and his refusal until after 1680 to countenance economies.

At the same time, Danby, recognising that MPs were becoming more organised in their opposition to official policies, began to seek to influence parliamentary opinion

---

3   J Miller, *James II: A Study in Kingship*, 1977, Wayland, pp 11–12.

in order to secure support for the government, particularly in voting further revenues. He used several methods, including payment to MPs of pensions drawn on the excise revenue, as well as writing to potential supporters to persuade them to attend sessions and to speak and vote in favour of government policy. In addition, he attempted to hamper his opponents' own organisation by such means as seeking to suppress coffee houses, now the fashionable places for men of affairs to gather.[4] More generally, he adopted policies designed to appease various factions and rewarded those who had remained faithful to the monarchy during the Civil War and Interregnum by appointing them or their heirs as lords-lieutenant and Justices of the Peace.

In foreign policy, Danby persuaded the king to abandon his former pro-French stance and move towards a military alliance with the Dutch. In this context, the Duke of York's elder daughter Mary, second in line to the throne after her father, was betrothed in October 1677 to William of Orange, a marriage alliance greeted with public rejoicing by anti-Catholics. Overall, the government remained unpopular, not least because an army was kept in being even after the conclusion of Britain's part in the Dutch War. The hatred and suspicion of standing armies engendered by the army's role in the events of 1648–60 cannot be exaggerated.

15.1.5 Crisis

The summer of 1678 produced another major crisis, the immediate trigger for which was the revelation of the 'Popish Plot'. Titus Oates, a fanatical Protestant, had earlier gained admission to Catholic seminaries in France and Spain by posing as a convert. Returning to England in August, he made a sworn deposition before a magistrate, Sir Edmund Berry Godfrey, alleging a Jesuit plot to shoot the king, accompanied by a Catholic uprising in Ireland and, possibly, a French invasion. The allegations were referred to the Privy Council, which rapidly established that neither Oates nor his allegations could be taken seriously. However, the tale played on all the greatest fears of the day and suspicions were only heightened when Godfrey disappeared on 12 October. Five days later, his body was found strangled and stabbed with his own sword, and it was generally assumed that he had been killed by Catholics to forestall potential revelations about the plot.[5] At the same time, the Privy Council investigation unearthed treasonable material in the correspondence of Edward Coleman, formerly secretary to the Duke of York. On 21 October, Parliament voted unanimously that there had been and still was a plot, and declared that anyone who doubted its existence was in peril of his life.

The inevitable wave of anti-Catholic hysteria followed, complete with rumours of French and Spanish landings, and Catholics assembling secret arsenals. The Duke of York's position was seriously compromised by the discovery of Coleman's correspondence. The king and Danby made limited concessions to placate Parliament,

4   Coffee first became widely available in the 1660s, along with chocolate and tea. Coffee houses sprang up in London and other major ports; socialising in them became a craze for those with sufficient money and time. Different coffee houses became fora for conducting various types of business. Most famously, Lloyd's coffee house became the centre of marine insurance business. Naturally, there were coffee houses where critics of the government gathered.

5   The Godfrey case has generated a considerable literature. See JP Kenyon, *The Popish Plot*, 1974, Penguin, Appendix A for a summary on the subject.

Charles assenting to a second Test Act which excluded Catholics from sitting in either House, although Danby's strategy of cultivating individual members made it possible to secure a narrow majority for a provision exempting the Duke of York from its effect. A Licensing Act imposed stringent censorship of printed material, requiring that it be approved by a bishop of the Church of England before publication.

However, in December, embarrassing revelations emerged regarding the secret Treaty of Dover and of the clauses which had hitherto remained concealed. On 21 December, the Commons resolved to draw up articles of impeachment against Danby. On 30 December, the king prorogued the session and, on 24 January, following precedents set by his grandfather and father, he dissolved the Cavalier Parliament in order to prevent further revelations about his relations with Louis XIV from emerging.

Three short-lived Parliaments sat during the next two years, their business dominated by attempts to pass a Bill excluding the Duke of York from the succession, which were in turn frustrated by the king's of his prerogative powers to prorogue Parliament. However, there was one lasting achievement of these brief Parliaments: the Habeas Corpus Act 1679. The Habeas Corpus Act 1640 had dealt with one potential loophole in the common law by declaring detention by order of king and Council to be susceptible to the writ. The 1679 Act dealt with abuses which had occurred in recent years by prohibiting evasion of the procedure by removing the prisoner to a place outside the jurisdiction of the English courts, and specified that there must be no delays in granting the writ.

15.1.6 The exclusion years

In the context of the exclusion issue, the political nation split clearly into organised camps for the first time. The exclusionists, or Whigs (from a traditional Scottish name for the Covenanters), had some ideological links with the Parliamentarians of the Civil War, since they claimed to stand for the ancient liberties of England, were generally friendly towards Protestant dissenters and were extremely hostile to bishops. Like their predecessors, the Whigs favoured an increase in the power and role of Parliament vis à vis the Crown. The anti-exclusionists were labelled Tories, from an old Irish term for Catholic rebels. They should not be confused with the modern Conservative Party, also familiarly known as Tories. Like the Whigs, they believed in a strong Parliament, but considered it to be threatened by dissenters rather than bishops. They were generally prepared to support the government and so the king and his ministers attempted to cultivate them and to place them in public offices in preference to the Whigs. They believed in hereditary monarchy to a much greater extent than the Whigs and also to a greater or lesser extent in Divine Right.

Both groupings drew support from the landed interest, though the Whigs also had support from merchants and the Tories were to a greater extent the representatives of the rural squirearchy. Both believed that political rights should be confined to the propertied classes. In this period, the Whigs were more effective in the propaganda war, securing Commons majorities for the Exclusion Bills of 1680 and 1681. However, they faced the problem that there was no obvious alternative heir to the Duke of York, an issue which all three Exclusion Bills glossed over. Charles was fond of his eldest illegitimate son, James, Duke of Monmouth, but, aware that Monmouth was a reckless, egotistical and empty-headed young man with little in the way of monarchical abilities, he was prepared to swear on oath before the Privy Council in

1680 that he had not married Monmouth's mother before his birth in 1649 or at all. The Duke of York's elder daughter, Mary, was now married to William of Orange and was entirely subservient to him. William had a claim in his own right as the son of Charles I's eldest daughter, but there were suspicions that he would drag Britain into a long and ruinously expensive war against Louis XIV.

A combination of circumstances put Charles II in a much stronger position in 1679–81 than his father had been in the early 1640s. He was not in such desperate need of money, since he did not have to provide for a war and was finally prepared to accept some limitations on his expenditure. A Covenanter rebellion in Scotland in 1679 was put down before becoming widespread, Ireland was quiescent and non-parliamentary revenues were continuing to rise as a result of general economic prosperity. Charles and his ministers were a good deal more adroit at handling Parliament than their predecessors had been. In any event, the Whigs could not call on the same extra-parliamentary support as their predecessors.

15.1.7 The end of the reign

After the dissolution of March 1681, Parliament did not meet again for four years, so depriving the Whigs of their main forum for opposing official policy. At the same time, Charles II and his ministers were able to use existing governmental machinery to reduce the Whigs' influence outside Parliament, by such means as removing Whigs from commissions of the peace and lord-lieutenancies, and reducing the independence of boroughs by means of *quo warranto* inquiries.

It will be remembered that as far back as the 1280s, Edward I had instituted *quo warranto* inquiries of his magnates in seeking to bring the whole of England within the scope of royal justice. The claims of boroughs to internal self-government rested on their charters, granted piecemeal over many centuries. From 1681 and increasingly from 1683, the Crown's lawyers demanded that numerous boroughs – in particular, those whose corporations were known to be strongly Whiggish – substantiate the authenticity of their charters. If technical flaws were found, as they frequently were, legal proceedings were brought in which the charter at issue was declared forfeit and was replaced by a new one which gave the Crown much greater influence over the appointment of office-holders. It has been calculated that 51 new charters were granted between 1681 and the death of Charles II in February 1685, 47 in the first three months of James II's reign, and a further 21 up to August 1686. This also gave the Crown some indirect influence over the future composition of the Commons, since the two MPs who represented each borough were generally elected by its corporation.

The courts continued to lack independence from the Crown. Since the first years of his reign, the king had taken care to appoint judges who accepted his policies and was prepared to use his powers of dismissal against those who showed too great a degree of independence. The criminal law could also be used against those whom the king and his government considered their most dangerous enemies. The Earl of Shaftesbury, now the leading Whig in the Lords, was sent to the Tower on charges of treason arising from his having, with others, taken an armed following to the 1681 Parliament, and escaped condemnation only because a grand jury nominated by two Whig sheriffs threw out the charges against him. The law of treason formed a useful weapon for governments at this time, since its procedures were very much weighted against defendants, who were forbidden legal advice and advance disclosure of the particulars of the charges or the identities of the witnesses against them.

As the hysteria arising from the Popish Plot receded, there was in any case a reaction against some of the more radical Whig proposals, and this was encouraged by the revelation of the Rye House Plot in June 1683. This was a far-fetched scheme to assassinate the king and the Duke of York as they drove through Newmarket to attend the races, but three prominent Whigs were allegedly implicated in it, two going to the block and the third committing suicide in the Tower. The intended beneficiary, the Duke of Monmouth, was privy to the plot, though he claimed that he had never intended the deaths of his father and uncle. Charles, ever-indulgent towards Monmouth, pardoned him but banished him from the country.

15.2   THE SECOND REVOLUTION 1685–1689

James II is the great bogeyman of the Whig interpretation of history. His despotism and his attempts to impose absolute monarchy and bigoted Catholicism on liberal Protestant Britain created the wave of popular revulsion and an invitation to William of Orange which led directly to the Revolution Settlement of 1688–89. The Settlement curbed for all time the potential for the monarch to abuse his or her powers and the Crown was subordinated to the final authority of Parliament. James's reputation is also irrevocably linked in national myth with the suppression of the popular rising led by his nephew, the Duke of Monmouth, and the activities of his Lord Chief Justice, George Jeffreys, in hanging the survivors of the Battle of Sedgemoor on charges of treason.

What did James do to attract such a disastrous image?

15.2.1 The accession of James II

After the hysterical opposition at the time of the Exclusion Crisis and his general unpopularity during his brother's reign, it seems initially surprising that the Duke of York succeeded without opposition as James II of England and Ireland and James VII of Scotland when Charles II died on 6 February 1685. He inherited a government which was financially secure and an efficient English army of 10,000 men, together with smaller forces in Scotland and Ireland. The first Parliament of his reign, predominantly Tory in composition, voted him the traditional revenues for life, though not without some opposition from some who favoured a time-limited grant only, and accompanied by resolutions in support of the Church of England and in favour of enforcing the penal laws against both Catholics and dissenters. At this stage, James's Catholicism does not seem to have caused particular problems.

The Duke of Monmouth landed on 11 June at Lyme Regis in Dorset in the guise of Protestant champion, but his rising failed to attract support outside the West Country or even from the gentry of those shires where there was support, and never became a serious threat. The regular army remained loyal and under two efficient commanders, one of them John Churchill, the future Duke of Marlborough, smashed Monmouth's motley assemblage of cloth workers and farmers when the Duke rashly attempted a night attack on the enemy camp at Sedgemoor on 5 July.[6] Of Monmouth's 5,000 men, about 1,400 were killed and Monmouth was taken prisoner while attempting to flee. The rising which Monmouth anticipated in Cheshire, under Lord Delamere, never materialised and a concurrent landing in Scotland by the 9th Earl of Argyll was easily put down. Both Duke and Earl were condemned by Act of Attainder and went to the block.[7] There followed the 'Bloody Assizes' under Jeffreys, as a result of which, some 300 lesser rebels were hanged, drawn and quartered, and a further 1,000 transported to the West Indies for life. The notoriety of the Bloody Assizes is largely retrospective, arising from the writings of early 18th century Whigs and radicals, and it would be quite unrealistic to see the activities of his Lord Chief Justice as a major cause of James II's downfall.[8]

If James did not attract positive enthusiasm on the part of his subjects, he was not initially an unpopular ruler. In any event, he was approaching 52 – Charles II had died at 54 – and it must have seemed unlikely that he would have a Catholic heir. Though his two wives had borne him 18 children, only his two daughters by Anne Hyde survived. Both were firmly Protestant, married to Protestant princes and could be expected to produce Protestant children. The reign of Catholic James would be no more than a brief interlude in a Protestant monarchy.

15.2.2 After the honeymoon

Far from James II attempting to impose Catholicism on his realms by force, his policy was one of religious toleration, though, like Mary I, he hoped that a populace free to follow their own consciences would move back into the Catholic fold. However, the public mood remained absolutely against toleration for Catholics, as James completely failed to recognise. Before long, he attempted to force toleration on his people by means which included prosecution of Anglican clergy opposed to his policy. Accepting that he could not immediately secure repeal of the Test Acts in Parliament, he attempted to bypass them by use of the prerogative and, in the longer term, to pack a future Parliament in order to obtain a majority in favour of repeal. This fatally undermined his position and when he proceeded with the prosecution of the Seven Bishops for seditious libel after they had refused to publish his second Declaration of Indulgence in their dioceses, his opponents proclaimed that he was seeking to impose absolutist government on the model of that of Louis XIV. The unexpected birth of a

---

6   The most detailed account of the affair can be found in Charles Chevenix Trench, *The Western Rising*, 1969, Longman, which concentrates on the military aspects, into which the author, a former professional soldier, has many valuable insights.

7   The Argyll attainder was lifted within a few years. Monmouth's remains in force, though his wife's dukedom of Buccleuch was not affected. A myth remains that a marriage certificate once existed to prove that Charles II did marry Monmouth's mother, making Monmouth's Buccleuch descendants the rightful British sovereigns.

8   The punishments meted out to the rebels were no more than those usual at that time. Those condemned were taken in arms against the Crown, so that, according to contemporary legal standards, they had no possible defence to the charge of treason. Those not taken in arms were the subject of a general pardon in March 1686. Jeffreys claimed later that he was merely applying the law as it stood, there being no provision for appeal at this time. A jury having found the rebels guilty, he had no option but to pronounce a death sentence, and it was then for the king to choose to exercise the prerogative of mercy. However, Jeffreys' efficiency left little time for pleas for clemency to be made, let alone considered; most of the condemned were executed within two days of sentence.

healthy male heir on 10 June 1688 had already raised the spectre of a long term Catholic succession and marked the beginning of the end.

During the short sitting of Parliament in November 1685, James announced that the additional regiments raised to deal with Monmouth would not be disbanded and that he had already given military commissions to Catholics despite the Test Acts. Further, George Saville, Marquess of Halifax, had been removed from the Privy Council for opposing this. Similar appointments followed, not only in the armed forces but in the judiciary and commissions of the peace, and to the lieutenancy of counties, by reliance on the 'dispensing power' to set aside the effect of the Test Acts in relation to the individuals concerned. By no means all the persons who benefited from the king's application of the dispensing power were Catholics; a significant proportion were Protestant dissenters, also excluded from public office by the Test Acts.

A deep suspicion of standing armies and of their being potential instruments of repression survived from the late 1640s and the Interregnum. Since the Restoration, Parliament had no direct influence over the regular regiments, which were raised as necessary and employed entirely on the basis of the prerogative. This was in contrast to the militia, governed by the Militia Act 1662 although commanded by the lords-lieutenant and deputy lieutenants of counties, who were appointed by the king and held office during his pleasure. The only source of parliamentary control over the regular army was the indirect one of authorising the raising of revenue to provide for the army. There was also no legal basis for the enforcement of military discipline, so the control exercised over the regular troops by their own officers was uncertain. Soldiers had an unfortunate reputation for drunkenness and disorderly behaviour at best, and the presence of large numbers in any particular locality was greatly feared by law-abiding citizens.

The army, doubled to around 20,000 by the new regiments raised to deal with Monmouth, was therefore not subject to any civilian authority except insofar as acts committed by soldiers constituted offences under the ordinary criminal law. Its reliability was not entirely certain, much depending on the respect and trust inspired by individual commanders, but the majority of its members had seen active service and certain regiments had developed a considerable reputation for toughness and fighting efficiency. Further, the organisation of the army, which was not so much a single entity but a collection of regiments, meant that the commanders of those regiments were their virtual owners. Should colonels of regiments remain loyal to the monarch and put his interests above all else, the army could prove a very effective instrument of repression indeed.

The militia, although much larger, was a less effective body, principally because of its lack of training, militia soldiers being mustered for only 12 days each year and much even of this time being devoted to administrative matters.[9] However, control of the militia had considerable symbolic importance and if Catholics were appointed as lords-lieutenant and had personal reason for gratitude towards King James for dispensing them from the provisions of the Test Acts, would the militia not also become a potential instrument of repression?

Was there, from the end of 1685 onwards, a growing fear that a standing army, with its officers, particularly its regimental commanders, predominantly Catholic,

9　Chevenix Trench, *op cit*, pp 103–09.

would force an unwilling populace back to Rome? Certainly, two of the greatest concerns of the period, fear of the political role of a standing army and of Catholicism, were two of the three planks of opposition to James II. The third was his use of extra-parliamentary measures to achieve his ends.

Opposition to James's new policy was only encouraged by events in Ireland, where the new Earl of Tyrconnell, Richard Talbot, a staunch Catholic and old associate of James's, had begun purging the Irish army of Protestants even before the death of Charles II. At the same time, fear of Catholicism and of the repressive tendencies of Catholic monarchs appeared to be entirely justified by the Revocation of the Edict of Nantes in October 1685 by Louis XIV, which greatly increased numbers of Huguenots seeking refuge in England. They tended to be people of education and industry, whose tales of persecution and narrow escapes from France, and the coincidence of religion between James II and Louis XIV, created a climate of fear that what was happening in France could happen in Britain.

The sharp deterioration in James's popularity was not arrested by the decision in the important case of *Godden v Hales* in June 1686.[10] Sir Edward Hales, a convert to Catholicism, was granted a colonel's commission despite failure to comply with the Test Acts. His coachman, Arthur Godden, brought an action against him and Hales appealed against his conviction on the basis of a dispensation under the Great Seal. As in the 1630s, the judiciary proved compliant towards the monarch: 11 of the 12 judges of the King's Bench upheld the appeal and the existence of the dispensing power.

15.2.3 James II's religious policy

At the same time, James II set about a personal campaign of persuasion towards his greater subjects, in the hope of leading them into the Roman fold, though anti-Catholicism was so deeply entrenched that he is only known to have made one significant convert even at a time when gaining the favour of the monarch was the way to office and success. Coercion followed the failure to persuade. In March 1686, the clergy were instructed to confine their sermons to matters contained in the official Anglican catechism and to avoid attacks on Rome. After the Bishop of London refused the king's order to suspend a rebellious cleric from preaching, James made use of the prerogative to create a Court of Ecclesiastical Commission, whose first act, in September 1686, was to suspend the bishop from his office.

With Anglican opinion increasingly alienated, James attempted to cultivate dissenters. In the course of 1686, he issued dispensations from the Test Acts to prominent Quakers such as William Penn, whom he used as his emissary to Holland in an attempt to persuade his heir presumptive, Mary, and her husband, William of Orange, to support his plans for repeal of the Test and Corporation Acts. Soon afterwards, James dismissed his two leading Anglican ministers.

On 4 April 1687, James II issued his Declaration of Indulgence, which by the royal prerogative suspended the penal laws and granted freedom of worship both in public and in private. Shortly afterwards, he announced the dissolution of the Parliament, which had been prorogued since November 1685, and his ensuing actions made it clear that he sought dissenter support for the repeal of the Test and Corporation Acts

---

10   11 St 1165.

as a *quid pro quo* of including them within the Declaration of Indulgence. Unfortunately for the king, his cultivation of dissenters did not win him their wholehearted support. Some objected on principle to use of the suspending power; others suspected that the king's espousal of general toleration was but a cloak for the future imposition of Catholicism on the country.

15.2.4 Crisis looms

Urgency was created on 27 April 1688 by the re-issue of the Declaration of Indulgence, coupled with an announcement by the king that he would not delay the summoning of a new Parliament beyond November. Tension developed further, ultimately to a 'now or never' point for James's political opponents, as the result of a number of unrelated circumstances which coincided in time. One was the situation in continental Europe, where a major war was expected to break out before the end of 1688. Louis XIV was seeking to install his own candidate as Archbishop of Cologne, one of the Electors of the Empire, and was pursuing a very tenuous claim to rule over the Palatinate. The Emperor, traditional rival of the French, had for some years been at war with the Ottoman Empire, his neighbour to the south-east, but this was clearly about to end, leaving Louis with only a brief window of opportunity before his enemies united against him under imperial leadership. Meanwhile, Anglo-Dutch relations had deteriorated sharply, bringing the possibility that James would emerge either as a direct ally of Louis XIV or, by making war on William of Orange, would neutralise Louis's leading enemy in western Europe.

In December 1687, it emerged publicly that James's queen, Mary of Modena, was pregnant, and by the spring of 1688, it was clear that the birth would occur shortly. It should not be assumed that the Whigs saw this as a significant threat, since none of Mary's 10 previous children had survived infancy. Even if the infant did confound expectations, there was a 50% chance of its being a girl, who would take her place in the succession behind her Protestant half-sisters. Even if the child proved to be a son, it was far from unlikely that the now relatively elderly father would die during his minority, so leaving his upbringing and the government of the realm to Protestant regents.

However, the Whigs began to make contingency plans. In May, the Whig leader, Edward Russell, went secretly to William of Orange, sounding him out as to whether he would be prepared to come to England with an army. William replied that he would not do so unless formally invited by leading men and that he could not in any case do so until after the death of the Great Elector, which was confidently expected at this time and would take his electorate out of the French orbit.[11]

Meanwhile, most of the Anglican clergy refused to obey the king's command to read the Declaration of Indulgence in their churches. On 18 May, the Archbishop of Canterbury, William Sancroft, and the Bishops of Bath and Wells, Chichester, Bristol, St Asaph, Ely and Peterborough petitioned the king to withdraw the Declaration, 'because that Declaration is founded upon such a dispensing power as hath often been

---

11 Friedrich Wilhelm of Brandenburg (1640–88) became known as the Great Elector in consequence of his successful policies of retrenchment after the Thirty Years War, which established the foundations of the military might of Brandenburg and later of the Prussian kingdom.

declared illegal in Parliament'.[12] This petition was widely distributed and James now made a fatal mistake. He had the Seven Bishops arraigned on charges of seditious libel, on the basis that it was illegal to put a petition to the king except via Parliament, which alone provided a channel of communication from subject to king.

Before the Seven Bishops came to trial, Mary of Modena gave birth to a healthy son, duly baptised James Francis Edward with the Pope as godfather and created Prince of Wales and Earl of Chester. Before long, the scurrilous rumour began that he was an impostor, that the queen's infant had been stillborn and that a child of low birth – a miller's son, according to Gilbert Burnet, the Whiggish Bishop of Salisbury – had been smuggled into the royal bedchamber in a warming pan. The only thing that gave any credence to the tale was that on an extremely hot day, a warming pan had been taken into the queen shortly after the birth but before the child was ceremonially shown to those assembled, as was the custom of the time.[13]

James II's position was now deteriorating rapidly. The trial of the Seven Bishops became a debate on the legality of the suspending and dispensing powers, as their legal representatives made the alleged illegality of the Declaration of Indulgence the core of their defence, rather than the narrower issue of whether their issue of the petition or its contents actually involved seditious libel.[14] Despite a pro-government summing up by Wright LCJ and a statement by Alibone J, a Catholic appointed in April 1687, that such a petition was 'next door to treason', two other judges (Powell and Holloway JJ) summed up in favour of the bishops. After a night's deliberation, the trial ended on 30 June in acquittal on all charges. The Seven Bishops became the heroes of the hour, as the Five Members had been in 1642, and were duly hailed in some quarters as martyrs for English liberty. Soon, Anglicans and Dissenters united in opposition to the king.

William of Orange's involvement in the affairs of England at this time has a distinct cloak-and-dagger air. The Great Elector died early in June, and the birth of the Prince of Wales and the contemporary practice of one ruler congratulating another in such circumstances gave William a convenient pretext for sending an emissary to England in order to obtain a letter of invitation to invade. This was dispatched on 30 June.

However, it is not at all clear what were the true intentions of William himself or of those who issued the invitation, none of whom were of major political importance other than the Earl of Danby, who currently held no public office. The general view of modern historians is that the English Whigs were not yet thinking in terms of the deposition of James II, but sought to force him to concede limitations on his powers. Indeed, their consensus is that the prime mover in the eventual deposition was William himself, though it is not clear whether he had yet formed this intention. Circumstantial evidence and the activities, so far as they are known, of William's

---

12 JP Kenyon, *The Stuart Constitution*, 2nd edn, 1986, CUP, pp 406–07. In fact, the Declaration relied on the suspending power, which had indeed been declared unlawful by Parliament in 1673, in relation to Charles II's Declaration of Indulgence in favour of Dissenters.

13 Royal births were then public events. It is estimated that more than 30 people were crowded into the queen's bedchamber and an adjoining antechamber on 10 June, making it highly unlikely that a substitution could have taken place unnoticed. In any case, the new Prince of Wales grew up with a strong physical resemblance to his official parents. In particular, he had the same black eyes as Mary of Modena.

14 12 St 416.

intelligence agents suggest that he may have been considering an invasion of England, with the intention of placing his wife on the throne, since the early 1680s.

15.2.5 Invasion

William III of Orange was the posthumous child of the *stadtholder* William II by his marriage to Mary, eldest sister of both Charles II and James II, and was heir to their thrones after James's daughters. The United Provinces, of which he was the first citizen, was not a unitary state, but a federation of the seven Netherlands provinces which had gained independence from Spain by the rebellion which began in the 1560s and was finally ended by the Peace of Westphalia of 1648. Its constitution provided that sovereignty vested in the seven provinces themselves, so that decisions of the States General, which had responsibility for foreign policy and defence against external enemies, required the approval of all the provinces. This was not a recipe for decisive military leadership or efficient mobilisation of national resources in time of war. However, during the revolt against Spain, the practice developed of seeking military leadership from the leading noble family of the region, the House of Orange, each Prince of Orange being appointed as *stadtholder* (governor) of five of the provinces and as military and naval commander-in-chief of the federation. Gradually, tensions developed as successive *stadtholders* sought to convert the federal republic into a centralised monarchy on the pattern of the major European states.[15] Following the death of William II in 1650, his appointments fell into abeyance until 1672, when the threat from Louis XIV persuaded the States General to offer them to his son.

At this point, William III embarked on the central purpose of his life: opposition to Louis XIV. With the decline of Spain as a major power, France was the main threat to the United Provinces and French power was steadily increasing through the first half of the 1680s. William was aware that the United Provinces could not defy Louis XIV alone, but his attempts before 1688 to create an effective coalition against France were unsuccessful. His position gave him limited powers and his policies were threatened by political opponents. After 1685, his prospects of achieving his aims improved, in part as a result of the Revocation of the Edict of Nantes, which caused a resurgence of anti-French feeling among the Dutch. In 1686, William organised the German states into an anti-French League of Augsburg and could expect military support from the Emperor once the Turkish war was concluded. William was anxious to bring England, the leading naval power of Europe apart from his own country, into the coalition. That prospect appeared in the summer of 1688 to be slipping away. Though James II had endeavoured to distance himself from Louis XIV, the mere fact that both monarchs were Catholics created an assumption that it was only a matter of time before they concluded a military alliance. In any case, deteriorating relations between Britain and the United Provinces due to commercial rivalries meant that a fourth Dutch War was becoming a distinct possibility. To pre-empt this danger by taking control of the three kingdoms therefore made very good political and military sense.

There was then an interlude while William raised the necessary army, his existing forces being committed to protecting the United Provinces. Time and tide on this occasion very definitely favoured the invader. In September, the potential French

---

15   See Miller, *op cit*, pp 131–32.

threat to the United Provinces was temporarily nullified by Louis XIV's invading the Palatinate. James II began to panic. Aware of William's intention to invade, he backtracked on his religious policy in the hope of regaining the favour of his Anglican subjects. He announced that the forthcoming elections would be free from government interference, restored officials and magistrates dismissed in the past two years, dissolved the Commission for Ecclesiastical Causes and opened negotiations with Archbishop Sancroft and other leading Anglicans in the hope of finding a way to toleration which was broadly acceptable. When the bishops rejected these overtures, James backtracked again, withdrew the writs for the Parliament planned for November and stood by the Declaration of Indulgence. His actions from then on were those of a man who was rapidly losing his nerve.

It was not until 30 October that the winds allowed the invasion fleet to sail. William's force, comprising an army 12,000 strong in 225 transports, escorted by 50 warships, was considerably largely than the Spanish Armada of exactly a century earlier, better organised and better led. It was also more fortunate with the weather, since an easterly 'Protestant wind' allowed it to sail but kept the English fleet bottled up in the Thames estuary. There is some evidence that William originally intended to land in Yorkshire, where Danby would rise in his support, but now he took advantage of the Protestant wind to reach the firmly anti-Catholic and anti-James West Country. He landed unopposed at Torbay, Devon, on 5 November, and from there marched to Exeter, where he established a secure base and set about the winning of the propaganda war. Shrewdly, at this stage, he declared that he sought only the election of a free Parliament and a full inquiry into the birth of the Prince of Wales, so portraying himself as the protector of the English against manipulation of the legislature and a spurious heir apparent.

Militarily, James II was in an awkward position. He could advance westwards, leaving London unguarded in his rear, or dig in around London, so surrendering the initiative and risking a loss of morale among his troops. He compromised by advancing as far as Salisbury, which he reached on 19 November. From then on, his position began to be undermined by desertions. Danby seized control of York and the Earl of Devonshire Nottingham. James's second daughter, Anne, fled from London and took refuge with Devonshire. On the advice of his army commander, the Earl of Feversham, the increasingly indecisive king returned to London, which he reached on 25 November, hoping to rally support there. Instead, more of his officers deserted to William. Most notable among the turncoats was John Churchill, the king's second-in-command, who only three years earlier had put down Monmouth's rebellion and was James's protégé and close personal friend.[16] Others included the king's son-in-law, Prince George of Denmark. These were joined by the Duke of Ormonde, the leading Irish peer, and Lord Drumlanrig, son of the Duke of Queensberry, who was the most powerful figure in Scotland. Each took his regiment with him.

James's position now strongly resembled that of Richard II nearly 300 years earlier. He could no longer rely on what remained of his army. Though its Catholic officers would presumably have remained loyal, they numbered only about 10% of the total, and great swathes of England were held by his enemies. Thoroughly demoralised,

---

16 Churchill's sister, Arabella Churchill, had been James's mistress and was the mother of his son, James FitzJames, Duke of Berwick. Military ability seems to have run in the family, since Churchill became the greatest commander of the age and Berwick was a Marshal of France and one of Louis XIV's more effective generals.

James was advised to negotiate, but, like Richard II and Edward II before him, he disintegrated under the pressure of events. On 10 December, with William's troops approaching London, he sent his queen and baby son to France, and the following day, King James II and VII, once the fighting Lord High Admiral of Lowestoft and Sole Bay, donned a disguise and fled.

William of Orange still denied any intention of seeking the crown for himself and proposed that the elections for Parliament should go forward and that the two armies should remain 40 miles from London while it sat. He gave specific assurances to his wife that her father's person should remain inviolate and offered James the protection of his own personal Guard.[17] Coward notes that a meeting of peers at the Guildhall after 11 December showed continuing support for James even among those who had recently suffered at his hands, including two of the Seven Bishops.[18]

James's initial attempt at flight, during which he flung the Great Seal into the Thames in the hope of preventing his enemies from governing,[19] ended when he was picked up by a group of fishermen at Faversham in Kent and returned captive to London. By this time, the capital had become prey to rioting and general hysteria. William, meanwhile, had reached Windsor and ordered James to leave London while his army restored order. Without William and his allies making any serious attempt to prevent him, James set out for France a second time on 22 December and arrived safely at the court of Louis XIV, where his queen and heir had already taken refuge, on Christmas Day.

15.2.6 Transfer of power

With James II out of the way, William of Orange summoned all the surviving members of Charles II's Parliaments then in London to a meeting on 23 December, at which it was agreed that he should send out letters under his personal seal for a parliament or 'convention' to assemble on 22 January. Meanwhile, he accepted a request that he should assume responsibility for public order and civil administration. William now stood in the same position as General Monck in 1660, with the very significant difference that Monck apparently had no intention of making himself head of state. In the interval before the Convention met, William took a number of steps which suggest that he did not regard himself as a mere caretaker. He lodged the Lord Chancellor, the notorious George Jeffreys, in the Tower and replaced all the judges appointed by James II. He also expelled the French ambassador, a deeply provocative act when Britain and France were not at war.

The Convention was faced with a difficult situation. How was the current vacuum in government to be dealt with? In 1660, the solution was simple: there was only one realistic candidate for the position of head of state, and Charles II's reputation was entirely benevolent, that of a dashing young man whose Declaration of Breda showed an intention to pursue policies of peace, reconciliation and moderation. James II was not by now viewed with any favour, but he was an anointed king and there were elements which were prepared to allow him to remain on the throne if suitable limitations on his power could be devised and he was prepared to accept them, or

---

17 JP Kenyon, *Stuart England*, 1985, Penguin, pp 251–52.
18 Coward, *op cit*, p 356.
19 Remarkably, it was caught a few days later in fishing nets and passed to William of Orange.

perhaps with William as regent. If James was no longer an acceptable sovereign, who was to replace him?

Republicanism, except among a few extremists, seems to have become thoroughly discredited after the Interregnum and the issue was whether James should remain king or William succeed him. On 28 January, the Commons resolved that the throne was now vacant, James having abdicated. The Lords, with a majority holding Tory views, refused to accept this, on the basis that an hereditary throne could not be vacant, since the word implied an elective element. The Earl of Rochester's proposal for a regency was rejected by three votes, after which certain Tory peers, led by Danby, put forward a solution which, conveniently, allowed them to proclaim their attachment to hereditary monarchy while repudiating both James II and his son. James, they maintained, had not abdicated, which required some form of formal renunciation. Instead, he had 'deserted' the throne. Further, his so called son was an impostor and his elder daughter was the rightful ruler.

There followed deadlock between Lords and Commons, the latter rejecting the Lords' amendments to the resolution of 28 January and the former reinstating them. On 3 February, Mary, who had now arrived from Holland, rejected Danby's proposal that she reign as queen regnant with William as her consort, and William declared that he was not prepared to be either regent or consort, but only king. At the same time, Mary's younger sister, Anne, postponed her rights of succession behind William's.

On 6 February, the Lords gave way, perhaps because of a real threat of mob violence in London, and accepted the inevitability of William as sovereign, rather than face the alternative of a lengthy interregnum and possible insurrection. It is also possible that the Lords wished to pre-empt an attempt by James II to re-establish himself while the vacuum continued, though this is highly speculative. The Lords insisted that the crown be offered to William and Mary jointly, each having full sovereignty. The Commons agreed, this solution was put to the pair, and on 14 February, they were duly proclaimed as William III and Mary II of England, Scotland, France and Ireland. The Tories, as well as accepting the myth of the 'warming pan baby', salved their consciences over their acceptance of a breach of the principle of truly hereditary succession by claiming that what was to become known as the Glorious Revolution had been divinely ordained, so that the new joint sovereigns indeed ruled by Divine Right. In any event, they argued, obedience was due to any government that secured security and protection for society. Those with particularly tender consciences could regard themselves as obeying William only as *de facto* king, while they continued to uphold James II as *de jure* king.[20]

John Locke's *Two Treatises on Civil Government*, published in 1690 but mainly written during the Exclusion Crisis, also offered a theoretical justification for James's removal. Locke upheld the traditional idea that the monarch should rule in the interests of his people, but took it a stage further. Power, whether legislative or executive, was granted on trust for the attainment of an end, and when that end was neglected or opposed, the power was forfeited. On the vexed but vital question of who or what had the power to judge when the monarch or executive acted contrary to their trust, Locke considered that 'the people' should be the judge and regarded resistance to the monarch in circumstances where the trust was forfeited as the final expression of the sovereignty of the people.

20   Coward, *op cit*, p 358.

15.2.7 The Bill of Rights

As well as settling the succession to the Crown, the Convention of 1689 had also to deal with the leading political issues of the day, which continued to be the powers of Crown and Parliament, both separately and vis à vis one another, and religion. On 29 January, the Commons appointed a committee to consider the rights of the subject, both those which already existed and those to be created by legislation to which the future monarch was to be required to agree before accepting the throne. Their report was completed by 3 February and became known as the Declaration of Rights. It took the traditional form of a condemnation of the 'unconstitutional' and 'illegal' actions of James II, followed by a programme of changes intended to prevent future monarchical abuses. These included guarantees for the continuance of Parliament, religious toleration for Protestants and proposals for reforms in chancery procedures and in treason trials. The importance of judicial independence was recognised by a call for judges no longer to be dismissible at pleasure, but appointed 'during good behaviour' and paid proper salaries.

The Convention declared itself a valid Parliament and for the first time applied the Test Acts to the monarch, by including their requirements in the coronation oath via the Coronation Oath Act 1689. The Mutiny Act provided a statutory basis for the existence of a standing army in peacetime and for military discipline, since it gave the monarch powers of trial by court-martial, but only for one year at a time. By contrast, the Navy, having avoided involvement in politics, was considered not to pose any constitutional threat. The Lord High Admiral was granted powers of court-martial in perpetuity by the Naval Discipline Act 1661 and this position was not altered.

However, the Bill of Rights passed in December 1689 gave effect only to some provisions of the Declaration of Rights. Ultimately, the Bill, like Magna Carta, formed a declaration of existing law, or what the Convention regarded as existing law. Its most important elements were the formal abolition of the suspending and dispensing powers, a clear statement that the raising of revenues for the Crown required grant of Parliament, as did the maintenance of a standing army in peacetime, and Article 9, which guaranteed freedom of speech in debates and other proceedings in Parliament. Fear of Catholicism was evident in Article 7, which allowed Protestants to carry arms in their own defence. The remaining provisions were vague statements of principle, requiring parliaments to be held 'frequently', prohibiting 'excessive' fines or surety for bail and 'cruel and unusual' punishments, and declaring that parliamentary elections ought to be free.

The Bill of Rights also dealt with the succession to William and Mary by confirming the postponement of Anne's claims until after the deaths of both William and Mary. Given that William had been in very indifferent health throughout his life, it may well have seemed unlikely that he would survive his wife. At this time, it may also have seemed that a Protestant succession was assured for the future, since in the summer of 1689, Anne followed Mary of Modena in giving birth to an apparently healthy son after a series of stillbirths, miscarriages and unviable infants.

A limited degree of religious toleration followed in the Toleration Act 1689, which granted freedom of worship to those who took the oaths of supremacy and allegiance and made the declaration against transubstantiation. Otherwise, the penal laws remained in force. Ironically enough, William III, the 'Protestant champion', rapidly attracted domestic suspicions in respect of both his Calvinism and his advocacy of toleration for all Protestants.

Many of the most contentious of the traditional powers of the Crown were left untouched by the Bill of Rights, since the monarch remained free to choose his own ministers and to make policy, particularly foreign policy. Though the maintenance of a standing army required renewal of the Mutiny Act every year, powers of control over troops remained in the hands of the Crown. That the Mutiny Act had to be renewed annually, however, meant that Parliament had to sit every year, so that never again could the monarch rule for long periods without summoning Parliament. At the same time, the monarch's powers of patronage remained intact and there remained no bar on office-holders sitting in either House, so that the new king was able to influence members of both Houses by controlling their access to public office.

The 'Revolution Settlement' of 1689 was thus incomplete. Some elements of the Declaration of Rights were not given effect at all and others remained outstanding until the Act of Settlement was passed in 1701. Why was this so? First, there was the innate conservatism of the majority of members of the Convention, whose concerns over constitutional matters were secondary to the desire to replace one monarch with another. Secondly, there was the desire of some of the leading Whigs – typical of a time when careers in public life were made or broken by royal favour – not to alienate the new monarch by making serious inroads into those elements of the prerogative which had not been central to the recent crisis.[21] This was particularly the case in relation to foreign policy, where William III made no secret of his intentions and indeed embarked on war against Louis XIV in the course of 1689.

---

21 See Coward, *op cit*, pp 360–61.

CHAPTER 16

THE REVOLUTION ENTRENCHED 1689–1707

16.1   SCOTLAND AND IRELAND 1689–91

The developments so far described applied only to England. The situation in Scotland and Ireland in 1689 and after was very different, and in both countries there remained a considerable rump of support for James II.

A Scottish Convention met on 14 March 1689 and its Presbyterian majority was instrumental in passing a Claim of Right and Articles of Grievances which were more sweeping than the English Declaration of Rights. They sought nothing less than an independent Scottish Parliament, the removal of the Lords of the Articles and the re-establishment of Presbyterian church government. Initially, the new king's ministers blocked the legislative changes required to put this programme into effect, but it soon became clear that William III needed the support of the Presbyterians. Viscount Dundee, Commander-in-Chief in Scotland, declared his continued support for James and managed to win the volatile Highland clans over to what was the first stirring of the Jacobite cause. Dundee had served under William on the continent and was well-practised at dealing with conditions in Scotland through his ruthless suppression of illegal conventicles. He seems to have had an unusual degree of personal charisma and the ability to persuade the fiercely independent Highland chiefs to rally to his cause. The situation became so serious that the new king had to delay his intended campaign against Louis XIV in order to deal with Dundee. William conceded the main Presbyterian demands, so that the Scottish Parliament, ironically enough, was in the last 18 years of its existence more independent of the Crown than ever before. Ironically too, the military danger was short-lived. Dundee won a brilliant victory at Killiecrankie on 27 July 1689, but was killed in the closing stages of the battle. The unreliability of Highland troops then worked in William's favour, as the clans, without anyone to unite them other than the distant figure of King James, abandoned the Jacobite cause for the time being. However, they left a powerful reputation for military might, and the possibility of their uniting again in the Jacobite cause was to exercise the minds of successive governments for many years to come.

William III's position in Ireland was also precarious. Government was in the hands of the Earl of Tyrconnell, who held Ireland for James at the time of the change of monarchs and welcomed him when he landed at Kinsale in February 1689, by another irony, the first monarch to set foot in that country since Richard II. The Test Acts did not apply in Ireland and the Irish Parliament, which met in Dublin in May, had no fewer than 218 Catholics in its House of Commons of 224 members. This 'Patriot Parliament', defying the strictures of Poynings' Law, proceeded to repeal much of the legislation passed under English influence since 1640, in particular restoring many estates confiscated from Catholics.

This produced a backlash among the Presbyterians of Ulster. The Siege of Londonderry had already begun in December 1688, when 12 'Apprentice Boys' slammed the city gates against a Catholic force led by the Earl of Antrim. The siege lasted until July, when the besiegers gave up their attempts to take the city and went away. Other Protestants followed the example of those of Londonderry and armed themselves. From Londonderry and Enniskillen, they appealed to William of Orange for support.

As had his predecessors, William recognised the danger of the French using Ireland as a springboard for invasion, but was not in a position to commit an army of any size until August. This army was inadequately supplied and soon fell prey to the common hazards of campaigning at that time. Bad weather, inadequate shelter, proximity to the Irish bogs and poor food combined to provide perfect conditions for disease, which killed off almost half the invading force.

In national myth, this time the mythology of Ulster Unionism, the deciding event was the Battle of the Boyne of 12 July 1690, where a largely mercenary army under the personal command of William of Orange defeated a mixed force of Frenchmen, German and Walloon mercenaries, and Catholic Irish, led by the French Comte de Lauzan in the name of King James. Fighting, however, continued for more than a year afterward, until Limerick surrendered to the Williamite forces on 3 October 1691. By this time, James was long gone, having fled from the Boyne in despair and returned to France, to spend the final 11 years of his life seeking solace in religious austerities.

William was interested in Ireland only in order to secure his rear while he made war on Louis XIV, and chose to support the Ulster Presbyterians only because they for their own reasons opposed the Catholics who sought to maintain James II. Yet, more than 300 years later, he remains the great hero and symbol of Ulster Protestant myth, along with the Apprentice Boys who shut the gates of Londonderry. Together, they saved Ireland from Catholic oppression; the myth ignores the unpalatable fact that the success of William of Orange led to a long period of Protestant oppression of the Catholic majority and deepened the existing divisions yet further. In any event, the Ulster Presbyterians of 1689–91 were not seeking to preserve Ireland's place in the United Kingdom – the United Kingdom did not then exist, and the Presbyterians had not so far shown any particular love for the Crown – but merely to preserve their own economic, social and religious position. The myth has proved far more pervasive than messy and ambiguous truth.

The constitutional position of Ireland was theoretically embodied in the Treaty of Limerick, negotiated in the autumn of 1691 between the leading generals on either side. This was relatively generous, in that it confirmed the religious settlement as it had been at the death of Charles II and allowed Catholics to hold office, as well as giving some protection to Catholic landowners. The Irish who had fought against William were permitted to leave the country and enter French service. However, the Treaty was entirely nullified by the English Parliament on the authority of Poynings' Law. In the sessions of 1690 and 1691, the Westminster Parliament formally repealed all the legislation passed by the Patriot Parliament and imposed a religious test on the English model on membership of the legislature and public offices. Catholics were thus excluded from Parliament, the army, government service, the law and the municipal corporations. Their right to buy, hold or bequeath land was severely restricted and, by 1702, only 14% of Irish land remained in Catholic hands. From its sitting in 1692 until the Union of 1801, the Irish Parliament was a Protestant body, and Ireland ruled by Protestants of the Anglican persuasion, the smallest of the three main groups in the population.

16.2   POST-REVOLUTION POLITICS

From 1691 almost until 1714, government and politics in Britain were dominated by the direct and indirect effects of continental war. After William of Orange declared war on Louis XIV in 1689, fighting continued until 1697. After a relatively short period of peace, the general European conflict known as the War of the Spanish Succession then occupied the years 1701–1712. It is this period of near-continuous war, and a crisis over the succession, which forms the context for the constitutional developments of the balance of the reign of William of Orange and the reign of Queen Anne.

That Britain was involved in land wars over such a lengthy period meant that the principle of a standing army came to be accepted, although a Mutiny Act had to be passed every year down to 1881, other than in time of war. The Acts allowed the maintenance of an army up to the numerical limit specified and, though at any time the conclusion of peace meant a considerable reduction in the size of the army, Britain has never been without a standing army since 1689. The demands of war, as always, put considerable pressure on public revenues and in the 1690s brought developments which have lasted until the present day. This was a crucial period in the hitherto haphazard organisation of public finance, bringing the creation of a Bank of England, a National Debt and a requirement in practice of annual sessions of Parliament so that the legislature could authorise the raising and spending of official revenues. This in turn gave rise to much more ordered scrutiny of public spending, originally in respect of the armed forces, but gradually widening into other spheres of governmental activity.

16.2.1 Financial developments

As has already been seen, official revenues were rarely able to finance all government expenditure, so that the Crown was for much of the period from the 14th century onwards in a state of permanent financial crisis. Financial pressures became acute in time of war, and financial difficulties were a major precipitating factor in political and constitutional crisis. From 1660, it was finally accepted that the king could not be expected to 'live off his own' and that the Crown must have regular sources of revenue from taxation, in addition to the traditional revenues which it had long enjoyed but which were clearly inadequate. By the end of the century, the main sources of Crown revenue, about half the total, were customs and excise and a land tax collected on the basis of regular assessments and created by a statute of 1692. At various times, the Stuart monarchs had attempted to ride out financial crises and avoid summoning parliaments by large-scale borrowing at interest, using their personal assets as security. This source of funds proved inadequate in the longer term and only delayed political crisis. From the 1660s, the Crown attempted to create a more reliable system of public credit and financial administration.

Charles II created a Treasury Commission to deal with aspects of Crown finance which did not fall directly under the auspices of the Exchequer. During the Second Dutch War (1665–67), the secretary of the Commission, Sir George Downing, made innovations which acted as precedents for more far-reaching changes brought in during the 1690s under pressure of renewed war. To encourage investors to lend to the Crown in order to finance the war, Downing sought to do two things: first, to ensure that money raised through loans was used for specified purposes only; second, by adopting procedures that gave greater certainty of repayment of the capital originally borrowed, by providing that those who lent first should be repaid first, and granting creditors legally enforceable payment orders. These developments were not entirely without setbacks – the Stop on the Exchequer of 1672 was a clear demonstration that the Crown was not always capable of keeping up interest payments on its debts – but they nevertheless presaged the changes which came into effect in the 1690s.

As a result of the war with France, the financial demands on the Crown after 1689 were greater than ever, the gap between permanent Crown income and expenditure reaching about £11.3 million. In 1693, Parliament authorised the king to borrow £1 million, to be repaid by annuities funded from new excise duties authorised by Parliament. In the following year, Parliament authorised the Crown to borrow £1.2 million at 8% interest. Again, this was to be repaid by specific duties authorised by Parliament. Further, the creditors were given authority to incorporate themselves as a bank and to make further loans on the security of parliamentary taxation. This was the origin of the Bank of England, and not only did the government pay interest on its loans at 8%, it paid £4,000 per year towards its administrative costs. Crown debt gradually evolved into the National Debt and from this point on, the violent fluctuations in the money supply available to the Crown smoothed out. Further, as investors could rely on repayment under parliamentary guarantees, they became increasingly willing to lend to the government. Coward considers this development to be of far-reaching importance in relation to foreign policy and to Britain's emergence as a major European power. Confident of adequate financial resources, William III, Anne and their Hanoverian successors were in a far better position than earlier monarchs to take a role on the continental stage.[1] That there was far less potential for conflict between Crown and Parliament over finance also meant that national politics became less confrontational than they had been during the 17th century and a pattern of development by evolution was able to establish itself.

William III was perhaps the last monarch who personally dictated policy, but his long absences abroad on campaign meant an increase in the authority of his ministers. The primacy of foreign affairs for much of the reign brought about a formal division of responsibilities between the two secretaries of state. For some time, the two had been responsible respectively for the northern and southern halves of England and Wales; now this division was extended to foreign affairs. The Secretary of State for the Southern Department, usually the senior, dealt with relations with France, Spain, the Mediterranean and the colonies, the Secretary of State for the Northern Department with Russia, the United Provinces, the German states and Scandinavia.[2]

At the same time, public administration was also developing and a permanent civil service was beginning to emerge in the personnel of the Treasury, the Navy Office, the offices of the Secretaries of State and a much-enlarged Customs and Excise controlled by the Treasury. By 1714, this civil service numbered about 12,000 members.[3] The old practice of 'franchising' the collection of Crown revenues disappeared after 1683, and with it some – though by no means all – potential for

1   B Coward, *The Stuart Age*, 1980, Longman, pp 453–55 sets out the financial history of the period in an admirably cogent form.
2   G Williams and JA Ramsden, *Ruling Britannia: A Political History of Britain 1688–1988*, 1990, Longman, p 20.
3   *Ibid*, p 21.

corruption in public office. The potential for official corruption was also reduced by the provision of more realistic salaries for office-holders.

The final elements of the Revolution Settlement remained to be put into place.

16.3   THE ACT OF SETTLEMENT

The Act of Settlement is known to the general public only as the source of the continued prohibition on the succession of a Roman Catholic or a person who 'shall marry' a Roman Catholic to the throne of the United Kingdom, regarded by many as discriminatory, divisive and completely outdated. The Act also enshrines the principle of male primogeniture in the royal succession, now also regarded as incompatible with modern monarchy. It was, however, a product of its own time and it is a matter of historical accident that its major provisions remain in force to the present day, not only in establishing the succession to the Crown, but of wider significance in establishing the constitutional independence of the judiciary of what is now the United Kingdom.

16.3.1 The succession

The immediate trigger for the passing of the Act was the death of the last surviving child of the future Queen Anne at the end of July 1700. Queen Mary had died childless in 1694 and William III showed no inclination to remarry. Anne therefore remained his heir. By her marriage to George of Denmark, she had produced six children, five of whom had died in infancy.[4] The sixth, William, Duke of Gloucester, born in 1689, just as the initial Revolution Settlement came into effect, seems to have been hydrocephalic and mentally retarded. Nevertheless, he was acclaimed during his brief life as a future Protestant champion on the model of William of Orange. By the time of his death, it was clear that his mother, who was not yet 40 but whose health had suffered dramatically as a result of her attempts to secure the succession, would have no more children and might well not live for much longer.

By contrast, Anne's Catholic half-brother, James Francis Edward, the 'warming pan baby' of 1688, was in good health and had a younger sister, born in 1692.[5] James II was still alive, though he no longer sought actively to return, having come to the belief that his downfall was God's punishment for his sins. He and his son retained the support of Louis XIV, despite the Treaty of Ryswick of 1697, by which Louis recognised William of Orange as monarch, and were regarded by a sizeable minority in Britain as the legitimate rulers. The prospect of a Jacobite restoration after the death of Anne, who could claim legitimacy as James's daughter and whose place in the succession was enshrined in the Bill of Rights, was genuine. Even if a Jacobite restoration did not come about, there was the alarming prospect of a future war for the crown. It should not be forgotten that the 1640s were within living memory and few could have been desirous of another lengthy war on home soil. The wars of the 1640s had been fought out during the last decade of the Thirty Years War, so that

---

4   A total of 18 pregnancies are reported, but some of these were almost certainly hysterical, as
      the unfortunate woman became increasingly desperate to produce living heirs.
5   She died unmarried in 1712.

continental rulers had not intervened on behalf of Charles I. At the close of the century, however, James II had French support and the political circumstances of the time meant that this was likely to take an active form. After all, it suited Louis XIV's purposes admirably to seek to destabilise William of Orange's crown.

Pressure for succession to be settled by legislation was further strengthened by the death of the Spanish king Carlos II in November 1700 without an obvious heir. This led directly to the War of the Spanish Succession, as Louis XIV and the Emperor Leopold I endeavoured to consolidate their positions in Europe by establishing their respective candidates on the Spanish throne,[6] and the remaining powers ranged themselves in support of one or the other.

Though there was some sentimental attachment to the House of Stuart, the view of those in power was that no Catholic should follow William and Anne on the throne to threaten the constitutional system put in place in 1689. A Protestant heir had to be found, one, moreover, who could claim dynastic legitimacy as a descendant of previous monarchs. But who was there? Charles II's issue were all illegitimate. The sisters of Charles II and James II had left a number of legitimate descendants, but all were Catholic. The Whigs had to go back another generation, to the descendants of Charles I's sister, Elizabeth, and the Elector Palatine, Frederick V. The majority of these were also Catholic, but included a surviving daughter, Sophia Dorothea, widow of the Elector Ernst August of Hanover. Not only was the Electress a Protestant, so were her eldest son, Georg Ludwig, now Elector, and a daughter. The Electress also had four Protestant grandchildren, considerably strengthening the prospects for Protestant succession in the long term.

Never mind that the Electress and her family had spent their entire lives on the continent and were strangers to the British Isles, they were Protestants and that was enough. The Act of Settlement duly vested the succession to the thrones of England, Scotland and Ireland in the Electress and her descendants, provided always that they were Protestant and did not marry a 'Papist'. The reigning monarch was required to maintain communion with the Church of England. In fact, the Hanoverians were Lutheran, but this was not considered a problem.

16.3.2 The judiciary

Other provisions of the Act of Settlement dealt with the major political concerns of the moment. William III was under considerable pressure, his foreign policy having proved expensive and less than entirely successful. The concerns of the Exclusion Crisis, that William would use his British kingdoms mainly as a means of continuing his struggle against Louis XIV, had proved amply justified. A number of William's

---

6   Carlos II (1665–1700), the last Habsburg ruler of Spain, is the supreme example of the hazards of dynastic inbreeding, and was a physical and mental invalid from birth. His death without issue had been anticipated for many years and much of the military and diplomatic history of the period turns ultimately on the question of the Spanish succession. Louis XIV's queen, Maria Theresa, was Carlos's sister, and Louis sought the Spanish Crown for his younger grandson, Philip, Duke of Anjou. The Emperor Leopold, son of Carlos's aunt, advanced the claims of his younger son, the Archduke Charles. Matters were complicated by Maria Theresa having renounced her rights over the Spanish throne at the time of her marriage, and Carlos having willed his throne to Philip of Anjou with the proviso that the French and Spanish Crowns should never be united. Not only Spain was at stake, but the Spanish Netherlands (modern Belgium) and the huge Spanish Empire in the New World – modern Latin America except Brazil, and large areas of the southern United States.

ministers had been unable to command support in Parliament and had been forced to resign. In order to obtain the passage of legislation dealing with the succession and, perhaps of more immediate concern, to persuade Parliament to vote large grants for the renewal of war, William was prepared to make concessions. Like the rest of the Act of Settlement, these concessions would only take effect on the death of Anne and therefore did not affect his own position.

The concession of lasting importance was the provision in the Act of Settlement that the higher judiciary – the judges of the High Court and above[7] – hold office 'during good behaviour' rather than at pleasure as previously, and so cannot be dismissed on the basis of royal or governmental disapproval of their actions. James II had dismissed 12 judges during his brief reign. Charles II had also suspended some judges from sitting and removed a Chief Justice from office by forcing him to retire.[8] William III had begun the appointment of judges during good behaviour as a regular practice, but had firmly resisted two attempts to enshrine it in statute, so that his acceptance of the provision was a significant climbdown. 'Good behaviour' is a vague phrase and has yet to be judicially defined, but is thought to confer a power of dismissal only in cases of misconduct.[9] Henceforth, a judge could only be dismissed by the monarch following an address by both Houses of Parliament, so that the co-operation of monarch and legislature was required in order to effect the dismissal of a judge. That this would in practice be extremely difficult to achieve is amply demonstrated by only one judge having been removed by these means in 300 years. This was Sir Jonah Barrington, a judge of the Irish courts who was found in 1830 to have misappropriated money belonging to litigants.

However, until 1707, even tenure during good behaviour was ended by the death of the monarch. On 'demise of the Crown', all judicial proceedings ceased and judicial power vested in the new king, who could then choose or not to re-appoint those judges who had held office on his predecessor's death. Queen Anne took this opportunity to remove some judges in 1702. By the Succession to the Crown Act 1707, patents of office remained effective for six months after the demise of the Crown and, since 1760, judges have enjoyed continuity in office irrespective of the identity of the monarch.[10] Further, judicial salaries became permanently authorised by the Act of Settlement, so were not subject to parliamentary approval. Parliament was therefore prevented from putting pressure on judges by threatening to withhold their salaries or from offering bribes in the form of salary increases.

The importance of these developments cannot be overstated. For much of the 17th century, the judges had tended to interpret the law on the basis of what was good for the Crown. Very few were prepared to risk dismissal by incurring the king's wrath. From the early 18th century, the judiciary increasingly applied and developed the law without fear or favour. This constitutional guarantee of independence is, admittedly,

---

7   In 1701, there were no county courts and hence no circuit judges. These enjoy less constitutional independence than their superiors, being dismissible by the Lord Chancellor on the basis of incapacity (s 17(4) of the Courts Act 1971). Even so, this power has been used only once, in the case of a circuit judge convicted in 1983 of smuggling quantities of whisky and cigarettes from the Channel Islands to England.

8   JH Baker, *An Introduction to English Legal History*, 3rd edn, 1990, Butterworths, p 192.

9   This does not cover conviction for all types of criminal offence, since no action was taken in the case of a High Court judge who pleaded guilty in 1975 to drink-driving. Arguably, misconduct means misconduct in office and criminal offences involving dishonesty.

10 Baker, *op cit*.

limited in its value as there is no prohibition on the putting of pressure on a judge to induce him to resign, whether over concerns about his competence or because he is perceived to have stepped out of line. Lord Chancellors have also on occasions issued public reprimands, generally in relation to extra-judicial statements. For example, in 1978, the then Lord Chancellor, Lord Rawlinson of Ewell, 'strongly deprecated' remarks made by Melford Stephenson J about the Sexual Offences Act 1967, which permitted homosexual acts by consenting males aged 21 or over in private.[11] More recently, Lord Irvine of Lairg criticised two High Court judges over views they had expressed on constitutional matters in a public lecture.

The remaining provisions of the Act of Settlement were designed to prevent future foreign-born monarchs from following those actions of William III which had aroused the most opposition during his reign in England, that is, his long war against Louis XIV and the measures taken to prosecute it. Following Anne's death, no monarch should leave the realm without parliamentary consent and no foreign-born monarch should without parliamentary consent take England into 'any War for the defence of any Dominions and Territories which do not belong to the Crown of England', so preventing England being drawn into a war for the defence of Hanover by the unchecked will of the monarch. No foreigner could be appointed to public office or sit in the English Parliament. This provision became a nullity in practice, since after 1714, those foreigners to whom it was likely to apply rapidly became naturalised British subjects. In any event, the Hanoverian monarchs tended to rely on men of British origin to a much greater extent than William III, whose patronage of Dutchmen who were reputed to share his bed became notorious.

16.4   THE ACTS OF UNION 1707

The last of the great legislative developments of the period, the final element in the constitutional skeleton put into place under William III and Anne, was the political union between England and Scotland which took effect in 1707. Although James I had been an enthusiast for union, no progress was made in this area, except briefly during the Interregnum. That union was imposed by conquest and did not survive the fall of the Commonwealth. Indeed, the politics of much of the 17th century tended to drive the two countries apart. There was deep mutual antipathy between Englishman and Scot, each considering himself superior to the other, and the institutions of his own country to be superior, not least in the perennially divisive sphere of religion.

Further, events from 1689 demonstrated that sentiments in favour of the Stuarts were considerably stronger in Scotland than in England. To exacerbate the potential danger, the Scots were far from being a united people; there was then as much mutual suspicion between Highlander and Lowlander as between Scot and Englishman, if not more. Political, economic and social power lay mainly in the Lowlands, where Presbyterianism was strongest, and the power of Lowland magnates was made still greater by the events of 1689–90. Excluded from real power as, in fact, they had always been, the Highland chiefs tended to tilt towards the Jacobite cause as a means of bolstering their own position and of preserving their traditional independence. Highland antipathy was worsened by religious differences and the use made of the

---

11   (1978) *The Times*, 6 July.

Campbell Earls of Argyll to enforce security in the Highlands, so re-opening old divisions between the Highland chiefs themselves. There was also significant opposition to William in the Lowlands from the Episcopalian minority.

The divisions between English and Scottish, and between Highlander and Lowlander, only intensified during the rest of William III's reign, so increasing concern over his own and his successors' security north of the Tweed. One factor was the Massacre of Glencoe of 13 February 1692, yet another of the events of the period that have found a place in national myth, though it has its origins in Highland-Lowland antipathy rather than Scottish-English conflict. Following Dundee's rising, William III's adviser on Scottish affairs, Sir John Dalrymple of Stair, persuaded the king to compel all Highland chiefs to take an oath of allegiance to William by 1 January 1692. Alexander Macdonald, or Alasdair Macdonald or MacIain, chief of the Macdonalds of Glencoe,[12] did not take the oath until five days after the deadline. On 13 February, Glencoe was subjected to a surprise night attack by government troops and some 40 of MacIain's dependants were killed in their beds. Final responsibility for the massacre has never been conclusively determined. Certainly, it was authorised from London by the king and Stair on the basis that MacIain had not taken the oath, but their information was incomplete, and there is a strong possibility that the fact that MacIain had taken the oath, albeit belatedly, was deliberately kept from them by his Lowland enemies.

It was therefore feared in England, justifiably, that on the death of Anne, the Scots, or a significant proportion of them, would resist the imposition of the alien Hanoverian dynasty and so end the union of Crowns and threaten English security. The threat was made worse by the Highlands being peculiarly difficult to control for geographical reasons.

The final trigger in the events leading to the Acts of Union was an economic one, the debacle of the 'Darien scheme', which left the Scottish state virtually bankrupt. One important development of the 17th century was the emergence of the great trading companies, created by royal charter and given monopolies of trade with particular areas, notably the East and West Indies and North America, where a number of them established colonies.

In 1695, a Company of Scotland was created by royal charter to trade to Africa and the East and West Indies and to found colonies in the parts of those areas not already under the sovereignty of a European ruler. Scotland was at this time in a state of economic crisis because of an English blockade which limited its trade with the continent, imposed as a result of the war against Louis XIV, and because the English Navigation Acts prevented Scotland from participating in English colonial trade. It was hoped that the new Company would rectify this. Scotland also wished to emphasise its position as a sovereign state independent of England by founding and developing its own colonies.

The Company of Scotland was not a success. The East India Company was able to prevent it from becoming active in its own sphere of influence and the new Company instead looked westwards, seeking to found a colony on the Isthmus of Darien in modern Panama in order to benefit from trade across both Atlantic and Pacific. Darien was within the Spanish colonial empire and the scheme was opposed by William III,

---

12 Alasdair Macdonald was the Gaelic version of his name, Alexander Macdonald the anglicised. MacIain was a title drawn from the half-legendary first chief of the clan.

who had no wish to encourage Spain to ally itself with France. He therefore forbade English merchants from investing in the Company or supplying the colony, and persuaded merchants in Amsterdam and Hamburg not to invest in the Company. Given that much of the Company's investment came from outside Scotland, this was a serious restriction on its viability. In any event, Darien is one of the least healthy areas in the world, much of it low-lying swamp which provides a perfect breeding ground for diseases such as malaria. 'New Caledonia' ran rapidly into serious difficulties. Some 3,000 colonists went out to Darien from the summer of 1698 onwards. By the end of 1700, almost all had succumbed to disease.

Though the failure of the expedition was probably inevitable, given the hostile environment of Darien and the failure of previous attempts to colonise the area, blame was laid at the door of William III and his ministers, who had refused repeated appeals for aid in order not to alienate the Spanish. The collapse of the Darien scheme was attributed in Scottish national mythology to English treachery and betrayal. It also had serious economic consequences, since up to a quarter of national capital had been invested in it, and the consequent crisis was exacerbated by a succession of poor harvests in the late 1690s, leading to a famine in which perhaps 5% of the Scottish population died.[13]

At the death of William III on 7 March 1702, English-Scottish relations were in a very poor state and did not improve. Shortly afterwards, the Scottish Privy Council took Scotland into the War of the Spanish Succession without reference to the Edinburgh Parliament. Though the Privy Councillors were themselves Scots, they had benefited greatly as individuals from royal patronage and tended to be thought of as dupes of the English Crown. The possibility that Scotland would not recognise the Hanoverian succession was reinforced when in 1703, the Scottish Parliament passed an Act of Security which provided that it had the power to nominate the successor to Queen Anne and that this would not be the same person as succeeded to the English crown unless:

> ... there be such conditions for government settled and enacted as may secure the honour and sovereignty of this crown and kingdom, the freedom, frequency and power of Parliaments, the religion, liberty and trade of the nation from English or from any foreign influence.

Though the Act limited the choice of successor to Protestant descendants of the House of Stuart, the Scottish Parliament were thus stating that the Hanoverians would be accepted in Scotland only if much wider demands were met, designed to ensure Scotland's complete constitutional independence from England. During the debates of 1703, the republican Andrew Fletcher of Saltoun indeed proposed that if Scotland did not choose a different monarch from England, then in dealing with Scottish affairs, the monarchy should be subordinated to the will of the Scottish Parliament. In either event, the prerogative should be strictly limited. Without the consent of the Scottish Parliament, the king should not make peace or war or conclude treaties, or issue general pardons. Places, offices and pensions should in future be given by Parliament, not the king, and there should be no standing army, whether in peace or in war, without the consent of Parliament. Finally:

---

13   M Lynch, *Scotland: A New History*, 1992, Pimlico, p 309.

If any king break in upon any of these conditions of government, he shall by the estates be declared to have forfeited the crown.

Though Saltoun's proposals were ignored by the members, the Lord Advocate, Lord Stuart of Goodtrees, was able to obtain a provision in the Act as passed that the continuation of the union of Crowns was conditional on Scotland being allowed free trade throughout the English colonies.

Not surprisingly, Queen Anne refused to assent to the Act and appointed a new royal commissioner, the Marquess of Tweeddale, to represent her in Scotland and bring the Scottish Parliament to heel. Tweeddale was no more successful than his predecessor and the Scottish Parliament passed the Act a second time the following year. This time Anne, at a time when English fortunes in the War of the Spanish Succession were apparently at a low ebb,[14] was persuaded to give her assent, omitting the free trade clause. Her ministers, headed by the Earl of Godolphin, decided that political union between England and Scotland was the only way to prevent a Jacobite restoration in Scotland on the queen's death. The War of the Spanish Succession continued; if the young James – 'the Pretender' to contemporaries[15] – managed to establish himself in Scotland with French aid, there was an obvious danger of Scotland being used as a springboard for a French invasion of England.

At the same time, relations between the two countries reached a new low when, at the instigation of the East India Company, the Royal Navy seized a ship belonging to the Company of Scotland which was attempting to run the English blockade of France. The English ship *Worcester* was seized in retaliation and the captain and two of his crew were hanged by the Scots on charges of piracy, the evidence for which was thin indeed.

In London, full governmental union was deemed essential in order to protect English security, but required the co-operation of the increasingly anti-English Edinburgh Parliament, which would have to legislate itself out of existence. England therefore put pressure on Scotland to acquiesce. In March 1705, an Aliens Act took effect containing a provision that unless by 25 December 1705, the Scottish Crown was settled on the House of Hanover, the import into England of all Scottish staple products (mainly coal, cattle and flax) would be banned and all Scots treated as aliens in England. Since by *Calvin's Case*, those Scots who held property in England could only protect that property through the courts on the basis that they were not aliens, this was a serious threat, especially to the moneyed classes. Less threateningly, the Act also requested that the Crown appoint commissioners to negotiate with the Scots for union.

Anti-English feeling continued to rise among the Scots in the Lowlands, encouraged by propaganda from both sides, to a point where the elite began to fear mob rule. Between that fear and the threat to their property and trading interests from the Aliens Act, the Scots elite caved in. When Parliament – its members, of course, drawn from this elite – opened on 28 June, the royal commissioner, Tweeddale, the Earl of Argyll, the Lord Privy Seal, the Earl of Queensberry, and the Lord Chancellor, Lord Seafield, persuaded the members to agree to the appointment of commissioners

---

14 The Battle of Blenheim, the first of the Duke of Marlborough's four great victories, had actually been fought, but the news had yet to reach London.

15 He became 'the Old Pretender' on the emergence of his son, Charles Edward, 'the Young Pretender', the Bonnie Prince Charlie of national myth.

to negotiate the terms of a future union, which would necessarily involve recognition of the Hanoverian succession.

Davies notes that the term 'union' had no precise meaning in the early 1700s and carried overtones of 'harmony', 'alliance' and 'co-operation' rather than constitutional integration, for which the terms 'incorporating union' or 'entire union' were used. He argues that those in Scotland who supported the latter were very much a minority; most Scots who supported union simply sought a treaty of co-operation with England. For that reason, the views of the commissioners who would negotiate the union – whatever the term was to mean – assumed a vital importance. On the proposal of the Duke of Hamilton, Parliament agreed by a majority of four that the commissioners should be chosen by Queen Anne, thereby putting the course of the negotiations outside its direct control. Davies states explicitly that Hamilton was bribed; he was shortly afterwards given an English dukedom, made a Knight of the Garter and the Thistle and appointed ambassador to Paris. Lynch uses the term 'collusion' but goes on to describe Hamilton's action – the Duke paraded himself in public as an anti-unionist – as 'a spectacular double-cross which made a Union Treaty possible'.[16]

Not surprisingly, the queen used her new-found power to appoint commissioners who favoured an incorporating union. The negotiations were brief; a draft Treaty was produced in 10 days and the Treaty in its final form in less than three months.

There remained the necessity for both Parliaments to approve the Treaty. Though debate on the matter in Edinburgh was stormy, the Treaty was eventually approved almost unchanged. Debate on Article I, dealing with the principle of an incorporating union, occupied a month, but this crucial Article was passed eventually by a comfortable majority. The other provisions caused little difficulty, even that in relation to religion, since the Scottish Parliament passed an Act, incorporated into the Treaty, to guarantee the continuation of Presbyterian church government. On 4 January 1707, the Scottish Parliament ratified the Treaty in its entirety by passing its Act of Union, matched by an Act of Union of the English Parliament.

Scottish historians have found it extremely difficult to accept that the Scottish Parliament should tamely vote itself out of existence and some have sought to explain this by large-scale bribery of its members by English ministers. This was certainly the view of many at that time, but Coward, with his customary caution, warns that the evidence is not conclusive. He prefers to rely on other factors, in particular the continuing economic crisis in Scotland, for which union offered a remedy through free access to England's foreign trade and to the more lucrative English markets without the hostile tariffs then in force. He also suggests that Scotland's experiences in the 1640s and 1650s, in particular in 1650–51, when Scotland recognised the young Charles II, could not have brought much enthusiasm for another war with England over the crown, particularly as it might well involve internal war between the Lowlands and Highlands. Further, the Treaty and subsequent Acts of Union guaranteed the independent continuance of the two institutions most cherished by the political class in Scotland: the Presbyterian church and the Scottish legal system.[17] Lynch also emphasises the economic factors in favour of union, noting that by 1700,

16 Davies, *The Isles,* 1999, Macmillan, p 579; Lynch, *op cit,* p 312.
17 Coward, *op cit,* pp 420–21.

half of Scotland's export trade was with England, though significantly reduced by the hostile climate of 1700–04. He adds, however, that the largest 'block vote' in the Scottish Parliament in favour of union came from the peerage, the most anglicised element in Scottish society. Though their economic interests were not uniformly promoted by union, the terms of the Treaty of Union preserved their position in local affairs and gave them a representation in the new Parliament of Great Britain which was out of proportion to their numbers and proportionately much greater than that of the Scottish populace.[18]

Much ink and rhetoric has been expended over the union in the past 300 years, Scottish nationalists seeing it as a sell-out to the English. However, looked at objectively, the framework put in place in 1707 is not entirely an unbalanced one. Certainly, England was the dominant partner, but this was inevitable given that there was in no realistic sense a marriage of equals. Quite simply, England was much the more populous, more developed and more prosperous of the two kingdoms, and Scotland's continuing economic crisis put its representatives in a weak bargaining position.

The Treaty of Union provided that England and Scotland were to become one country, to be known as the United Kingdom of Great Britain, and guaranteed the Hanoverian succession to a single crown. The new Parliament of Great Britain would include 16 Scottish peers, elected by their fellows for the duration of each Parliament, and 45 MPs. This representation was not proportionate to the Scottish element in the British population, and this had been insisted upon by the English negotiators, but was rather greater than the Scottish contribution to Crown revenues warranted. However, this representation was distinctly unbalanced, in that the Scottish franchise was very narrow, with about 3,000 voters in a population of something over one million.[19] The Scottish peerage had additional representation, in that those few peers who also held English titles were able to sit in the new House of Lords by virtue of their English titles. However, all English peers were entitled to sit in the Lords, not simply a limited number of representative peers.[20] By Article 18, laws concerning the regulation of trade and customs and excise duties were to be uniform throughout Great Britain. Subject to this, all laws in Scotland were to remain in force:

> … but alterable by the Parliament of Great Britain, with this difference betwixt the laws concerning public right, policy and civil government, and those which concern private right; that the laws which concern public right, policy and civil government may be made the same throughout the whole United Kingdom, but that no alteration may be made in laws which concern private right except for evident utility of the subjects within Scotland.[21]

On the basis of this, it has been argued by a number of Scottish writers that, contrary to the general principle of parliamentary supremacy embodied in the British constitution, the powers of Parliament have since 1707 been limited in respect of

18 Lynch, *op cit*, pp 313–14.
19 The electorate of England and Wales was then about 300,000 of some 5.5 million. Williams and Ramsden, *op cit*, pp 41–42.
20 From 1707, new peerages were 'of Great Britain' and carried a seat in the Lords. However, the distinction between pre-1707 peerages of England and Scotland was only finally dealt with by s 4 of the Peerage Act 1963, which entitled all Scottish peers to sit in the Lords.
21 Article 18. See AW Bradley and KD Ewing, *Constitutional and Administrative Law*, 12th edn, 1997, Longman, p 79.

Scottish affairs by the terms of the Treaty of Union. However, it must be said that the Scottish courts have maintained silence on this matter, so that these arguments are based on inferences from omissions, rather than anything more explicit.[22]

The separateness of the Scottish legal system was preserved by Article 19, which provided that the higher Scottish courts, the Court of Session and the Court of Justiciary were to remain 'for all time coming' as constituted at the time of its ratification, and no Scottish cause was to be capable of being heard by the English higher courts (Queen's Bench, Chancery and Common Pleas) or any other court sitting in Westminster Hall. No reference was made to the legal jurisdiction of the House of Lords, which as early as 1711, left the way open for the Lords to develop an appellate jurisdiction in respect of Scottish civil matters.[23] Further, the guarantee contained in Article 19 was limited, in that the Parliament of Great Britain had a residual power to make changes 'for the better administration of justice'.

Aside from the debate which still rages over its effect, Article 18 provided for an economic union between England and Scotland, with free trade between the two countries and common customs tariffs in respect of overseas trade. Scotland's official debts were written off and the country was to receive a cash payment of £398,085 10s – the 'Equivalent' – as compensation for taking on a share of the English National Debt. Part of this sum was to be used to compensate victims of the Darien scheme.

On 1 May 1707, the new Parliament assembled, marking the point at which the two Acts of Union took effect. They and the Treaty of Union remain in force. However, their effects were limited almost immediately by a number of legislative changes during the latter half of the reign of Queen Anne. The Treason Act 1708 reconciled the Scottish law of treason with that of England, in the light of an attempted French invasion in March of that year in support of the Pretender. At the same time, the Scottish Privy Council, which had been unaffected by the Acts of Union, was abolished, not by Queen Anne or her ministers, who were content that it should remain in being, but at the behest of the Marquess of Tweeddale, now one of the 16 representative peers, and his allies in the new House of Commons, who saw it as the instrument of their political enemies. In March 1712, Parliament passed a Toleration Act which granted greater freedom to the Episcopalian minority in Scotland, so striking indirectly at the position of the Presbyterian church which was also guaranteed under the Treaty of Union. The economic advantages of union were also less obvious in the first years after 1707 than had been predicted, as a result of new duties which affected Scotland to a greater extent than England. However, the union survived, if only as the lesser of two evils in the eyes of the Scottish elite, particularly in the light of the attempted invasion of 1708 and the serious Jacobite insurrection of 1715.[24] Further, the Treaty of Union and its ratifying Acts contained no mechanisms for dissolving the union, so that this could be achieved, if at all, only through institutions dominated by the English and English interests.

One more element of the lasting constitutional structure was put into place at this time, though this was not appreciated for a great many years. In 1708, a Scottish Militia Bill, intended to create a militia in Scotland on the same lines as that which

---

22　See Bradley and Ewing, *ibid*, pp 79–82 for a summary of the arguments.

23　*Greenshiels v Magistrates of Edinburgh* (1711) 1 Rob 12. It was held that the House of Lords fell outside the provisions of Article 19, as it was not a court within Westminster Hall.

24　Coward, *op cit*, p 422.

existed in England, was passed by both Houses of Parliament, and duly presented to Queen Anne for the royal assent. On the advice of her ministers, she refused assent. Not until George IV was faced in 1829 with a Catholic Emancipation Bill of which he strongly disapproved did the monarch again consider refusing the royal assent and on that occasion, he was advised that he should not thwart the will of Parliament in such a way. In the intervening period, and effectively by omission, a constitutional convention had developed, of no legal force but nevertheless binding in practice, that the monarch does not refuse assent to Bills passed by both Houses.

CHAPTER 17

THE EARLY 18TH CENTURY

17.1 INTRODUCTION

After the dramatic events of the previous 100 years, the 18th century was a time largely of constitutional development by evolution. Britain emerged as a regular player on the European political scene, not least because after 1714, the monarch was also ruler of a strategically important German state, and her diplomatic and military activity began to be influenced by her interests as a colonial power. The practice of government was therefore heavily influenced by foreign policy considerations, the need to ensure the efficiency of the army and Royal Navy, and official finance. It is no accident that the ministerial offices which had emerged before 1700 and became firmly established during the succeeding century were all concerned with foreign policy, the armed services and government finance. Though the two Secretaries of State had a domestic role, their main sphere was foreign affairs and not until 1782 was the office of Home Secretary created.

The 18th century was the period in which the office of Prime Minister emerged, along with the practice of Cabinet government. Crown patronage began slowly to decline, to be replaced by the power of factions, so that the focus of political life moved from the court to Parliament. It was also a period when many of the practices of government first emerged, not least the use of patronage and the honours system for openly partisan purposes. Although the monarch's power also began to decline, the process was very much a gradual one. Necessarily, new and established practices overlapped. In particular, the court remained important as a channel of communication with the monarch, so that appointments to court positions came to be made on factional lines.

By 1702, the main framework of the British constitution was in place, not least an effective system of public finance. In consequence, the periodic crises precipitated by monarchical need for money which had characterised national politics over many centuries largely disappeared as triggers for change. To a much greater extent than hitherto, the process of constitutional evolution involved consensus and the establishment of settled practices which were accepted as proper by politicians of all persuasions. This is not to say that crises did not occur, but they were much less violent and no longer involved recourse to arms, as Parliament and the press became the accepted arenas for expression of views.

After 1714, the Whigs had a near-monopoly of ministerial office for much of the century. The Whig oligarchy began to break up in the 1760s and at the same time, radicalism began to re-emerge as a political force. However, the radicals did not become a force in Parliament until much later, nor was there any great pressure on mainstream political figures to adopt radical ideas or to 'buy off' the radicals with limited change. Power vested in a relatively homogenous ruling class, with a homogeneity of views on what was desirable in a constitutional system.

The emergence of a professional political class continued and it became accepted through practice that ministers were chosen from members of one or other House of Parliament. Before 1600, few great figures in public life sat in Parliament, and those who did were peers who derived their power and influence from elsewhere. In part, this was because Parliament sat only for short periods and at irregular intervals. From the late 1620s, we see individual members of the Commons emerging as significant figures. This pattern continued after the Restoration, though the most prominent parliamentarians were as likely to be in the Lords as the Commons.

Though it had been the case from Tudor times, if not earlier, that peers were appointed as ministers, or trusted ministers were rewarded with peerages, it was only during the 18th century that ministers began to be appointed as a regular practice from among the members of the Commons. The practical realities of politics made it increasingly necessary for a Prime Minister to be able to rely on the support of a majority in the House of Commons, but for much of the period, governments were dominated by members of the Lords.

As previously, an important factor in these developments was the personality and abilities of the reigning monarch, along with a governmental system of increasing complexity which required greater professionalism on the part of those who operated it. Queen Anne did not possess the commanding personality of an Elizabeth I, nor her ability to manipulate, and was in poor health throughout her reign. In consequence, it was her advisors who dictated policy. This pattern continued and was further developed under George I, who spent long periods in Hanover. It was in his reign that the office of Prime Minister first emerged. Gradually, there was a permanent shift of power, so that it came to be the Prime Minister who initiated policy and in all practical senses exercised supreme executive power, not the monarch.

During the 17th century, the first long term political and parliamentary groupings had emerged, acquiring more specific identities and the labels of Whigs and Tories during the Exclusion Crisis of 1679–83. From the second half of Anne's reign, governments, intermittently at least, were structured on clear factional lines. Though both Whigs and Tories drew their membership and support from the propertied classes, the economic and social developments which took place in the 1690s and early 1700s created a real as well as an ideological distinction between them.

17.2 ENGLISH SOCIETY AND THE POLITICAL NATION

In 1695–96, Gregory King published the earliest systematic attempt at a demographic study of the English population and the contribution of different groups to national wealth. He estimated the total population of England to be slightly more than 5.5 million, in 1.36 million families. He divided the population into families increasing or decreasing national wealth, then sub-divided each band into various categories. Heading the complex social pyramid were the 160 peers, their families and other landowners whose estates exceeded 10,000 acres, who between them owned some 20% of the cultivated land and gained their income mainly from rents, supplemented by the rewards of public office. There were then some 15,000 gentry families, again living mainly off rents, as did the 150,000 lesser freeholders. Others whose economic activities increased the nation's wealth included the clergy, professional men, officers of the army and navy, merchants, traders and craftsmen. These categories totalled some 2,675,520 people, slightly fewer than the 2,825,000 common seamen, labouring people and outservants, cottagers, paupers and vagrants who decreased the nation's wealth.[1]

Perhaps the greatest flaw in King's study is that he under-estimated the numbers of merchants and traders and others whose income derived from commercial activity, and the size of their incomes. This in turn led to his under-estimating the contribution of the commercial classes to national wealth at a time of boom, particularly in overseas trade. Until the middle years of the 17th century, England's foreign trade was dominated by the cloth industry, which produced some 80% of English exports in the 1600s, but after 1660, there was considerable diversification, in part reflecting the creation of overseas colonies and trade in new commodities such as sugar, tea, coffee and tobacco. The emergence of the Bank of England and the great joint stock companies provided the commercial classes with new and very lucrative opportunities for investment. At the same time, the poor harvests of the 1690s led to a decline in incomes from land, while the burden of the land tax, levied at 4s in the pound for most of the period 1692–1713, fell much more heavily on the landowners than on the commercial classes.

For most of William III's reign, government was dominated by Whigs, who tended to pursue policies favourable to commercial interests. Further, the Tories were concerned to protect the Church of England to which the majority of their supporters belonged, whereas the commercial classes included a significant proportion of Dissenters. In consequence, the Whigs became increasingly the party of the commercial and professional classes, while the Tories were dominated by landed interests, particularly the lesser rural gentry whose position was most at risk from social change, though it must be emphasised that there was never a complete split between the two.

17.3   QUEEN ANNE 1702–14

While the Whigs remained relatively united until the 1720s, the Tories after 1701 were divided over the Hanoverian succession and religious matters. Since Roman Catholics were politically emasculated by the Test Acts, and the small proportion that remained also opposed the Hanoverian succession, the more extreme 'high' Tories saw the main threat to the Church of England as coming from the Dissenters.

Under Anne, the Tories gained ministerial office to a much greater extent than hitherto, but for much of the remainder of the century, they were largely in opposition and under suspicion of espousing the Jacobite cause. The queen was temperamentally inclined towards the Tories, but the political and military situation of the first years of her reign, dominated by the War of the Spanish Succession, required a policy of moderation in domestic affairs. The Duke of Marlborough, Captain General (Commander-in-Chief) of the Armed Forces, was moderately Tory in his views, but recognised the need to secure Whig support for England's involvement in the war, which reached its peak in the period 1704–06. This was a war on an unprecedented scale, involving British troops in campaigning in Flanders, Germany as far south as

---

1   *A Scheme of the Income and Expense of the Several Families of England Calculated for the Year 1688.* See B Coward, *The Stuart Age*, 1980, Longman, pp 482–85; and G Williams and JA Ramsden, *Ruling Britannia: A Political History of Britain 1688–1988*, 1990, Longman, p 26.

the Danube, Spain, North America and the Caribbean, and cost the British Crown some £4 million per year. The support of the commercial classes was imperative. As a result, the early years of Anne's reign saw what was effectively coalition government centred on Marlborough and the Lord Treasurer, the Earl of Godolphin, its ministers drawn from the Whigs and more moderate Tories. Marlborough and Godolphin both sat in the Lords, and Marlborough was in any case usually abroad with his armies, but they recognised the need to influence the House in order to secure the necessary legislation for the war effort. They therefore obtained office for their supporters in the Commons, particularly two moderate Tories: Robert Harley, the Speaker (not yet a non-partisan office), who became Secretary of State for the Northern Department, and Henry St John, appointed to the new post of Secretary of State for War.

At this time, the Whig-Tory dichotomy at ministerial level was not absolute; indeed, Godolphin remained aloof from party ties. Rather, the divisions between the two groups expressed themselves in vicious verbal battles within Parliament, attempts by Tories to infiltrate themselves into the boards of the joint stock companies so as to undermine a principal area of Whig strength, and a propaganda war in the newspapers and periodicals which had emerged since the Licensing Act of 1678 lapsed in 1695.

From 1708, the coalition became increasingly isolated from mainstream political opinion, as the course of events, in particular a popular desire for an end to the war, ceased to favour them, and public and political opinion became more sharply polarised. Three of Marlborough's four great victories came in the years 1704–08 and were followed by attempts to negotiate peace with the now ageing Louis XIV, who by the summer of 1709 was willing to concede all the allied demands except that which required him to use French troops to force his grandson, Philip of Anjou, out of Spain. Marlborough's fourth victory, Malplaquet, came in September 1709, but allied casualties were greater than French, and this only increased demands for an end to the war on the grounds that further campaigning would serve no purpose. There was also deepening suspicion of those who were making fortunes out of the war, mainly London financiers, and often Dissenters or those of Jewish or Huguenot origins. The leading Tories became more extreme in their views and the division between moderate and high Tories became much more marked.

The impeachment of Dr Sacheverell for an allegedly seditious sermon and its reverberations in 1709–10 brought down the coalition. Harley replaced Godolphin as Lord Treasurer and for the rest of the reign, the government was composed of Tories. Sacheverell's impeachment, along with other events of the time, demonstrated the need for ministers to have the support of a majority of members of both Houses, and by this stage, a 'party' machinery was beginning to develop. This machinery was heavily based on traditional ties such as patronage, but also involved the emergence of a political press on partisan lines. The *Review*, which first appeared in 1704 and was edited by Daniel Defoe, best known today as author of *Gulliver's Travels* (itself a political allegory) but in his own time a leading propagandist, adopted a pro-government stance under a cloak of impartiality, but many more lost no opportunity to 'smear' their publishers' political enemies. At the same time, the court continued to have a vital political rule. Although the mechanisms of Cabinet government were emerging in embryonic form, with monarchs since Charles II having regular meetings with their ministers as a body, courtiers were still persons of enormous political influence, as they controlled access to the monarch.

Queen Anne's reign also saw use being made of the royal prerogative for partisan purposes. One aspect of the prerogative was the power of appointment to commissions in the army. This was not only important in the military context, but was a highly significant form of patronage, since colonelcies of regiments brought their holders large financial gains. As Captain General, Marlborough insisted that this power be exercised solely on his recommendation, something which his political enemies regarded as a usurpation of prerogative powers. This prompted a major crisis early in 1710.[2]

A more obvious use of the prerogative for avowedly political and partisan ends came in 1712, when the queen was persuaded by Harley (created Earl of Oxford in 1711) and St John (created Viscount Bolingbroke in 1712) to create 12 additional Tory peers to establish a sufficient majority in the House of Lords for the making of the Treaty of Utrecht, then under negotiation between Britain, the Netherlands and France. From 1710, Harley's government had been seeking an end to the war, particularly after it became clear that the Emperor Joseph I, who had earlier succeeded Leopold, would have no son, so that his brother, Archduke Charles, already the allied candidate for the Spanish throne, would in due course become Emperor. This removed a major justification for Britain's role in the war. Why resist Bourbon rule over Spain when the only alternative was imperial rule, so reviving the 16th century transcontinental empire of Charles V?

The peace negotiations dragged on for over two years. Britain accepted the Bourbon succession in Spain and received in return recognition of the Hanoverian succession, permanent possession of Gibraltar, captured in 1704, Minorca, St Kitts in the West Indies, Nova Scotia, Newfoundland and Hudson Bay, together with a 30 year monopoly of trade with Spain's American empire. These terms were generous and compensated the Allies for the Bourbon succession by breaking up the Spanish Empire in Europe, all the Habsburg possessions outside Spain passing to the Emperor. Still the peace met considerable opposition in Britain. The Tories had only recently assured the public that they would not accept Philip of Anjou on the Spanish throne; now they reneged on this. Although Philip was prepared to renounce all claims to the French throne, so preventing the union of Crowns between France and Spain which the Allies had feared, that renunciation was very insecure. By the end of 1712, only two lives stood between Philip and the French Crown after a series of disasters hit the Bourbon dynasty in the space of little more than a year. Louis XIV's heir was now a sickly two year old great-grandson, and after him, Philip was Louis's only legitimate descendant in the male line.[3]

Further, the proposed Treaty represented a direct betrayal of an earlier British promise to her allies not to make a separate peace and it was therefore opposed by the Elector Georg Ludwig of Hanover, heir to the British throne after his mother. Nor did the British government gain imperial acceptance of the Hanoverian succession, since the Empire was not a party to the negotiations. Queen Anne was unlikely to live much longer and the Electress Sophia was over 80 years old. The Elector was likely to become king within a short time and there was recognition among British politicians

2   WA Speck, *The Birth of Britain*, 1994, Blackwell, pp 169–70.
3   Salic law prevailed in France, so that the throne could be inherited neither by nor through a female. First, Louis XIV's only legitimate son, the Dauphin Louis, died of smallpox, and within months, the Dauphin's elder son, Philip's only brother, succumbed to measles, along with his own elder son.

that antagonising him was not the way to secure offices and honours in the future. In addition, certain Whigs were concerned that an end to the war would encourage France and Spain to give active support to the Pretender, raising the spectre of a possible invasion on Anne's death.

On 7 December 1711, the Whigs obtained, by a majority of one, a Lords resolution condemning peace 'without Spain'. Harley acted swiftly and persuaded the queen to create 12 Tory peers whose votes were sufficient to reverse the resolution. He then marshalled the support of a majority of both Houses against the Whigs and the few 'Hanoverian Tories', and secured a series of votes which endorsed his government's peace policy. The Treaty of Utrecht was duly concluded in April 1713 and a precedent was set by which the powers of the monarch as fountain of honour could be used for avowedly partisan political purposes, and solely in order to manipulate Parliament for the purposes of the government of the day.

Tory supremacy did not last long. Once the Treaty of Utrecht was concluded, the focus of political attention turned from the Spanish to the British succession. Queen Anne was seriously ill in December 1713; though she recovered, her health was more precarious than ever. While the Whigs were united in favour of the Hanoverian succession, the Tories were deeply divided. Jacobite Tories were in a minority, but were a sizeable minority, and a further substantial group was undecided. Their leaders at this point behaved equivocally; both Harley and Bolingbroke made contact with the Pretender in the winter of 1713–14. It is not clear whether either actually favoured a Jacobite restoration or was simply 'hedging his bets'. The Duke of Marlborough, now out of office but still much respected, carried on a highly equivocal correspondence with the Duke of Berwick, his nephew but also half-brother to the Pretender. More serious for the Tories was the breakdown in relations between Harley and Bolingbroke, whose rivalry, which had smouldered for a number of years, turned to open warfare in the summer of 1713.

In March 1714, the Pretender publicly announced that he would not change his religion. Bolingbroke then set about uniting the Tories behind him and sought to weaken Harley's influence over the queen. His overall intention seems to have been to put himself into an unassailable position within Parliament and at court, and to purge his opponents from public office and replace them with his allies, so that by the time the Electress or her son succeeded to the throne, the Tories under Bolingbroke's leadership would dominate public life.

However, Bolingbroke's scheming failed for three reasons: first, the Tories remained disunited, principally because of suspicions over his contacts with the Pretender; second, the queen disliked him and resisted his attempts to influence her; third, by what was more or less a matter of chance. By the time the queen dismissed Harley as Lord Treasurer on 27 July 1714 at the behest of the Whigs, she was mortally ill, and lapsed into a coma on 30 July without naming Bolingbroke as successor. On the initiative of the Lord Chancellor, Viscount Harcourt, the Earl of Shrewsbury, one of the 'immortal seven' who had issued the invitation to William of Orange in 1688, was appointed Lord Treasurer by the Privy Council. On 1 August, the queen died and the Act of Settlement took effect.

17.4 THE EMERGENCE OF THE WHIG OLIGARCHY

Necessarily, preparations were made during Anne's reign for the accession of a foreign-born monarch, who would take some time to arrive in Britain after the queen's death. An Act of 1705 naturalised the Electress Sophia and the issue of her body 'whenever born', provided that they were not and did not become or marry a Roman Catholic,[4] an Act which would remain in force until its repeal by the British Nationality Act 1948 and would produce the unintended consequence that several hundred members of European royalty, including a number of foreign monarchs, were or in some cases are technically British nationals.[5] The Succession to the Crown Act 1707 made provision for the continuance of government in the critical period before the new monarch could arrive from Hanover and physically occupy the throne. For the first time, Parliament would not be dissolved on the demise of the Crown, but would remain in being for six months afterwards unless dissolved earlier by a legitimate monarch. Office holders would similarly retain their positions for six months and a Regency Council would govern on behalf of the new ruler.

Following Anne's death, the mechanism operated smoothly and the House of Hanover succeeded with as little active opposition as the House of Stuart had in 1603. The Electress having died in June, the Elector Georg Ludwig was proclaimed King of Great Britain and Ireland as George I, and arrived in England on 18 September. It was perhaps fortunate that the French and Spanish had made no preparations to give military support to the Pretender on the queen's death. By the time James landed in Scotland with a French army at the end of 1715, the political landscape had changed and the Jacobite threat to the new king's security, although a source of serious alarm then and later, never assumed major proportions.

Following George I's arrival, the government became overwhelmingly Whig in composition. The new king was an admirer of William III; he had committed 12,000 Hanoverian troops to the allied cause in the War of the Spanish Succession and, as predicted, disapproved of the Tory government's making of a separate peace. As was inevitable, since he was a stranger to Britain and spoke little English, he was heavily influenced initially by his Hanoverian advisers, who themselves favoured the Whigs for foreign policy reasons. He also suspected the Tories of Jacobite leanings. Even before his arrival in Britain, he dismissed Bolingbroke, and the Whig ministry he appointed proceeded to purge Tories from the ranks of office-holders. Before the general election of February 1715, 22 of the 42 lords-lieutenant were removed from office and replaced by Whigs. The Whigs took the opportunity to mount a smear campaign against the Tories, firmly identifying them with Jacobitism.

The Tories were in any case in a poor position as a result of the feud between Oxford and Bolingbroke. The election left the Whigs with a comfortable majority of 372 to 186, and the actions of some Tories thereafter only played further into Whig hands, as Bolingbroke fled to the continent and offered his services to the Pretender. There was rioting in the Jacobite cause in London and in the Welsh border counties, considered serious enough for Parliament to suspend habeas corpus on 21 July, effectively giving a power to imprison without trial and to rush through the Riot Act.

---

4   Princess Sophia's Naturalisation Act 1705, 4 & 5 Anne c 4 or c 16.
5   See AE Lyon, 'For he is an English man; the unforeseen consequences of Princess Sophia's Naturalisation Act 1705' (1999) 20 Statute Law Review, pp 174–84.

This was Britain's first statutory public order measure and gave lords-lieutenant the power to use troops against rioters if they failed to obey an order to disperse. Both Harley and the absent Bolingbroke were impeached and the former was sent to the Tower.

In September, the Earl of Mar raised the Pretender's standard at Braemar and by November had 10,000 men bearing arms in the Jacobite cause. Though the Pretender himself landed in Scotland on 22 December, Louis XIV had died in August and the regents acting for the infant Louis XV did not provide troops. Mar delayed too long before moving south of the Tay, giving the government sufficient time to raise additional troops, arrest known Jacobites in England and send troops to areas where Jacobite sympathies were known to be strong. In the end, the Jacobite rising in England was confined mainly to Catholics in the northern counties and was turned back by superior government forces at Preston. The Scottish rebels fared no better and were ultimately left to their own devices by the Pretender, who re-embarked for France on 4 February 1716. Thereafter, the French regents failed to provide him with support for any further military endeavours and, having entered into an alliance with Britain in 1716, ceased to recognise him as *de jure* king. The Pretender then took up residence in Rome at the invitation of the Pope, remaining there for the rest of his life.

The debacle of the 'Fifteen' left the Whigs in an unassailable position, able to continue the purging of their political enemies from Parliament and from positions of influence on the basis of real or imagined Jacobite leanings. Further, the life of the 1715 Parliament was prolonged from three years to seven by the passing of a Septennial Act in December 1716, which left the 1715 Parliament in existence until February 1722. In the event, this enabled the Whigs to weather the power struggle between its leaders which was a feature of the years 1717–21, without the Tories having the opportunity to profit via a general election.[6]

Though the Tories were thus neutralised, why were the Whigs able to gain and maintain a monopoly of power in the 18th century? Both parties represented the propertied interests, and their policies benefited the propertied classes; in matters to do with property and the economy, there was considerable uniformity between them. The radicalism of the 1640s and 1650s, and its demands for far-reaching social change, was no longer a significant political force. Though the continuing commercial boom until the 1720s brought greater prosperity and thus a larger proportion of the population within the electorate, there was no serious demand for changes in the parliamentary system, either by widening the franchise or by re-distributing seats so as to reflect population distribution. Though there was public disorder on single issues at various times, such as that over the Militia Act of 1757, radicalism did not re-emerge with any significance until the appearance of John Wilkes in the 1760s. Why this was so remains unclear.

At the same time, following the South Sea Bubble of 1720, there was a long period of economic prosperity and general peace in Europe until 1740. Neither Whigs nor Tories sought to make any change in the basic structures of society, which remained rigidly hierarchical, although there was considerable social mobility at an individual level. Those who prospered became absorbed into the higher levels of society and adopted the ways of those who had been their betters, symbolised by their purchases of country estates, rather than seeking to change that society.

6   See F O'Gorman, *The Long Eighteenth Century: British Political and Social History, 1688–1832*, 1997, Arnold, pp 66–68.

Geoffrey Holmes and Daniel Szechi have looked in some detail at the composition of both Parliaments and Cabinets, and have noted a distinct shift in favour of aristocrats after 1688. From the 1690s until the 1720s, members of the Commons consistently held about a third of Cabinet posts, frequently among the most important of them; from 1693 to 1720, one if not both of the two Secretaryships of State was invariably held by a commoner. By contrast, there were more Dukes in Henry Pelham's Cabinet of November 1744 than there had been in the entire English peerage in 1688, if the bastards of Charles II and James II are omitted. Further, in the course of the century, an increasing proportion of MPs were closely linked to the peerage by blood or marriage. An uncertain but high proportion of other MPs were in some way dependent on peers.[7]

17.5   THE EMERGENCE OF A PRIME MINISTER

In hindsight, the most momentous event of George I's reign was the appointment of Sir Robert Walpole as First Lord of the Treasury and Chancellor of the Exchequer in April 1721. He was to retain them continuously until 1742 and would be recognised in retrospect as the first British Prime Minister. Since the time of Charles II, the practice of Cabinet government had been gradually evolving, the monarch chairing regular meetings of ministers when in London. During 1717, George I virtually ceased to attend these meetings and the role of chairman was from 1721 taken over by Walpole, whose long period in power meant that this became a regular feature of government practice. At the same time, Walpole, unprecedentedly for a leading minister, exercised effective leadership over the House of Commons and became able to ensure its compliance to his will.

This is not to say that from 1721, the king ceased to have any influence over policy. That he was simultaneously ruler of a continental state, and the Pretender needed to be kept isolated from the support of the major Catholic powers, meant that foreign affairs assumed still greater importance. Both George I and George II were personally involved in foreign policy and kept control of military patronage in their own hands. Furthermore, the importance attached by contemporaries to the political role of the monarch, and the poor relationship between George I and his only son, now Prince of Wales, meant that the political opposition – for much of the period within the Whig ranks rather than external – tended to cluster round the heir apparent with the long term aim of benefiting from his accession. This was a pattern which continued intermittently up to 1820, as the Hanoverian kings and their heirs remained on terms which ranged from merely bad to proverbially dreadful.[8]

Walpole, by origin a Norfolk squire, had entered the Commons in 1701 and gained very wide-ranging ministerial experience before 1721. His origins, along with his pragmatic and cautious attitudes and fiscal policies, gave him the confidence of the rural landowning class, but he also developed strong links with the London commercial class into which he married. Perhaps most significant in creating his hold

---

7   G Holmes and D Szechi, *The Age of Oligarchy: Pre-Industrial Britain*, 1993, Longman, pp 36–42.

8   It is not clear why father-son relationships among the Hanoverians were so unhappy, though an obvious factor is the accident of biology which meant that all five kings of the dynasty were relatively long-lived and, except for George IV and William IV, neither of whom had legitimate sons, their heirs had many years of adult life with position but no real power.

on power was his success in dealing with the crisis caused by the 'South Sea Bubble', which erupted in 1720 when Walpole held the relatively minor office of Paymaster-General.

The South Sea Company was founded by Harley in 1711, ostensibly to exploit the trading rights which his government expected to gain from the Spanish Empire, but in reality to profit from the National Debt and to counter-balance the Whig-dominated Bank of England and East India Company. Initially, it was highly successful, and in the period 1717–20, it negotiated with the government to take over £31 million of the National Debt, then in the hands of private investors who were being repaid by the government via high interest annuities. In order to persuade these investors to part with their annuities in return for South Sea stock, the Company offered them interest at 5% per annum up to 1727 and 4% thereafter. The South Sea directors created an atmosphere in which investors were prepared to pay any price for South Sea stock, which rose from £100 at the beginning of 1720 to £1,050 by the end of June. Such frenzied buying could not continue; some of the larger investors sold and this precipitated a run on South Sea stock, which went into freefall in September. This created a wave of backbiting and recrimination towards the government and allegations of corruption and criminality in high places, in a fashion which has occurred many times since, but never to the same extent.

Walpole resisted the opportunity to attack his political enemies and instead made himself indispensable to the political system.[9] He persuaded the Bank of England and the East India Company each to take over £9 million worth of South Sea stock, bringing the freefall to an end, and worked out a scheme for compensating investors. In the process, Walpole established a reputation not only as a very safe pair of hands, but also as an honest man.[10] Indeed, public confidence in the Whigs was only briefly interrupted, and they were returned in the 1722 election with an even larger majority than previously.

Williams and Ramsden note that since the end of the 17th century, the head of the Treasury had emerged as the crucial link between the legislature and the executive, since after the Bill of Rights, much of government financial activity required parliamentary approval, and so the head was in the natural position from which to exercise dominance over his fellow ministers. However, no minister before Walpole enjoyed such a long period in office. Further, the majority of Walpole's predecessors had sat in the Lords for all or part of their tenure and so were unable to become the dominant figure in the Commons that Walpole made himself by the assiduous use of his powers of patronage and abilities as a manager.[11] Why Walpole preferred to remain in the Commons throughout his active career is a matter of some debate among historians, but certainly it was to his advantage in the financial sphere, since not only could official revenues only be raised with the assent of Parliament, but by this date, it was the norm for financial legislation to begin its passage there. He also benefited from the fortuitous deaths of most of his main Whig rivals in the period 1721–27.

---

9   Williams and Ramsden, *op cit*, p 59.
10 That Walpole was himself a South Sea investor did not emerge at the time. O'Gorman, *op cit*, pp 70–71.
11 Williams and Ramsden, *op cit*, pp 60–61.

By now, George I's Hanoverian advisers had ceased to be a major force in British politics, as the king came to know and to trust his British ministers. Even so, Walpole's position was not unassailable and he depended on being able to play the court as well as Parliament. This was demonstrated on George II's accession, when he appeared inclined to replace Walpole, who had earlier incurred his enmity, with Spencer Compton, treasurer of his household as Prince of Wales. Walpole had for some years been cultivating the new queen, Caroline of Anspach,[12] and she at once went to work on his behalf. By this time, the financing of the royal household, once inseparable from general public finance, was achieved via a Civil List, voted by Parliament at the beginning of each reign.[13] At the helm in the Treasury, Walpole obtained for George II the largest Civil List yet, and so demonstrated his abilities, just as Compton failed to compose a satisfactory Speech from the Throne for the State Opening of Parliament.[14] George II therefore confirmed Walpole in office and his omnipotence continued for a further 15 years, although his position became less assured as time went on.

Walpole made full use of the patronage which went with his position not only to cement his own hold on power, but also to consolidate the position of the Whigs. As First Lord of the Treasury and Chancellor of the Exchequer, and the king's personal adviser and political confidant, he had unrivalled access to sources of patronage and used these to secure support both at court and in both Houses. When bishoprics fell vacant, as no fewer than six did in 1723, he was able to persuade the king to fill them with Whig-inclined clerics. Equally, he held out prospects of office to peers who might be encouraged to speak and vote on Whig lines, and of peerages to loyal Whigs outside the Lords. O'Gorman estimates that in the years 1689–1714, the two parties were roughly equal in the Lords. By the mid-1720s, consistent Tory voters were down to about 20% of the 200-odd members. In the Commons, Walpole again made full use of his powers of patronage. Since office-holders were not generally precluded from sitting as MPs, he distributed offices among his supporters and also persuaded the king to revive the Order of the Bath, which provided him with a further valuable source of patronage.

At the same time, Walpole continued to stigmatise the Tories as Jacobites and, in rewarding his supporters, he deprived Tories of office and influence at both local and national level. Further, a moderate policy in religious matters, aided by the absence of Tories as a major force in Parliament, ensured the Whigs of Dissenter support without alienating the Church of England.

Finally, Walpole, having restored economic stability and commercial confidence at the time of the South Sea Bubble, was able to continue that stability, aided by several years of good harvests and by a general peace in Europe. Seeking to shift the burden of taxation from land to indirect taxation, Walpole increased efficiency in the collection of revenue from foreign trade and reduced smuggling by introducing a system of bonded warehouses in the major ports.

Meanwhile, Whig dominance in Scotland and Ireland was, if anything, even more complete than in England. The Scottish members in the Commons and Scottish

---

12   To a point where Walpole's enemies spread rumours that they were lovers.

13   This practice began in 1689, though initially, the Civil List was expected to cover the salaries of ministers, judges and other public officials, as well as the more obvious expenses of the royal family and their households. See V Bogdanor, *The Monarchy and the Constitution*, 1995, Clarendon, p 183.

14   Admittedly, Compton was fully aware of his own unsuitability for high office.

representative peers in the Lords were for most of the period 1720–42 among the pillars of Walpole's control over Parliament. Day-to-day power over Scotland was exercised effectively through the Campbell faction, headed by the 2nd Duke of Argyll. Apart from rioting in Glasgow over the introduction of a Malt Tax in 1725 and the Porteous Riots of 1736, when a mob of 4,000 broke into Edinburgh prison and lynched a Captain Porteous, whom they held responsible for the execution of a smuggler, there were no serious disturbances between the Jacobite risings of 1715 and 1745.

The general election of 1715 returned a solid Whig majority to the Dublin Parliament and as neither the Triennial nor the Septennial Act applied to Ireland, there was no further Irish election until the demise of the Crown in 1727. Poynings' Law required all legislation passed in Dublin to be approved at Westminster; by the Declaratory Act of 1719, Westminster took upon itself to legislate directly for Ireland and to hear appeals from the Irish courts. Following a flurry of opposition in 1722 to the introduction of a new copper coinage for Ireland in a manner which would provide handsome profits for Englishmen, Walpole ensured that the activities of the Irish Parliament were supervised by 'undertakers' whose loyalty to him was secured by the exercise of patronage in their favour. This system was so successful that Ireland remained quiescent until the 1760s.

From the late 1730s, Walpole's power was clearly on the wane. In 1737, Frederick, Prince of Wales, quarrelled with his father over his financial provision and sought the aid of the parliamentary opposition to persuade the government to increase it. George II, whose support had been an important factor in enabling Walpole to survive the crisis of 1733, was sufficiently enraged at his son's conduct to expel him from St James's Palace, whereupon Frederick set up a rival court which became a focus for political opponents of the government until his death in 1751. This development was a serious threat to any government. As O'Gorman reminds us, no longer could the opposition be dismissed by the government and its supporters as unpatriotic, or even as Jacobite in sympathy, and they themselves could argue persuasively that they were acting in the best interests of the House of Hanover.[15]

At the same time, the deteriorating international situation acted against the interests of Walpole, who owed his hold on power in no small measure to his policy of peace, stability and low taxes. Differences with Spain over trade to the West Indies led ultimately to the outbreak of the celebrated War of Jenkins' Ear in October 1739, so called because the final trigger was the Spanish seizure of a British merchant ship commanded by a Captain Jenkins, and the cutting off of one of Jenkins's ears as punishment for alleged illegal trading in the Caribbean. Walpole's policy of negotiation with Spain having failed, he had lost considerable political face.

1740 brought the second general European war of the 18th century, once again triggered by conflict over royal succession. When the Emperor Joseph I died in 1718, leaving two daughters but no son, he was succeeded by his brother as Charles VI. Charles too had only daughters but, unlike his brother, had no close male relations. He therefore sought to make his elder daughter, Maria Theresa, his heir in the Habsburg hereditary lands, and to have her husband, Franz Stephan of Lorraine, follow him as Emperor. Although since the 15th century, it had in practice been a Habsburg possession, the Imperial Crown was elective and Charles's diplomacy for much of his reign was therefore directed towards gaining the support of the Electors and

---

15 O'Gorman, *op cit*, p 82.

guarantees from other powers for his plan, known as the 'Pragmatic Sanction'. Britain guaranteed this in 1731 and was among the powers to which Maria Theresa appealed for aid following Charles's death in October 1740. Charles Albert, Elector of Bavaria, put himself forward as an alternative candidate and was supported by France. At the same time, the new King of Prussia, Frederick II, saw an opportunity to benefit from the uncertainties over the Austrian succession and invaded the neighbouring Austrian province of Silesia.

Under the Septennial Act, a general election was necessary in May 1741. The Walpole Whig majority, already reduced in 1734, was cut still further. Walpole hung on a further nine months, though the military course of the war went against Britain for the rest of 1741. At the same time, George II as Elector of Hanover was pursuing a policy which entirely contradicted that of his British ministers, negotiating Hanoverian neutrality in the war but committing himself to supporting Charles Albert in the forthcoming imperial election.

None of this assisted Walpole, and the fine balance in the Commons created by the 1741 election was tilted inexorably against him when decisions were made by Parliament in disputes over elections to individual seats. Williams and Ramsden regard defeat in votes on election petitions as the 18th century equivalent of votes of no confidence in the government, since a government having the confidence of a majority of MPs could be expected to win each one. Certainly, after the seventh successive defeat in such a vote, Walpole resigned on 2 February 1742, despite retaining the confidence of the Crown and having a safe majority in the Lords. Ministers held office from the king and acted in the king's name, but Walpole's fall demonstrates a recognition that in the practical sphere, a minister could not remain in power without sufficient support in the Commons to be able to carry his policy through.

17.6   GOVERNMENT POST-WALPOLE

After Walpole's fall, it was to be some years before a single individual again established such a position of dominance over his fellow ministers to be realistically viewed as a Prime Minister. For many years, except in 1746–54, when there was a stable ministry under Henry Pelham, government was in a state of flux, with frequent changes of personnel. However, the Whigs retained their hold on power. Indeed, the period 1742–63 saw the Whig oligarchy reach the peak of its dominance, 90% of Commons seats going to Whigs without any opponent standing. Peers, their close relations, clients and allies dominated not only Parliament but also the key local offices of lord-lieutenant and Justice of the Peace. Much the largest occupational group in the Commons was composed of landowners, some two-thirds of the total membership. The other main groups were lawyers, merchants and officers of the army and navy, each numbering 50–60 in 1761.[16] Parliamentary business, apart from matters relating to foreign affairs and supply, was dominated by legislation concerned with private rights over property. The 18th century was a time of modernisation of ancient practices in agriculture. This is reflected in the large number of Enclosure Acts passed, almost always at the behest of a landowner or group of landowners, to allow

---

16   See Williams and Ramsden, *op cit*, pp 74–76.

the enclosure of the open fields which had existed in large areas of rural England for centuries and had been farmed on a semi-communal basis. At the same time, desire among the propertied and prosperous classes for better transport led to the creation of turnpike trusts, which took responsibility for building and maintaining sections of road and financed their activities by charging tolls. The transfer of existing roads to turnpike trusts required legislation, so that Turnpike Acts accounted for a similarly high volume of parliamentary business.

The dichotomy between the foreign policies of Britain and Hanover, the only serious division between the two which occurred in the 120 years of the union of sovereignty, was ended in 1743 when Hanover joined with Britain in supporting Maria Theresa. George II, having cast his vote as Elector of Hanover in favour of Charles Albert the previous year, now led a 'Pragmatic Army' composed of British, Hanoverian, Austrian and Hessian troops to victory over the French at the Battle of Dettingen in June, the last occasion on which a British monarch commanded troops in battle.

17.6.1 The Forty-Five

Though control of government shifted in this period between different factions and alliances among the Whigs, the unshakeable Whig dominance led the most extreme among the Tories, disillusioned with their prospects of obtaining positions of power under the current regime, to turn a second time to the Pretender James. Six, including two peers, invited him in April 1743 to invade. Since Jacobitism proved a complete failure and, after 1745, increasingly the province of a few diehards as the Old Pretender maintained his small court-in-exile in Rome and the Young Pretender ruined his health and credibility with drink and debauchery, it is easy to forget that in the eyes of contemporaries, it presented a serious danger and was an important factor in the domestic and foreign politics of the day. Holmes and Szechi note that the risings of 1715 and 1745 were the major episodes in a regular serious of conspiracies which occupied the years 1692–1760. Seven abortive invasions by James II, his son or grandson or their foreign allies on their behalf took place, foiled by the vigilance of the Royal Navy and/or bad weather.[17]

The invasion which followed the invitation of 1743 did not take place for two years, the interval being occupied by the Pretender in soliciting French backing, although in the end, the French, facing an efficient Royal Navy blockade in the Channel, preferred to await the outcome of events and invade only if the Jacobites proved an effective threat to the Hanoverian regime. On 23 July 1745, the Pretender's elder son, Charles Edward Stuart, 'Bonnie Prince Charlie' to romantics ever since, landed on the Hebridean island of Eriskay with seven companions and a quantity of French muskets. He reached the Scottish mainland two days later, where he claimed the land for his father as James III and declared himself Regent.

By accident, his landing occurred at a singularly inopportune moment for the government. The King was in Hanover and the bulk of the regular army was on the continent, along with most of the irregular Highland companies formed in recent years to keep order among the clans. Only a few thousand second-rate troops were stationed in Scotland. The Disarming Acts, passed after 1715 to emasculate the

---

17 Holmes and Szechi, *op cit*, p 97.

military strength of the clans, had proved most effective among the Hanoverian clans such as the Campbells. General George Augustus Wade, recently retired as Commander-in-Chief in Scotland, had expended much money and the energy of his troops in building roads to enable government forces to move swiftly to quell trouble in the Highlands. Now it was the Jacobites who made use of Wade's roads, as the Young Pretender gathered support in the north of Scotland, evaded a pursuit through the Highlands by Lieutenant-General Sir John Cope, captured Edinburgh and finally surprised and defeated Cope's small force at Prestonpans on 21 September.

At this point, the shaky foundations of Charles Edward's strategy began to emerge. Assuring his military commanders, Lord George Murray and the Duke of Perth, that the French were about to invade and the English Tories would rise in his cause, he led a force of about 4,500 into England early in November. This was not only undisciplined, ill-equipped and of poor quality, whatever the bravery of its members, but it also suffered from divided command. Neither Murray nor Perth was willing to concede place to the other, so that a compromise was worked out whereby each exercised overall command on alternate days. Without meeting opposition, Charles Edward reached Derby on 4 December where, unable any longer to persuade Murray and others that his claims were correct and having failed to attract many Englishmen to his cause, he agreed to withdraw to Scotland.

Pursued north by a regular army withdrawn from the continent to deal with the emergency and commanded with efficiency but little humanity by the king's second son, William, Duke of Cumberland, the Young Pretender was defeated at Culloden Moor, near Inverness, on 16 April 1746. Davies makes the point that there was no need for Charles Edward to fight a pitched battle[18] and it is possible that his followers could by guerrilla means have caused immense difficulties for the government and tied down large numbers of troops for an indefinite period. No longer on good terms with the capable and experienced Murray, Charles Edward chose to stand and fight, with results that were all too predictable. Facing a seasoned and well-equipped army of more than twice their numbers, most of the half-starved clansmen were killed or taken prisoner. Charles Edward escaped, to spend several months as a fugitive before finding a ship to convey him back to France. After the failure of his enterprise, he declined rapidly into alcoholism, becoming completely estranged from his father. The once 'bonnie' Prince Charles Edward had no legitimate children, and with his death in 1788 died any hope of a Stuart restoration.[19]

In national myth, the 'Forty-Five' is presented as Scotland against England, the gallant young Charles against the stodgy German George II and 'Butcher' Cumberland. As usual, the reality was much more complex. Far from being united in the Jacobite cause, Scotland was divided between Jacobitism, loyalty to the government and a majority which preferred to sit on the fence and await the outcome of events. Such a significant institution as Glasgow University declared its loyalty to

18 N Davies, *The Isles*, 1999, Macmillan, pp 626–28.

19 On his death, the by now nominal Stuart claim passed to his brother, Henry Benedict, titular Duke of York and a Cardinal of the Roman Catholic church, who was proclaimed Henry IX of Great Britain and Ireland by his supporters. Though the Cardinal insisted on being accorded royal honours, he did not press his claim. After the papal court was driven from Rome by Napoleon Bonaparte in 1803, he accepted a pension from George III, though he refused to recognise him as anything more than Elector of Hanover. When the Cardinal died in 1807, the Stuart claim was inherited by the descendants of Charles I's daughter, Henrietta Anne, Duchess of Orleans, and now vests in the Wittelsbach Dukes of Bavaria.

the government and awarded Cumberland an honorary doctorate of laws even before Culloden. Only a small minority even among the traditionally Jacobite clans ever took up arms on behalf of Charles Edward, and about half of the 9,000 men who fought under Cumberland at Culloden were themselves Scots, mainly serving in the Lowland regiments which had remained loyal to the Crown ever since 1688. There is truth, however, in the traditional picture of brutality in Scotland after 1745, with systematic efforts to destroy the traditional clan structure and the prohibition of such symbols of highland identity as bagpipes and the wearing of tartan.

17.6.2 Foreign affairs

Foreign policy loomed large in the governmental concerns of the 1740s and 1750s, which saw not only the War of the Austrian Succession, which ended in stalemate in 1748, but the first part of the Seven Years War of 1756–63, whose genesis lay in 'unfinished business' left over from the earlier conflict. The latter was the first truly global conflict, embracing the colonial possessions of the great powers not only in North America and the West Indies, but also in India, where an East India Company army under Robert Clive ousted the French from Bengal, so that Britain became the only European power with significant possessions in the sub-continent. Thereafter, although the great expansion of British territory did not come about until the 19th century, India was entirely a British sphere of influence.

CHAPTER 18

THE LATER 18TH CENTURY

18.1 INTRODUCTION

Some 50 years after John Locke composed his *Two Treatises of Government* in 1731, the French jurist Montesquieu drew on his ideas to create the doctrine of the separation of powers, which has been of supreme importance in constitutional thinking since:

> There would be an end to everything, were the same man, or the same body, whether of the nobles or of the people, to exercise those three powers, that of enacting laws, that of executing the public resolutions, and of trying the cases of individuals.[1]

The three powers must therefore be exercised by separate bodies. In order that no one body may gain a pre-eminent position over the other two, there must be a system of checks and balances between them. Given that Montesquieu, in setting out his theory, contrasted the balanced constitution which he believed Britain enjoyed and which protected the liberties of the subject with the absolutist regimes of France and other major European powers, in which all power vested ultimately in the monarch and his narrow coterie of advisors, it is ironic that he wrote at a time when the British governmental system was more closely controlled by one party, and indeed by one man, Walpole, than at any other time before the late 20th century.

Today, George III (1760–1820) is known to non-specialists principally as a sufferer from the rare metabolic disorder porphyria, which in its acute phases gave him the appearance of extreme mental disorder brought to a popular audience in the film *The Madness of King George*. He has intermittently been pilloried as the main cause of Britain's loss of her American colonies, and by Americans as the tyrant from whom they won their freedom. To students of the constitution, his 60 year reign is important as the period in which the Whig oligarchy broke down and was challenged from without by the re-emergence of radicalism as a social and political force. It was, however, many years before this led to structural change. Of more immediate significance was the American Revolution, which created an independent state from 13 of the British colonies on the North American mainland, with a written constitution drawing on both the existing British constitution and the philosophical and political concepts of the French Enlightenment. The American 'Founding Fathers' in turn gave inspiration to the French revolutionaries of 1789 onwards and to later generations of British radicals.

18.2 EARLY TENSIONS

George I had left the direction of British government largely to his ministers, as, to a lesser extent, had George II. George III was not only much less interested in Hanover, which he rarely visited and whose government he left to viceroys, he was keen to stamp his influence on British affairs and restore the pre-eminence of the monarch

---

1   Montesquieu, *De l'Esprit des Lois*, Book XI, Chapter 6, quoted in AW Bradley and KD Ewing, *Constitutional and Administrative Law*, 12th edn, 1997, Longman, p 90.

over his ministers. In March 1761, as the general election following the demise of the Crown proceeded, he appointed his close friend and mentor, John Stuart, 3rd Earl of Bute, to the vital post of Secretary of State for the Northern Department, despite Bute's complete lack of ministerial experience. The new king also attempted to counter the power of the Whig grandees by giving offices in the Royal Household to six leading Tories and seeking to persuade exiled Jacobites to return to Great Britain, either, according to admirers, in order that he could be and be seen to be a king to all his subjects, not just the Whigs, or, to detractors such as Edmund Burke, writing in 1770, to place willing tools of monarchical ambition in high places so as to advance the royal prerogative at the expense of traditional English liberties.[2]

Whatever his motivation, George III's efforts to lessen the Whig grip on all aspects of political life was a complete failure. Holmes and Szechi go as far as to say that these acts of royal kindness destroyed the Tory party as an organised force in a way that 46 years in the political wilderness had failed to do. However, some Tory concepts, particularly reverence for the Anglican Church, became absorbed into Whig political thinking, along with the importance of maintaining the established order.[3]

George III's desire to restore the monarch's pre-eminent role in government led to the emergence of a new political faction within the Whig oligarchy, known as the 'King's Friends'. At the same time, the traditional factions based on dependence on the leading Whig aristocrats, such as the Duke of Newcastle, continued in being, but the proportion of 'independent country gentlemen' and their significance as a parliamentary force increased, so that in the late 18th century, they were usually crucial to the survival or fall of any ministry. Holmes and Szechi have calculated that every House of Commons returned in the 20 years from 1763 contained up to 300 members of varying degrees of independence, most of them gentlemen and provincial bourgeois of modest means who were prepared to put the interests of their friends, neighbours and locality above the prospect of office. Given that these Independents formed about half the membership of a House of 558, their role was crucial.

For the time being, although it was the Independents who frequently held the balance of power and had the ability to break a ministry if they chose, it was the aristocratic factions that actually formed the shifting ministries of the 1760s – in that decade, there were six changes of first minister, and 16 of one or other Secretary of State – just as they had done since Walpole's fall. At the same time, the placemen, civil servants and courtiers who sat in Parliament came to take the lead from the king, rather than from the leading minister.

The king's insistence on appointing Bute as Secretary of State created tensions within the Cabinet, only increased by difficulties over Spain as the Seven Years War continued. Charles III succeeded to the Spanish throne in 1759 and warned Britain then that Spain would not stand by while the northern European powers overturned the equilibrium created by the Treaty of Utrecht. In August 1761, he entered into a secret compact with his Bourbon cousin, Louis XV of France, rumours of which led William Pitt the Elder, then Secretary of State for War, to demand pre-emptive strikes by the Royal Navy against the Spanish treasure fleets. When the Cabinet did not support him, Pitt resigned. In May 1762, Newcastle resigned over the issue of

---

2   G Holmes and D Szechi, *The Age of Oligarchy: Pre-Industrial Britain*, 1993, Longman, pp 277–79.
3   *Ibid*, pp 279–80.

subsidies to Prussia, whereupon the king appointed Bute to replace him as First Lord of the Treasury, with the intention of concluding an early peace.[4]

The Treaty of Paris, which concluded the Seven Years War, proved to be of enormous importance in the genesis of the British Empire. Britain gained Canada and Louisiana from France, and Florida from Spain, so obtaining the whole of the North American mainland east of the Mississippi, together with the Caribbean islands of Grenada, St Vincent, Dominica and Tobago. However, the peace terms were unpopular in the extreme, since in the interests of creating a workable balance of power for the future, Britain gave up many wartime conquests. Not surprisingly, this 'surrender' was condemned by Pitt and Newcastle, now out of office but extremely influential. However, Henry Fox, Bute's leading Commons ally, was able to gain the support of sufficient of the Independents to defeat 'the young friends of the Duke of Newcastle' by a majority of 319 to 65 on a motion of whether or not to accept the peace terms. This success led the king and Bute to purge Newcastle's supporters from their offices, at both national and local level, a demonstration that George III now considered himself very firmly in the saddle.

Despite this early victory, Bute's ministry did not last much longer. The expense of the Seven Years War had caused the National Debt to reach an unprecedented £140 million, so much that interest payments absorbed half Britain's peacetime revenues. Various fiscal measures were employed to increase revenues, including an increased excise on cider. Bute was burned in effigy in the cider-producing counties of the West Country and Herefordshire, where there was widespread rioting, along with disturbances elsewhere triggered by poor harvests and increased unemployment. Bute resigned in April 1763, to be succeeded by George Grenville, hitherto Chancellor of the Exchequer. It was Grenville who sowed the wind in the form of the Stamp Act of 1765 that was to reap the whirlwind of the American Revolution. However, before armed resistance began in the American colonies, there was a challenge to the established order at home.

18.3 'WILKES AND LIBERTY'

Shortly before the end of the Seven Years War, John Wilkes, a hitherto unimportant MP, founded an anti-Bute newspaper, the *North Briton*. Early in 1763, this published allegations of an affair between Bute and the king's mother. This was followed by Issue 45, which attacked the Treaty of Paris and the king's speech supporting it. Grenville's government sought to quash this opposition by issuing a general warrant to four named King's Messengers on 26 April for the arrest of all those connected with the publication of Issue 45, any search necessary for this purpose and the seizure of

---

4   By the end of 1761, Prussia, Britain's main ally, had been brought to her knees by a war on two fronts against Austria and Russia. So parlous was his position that Frederick II considered ever after that his throne and country had been saved by the death of the Russian Empress Elizabeth on Christmas Day. Her successor, Peter III, was first and foremost a German prince with little attachment to Russia, but boundless admiration for Frederick. He therefore sought an immediate peace, which was concluded before he was deposed in a Palace coup headed by his Empress, born Sophia of Anhalt-Zerbst but known to history as Catherine the Great. Such was the importance of this event in German national myth that Adolf Hitler believed that the death of President Franklin Roosevelt on 13 April 1945 would be his salvation, just as the death of Elizabeth had been, for the Americans would then sue for peace.

papers in the possession of the persons concerned.[5] Acting on this authority, the King's Messengers arrested Wilkes on 30 April.

Wilkes's allies swung into action, making application for habeas corpus against the King's Messengers within an hour of his arrest. This was foiled in a fashion officially illegal by the two Secretaries of State, who ordered Wilkes's committal to the Tower before a writ of habeas corpus could be issued. Serjeant Glynn, acting for Wilkes, then made further application, this time against the Constable of the Tower, alleging that the warrant of commitment to the Tower was defective and, of much wider significance, that as a Member of Parliament, Wilkes enjoyed freedom from arrest in all matters other than treason, felony and breach of the peace. Seditious libel, of which he was accused, was none of these. The judges agreed with Glynn. A libel was not a breach of the peace; it did no more than tend to a breach of the peace. Specifically, the judges overruled the decision in the *Seven Bishops' Case* that a libeller could be required to give surety against a breach of the peace and ordered Wilkes's immediate release.

R v Wilkes[6] established that Members of either House of Parliament enjoyed the privilege of freedom from arrest in a very limited range of criminal matters concerned only with the publication of opinions. This supplemented the freedom of speech conferred by Article 9 of the Bill of Rights in relation to debates and proceedings in Parliament. In practice, this freedom from arrest was of small importance, since Parliament, as soon as it re-assembled in November 1763, resolved that parliamentary privilege should no longer apply to give Members effective immunity from criminal proceedings. The loophole created by Wilkes's earlier legal victory was thus plugged. What is much more significant is that in the 1760s, the courts were for the first time prepared to give the liberty of the individual priority over the interests of the government of the day.

Some months before the issue of the general warrant against the publishers of the *North Briton*, analogous warrants were issued to the same King's Messengers in respect of publishers of similar allegations in other anti-government newspapers. One of those named in such a warrant, which purported to authorise the searching of his house and seizure of his papers, was John Entick. On 11 November 1762, the King's Messengers went to Entick's house in Stepney and ransacked it in search of seditious materials. Entick afterwards sued the King's Messengers for damages; by entering and searching his house without his permission and without lawful authority in any other form, they had trespassed on his land. The King's Messengers sought to rely on the authority conferred by the general warrant.

General warrants had been issued by successive Secretaries of State for many years without any legal challenge, but the Lord Chief Justice of Common Pleas, Lord Camden, now held the warrant defective. On the narrow point, the warrant was incapable of conferring authority for the King's Messengers to enter upon Entick's land, so that they were liable to him in damages. Ministers did not have power to issue any form of warrant save in respect of alleged treason. More broadly, Lord Camden ruled that under English law, any invasion of private property was lawful

---

5   The principal role of King's Messengers was (and remains) to take confidential government documents to and from British ambassadors abroad, but in the days before police forces, they were frequently used for other 'sensitive' tasks both in Britain and overseas.

6   (1763) 2 Wils 151.

where there was positive legal authority. More significantly still, the powers of ministers existed only insofar as they were granted by common law, statute or the prerogative. Ministers could not appeal to arguments of 'state necessity' to legitimise actions which would otherwise have no legal authority. The government had no special powers and could it claim such powers merely because it was the government.[7] This ruling is one of the foundation stones of such checks and balances as exist within the British constitution to restrain abuses by the executive. The case was followed in 1766 by parliamentary legislation to prohibit general warrants.

It was already established law that Parliament was entitled to determine its own composition. Recognising that Parliament was likely to expel him and that he would therefore lose his freedom from arrest, Wilkes fled to France in December 1763 after being wounded in a duel with one of Bute's supporters. Under ancient law, Wilkes thus rendered himself liable to outlawry, with consequent forfeiture of his goods and chattels and the profits of his real property. But, before leaving England, Wilkes had sought to turn what was in essence the predicament of a single individual on a narrow set of facts into a matter in which the liberty of all Englishmen was at stake, orchestrating the non-enfranchised majority of the population so that he created a mass challenge to the oligarchical politics of the 18th century.

As had Hampden and others, Wilkes sought to use the law and its technicalities as a weapon. As an outlaw, however, he was subject to perpetual imprisonment if he set foot again on English soil, and was in any case liable to be tried for seditious libel, with heavy penalties if he was found guilty. If he became an MP again, he could once more claim parliamentary privilege to evade the criminal proceedings against him, since the change in the law was not retrospective. As to his outlawry, Wilkes obtained an assurance from the authorities that they would not exercise their powers of arrest over him provided that he surrendered to the court on the first day of the Easter term 1768. On that day, he duly surrendered himself, but pleaded for his outlawry to be reversed.

Serjeant Glynn again acted for Wilkes and argued on a number of procedural grounds that his outlawry was void. Lord Mansfield LCJ disallowed all Glynn's arguments, but found a highly technical error in the proceedings and held Wilkes's outlawry to be void. Failing to win a seat in the City of London, Wilkes then stood in Middlesex, where a high proportion of the electorate were 40 shilling freeholders. Though he had hitherto drawn his most effective support from the political classes, he now set out to court the far more numerous but hitherto much less influential persons of modest means, in particular the urban tradesmen and petty bourgeoisie. Wilkes gained one of the two seats by a large majority and demonstrations followed in the capital in his support. The government were already concerned at the strikes and food riots which were taking place in London in consequence of worsening economic conditions, and a detachment of the Scots Guards opened fire on a Wilkite demonstration in St George's Fields, killing seven demonstrators and bystanders and wounding at least 15.

Wilkes accused the government of planning the 'massacre' of St George's Fields, and proceedings were taken to expel him from the Commons, as well as his being sentenced for various criminal offences to 22 months' imprisonment and a fine of £1,000. Twice Wilkes was expelled from the Commons, only to be re-elected

---

7   *Entick v Carrington* (1765) 19 St Tr 1029.

unopposed before a rival candidate could be found. At the third by-election, the rival candidate was declared elected even though Wilkes obtained four times the number of votes.

Wilkes appealed to the people, claiming that the government's handling of his case demonstrated a sinister intention to suppress the liberties enjoyed by Englishmen in general. 'Wilkes and Liberty' became the political slogan of the moment, and large numbers of small tradesmen and wage-earners turned out to hear Wilkes speak and to demonstrate in his support. Following the example set by Wilkes, challenges to existing law through the courts became a regular practice. The emergence of a substantial number of provincial newspapers in the past 50 years meant that the views and activities of Wilkes and his leading supporters were widely reported, so that Wilkite clubs were formed in various major towns, and in London itself, a Society for the Supporters of the Bill of Rights was formed, composed of radical lawyers, merchants and professional men who sought large-scale political reform in order to maintain the proper spirit of the Glorious Revolution. Their particular desires were for shorter parliaments, even annual parliaments, abolition of the rotten boroughs, reform of the system of office-holding and voting by secret ballot so as to restrict opportunities for electoral corruption.

But although the activities of Wilkes and the Wilkites alarmed successive ministries and gained Wilkes acclaim as a popular martyr, they did not succeed in becoming part of the political mainstream in sufficient numbers to achieve their aims. MPs who did espouse certain radical ideas, particularly the widening of the franchise, were too few for their views to be carried into effect. Opposition to the government from within Parliament was still essentially self-seeking, as MPs sought to benefit from the existing system rather than to change it. It was not for another half-century that parliamentary reform became a goal of substantial elements within the existing system, and then largely for pragmatic rather than idealistic reasons.

All the same, the relatively united front that the Whigs had previously presented broke down as the outside forces which had kept the different elements within Whiggism together disappeared. The Tories disappeared as a political force in the early 1760s. On 1 January 1766, James Francis Edward Stuart, titular James III and VIII, died in Rome at the age of 77. The Old Pretender had been born heir apparent to the thrones of England, Scotland and Ireland, and though he spent only a few months of his life on British soil, his claims had a greater legitimacy in the British mind than those of his son, who now proclaimed himself Charles III. James had also enjoyed a degree of support from the Catholic powers of the continent. His son did not. Neither France nor the papacy was prepared to recognise the new Jacobite monarch, still less to aid him in further attempts to gain the throne, so that more and more, Jacobitism ceased to be a real and active force, whatever sentimental attachment to the Stuart dynasty survived.

Freed from fear of a widespread and influential Jacobite fifth column in Britain, as well as from fear of the Tories, divisions among the Whigs became evident. Some saw the political role of George III as marking the beginning of an attempt to return to the absolutism of James II. The demise of the Tories removed one reason for objecting to change in the existing electoral system, so that some influential figures such as Charles James Fox took up 'reform' ideas, adding another element to the instability of government in this period.

18.4   THE AMERICAN REVOLUTION

A more effective challenge to governmental authority emerged across the Atlantic. The British had begun to establish permanent settlements early in the 17th century. By the middle of the 18th century, the 13 colonies on the North American mainland south of present-day Canada had developed much of the apparatus of civilised Europe. They had courts, both civil and criminal, universities, newspapers and printing presses, and legislative assemblies whose powers and relationship with Westminster were not precisely delimited, but whose membership was more broadly based than that of the British Parliament. The members of those legislatures were part of an elite, as in Britain, but an elite based to a greater extent on ability, education and endeavour than any in Europe. An increasing proportion of their populations had been born in the Americas or had emigrated from some European state other than Britain, so that ties of blood and sentiment to the British Crown were loosening. The British conquest of Quebec during the Seven Years War, in which colonial militias had fought alongside British regular troops, had removed the main external threat to the Thirteen Colonies, lessening reasons for reliance on Britain and at the same time increasing the pride and confidence of the colonists themselves. To a much greater extent than in Scotland, Wales and Ireland, the British Crown was literally a distant thing.

Just as opinion in the Thirteen Colonies was beginning to move towards greater self-sufficiency and self-government, the British were seeking to exert greater control. As so often, the primary reason was financial. With the National Debt at unprecedented levels, successive short-lived ministries in the period 1763–70 sought both to reduce costs and increase revenue. George Grenville, the Earl of Bute's successor, came to the apparently uncontroversial conclusion that the American colonies ought as far as possible to become self-financing in matters of defence. Though the French threat from the north had been removed, the early 1760s brought an upsurge in Indian hostility towards the colonists. Clearly, it remained necessary to maintain a regular army in North America, at a strength set at some 8,000 men. Grenville sought to raise sufficient revenue from the colonies themselves in order to cover the costs of providing this army, by means of a type conventional at this time.

However, when the Plantation Act of 1764, known as the Sugar Act, imposed for the first time a duty (3d per gallon) on imports of foreign molasses into the colonies, and the Act's preamble made clear that this was intended as a revenue-raising measure rather than merely to regulate trade, a cry was taken up with greater enthusiasm even than 'Wilkes and Liberty'. Previous practice, though there was no legislation on this point, was that the American colonies were taxed on the basis of measures passed by their own assemblies. Now, the Westminster Parliament, in which the colonists were not represented and which sat 3,500 miles away in a country that the majority of them had never seen, was seeking to tax the Thirteen Colonies directly. 'No taxation without representation' was now claimed, unprecedentedly, as one of the inalienable rights of all free-born Englishmen, the colonists claiming authority for this proposition in Magna Carta, the Bill of Rights and the writings of John Locke.[8] Once again, national myth was beginning to emerge as a potent political force.

---

8   G Williams and JA Ramsden, *Ruling Britannia: A Political History of Britain 1688–1988*, 1990, Longman, p 101.

When the molasses duty failed to produce sufficient revenue to cover the costs of garrisoning the Thirteen Colonies, Grenville's government persuaded Parliament to pass the Stamp Act in 1765. This extended to the American Colonies the duty which had been applied in England since 1694 to legal and commercial transactions and printed materials such as newspapers, a move which again seemed uncontroversial to British political opinion. After all, it did no more than place the Americans in the same position as their British brothers, most of them also excluded from the franchise.

Unlike the molasses duty, the duty on commercial and legal transactions could not be avoided by a change in purchasing habits. Failure to pay the duty and to have a document duly stamped rendered it inadmissible as evidence in any court, and the underlying transaction as therefore unenforceable. Neither could the duty be explained away as a trade regulation measure. It was a means of raising revenue and nothing else, doubling the average annual tax burden on each free American colonist.[9]

The Virginia Assembly passed a series of resolutions condemning the Stamp Act on constitutional grounds, and the Act gave the colonies reason to cleave more closely together than hitherto. It affected in particular merchants, printers and lawyers, and so the most educated and influential groups. It also affected plantation-based southern colonies as much as those of the north. Previously, the colonies, having grown up in isolation from one another and from widely differing roots, had guarded their separateness. Now, most of the colonial assemblies followed the Virginian lead and representatives from nine colonies met in New York as the 'Stamp Act Congress', to co-ordinate opposition to the Act, passing a motion accepting parliamentary legislation, but not taxation. Already, in the summer of 1765, there was a direct threat to British authority in the northern colonies, with violent attacks on Stamp Act officials and violent demonstrations in several cities, led by agitators calling themselves the 'Sons of Liberty'. American merchants agreed among themselves not to import British goods. The colonial militias refused to act against the rioters and no regular troops were available to carry out internal security duties in the cities. Necessarily, news took time to cross the Atlantic, a six week voyage at best, and British opinion, with the average annual tax burden running at 26 shillings per head, as against one shilling in the American colonies before the Stamp Act, was not favourable to the protesters. It was not until early in 1766 that the Grenville government, now in serious difficulties at home, responded to the American crisis.

The solution was designed to appease the colonists, but at the same time to emphasise that the British government and Parliament held sovereign power over the Thirteen Colonies. The Stamp Act was repealed and the duty on molasses was cut to 1d per gallon. At the same time, however, the new government of the Marquess of Rockingham obtained a Declaratory Act confirming Parliament's power to legislate for the American colonies. This climbdown was not popular in Britain, where George III and a number of senior political figures were avowedly hostile, and though the repeal of the Stamp Act was sufficient to damp down the colonial fires for the time being, the crisis of 1765 was only the beginning.

Governmental instability continued, as did the financial crisis. The Rockingham government lasted only a few months before the Elder Pitt, now Earl of Chatham, emerged as the new head of the administration. Charles Townshend, his Chancellor of the Exchequer, gave his name to a series of fiscal measures which set off the next

---

9   Holmes and Szechi, *op, cit*, p 285.

episode of colonial opposition to the Crown. Garrisoning America was proving yet more expensive than anticipated. The colonists had made clear their opposition to measures directed solely at raising revenue, and Townshend therefore chose to proceed by means of customs tariffs, which could be dressed up as measures to protect trade. New duties were imposed on imports of paper, glass, paint and tea, applicable to the American colonies as much as to Britain. Further, no longer was only the defence of America to be financed by the colonists, but the whole of the colonial administration.

In 1765–66, the colonists had been prepared, reluctantly, to accept the necessity for taxation as a means of regulating trade, but not for raising of revenue alone. In 1767, 'No taxation without representation' meant just that. Chatham's government was prepared to use force to implement the new tariffs, sending a small occupation army and naval squadron to Boston. This was enough to persuade the colonists to accept another compromise, that the tariffs were suspended in return for the explicit assent by the colonial legislatures to the right of the British Parliament to tax and legislate. Reluctantly, the legislatures accepted, but the merchants, encouraged by hard-liners such as Thomas Jefferson and John Adams, stepped up the trade blockade, so that at the beginning of 1770, when Lord North became head of another new ministry, the consequent loss to the British economy was estimated at £700,000 per year.

North, who had been Chancellor of the Exchequer in the previous ministry and whose main strength lay in financial administration, decided to redress the financial balance between Britain and the Thirteen Colonies a little, and at the same time to re-assert British control over its American subjects, by ending the suspension of the tariff on tea. It is not clear whether the riot which led to the Boston 'massacre' of 5 March 1770, when British troops opened fire on a crowd in Boston, was actually triggered by news of the new tax, but this use of military force is seen by some historians as the first armed act of the American Revolution.

At the end of 1773, Boston, one of the major commercial centres of the Thirteen Colonies, was also the venue for the next major confrontation. North's government had agreed that the East India Company should become the main exporter of tea to the colonies, with an advantageous position as regards tariffs. This attempt to prop up the now-ailing Company was seen by American merchants as a threat to their own position and by militants as another plot to deprive the colonists of their constitutional rights. The militants began a campaign of intimidation against merchant ships carrying the Company's tea, and in December, a group known as the Massachusetts Patriots boarded one such ship in Boston Harbour and threw its cargo overboard in the celebrated 'Boston Tea Party'.

This was seen in Britain as open and insulting defiance of the British government. North reacted with a series of coercive measures, including the closure of Boston Harbour until compensation was paid and the suspension of the Massachusetts charter while amendments were made in order to increase the powers of the Governor vis à vis the Assembly.

At the same time (March–May 1774), but independently of the troubles in Massachusetts, Parliament passed the Quebec Act as a framework for the future government of Canada. This framework was designed to appeal to the French-speakers who formed the majority of Canada's population, being closer to French institutions than to those of the British colonies further south. Canada was not to have an elected legislature, but a legislative council with members appointed by the Crown.

French law would prevail in civil matters, Catholics were included on the legislative council and Catholic priests were to receive tithes. To many Americans, this was a repressive and Popish measure, creating just the sort of despotism they or their forebears had crossed the Atlantic to escape.

Events moved rapidly and to the increasing disadvantage of the British government. The attempt to isolate Massachusetts failed as the other colonies sent men and arms, and the British commander in Massachusetts, General Thomas Gage, was rapidly bottled up inside Boston with his regular troops. In September 1774, representatives of the Thirteen Colonies met at Philadelphia as the Continental Congress to protest against the British actions over Massachusetts and to co-ordinate future action. This marked the point where the colonies began to act together in matters of policy and radical elements took over the initiative from the more conservative. The Continental Congress drew up a Declaration of Rights, which conceded that Parliament had power to regulate commerce within the British Empire, but condemned measures designed purely to raise revenue. It called for the repeal of a number of Acts, notably the Quebec Act and the 'Coercive Acts' imposed since the Boston Tea Party, and broke off commercial ties with Britain. In that same winter of 1774–75, a Patriot militia was formed in Massachusetts.

The king, his government and the majority of MPs took the view that the colonists must be mastered or they would themselves become the masters, although there were those in Britain who supported the stance taken by the Americans. The radical Tom Paine in his *Common Sense* mounted a sustained attack on the king and on the whole concept of hereditary monarchy, and the MP Edmund Burke argued in Parliament that the use of force in support of Parliament's claims to sovereignty was futile and that there should be a return to the pre-1764 position where colonial taxation was a matter for the colonial assemblies.

A final attempt at conciliation and compromise was made in February 1775, when North offered concessions on taxation provided that the assemblies voted sufficient funds to the government to make the Thirteen Colonies self-financing, but insisted that Parliament had and would continue to have legislative supremacy over British North America. Once again, time had to be allowed for these proposals to cross the Atlantic. By April, when they reached the colonies, events had intervened. General Gage meanwhile attempted to make a show of strength by seizing a Patriot arms depot at Concord. Part way between Boston and Concord, his troops found their way opposed by a body of Patriot militia at Lexington. Shots were fired and in the ensuing fight, some 400 men were killed or wounded. A further armed confrontation followed in June at Bunker Hill, when 2,000 men of the Boston garrison stormed a militia redoubt, with the loss of nearly half their strength. Since the entire Boston garrison had numbered only 5,000, there could be no more sorties and, thenceforth, the military initiative largely lay with the Americans.

A Second Continental Congress met in May, with opinion divided between moderates and hard-liners, but drifting rapidly towards a firm desire for independence. No action was taken by the British government until after the Continental Congress issued the Declaration of Independence of 4 July 1776. Since Bunker Hill, the Boston garrison had been under virtual siege by the local militia and the first American regular army, raised on the orders of the Continental Congress under the command of George Washington, a wealthy Virginia aristocrat who had learned the soldier's trade under British command, in the Virginia militia against the French during the Seven Years War.

Holmes and Szechi make the point that there was no unity of opinion or policy on either side of the Atlantic.[10] Though the Thirteen Colonies were beginning to act in consort, they remained very different from one another; they were neither united in their grievances, nor did their leaders share the same vision for the future. Throughout the Revolutionary War of 1775–82, a significant minority of their citizens, estimated at 19% of the white population, remained loyal to the British Crown, serving under British command and later leaving for Canada in order to remain under British rule. At the same time, a strong segment of the British political nation supported the colonists' aspirations and there was a mutual exchange of ideas between radicals, such as Thomas Paine, and the leading colonial thinkers, such as Thomas Jefferson. British radicals found much to admire in the societies and institutions of the Thirteen Colonies, where there was a far greater degree of religious and press freedom as well as less inequality of birth – liberals on both sides of the Atlantic tended to ignore the existence of a large slave population in the southern colonies.

Britain's defeat in the American war was inevitable for a number of reasons. There was the huge distance between the government at Westminster and the actual theatre of war, which meant that the political leadership could not respond quickly and effectively to changing conditions. It was almost a year before there was any reinforcement of Gage's small force in Boston, by which time, the Continental Congress had raised a considerable army and ensured that it was trained in the latest European methods. In consequence, the British missed the opportunity to gain the quick victory which was their main chance of success.

Further, Britain simply did not have the resources to fight a major war without effective allies. Holmes and Szechi stress that all its external wars for more than a century, except the brief War of Jenkins' Ear of 1739–40, had been fought in alliance with one or more of the major continental powers, so that Britain had not had to fight major land and naval campaigns at the same time. Britain did not then have the human or economic resources to maintain both a large army and a large navy, and the European power politics of the third quarter of the 18th century meant that none of the major powers was prepared to come to Britain's aid. To make matters worse, for reasons of old scores and their own advantage rather than any ideological commitment to the colonists' cause, France in 1777 and Spain in 1779 chose to enter the war on the side of the rebels, making it necessary for Britain to protect her possessions in the West Indies and reinforce military and naval forces in the Mediterranean and in India.

Inexperienced the Continental Army may have been, but it was built around a nucleus of men such as Washington who had served under British command. The much more numerous militias were less well-trained for conventional 18th century warfare, but ideally suited to guerrilla activity and pinning down regular garrisons. The Americans had much the greater numbers – some 200,000 men in arms in the course of the war against British regular forces of no more than 20,000 – and the enormous advantage of fighting on home soil and familiar terrain. The internal geography of North America, as well as the vast distances from Europe, was against

---

10   Holmes and Szechi, *op cit*, pp 301–05.

the British. Not only did it frequently take six months for troops and supplies to be gathered in Britain and cross the Atlantic, but large areas of the Thirteen Colonies were heavily wooded with few river-crossings. This made movement of large numbers of troops slow and difficult, and gave the Americans ideal opportunities to mount ambushes and blockade movements of supplies. The British could only hold what they could physically occupy and there were simply not enough of them to occupy very much or to take the offensive. In any case, the society and institutions of the Thirteen Colonies were not centralised. The colonists had no capital city whose capture would emasculate their government and cause a serious loss of morale in addition. When a town or fortress was captured by the British, the Americans simply went on fighting.[11]

18.5   IRELAND

Objections to existing constitutional arrangements were also emerging in Ireland. Theoretically a sovereign state, Ireland was in many ways a colony with less internal autonomy than those of North America. Under Poynings' Law, still in force after almost 300 years, the Irish Parliament could not pass binding legislation without reference to Britain, and the Declaratory Act of 1719 gave Westminster power to pass legislation for Ireland with or without reference to Dublin. In practice, the powers of Westminster were employed to preserve the status quo, and particularly to prevent Irish trade and industry from affecting the prosperity of the British commercial classes. Elections were necessary only on the demise of the Crown, so there was none during the 33 year reign of George II; had the system remained unreformed, there would have been none between 1760 and 1820. In any event, Parliament was only summoned every two years, not annually as was now well-established in Britain. Executive power was vested in a Viceroy or lord-lieutenant, generally an absentee, and during his absences, political affairs were placed in the hands of a small cabal of magnates known as 'undertakers', who benefited from exercising some of the Viceroy's powers of patronage. The disabilities imposed on the Catholics and Presbyterians under William III remained in force, so that the franchise and such power as the Dublin Parliament had were confined to the members of the smallest of the three main religious denominations, the Church of Ireland.

Though the Protestants held the reins of power in every walk of life, there were those among them desirous of change. In the 1760s, a number of Protestant MPs advocated legislative changes on the model of those already effective in Britain, notably regular elections, a Habeas Corpus Act and judges holding office during good behaviour. They also called for Ireland to have commercial equality with Britain rather than be subject to unfavourable tariffs in order to protect British interests. These demands were moderate indeed, but only one was actually put into effect, the Octennial Act, making the Dublin Parliament subject to regular elections, the first in 1769.

The American war had serious effects on the Irish economy by closing off important markets and putting a temporary end to emigration. In 1778, the North government attempted to remove some of the restrictions on Ireland's foreign trade, but change was blocked by British MPs. As had the Americans, the Irish reacted with

---

11   Holmes and Szechi, *op cit*, pp 305–14.

threats of a boycott, and the Dublin Parliament voted supply for only six months, instead of the two years before its next sitting. Like the Americans, the Irish had a volunteer militia in arms, raised to counter a possible French invasion, and its existence perhaps persuaded North and his ministers to compromise for the time being. Limited trade concessions by the government bought off the crisis, but, as in America, the wind of change was stirring.

18.6   EARLY RADICALISM

By the late 1770s, the movement in Britain for parliamentary reform had become solidly based. Christopher Wyvill, a wealthy Yorkshire clergyman, summoned the gentry of the county to a meeting in December 1779 to protest against high wartime taxation and excessive taxation. He and his supporters believed that governmental corruption could be destroyed by restoring the independence of the Commons from the executive and making MPs more accountable to the electorate. In order to secure their objectives, which included triennial parliaments, the abolition of rotten boroughs and the re-distribution of seats, Wyvill and his followers organised a series of petitions to Parliament. These had no direct effect, but established petitions as a means of making Parliament aware of the views of the electorate, the culmination of which were the Chartist petitions of the 1840s. Another leading radical from establishment roots was Major John Cartwright, who began a 50 year career in reform politics in 1776 with his book, *Take Your Choice*, in which he argued the case for universal suffrage, annual parliaments, secret ballots and equal member constituencies.[12]

At the same time, opponents of the North government within Parliament were adopting some of the ideas of the radicals for ideological reasons and in their own interest, in particular the greater separation of legislature and executive, and greater independence of the Commons, by the abolition of certain offices and the prevention of office-holders and persons holding government contracts from sitting in the Commons. An 'Economical Reform' movement emerged, headed by Edmund Burke, the Marquess of Rockingham and the Earl of Shelburne, which attempted to force a reduction in government spending by the abolition of obsolete offices and the separate administrations of the Duchies of Cornwall and Lancaster and the County Palatine of Chester.[13]

During the 1770s, the radicals moved carefully and avoided stirring up the kind of heated opposition that Wilkes and his activities had inspired. They set themselves against inciting riots and demonstrations, and instead concentrated on appeals to reason and better nature. However, the first signs of reaction to even moderate reform came in June 1780. Two years earlier, the North government had persuaded Parliament to pass a very limited Catholic Relief Act, enabling Catholics to hold commissions in the army on the taking of an oath of allegiance and to buy and inherit land. This was not popular with traditionalists, not least because from 1777, Britain was once again at war with Catholic France and from 1779 with Catholic Spain. In order to intimidate Parliament into repeal, Lord George Gordon, leader of a 'Protestant Association', led his supporters in a march to Westminster. The

12   F O'Gorman, *The Long Eighteenth Century: British Political and Social History, 1688–1832*, 1997, Arnold, p 228.
13   *Ibid*, p 229.

demonstration soon got out of hand and various demonstrators and their criminal hangers-on began attacking Catholic premises in a manner not seen for many years. A week of mob violence followed, considered by some writers the most serious ever on the British mainland. The Gordon Riots left 300 dead and were only quelled by troops moved in from outside London with orders to open fire on rioters without the formalities required by the Riot Act.[14]

18.7   THE CRISIS OF 1782–84

After Lord Cornwallis's surrender at Yorktown on 17 October 1781, the American war was effectively over. This defeat, along with the loss of Minorca to Spain the following March, brought down North's government after 12 years. There followed two years when no ministry was able to gain sufficient parliamentary support to function effectively, and George III's serious illness set off a constitutional crisis and calls for the abolition of the monarchy. Following North's resignation, the realities of politics forced George III to appoint the Marquess of Rockingham as First Lord of the Treasury and to invite him to form a government, for all that Rockingham had during the latter years of the North government been a persistent critic of government spending and of the king's political role. To make matters worse, Rockingham and his allies accepted the independence of the American colonies as inevitable, a position diametrically opposed to the king's. Confrontation soon followed over the constitutional relationship between king and ministers.

Until now, the ministers had been chosen by the king, who had regard to the support any potential first minister could command in Parliament, but did not treat this as the deciding factor in his choice. Rather, the choice of minister was based on a number of factors, which included the king's personal views as well as his assessment of the abilities of the person concerned. Once ministers were appointed, their relationship with the king had largely taken the form of a partnership, in which the king was, ultimately, the senior partner. His ministers advised him and he could require them to act on his will, as had been seen in foreign policy under George II, when the king's interests as Elector of Hanover conflicted with his ministers' assessment of the interests of Britain. In the crisis of 1782–83, there was a clear movement, though incomplete, towards a position where not only was choice of ministers to be determined by the degree of parliamentary support a candidate could command, but the ministers in the final analysis had the upper hand, so that the king could be required to give way and act according to their advice, for all that he found it unpalatable.

Reluctantly, the king accepted Rockingham's demand that negotiations with the colonists should begin. Rockingham was at the head of the government for only three months before he died on 1 July 1782, but a significant achievement of his brief tenure was the removal of the worst excesses of the constitutional relationship between Great Britain and Ireland. In April, inspired by the changed political situation at home and the success of the American colonists, the Irish House of Commons demanded fundamental changes to the existing domination of Westminster over Ireland. Aware that the Irish militia now numbered 40,000 men, considerably more than the small

---

14   See Williams and Ramsden, *op cit*, p 118.

regular garrison, and might be prepared to follow American examples, the new government was prepared to concede limited changes. Poynings' Law was modified to remove the powers of the Privy Council to initiate Irish legislation. A Renunciation Act repealed the Declaratory Act and so ended Westminster's power to legislate directly. Irish judges now followed their mainland brethren in being given tenure during good behaviour. A Catholic Relief Act removed some of the disabilities affecting Roman Catholics, though they remained excluded from Parliament, the major offices and the franchise. However, Poynings' Law remained on the statute book, albeit in its modified form, and the position and powers of the Viceroy remained unchanged.

After Rockingham's death, the king was initially able to exert his political authority by appointing the Earl of Shelburne to succeed him, rather than the senior surviving Rockinghamite, the Duke of Portland. Shelburne, though Rockingham's Home Secretary and a fellow proponent of Economical Reform, believed that a king was entitled to choose his own ministers and was on that basis acceptable to George III. However, he also recognised the need for a realistic and considered peace. Indeed, Shelburne believed that Britain's interests in North America were best served by allowing the colonists independence on generous terms, not least because he saw this as the best means of preventing the new United States from becoming a Bourbon client.

Realistic Shelburne's stance on the peace terms might have been – and the other elements of the peace were generally favourable to Britain[15] – but, once again, they were deeply unpopular at home. Charles James Fox, who had been Rockingham's Foreign Secretary before resigning over the concessions to the Americans, now entered into an unexpected alliance with Lord North, hitherto an inveterate enemy, based on their shared opposition to the peace terms. After the new alliance defeated the government in a vote on the acceptance of the terms, Shelburne resigned on 24 February 1783.

There followed more than a month when there was no effective ministry in office. The king attempted to persuade William Pitt the Younger, who had been Shelburne's Chancellor of the Exchequer, to lead a government, but Pitt consistently refused. Much of George III's conduct during this period was motivated by his personal loathing for Fox, whom he regarded as an unsavoury influence on the Prince of Wales, then approaching his majority and showing disturbing signs of a licentiousness which had appalled the king when he earlier witnessed it in his uncles. This personal dislike was built on a foundation of disapproval of Fox's political views and of his venomous attacks on the government during the American war, which had been led by Lord North.[16] Government by coalition was common enough in the 18th century, but the depth of earlier divisions between the followers of Fox and North, and the vehemence of Fox's wartime attacks on North and his then ministers, made the new alliance seem uniquely lacking in integrity in any form.

Nominally, the Fox-North coalition was headed by the Duke of Portland, who struck a further blow against George III's sense of constitutional proprieties and his independence in matters of prerogative (of which he regarded his unrestricted choice

---

15 Britain ceded Tobago and a small strip of land near Pondicherry to France, but France withdrew from her other wartime gains. Spain kept Florida and Minorca, but Britain retained Gibraltar, the restoration of which had been the chief Spanish war aim.

16 Williams and Ramsden, *op cit*, p 125.

of ministers as the single most significant element) by informing the king that he would only accept office if the king accepted his choice of the seven leading ministers and allowed him a free hand in selecting the remainder. The seven Portland named included Fox. The king reacted by drafting a statement of abdication, in which he announced that he would retire to Hanover rather than 'submitting to being a cipher in the trammels of any self-created band'.[17] A few days later, however, he climbed down and sent for Portland, though he wrote at the time that the new ministry would not have 'either my favour or my confidence'. In the circumstances, a direct confrontation between king and ministers was inevitable, and before long, it came.

Among Fox's responsibilities as Foreign Secretary was that of India. During the Seven Years War, the East India Company had acquired control of large areas of territory formerly held by the French or by various Indian princes. In 1765, in the immediate aftermath of the war, the Mogul Emperor also granted the Company the rights of revenue collection in Bengal, where it now held exclusive sway. So far had the Company moved from its roots as a trading organisation that the collection of revenue had become in recent years its most profitable activity. Unfortunately, the Company did not have the infrastructure to handle its new responsibilities and its servants had unrivalled opportunity to profit by corrupt exercise of their offices. In 1773, Lord North's government had passed a Regulating Act in order to impose some control over the Company's administration of its territories in India, creating a Governor-General and Council in Bengal, with some powers over the other presidencies of Madras and Bombay. Fox's India Bill, introduced into Parliament at the end of 1783, proposed a Board of seven Commissioners in London, which would run the affairs of India and control appointments to the Company's administration. What ensured the king's opposition to the Bill was that all the persons named in the Bill as future Commissioners were supporters of the Fox-North coalition, so that the Bill appeared to be a cynical exercise in patronage. The coalition was strong enough in the Commons for the Bill to pass its Second Reading by a comfortable majority of 229 to 120, despite a sustained attack by Pitt. At this point, the king, with the possible connivance of Pitt himself, informed the Lords that those peers who voted in favour of the Bill 'were not only not his friends but he should consider them as his enemies'.[18] On 17 December, the government, which normally had a majority in the Lords, was defeated there on the India Bill for the second time. The following day, the king dismissed the Portland government and sent for Pitt.

William Pitt the Younger, who now became Britain's youngest ever Prime Minister at the age of 24, was now at the head of a government but, unprecedentedly, took office without the support of a majority of MPs. Opinion of the day was that the new ministry would not even survive the Christmas recess, so that it became known as the 'mince pie administration', but Pitt and his followers hung on until April. During this time, government was deadlocked, with the Cabinet unable to get its measures through the Commons and losing several votes of no confidence but refusing to resign. However, Pitt had the unflagging support of the king and widespread support in the country as a whole. Fox-North MPs began to desert their leaders, so that by 8 March 1784, the imbalance between government and opposition had fallen from over

---

17 Williams and Ramsden, *op cit*, p 124.

18 Correspondence of George III, Vol 19, cited in CC O'Brien, *The Great Melody: A Thematic Biography of Edmund Burke*, 1982, Minerva, p 330. See Williams and Ramsden, *op cit*, pp 126–27; V Bogdanor, *The Monarchy and the Constitution*, 1995, Clarendon, p 12.

100 MPs to one. The king then dissolved Parliament, which under the Septennial Act still had three years to run, and a general election took place in April, at which the Pittite faction gained a clear majority.

This was one of the first occasions on which a dissolution of Parliament took place at the behest of a government, before the statutory end of a parliamentary term, so triggering a general election at a time calculated by that government to be most apposite for its purpose, a weapon which has become a regular part of the political armoury in the years since. Pitt also had the great, perhaps crucial advantage of the king's support, along with a reputation for personal integrity and commitment to reform, and the further advantage of being the son and namesake of Pitt the Elder, who, more than 20 years after steering Britain to the successes of the Seven Years War, had become surrounded by an aura not unlike that which has attached to Winston Churchill.

Bogdanor also considers the position which Pitt held after his election success to be unprecedented. As the hated Fox remained his only realistic rival for the highest office, the king was effectively prevented from dismissing Pitt as he had dismissed Portland and others of his predecessors. This gave Pitt a vastly greater degree of independence from the monarch, though this independence was by no means absolute. Although the balance of power in the partnership was changing, with accountability to Parliament and to the electorate gaining in importance, the relationship between Prime Minister and monarch remained one of partnership. The overwhelming dominance of the Prime Minister had not yet arrived.

The crisis also brought about more concrete division between government and opposition, though the term 'His Majesty's Opposition' did not appear until the 1820s. Fox, an apostle of the principle that the main function of an opposition is to oppose, recognised that to be effective, an opposition must be organised. It was among the 140 or so MPs who made up the opposition under Fox and Portland that the role of party whip first appeared, and steps were also taken to raise additional party funds and to develop an embryonic party machinery, though by modern standards, the Foxite Whigs remained a disparate and disorganised group without effective party discipline. Pitt, by contrast, gained his support in the traditional fashion of first ministers, from his own personal supporters, office-holders and those of the independents who accepted his claims to rule in the national interest.[19]

18.8   CHANGE UNDER PITT

Pitt emerged from the 1784 election facing serious difficulties, not least the continuing financial crisis. Despite all the various attempts to stabilise public finances, under the pressures of the American war, the National Debt had doubled and more than half of the government's annual revenue was now swallowed up by interest charges. A major achievement of Pitt's first years in power was a rationalisation of public finances, building on foundations set in North's time. As is true of many aspects of the British constitutional system, the structures for collecting, handling and auditing official revenues had grown up in haphazard fashion. By 1784, 11 different forms of loan stock were supplied from 103 separate accounts, leading to duplication, expense and

19   Williams and Ramsden, *op cit*, p 140.

waste in administration, not to mention corruption. In 1787, Pitt created the Consolidated Fund, unifying and rationalising the disparate systems, and at the same time, the administration of the Sinking Fund set up by Walpole was made more rigid and was placed under the supervision of statutory commissioners, so that the ministerial practice of raiding the Sinking Fund for short term reasons could not continue.

Pitt's attempt at a limited degree of parliamentary reform was, however, a failure. He had been a moderate advocate of reform throughout his time in the Commons, espousing Wyvill's campaign for the abolition of rotten boroughs and an increase in the number of county seats. His Bill of April 1785 proposed the abolition of 36 rotten boroughs and the re-distribution of the seats thus freed among the counties and to London, which had a rapidly-expanding and seriously under-represented population. This measure was defeated by 248 votes to 174, and O'Gorman identifies four reasons for this defeat, which he considers reflect the main difficulties of the reform movement in this period.[20]

First, the disenfranchisement of rotten boroughs represented an attack on the property rights which were at the centre of the concerns of the political nation in the 18th century. Second, though Pitt's proposal was apparently moderate and limited, its effects would have been considerable since, according to Wyvill's own estimate, about 100,000 electors would be added to 300,000. The third and fourth reasons had more to do with the political realities of the day. Wyvill's links with Pitt had alienated Fox and his supporters, and the petitioning movement which had developed under Wyvill's aegis had lost much of its initial impetus.

In any event, the reform movement was very shortly to be dealt a major blow, whose effects would be long-lasting and would remove any prospect of progress for a generation. This was the outbreak of the French Revolution in the summer of 1789.

18.9   THE MADNESS OF KING GEORGE

First, however, the powers of the monarch re-emerged as a major political issue in 1788 as a result of George III's serious illness and temporary lapse into insanity. The king's malady has been posthumously diagnosed as variegate porphyria, a rare and hereditary metabolic disorder, though the evidence is not wholly conclusive.[21] He became ill early in June 1788 with what was described as a bilious fever and appeared to recover after taking the waters at Cheltenham. However, physical illness recurred in August and towards the end of October, the king's condition deteriorated alarmingly, with the emergence of hallucinations, agitation, incessant talking for hours at a time and relentless over-activity. Whatever the precise cause of the king's condition, he rapidly became quite incapable of fulfilling his responsibilities as monarch and was likely to remain so for a period whose duration could not be predicted. Clearly, a regency was necessary, with the possibility that it would last for the remainder of the king's life.

---

20 O'Gorman, *op cit*, pp 230–31.

21 For a discussion of George III's illness and its possible causes, see VHH Green, *The Madness of Kings*, 1993, Sutton, pp 189–205. Very recent researchers have attempted to obtain conclusive evidence of porphyria among the king's descendants through DNA samples and close scrutiny of medical documents, with varying degrees of success. See JCG Rohl, DW Hunt and M Warren, *Purple Secret*, 1998, Bantam.

Not surprisingly, Fox saw the situation as a means of removing Pitt from power. The Prince of Wales, aged 26, had already amply justified his father's forebodings by adopting a profligate lifestyle and contracting an invalid marriage in contravention of the Royal Marriages Act. On bad terms with his father in Hanoverian fashion, he continued his association with Fox and opposed many of Pitt's policies. As heir apparent, the Prince was the obvious candidate for the position of Regent, though an analogous situation had never previously occurred, so that there were no precedents to be appealed to.[22] As Regent, the Prince was likely before long to come into irreconcilable conflict with Pitt. He would then use prerogative powers to dismiss Pitt and his ministers, and replace them with Fox and his leading followers. Not surprisingly, Fox called for the immediate introduction of a Regency Bill in terms which would give the Prince of Wales unrestricted powers.

Pitt, by contrast, hoped that the king would recover his mental faculties within a short time and resume the reins of government. The obvious difficulty, quite apart from the uncertain duration of the king's incapacity, was that no Bill, including, of course, a Regency Bill, could become law without the royal assent, so that some resolution of the situation could not be delayed. Pitt therefore introduced a Bill into the Commons providing that the Prince of Wales should be Regent, but with restricted powers. Perhaps surprisingly, since under its terms the Prince would not have been prevented from dismissing the existing ministers and replacing them with Whigs, Fox and his supporters opposed the Bill, arguing that the limitations on his power which, *inter alia*, prevented him from making peers represented improper derogations from royal power. Contrary to traditional Whig doctrine, they argued that the Prince of Wales had an absolute hereditary right to succeed to the throne and an absolute right as Regent to stand in his father's shoes. The delay caused by their opposition to the Bill played into the government's hands. Although the death of the Speaker on 2 January 1789 brought a new urgency to the situation, since the appointment of a new Speaker had to be confirmed by the monarch, by the time the Bill completed its passage through the Commons on 12 February, the king was showing clear signs of recovery. Interestingly, Bogdanor states that the Bill actually became law, the royal assent being assumed by a legal fiction to have been granted, but he does not cite any authority for this.[23]

18.10 FALLOUT FROM THE FRENCH REVOLUTION

Initially, the reaction of the British political nation to the early stages of the French Revolution was generally favourable. The fall of the Bastille, the abolition of feudalism by the new National Assembly and the establishment of constitutional monarchy in place of the previous royal absolutism were seen by the traditionally-minded as a parallel to the Glorious Revolution of a century earlier, and by the more radical and idealistic as the beginning of a new age of enlightenment and benevolence. As the American colonists had created a constitution based on the high ideals of the French Enlightenment, giving effect to Montesquieu's philosophy of the separation of powers

22 The nearest parallel can be found in the intermittent incapacity of Henry VI in 1453–59.
23 Bogdanor, *op cit*, p 46. For the crisis as a whole, see O'Gorman, *op cit*, pp 220–21; and Green, *op cit*, pp 190–97.

in order to prevent domination of government by any one of its three organs, so the revolutionaries in France would do the same.

However, within three years, the Revolution began its descent into the Terror, with the abolition of the monarchy in August 1792 and the imprisonment of Louis XVI, his family and others declared to be enemies of the regime. In September, the new French government, already at war with Austria and Prussia, declared its opposition to traditional structures by issuing a decree calling on the peoples of Europe to follow the French example and rise against their oppressors, much as 200 years earlier, the papacy had encouraged the Roman Catholics of England to rise against Elizabeth I. On 21 January 1793, Louis XVI went to the guillotine. On 1 February, the revolutionaries declared war on Britain.

By now, the initial unity of views about the French Revolution had disappeared, to be replaced by polarisation. Edmund Burke, in his *Reflections on the Revolution in France*, published in the autumn of 1790, regarded the Revolution not as a triumph of the majority of the populace, but the consequence of a minority conspiracy. Tom Paine's *Rights of Man*, published in two parts as a riposte to Burke, attacked all traditional institutions, not least hereditary monarchy, arguing that the French had shown the way ahead by developing a new political structure from a basis of natural rights. Previously, the majority of reformers had in traditional fashion seen the way forward in a return to the purity of an idealised earlier era. The more radical advocates of reform now took up Paine's ideas, demanding the replacement of existing governmental institutions with new ones on the French model. Perhaps the most influential advocate of Painite ideas was the London Corresponding Society, founded in January 1792 by a London shoemaker, Thomas Hardy. The Society sought lower taxes, cheaper food, better education and proclaimed that politics should be available to all. It attacked not only the traditional radical target of corruption in high places, but also privilege and unearned wealth, so establishing itself as a threat to the established order.

That new institutions and a constitutional system based on ideas of equality and the innate nobility of man could be created by agreement and without provoking extremes of violent repression had been amply demonstrated by the Americans, whose new constitution had been created in the name of 'the People' in 1787. The Americans were an ocean away and apparently content with what they had; at this time, they were no threat either to the remaining British possessions in North America or to the government and constitution of Great Britain itself. The French, by contrast, were not only waging successful war against two of the great European powers, but were urging the subjects of George III to embark on violent revolution themselves. In consequence, the reaction of Pitt's government to the new radicalism strongly resembled that of Elizabeth I and her advisers to Catholicism.

Established reformers were themselves alarmed at the new extremism, or appearance of extremism, particularly in a time when bad harvests and economic decline had brought a renewal of social unrest. Even if the London Corresponding Society was never more than 10,000 strong and simply sought to disseminate the new ideas via the printed word, those new ideas were a clear threat to the traditional order. Thomas Spence sought the nationalising of agricultural land, William Frend questioned the existence of the Established Church and Mary Wollstonecraft sought equality of the sexes. In Establishment eyes, such ideas were dangerous in themselves, far more so if they reached the uneducated and unstable. When this fear of Britain descending into the same Terror and destruction of traditional institutions as France is understood, it ceases to be surprising that over the years 1793 to 1815, when Britain was almost continuously at war with France, and for a considerable period afterwards, the attitude of successive governments to any form of opposition to the status quo was repressive in the extreme. Nor is it surprising that, with the needs of war at the centre of affairs for the next 20 years, the government's own proposals for reform were put to one side.

At the same time, there was increasing division among the radicals themselves. The reform movement in England before 1789 was mainly a middle class affair, inspired by the myths of the Glorious Revolution, the writings of such intellectuals as Adam Smith and David Hume, and the ideas of the French Enlightenment. They sought to remove the abuses which existed within the established order, not to destroy that order. To them, the extremism and violence into which the initially moderate and principled French Revolution descended brought disillusionment and they moved to dissociate themselves from the new breed of working class revolutionary who was now emerging to seek the destruction of the social and political order of the day by any means.

In the early years of the war, the armies of revolutionary France were overwhelmingly successful on land, occupying Holland and Italy, forcing Austria to abandon the Austrian Netherlands and Prussia its territories on the west bank of the Rhine. British arms suffered a serious reverse in Holland in 1792 and though the Royal Navy was able to defeat the French on a number of occasions, these successes took place far from home and out of the main theatre of war. That armies of untrained volunteers could defeat those of the greatest European military powers only brought further alarm on the part of the government.

In May 1792, a royal proclamation instructed magistrates to be on their guard against seditious writings, and 18 months later, the militia were called out to deal with a perceived threat of internal disruption. Some Painite radicals sought a National Convention on the new French model, and their attempt to create one at Edinburgh in November 1793 as a rival to Parliament was one of the factors which led to the suspension of habeas corpus in May 1794 and the prosecution of certain radical leaders for high treason. Rioting arising from poor harvests and rising prices included violent demonstrations against the king and Pitt at the State Opening of Parliament in October 1795. The government took further measures against the radicals by the Seditious Meetings Act, prohibiting unauthorised meetings of more than 50 persons, and the Treasonable Practices Act, which declared any criticism of king or government to be treasonable. Two years later, the naval mutinies at Spithead and the Nore, which confined large sections of the British fleet to their harbours for a lengthy period, and the proclamation by the leaders of the Nore mutineers of a 'floating republic', led to further stern measures.[24] Stamp duty on newspapers was raised from 2d to 3s 5d, and an Incitement to Mutiny Act was passed to prohibit the seducing of members of the Armed Forces from their duty and allegiance to the Crown, or the inciting of members of the Armed Forces into committing acts of mutiny.

It might be argued that the savage repression of the radical movement was counter-productive. True, the suspension of habeas corpus enabled the government to

---

24 The mutinies were not inspired by radical agitation so much as by the appalling conditions in which Royal Navy seamen of the day were expected to serve. Indeed, the Spithead mutineers protested their loyalty to the Crown and were persuaded to return peacefully to their duties by the intervention of the much respected Admiral Lord Howe.

detain indefinitely a number of radical leaders without trial and so remove any influence they might have had, and various radical groups ceased to exist, some of their members fleeing abroad. However, a hard core remained underground and had nothing to lose by extreme action. This is exactly what happened in Ireland in 1798, where that which the government most greatly feared came to pass, when a local insurrection was combined with a French invasion.

18.11 IRELAND 1797–1801

The United Irishmen movement began as an Irish cousin of the more moderate English and Scottish radical groups, seeking parliamentary reform and equal rights between men of different religious denominations. It was most numerous among the Presbyterians of Belfast and liberal Protestants and Catholics in Dublin. Some of its original aims were achieved in 1792–93 when Pitt, concerned, as many before him, about the possibility of the French invading Ireland and gaining support among disaffected elements in the population, persuaded the Dublin government to bring in a number of Catholic relief measures. Catholics could now own property, serve on juries, carry arms, enter university and hold some legal and judicial offices. They were also admitted to the franchise, though still excluded from sitting in Parliament. In any event, since the franchise remained based on a property qualification and the other rights in practice affected only the very small number of Catholics who had the wealth and education to make use of them, the position of the mass of the population remained unchanged.

With most of the aims of the moderates achieved, though not as a result of United Irish campaigning so much as the needs of the British government of the moment, the movement became the preserve of extremists, who sought nothing less than complete independence from Britain. Some time in 1796, one of its leaders, Theobald Wolfe Tone, a Dublin Protestant, travelled secretly to Paris and persuaded the French to mount a large-scale naval expedition to Ireland. As with several earlier Jacobite expeditions, the weather now came to the rescue of the British government. The French force was dispersed by December storms off Bantry Bay. A further French expedition took place in August 1798, when a small force landed at Killala, County Mayo. This was defeated by government troops and the local risings intended to coincide with the invasion were suppressed with the same ruthlessness as 'Butcher' Cumberland had employed in Scotland 50 years earlier. Some 12,000 people were killed. Wolfe Tone was captured in County Wexford, scene of the worst fighting, wearing a French uniform and was duly condemned to death for high treason, but committed suicide while awaiting execution.

The suppression of the 1798 rebellion led to further measures against radicals on the British mainland, a society of United Englishmen having been revealed with links to the Irish group and to the London Corresponding Society. Habeas corpus was again suspended, most of the remaining radical societies were declared unlawful and their assets were seized. The Combination Acts declared all associations of working men and all meetings for political purposes of more than four persons to be illegal. At the same time, the Pitt government concluded that the current constitutional position of Ireland could not be sustained and set in train a process towards union.

Although the rebellion of 1798 had been crushed and the French invasion was a small-scale affair, the threat of further invasion and of Ireland being used as a stepping stone to the British mainland remained serious. Revolutionary France continued its military success. Only the Royal Navy's blockade of the Channel prevented a French invasion, but the main French fleet had not yet been brought to battle and an Army of England had spent part of 1798 encamped on the Channel coast, before being diverted to Egypt under its remarkable commander, the 29 year old Corsican, Napoleon Bonaparte. The corrupt regime of the Mameluke sultans who ruled Egypt was crushed in a few months, and though the French Mediterranean fleet was destroyed by Admiral Lord Nelson at the Battle of the Nile in August 1798, the French Army was again free for an invasion of England. Pitt recognised that those who held power in Dublin formed a narrow and entirely unrepresentative oligarchy, and were hated for political or religious reasons by the great bulk of the population.

As in the case of Scotland a century earlier, the Irish Parliament would have to pass an Act of Union and vote itself out of existence, so that a campaign to win over the support of Irish MPs and peers was set in train by the lord-lieutenant and his advisers, notably Lord Castlereagh, Chief Secretary to the lord-lieutenant, and at the beginning of a political career which was to see him presiding over the Congress of Vienna. Pitt recognised that for the union to be acceptable to the Catholic majority, and so draw them away from potential support for France, it would have to be accompanied by the removal of the religious test in all remaining areas and reform of the tithe system, by which both Catholics and Presbyterians were required to support financially the Church of Ireland, of which they were not members.

To a greater extent than its Scottish equivalent, which was ultimately the product of negotiation, even if the English were much the stronger negotiators, the Irish Union involved terms imposed by Westminster. Ireland was to be represented by 100 MPs and 28 peers, as in Scotland, an under-representation in terms of population, plus the Church of Ireland Archbishop of Armagh and three bishops.[25] The Church of Ireland was established in the same way as the Church of England on the mainland, this being specifically stated to be an essential and fundamental part of the Union. All trade within the new United Kingdom of Great Britain and Ireland was to be free, though this greatly favoured English manufacturing, and Ireland would retain its separate legal system, though there were no restrictions on the powers of the new Parliament of the United Kingdom to legislate for Ireland.

However, Pitt's plan for complete Catholic emancipation, allowing Catholics to sit at Westminster, did not come to fruition. The leading Irish Catholics seem to have believed that they had received assurances that the Union would not go ahead without emancipation, but no such measures had been introduced in Parliament when the Union took effect on 1 January 1801, so that there was no pressure on Pitt's government to obtain the necessary legislation. About half of Pitt's Cabinet opposed the plan in any case and, fatally for Pitt, so did George III himself. Faced with an impasse, Pitt and most of his senior ministers resigned in February, and with him went any prospect of moderate reform, even for reasons of government expediency, until after the conclusion of the wars.

---

25   There was and remains also a Catholic Archbishop of Armagh.

CHAPTER 19

THE REFORM ERA

19.1 INTRODUCTION

The 19th century, or the two-thirds from 1830 onwards, was the period in which the work of government began to expand beyond the traditional concerns of foreign policy, defence of the realm and national security, and administration of justice. By extension of the franchise and modernisation of constituency structure, the House of Commons was converted from a body largely composed of members of the aristocracy and their clients, representing the interests of only a small portion of the population, into a legislature with some claim, however imperfect, to reflect the popular will. This led in turn to government accepting a responsibility to act in spheres now thought central to its work – education, health, employment and housing. In the same period, the principle was also established that the monarch would not refuse royal assent to Bills passed by Parliament, and the balance of power in the relationship between sovereign and Prime Minister began to tilt to an ever-increasing extent in the latter's favour.

One obvious question is why it was in the 1830s that a parliamentary system which had remained essentially unaltered from medieval times began to be modernised – why had it taken so long?

The question is best answered by considering the political and social background of the early part of the century, in which war, the needs of war and the difficult aftermath of war absorbed all the attentions of government, and for much of the period, there was fear of violent revolution on the French model. In the four years from 1828, the specific political climate of the day meant that a measure of reform became expedient. Not only were there major changes to the franchise, but also the final abolition of the penal laws against Catholics.

19.2 THE NAPOLEONIC WARS

A temporary break in the European war came via the Treaty of Amiens of March 1802. The settlement was not expected even then to produce an enduring peace, and war was renewed in May 1803. There was peace again from May 1814 to March 1815, when the Bourbon monarchy was restored in France and the Congress of Vienna met to redraw the map of Europe, and a further renewal of war in the 'Hundred Days' between Napoleon's escape from Elba and final defeat at Waterloo.

French plans to invade Britain were ended by the naval victory at Trafalgar in October 1805. Britain remained the leading naval power for the rest of the war and played an increasingly important role on land from 1808. For a time, Britain was without allies, as Austria, Prussia and Russia were successively defeated in 1805–07 and concluded peace terms which accepted Napoleon's conquests and domination of Europe. From 1808 until Napoleon's invasion of Russia in the summer of 1812, Britain's only allies were Spain and Portugal, both second-rate powers and under French occupation.

It was a situation paralleled in 1940–41 and, in a similar way to Hitler, Napoleon attempted to starve Britain out. Deprived by the Royal Navy of the ability to invade Britain, Napoleon introduced the 'Continental System' in 1806–07. France and her dependencies (now most of mainland Europe) were forbidden to trade with Britain and her colonies, and European ports were closed to British shipping. Britain retaliated by blockading all ports attempting to exclude British ships and goods, and prohibited all trade between territories under French control overseas. This blockade was enforced not only by the seizure of enemy ships, but also by the searching of neutral ships bound to or from continental ports, their diversion to British-controlled ports and seizure of their cargoes.[1] Given Britain's command of the seas, the blockade formed a highly effective weapon of war. However, it caused serious hardships at home and added to a general economic depression which developed from 1811. This was worst in Lancashire, where the expanding cotton industry gained most of its raw material from the southern United States, subject to the blockade as a neutral country. To make matters worse, the Americans first adopted a policy of 'non-intercourse' with Britain and then declared war in the summer of 1812, cutting off the supply of raw cotton for the next two years. There was another wave of popular unrest, particularly in manufacturing districts, and renewed fear of bloody revolution as the wars entered their critical final phase.

The Younger Pitt was Prime Minister from 1784 to 1801 and from 1804 until his death in January 1806. Pitt's death, and that of Charles James Fox in September of the same year, can, in the trite phrase, be said to mark the end of an era. Thereafter, slowly and haltingly, with many reverses, politics began to be based on party rather than person. The old groupings around individuals, and ministries based on the support that individuals could command, gradually disappeared until in the mid-19th century, party government in the modern fashion emerged.

It is then that the party labels of Whig and Tory began to re-emerge, the latter being applied to the political successors of Pitt. The new Tories, like the old, stressed the importance of loyalty to the monarchy and the maintenance of links between church and state, considering the two indivisible. They were therefore strongly opposed to any change which might weaken the position of the Church of England. Though Pitt had once been an advocate of parliamentary reform and in more recent years had for pragmatic reasons favoured measures which would have allowed Catholics to sit in Parliament, he had, through fear of revolution, adopted repressive domestic policies. The new Tories followed his example in their opposition to reform and were also deeply hostile to Catholic emancipation. When, in order to pre-empt threatened discontent in Ireland, the short-lived Ministry of All the Talents of 1806–07 proposed concessions to Catholics which would allow them to reach senior rank in the Armed Forces, George III declared that his ministers were threatening his freedom to act in consistency with the Coronation Oath, which required him to maintain and protect the Reformed Protestant religion, and commanded the ministers to promise not to raise the issue of Catholic emancipation with him again. When the ministers refused to make such a promise, the king dismissed them in his last major political act before he became incurably insane at the end of 1810.

---

1   Blockade is an entirely lawful form of naval warfare, provided steps are taken to ensure the safety of the crews of merchant ships and any passengers.

The Whig-dominated Ministry of All the Talents was succeeded by a largely Tory administration under the 3rd Duke of Portland. Although Portland obtained a dissolution of Parliament and a substantial majority at the election which followed, his government was never entirely secure, suffering from the bitter personal feud between George Canning, the Foreign Secretary, and Lord Castlereagh, Secretary of State for War, which climaxed in their fighting a duel with pistols in 1809. Portland became fatally ill towards the end of 1809 and was replaced by Spencer Perceval, who in May 1812 gained the melancholy distinction of being the only British Prime Minister to be murdered while in office.[2]

Perceval took office at a time when Britain's military fortunes were at a low ebb and there was increasing criticism of governmental incompetence and corruption. His main success came in the smooth passage of a Regency Bill through Parliament on similar terms to those of 1788, giving the Prince of Wales full powers of appointment and dismissal of ministers and of dissolving Parliament, but restricting his freedom to create peers. The queen was given custody of the king, who thereafter resided quietly at Windsor, where he died, virtually forgotten, in 1820. The Act took effect early in 1811, but if the remaining Foxite Whigs hoped for gains at the hands of their old ally, they were doomed to disappointment. Following Perceval's death, he was replaced by his close ally, the Earl of Liverpool, at the head of a largely unchanged ministry.

Liverpool's government remained in office until 1827, gradually becoming more completely Tory in its composition. Liverpool, like Perceval, came to power at a time of enormous difficulty. Though the Royal Navy had by now secured possession of most of the overseas possessions of France and Holland, Napoleon remained master of Europe. It was not until later in the same year that Wellington achieved the first of his major victories and went firmly onto the offensive in Spain, and Napoleon made the fatal mistake – repeated by Hitler – of believing that he could defeat Russia decisively by taking Moscow. With winter coming on, his troops unable to live off the land in their usual fashion and his lines of communication hopelessly over-stretched, Napoleon ordered a retreat. In his rear, he left an intact Russian army, and a Prussian corps diverted to besiege Riga, whose commander soon concluded the Convention of Tauroggen, which bound his country, under French occupation since 1806, to make war against France. Early in 1813, Austria was added to the new alliance of Britain, Russia and Prussia, which then went on the offensive. Early in 1814, Wellington crossed the Pyrenees, to reach Toulouse before France sued for peace and the allies exiled Napoleon to the Mediterranean island of Elba.

Successful though the war had been, it was not finally over, since Napoleon escaped from Elba in March 1815, raised another army and was only finally defeated at Waterloo on 18 June. In the same way as its 18th century predecessors had done and subsequent wars were to do, it left Britain in financial crisis. War expenditure between 1793 and 1815 totalled £1,658 million. Taxation reached 20% and government spending accounted for 29% of national income in 1814. At the same time, there was a large and continuing increase in population, for reasons which are imperfectly

---

2   Perceval's murderer was John Bellingham, a deranged man who held a grudge against the government after judging that the British ambassador in St Petersburg had failed to render him sufficient assistance in litigation concerning investments in Russia. Bellingham insisted that the Prime Minister be present at the inaugural meeting of a parliamentary committee convened to inquire into the matter, and shot Perceval as he made his way to the committee room. See L Stephen (ed), *Dictionary of National Biography*, 1885–1900, OUP.

understood, a series of disastrous harvests and difficulties in securing imports of foreign grain. All this led to high food prices – in 1812, the price of wheat averaged 126s 6d per quarter, more than twice that of better years.[3] Industry, particularly iron and steel and armaments, had profited immensely from the war and, with a return to the much lower demands of peacetime, depression inevitably followed. To add to the social and economic difficulties, there were large numbers of servicemen, many of them disabled, thrown onto a difficult labour market as the army and navy were reduced to peacetime strengths.

19.3   RADICALISM AND UNREST

Calls for reform had re-emerged in recent years, in a context not only of traditional concerns about official corruption, but a more idealistic desire to improve the condition of man. This was not only an expression of the ideas of the French Enlightenment, but also of a social conscience which had a strong religious basis. It is no accident that a quite disproportionate number of 19th century social reformers were Quakers, and a number of others were Methodists and Evangelical Anglicans.

Methodism began in the 1740s in the attempts of John Wesley and other preachers to remedy the Anglican church's neglect of its spiritual and pastoral role. Gradually, it became an organised movement separate from the Anglican church, with its own clergy and places of worship, and was strongest among the upper levels of the working classes, such as skilled manual workers and small traders. It emphasised the education of its members, initially so that they could read the scriptures for themselves, and general self-improvement and responsibility to one's fellow men. A little later came Evangelism, which remained within the Established Church. It emphasised personal faith and the superiority of the Bible over sacraments and ceremony, and found secular expression in the desire of its adherents to do good in the world.

Alongside religiously-inspired campaigning on issues of social importance came renewed calls for political reform. However, the attempts of middle class radicals to bring about reform through appeals to logic and reason were seriously hampered by the re-emergence of mass disorder in 1811–12. The activities of the Luddites have been much discussed by historians, and their motivation hotly debated, along with their links (or the absence of them) to the working class protesters of the 1790s. What is certain is that there was a wave of machine breaking and violence in Nottinghamshire, Lancashire and Yorkshire, apparently as a protest against the high rents charged for the frames used by framework knitters and the looms used by handloom weavers, and more generally against the introduction of new machinery which allowed skilled labour to be replaced by unskilled. This coincided with food riots following poor harvests and seems to have caused alarm among the establishment, not least because there were instances of quasi-military drilling and oath-taking and attacks on militia depots. 15,000 troops were sent to Yorkshire and a further 2,000 to Nottinghamshire.

Though the disorder subsided from the peak of 1812, it re-emerged with the end of the war. The government reacted to the continuing fluctuations in grain prices by a measure to protect the landed interest from the threat to their income caused by falling

3   See N Gash, *Aristocracy and People, England 1815–1865*, 1979, Arnold, p 366.

prices. This was the notorious Corn Law of 1815, which forbade the import of foreign corn while the price of British corn remained below 80s per quarter, a figure established by a select committee as the minimum necessary to provide adequate remuneration for British farmers. This kept the price of corn, and hence of bread, much the most important element in working class diets, artificially high. The Bill's passage provoked serious rioting in London and, O'Gorman suggests, gave rise to class antagonism in that it demonstrated that the government were prepared to adopt protectionist measures for the benefit of the landed class, but left the poor to the uncertainties of the free market.

An exceptionally wet summer led to another failed harvest in 1816, as a result of which, wheat prices again topped 100s a quarter and there were further outbreaks of serious rioting, coinciding with an orchestrated campaign by the middle class radicals for parliamentary reform and against government financial policy. Though the war was over, the burden of taxation remained very high, the more so in the context of economic depression. Whereas government revenue before 1793 had been £16–17 million annually, it now stood at over £50 million, 80% required for interest payments on the National Debt.[4] For the first time since the 1790s, the usual tactics of petitioning, pamphlets and correspondence were supplemented with public meetings, notably those held at Spa Fields, London in November and December 1816 and addressed by the charismatic Henry 'Orator' Hunt, who insisted that the prevailing economic distress was directly related to the political system. Memories of the Terror were still fresh and the murder of Spencer Perceval was a very recent event. Government and establishment became increasingly alarmed.

As in the 1790s, the government began to fear organised plots and insurrections, though there was no longer any danger of a French invasion, and their fears were not entirely unjustified by events. One group of conspirators looted gunsmith's shops and attempted to storm the Tower of London. Though quickly arrested, they were acquitted on a technicality at trial. Their leaders, Arthur Thistlewood and James Watson, continued their plotting, their activities culminating in the Cato Street Conspiracy of February 1820, in which they sought to murder Lord Liverpool and his Cabinet at dinner. Like the Gunpowder Plot, the conspiracy was infiltrated by spies and *agents provocateurs* at an early stage and never became a serious threat, but it fuelled the official paranoia which was a feature of the day.

The apparent threat of serious insurrection led each House of Parliament to set up a secret committee in February 1817 to consider the evidence of sedition reported by magistrates to the Home Office. The committees reported later in the same month that an organised revolutionary movement centred on London was in existence, some of its elements operating in the guise of societies seeking parliamentary reform. Whether such a movement truly existed is, yet again, a matter of debate; the multiplicity of small radical groups and the lack of co-ordination between them would suggest that it did not. What is important is that the political establishment believed in its existence. The government obtained legislation suspending habeas corpus in respect of persons suspected of treason, creating compulsory licensing of rooms used for political meetings, prohibiting meetings of more than 50 persons without prior approval from magistrates and making incitement to mutiny in the Armed Forces a capital offence. Against this background, the motion for a select committee on parliamentary reform

---

4   *Ibid*, pp 102–04.

brought by the moderate radical MP Sir Francis Burdett in May was defeated by 266 to 77. Even the many Whigs of a reforming persuasion were strongly opposed to popular agitation and also to the power without responsibility connotated by suffrage unrestricted by a property qualification.

The powers granted by the 1817 legislation were exercised with considerable circumspection. 44 people were arrested on suspicion of treason; except for one who died during his imprisonment, all were released by January 1818. Mass meetings of radicals resumed early in 1819. 'Orator' Hunt blamed the sufferings of the people on the failings of the government and called on Englishmen to claim their rights to equality on the basis of the *Declaration of the Rights of Man*, universal manhood suffrage and an end to the Corn Law. A series of mass meetings followed in the industrial areas of the north and Midlands. At the same time, there was a revival of the 'National Convention' movement of the 1790s in those manufacturing centres which as yet had no parliamentary representation. This was seen by the establishment as a treasonable attempt to set up a rival legislature to Parliament, and the government reacted with a royal proclamation against illegal meetings. Informed that such a meeting was to be held at St Peter's Fields, Manchester on 9 August, at which 'Orator' Hunt would speak, the local magistrates issued a warning to the organisers, who postponed the meeting for a week and declared that their purpose was not to elect a representative, but merely to 'consider the propriety of adopting legal and effective measures to obtain a reform of Parliament'.

As with many instances of apparent bloody repression, the 'Peterloo massacre' of 16 August 1819 was more the result of muddle and incompetence than deliberate policy. On the morning of the meeting, seeing the size of the crowd that was gathering, and considering Hunt to be a dangerous rabble-rouser, the magistrates issued a warrant for his arrest before he was due to speak, on grounds of the threat to the peace. Given that there was no police force and the crowd was large – some 60,000 – and potentially volatile, the magistrates called for the assistance of the 15th Hussars, who were quartered in the vicinity, and the local yeomanry. Mounted police work, particularly in crowd control, is highly specialist and requires thorough training of horses, essentially nervous creatures which react badly to sudden noise and movement. Neither the 15th Hussars nor the yeomanry had anything approaching the necessary training, and the yeomanry were in addition ill-organised and ill-disciplined. Sent to arrest Hunt, the yeomanry were rapidly surrounded by the crowd. Believing them to be under attack, the magistrates sent in the Hussars to rescue them. By the time order was restored, 11 people were dead and some 400 injured, a high proportion probably as a result of panic in the crowd.[5] Gash makes it clear that although the magistrates made a serious error of judgment in choosing to arrest Hunt at the meeting rather than beforehand, they were far from unjustified in their concern for public order.[6]

Perhaps surprisingly, Peterloo did not provoke immediate reaction from either the government or the radicals. Meetings continued; one in Glasgow, which went ahead

---

5   Incidents at football stadiums in recent years have amply demonstrated the lethal consequences of panic among large crowds in confined spaces. The Hillsborough disaster of April 1989, in which 98 people were killed, is the most notorious.

6   See Gash, *op cit*, pp 88–96 for details on Peterloo and its general context. See also Lord Denning, *Landmarks in the Law*, 1984, Butterworths, pp 153–64 for a polemical account of the legal issues involved in the arrest of Hunt.

despite a magistrates' warning, was followed by a general riot which lasted several days. Rather than the angry reaction to Peterloo which might have been expected, there was a gradual reduction in mass political activity, possibly as a consequence of a better harvest and the resulting amelioration of economic conditions. Apart from the hard-line Home Secretary, Lord Sidmouth, no minister pressed for further anti-radical legislation until after the Whigs chose to make political capital from Peterloo. For some years, the Whigs had been very much in opposition; there was also a developing division between traditional Whig 'grandees' on the 18th century model and the more modern and socially aware 'progressive' Whigs, such as William Wilberforce. Whig politicians criticised the government's response to Peterloo and called for an inquiry into the affair, a suggestion quickly condemned by the Prince Regent. Earl Fitzwilliam, lord-lieutenant of Yorkshire and among the most prominent of the Whig grandees, supported a local resolution for an inquiry which also condemned the government. This was an improper act on Fitzwilliam's part, since, as lord-lieutenant, he was the local agent of the Crown. He was promptly removed from office and both government and opposition closed ranks.

As with more modern political leaders in times of crisis, Lord Liverpool and his government had to be seen to be doing something to deal with the perceived threat of insurrection. They were also faced with the sudden re-emergence of effective opposition. Parliament was recalled and the Whigs were placated with a full debate on Peterloo, at which a Whig motion for an inquiry was defeated after most of the remaining independents chose to ally with the government. Emergency legislation was passed, again with strong support from the independents.

The Six Acts of 1819 have, like Peterloo, a sinister reputation as another high peak in official repression of protest, but only two involved direct interference with the liberties of individuals, giving magistrates in specified towns power to search private premises for arms and prohibiting mass meetings for political purposes without prior authorisation. Three attempted to close loopholes in the existing law by preventing evasion of stamp duty on newspapers, providing for the destruction of publications found by the courts to contain blasphemous and seditious libels, and reducing the means by which those accused of criminal offences could delay being brought to trial. The final Act prohibited unauthorised military organisations and training. Research indicates that the legislation was little used and was largely ineffective.

19.4   THE DRIFT TOWARDS REFORM

In its last five years, from 1822 to 1827, the Liverpool government, with the senior Cabinet posts occupied by men of more liberal tendencies than hitherto, began to move cautiously in the direction of change and modernisation, though not yet to support for parliamentary reform. Developments in Ireland brought renewed pressure for Catholic emancipation, the issue which had led George III to dismiss two governments. In 1823, Daniel O'Connell, a prominent Irish lawyer, formed a Catholic Association, with the intention of drawing together opposition to anti-Catholic legislation, and this rapidly caught the imagination of the Irish populace, becoming a mass movement financed by a 'Catholic Rent' of 1d per month and developing a nationalist as well as a Catholic agenda. The Catholic question was such a divisive issue among the Tories that as far back as 1812, Lord Liverpool and his Cabinet had agreed to adopt a 'neutral' position. There would be no official government policy, but if the issue was raised in Parliament, individual ministers were free to speak and vote as they wished. By this means, Liverpool was able to prevent his Cabinet becoming hopelessly divided, but the Catholic question remained extremely controversial, not least because of continued royal opposition to change.

19.4.1 Sir Robert Peel

As Home Secretary under Liverpool from 1821, Sir Robert Peel set about a rationalisation of the criminal law, which had developed over many centuries in a fashion impressive largely in its lack of coherence. There were more than 200 capital crimes, creations of the common law or of statutes passed in response to specific concerns, and the criminal justice system had developed little since medieval times. In the same way, the problems of preventing and detecting crime with which medieval monarchs had grappled had not been addressed in any systematic way. The most conspicuous vacuum was the absence of any police force other than the men of the customs and excise, constables appointed by the borough corporations and parish watchmen of low efficiency.

Penal reform was an area in which the burgeoning social conscience of the day expressed itself, but change had hitherto been blocked by Peel's predecessor, Lord Sidmouth. However, concern within Parliament led to the appointment in 1819 of an investigatory committee and, on becoming Home Secretary, Peel proceeded with changes based on its recommendations. No fewer than 278 statutes were repealed and the remaining statutory provisions were consolidated into eight new Acts. The number of capital offences was very considerably reduced and, in consequence, the number of executions averaged 61 annually in the years 1822–26 as against 108 in 1817–21.

In a context of rising crime despite improvements in the economic situation since 1820, Peel's philosophy gave equal weight to the improvement of mechanisms for preventing crime, apprehending offenders and maintaining public order. The use of troops in a public order rule was unpopular and largely ineffective, and there were doubts about the army's reliability following a mutiny among the Foot Guards in 1820. However, Peel faced the difficulty that uniformed police forces, and particularly national police forces such as the French *gendarmerie*, were regarded by many as instruments of government repression and so were incompatible with the English tradition of liberty. It was not until 1829 that Peel was able to secure the creation of the Metropolitan Police, for which he is now chiefly remembered, and then only because there was no coherent civic authority in London, so that the Home Secretary did not have to face opposition from local government bodies.

19.4.2 Catholic emancipation

As Peel continued his rationalisation of the criminal law, he, along with the rest of the government, became embroiled in a new crisis over Catholic emancipation, which eventually brought about the collapse of Lord Liverpool's administration. Prior to 1822, the Cabinet was dominated by those opposed to change, the 'Protestants'; Lord Castlereagh was the only senior minister in favour of Catholic emancipation. In 1825, after two earlier and more limited Bills had been rejected by the Lords, Sir Francis Burdett introduced a comprehensive Catholic relief Bill. When this passed its third reading in May, Peel, now the leading 'Protestant' in the Commons and faced with opposition from all his senior colleagues except Liverpool, offered his resignation, considering his position to be an embarrassment to himself and to the government to which he belonged.[7] Liverpool then concluded that the 'Protestant' party in the government would be so reduced that he could not continue as Prime Minister, though he was persuaded by the other leading Tory peers not to resign and so precipitate the collapse of the government.

Burdett's Bill was defeated in the Lords, not least because of an angrily hostile speech by the Duke of York, then heir presumptive to the throne,[8] on one of the last occasions in which a member of the royal family involved themselves directly in an issue of political controversy. Canning now demanded that the Cabinet abandon its 'neutral' stance and endorse Catholic emancipation. Again, there were threats of resignation before he was persuaded to back down in the interests of continued unity, but that unity was now increasingly precarious.

The government was returned to power in the 1826 election, but Liverpool then had a stroke and resigned, dying the following year. There followed a period in which three Tory Prime Ministers succeeded one another in less than a year as their party struggled to hold on to power. No single minister enjoyed support from the majority of the Cabinet, and the king's appointment of Canning precipitated wholesale resignations. Canning attempted to retain power by persuading some of the leading Whigs to enter a coalition, but died in August after four months in office. His successor, Viscount Goderich, proved incapable of holding together the administration, so that the king replaced him with the Duke of Wellington early in 1828.

Wellington's appointment was in some ways a compromise, in other ways the appointment of a strong man capable of re-establishing support for the government after the difficulties of the past year. He had never held political office, but as the nation's most distinguished soldier since Marlborough, he enjoyed enormous respect. Moreover, he was not associated with any of those Tories who had been discredited by recent events. However, he did not possess Liverpool's political skills and was viewed with suspicion in a country which remembered that its only previous military head of government was Oliver Cromwell.

Events rapidly demonstrated that the Tories had become irredeemably divided over Catholic emancipation. Once more, it was the situation in Ireland which persuaded sufficient of the opponents of change to end their opposition and allow the 1829 Bill to pass the Lords, where several previous Bills had foundered. Catholics on the British mainland were a small and politically mute minority, whereas they were over two-thirds of the Irish population, forming a clear majority everywhere except Ulster. In Establishment eyes, they were a potentially volatile and dangerous majority. In 1828, Daniel O'Connell, leader of the Catholic Association, stood as a candidate in a by-election in County Clare and, thanks to the overwhelming support of the 40s freeholders, polled more than two-thirds of the vote despite being barred from taking his seat. The lord-lieutenant warned that the same could happen in scores of Irish

---

7 This represents an early example of the constitutional convention that a minister unable for reasons of conscience to support government policy should resign in order to preserve Cabinet collective responsibility.

8 He died in 1827, so that it was the next brother, the Duke of Clarence, who eventually succeeded as William IV.

constituencies at the next general election and that O'Connell was in a position to lead his followers into open rebellion.

Though previously opposed to Catholic emancipation, Peel now introduced a government Bill into Parliament which would repeal all remaining provisions of the penal laws. This not only allowed Catholics to sit in Parliament, but opened all offices to them, except those which represented or were directly linked with the Crown, though in legislation passed at the same time, the 40s freehold was abolished in Ireland and the Catholic Association was suppressed.

On Peel's plea of necessity, the Bill was passed by large majorities in both Houses and was presented to the king for the royal assent. It was just over 120 years since Queen Anne refused her assent to the Scottish Militia Bill. No Bill to which the monarch was known to be opposed had reached this stage since, so that the issue of whether the monarch retained power to refuse assent had not arisen. That George IV, while unhappy at some of the actions of his ministers, was reluctant to oppose them openly had been demonstrated in 1824 when he pleaded gout and the loss of his false teeth to avoid the necessity of reading a speech to both Houses prepared by Canning and announcing the recognition of three South American republics which had separated themselves by rebellion from the old Spanish Empire.[9]

A precedent was set for the future when George IV, however reluctantly and amid threats of abdication, gave effect to the policy of the government which ruled in his name by giving the royal assent to the 1829 Bill. Sir Walter Bagehot, writing in 1865–67, stated categorically that the monarch no longer had the power of veto over legislation passed by both Houses through a refusal of the royal assent,[10] but in 1913–14, George V believed that he would be acting within his powers if in defined circumstances, he refused assent to the Home Rule Bill, and seems to have been prepared to do so.[11] 1829 marks a watershed, the last occasion on which there was a real and substantial possibility that the monarch would refuse assent by reason of personal opposition.

19.5   THE GREAT REFORM ACT

Though the Catholic Emancipation Act passed into law, a significant proportion of Tories voted against it. They saw the Act as a betrayal of principle by Wellington and Peel, both of whom had previously opposed emancipation but now acted solely on the basis of expediency. Further, the executive had ridden roughshod over the wishes of the majority of the electorate who, during the passage of the Bill, had expressed clear opposition. The 9th Earl of Winchilsea went so far as to challenge Wellington to a duel with pistols, calling him the greatest threat to English liberty since Cromwell.[12] Perhaps at first sight surprisingly, the hard-line 'Ultra' Tories who had opposed emancipation began to see advantages in a reform of Parliament which would free

9   V Bogdanor, *The Monarchy and the Constitution*, 1995, Clarendon, p 15.

10   W Bagehot (M Taylor (ed)), *The English Constitution*, 2001, OUP, p 53.

11   See further below, pp 382–83.

12   The duel took place on Battersea Common on 21 March 1821. Both parties deliberately fired wide. See Elizabeth Longford, *Wellington: Pillar of State*, 1972, Weidenfeld & Nicholson, pp 235–39.

members from domination by the government and those who controlled the boroughs.

Although the Tories formed a majority of the Commons returned in the 1830 General Election, Wellington's government, without the support of the 'Ultras' and the Canningites, rested on such unstable foundations that it was only a matter of time before it fell, as it did when Parliament assembled in November for the new session. The radical Henry Brougham had been elected an MP for Yorkshire on a pledge to introduce a reform Bill and the government lost on a motion introduced by Wellington himself that there was no need to change 'the system of representation'. Seeing this as the vote of no confidence that it was, the government resigned at once.

The Whigs were the minority party in the Commons and were divided among themselves. However, none of the Tory leaders could either command a majority in the Commons or form a united Cabinet, so that the new king, William IV, turned to the Whigs, selecting Charles Grey, 2nd Earl Grey, as the head of a coalition which represented all the leading elements other than the Ultras. Though by origin very much a Whig grandee, Grey considered that the existing electoral system remained defensible only if it produced governments which were both effective and acceptable to public opinion. Generally speaking, the system had worked, at least in providing governments which had been able to function effectively. However, public opinion had become deeply hostile to the system, as manifested by intermittent violence among the masses, and the more reasoned campaign for change which had been going on since the 1760s. Events since Lord Liverpool's resignation now demonstrated that the existing system could no longer be relied on to produce effective government. Reform had become a necessity, and to delay the inevitable any longer would be counter-productive.

The impetus for reform was strengthened by a revival of agitation, prompted by economic difficulties and disillusionment with the existing political system. Once again, a poor harvest and rising food prices brought a revival of mass meetings and the emergence of new radical groups along the lines of the Catholic Association (complete with 'Radical rent') on the one hand, and rioting and machine-breaking on the other.

As had previous governments, the Grey Cabinet took stern measures to deal with the disturbances, establishing special commissions to try the rioters, numbers of whom were sentenced to death or transportation. However, Grey also instructed a team which included the leading two Whig radicals, the Earl of Durham and Lord John Russell, to draft a Bill which would satisfy the demands of public opinion for parliamentary reform, at least among the middle classes who would be the main beneficiaries, and separate them from the working classes, who were regarded as a danger to government stability, while retaining a franchise based on a property qualification and the existing constituency structure.

For Grey, the three cardinal principles of reform were the disenfranchisement of rotten boroughs, enfranchisement of the new towns and a common £10 franchise. There was also a need to reduce the scope for bribery and intimidation of voters. What was intended was not the replacement of the existing system, but its modernisation and improvement.

19.5.1 The Bill

The Reform Bill of 1831, affecting England and Wales only and introduced into the Commons by Russell in March, was therefore essentially conservative. The existing confusion of borough franchises would be replaced by a uniform franchise which gave the vote to all male householders who owned or rented property worth £10 per year and paid rates. The county franchise remained based on the 40s freehold. 60 rotten boroughs would be abolished and 47 others would have their representation reduced from two members to one, making 167 seats available for re-distribution. Some of these would go to 34 of the new towns, now to be represented for the first time, and the remainder used to give each of the counties an additional member. Procedural changes included the provision of an official register of electors, an increased number of polling places and the limiting of the duration of polls to two days. The draft Bill also proposed the introduction of secret ballots and a reduction in the maximum life of a Parliament from seven years to five, but these provisions were removed by the Cabinet before the Bill went before Parliament.

Similar Bills were introduced for Scotland and Ireland, again establishing a uniform £10 franchise in the boroughs. The Scottish Bill was the most far-reaching of the three, since the changes would increase the number of voters from a paltry 4,500, spread over 30 counties and 15 burghs, to about 65,000, still a fraction of the population, but a considerably greater fraction. In Ireland, there would be little actual increase in the electorate, since Irish property values were generally much lower than elsewhere. Given that Catholics formed the bulk of the poorest segment of the population, the extension of the franchise to Catholics under the 1829 Act also brought little change in the composition of the electorate.

19.5.2 The struggle in Parliament

That the English Bill was intensely controversial is only too clearly demonstrated by its being carried in the Commons by a single vote. Unlike Catholic emancipation, parliamentary reform was not an all-or-nothing measure, which MPs either favoured or did not. It was an issue over which there were many shades of opinion, based both on principle and on self-interest. Some of the opposition to the Bill came from MPs who believed that it did not go far enough, though there were others, almost exclusively among the Tories, who held out for the existing system. This was an age deeply suspicious of anything that smacked of power without responsibility and held that anyone without a stake in the country via ownership of property could not be trusted to cast a vote in the interests of the country. Advocates of the system as it was believed that change would upset the fine balance of the constitution by weakening the discretionary powers of the Crown and the position of the House of Lords, and giving excessive influence to the electorate. Ultimately, that could only produce weaker government. Further, the Reform Bill, though itself limited, would be the beginning of a process which could only end in the abolition of all aristocratic privilege, with serious knock-on effects for the sanctity of property.[13]

There were, of course, other reasons for concern about the Reform Bill. Its re-distribution of seats was a broad brush, which made the pattern of constituencies

13 See Gash, *op cit*, pp 147–50.

rather less unrepresentative but fell far short of introducing a system based on actual population distribution. Though the procedural changes were well-meant and ultimately useful, there remained enormous scope for exerting improper influence over voters, and it was many years before the vital step was taken to introduce secret ballots.

The Bill was carried on its second reading, but the government was defeated at the committee stage on what it regarded as issues of principle, so that Grey requested a dissolution, which the king granted. For the first time in British political history, a British government sought a mandate from the electorate for a flagship policy. The government gained a clear majority of seats, the opposition only winning strong support in those very boroughs which would lose all or part of their representation if the Bill went through. Armed with this clear vote of confidence at the bar of public opinion, Grey's government re-introduced the Bill at the beginning of the new Parliament and this time, the Bill passed its second reading by a comfortable majority. However, Tories were much in the majority in the Lords, where the Bill was rejected in October 1831. Using the precedent set 120 years earlier over the Treaty of Utrecht, Grey sought the creation of additional Whig peers. William IV was far less partisan politically than either his father or his elder brother. He seems not to have been hostile to the Reform Bill as such, but he was reluctant to allow the Royal Prerogative to be used as an instrument to force it through. He refused Grey's request.

This produced deadlock. There were serious outbreaks of rioting in Nottingham, Derby and Bristol as pro-reform mobs went on the rampage, and several hundred people were killed. There were calls for vigilante organisations to be set up, a prospect which alarmed the government, and a royal proclamation was issued to proscribe such organisations. Some aristocrats were sufficiently concerned to begin fortifying their country houses and laying in supplies of weapons and ammunition for the first time since the 17th century.

The political stalemate continued until May 1832, when, as rioting and agitation continued, Grey's government resigned. For a second time, a monarch sent for the Duke of Wellington in the hope that he could form a working ministry, specifically to find a way of passing a reform measure sufficient to appease the public mood without misuse of the prerogative of creating peers.

Wellington proved unable to form a ministry and the country moved further towards wholesale insurrection. Not only was there the prospect of yet more serious rioting; notices appeared in shops promising that no taxes would be paid until the Reform Bill was passed which, along with calls by one middle class radical association for a run on gold, brought the possibility of a campaign of civil disobedience among a significant segment of the propertied classes. Whereas previous fears of revolution had brought calls for the establishment to stand firm, now the mood, perhaps influenced by the bloodless revolution in France which had forced the abdication of Charles X two years earlier, was in favour of change before it was too late. Faced with this, William IV gave way. He recalled Grey on the basis that no one else was in a position to form a government, and agreed to the creation of the necessary peers if the Bill was again blocked in the Lords.

As would happen in 1911, the Tory majority in the Lords was prepared to back down rather than have the Upper House dominated by parvenu political appointees.

A high proportion of them absented themselves from the vote on the third reading and the Reform Bill was duly passed, being granted royal assent on 7 June 1832.

19.5.3 Reform takes effect

In its final form, the 1832 Act retained the 40s franchise in the counties and added persons leasing property of equivalent value and tenants-at-will paying at least £50 in annual rent. The voting qualification in the boroughs required occupation of property set at £10 per annum. Boroughs with fewer than 2,000 inhabitants lost all parliamentary representation, those between 2,000 and 4,000 were reduced to one member and boroughs with larger populations were now to have two members.

The impact of the new legislation on the size and composition of the electorate is difficult to gauge. The registered electorate totalled 633,000 in 1833, but in the absence of an earlier register, it is impossible to know how much of an increase this was, estimates varying from 50% to 80%. Since the franchise remained based on a property qualification, the working classes did not benefit, except in those areas where property values were high enough to bring small numbers within the £10 limit. Only some 20% of the adult male population were eligible to vote in England and Wales, and about 14% in Scotland.

Though the re-distribution of seats had brought some improvement, there was still great variation in the size of constituencies and an imbalance in representation between different parts of the country. In particular, the southern counties, having many more boroughs, were better represented than those of the north. The possibility of undue influence by landowners and other prominent figures over local voters was not removed, and Gash goes so far to suggest that with the increased numbers of contested elections after 1832, the incidence of corrupt election practices may actually have increased.[14] In Scotland, the impact of the re-distribution of seats was greater, the changes increasing the number of burgh seats from 15 to 23 and producing an average electorate of about 1,300 in each of the Scottish urban seats and 1,100 in the county seats. Ireland had already been subjected to a re-distribution of representation in the Act of Union, so that the 1832 legislation made only minor changes.

19.6   CHANGE IN LOCAL GOVERNMENT

The next few years saw the Whigs falling rapidly into difficulties as a result of disunity within their own ranks, though important pieces of legislation were passed in this period. In the area of constitutional development, much the most significant change was the Municipal Corporations Act of 1835, essentially an application of the principles underlying the Reform Act to local government, bringing the modernisation of a system which had remained largely unchanged since medieval times.

At county level, governmental responsibilities, mainly coercive in nature, were exercised by the magistrates. In particular, magistrates retained their power to deal with civil disturbance under the terms of the Riot Act. Government of the older towns remained based on borough charters granted piecemeal by medieval kings. There

---

14 Gash, *op cit*, p 152.

were common features, most notably that membership of many borough corporations – known as 'close' corporations – was based on nomination from within, so that they tended to become self-perpetuating oligarchies of merchants, manufacturers and urban gentry, without accountability or responsibility to the populations they served. In the absence of serious corruption, this was not necessarily a major disadvantage, since the responsibilities of these corporations had remained fossilised according to the terms of the charters. The new public services which had emerged since the early 18th century were largely set up through private Acts of Parliament and their management was entrusted to specialist bodies which existed independently of the town corporations: street commissioners, water boards, harbour trustees, watch committees, paving and lighting authorities.

The result was a patchwork of overlapping and conflicting jurisdictions which supplemented the old town corporations. Further, in the new industrial towns such as Manchester, which had grown with enormous rapidity over the space of a generation or so, the system of local government was based on structures created when they were still villages, with a variety of specialist bodies of the new type grafted on.

At the lowest level of the local government structure was the parish, the principal unit in rural areas and in unincorporated towns such as Manchester, and based on the long-established ecclesiastical parishes. Its functions included fixing rates, administration of the Poor Law, upkeep of the parish church and of roads passing through the parish, and the appointment of churchwardens and overseers of the poor. The ruling body was the parish meeting, known as the vestry from the practice of holding its sessions in the church vestry, but there was no uniformity of structure. In the closed vestry, the meeting comprised the parish clergy and wealthier inhabitants, a self-perpetuating oligarchy similar to the closed corporation. By contrast, the open vestry comprised all male householders or could even be open to all adult males.

In traditional British fashion, this ramshackle structure managed to function, but it was under increasing criticism, and demands for change and rationalisation were becoming more strident. The close corporations lost their direct power of election of MPs in 1832, but they retained sufficient influence to be a target of the Whig reformers for party reasons (they tended to be Tory-dominated), as well as on principled grounds of improving the efficiency of local government. There was also the new anomaly, arising from the Reform Act, that many of those now enfranchised at national level had no vote in borough elections.

The government acted first in Scotland, where the burgh corporations were more narrowly closed than in England, and there was a strong and united middle class reform movement. Two Acts were passed in 1833, creating a system of town councils elected on the basis of the £10 franchise.

In England, the reform was more controversial and the process much more prolonged. A Royal Commission was set up in the summer of 1833 in order that the changes could be justified on the basis of removal of existing abuses. This commission was dominated by radicals and, pre-judging the situation rather than embarking on an objective examination, duly reported a picture of inadequacy at best, and widespread corruption.

By this time, the Grey government had fallen, as a result of differences within the ruling coalition over Ireland, where the threat of a violent rising continued. On Grey's resignation in July 1834, Lord Melbourne became Prime Minister, but was unable to form an effective government. In December, William IV dismissed him and his ministers and installed Sir Robert Peel at the head of a Tory ministry. By this time, the proportion of courtiers and office-holders in the Commons was not enough to keep a government in power, and although the Tories considerably increased their representation at the election called in January 1835, the Peel government lasted only until May, when the king again sent for Melbourne. However, it was in this interim period between two Whig ministries that the Municipal Corporations Bill, introduced by the Peel government, went through the Commons.

As in the case of Catholic emancipation in 1829, Peel accepted the inevitability of change in local government, but once again, a government measure came close to foundering in the Lords, so that the Bill was extensively amended and became more modest than originally intended. Although the local franchise was extended to all male householders who paid rates, this did not in practice extend the franchise to the working classes, since few working class householders paid rates. Most rented their accommodation, the landlord taking responsibility for the rates and the tenant meeting the cost through his rent. Property qualifications were imposed for councillors themselves, who were to be subject to election every three years. Borough magistrates, instead of being chosen from within the corporations as previously, would now be nominated by the Crown.

Structurally too, the 1835 Act was limited. It imposed direct elections on the existing 178 borough corporations, making them accountable to their ratepayers, but the great majority of the specific-issue bodies were unaffected, so that the existing piecemeal system of local government remained intact. However, the Act created a procedure by which the new towns could become incorporated and so gain corporations on the new model. Perhaps most significantly in the long term, the Act required corporations to set up police forces on the model of the Metropolitan Police and to be paid from rates.

CHAPTER 20

AN INCREASING ROLE FOR GOVERNMENT

20.1   INTRODUCTION

The changes introduced in 1832 were the beginning of a process, not finally completed until 1928, whereby the franchise was extended to all adults of both sexes, and Parliament and government gradually became more representative of the popular will and the concerns of the public as a whole. At the same time, a social conscience which had strong religious foundations and a desire for greater efficiency, led to the expansion of the work of government for the first time into areas which are now regarded as central, including health, education and housing. However, early legislation was limited in scope for a number of reasons, not least that the mood of the day was largely against compulsion, so that the new powers granted to public bodies tended to be enabling only, and compromise was often necessary to appease vested interests in order to get the legislation through Parliament. Legislation was in any case piecemeal, since Bills were introduced in Parliament to deal with specific concerns, and it was not until later that comprehensive packages became common. The mine and factory legislation of the 1830s and 1840s provides a convenient example.

20.2   EARLY STEPS IN SOCIAL REFORM

There were two prime movers for industrial legislation. One was Robert Owen, a self-made Scottish industrialist turned social reformer who set out to demonstrate that improved working and living conditions brought advantage to factory owners as well as their workers. Owen's model cotton mill and workers' housing project at New Lanark, near Glasgow, in the early 1820s attracted few imitators, and he turned to encouraging industrial workers to help themselves via the formation of trade unions. The second was Anthony Ashley Cooper, 7th Earl of Shaftesbury from 1851 and previously a Tory MP for Dorset. His inspiration for industrial reform came from religiously-based humanitarianism and old-fashioned aristocratic paternalism.

Shaftesbury's earliest work concerned 'climbing boys' – employed to clean chimneys from inside, and often no more than seven or eight years old so as to be small enough for the work. This dangerous and frequently fatal trade was condemned by Charles Kingsley in his novel *The Water Babies*, and Shaftesbury led a successful parliamentary campaign to prohibit it before turning his attention to the employment of children in mines and factories. The evangelical Christianity of the time had a strong sentimental flavour and Shaftesbury's work on behalf of children attracted a great deal of support, though attempts to improve the position of all workers foundered repeatedly on the hostility of vested interests and an emerging philosophy of the free market as the means to improve living and working conditions.

Though the legislation which reached the statute book was of great value to those it did protect, some represented essentially a gesture to the social conscience of the day. In 1842, Shaftesbury secured the passage of a Coal Mines Act prohibiting the employment of women, girls, and boys under 10 underground. However, according to the 1841 census, women and girls constituted only some 2% of those employed underground. The first factory legislation also affected only women and children, leaving the working conditions of adult males virtually unchanged, in part because of the compromises required to get the legislation through both Houses.

In any event, mine and factory legislation dealt only with mines and factories. Though industry employed increasing numbers of people, throughout the 19th century, very large groups continued to be employed in agriculture and, in particular, domestic service. Their working lives were to remain unregulated, except for the introduction of a minimum agricultural wage and legislation to give some security of tenure to agricultural workers with tied accommodation. The first comprehensive piece of health and safety legislation, covering all forms of workplace, did not come into effect until 1976, limits on working hours intended to apply generally only in 1999, and then as the result of a European Community directive.

Education was now emerging for the first time as an area of governmental activity, on the basis that the state ought to oversee the rearing of workers' children in religion and industry. Hitherto, schools had been created in a haphazard fashion, mainly under the auspices of the churches and local charitable organisations. More recently, the educational activities of the Church of England and the non-conformists had become focused on two agencies, each of which founded and ran elementary schools throughout England, the National Society for the Anglican church and the British and Foreign Society for the non-conformists. In 1833, the Grey government began the practice of paying a modest annual grant to each of these societies. This very rapidly became a major bone of contention, and education became the main battleground between the Anglican and non-conformist churches. This conflict carried over into secular politics, since the Tories remained upholders of the Anglican church and the Whigs derived a significant proportion of their support from non-conformists. At the same time, pressure began to grow for a state system of education along secular lines.

In 1839, Lord Melbourne's government proposed to equalise the grants paid to the two societies, to make grants available to other schools, including Catholic schools, to create non-denominational schools for teacher training and to place state participation in education under the supervision of a committee of the Privy Council, composed entirely of laymen. Though this was intended as a compromise that would satisfy both the main religious groups, there were three novel features which infuriated the Anglican establishment: equality of treatment for non-conformity, greater state control and the first movements towards secular education. Faced with protests from outside Parliament and the loss of its shaky majority, the government dropped the most contentious proposals. In 1843, the Peel government which replaced Melbourne's was forced by a combination of non-conformist and Catholic opinion to drop a Factory Education Bill that included compulsory school for child factory workers under the auspices of the Anglican church. These successive confrontations over education demonstrated only too clearly that religion remained a most powerful force in the politics of the day and that an insecure government could potentially be brought down by religiously-inspired opposition.

Overall, the changes made in this period were valuable and ground-breaking in that, for the first time and however imperfectly, a government took upon itself responsibility for the well being of the entire populace, in addition to the interests of the Crown and the control, where necessary, of elements hostile to the status quo. That innovations in all three spheres of change – governmental, religious and social – were limited and did little to improve the lives of large segments of the British population goes far to explain the popular restiveness which characterises the late 1830s and much of the 1840s, and found expression in the movement for more extensive governmental reform known as Chartism, and in the beginnings of what was to become an effective trade union movement.

20.3   CHANGE IN POLITICAL PRACTICE

It is also in this period that we see the House of Lords for the first time acting in a concerted fashion against the policy of the government of the day. Hitherto, the Lords had on occasions blocked specific legislation passed by the Commons, in particular, Bills for Catholic emancipation, but had not generally been hostile to the policies of a government in power, taking the view that they should not oppose the actions of ministers who had the king's confidence and acted on his behalf.[1] From 1831, with distance between monarch and ministers becoming apparent,[2] we see the rejection or emasculation of a number of pieces of government legislation by vested interests making use of their strength in the Upper House. This would re-emerge with full force in the confrontation between the House of Lords and the Liberal government of 1909–11.

This hostility from vested interests, most directly expressed in the House of Lords, is a reason why Grey's government fell in 1834 and its successors failed to replicate its zeal for change and modernisation. For some years thereafter, neither party had sufficient strength to be able to govern without some degree of compromise and co-operation with different elements in their own ranks, if not with the opposition.

It is to the same period that Bogdanor dates the beginning of the final triumph of party over factionalism. With the expansion of the franchise and the abolition of boroughs controlled by a single landowner or small group of landowners, or by closed corporations, party replaced interest as a source of power, and ideology replaced patronage as the tie between ministers and members, and between members themselves. Further, the two parties had to create policy and ideology which would appeal to voters, something first seen in Peel's *Tamworth Manifesto* to the Tories of 1834, and had to develop party organisation and party discipline. Traditionally, the ability of a government to remain in power depended on the ability of the Prime Minister to hold the support of the monarch. By the 1830s, it became necessary to have the support of the Commons. Though William IV dismissed Melbourne in 1834 and sent for Peel, the latter, knowing he could not command a majority in the Commons, accepted office with reluctance and on the basis that a dissolution and general election would follow.

The events of the early months of 1835, after Peel failed to gain a majority at the election, demonstrated that a ministry could not remain in power if it lacked the ability to carry a majority of the Commons, for all that Peel continued to enjoy the full confidence of the king. The concurrent growth of party meant that the sovereign ceased to have any alternative to his ministers for the time being, short of precipitating a general election by a dissolution of Parliament, something which might very easily backfire by giving a clear majority to the 'wrong' party. He could no longer turn to an

---

1   N Gash, *Aristocracy and People, England 1815–1865*, 1979, Arnold, pp 171–72.
2   See above, pp 323–26.

alternative faction. In May 1835, following Peel's resignation, William IV had to recall Melbourne, for all that he had previously declared that he could have no confidence in a Whig Prime Minister.

Therefore, the monarch increasingly had no option but to accept the advice of his ministers for the time being, and use such powers as he retained in order to give effect to the policies of those ministers. December 1834 therefore stands as the last occasion on which a monarch dismissed a government.[3] Nevertheless, when Lord Melbourne and his ministers resigned in May 1839 after their majority shrank to almost nothing on a vote to suspend the constitution of Jamaica, Queen Victoria summoned Peel to form an administration. When Peel insisted that, as a mark of confidence, the queen should dismiss all ladies-in-waiting who were related to Melbourne's ministers, and she refused to do so, Peel concluded that without the monarch's confidence, he could not form an effective administration. The queen then recalled Melbourne, who managed to remain in office until the next election in 1841, which gave Peel a clear majority.[4]

At about the same time, the new terms 'Liberal' and 'Conservative' began to appear as party labels, though initially as a supplement to the traditional Whig and Tory, which did not finally disappear until much later and remained in use for a time as descriptions of particular political stances. The Liberals originally emerged as an alliance of Whigs, radicals and Irish members, the Conservatives as a combination of traditional Toryism and the newer practices of Lord Liverpool's administration, both groupings gradually coalescing into formal parties. However, the new parties remained loose by comparison with those of more recent times. Party discipline in the sense found later did not exist in the 1830s, when MPs still stressed their personal independence and whipping was in its infancy. There was no formal party structure or party leadership. Prime Ministers, even if they commanded a majority in the Commons, therefore had to move carefully in order to maintain the support of 'their' MPs and, as in the controversy over education in 1839, could easily find themselves threatened with the loss of any effective majority.[5]

The new dichotomy did not last long. A decade later, conflicting views within the Conservative ranks over free trade caused Peel's government to collapse and the party to split permanently. For some 20 years thereafter, the rump which continued to call itself Conservative and consider itself the repository of the Conservative tradition was insufficiently strong to command a parliamentary majority, while the 'Peelites' hesitated to amalgamate with the Liberals, though they were usually prepared to co-operate with them. This co-operation formed the basis of several coalitions but on occasions broke down, which meant that more than once, Queen Victoria asked one or other of the leading Liberals to form a government, but he found himself unable to persuade a sufficient number of potential ministers to serve under him. This was the case in 1855 when, following the resignation of Lord Aberdeen, Lord John Russell was unable to form a government, and the queen then sent for his great rival, Lord Palmerston. It has been suggested that the queen knew very well that Russell did not have the necessary support and was merely 'going through the motions' in sending for him, as he had seniority over Palmerston in terms of experience.[6]

3	V Bogdanor, *The Monarchy and the Constitution*, 1995, Clarendon, pp 17–19.
4	*Ibid*, pp 19–20.
5	See Gash, *op cit*, p 164.
6	Gash, *op cit*, p 263.

20.4   CHARTISM

Some historians have seen the 1820s and 1830s as a time of constitutional revolution. However, certain of the developments only appear revolutionary in hindsight, and the 'flagship' change, the Reform Act itself, was much too limited in its scope to satisfy the aspirations of more than a narrow range of opinion. From disappointment with the scope of the reform which had been achieved, combined with resentment over economic distress, came Chartism.

'Chartism' is an umbrella term for a broad and amorphous movement, embracing the traditional lower middle class reformers who were seeking to persuade the establishment of the logic of universal suffrage and all that had been argued for since the 1770s, and the mass protesters who had first emerged in the 1790s. Once again, it was the apparent threat they posed to vested interests, particularly the threat of violent disorder, which engendered hostility among those who held power. Though all their aims but one – that of annual parliaments – were eventually achieved, this occurred on a piecemeal basis and over a lengthy period. The success of what can fairly be termed the first single-issue modern pressure group, the Anti-Corn Law League, in bringing about change in the law showed the way forward in the political sphere. Following the failure of Chartism, working class agitation became channelled into an emerging trade union movement, itself based on organisation within specific occupations, working largely independently of one another.

Perhaps the greatest single working class grievance was the New Poor Law, introduced by the Poor Law Amendment Act 1834. Levels of expenditure on poor relief, funded by a Poor Rate charged on householders, greatly increased from the 1790s. In 1831–32, expenditure on poor relief totalled some £7 million, around 80% of local government spending.[7] This resulted from a combination of many factors, not least the continuing increase in population, which meant that absolute numbers of people in poverty were far greater than they had been in the 18th century. However, opinion of the day, which stressed the benefits of thrift and 'self-help', simplistically attributed poverty among the able-bodied largely to idleness, taking the view that if the lower classes were prepared to support themselves, they could. They were supported in this view by the findings of the Royal Commission on the Poor Law set up by Grey's government in 1832, which condemned the existing system of poor relief, based since the 1790s on the subsidising of wages, as an incentive to idleness. The Commission recommended fundamental changes in order to remove this incentive and to promote efficiency, uniformity and economy in administration.

Under the 1834 Act, responsibility for the administration of the Poor Law was transferred from the parishes to 'Unions' covering a number of parishes and with an elected membership, supervised by a central Poor Law Commission. Each Union was responsible for building and operating a workhouse. Though limited 'outdoor' relief would continue to be available to other groups, henceforth, poor relief was only available to the able-bodied within those workhouses, where conditions were deliberately bleak so as to discourage the seeking of relief. In practice, the system was not applied as uniformly across the country as its creators intended, but it nevertheless inspired the furious hatred of the working classes of the day and became a target of both working class agitation and philanthropic opinion.

---

7   Gash, *op cit*, p 195.

Chartism took its name from the 'People's Charter' produced in 1837 by the London Working Men's Association, a long-established reformist body, and accepted in 1838 as the campaigning agenda for a range of radical, trade union and anti-Poor Law organisations. The Charter set out 'Six Points', all of which were familiar aims of reformers since the 1770s:

(1) universal male suffrage ('manhood suffrage');

(2) annual parliaments;

(3) secret ballots;

(4) equal electoral districts;

(5) abolition of property qualifications for MPs;

(6) payment of MPs, to make it possible for those without private means to enter Parliament.

A petition was drawn up, calling for the Six Points to be embodied in a new Reform Bill, and was submitted to Parliament in 1837. Though there was nothing new about the aims of the Chartists, what was unprecedented was that Chartism became an umbrella for a very wide range of aspirations among the working classes and the lower echelons of the middle classes, and brought a new co-ordination of activity between a range of campaigning bodies. Chartism seems to have found its appeal in disillusionment over the effects of the 1832 Act (which seemed in reality to have changed nothing), economic distress and resentment over the New Poor Law. A further cause of resentment was the Corn Law, twice modified since 1815 but still very much favouring the agricultural interest and fostering increased food prices in times of scarcity. The gaining of parliamentary representation for non-enfranchised groups was seen not only as an end in itself on ideological grounds, but as the means to the resolution of the economic and social problems of those groups by giving them direct representation in Parliament. If the Six Points could be achieved, government in the interests of the working classes must follow.

1837 saw the beginnings of a recession which was to be the worst of the century on the British mainland, and lasted until 1843 and later. The general election which followed the death of William IV, the last to be prompted by the demise of the Crown, saw a reduction in the small Whig majority which had brought Lord Melbourne to power two years earlier, and Melbourne's government concluded that further parliamentary reform would alienate the existing electorate. When three radical demands – secret ballots, triennial parliaments and extension of the franchise – were put to the Commons at the end of the year, they were firmly opposed by the Leader of the House on behalf of the government. Only one was put to the Commons, to be defeated by 509 votes to 20.

To Williams and Ramsden, this crushing defeat demonstrated to the Chartists that the foundations of aristocratic power remained intact and they could hope for little from the government of the day.[8] Further, the social changes of the past century had caused a dislocation of the social order, so that ties of deference and dependence towards landowners and a sense of responsibility from the landowners towards those resident on their land, or between traditional employers and their workers, who for centuries lived under the same roof and ate at the same table, no longer existed on any

8　 G Williams and JA Ramsden, *Ruling Britannia: A Political History of Britain 1688–1988*, 1990, Longman, p 214.

scale. Increasingly, large portions of the working class population were physically separated from the better-off, living in overcrowded conditions in areas of cheap housing thrown up around the new factories, while those who could lived elsewhere. The time was ripe for the emergence of a distinctive working class consciousness and an antagonism towards the moneyed classes.

British society, particularly in England, had always been highly stratified, but now each of the strata was developing sub-strata, as industrial development brought the growth of new trades and professions. This had two consequences. One was a greater and more conspicuous divide between haves and have-nots, as some groups prospered while established industries such as handloom weaving declined sharply, and unemployment increased as a result of mechanisation. Poverty had always existed, but the pre-1834 Poor Law had provided a relatively benevolent safety net for those unemployed or under-employed and their families. Post-1834, this largely ceased, at least for the able-bodied male poor, who were in any case much more numerous as a result of population growth. At the same time, the new middle classes and skilled manual workers were gaining in prosperity and benefiting from increasing access to education, but lacked political influence.

Chartism offered a solution which fitted the concerns of all these various elements. In addition, the Irish who followed Feargus O'Connor, the leading Chartist figurehead and the most prominent radical of the day, saw in Chartism an opportunity to bring about an end to the Union, and non-conformists saw a way to end the continuing Anglican supremacy.

The summer of 1839 saw the first of three petitions to the Commons, but the Chartist leadership failed to give a firm lead to its supporters in order to co-ordinate activity among the various groups, nor did they have any coherent plans to be given effect if the petition was ignored, as it was. Although there were rumours of mass insurrection and calls for a general strike in the form of a 'national holiday', nothing much actually happened, other than the 'Newport Rising' of November, a mysterious affair in which some 20 Chartists were killed. The government avoided playing into Chartist hands by adopting a policy of moderation in relation to the threat to law and order, so that the cause had few martyrs.

A much larger Chartist petition was presented to Parliament in 1842 and included a demand for the abolition of the 1834 Poor Law and the Irish Union. Again, the government took little notice and from then on, the Chartists, though their numbers remained large, were increasingly sidelined as a political force. The aggressive nature of some manifestations of Chartism, including strikes and mob violence in industrial areas, repelled many who might have sympathised with the Chartists' political aims. By no means all the violence which occurred in the summer of 1842 was necessarily Chartist-inspired, as distinct from a more or less spontaneous response to economic distress. However, it coincided in time, and was linked in the minds of many with the speeches and writings of leading Chartists such as O'Connor, and led many members of the middle classes to conclude that such activities only proved that the working classes were not fit to receive the franchise. For others, including many traditional reformist groups who considered the 'household franchise' – extension of the franchise to all adult male householders, so that each household had a parliamentary vote – to be the proper end, the Six Points were, quite simply, too radical.

As in 1839, but on a much larger scale, the government was also able to deal with the threat to law and order in a manner which combined efficiency with moderation, and avoided creating political martyrs. They were aided by the emergence of effective police forces and by the development of railways, which enabled troops to be removed rapidly to trouble spots when necessary.

The final Chartist petition in April 1848 coincided with the outbreak of revolution across Europe, and the apparent threat to property and to the status quo sounded the final death knell of the mass movement for parliamentary reform. The Chartist procession never reached Westminster, being forced back at a barricade erected across Kennington Common by troops and police. Prevented from reaching the Houses of Parliament, the Chartists quietly dispersed.

Chartism was ultimately a failure, though it caused considerable alarm to the government, given the coincidence of large numbers of people, inflammatory political rhetoric, violence and the lurking fear of revolution which had existed since the 1790s. Crucially, perhaps, the Chartists failed to gain support within Parliament and lacked a unified or efficient command structure. The failure of Chartism spelled the end of mass action involving both the middle classes and working classes, who for the remainder of the century and for some time after saw their aspirations as separate and different. That a protest movement, carefully organised and seeking a clear goal, could achieve its objectives was demonstrated at the same time by the success of the middle class campaigners for the repeal of the Corn Laws.

Chartism was as much as anything a victim of its times. In 1841, Lord Melbourne's Whig government was replaced by a Conservative administration headed by Sir Robert Peel. Rather than being interventionist in relation to social problems, the Peelite Tories, like the Thatcherites of 140 years later, followed the leading economic thinkers of their time in believing that an increase in national prosperity would bring a natural end to many of these difficulties, and sought to create conditions in which commerce and industry would flourish. In particular, Peel, initially a supporter of the traditional policy of aiding British producers by means of protective tariffs, was gradually converted for pragmatic reasons to advocacy of their abolition. The first half of the 1840s was a time of economic depression, for the first time affecting industry to a greater extent than agriculture. Measures to reverse this, largely through the abandonment of protectionist duties so as to provide British industry with cheaper raw materials and alleviate the hardships of the poor through lower food prices, occupied the attentions of Peel's government rather than parliamentary reform. The later 1840s saw the Irish famine and, again, government efforts were concentrated on alleviating this crisis.

Finally, for 20 years after Peel's government fell, no ministry had a sufficiently large majority to push through major changes, even had the will been there. In any event, the will was not there. The traditional fears of revolution and of the dangers of power without responsibility continued to be powerful influences on the political establishment of the day. There was a strong current of feeling that although the changes of 1832 had been necessary and proper, they were all that was necessary; further change would only result in destabilisation and weakness.

20.5   FINANCIAL CHANGE UNDER PEEL

The Melbourne government fell finally in 1841 when it was unable to obtain a Commons majority for its financial measures. The ensuing election gave the

Conservatives a majority of some 80 seats, which enabled the government to press ahead with far-reaching financial changes. An income tax had been introduced during the Napoleonic Wars but, since 1816, successive governments mainly relied on tariffs to raise revenue. This proved unsuccessful, so that Peel and his Chancellor of the Exchequer, Henry Goulburn, now re-introduced income tax, the first time it had been imposed in peacetime. This was regarded as a deeply radical, not to say revolutionary step, placing a significant burden of taxation on the better-off, but aroused comparatively little opposition. The rate was set at 7d in the pound in order to produce a budget surplus which would make substantial reductions in tariffs possible, and reductions then followed in import duties on some 750 types of goods.

Inevitably, this policy did not produce an immediate improvement in economic conditions – indeed, the crisis deepened before the situation began to improve. This period saw the second Chartist petition and widespread industrial unrest as employers attempted to impose pay cuts on their workforces.

That the economic depression affected manufacturing far more severely than agriculture was one of the reasons why Peel's government pressed ahead with the repeal of the Corn Laws in 1846. Another was the campaigning of the Anti-Corn Law League and analogous bodies. There had been some association between the anti-Corn Law movement and the Chartists in the early days of Chartism, but the relationship between the two was uneasy.[9] From 1841, the League sought to gain the moral high ground by attracting the support of non-conformist clergy. This gave the League a solid base of support among non-conformists of the lower middle classes, many of whom had been enfranchised in 1832, so that a number of the League's supporters, including its leader, Richard Cobden, were elected to Parliament at the 1841 election. The League thus had the direct influence in the Commons which the Chartists lacked, at a time when a ministry with inherent sympathy for its aims took office.

In subsequent years, Peel's policy moved further towards complete abolition of the Corn Laws, but he faced opposition from the landed interest within his own party, which was ultimately to split the party irreparably. By 1845, tariff reform meant that corn was the only staple item still subject to high levels of protection, and cheap food imports had not brought about the economic disaster forecast by some traditionalist economists, strengthening the Anti-Corn Law League's argument that the Corn Laws existed primarily for the benefit of a minority landed interest rather than the nation as a whole. At the same time, the League refined its organisation, creating regional offices to collect and distribute funds and to distribute literature. It also took full advantage of recent developments; the penny post of 1840 which enabled wider distribution of League literature; the new electoral register for the targeting of voters; and the railways for national speaking tours by League leaders. However, the final nail in the coffin of the Corn Laws was not the activity of the League, but the Irish famine.

20.6   THE IRISH POTATO FAMINE

From the 1830s, the problem of Ireland loomed steadily larger as an issue in British national politics. This period saw the growth of widespread opposition to the Union

---

9   See Gash, *op cit*, p 222.

of 1801, as well as the growth of movements which at first concerned themselves with the remedying of specific grievances, but increasingly sought an end to the Union as it was, generally through Home Rule, but in some cases by complete independence. In 1797, Irish independence had been the aim of a minority of extremists and there was no concerted opposition to the imposition of Union; however, increasingly through the 19th century, the Home Rule campaign became part of the political mainstream.

Catholic emancipation and the 1832 reform had little practical effect in Ireland. The principal bones of contention remained intact, notably the vast economic inequality between Ireland and the British mainland, the disproportionate advantages given to the minority Church of Ireland under the existing constitutional arrangements, and the gulf between rulers and ruled. Melbourne's government depended on support from O'Connell and other Irish Catholic members to remain in power, so that church reform in Ireland assumed enormous political importance, even more so than in England.

The specific issues were tithes, now the subject of a concerted campaign of opposition, and the related matter of the introduction of a power for Parliament to appropriate part of the tithe revenue of the Church of Ireland for other purposes. The two issues were political and constitutional as well as religious, raising the question of the autonomy of the Church and the terms of the Union, which had guaranteed the permanent establishment of the Church. They were more controversial still because the Church of Ireland gained the bulk of its tithe income from non-members, a significant proportion of whom were living at or below subsistence level. The Grey government introduced an Irish Church Act, which streamlined the existing top-heavy structure by abolishing 10 of the 18 bishoprics. However, the inclusion in the Irish Tithes Bill of 1834 of a provision to permit appropriation caused several of Grey's ministers to resign and Grey himself to retire, precipitating the chain of events which led to William IV's dismissal of the government in November.

There was then a relative lull until the 1840s, when Daniel O'Connell took up the anti-Union cause, founding a Repeal Association which rapidly gained large-scale support among the Catholic population and from the Catholic church. This in turn had sufficient influence on the various elements underlying Chartism for a demand for repeal of the Union to be included in the petition of 1842. Peel recognised the dangers of the situation and made attempts to deal with what he saw as the main obstacle to good government over Ireland: poor relations between landlord and tenant, and between the British government and the Catholic middle class. The situation was then irredeemably altered by the famine.

Though Ireland had a flourishing linen industry and an emerging shipbuilding industry in the north, both dominated by Protestants, it was mainly an agricultural country. This produced an increasing disparity with the British mainland. Within Ireland, there was a further sharp disparity between the efficient commercial agriculture which existed in some areas and the subsistence economy holding sway over much of the country. Like the mainland, Ireland had been subject to unprecedented population growth in recent years. The population had doubled in the previous half-century and now stood at more than eight million. Combined with the traditional system of land tenure, this meant that the small plots of land on which many families subsisted were sub-divided to a point where the crops they produced could no longer reliably support those families. There was heavy reliance on potatoes, cheap, nutritious, filling and better adapted to the prevailing climatic conditions than grain. The nature of the economy, with high levels of unemployment and under-employment, meant that large-scale poverty was endemic, particularly among the Catholic majority. It was officially estimated that about 30% of the population were in distress for at least part of the year. Nevertheless, the 1834 Poor Law, which pre-supposed the existence of regular full time employment available to all those prepared to work, had been imposed on Ireland on the same terms as the rest of the United Kingdom.[10]

Peel's government created a commission to investigate the land question and at the same time introduced a package of measures to placate the Catholic church and erode the basis for its supporting O'Connell and his Repealers. This created uproar within Parliament and outside. Despite Catholic emancipation, anti-Catholic feeling was stronger than it had been, partly for political reasons – the aggressive tactics of O'Connell and his supporters – and because of the rapid growth of evangelical Protestantism in the intervening period.

As divisions among the Conservatives deepened when the 1845 budget introduced further tariff reform measures, blight affected a significant proportion of the 1845 potato crop. In England and Scotland, where agriculture was diversified, this brought increased prices and some shortages. In Ireland, where about a third of the crop was lost and where potatoes formed the staple diet of many, it was a catastrophe on a huge scale, the more so as blight is caused by an organism which, in the absence of effective techniques to counter it, remains in the soil. Figures quoted by Williams and Ramsden demonstrate this very clearly. From an estimated 14.862 million tons in 1844, the last 'clean' year, the yield fell to 2.999 million tons in 1846 and 2.046 million tons in 1847. After 1847, the worst effects of the blight began to recede, but the yield of 1849 barely exceeded four million tons.[11]

This natural disaster was completely unexpected. The full effects of the blight took some time to become apparent, but only strengthened agitation for the repeal of the Corn Laws. It was demanded that not only should unrestricted imports of foreign corn be permitted, but that the state should supply corn to the Irish. Peel called for the total repeal of duties on all items necessary to subsistence, including foodstuffs, a demand that split his party and his Cabinet.

A high proportion of Tory MPs represented the landed interest, considering that the Corn Laws were necessary to protect British agriculture from foreign competition and that Peel was surrendering to the agitation of the Anti-Corn Law League, using events in Ireland as a convenient pretext to force through repeal. To his opponents, Peel, once a protectionist, who had previously changed his stance on another issue of fundamental importance to Tories, Catholic emancipation, was also guilty of hypocrisy and determined to follow his own views regardless of those of his party. In any event, they argued, a reduction in the price of bread accruing from the repeal of the Corn Laws would not prevent starvation among the Irish, since those in the most acute distress had no money with which to buy bread.

Peel had been Chief Secretary for Ireland early in his political career and so had a good knowledge of the realities of the Irish economy. In his view, the only way to prevent widespread starvation and disease was large-scale famine relief at the

---

10 Williams and Ramsden, *op cit*, p 223.
11 Williams and Ramsden, *op cit*, p 229.

taxpayers' expense. Complete repeal of the Corn Laws was a necessary part of such a scheme.

Peel managed to secure the phased abolition of the Corn Laws over a three year period, but the Conservatives became hopelessly divided over the issue and, on Peel's resignation in June 1846, they were replaced by a Liberal ministry under Lord John Russell, which now faced the enormous burden of dealing with the effects of the famine. Peel had already begun a programme of relief with the purchasing of £100,000 worth of maize from America and the opening of food depots, but this was quite insufficient to deal with the consequences of the almost complete failure of the 1846 potato crop.

The Russell government accepted that economic conditions in Ireland were not the same as in England, and that large-scale under-employment presented a unique difficulty. It created a programme of labour-intensive public works, particularly the building of roads, so that the supplies which were beginning to be imported could be more efficiently transported and the destitute could earn sufficient money to feed themselves. This was financed by the Treasury, but, necessarily, the public works took time to be set up, and in the free market of the day, the acute scarcity of food meant a huge rise in prices. In 1847, the government reluctantly accepted the necessity of outdoor relief and started to provide soup kitchens, but, again, the policy took time to be put into effect. In any case, the mechanisms which existed were inadequate to cope with the unprecedented scale of need.

Of the 8 million Irish living in 1845, about a million died in the following five years from the direct effects of the famine. A further million emigrated before 1852 and high rates of emigration continued for the rest of the century. Combined with a sharp reduction in the birth rate, as healthy young adults formed the majority of emigrants, this meant that the population fell by almost half in the period up to 1914, to 5.5 million in 1871 and to 4.5 million in 1901.

In purely economic terms, the long term effects of the famine were largely beneficial. The fall in population meant that small landholdings were consolidated, there was less pressure to produce basic foodstuffs and labour was more expensive, so that emphasis shifted from production of potatoes and grain to livestock, particularly dairying. A degree of impetus was given to this change by unprecedented legislation in 1848 and 1849 to facilitate the sale of landed estates to purchasers prepared to work them more efficiently than their existing owners. The second of two Acts effectively created a system of compulsory sale by establishing a court of three salaried commissioners, with powers to authorise the sale of Irish estates and to divide the proceeds on an equitable basis among those with interests in the property.[12]

The political effects were, however, serious and long lasting. Both in Ireland and among emigrants, there developed a lasting resentment against the British government for the failure to deal effectively with the famine and a potent national and international myth that this was the result of deliberate policy, which remains today and motivates support for the IRA and other terrorist organisations.

---

12   See N McCord, *British History 1815–1906*, 1991, OUP, p 183.

20.7   CHANGE AND PROGRESS 1846–67

Peel's government was the last ministry to hold an overall Commons majority for some 20 years. The Conservatives divided permanently over the repeal of the Corn Laws. The 'protectionist' majority, some 240 MPs, retained the party label under the leadership first of the Earl of Derby and later of Benjamin Disraeli, who emerged as their most prominent figure after Peel's death in 1850. The 'Peelite' minority of about 120 worked in somewhat uneasy co-operation with the Liberals up to 1865, but did not merge with them until that year.

Though none of the governments of this period had the same enthusiasm for change and modernisation as those of Grey or Peel, nonetheless, there was a continued momentum in favour of social legislation, notably in education and public health, and more generally in giving increased powers to local authorities to deal with problems of the day. As yet, the prevailing philosophy was in favour of encouraging self-reliance and voluntary effort. State intervention was resorted to only where this proved inadequate or left serious gaps in coverage. Public health and education were areas in which a religiously-inspired sense of responsibility for the less fortunate was a major political influence, along with a rising national pride among the middle classes that included a general desire for 'improvement' both for themselves and for the 'deserving' among the lower classes. Much was achieved by voluntary fund-raising in the founding and operating of hospitals and dispensaries.[13] The 'improving' strain in the Victorian mindset was also greatly concerned with raising standards of morality, which it saw as strongly linked with living conditions. Wholeness in living conditions would create a new wholesomeness in popular morals.

Equally, and separately from the work of the two main religious societies in founding and running schools, there was much activity in creating learned societies at local and national level, a development which had begun earlier in the century, adult educational facilities and subscription libraries. Political pragmatism played an important role in state intervention. Elementary education, well-grounded in the Scriptures and emphasising the importance of hard work and obedience, was seen as a force for curbing the dangerous propensities of the working classes, as well as providing the country's industries with a suitably qualified and literate workforce. Equally, better living conditions in the towns not only benefited the residents generally, but removed or limited some of the grievances which gave rise to disorder.

The necessity of the government's playing a role in the sphere of public health and sanitation was first officially recognised by the Poor Law Commission, created under the 1834 Poor Law. The 1832 Royal Commission on the Poor Law was the first large-scale example of what was to become the common practice of the Victorian era of basing change on the findings of an official commission of inquiry. The Poor Law Commission's *Report into the Sanitary Condition of the Labouring Population*, published in 1842, identified the needs of the new towns at their most elementary: clean water and proper sewage facilities. At the same time, the system of civil registration of deaths introduced in 1837 was beginning to produce reasonably reliable statistics on numbers and causes of deaths, and demonstrating the very high incidence in the new towns of diseases such as cholera and typhoid, which were then believed to be caused by

---

13 *Ibid*, pp 242–43.

atmospheric contagion and general lack of cleanliness.[14] A Public Health Act of 1848 created a central Board of Health and authorised each borough authority to appoint a Medical Officer of Health. The Board of Health was given enabling powers to create local Boards of Health at the request of 10% of the ratepayers of the boroughs concerned, and compulsory powers in boroughs where the annual death rate exceeded 23 per 1,000. Such Boards were elected by ratepayers and had powers to regulate water supply, sewage and street paving, and to levy rates for those purposes.

The legislation gave the local Boards enabling powers only, but considerable use was made of its provisions. By 1865, Gash notes, no fewer than 570 local authorities had made use of powers under the 1848 Act or the more general 1858 Act, encouraged by a system by which central government made loans available for public health and sanitation purposes, a total of some £10 million being lent in the period 1848–71.[15] Compulsion was occasionally used where deemed appropriate, though not necessarily where it was most needed. Smallpox had been a major scourge of the 18th century, when it is estimated to have caused about one-sixth of all deaths in Britain. An effective and safe means of vaccination had become available towards the end of the century, and an Act of 1840 aimed to encourage voluntary vaccination. This, however, had little effect, quite possibly because there was already a very high take-up of vaccination, and an Act of 1853 imposed a system of compulsory vaccination of infants, with fines for non-compliance. This lasted in various forms until after the Second World War, although by 1850, smallpox caused no more than 1–2% of deaths.

Although the national Board of Health was abolished in 1858, most of its powers were transferred to the Privy Council Office, and the new Chief Medical Officer of Health, Dr John Simon, set in train a series of investigations and reports into specific diseases which he and his staff were able to use to persuade local authorities of the need for improvement and the idea of public health as a duty of society.

Steps were also taken to improve standards in medicine, nursing and midwifery, which were entirely unregulated prior to this period. In medicine, there was traditionally a sharp division between physicians, generally university graduates, and surgeons, who received their training by apprenticeships. In addition, there were apothecaries, in some ways analogous to the modern general practitioner, who had their own professional body and system of training. There were also a large number of 'quacks' without formal training, peddling remedies which ranged from the efficacious through the merely ineffective to the downright dangerous. This unsatisfactory situation began to be resolved, after a select committee investigation, by statutory controls on pharmacists from 1852 and the creation of a statutory Medical Register in 1858, along with a General Medical Council with powers of regulation and professional discipline. This resulted in the establishment for the first time of minimum standards of entry to the medical profession, together with a rigorous system of training. At the same time, the professional bodies – the Royal College of

---

14 At this time, it was not fully understood that diseases were caused and spread by microbes rather than directly by dirt or 'bad air', and rival theories held sway until the 1880s, when the microbiologist Robert Koch isolated the bacteria which caused a number of specific diseases. For example, it was commonly held that cholera, of which there were a number of epidemics in Britain in the 1840s, was spread by an invisible cloud passing at night some two feet above the ground, hence the frequency with which people went to bed apparently healthy and woke stricken with the disease.

15 Gash, *op cit*, pp 341–43.

Physicians and the Royal College of Surgeons – began to co-operate to a much greater extent than they had previously and adopted a more pro-active role in setting and maintaining standards. As new specialist areas of medicine were created, additional professional bodies emerged to regulate them.[16]

The 1850s and 1860s were decades of considerable activity in relation to 'nuisance removal', which was concerned in particular with sewage and refuse from trades such as tanning, and a number of Acts were passed to deal with specific areas of concern and to permit the creation of nuisance authorities. A Sewage Utilisation Act created a national network of sewage authorities in 1865, and marked a turning point in that it applied uniformly across the United Kingdom and to rural as well as urban areas.

Legislation specifically concerned with housing was instituted in 1851 with two Acts to regulate common lodging houses, considered by respectable Victorian society to be cesspools of filth and immorality, and to permit borough authorities to set up common lodging houses on their own initiative. That the expanding population created difficulties over disposal of the dead was recognised by a series of Burial Acts to authorise the provision of municipal cemeteries and to permit the cremation of human remains.

20.8   GOVERNMENTAL CHANGE

A traditional area of concern to modernisers was the efficiency of national administration. Although a considerable number of offices had been abolished since the 1770s in successive drives against wastage and opportunities for corruption, the Civil Service remained essentially unchanged. One of the innovations made by Lord Aberdeen's coalition government, which held office from 1852 until 1855, was the establishment of the Northcote-Trevelyan Committee to investigate the civil service. Its proposals, published in 1855, were designed to:

(a) lessen the cost and increase the effectiveness of government;

(b) separate higher administrative work from clerical work;

(c) lessen aristocratic control of the civil service by reducing patronage;

(d) introduce open competition for entry and promotion by merit.[17]

These recommendations were not brought fully into effect until 1870, during Gladstone's first ministry, but from then on, entry into the civil service was based on competitive examination and progress within the service was then to be based on merit rather than on patronage. In the intervening period, each minister had power to nominate individuals to posts in the appropriate government department, and the newly-created Civil Service Commission conducted an examination to confirm

---

16   Though in most cases there was no state intervention, this was an era when a great number of professional bodies were founded, not least because of disputes between different groups. For example, an Institute of Civil Engineers was founded early in the century for civilian engineers, as distinct from the military engineers of the Royal Engineers. This later refused to accept as members those early railway pioneers whose expertise was with machinery rather than roads, canals, bridges and railway track, and, headed by George and Robert Stephenson, they formed themselves into a separate Institution of Mechanical Engineers in 1847. Further technical developments and professional disputes spawned an Institute of Marine Engineers and Electrical Engineers in the 1870s.

17   D Read, *England 1868–1914: The Age of Urban Democracy*, 1979, Longman, pp 134–35.

suitability. However, the standard of examinations in this period was a matter for the departments themselves and there was no requirement for them to be particularly demanding; Professor Norman McCord notes that one department was content to set an examination of a standard only a little higher than that expected of 14 year old boys of poor education.[18] Even after 1870, there was no attempt to broaden the social composition of the Civil Service, whose members continued to be drawn from the upper and upper-middle classes, as they alone had the necessary education.

The extension of the activities of government from the early 1830s brought the creation of new governmental bodies such as the Poor Law Commission, increases in government spending to £70 million by 1860 and £81 million by 1880, and the creation of new parliamentary machinery to scrutinise that spending. A House of Commons Public Accounts Committee was created in 1861 and was made into a permanent body the following year. The Exchequer and Audit Department Act gave the Comptroller and Auditor-General tenure of office which was fully protected from government interference and which required him to draw the attention of the Commons to shortcomings in official accounts. At the same time, the Treasury embarked on an internal efficiency drive and greatly strengthened its procedures for examining and authorising the spending of the various government departments. By 1887–88, FW Maitland felt able to declare, somewhat sweepingly, in the lectures which form the basis for his book that 'nothing whatever can be done which in any way involves the expenditure of public money without the consent of the Treasury'.[19]

The poor performance of the Armed Services during the Crimean War led to attempts to rationalise the chaotic system of army administration which, in the usual British fashion, had developed in haphazard fashion and remained fossilised. Before changes made by Palmerston's government in 1855, the cavalry and infantry came under the authority of the Commander-in-Chief, but artillery, fortifications and barracks came under a separate Master-General of the Ordnance. Supply and transport were dealt with by the Treasury. The militia, much less important than in the days before a standing army, but retaining a significant home defence role, was the responsibility of the Home Office. At Cabinet level, the Secretary of State for War had divided loyalties, since his portfolio also included the colonies. From 1855, there was a full time Secretary of State for War and responsibility for most military matters became vested in the Commander-in-Chief and a unified War Office.

20.9   LAW AND ORDER

Though the boroughs had been required to create police forces by the Municipal Corporations Act 1835, this brought little short term benefit, since criminals tended to concentrate their activities in rural areas where the traditional parish constables represented the only concession to the maintenance of law and order. A Rural Police Act of 1839 attempted to remedy the situation, but merely enabled county magistrates to set up police forces. By 1853, only 22 counties, barely half the total, had actually set up police forces, and the efficiency of these and the borough forces – of which there were over 200 – was very variable. A Police Act in 1856 therefore required the

---

18   McCord, *op cit*, p 293.
19   FW Maitland, *The Constitutional History of England*, 1908, CUP, p 409.

establishment of a police force on the model of the original Metropolitan Police in every county in England and Wales, and sought to balance central and local control and ensure efficiency by providing for central grants to forces towards the cost of pay and uniforms, provided standards enforced by Home Office inspectors were met.

In this period, Britain was gradually becoming a more orderly society in any case, for reasons which include the greater influence of the churches, increased access to education and improved living conditions. After the 1840s, large-scale mob violence was increasingly a rarity. Gash notes that traditional entertainments of a brutal kind, such as prize-fighting, cock-fighting and bull-baiting, gradually became less popular, though even in the 1840s, the new railway companies were providing cheap excursion fares to executions and 100,000 people are said to have observed the hanging of a particularly notorious murderer in Liverpool in 1849. Admittedly, executions were acquiring a novelty value because of their rarity. Changes in criminal justice reduced the number of capital crimes to four by 1841. Thereafter, it was in practice only murderers who were hanged, since cases of treason, piracy and arson in royal dockyards were rare. In 1846, there were six executions; in 1849, 15.

CHAPTER 21

THE LATER 19TH CENTURY

21.1   INTRODUCTION

Though there was a continuing increase in government involvement in different areas of national life in the 20 years of coalition governments, the next major period of change began in the late 1860s. This involved a second extension of the franchise in 1867 and the interventionist activity of Gladstone's first ministry of 1868–74.

21.2   THE SECOND REFORM ACT

As in 1832, the 1867 reform came about because the government of the day considered it appropriate, rather than as a direct consequence of popular agitation. Indeed, since the final failure of Chartism in 1848, parliamentary reform had ceased to be a particularly contentious issue. The energies of working class radicals were largely diverted into trade union activity, and a surge of anti-aristocratic feeling and hostility to the current political system resulting from the early military failures of the Crimean War of 1854–56 had spent itself before the end of the decade.

Among the disparate threads making up mid-19th century Liberalism was support for the household franchise, most prominently expressed by Lord John Russell. At the same time, the more populist Liberals were recognising that the extension of the franchise was likely to tip the balance of the national vote in their favour, as had occurred in 1832. The fear of the working class mob was also receding as the violent disturbances of the early 1840s and before faded from the national memory, and the religiously-inspired temperance movement gained a strong hold among the upper levels of the working class, along with a pattern of recreation and 'respectability' associated with church and chapel-going. A major source of objection to the widening of the franchise was therefore losing its strength.

The developing political mood in favour of a broader franchise was recognised by the Conservatives during their brief period in office in 1858–59. A Bill was introduced which sought to widen the franchise while promoting their party interests by proposing what the veteran radical John Bright termed 'fancy franchises', giving the vote to groups defined by occupation and educational qualifications – clergy, doctors, schoolmasters, university graduates and government pensioners – together with persons holding government stocks or £60 in savings. Given that many members of these groups must already have qualified for the vote, it is unlikely that the Bill would have had much effect in practice, more particularly as 40s freeholders living in boroughs would have been excluded for the first time from the county vote. In any case, it was defeated by an alliance of members who thought it went too far and others who rejected it as not going far enough.

However, by a change in 1858 which passed almost unnoticed at the time, for all that it formed one of the Chartist Six Points, the property qualification for MPs was abolished. This made it possible, in theory, for any man to stand for Parliament and to sit if elected, but until a parliamentary salary was introduced in 1905, this change had little practical effect, since only those who had sufficient income from other sources, coupled with sufficient time to devote to parliamentary activity, were in a position to seek election.[1]

Though popular interest in the matter had faded, neatly symbolised by a *Punch* cartoon of March 1859 showing the two party leaders in the Commons, Russell and Disraeli, together with Bright, attempting to prod a sleeping British lion into activity with goads marked 'Reform', there was a general mood on both sides of the Commons in favour of some extension of the franchise. In particular, Gladstone, who with his fellow Peelites had now joined the Liberals, was a firm supporter of an extension to include the skilled working classes, on the basis of their sober lifestyle and contribution towards national prosperity. The Conservatives, for their part, had been largely excluded from government for the past 20 years and no longer had much attachment to the existing system. However, there was a lack of overall agreement on the form a new reform should take.

Movement came finally in 1866, when Gladstone, Leader of the Commons under Russell, introduced a Bill reducing the borough qualification from £10 to £7, and that for tenants-at-will in counties from £50 in rent to £14. Two new categories covered men who were not householders but either lived in expensive lodgings – generally unmarried professional men – or had at least £50 in a savings bank. The Russell Cabinet estimated that the scheme would create some 400,000 additional voters. In addition, there would be some re-distribution of seats. The Liberals were divided, Gladstone's attempts to garner support from the Conservatives failed and the Russell government fell.

Ironically after the recent apathy, the failure of the 1866 Bill provoked a revival of popular agitation for extension of the franchise, with rioting in Hyde Park and a Reform League orchestrating a campaign of public meetings and petitions. With the Liberals divided, the new Conservative minority government, once more led by Lord Derby, saw an opportunity to gain the political advantage by introducing their own reform Bill. At this point, initiative passed to the calculating and tactically astute Benjamin Disraeli, who persuaded Derby that the party interest would best be served by a Bill creating a household franchise at a level of property values calculated to include the skilled manual workers. Disraeli was confident of his ability to persuade the Conservatives to support a Bill in these terms – after 20 years largely in opposition, the Conservatives were ahead of the Liberals in fostering party loyalties – and he was prepared to accept amendments from the more radical elements among the Liberals provided the overall Bill was carried.

Disraeli's strategy was successful and the Bill duly became law as the Representation of the People Act 1867. It was drawn largely on the same terms as the abortive Liberal Bill, but introduced a significant working class element into the electorate for the first time by making all householders liable for their own rates. This meant that about half a million persons who met the new £7 qualification but would have been excluded from the franchise as non-ratepayers were added to the electorate.[2] Effectively, the 1867 Act introduced a household franchise in England and Wales and, with parallel Acts covering Scotland and Ireland, increased the size of the

---

1   It was recognised that MPs, other than 'gentlemen of independent means', had occupations independently of their sitting in Parliament, and the working hours of Parliament, so much criticised today, reflect this.

2   N McCord, *British History 1815–1906*, 1991, OUP, pp 258–59.

electorate to some 2.5 million, about one-third of all adult males in Great Britain, though a smaller proportion in Ireland. McCord notes that the effect of the Act was greatest in the new towns: in Leeds, the electorate increased fourfold and in Blackburn fivefold. There was a clear shift in the social composition of the urban electorate in favour of the working class, although the effect was less marked in the counties.[3] In addition, there was a new allocation of seats, the larger cities such as Birmingham being given a third member. Finally, the traditional dissolution of Parliament on the demise of the Crown was abolished.

Some elements of the 1867 Act were intended to favour the Conservatives, but, nevertheless, the Liberals achieved power in the election of December 1868 with the overall majority which enabled Gladstone to adopt a progressive agenda, although limits were placed on the scope of change by the need to preserve party unity. 1868 is also considered by a number of historians as marking a further significant constitutional change. From the 1830s, a succession of Prime Ministers had accepted that their governments could not survive in office without the support of a majority of the Commons, but had not resigned after losing a general election; rather, they had waited to lose a vote in Parliament. In 1868, Disraeli, who succeeded Derby as Prime Minister earlier in the year, resigned immediately the election result became known and advised Queen Victoria to send for Gladstone.

21.3   CHANGE UNDER GLADSTONE

Gladstone's first ministry was responsible for several important pieces of legislation in education, the Armed Services and the judicial system. None of it was unprecedented; in each of these spheres, there had been previous government intervention to deal with specific problems, but each was greater in its scale than any which had occurred previously. Williams and Ramsden note that not only had the strength of evangelical Protestantism, both Anglican and non-conformist, continued to develop since the 1840s, but by the late 1860s, those who had become enthusiastic converts as young men were reaching senior positions.[4] The evangelical social conscience was therefore a powerful influence on the actions of government.

21.3.1 The School Boards

The Education Act 1870 broke new ground by creating the first state-funded and state-run elementary schools. The voluntary bodies received government grants from 1833 and state influence over them had gradually been extended over the intervening period, first by linking levels of grant to school attendance, and then from the 1860s by 'payment by results', whereby payment of a portion of the grant was conditional on a set proportion of pupils reaching the prescribed standards in tests carried out annually by inspectors appointed by the Privy Council Committee on Education.

The 1870 Act created a procedure under which a School Board could be elected by ratepayers in a locality in defined circumstances involving the inability of the voluntary bodies to provide adequate school provision. Such a School Board – yet

3   *Ibid*, pp 259–60.
4   G Williams and JA Ramsden, *Ruling Britannia: A Political History of Britain 1688–1988*, 1990, Longman, p 274.

another of the specific issue bodies created by Victorian statutes – had power to levy a rate to finance the building and operating of its own schools. Although the Act was intended only as a means of supplementing the activity of the voluntary bodies, in practice, the School Boards were responsible for a steadily increasing proportion of new schools after 1870, since their powers to levy rates gave them access to far greater funds than the religious societies.

21.3.2 The army

In 1861, as part of attempts to curb excessive government spending, the Commons demanded a reduction in military garrisons overseas, resolving in a significant debate that self-governing colonies ought to defend themselves. Further, the Indian Mutiny of 1857–58 and the Maori Wars in New Zealand had demonstrated all too clearly the inefficiency of the prevailing system in defending Britain's overseas possessions. Garrisons were too thinly spread to be effective in nipping insurrections in the bud and there had been much delay in concentrating troops in sufficient numbers to put down rebellion. The Indian Mutiny, indeed, had shown the appalling vulnerability of small, isolated (and complacent) garrisons to unrest among an armed and organised populace.[5] Improvements in transport – railways, the steamship, the opening of the Suez Canal in 1869 – and in communications, in particular the electric telegraph, meant that it was becoming more efficient to concentrate troops in a smaller number of outposts. Given that in the 1860s, self-governing colonies were only just beginning to emerge – Canada was the first, in 1867 – and there was no particular governmental will on the issue, little was done to change existing practices until the Liberals came to power in 1868, but over the next decade, British troops were largely withdrawn from Canada, Australia and New Zealand, which now had their own small regular armies, supplemented by much larger militias.

A major symbolic change came in 1870, when Gladstone's Secretary of State for War, Edward Cardwell, obtained the abolition of commissioning by purchase, in the teeth of such opposition in Parliament that a Bill dealing with the matter had to be dropped and the change made by invoking prerogative powers. The change was largely symbolic for two reasons. First, by no means all commissions had been subject to purchase. Second, the change, like the introduction of competitive examinations for the Civil Service, made little difference to the social composition of the officer corps, since rates of pay remained low and private incomes were in practice required in the majority of regiments. Nevertheless, 1870 marked the beginning of a gradual move towards greater professionalism. Cardwell also introduced short-service enlistment for other ranks, who thenceforth could elect to serve for as little as six years, rather than for life, which not only encouraged enlistment, but also allowed the building-up of a trained reserve.[6]

---

5   The insurrection began among Indian troops serving in the East India Company's Bengal Army, when the Meerut garrison rose on 10 May 1857 and massacred their British officers and their families. Similar risings followed elsewhere over the next few weeks and left the mutineers, joined by some of the Indian princes, in control of much of northern India. The suppression of the Mutiny took well over a year and required the despatch of large numbers of troops from Britain.

6   Even so, soldiering continued to lack appeal to the respectable working classes. When William Robertson, son of a Lincolnshire tailor, joined the 16th Lancers in 1877, his mother tearfully declared that she would sooner see him dead than in a red coat. Robertson, however, was an early beneficiary of the Cardwell reforms, becoming the only man ever to rise from Private to Field Marshal through every rank in between.

21.3.3 The judicial system

The most far-reaching change introduced by Gladstone's first ministry was the rationalisation of the judicial system given effect by the Judicature Acts 1873–75. By the 19th century, there was a relatively coherent system of criminal jurisdiction, the county assizes and quarter sessions, presided over by judges on circuit, dealing with the more serious matters involving trial by jury, and local magistrates with lesser matters, though the limits of their respective jurisdictions were undefined and the system was generally inefficient and lacking in objectivity, operated by the privileged classes and to a greater or lesser extent in their own interests.

The administration of civil justice was considerably less satisfactory, with overlapping and competing jurisdictions, as courts had emerged over the centuries with no attempt to set the boundaries of their authority or to define the relationships between them. In particular, there was no longer any clear division in types of work between the Courts of Exchequer, King's Bench and Common Pleas. In practice, this largely benefited the King's Bench, which emerged as the most important of the common law courts. Division between the common law and equity had also become less marked, and equity had come to be seen not as a separate system governed by the dictates of conscience, but as a gloss on the common law with its own set of rules. Blackstone, writing in 1768, saw little difference between the two systems.[7] However, the formal division remained intact, so that a litigant who sought a combination of legal and equitable remedies – damages together with an injunction, for example – had to bring separate actions in one or other of the common law courts and in the Court of Chancery. An Admiralty Court had also emerged at the end of the medieval period and this gradually acquired authority in wider commercial matters, though, once more, the limits of that jurisdiction remained undefined.

Changes earlier in the century had created further courts. Until 1857, wills and intestacies, and divorce and other matters related to marriage, were the responsibility of the ecclesiastical courts. In that year, as part of the general dismantling of the exclusive authority of the Church of England in secular affairs that had begun in the 1830s, these matters were respectively transferred to a new Court of Probate and Court for Divorce and Matrimonial Causes. The jurisdiction of the ecclesiastical courts was limited to matters directly concerning the church and its clergy, notably church discipline and the fabric of church buildings.

All the ancient courts sat at Westminster and litigation in them was neither simple, cheap nor quick. Although some boroughs maintained local courts with jurisdiction in certain matters, there was very little in the way of access to justice for the majority of the population. An attempt was made to remedy the situation by the County Courts Act 1846, passed in the teeth of opposition from the vested interests of the legal profession, which set up a framework of local courts to deal with claims of limited monetary value that survives in its essentials today.

When the Liberals came to power in 1868, there were thus no fewer than seven higher civil courts, together with the assizes for criminal matters and the county courts. Not all were subject to appellate jurisdiction, which was vested in the Exchequer Chamber for common law matters, the Lords Justices in Chancery for

---

7 JR Spencer, *Jackson's Machinery of Justice*, 8th edn, 1989, CUP, p 7.

Chancery matters and the Privy Council for Admiralty matters. As yet, there was no provision for criminal appeals.

Following two reports by a Judicature Commission, the Judicature Acts created a unified Supreme Court of Judicature comprising of a High Court and a Court of Appeal, the latter with appellate jurisdiction over all matters heard by the former. The High Court was then organised into Queen's Bench, Common Pleas and Exchequer Divisions, the latter two absorbed into the former in 1881, to deal with common law matters, together with the Chancery Division, dealing in particular with matters involving land, and the Probate, Divorce and Admiralty Division. All were given power to award both legal and equitable remedies. The assizes also formed part of the High Court and, from 1876, the House of Lords became the final court of appeal for Great Britain, retaining original jurisdiction in trial 'at the bar' for treason, a relic of the old law of attainder, and of peers for criminal offences.

The system created by the Judicature Acts remains largely intact. In 1971, the Probate, Divorce and Admiralty Division was dismantled, mainly in view of the enormous increase in matrimonial causes and litigation involving children in the second half of the 20th century, and the need for a specialist corps of judges to deal with them. Probate work was transferred to the Chancery Division and Admiralty work was given a more logical home in the Queen's Bench Division. The rump was re-named the Family Division. In the following year, 1972, the centuries-old assizes and quarter sessions were replaced by a Crown Court, sitting, like the High Court, in various parts of the country and each having its resident circuit judge, though High Court judges of the Queen's Bench Division continue to travel on circuit to preside over trials for the most serious offences.

21.3.4 Local government

That the mishmash of different authorities within a small area having responsibilities for different functions was a source of inefficiency was beginning to be recognised, though it was not for a number of years to come that most of these bodies were absorbed into multi-functional county and borough councils. Gladstone's government sought to bring some cohesion and consistency to the system by the creation in 1871 of a Local Government Board, which took over the functions of the Poor Law Commission and the majority of the local government functions, including education and public health, of the Privy Council and Home Office. This was not an unqualified success, since the different sections within the LGB retained a good deal of autonomy, and the Poor Law section tended to dominate the remainder. Indeed, the low priority given to public health led Dr John Simon to retire in despair as head of the Medical Department in 1876.

21.4 THE CONSERVATIVES IN POWER

Since their defeat in 1868, the Conservatives under Disraeli had worked hard to build the first coherent party organisation in British history and a solid base of support among newly-enfranchised groups, stressing that it had been the Conservatives, and not the Liberals, for all their progressive reputation, who had secured the vote for the working classes. Given the widening of the franchise, it was recognised that there would be a significant future reduction in uncontested seats, so that the party had not only to woo voters but to select suitable candidates, a task which had hitherto been carried out mainly by party whips and traditionally Conservative organisations such as the Carlton Club. A Conservative Central Office with a full time staff was created in 1870. Local Conservative voters were encouraged to form themselves into associations administered by paid agents, sending representatives to a party conference, and co-ordinated by a National Union of Conservative Associations set up in 1867. This development was only encouraged by the introduction of the secret ballot in 1872.

These tactics were successful and the Conservatives came to power in the 1874 election with an overall majority of some 50 seats. Demoralised and disillusioned, Gladstone handed over the Liberal leadership in the Commons to the Marquess of Hartington.[8]

Having come to power with the support of the working classes, the Conservatives passed a number of pieces of social legislation, some building on work already carried out by their predecessors; indeed, the Factory Act of 1874 originated in a Liberal Bill and was enacted largely in that form. The Public Health Act 1875 was mainly a consolidation of previous piecemeal legislation, though in setting down clearly the functions of the various bodies with public health responsibilities, it greatly aided the enforcement of sanitary law. However, the Artisans' Dwelling Act of the same year did break significant new ground in authorising the compulsory purchase of property for the purposes of slum clearance and the construction of what would now be termed 'social housing' at ratepayers' expense. Unfortunately, there was no requirement to exercise the slum clearance powers in conjunction with the powers to provide replacement housing. In consequence, the former were mainly used for re-development of town centres to give effect to an emerging spirit of civic pride, as, for example, in Birmingham.[9]

21.5 THE 1880s

After 1875, the Conservative government turned its attention increasingly to foreign affairs. Further interventionist activity had to wait until the Liberals returned to power in 1880. This was on a smaller scale than in Gladstone's earlier ministry, for a number of reasons, including, again, the dominance of foreign affairs, the Irish issue, which reached its 19th century peak in this period, disunity among the Liberals and the activities of the Conservative 'Fourth Party' led by Lord Randolph Churchill[10] who, unhappy with the passivity of the Conservative leader in the Commons, Sir Stafford Northcote,[11] took every opportunity to embarrass the government, so disrupting the legislative programme by using up parliamentary time.

Chief among the changes which did take effect were the second tranche of Cardwell's army reforms, which gave the British Army a basic shape which it retained until the 1950s, and three pieces of electoral reform legislation, which together sought to reduce the scope for bribery and intimidation of voters, to extend the franchise

---

8   Hartington held his title by courtesy as heir to the 7th Duke of Devonshire, and so sat in the Commons.
9   D Read, *England 1868–1914: The Age of Urban Democracy*, 1979, Longman, pp 56–57.
10   Father of Sir Winston Churchill.
11   The Conservative leader, the 3rd Marquess of Salisbury, sat in the Lords.

changes of 1867 to the counties as well as the boroughs, and to link representation to population for the first time.

21.5.1 Electoral reform

Though the secret ballot had been introduced in 1872, there remained much concern about corrupt election practices. Indeed, evidence suggests that spending by parliamentary candidates to attract voters to their cause by legitimate and illegitimate means was now higher than ever, and elections continued to be attended by heavy drinking and violence. In order to prevent such abuses and to create a more level playing field for individual candidates and the parties they represented, Gladstone obtained the passage of the Corrupt and Illegal Practices (Prevention) Act 1883, which effectively restricted election spending in each constituency to £1,000 for every 5,000 voters, and limited the number of paid party workers. Breach of the limits and other forms of electoral malpractice became punishable by imprisonment for up to two years and disqualification from sitting in Parliament.[12] Read notes that the number of successful petitions for election bribery immediately dropped sharply, from 16 in 1880 to three in 1885.[13]

However, since the limitations dealt largely with spending in the name of individual candidates and at constituency level at election time only, there was nothing in the legislation which prohibited generosity by sitting MPs and prospective candidates to local organisations in the relevant constituency, or the raising of funds by the central party organisation and its spending at national level. Further, there was and remains nothing in the legislation to prevent a party, on coming to power, from rewarding the makers of large donations to central funds by persuading the monarch to grant them peerages and knighthoods, an abuse which continues today in increasingly blatant fashion.[14] Equally, the 1880s and 1890s saw the appearance of the first 'press barons', the ennobled proprietors of national newspapers which adopted a particular political stance.

The Representation of the People Act 1884 was initially opposed by the Conservatives, but their resistance ceased when Gladstone agreed at the urging of Lord Salisbury to give effect to a re-distribution of seats, which the Conservatives considered would favour them. The Act recognised the anomaly that many urban householders of modest means, whose right to vote was based on the renting of property worth £7 per year, would not qualify to vote should they move outside the boundaries of a borough. By imposing the £7 voting qualification in the county constituencies, the 1884 Act extended the franchise to working class householders in rural areas, including the majority of agricultural labourers, and to about two-thirds of the adult male population. The change was particularly marked in Ireland, where the urban population was small and property values were low, so that the 1867 Act had had little effect. The newly-enfranchised population of rural Ireland tended, a generation after the great famine, to be anti-English in their sympathies, and their

---

12 The regime introduced by the 1883 Act remains in force today, although it has been the subject of criticism for its complexity.

13 Read, *op cit*, p 313.

14 See M Pugh, *State and Society: British Political and Social History 1870–1992*, 1994, Arnold, p 23. Recent examples of the giving of peerages in return for financial reward are too numerous to mention.

support was instrumental in giving Parnell's Home Rulers the bulk of Irish seats and so the overall balance of power at the next general election in November 1885. The franchise was also extended to male occupiers of lodgings worth £10 per year.

However, there was still no general conception of the franchise as a universal right, rather than a privilege for the responsible and deserving. Adult males living under the parental roof remained excluded, as did living-in servants and paupers – until 1885, any person who entered the workhouse was automatically deprived of the franchise.

Women's suffrage had begun to emerge as an issue in the 1860s, but attracted no popular or parliamentary support, and its proponents were divided among themselves as to whether it should be accorded to married women, who were arguably represented via the votes of their husbands, or only to spinsters and widows.[15] The 1867 Act as passed made no reference to gender, and in *Chorlton v Lings*, a woman who met the householder qualification argued that Parliament, by failing to exclude women from the franchise expressly, had impliedly granted them the vote. However, the Court of Common Pleas held that this could not have been Parliament's intention; had Parliament intended to go against established constitutional values, they would have done so expressly.[16] Several Private Members' Bills were introduced in the years after *Chorlton*, but none attracted more than a handful of votes.

It was also entirely possible for one man to qualify for more than one vote. Not only did all university graduates have an additional vote, a man with both residential and business property acquired votes in respect of both, and the same person might possess 40s freeholds in more than one county. Read estimates that there may have been more than half a million such 'plural voters' in 1914.[17] Plural voting did not finally disappear until the 1950s.

The following year, a Redistribution Act was passed pursuant to the agreement between Gladstone and Salisbury. This re-distributed the seats of 142 boroughs with populations of fewer than 15,000 among the counties and the most populous boroughs, where the old units were split up into single-member constituencies reflecting size of population, approximately one seat per 50,000 people. Liverpool was now split into nine constituencies, and Manchester into six. Lancashire acquired 15 additional MPs and the West Riding of Yorkshire 13. 39 seats were transferred to the London boroughs.

Although the 1883–85 legislation did nothing to change the composition of Parliament, in that MPs of both the main parties continued to be drawn from the upper and upper-middle classes, the 1870s and 1880s saw moves by governments of both political persuasions to increase their control over Parliament. Already in 1868–74, Gladstone had introduced additional sittings in order to accommodate government business, and government control tightened noticeably as the tactics of the 'Fourth Party' and Irish Party demonstrated government vulnerability to deliberate time-wasting. Shortly before losing power in 1880, Disraeli's government obtained a standing order giving the Speaker power to suspend individual members for a variety of minor misdemeanours. After a debate which lasted from 3.45 pm on

---

15   See Read, *op cit*, pp 42–44, 310–11.

16   (1868) LR 4 CP 374.

17   Read, *op cit*, p 311.

31 January 1881 until it was terminated by the Speaker at 9.30 on the morning of 2 February, the Speaker was formally given power to close a debate and call a vote and, from 1887, any member was permitted to move for closure with the consent of the Speaker. The 'guillotine', restricting time for debate on particular Bills by allowing a resolution to be moved for a vote – since the government normally had a majority, it could be confident that the resolution would be passed – also appeared for the first time in 1887,[18] and by 1902, the opposition were complaining that the Conservative government under AJ Balfour were seeking to run the Commons according to a railway timetable. All this reduced the ability of the opposition to oppose the government of the day, and in particular the ability of private members to exert real influence.[19]

21.5.2 New constitutional issues

That there was now a relatively representative electoral system gave rise to new constitutional questions. First, to what extent was a government required to give effect to the will of the people as expressed in a general election? In particular, was a popular mandate required for legislation of a particularly controversial nature? Second, what was the role of the unelected House of Lords and what was its relationship to the Commons?

Walter Bagehot, writing in the period May 1865 to January 1867, shortly before the second Reform Act, considered that the prime function of the House of Commons was to choose a Cabinet. The Cabinet was the key to the effective functioning of the constitution, since it created a near-complete union of executive and legislative power. As the Cabinet depended on the confidence of the Commons both to give effect to its policy and to remain in power, the House was in a real sense an electoral body. In order to choose a Cabinet which was strong and capable of governing effectively, MPs had to be capable of making suitable choices, based on the need for firm government in the national interest, and independently of the view of their constituents. Though Bagehot was a supporter of the extension of the franchise on the 1867 terms, he considered that the imposition of manhood suffrage, as advocated by the Chartists, would weaken the ability of the Commons to perform this function effectively.[20]

AV Dicey, whose *Law of the Constitution* appeared in 1885, was rather more inclined towards the idea of government at the will of the people, going so far as to

---

18 The guillotine has become a regular weapon in the governmental armoury, being used in cynical fashion in relation to the most controversial Bills, which would otherwise be subject to extremely lengthy debate. A good recent example is that applied in respect of the Anti-Terrorism, Crime and Security Bill 2001, hastily cobbled together in the wake of the terrorist attacks of September 11th and giving powers which included provision for the detention without trial of non-British persons suspected of a wide and nebulous range of links to international terrorist groups, in circumstances where there is no prospect of conviction for any offence, very largely because the Human Rights Act 1998, enacted by the same government, prevents their deportation on grounds of national security. The Bill aroused immense controversy, not least because its provisions did not apply to domestic terrorist groups such as those active in Northern Ireland. It was introduced in the Commons on 27 November, the government demanding that it be enacted before Parliament rose for the Christmas recess. Despite defeats on a number of specific points in the House of Lords, the Bill completed its stages substantially unaltered and was granted the royal assent on 14 December, becoming law immediately. The first arrests made under the Act came as early as 19 December.

19 Read, *op cit*, pp 314–16.

20 W Bagehot, *The English Constitution*, 2001, OUP, pp 11–14, 100, 109–11.

advocate referenda, as practised in countries such as Switzerland, on the most significant issues. However, he too was opposed to extension of the franchise, in particular to votes for women, since they would tend to form a block vote in pursuit of gender-discriminatory policies, so denying Parliament its claim to sovereignty based on the will of all and the interest of all, the more so as women formed a small majority in the adult population.[21]

However, the idea that governments ought to give effect to the popular will was largely rejected by the politicians of the day. Gladstone was firmly opposed to the idea that he was under mandate to the electorate and emphasised the right of governments to introduce legislation on any matters, including the most contentious, without seeking prior approval from the electorate.[22] By contrast, the House of Lords, with a large Conservative majority, seems to have seized on the idea that it was constitutionally proper for them to reject Liberal legislation on the basis that the electorate ought to be consulted. Whether this was a matter of principle or not, it was certainly convenient for the Conservatives, who now had a second line of attack when in opposition in the Commons. Read notes that the Conservative peers were able to defeat or alter fundamentally major government Bills in every Liberal administration from 1868 to 1914.

Aware that they could not hope to command a majority in the Lords unless the monarch could be persuaded deliberately to create large numbers of Liberal peers, the Liberals began in the 1880s to consider possibilities for change, in the form either of a re-structuring of membership or, as advocated by John Bright in 1883 and finally adopted in the Parliament Acts, restricting the power of the Lords to that of delaying legislation only.[23] In 1888, both Lord Salisbury, as Conservative Prime Minister, and Lord Rosebery, a future Liberal Prime Minister, proposed the introduction of life peers specifically for political purposes, but this was not followed up, although Lords of Appeal in Ordinary, the 'law lords' carrying out the judicial functions of the House, were already appointed for life.[24]

21.6   IRELAND 1867–93

The problem of Ireland also began to emerge as a major political issue in the late 1860s. Quite simply, the structural problems which existed there had never been addressed by any government. Political power remained in the hands of an aristocracy and gentry which was Church of Ireland in religion and English and Anglo-Norman in origin. Governmental power was vested in a resident Viceroy, the former lord-lieutenant, invariably a senior member of the English peerage, and a Chief Secretary with a seat in the Cabinet who divided his time between Dublin and Westminster. Economic power in rural areas was also largely in the hands of the aristocracy and gentry, frequently as absentee landlords, while the linen and

---

21   See I Loveland, *Constitutional Law: A Critical Introduction*, 1996, Butterworths, p 257.

22   Read, *op cit*, p 318.

23   Read, *op cit*, pp 318–19.

24   As the appellate responsibilities of the House of Lords became wider, there were insufficient hereditary peers with the necessary judicial expertise, and the granting of hereditary peerages to eminent lawyers was considered improper except in the case of appointees to the office of Lord Chancellor who, before 1958, were normally created viscounts.

shipbuilding industries of the north were dominated by the Presbyterian descendants of James I's plantations.

Those changes which had been made by successive governments were small-scale and did not affect the basic social, economic and political structure. Further, such changes brought little benefit to the majority Catholic population. The governments which held office from 1846 to 1868 were either coalitions or lacked overall majorities, and so had to follow a middle course between different elements in both Houses in order to retain sufficient support to govern. Several Cabinets included Irish landowners who benefited from the status quo. Notable among them was Lord Palmerston, Prime Minister in 1855–58 and again in 1859–65, Foreign Secretary under Russell and a landowner in County Sligo, which, before the potato famine, was an area largely of subsistence agriculture. He was hostile to the land reformers on the basis that any increase in tenants' rights reduced the rights of the landlords, and was strongly anti-Catholic in his personal views.

The influence of Irish emigrants to North America began to be felt in the 1860s, when 'Fenian' clubs formed among them began to agitate for an Irish uprising and committed acts of terrorism on the British mainland that included the murder of a police sergeant in Manchester and a bomb in a factory in London that caused a number of deaths. At this stage, they attracted little support in Ireland, but a strong undercurrent of disaffection was becoming apparent, particularly in rural areas, over the conduct of landlords towards their tenants. A Land League was formed to campaign for fair rents, security of tenure and freedom for tenants to sell their leases.

At the same time, there were divisions within the Liberal ranks on the main domestic issues, between Whiggish traditionalists, mainly from landowning backgrounds, and the popular Liberalism which had emerged among the middle classes in the manufacturing towns and was strongly linked with non-conformity. A number of times in his political career, Gladstone seized on a single issue as a means to unite his party. Lord John Russell, now Earl Russell, urged action to deal with the anomalous position of the Church of Ireland in order to cut the ground from beneath the feet of the Fenians, and Gladstone chose this as the issue on which to unite the Liberals. The Irish Church Act, disestablishing the Church of Ireland, was passed in 1869, but a land reform Bill designed to deal with the worst abuses of the landlords was much reduced in its effect by the compromises needed to get it through Parliament, and the resulting Act had little practical value.

Gladstone's attempt in 1873 to found a third university in Ireland, primarily for Roman Catholics, met heavy opposition, and after the relevant Bill was defeated at its second reading, the government resigned. The Queen invited Disraeli to form a government, but he refused, on the grounds that the Liberals had been defeated by a temporary alliance not representative of the true working of the political system. After a brief hiatus not untypical of the 19th century, the Liberals returned to office, but their majority was increasingly eroded by by-election defeats over the remaining months of 1873.

Gladstone's second ministry, from 1880, is principally remembered today for its thwarted attempt to introduce Irish Home Rule. The strength of Irish disaffection and the extent to which the nationalist demand for Home Rule via a recreated Irish parliament with full powers existed was demonstrated in the 1874 and 1880 elections. Each returned some 60 members for Irish constituencies who supported Home Rule and formed a distinct Irish Party. Neither Liberals nor Conservatives could claim significant support outside Protestant-dominated Ulster. The 1874 election brought an overall Conservative majority of sufficient size that Disraeli did not need to woo the Irish members, so that Ireland was effectively put to one side in that period. From 1880, however, the position was very different.

The early 1880s saw a world depression in agriculture, which had serious effects in Ireland. Evictions of tenants unable to pay their rents, the main concern of the Land League, greatly increased and were met by a campaign of violence, including the murder of the Chief Secretary, Lord Frederick Cavendish, and Thomas Burke, his Permanent Secretary, who were attacked and had their throats cut with surgical knives while they were walking in Phoenix Park, Dublin on 6 May 1882. Charles Stuart Parnell, leader of the Irish Party, sought to use the crisis as a political bargaining counter and was arrested and briefly imprisoned on the grounds that the violence had been provoked by his speeches. Gladstone took the opportunity to force a Land Act through Parliament, which largely conceded the demands of the Land League and which stemmed the crisis for the time being. However, the 1885 election, called at short notice after the government ran into increasing difficulties, gave Parnell the balance of power, and he offered the support of his MPs to the party which would press ahead with Home Rule.

Gladstone, hoping that Home Rule would prove the unifying issue for the Liberals that disestablishment had been in 1868–69, grasped the nettle and introduced a Home Rule Bill which provided that Irish MPs would be excluded from Westminster and would sit in a new assembly in Dublin with powers in defined areas. Ireland would in future contribute one-fifteenth of national expenditure to cover matters such as defence, foreign policy, currency, trade regulation and the Post Office, which remained the responsibility of Westminster. Though there was increasing hostility between the Protestants of Ulster and the Catholic majority, no specific provision was made for their separate treatment – such that Lord Randolph Churchill played the 'Ulster card' and claimed that Gladstone sought to sacrifice loyal Protestants to their Catholic enemies.

Gladstone's stratagem backfired badly. Not only was the Bill defeated in the Commons as the result of a rebellion among Liberal MPs, 93 of whom voted against the government, but the two factions opposing Gladstone, the radicals led by Joseph Chamberlain and the traditionalists under Lord Hartington, elder brother of Lord Frederick Cavendish, seceded from the main Liberal Party and fought the ensuing general election as Liberal Unionists with a separate party organisation. In alliance with the Conservatives, they adopted a platform of preserving the Union and safeguarding the Empire. This had considerable appeal to voters on the British mainland and the new alliance achieved power with Lord Salisbury as Prime Minister.[25]

From this point, the tide of events moved away from Home Rule, much as it had moved to the disadvantage of Chartism during the 1840s. Except for the years 1892–95, the Conservatives, who were firmly opposed to Home Rule since it threatened the integrity of the United Kingdom, held power continuously until 1905. Indeed, Lord Salisbury famously declared the Irish to be as fit for self-government as the Hottentots of South Africa.[26] After the failure of 1885–86, Parnell was less able to

---

25 Disraeli had died in 1883.
26 Quoted in Pugh, *op cit*, p 79.

command support among Irish MPs and was brought low in 1889 by scandalous revelations about his private life, when he was cited as co-respondent in a divorce action brought against the woman with whom he had been living since 1881 and had three children. It must be recalled that in the 19th century, both divorce and cohabitation were rarities, and the disclosure that Parnell was living with a married woman outraged contemporary opinion, both among the Irish Catholics who had hitherto supported his political aims and on the mainland. Parnell resigned as leader of the Irish Party and died two years later. Soon after, the Irish Party split and expression of Irish nationalism moved into new manifestations. One was a revival of Gaelic culture and the Gaelic language, in which writers such as WB Yeats were prominent. The other, coming a little later and slower to show its hand, was a terrorist movement, the Irish Republican Brotherhood, whose founders concluded that British politicians would never concede Home Rule via the ballot box.

Gladstone remained a firm advocate of Home Rule and introduced a second Bill on returning to office in 1892. Indeed, he was now over 80 years old and was only persuaded by his party to continue as their leader because of the opportunity it gave him to press for Home Rule. This Bill obtained a majority in the Commons, but was heavily defeated in the Lords. There, for the time being, the matter rested.

21.7   LOCAL GOVERNMENT FROM 1885

The third tranche of parliamentary reform in 1883–85 prompted a re-structuring of local government, much as had the original Reform Act. In 1888, a Local Government Act belatedly introduced a system of elected county councils to take over the governmental responsibilities of the magistrates, other than policing, together with 61 county borough councils, separate from both the counties and the existing boroughs, mainly in towns with more than 50,000 inhabitants. A London County Council was created to replace the existing unwieldy and chaotic structure in the capital, so giving the city which was then the largest in the world, as well as the capital of an empire covering a quarter of the globe, a coherent governmental structure for the first time.

The County Electors Act of the same year created a common franchise for both the new councils and existing borough councils, based on one year's residence, one year's occupation or one year's ratepaying. This was rather broader than the parliamentary franchise and about three-quarters of adult men and a much smaller but still significant proportion of women, varying between 10 and 15% in different areas, qualified.[27]

In 1894, the Liberal government under Lord Rosebery abolished most of the existing miscellany of single-function authorities and replaced them with a reasonably coherent system of rural and urban district councils and parish councils, each with defined responsibilities in a specific geographical area. School Boards remained in

---

27 Women had first gained a local franchise in the boroughs in 1869 and at about the same time began to be elected to offices at local level, initially to School Boards. A woman was elected as a Poor Law guardian in 1875, and two to the new London County Council in 1889, though the legislation which created the Council specifically disqualified women and they were removed after legal action. After the property qualification for Poor Law guardians was abolished in 1894, women guardians became much more numerous, and the future Suffragette leader, Emmeline Pankhurst, was one of a number who gained their early political experience in this role.

being until 1902, however, along with the vast Poor Law system, which was intact in its essentials until 1929 and which now had very extensive responsibilities in relation to the health of the poor.

In 1899, again under the Conservatives, 28 Metropolitan Borough Councils were created in London, and certain of the London County Council's existing responsibilities devolved to them, so that local government in London mirrored that of the rest of the United Kingdom. In part, this change was made for political reasons; the Conservatives wished to break the power of the 'Progressive' bloc, a loose alliance of a range of non-Conservative groups from Liberal Unionists to Fabian Socialists, which was achieving a position of dominance, with Lord Rosebery as Council Chairman.[28]

21.8   THE BEGINNINGS OF THE LABOUR PARTY

As the 19th century drew to a close, much of the detailed structure of the British constitutional system was now in place, by a process largely of peaceful evolution since the 1820s. Parliament was a relatively representative body, with the extension of the franchise and the creation of a system of constituencies which reflected population distribution. Its workings had changed very considerably, with the triumph of party over personality. The spheres of government involvement had expanded enormously, with a recognition that the state had a role to play in matters of social welfare, and the putting in place of a coherent system of local government.

As yet, the working classes, though a proportion of them now held the franchise and so were in a position to influence government, were not directly represented in Parliament, membership of which was still the preserve of the upper and middle classes. Some constituencies, particularly in Yorkshire and Lancashire, were overwhelmingly working class in population, but the working class vote was shared between the Conservatives and the Liberals. Both the main parties, more particularly the Liberals, had some elements of policy which favoured the working classes, but the Liberals in particular were a 'broad church', embracing a very wide range of political opinion and united only in a vague concept of promotion of individual freedom and support for continued free trade. The lacuna was filled after 1893 through the formation of the Independent Labour Party.

A few trade unionists sat in Parliament from the 1860s on 'Lib-Lab' tickets after standing for election unopposed by local Liberals. None achieved any prominence in the Commons, and Liberal constituency associations in any case shied away from adopting working class candidates. The expense of fighting elections was also a problem – in the 'Khaki Election' of 1900, an average of £776 was spent per candidate, at a time when the bulk of the population earned less than the income tax threshold of

---

28   Read, *op cit*, p 338.

£160 per year,[29] and 28–30% were estimated to live below a poverty line set by Seebohm Rowntree at 22s per week for a family of five.[30]

The formation of a political party specifically for the working classes had been discussed for a number of years, but the decisive step was finally taken in January 1893. The Independent Labour Party (ILP) was headed by James Keir Hardie, who had been elected as MP for the largely working class constituency of West Ham the previous year, and had its roots in a network of socialist clubs which had sprung up in the cotton and wool areas of Lancashire and Yorkshire in recent years. The new party defined its object as the 'collective ownership of the means of production, distribution and exchange', but its leaders recognised the need for a moderate and non-doctrinaire approach to politics, not only to win the votes of trade union members but to gain financial support from the trade unions as institutions. The early policies and tactics of the ILP were therefore not greatly different from those of the working class Liberals, but of 28 candidates fielded by the ILP at the 1895 election, none was elected, Hardie himself losing his seat.

However, over the next decade, ILP members began to be elected to local councils and School Boards. In 1900, there were 63 ILP members of town councils; in 1905, there were 153. At the same time, the continuing refusal of local Liberal parties to select working class candidates encouraged some trade union leaders to see advantage in the ILP's campaign for independent working class parliamentary representation.

---

29 See Williams and Ramsden, *op cit*, p 317. Professor Martin Pugh estimates that there were about a million taxpayers at the time of Lloyd George's 1909 Budget. See Pugh, *op cit*, pp 117–18.

30 Rowntree, a member of the Quaker chocolate family, was one of several individuals who set out to assess the true extent and causes of poverty on an objective and systematic basis from the 1880s onwards, producing *Poverty: A Study of Town Life*, dealing with conditions in York, in 1901. See Pugh, *op cit*, pp 43–44.

CHAPTER 22

QUEEN VICTORIA AND THE EMERGENCE OF CONSTITUTIONAL MONARCHY

22.1   INTRODUCTION

As the 20th century dawned, there occurred a change of huge symbolic importance when Queen Victoria died on 22 January 1901 after a reign of 63 years, the longest in British history and exceeded by those of only two continental monarchs.[1] Her reign was of huge importance in the evolution of the monarchy from an institution with a significant active role in national politics to one which functioned largely on a symbolic level as a focus for national unity and patriotism.

Prior to Victoria's reign, any government had been in a real sense His Majesty's Government. The monarch's will governed the appointment of ministers, though this was tempered by recognition of the need for ministers to enjoy the confidence of the House of Commons. A monarch who found himself at odds with his ministers over policy could dismiss those ministers and appoint their political rivals to replace them, or dissolve Parliament of his own volition and so force a general election. Bogdanor observes that before 1841, general elections tended to come after changes of government rather than before; the purpose of an election was essentially to endorse the sovereign's choice of Prime Minister.

A dissolution was the personal act of a monarch and it was considered dishonourable for a Prime Minister to seek a dissolution unless there was a real prospect that he would increase his Commons majority at the consequent election. Victoria's immediate predecessor, William IV, became the last monarch to dismiss a ministry in 1834, though he shortly afterwards accepted that his preferred Prime Minister, Sir Robert Peel, could not maintain the confidence of the House and recalled Lord Melbourne. 1841 marked another watershed, when Melbourne insisted on a dissolution after his government lost a no confidence motion. He did so despite the urging of Prince Albert, who had married Victoria the previous year and who now informed him that such an action was constitutionally improper. Lord Brougham, a former Lord Chancellor, indeed declared a dissolution for the purpose of ascertaining national opinion through a general election to be 'wholly unworthy of notice' and 'perverting to the mere purposes of party the exercise of by far the most eminent of the Royal Prerogatives'.[2] Previously, a Prime Minister in such a position had resigned, allowing the monarch to choose an alternative Prime Minister without an election. There is evidence that Victoria felt personally humiliated when the election result left her with no realistic alternative to Peel.

Bogdanor makes clear a paradox that encapsulates the change. Peel became Prime Minister in 1841 largely by the will of the electorate. However, like his predecessors, he considered himself to be primarily the servant of the monarch, and his failure to accept the party will over the Corn Laws or to seek a compromise acceptable to the party brought about his own downfall and the irreparable splitting of the Conservatives.[3]

---

1   Louis XIV (1643–1715) and Franz Josef of Austria-Hungary (1848–1916).
2   AC Benson and Viscount Esher (eds), *Letters of Queen Victoria*, 1st ser, 1907, John Murray, p 369.
3   V Bogdanor, *The Monarchy and the Constitution*, 1995, Clarendon, pp 22–23.

22.2   VICTORIA'S EARLY YEARS

Though the process by which the direct political power of the monarch largely disappeared was underway before Victoria's accession, much occurred during her own reign to confirm and even accelerate this trend. Bogdanor divides the reign into four phases. During the second period, from 1841 to 1868, the potential for royal influence was at its greatest, particularly during the era of coalition governments after 1846. For much of this time, he considers, Prince Albert was almost a joint sovereign with Victoria, having access to Cabinet papers, being present at the Prime Minister's audiences with the queen (a unique privilege)[4] and exercising an unofficial though powerful influence behind the scenes.

Bogdanor gives Albert the credit for introducing the concept of the monarch as a figure independent of party politics; his purpose in doing so was to strengthen the role of the sovereign. To Albert, the sovereign alone represented the state and was in a unique position to use his or her powers for the good of the state, since all politicians were partisan. Remaining above party politics enabled the sovereign to play an active role in government, particularly in foreign policy.[5]

At times, Albert was prepared to give expression to views which conflicted directly with those of his wife's ministers, as in 1843, when he criticised Peel's policies in a letter to his cousin, the King of Portugal.[6] Such behaviour by a person who held no official position and was not even British by birth could have led to a direct confrontation between monarch and ministers, as had occurred in previous reigns. Albert was by no means a popular figure; his earnestness and formidable intellectual powers appear to have alienated his adopted countrymen, and successive governments refused to permit Victoria to give him any formal public role. That it did not lead to crisis was due in considerable measure to the accident that much of the period of Albert's influence coincided with the era of coalition government, which allowed the queen an active role in the selection of Prime Ministers.

22.3   THE WIDOW OF WINDSOR

After Prince Albert's death on 14 December 1861, the queen withdrew completely from public life and for many years was a virtual recluse. Though she continued to read Cabinet papers and receive ministers in audience, she did not even open Parliament.[7] The monarchy had enjoyed a considerable upsurge in popularity since 1837, due mainly to the sentimental appeal of an attractive young woman monarch of irreproachable moral character after a succession of elderly and frequently dissolute men. A reaction now occurred. For the first time, a republican movement appeared in the United Kingdom – despite the unpopularity of individual Hanoverian monarchs, there seems to have been no serious hostility to the institution of monarchy previously.

---

4   No third party is present at the Prime Minister's audiences with the sovereign and no official record is kept of discussions.

5   Bogdanor, *op cit*, p 25.

6   Bogdanor, *op cit*, p 25.

7   The present queen has been quoted as saying that the State Opening of Parliament is her most significant public duty each year, symbolising the ties between Crown, Parliament and people.

A London Republican Club was formed and attracted 18,000 members to its meeting in 1871. Charles Bradlaugh, one of the most controversial public figures of the day, published a pamphlet entitled 'The Impeachment of the House of Brunswick'[8] and in November 1871, the radical MP Sir Charles Dilke became the first member of either House of Parliament to declare himself a republican since the Restoration. Joseph Chamberlain, then Mayor of Birmingham but a prominent figure in national politics from his election to Parliament in 1876, also professed republicanism, incurring the queen's lasting enmity.

Fate then took a hand. In December, the Prince of Wales contracted typhoid and was gravely ill for several days. By the time a thanksgiving service was held in St Paul's in February 1872 to mark his recovery, the heat seems to have gone out of republicanism, which in any case had its roots more in impatience with the failure of the queen to appear in public than with any active desire for an end to the monarchy. Dilke's attempt in March 1872 to move a Commons motion for an inquiry into the Civil List received support from only two other members. Chamberlain received the Prince and Princess of Wales when they visited Birmingham in 1874, and in 1882, Dilke publicly repudiated his republican views, describing them as 'opinions of political infancy'.[9]

22.4   A MODERN MONARCHY

From the early 1870s, political opinion increasingly stressed the importance of the mystical and ceremonial aspects of monarchy, proofs of the sovereign's separateness from day-to-day politics and their role as focus for popular patriotism. Bagehot, writing during Queen Victoria's seclusion and much influenced by the events of his day, stressed that to be effective, a monarchy must be visible, and argued that Victoria had done as much harm to the institution by her withdrawal from the world as had any of her predecessors by their profligacy.[10] Disraeli is normally credited with persuading her to emerge into the public eye once more. By the end of the 1860s, the queen and the Conservative leader enjoyed a close personal relationship, and Disraeli employed a brand of charm to which his sovereign was peculiarly susceptible in support of his own astute reading of the mood of the day. In 1876, he persuaded the queen to accept the title of Empress of India,[11] an empty gesture where India itself was concerned, but one which brought her back into public view.

It is no accident, but as a result of deliberate policy that the last 20 or so years of the 19th century are so closely associated in British national myth with Queen Victoria herself. When one thinks of the 19th century, an early image which forms in the mind is of flickering and jerky film of the Diamond Jubilee of 1897 and then of the gun carriage bearing Victoria's coffin. Her own public appearances remained rare, but they were carefully choreographed so as to maximise the religious and ceremonial elements, in particular the links between the monarch and the Armed Forces, and between monarch and Empire, the latter of supreme importance in the development of the concept of a British Empire as a single entity.

8   The Electors of Hanover were also Dukes of Brunswick-Luneberg.
9   For this period, see Bogdanor, *op cit*, pp 28–29.
10   Bogdanor, *op cit*, pp 29–30.
11   Given effect by the Royal Titles Act 1876.

Meanwhile, the second and third generations of the royal family were developing the public role of the monarchy in the ways which are now indelibly associated with it. Prior to Victoria's reign, there was no particular role for members of the royal family other than the sovereign and his consort, and the Prince of Wales as an unofficial focus of political opposition during the 18th century. Most male Hanoverians spent periods in the army, but otherwise followed their own inclinations, all too frequently in the direction of dissipation, though George III and his queen began to give the royal family a role in the charitable sphere.[12] Though Victoria refused to allow her eldest son any public position, despite repeated suggestions that she should do so, her second son, Alfred, Duke of Edinburgh, went into the Royal Navy, and the third son, Arthur, Duke of Connaught, into the army. All three travelled extensively in British possessions abroad and in doing so encouraged a sense of Britishness among the peoples of the Empire.[13]

Three of the queen's daughters remained in Britain after their marriages and embraced the contemporary enthusiasm for philanthropy, in particular, Helena, Princess Christian of Schleswig-Holstein, who was a leading figure in the movement to establish nursing as a profession.[14] Some members of the royal family served, like the queen herself, as models of domestic propriety, and those, like the Prince of Wales, whose habits did not fit them for such a role were more discreet in their behaviour than George IV and his brothers had been.

After 1870, in Bogdanor's fourth phase, Queen Victoria adopted a more politically partisan stance in her dealings with her ministers, though this did not become public at that time. Not only did she enjoy a more cordial personal relationship with Disraeli than with Gladstone over the 15 years in which they alternated in Downing Street, but she was hostile to the Liberal foreign policies of the day. Gladstone was generally anti-imperialist and the queen interpreted this as hostility to the extension of her own rule and as a willingness to surrender British territory abroad.[15] Further, she disapproved of some of the methods used by Gladstone in attacking Disraeli's policy in relation to the decaying Ottoman Empire in the late 1870s; seeking to arouse popular feeling against the government was a tactic associated with radicals, not with sober statesmen suitable for the highest offices.

Bogdanor goes so far as to claim that Victoria intrigued with the Unionist elements among the Liberals and encouraged them to form a coalition with the Conservatives in order to frustrate Gladstone's plans for Home Rule in 1885–86, though he does not consider the extent of any role played by the queen in the split between the 'Gladstonean' Liberals and the Liberal Unionists which followed.

---

12 Herself the mother of 15 children, Queen Charlotte was particularly associated with the provision of maternity facilities.

13 The fourth son, Leopold, Duke of Albany (1853–84), was prevented by haemophilia from pursuing an active career.

14 Those who assume that Diana, Princess of Wales was the only royal person with highly developed charitable instincts should read *My Memories of Six Reigns* by Princess Christian's younger daughter, Princess Marie Louise (1956, Cassell). After her German husband obtained an annulment of their marriage in 1901, Marie Louise (1872–1956) was told by her mother not to mope but to throw herself into good works, and did so for the rest of her life. *Inter alia*, she set up a club to provide accommodation and recreational facilities for working class girls in the East End of London, and organised maternity and child health clinics in the same area.

15 See Bogdanor, *op cit*, pp 30–35.

This seems to have been the period in which royal hostility to Gladstone's government was at its most marked; earlier in 1885, the queen had reacted to the news of the death of General Gordon in Khartoum by sending a telegram to the Prime Minister in which she blamed government negligence for Gordon's death.[16]

However, at the same time, her freedom to select a Prime Minister, or to veto a Prime Minister's choice of his Cabinet, on the basis of personal preference disappeared, though she might exercise a casting vote when there was more than one realistic candidate within the majority party. Bogdanor contrasts the position after the 1880 election, when Victoria initially sent for Lord Hartington, officially the Liberal leader in the Commons, but had to accept Gladstone when the leading Liberals made it clear that they would serve under no one else, and on Gladstone's resignation in 1894, when, the queen seems to have favoured Earl Spencer, and the majority of Liberal MPs Sir William Harcourt. Eventually, Victoria sent for Lord Rosebery, who seems to have been the choice of the Cabinet, and her decision was apparently accepted by all concerned as entirely proper.[17] Despite her dislike of Chamberlain and Dilke, prompted by their early republican views, the queen was also unable to prevent their being appointed to Cabinet positions, though successive Prime Ministers avoided giving them offices which involved direct contact with the monarch. The only person over whose appointment the queen seems successfully to have exercised a veto was Henry Labouchere, who had once publicly insulted the royal family.

Victoria's death in 1901 left the process by which the monarchy separated itself from party politics and adopted the non-partisan position of today incomplete. This process was completed by her grandson and successor-but-one, George V.

---

16 Major General Charles Gordon was one of several Victorian military figures who became national heroes in a way difficult to comprehend today. As Britain attempted to extend control over the Nile upstream from Egypt, Gordon and a force of Sudanese irregulars were besieged in Khartoum by a charismatic religious leader known as the Mahdi. A relief expedition despatched late in the day failed to reach Khartoum before it fell and Gordon was killed on the steps of his headquarters on 30 January 1885. Some indication of the extent to which the affair caught the popular imagination is given by the fact that my maternal grandfather, born to struggling lower middle class parents in Nottingham, was named after the Chief of Staff of the relief expedition, news of whose death from wounds reached Britain on the day of his birth.

17 Spencer was later to declare that he would not have accepted office had it been offered and it is entirely possible that the existing Cabinet would have refused to serve under Harcourt, who was a difficult man and had antagonised many of his colleagues. See Bogdanor, *op cit*, pp 31, 33.

CHAPTER 23

TWO CONSTITUTIONAL CRISES: 1906–14

23.1 INTRODUCTION

Constitutionally speaking, the 20th century could be said to begin in January 1906, on the election of a Liberal Government with what became an ambitiously progressive agenda. A number of developments which had occurred by evolution in the last decades of the previous century then came together, to produce a full-blown crisis over the relationship between Lords and Commons, and a second prompted by the government's attempt to establish Home Rule in Ireland.

23.2 PRELUDE TO CRISIS

Two early developments concerned the office of Prime Minister. This was now so firmly established, and the dominance of the Prime Minister over government so clear, that its existence was formally recognised by an instrument under the prerogative in 1905 that accorded the Prime Minister a place in the official table of precedence by virtue of his office.

A Conservative government had held power since the 1895 election, headed by Lord Salisbury, and was composed almost entirely of patricians – all but two of the Cabinet were peers or large landowners. Salisbury, who retired in 1902, proved to be the last British Prime Minister to sit in the House of Lords, although a constitutional convention to the effect that a Prime Minister ought to sit in the Commons did not become established until much later.

As the century dawned, Britain was at war with the Boer republics of South Africa,[1] a conflict which dragged on until May 1902. As in many wars before and since, the initial stages went badly for Great Britain, as the Boers invaded Natal in October 1899 and inflicted a series of defeats on its British garrison in the notorious 'Black Week' of December. By January, the only British troops left in northern Natal were besieged in the small towns of Kimberley, Mafeking and Ladysmith. Although the British took the offensive as soon as reinforcements arrived, capturing both the Boer capitals within a few months and imposing British rule over both republics before the end of the year, the Boers failed to surrender as expected, and continued

---

1   The earliest Europeans in South Africa were the Dutch, who settled in the Cape from the 1620s, and were later joined by Huguenots leaving France. The Cape became a British possession during the Napoleonic Wars and as the British spread across Cape Colony and Natal in the 1820s and 1830s, imposing British-style government, the more independent-minded descendants of the Dutch and Huguenots made the 'Great Trek' north and created what Britain later recognised as the republics of the Transvaal and the Orange Free State. The Boers were mainly farmers, but the discovery in 1886 of gold in the Transvaal brought an influx of new settlers, known as *uitlanders*. At the same time, the British South Africa Company established new British settlements north of the Transvaal, in what are now Zambia and Zimbabwe, so that the Boer republics found themselves increasingly hemmed in. As Prime Minister of Cape Colony, Cecil Rhodes sought to establish Great Britain as the dominant power in Africa and in particular to curb the independence of the Transvaal, using the Transvaal's denial of equal voting rights to the *uitlanders* as a lever. The refusal of either side to give way over the *uitlanders* led finally to a declaration of war.

fighting as guerrillas.[2] 450,000 soldiers from Britain and the Dominions were deployed in South Africa, of whom 6,000 were killed and 16,000 died of disease. How was it, public opinion demanded, that the greatest nation in the world had taken so long, and the lives of so many of its finest young men, to subdue a few thousand farmers?

The war exposed a number of weaknesses in the existing governmental system and, in particular, brought demands for greatly increased state intervention to improve the health of the nation, as the poor physique of numerous men offering themselves for military service became apparent. In Manchester, 8,000 volunteers out of 11,000 failed to satisfy a relatively modest medical standard[3] and Major-General JF Maurice claimed in 1902 that some 60% of Englishmen were physically unfit for military service.[4]

23.2.1 Social reform

Education was one of the beneficiaries of the post-war mood, as there was an acceptance of the need to improve standards in order to make Britain better able to compete with its trading rivals and to fight future wars. Particular attention was paid to Germany, which already had an established system of technical education at secondary level and was emerging as Britain's main European rival. As well as German industrial growth, there was concern over the expansion of the previously tiny German Navy, the possibility that it would grow large enough to compete with the Royal Navy, which then dwarfed all others, and the expansionist ambitions of Kaiser Wilhelm II (1888–1918).

In Britain, elementary education had been compulsory up to age 13 since 1891, and elementary school fees were abolished at the same time, but neither the School Boards nor the voluntary societies had power to provide any form of secondary education. This was available only in the public schools and the relatively small number of grammar schools that had grown up in piecemeal fashion and provided for a mainly middle class clientele. Some School Boards created what were known as higher grade schools or provided secondary education through evening classes, but the lacuna in the law emerged in 1900 when, in a test action brought by the Vice President of the Privy Council Committee on Education, the courts ruled that the Board's expenditure on secondary education was unlawful insofar as it was met from the rates.

---

2   The two Boer republics maintained very small numbers of regular troops. However, all adult white male citizens were liable to serve in 'commandos', which operated as small mounted units armed with the highly effective Mauser rifle. The Boers used their greatly superior manoeuvrability and their operating in friendly territory to full advantage. It was only when the British commanders adopted a strategy of confining the commandos within limited areas by means of fortified blockhouses and barbed wire that the Boers began to be worn down. At the same time, the British moved the civilian populations of those areas into 'concentration camps' in order to deprive the commandos of easy access to supplies. Many thousands died in the camps, mainly as a result of British inefficiency and neglect to provide adequate supplies of food and water rather than any deliberate policy, but, as in Ireland, the affair left an ugly legacy of hatred and bitterness.

3   G Williams and JA Ramsden, *Ruling Britannia: A Political History of Britain 1688–1988*, 1990, Longman, p 335.

4   D Read, *England 1868–1914: The Age of Urban Democracy*, 1979, Longman, p 408.

The Education Act 1902, piloted through the Commons by Salisbury's successor, AJ Balfour, therefore gave county councils and county borough councils power to provide secondary education for pupils aged 11 and upwards, financed from rates, a central government grant and modest fees. Secondary education, according to regulations produced by the new Board of Education in 1904, should involve a broad general curriculum, with the emphasis on arts subjects, with compulsory Latin, but also compulsory science and mathematics. It was envisaged that a proportion of pupils would remain at school beyond the age of 13, and would afterwards move into professional, managerial and technical occupations.

The Conservatives also greatly simplified the confused system of educational administration. In 1900, the responsibilities of the central bodies involved in education (the Privy Council Committee of Education, the Science and Art Department and the Charity Commissioners) were transferred to a new Board of Education, headed by a President who became effectively a Minister of Education. By the 1902 Act, the School Boards were abolished and their role was transferred to the county and county borough councils. Further, the existing voluntary schools would now be financed from rates and the management body of each of these schools would include local authority representatives. These parts of the Act were deeply unpopular with the churches, but the provisions on secondary education proved highly effective. Between 1905 and 1914, the number of secondary schools inspected by HM Inspectors rose from 575 to 1,027 and the pupils they educated from 94,698 to 187,647. Modern research suggests that the main beneficiaries of the availability of secondary education were the lower middle classes, even after 1908 when the Liberals established what later became the 'Eleven Plus' by offering a larger grant to schools which offered 25% of their places free of fees on the basis of a competitive examination.[5]

Though the Liberal government of 1906 onwards is given credit for instituting social welfare provisions designed to improve the health of individuals directly, the foundations were laid by the Conservatives. In 1903, Balfour's government set up an Inter-Departmental Committee on Physical Deterioration which, over the following year, assembled much expert evidence on matters affecting working class health, such as air pollution, poor working conditions, nutrition and care of infants, and concluded that central government action was essential, in particular the institution of a system of regular medical inspections for schoolchildren and the provision of school meals to give pupils from poor backgrounds one meal a day of a reasonable nutritional standard. Whether the Conservatives would have instituted policies similar to those of the Liberals after 1906 remains unclear. Balfour's government became increasingly divided over the issue of tariffs and he finally resigned in December 1905. A Liberal administration briefly took office under Sir Henry Campbell-Bannerman, who had unexpectedly been chosen as Liberal leader in 1899 on the basis of his ability to persuade people to put aside their differences and work together.

The Liberals had been out of office for 16 of the past 19 years and were deeply divided internally during the South African War, with a strong anti-war faction labelled Pro-Boers. Campbell-Bannerman managed to persuade the Pro-Boers to focus their concern on specific policies adopted in the prosecution of the war, in particular the concentration camps, and the ending of the war enabled him to reunite the party on a platform of opposition to the 1902 Education Act and to the introduction of

---

5   For the 1902 Act generally, see *ibid*, pp 433–36.

tariffs. As with the Labour Party in 1945 and again in 1997, the Liberals also benefited from a sense among voters that the existing government had been in power long enough. The Liberals were returned with 400 seats, as against 269 for all the other parties, on a turnout of 83.2%.[6] More than 200 of the Liberal MPs entered Parliament for the first time, and among the Cabinet which continued in office was the former Pro-Boer, David Lloyd George.

Though the 1906 government is remembered now for its social reforms and the crisis brought about by Lloyd George's schemes for financing them, the Liberals did not fight the election on a progressive platform. The reforming agenda emerged slowly and early legislation was limited to giving effect to measures already pre-figured. Campbell-Bannerman, already 69 when he became Prime Minister, was dogged by poor health throughout his tenure. He resigned in April 1908 and was replaced by Herbert Asquith. Lloyd George succeeded Asquith as Chancellor of the Exchequer and Winston Churchill became President of the Board of Trade. The appointment of these three marked the beginning of the Liberal government's progressive phase.

Asquith was not himself a progressive, but he recognised a need to maintain Liberal strength in the face of Conservative and Labour successes in by-elections and a Conservative takeover of the London County Council in the local elections of 1907. He was therefore prepared to adopt a much more progressive social policy than Campbell-Bannerman. Lloyd George was a radical of humble origins; he had largely been brought up by an uncle who was a shoemaker and Baptist lay preacher in Criccieth, Carnarvonshire. Encouraged by his uncle, a self-educated man with a strong belief in self-improvement and social responsibility, Lloyd George qualified as a solicitor and built up a thriving practice before being elected to Parliament in 1890.

Winston Churchill came from a very different background. Born in Blenheim Palace and educated at Harrow, he was the son of Lord Randolph Churchill and a grandson of the 7th Duke of Marlborough. After serving for a short time in the 4th Hussars, he turned to journalism, in which he displayed unusual talents as a war correspondent. While Lloyd George was coming to prominence through his outspoken opposition to the South African War, Churchill made himself a national hero by escaping from a prison camp in Pretoria in December 1899 and reaching neutral territory in what is now Mozambique. On a tide of popular enthusiasm, he was elected to Parliament as a Conservative in the 'Khaki Election' of 1900, but crossed the Commons floor to the Liberals in 1904 over the tariff question. A commentator of the day remarked that Churchill tended to sudden enthusiasms. In 1908, his enthusiasm was for alleviating the effects of poverty and he became a close ally of Lloyd George in the campaign for social insurance.

By now, the principle of state old age pensions had been widely accepted, partly for fiscal reasons – a considerable proportion of persons in receipt of poor relief were aged 65 or over, and pensions financed by social insurance would bring considerable savings in Poor Law expenditure. Even if a non-contributory system were adopted, such persons were already supported at public expense, so there would be no additional cost to the Exchequer. Further, the work of social researchers had demonstrated that many old people who were not receiving poor relief were being supported by their families, and that the financial burden of supporting elderly

---

6   This compares with a turnout of 51% in the election of 7 June 2001.

parents while at the same time bringing up children was a significant factor in the incidence of malnutrition among working class children. Finally, it was increasingly recognised that individuals on modest incomes could not be expected to save sufficiently to provide for their old age entirely from their own resources.

Though the principle of old age pensions was accepted, there was much dispute about the form to be adopted, not least because of fears that a non-contributory system would act as a disincentive to thrift. The scheme adopted in 1908, planned by Asquith but executed by Lloyd George, was therefore a compromise. Individuals over 70 were granted a non-contributory pension of 5s per week, and married couples were granted 7s 6d. So that personal saving and membership of friendly societies was not unduly discouraged, but there was no unnecessary expenditure on persons who could support themselves, the full pension was payable only to those with annual incomes below £21. By 1912–13, almost one million old people were receiving pensions totalling £12.3 million, and outdoor relief for persons of pensionable age had almost disappeared.[7]

At the same time, Churchill addressed the problem of unemployment by setting in train the creation of labour exchanges as a practical means of enabling the unemployed to find work and so reducing the length of time they spent between jobs. As did Lloyd George, he recognised a need for unemployment insurance to provide an income for periods between jobs, and for sickness insurance to deal with temporary incapacity to work.[8] The National Insurance Act 1911 created compulsory sickness insurance for all manual workers and allowed all employed persons earning less than the income tax threshold of £160 a year to join the scheme voluntarily. The total contribution per person was 9d per week, 4d from the worker, 3d from the employer and 2d from the state. In return, the worker was entitled when incapable of work to 10s per week for 13 weeks, and 5s for 13 weeks, up to a maximum of 26 weeks in any one year, plus free treatment from a doctor, though not hospital treatment. In addition, the scheme provided unemployment benefits for engineering, building and shipyard workers, whose occupations were particularly liable to cyclical slumps.

23.3   LLOYD GEORGE'S BUDGET

Necessarily, these policies were expensive. At the same time, a trade recession reduced tax revenue and increased unemployment, and concern over the expansion of the German Navy led Asquith to commit the government to the building of eight new battleships. In his first budget, in March 1909, Lloyd George had therefore to find additional sources of income without, however, any retreat from the Liberals' continuing commitment to free trade. In addition to the need to raise revenue, Lloyd George may have adopted a deliberate policy of pushing the House of Lords to declare itself.

The Lords was overwhelmingly dominated by Conservatives – 472 in 1910 as against 105 Liberals and a small number of independent 'cross-benchers'. On a number of occasions in 1906–07, they had passed wrecking amendments and forced the government to withdraw a major Education Bill. On 24 June 1907, Campbell-

---

7   Read, *op cit*, p 465.
8   Long term incapacity continued to be dealt with via the Poor Law up to 1929.

Bannerman secured the passage of a Commons resolution in favour in principle of reducing the power of the Lords to that only of delaying legislation, as had been recommended by John Bright in 1883.[9] After this, the Conservative peers were more circumspect, but it is possible that Lloyd George saw confrontation as a way to enhance the Liberal position by bringing about the permanent emasculation of a chamber in which they were unlikely ever to gain a majority by means other than the deliberate mass creation of Liberal peers. At any rate, the Welsh firebrand sought to characterise the House as a bastion of class privilege, whose members were more concerned to preserve their own position than with the national interest. In an early exercise in political 'spin', he assiduously promoted his budget as a 'People's Budget'.[10]

The focus of the 1909 budget was on taxing the most prosperous in the land and on creating mechanisms for taxing the vast capital assets of the great landowners, a long established ambition of radical Liberals. The budget left tax incidence unchanged at 1s in the pound on earned incomes below £3,000 per year, but raised rates on all unearned income and earned income between £3,000 and £5,000 to 1s 2d. A super tax of 6d was added where income exceeded £5,000. To modern eyes, these figures appear modest in the extreme, but in the climate of 1909, the well-off considered them extortionate. Lloyd George increased death duties, which mainly affected the better-off, and announced a range of new taxes on land, aimed particularly at landowners who benefited from mineral deposits and high land values due to development potential. To add insult to injury in the eyes of the landowners, a new inquisitorial system of land valuation was to be introduced.

Many of the greatest landowners were peers, or closely related to peers, so that the budget represented a direct attack on their position. More generally, it was an attack on property rights and even in the Commons, the budget was sufficiently controversial for 70 days to be occupied in debate before the Finance Bill embodying it was passed.

It was a long established constitutional convention that the Lords would not oppose money Bills passed by the Commons, but Lloyd George set about provoking the Lords into outright rejection of the Finance Bill, attacking the Conservative peers for wanting a strong Navy without having to pay for it, and as parasites living off the endeavours of both employers and workers. Condemnation came not only from the Conservatives, but from the much-respected former Liberal Prime Minister Lord Rosebery, who described the budget as 'inquisitorial, tyrannical and socialistic'.[11] At this point, AJ Balfour, still Conservative leader, agreed with the Marquess of Lansdowne, the Conservative leader in the Lords, that the Conservative peers should reject the Finance Bill. This they did on 30 November 1909.

---

9   Read, *op cit*, p 451.
10 See Read, *op cit*, p 467; and M Pugh, *State and Society: British Political and Social History 1870–1992*, 1994, Arnold, pp 124–25.
11 Cited in I Loveland, *Constitutional Law: A Critical Introduction*, 1996, Butterworths, p 200.

23.4   THE CRISIS BEGINS

Parliament had refused the government supply, making it impossible for the Liberals to continue in office. In any case, the Lords rejection motion declared 'That this House is not justified in giving its consent to the Bill until it has been submitted to the judgment of the country', so proclaiming the Conservative peers' own stance on constitutional probity. Asquith sought a dissolution from King Edward VII and a general election followed in January 1910, fought by the Liberals on a 'Peers versus People' platform, by the Conservatives on the dangerous nature of the budget, described by Lansdowne as 'a monument of reckless and improvident finance',[12] and on the unwisdom of seeking to please the mass of the voters.[13] Asquith announced on 10 December 1909 that it was now insufficient for the Lords to accept the Finance Bill; some means of limiting their power to reject legislation passed by the Commons must follow.

Loveland considers in some detail which of the two opposing factions could properly said to be acting 'unconstitutionally'. He suggests that it is simplistic to assume that the Liberals had democracy on their side. The Liberal victory in 1905 was derived from a franchise which excluded considerably more than half the adult population, and the Liberal share of the vote did not exceed 55%.[14] On Diceyean arguments, the existing parliamentary structure established by the Revolution Settlement existed to prevent the enactment of factionalist legislation such as the 1909 Finance Bill, which was deliberately intended to promote the interests of one segment of the population at the expense of another. On that basis, the Lords, in rejecting the Bill, could be said to be giving effect to the true spirit of the British constitutional system.[15] The argument is interesting, but unconvincing, in that a substantial proportion of Conservative peers appear to have been motivated in the first place by self-interest.

That the immediate issues had gripped the public imagination is made clear by the still-record election turnout of 86.8%. The electorate gave the Liberals a mandate to proceed with the budget and with constitutional change, but only just. They gained 50.5% of the vote, giving them 275 seats, a bare majority of two over the Conservatives (241) and Liberal Unionists (32), so that the government had to rely on Labour and the Irish Nationalists in order to maintain an effective majority. On 14 April, Asquith introduced a Parliament Bill which abolished all powers of the Lords over money Bills and their power of veto over other Bills, though it allowed the Lords a power of delay for up to two years. It also provided for the reduction of the life of a parliament from seven years to five.

Necessarily, the Bill had to be passed by the Lords themselves in order to become law, and Asquith, anticipating its rejection, informed the Upper House that if its members rejected the Bill, he would again go to the country, seeking a clear mandate.[16] Even before the January election, Asquith had regard to the precedents of

---

12   *Ibid.*

13   Read, *op cit*, p 468.

14   It may be noted that few governments since have gained a majority of votes cast, and the extent to which governments are truly representative of the popular will must be increasingly in doubt as election turnouts have fallen from the high levels of the early 20th century.

15   Loveland, *op cit*, pp 202–03.

16   Read, *op cit*, p 469.

1711–12, when Queen Anne had made use of her prerogative of creating peers in order to enable the government to achieve peace in the War of the Spanish Succession, and of 1832, when William IV had been prepared, reluctantly, to act in the same way in order to obtain the passage of the Reform Bill. However, when in December 1909, Asquith sought the views of Edward VII on the matter, he was informed that the king was not prepared to use the prerogative in this manner, even if the forthcoming election returned a Liberal government. The king, through his private secretary, Lord Knollys, told Asquith that a second general election would be required in order to give an unambiguous mandate to 'swamp' the Lords with Liberal peers for the purpose of passing a Parliament Bill.

Asquith and his government now came under pressure from the Irish Nationalists. Having spent a period in the doldrums after Parnell's fall, they had re-emerged as a political force under the leadership of John Redmond and were anxious to prevent the Lords from blocking a further Home Rule Bill. In introducing the Parliament Bill, Asquith therefore declared that if the Bill were rejected by the Lords, he would seek a dissolution and election for a second time, with the implication, albeit unspoken, that before that election, he would seek an undertaking from the king that in the event of a Liberal victory, sufficient peers would be created to give the government a majority in the Lords for the Bill.

23.5   THE CRISIS DEEPENS

The Lords then passed the Finance Bill, accepting that the election had given the Liberals a mandate for their budget, but before the Parliament Bill completed its stages in the Commons, Edward VII died on 6 May 1910. All parties agreed, in deference to his successor, George V, to meet in a constitutional conference and attempt to resolve their differences amicably. By November, however, it was clear that a negotiated solution was impossible, mainly because of Conservative opposition to Home Rule and their insistence that major constitutional legislation should be the subject of a national referendum if twice rejected by the Lords.

Asquith, appreciating that a second general election was inevitable, then sought what George V regarded as 'constitutional guarantees' and what the Prime Minister believed to be no more than a hypothetical understanding on the creation of peers. Bogdanor goes into the role played by the king during the events of 1910–11 and the ensuing crisis over Home Rule in considerable detail,[17] making it clear that he was at all times in a most difficult position, not least because of his political inexperience, and demonstrated a very high degree of personal and political integrity throughout this period. Whereas a bare 20 years earlier, Queen Victoria had on occasions manifested considerable partisanship and been prepared to cause embarrassment to her ministers over, for example, the Gordon relief expedition, George V considered it essential that he remain neutral as between the opposing parties. In his view, his constitutional position required him to act on the advice of his ministers, but his neutrality would be seriously compromised if he gave the guarantees sought by Asquith, since that would represent an implied endorsement of the Liberal election programme. The king

---

17   V Bogdanor, *The Monarchy and the Constitution*, 1995, Clarendon, pp 115–21.

therefore considered that his only proper course was to wait until the situation postulated by Asquith actually arose.

However, the Cabinet was not prepared to accept this, partly through concern about losing face, but also, Bogdanor feels, because they did not entirely trust the new king to use his prerogative powers in their interest. He had in 1908, while still Prince of Wales, remarked to Churchill in the course of a dinner party that Asquith, who came from a family of West Riding wool manufacturers, was 'not quite a gentleman', and at about the same time had said to the permanent secretary at the Treasury that he could not think how the latter could 'go on serving that damned fellow Lloyd George'.[18]

Matters were made worse for the king at this point by a disagreement between his two private secretaries. Both had considerable experience, much more so than the king, but they held opposing political views. Lord Knollys, a Liberal, believed that the government's advice should be accepted, even though he had earlier told King Edward that it would better that he abdicate rather than accept Asquith's request for guarantees. Sir Arthur Bigge, a Conservative, was of the view that the king should continue to refuse to make any hypothetical promise. Knollys claimed that in the circumstances which now pertained, he would have advised Edward VII to give the guarantees and that there was no alternative government available should he think to dismiss the Liberals.

Here Knollys may have behaved with considerably less integrity than his master. Bogdanor suggests that Balfour might well have been willing to form a government in the circumstances, if only to prevent the king from being put under further pressure to give guarantees that the leading Conservatives considered to be unconstitutional. Though it is not clear whether Knollys was aware of Balfour's precise views, Bogdanor states unequivocally that Knollys 'hid from the king' details of a meeting in April 1910, just before the death of Edward VII, at which Balfour had apparently indicated that he would be prepared to take office should the Liberals resign.[19] At this point, on 16 November 1910, George V agreed with great reluctance to Asquith's demand and to a dissolution of Parliament, though he insisted that the Parliament Bill be submitted to the Lords before the election and that the undertaking to create peers be kept secret.

The election of December 1910 left the balance of the House of Commons unchanged. Asquith then re-introduced the Parliament Bill in the Commons, apparently hoping that a mass creation of peers would prove unnecessary. Once the undertaking was made public, Balfour concluded that, tactically, it would be better for the Conservative peers to accept the Bill than to continue opposing it. If the Bill were rejected, the Lords would be swamped with Liberal peers, who would have a sufficient majority to pass the anticipated Home Rule Bill at the first attempt and

---

18 Bogdanor, *ibid*, p 67. George V was a plain-speaking and straightforward man. Unlike his father, he was not known for his diplomatic skills and, in the light of future events, it seems likely that the Liberal Cabinet attached far more importance to these off-the-cuff remarks than they actually merited.

19 Unfortunately, Bogdanor does not cite any authority for this extremely interesting point, nor for his statement that George V believed for the rest of his life that Knollys, along with the ministers who had taken advantage of his inexperience, had not treated him fairly at this juncture. Of course, it is entirely possible that Balfour's stance had changed in the intervening seven months, but there seems to have been no attempt to establish the precise position.

without substantive amendment. If the Lords accepted the Bill, however, they could delay the Bill as a whole for up to two years and, with a continuing large Conservative majority, make significant amendments and so limit the damage caused to the integrity of the United Kingdom.

In May, Lord Lansdowne and a group of moderate Conservative peers sought a way out of the crisis by introducing a Bill which left the powers of the House of Lords unchanged, but altered its composition with the intention of giving it a legitimacy equal to that of the Commons, increasing the expertise of its members and converting it from an aristocratic to a meritocratic assembly. The Bill envisaged a second chamber of 350 members. Hereditary peers would no longer have automatic membership, but one-third of the 350 would be 'Lords of Parliament', peers who had previously held major public office. A further one-third would be elected by MPs and the remainder would be appointed by the government in proportion to party strengths in the Commons. The Lords of Parliament would provide the independent element necessary to free the House of Lords from the stigma of its unrepresentative nature, and the House as a whole would have legitimacy to reject 'factionalist' legislation. However, Asquith and his ministers rejected the proposals on grounds very similar to those on which governments of recent times have opposed the creation of a representative or 'expert' Upper House: that such a body would be better placed to obstruct government policy.[20]

With a high degree of abstention on the part of peers such as Lansdowne, who continued to oppose the Parliament Bill in principle, the bishops dividing equally and a number of Conservatives voting with the Liberals for fear of an influx of parvenus into the peerage, the Bill was passed on 10 August.

Bogdanor challenges the view of most previous writers that George V was bound to give the guarantees and that Knollys was justified in omitting to inform him of the details of the April meeting in order to prevent the inexperienced king from making a mistake which could have had serious adverse consequences for the monarchy. This view postulates that the government would have resigned had the king continued to refuse the guarantees, that the king would then have appointed Balfour and that a dissolution of Parliament would have followed, since the Conservatives were a minority in the Commons and were not in a position to attract sufficient support from other parties to create a working majority. The king would then be placed in an apparently partisan position, being prepared to grant a dissolution to the Conservatives after implicitly refusing a dissolution to the Liberals by denying them the guarantees that they sought as part of a 'dissolution package'. The situation would be made more serious yet by an appearance that the king had dismissed a Liberal government which had the confidence of the electorate, and replaced it with a Conservative government which did not.

Bogdanor considers this analysis to be flawed. George V was prepared at all times to follow the advice of his ministers, and accepted that he was bound to do so, and to assent to their request for a dissolution in December 1910. He argues that the king was not bound to undertake to use his prerogative in a particular manner in hypothetical circumstances, and notes in particular that the result of the forthcoming election could not be predicted, nor could the form in which the Parliament Bill might be presented to the Lords, given the possibility of extensive amendments in the Commons.[21]

20 Loveland, *op cit*, p 203.
21 Bogdanor, *op cit*, pp 117–19.

It is not without a certain irony that the Parliament Act 1911, as finally passed, was envisaged by its creators as an interim measure, pending a re-structuring of the House of Lords. The government appointed a commission headed by Viscount Bryce, a future architect of the League of Nations, to investigate the role of the second chamber and to make recommendations for its future composition, though these were never acted upon. The 1911 Act has remained in its original form, amended only to reduce the period of possible delay to one year. The Lords lost all power over money Bills, and in the case of other Bills, the provisions of the Act allowed the Lords to be bypassed. If, having been rejected by the Lords, a Bill was passed by the Commons in two subsequent sessions of Parliament, it could be presented for the royal assent notwithstanding its failure to be passed by both Houses. The only exception was a Bill to extend the life of a Parliament beyond seven years (since reduced to five years).

Events since have shown that until recent years, the powers created by the Parliament Act, either in its original form or in the amended form of 1949, were used rarely and only in the case of Bills of major significance:

(a) the disestablishment of the Church in Wales 1914;

(b) Irish Home Rule 1914;

(c) the nationalisation of the steel industry;

(d) the Parliament Act 1949.

The Thatcher government then used the mechanism to obtain the passage of the War Crimes Act 1991, which was initially rejected by the Lords for the principled reason that it effectively conferred retrospective criminal liability on a particular class of persons.[22] The government considered that the Act merely closed a loophole in the existing law and did not so much create retrospective liability as a mechanism by which the persons affected could be tried in respect of matters which had constituted offences under the law of civilised countries at the relevant time. The 1997 Labour government has frequently used the powers of the Parliament Acts, largely, it appears, for reasons of convenience rather than principle, and not to enable the passage of complete Bills but to override amendments inserted by the Lords. For example, the Lords amended the provision of the European Parliamentary Elections Bill 1998 introducing proportional representation in European elections on a 'party list' rather than a named candidate basis no fewer than six times, the Parliament Acts being invoked as soon as the provision was rejected for the final time at the beginning of the 1998–99 parliamentary session. Whether this practice will continue remains to be seen.[23]

23.6   THE IRISH QUESTION

This crisis was almost immediately followed by a second. In pressing forward the Parliament Bill, Asquith had himself been placed under pressure by the Irish

---

22 Persons who were not within the jurisdiction of the United Kingdom courts at the material time since they were not then British subjects and the alleged offences took place overseas.

23 A Parliament Acts (Amendment) Bill was introduced into the House of Lords on 14 November 2001 by the former Master of the Rolls, Lord Donaldson of Lymington, in order to reduce the potential for abuse by restricting the use of the Parliament Acts mechanism to third and subsequent sessions of any Parliament.

Nationalists on whose support the government depended. In 1912, he accordingly introduced a third Home Rule Bill, more limited than that of 1886, since it retained Irish representation at Westminster and reserved a greater number of matters to the United Kingdom Parliament. He attempted to counter the Conservative view that Home Rule for Ireland would lead inevitably to the break-up of the United Kingdom by arguing that devolution of some of the powers of the existing Parliament could only bring greater efficiency, and emphasised the existence of some 20 self-governing legislatures owing allegiance to the Crown in various parts of the British Empire, notably the 'white dominions' of Canada, New Zealand, Australia and South Africa, the last created as recently as 1910 by the union of the Cape and Natal with the former Boer republics, demonstrating, Asquith claimed, that it was possible to make friends of former enemies.

The Bill was rejected by the Lords, whose Conservative majority remained overwhelming. Not only were the Conservatives opposed to Home Rule as a matter of principle, the situation was gravely complicated by the division between Ulster and the rest of Ireland that had emerged much more strongly since the 1880s. Over much of Ireland, Unionists were a small and scattered minority, but in Ulster – modern Northern Ireland plus the counties of Donegal, Cavan and Monaghan – they formed a majority and were a generally more prosperous and better-educated group than the Nationalists. They were supported in their wish to remain within the Union by the Conservatives, who in this period absorbed the remaining Liberal Unionists. A proportion of Conservatives were prepared to accept that Home Rule for the rest of Ireland was inevitable, but considered that imposing Home Rule on Ulster against the wishes of the majority of its people was contrary to the emerging ideology of national self-determination and tantamount to expelling from the United Kingdom persons who did not desire special treatment, but simply wished to retain their existing position.[24]

It now became clear that a proportion of Ulster Unionists were prepared to take up arms against the British government in order to resist rule from Dublin, so that the Home Rule issue raised the spectre of serious disorder at best, if not civil war. In any event, argued Andrew Bonar Law, the new Conservative leader, the Liberals had no election mandate for Home Rule, and such a major constitutional change should not be pursued without a further general election. For their part, the Liberals claimed that there had been public discussion of Home Rule at the time of both elections in 1910, that to allow the Conservatives to force a general election on the issue would give the Opposition an effective right of veto over a government, and that in any event, a popular mandate for Home Rule might not persuade the extreme Unionists in Ulster to abandon the possibility of armed resistance.

Under the Parliament Act, the Home Rule Bill could become law after being passed by the Commons in the next two sessions of Parliament, and thus before the end of 1914, but in the intervening period, the situation deteriorated markedly. Irish Nationalists considered that the Bill did not go far enough and was in itself only an initial step, strengthening Conservative fears that Home Rule would lead to the break-up of the United Kingdom.

On 28 September 1912, a public ceremony took place in Belfast City Hall at which Unionists were asked to sign a Covenant to use 'all means which may be found

---

24   Bogdanor, *op cit*, pp 122–23.

necessary to defeat the setting up of a Home Rule Parliament in Ireland'. Eventually, some 250,000 Unionists subscribed to this open-ended commitment to force and about 35,000 of them joined an Ulster Volunteer Force led by Sir Edward Carson, one of the leading barristers of the day, which began to train with rifles imported from Germany. Given that any action would have been treasonable under the 1351 Statute as armed rebellion against the Crown, there is considerable irony in their protestations of unswerving loyalty. The government seems not to have made any serious attempt to prevent these sinister developments, apparently hoping that Carson and his followers were bluffing, and perhaps afraid that any action to suppress the private army would set off the violence they hoped would never happen. To make matters worse, there was considerable and justified concern as to whether the British Army, if called upon to act in aid of the civil power in Ulster, would actually do so. A significant proportion of its officers had family connections with Ulster and sympathies were generally with the Unionists. This concern was only heightened when in March 1914, a British Covenant was launched and its first signatories included the much respected Field Marshal Earl Roberts of Kandahar. At the same time, 57 officers of the cavalry brigade serving at the Curragh, near Dublin, declared that they would resign their commissions if called upon to act against Carson's volunteers.[25]

An issue of constitutional principle also emerged. On the basis that the Parliament Act was an interim measure only, the Conservatives argued that the normal structure of the constitution was in suspension pending the re-structuring of the Upper House. Until a 'popular' second chamber replaced the Lords, the normal checks and balances which existed by constitutional convention did not exist and the king had the power either to refuse assent to the Home Rule Bill or, if the ministers continued to refuse a general election before the Bill became law, to dismiss them. The Conservatives concluded that the proper course was to force a general election; furthermore, since the government was acting unconstitutionally, they were entitled to use means going beyond those of normal parliamentary opposition in order to do so. Again, Bogdanor goes into this issue in detail,[26] showing that the king was gravely concerned at the constitutional propriety of his government's actions in seeking to give effect to the Home Rule Bill on the authority of the Commons alone and without a prior popular mandate. From papers produced in this period, it emerges that George V believed not only that his constitutional position had been altered by the Parliament Act, at least in the interim period before the re-structuring of the Lords, but also that the Act had rendered obsolete those precedents on which he would have relied in exercising the relevant prerogatives.

In the face of the government's intransigence, Bonar Law and other senior Conservatives concluded that the role of the monarch was crucial since, in practice, an election could only be forced if either the king refused to give the royal assent to the Home Rule Bill, so that Asquith would seek a dissolution, or the king dismissed the government, in which case, Asquith's successor would have no option but to seek a dissolution. Indeed, now that the power of veto over legislation had been removed from the House of Lords, the sovereign was the sole guardian of the integrity of the constitution against a government seeking to act in an improper fashion. Whether the king retained power to dissolve Parliament and so precipitate a general election

---

25 Read, *op cit*, p 507.
26 Bogdanor, *op cit*, pp 123–35.

against the will of his government was in dispute. Sir William Anson, a leading constitutional thinker, considered that he did. The Liberals claimed that one consequence of the Parliament Act was that the Lords had lost any power to decide upon a dissolution, that the sovereign's power to do so was in abeyance through disuse and that sole power in this regard rested with the government.

Once again, King George V was faced with a major dilemma, made much worse by his position as head of the Armed Forces and the very real threat of armed conflict over Home Rule. He acted throughout the crisis in an exemplary fashion, establishing a model of constitutional propriety for his successors. Not only were the Unionists arming in Ulster, nationalist Irish Volunteers were following suit elsewhere. Whichever way he acted or omitted to act, the political neutrality which he regarded as an essential part of his constitutional role would be compromised. If he assented to the Bill, he would be subjecting a proportion of his subjects to Home Rule against their express will and might well precipitate a civil war. If he did so without a prior general election, he would, he and a responsible body of opinion believed, be acting unconstitutionally. If he did not or he dismissed the government, he would, in the eyes of his government and a second responsible body of opinion, be acting unconstitutionally in relying on prerogatives which no longer existed. In either event, the monarchy would be damaged.

A memorandum produced by Lord Stamfordham, the former Arthur Bigge and from 1913 the king's sole private secretary,[27] demonstrates that George V's paramount concern at all times was that civil war over Ulster should be avoided. In his view, Ulster should be excluded from the Bill, and the Conservatives should accept Home Rule for the remainder of Ireland. If a consensual settlement could not be reached, there must be a general election or, failing that, a referendum on the issue.

Partly as a result of Stamfordham's influence, a number of meetings took place between Asquith and Bonar Law during the winter of 1913–14, but without agreement. On 9 March 1914, while introducing the Bill in the Commons for the third time, Asquith raised the possibility of an additional Bill to postpone the application of Home Rule to Ulster for six years, which meant two general elections must take place before it took effect in Ulster. This suggestion was bluntly rejected by Carson as 'sentence of death with a stay of execution for six years'.[28] At the same time, Asquith also raised the possibility for a referendum on the inclusion of Ulster in the Home Rule Bill, but on 19 March, he refused the king's suggestion that a referendum take place on the Bill as a whole.

An impasse had now been reached, since no settlement had been achieved by negotiation and Asquith continued to reject a general election or referendum. Bogdanor considers that of the two prerogatives which the king might have utilised, that of dismissing the government was the less extreme, since it did not entail disregard of ministerial advice. This seems a curious interpretation, since the king would dismiss his ministers on the basis that he was not prepared to accept their advice and could no longer work with them.

On the information available, the king seems to have been inclined towards a dismissal of the government, if the situation required him to force an election, rather than refusal of assent, though it remains unclear to what extent he was prepared to act

---

27   Cited in Bogdanor, *op cit*, p 127.
28   See Read, *op cit*, p 508.

rather than merely to threaten. Certainly, he believed himself entitled to act, though in the event, the question was not tested. In June, Asquith introduced the amending Bill into the Commons, having on 9 May assured the king that he would not seek royal assent to the Home Rule Bill without the amending Bill. The king clearly remained concerned on this point, since he sought further assurances from two senior ministers.

Under the influence of the king, a further attempt at negotiation followed, with a conference at Buckingham Palace on 21–24 July between the leading protagonists. All were now prepared to accept the principle of excluding Ulster from Home Rule, but the talks broke down over whether the area to be excluded should include two counties where Protestants and Catholics were almost equal in numbers.

Meanwhile, a 19 year old Bosnian Serb named Gavrilo Princip had murdered Archduke Franz Ferdinand, heir presumptive to the Austrian throne, in the Bosnian city of Sarajevo on 28 June. This exacerbated long standing tensions in Europe and precipitated an Austrian ultimatum to Serbia, whose secret service was believed by the Austrian government to be responsible for the assassination. The ultimatum was couched in such terms that, had it been accepted, Serbia would have ceased in practice to be an independent state. On 24 July, as the Buckingham Palace Conference broke up, Serbia rejected the ultimatum and on 28 July, Austria duly declared war on Serbia. In consequence of a series of alliances between the continental powers, Russia mobilised in order to protect Serbia; Germany, allied to Austria, delivered an ultimatum to Russia. When this was ignored, Germany launched a pre-emptive strike on Russia's ally, France. The German war plan required an advance through Belgium. As a guarantor since 1839 of Belgian neutrality, Britain delivered an ultimatum to Germany. When this expired at midnight on 3 August, Britain declared war on Germany and her allies.

On 30 July, Asquith postponed discussion on the amending Bill and instead introduced a Bill suspending the imposition of Home Rule until after the war, promising that there would be no coercion over Ulster. Though the king remained deeply unhappy and continued to advocate a consensual settlement, he assented to the Home Rule Bill in September. He considered that Asquith had acted improperly, if not deceitfully, in presenting the Bill to him without the amending Bill and contrary to the assurances given earlier, but it appears that he was persuaded that he would not in the changed circumstances be justified in refusing assent, since there would as a matter of reality be an amending Bill, a general election and full debate on the issue of Home Rule before the Home Rule Act came into force.

It is of interest to speculate on the king's view of the likely duration of the war. The popular view that the war would be 'over by Christmas' was not shared by the government. Lord Kitchener, newly appointed Secretary of State for War, announced in August 1914 the raising of a 'New Army' of 100,000 men, who would enlist for three years or the duration of the war. The Parliament Act had reduced the maximum duration of a Parliament to five years, meaning that a general election should take place in December 1915. However, the law allows a Parliament to extend its own life by a maximum of one year at a time in time of war; the 1911 Parliament did so on three occasions before an election finally took place in December 1918. Had the war come to an end before December 1915, it seems possible that in the intervening period, the government could have sought to give effect to Home Rule in advance of an election and so triggered a renewal of the constitutional crisis.

Carson's Ulster Volunteer Force enlisted en masse in the British Army and, as the 36th (Ulster) Division, fought on the Western Front throughout the war. Large numbers of Catholics, including some former Irish Volunteers, also served under the British Crown. By the summer of 1916, 130,000 Irishmen of both religious groups were serving soldiers. Though the mainstream Irish Nationalists were prepared, if reluctantly, to accept the postponement of Home Rule, the extremist elements within the nationalist movement were not. Before the end of 1914, Sir Roger Casement – ironically a Protestant who had achieved distinction in the British Consular Service – travelled to Germany and attempted to subvert Irish prisoners of war into joining an Irish Brigade in the German Army. Casement's efforts garnered no more than a handful of recruits, the great majority of Irish prisoners angrily rejecting his overtures. However, Patrick Pearse and other militants, now seeking a fully independent Irish republic with immediate effect, began to plan a rising to begin in Dublin at Easter 1916, and Casement obtained a quantity of weapons from the German government for this purpose. British Naval Intelligence became aware of the planned shipment of these weapons at an early stage; the ship in which they were transported was apprehended at sea by the Royal Navy and Casement was arrested near Tralee shortly after being landed there by U-boat. The rising went ahead on 24 April, but was rapidly put down amid heavy casualties on both sides. Martial law was declared and Pearse and 14 others were court-martialled and executed by firing squad. Casement was convicted of high treason and, despite an extensive campaign for clemency, was hanged on 3 August.

The vigorous suppression of the Easter Rising and the 'martyrdom' of its leaders created a backlash among nationalists, and the large-scale insurrection that had been dreaded for so long followed, but among the Catholics of the south rather than the Ulstermen. Home Rule was no longer enough; complete autonomy was sought, if not an independent republic. At the same time, the acceptance among the Allied powers that the principle of national self-determination should be a major facet of the post-war settlement made it increasingly difficult for the British to justify their previous stance over Ireland.[29] In the 1918 election, 78 of the 104 Irish seats went to the republicans of Sinn Fein ('Ourselves Alone'), for all that they had made it clear during the campaign that they would not take their seats if elected, since that would mean swearing allegiance to the British Crown.

The Sinn Fein candidates assembled in Dublin and proclaimed themselves as the parliament (or *Dail*) of an independent Irish republic, and a long and bitter campaign, marked by murder and atrocities on both sides, occupied the period 1919–21. Finally, in an Anglo-Irish Treaty negotiated between the British government and representatives of the Dail headed by Michael Collins, both sides accepted a compromise. The six Protestant-majority counties of Ulster would remain within the United Kingdom under a modified form of Home Rule, while the remaining 26 counties were granted dominion status as the Irish Free State. The Treaty was ratified by Parliament in 1922 in the Government of Ireland Act.

However, a second civil war then broke out between Collins and his adherents on the one hand and extremists headed by Eamon de Valera on the other, who continued to seek a fully independent republic embracing the entire island. The latter triumphed.

---

29 National self-determination was one of the 'Fourteen Points' espoused by the Allies at the behest of the American President Woodrow Wilson, and was applied in particular to the peace settlement with the former Austro-Hungarian Empire.

In 1931, the Statute of Westminster gave the Free State, along with the other dominions, virtual autonomy, and in 1933, de Valera's government made use of this to convert the Free State into a de facto republic. The Governor General was stripped of his powers, Irish citizens were deprived of their status as British subjects and appeals to the Privy Council ended. A new constitution, largely drafted by de Valera, was adopted in 1937. The Free State remained neutral during the Second World War, although considerable numbers of Irishmen served in the British forces. Finally, in 1949, de Valera's government formally declared the Free State a republic and withdrew from the British Commonwealth. Conflict over Northern Ireland continues and at the time of writing, the situation is far from resolved.

CHAPTER 24

REPRESENTATION OF THE PEOPLE SINCE 1900

24.1   WOMEN'S SUFFRAGE

The legal and social position of women gradually improved over the last two decades of the 19th century and the first decade of the 20th to one of less extreme inequality with men. In particular, the Married Women's Property Act 1882 enabled women to retain control of their own assets after marriage, and career opportunities were emerging for middle class women and the better-educated among the working classes in spheres such as teaching and nursing. Women were also increasingly involved in local government as members of county and borough councils and Poor Law guardians. These changes undermined the traditional view that women's suffrage was inappropriate and it became increasingly difficult to justify the failure to accord votes to women on the same terms as men.

Professor Pugh considers that by 1906, the political will, particularly among the large Liberal majority in the House of Commons, was in favour of women's suffrage in principle, though they did not accord it a high legislative priority and there was no agreement on the terms on which women should be granted the franchise. Neither of the two main parties was united on the women's suffrage issue. Labour did not commit themselves, since some members feared that granting votes to women would hinder their campaign for universal male suffrage.

Since the 1880s, an assortment of groups had campaigned for women's suffrage by the established methods of oral and written persuasion. These were brought together in 1897 under the umbrella of a National Union of Women's Suffrage Societies (NUWSS). In 1903, Emmeline Pankhurst and her daughters, Christabel and Sylvia, formed the Women's Social and Political Union (WSPU). In 1905, concluding that insufficient notice was being paid to women's suffrage, the Pankhursts embarked on a campaign of militancy to publicise their cause. They interrupted meetings, demanding that speakers commit themselves to women's suffrage. They created disturbances and, when arrested and convicted for breach of the peace, they followed the example set by John Wilkes in refusing to pay fines and being committed to prison for default. From disrupting meetings, the Suffragettes – the term coined by the *Daily Mail* to distinguish the WSPU from more moderate Suffragists – graduated to breaking the windows of politicians' houses, arson in public buildings and other acts of criminal damage. When imprisoned for their offences, they went on hunger strike in the hope of being released on medical grounds. All this, Pugh considers, was grist to the mill of opponents.[1] That the Suffragettes, mainly well-educated women from 'good' backgrounds – Mrs Pankhurst was the daughter of a doctor and the widow of a barrister – could behave in such a manner only demonstrated that women were not equipped for the responsibilities of the franchise. Even those broadly in favour of women's suffrage were repelled by the violence and contempt for existing law manifested by some among the Suffragettes.

---

1   M Pugh, *State and Society: British Political and Social History 1870–1992*, 1994, Arnold, pp 134–36. See also D Read, *England 1868–1914: The Age of Urban Democracy*, 1979, Longman, pp 500–04.

However, although the Pankhursts attracted few adherents and the WSPU itself split on no fewer than three occasions, the issue did achieve a greatly enhanced place in the public and political consciousness, and by 1914, the NUWSS, which had at all times eschewed militancy, embraced some 300 groups with a total membership of about 50,000.

In 1912, the Liberal Cabinet agreed to an amendment to its Franchise and Registration Bill which would have given some women the vote, and the Commons accepted this on a free vote. However, the Speaker then ruled that the amendment fundamentally altered the character of the Bill and was therefore contrary to parliamentary procedure. This decision was followed by an upsurge in Suffragette militancy. Most famously, Emily Wilding Davison attempted to disrupt the 1913 Derby by running onto the course and into the path of the king's horse and died from her injuries. The horse and rider were also injured, and public sympathy largely lay with them. Mrs Pankhurst was then involved in a conspiracy which brought about an explosion in a house being built for Lloyd George, and was sentenced to three years' imprisonment. Earlier, the government had attempted to deal with the hunger strikes by making use of forcible feeding, but this attracted so much adverse publicity that the Home Secretary sponsored the so called 'Cat and Mouse' Act, which allowed for the temporary release of hunger strikers and their re-imprisonment once they were fit for renewed incarceration.

As with Irish Home Rule, the First World War intervened before matters proceeded further. Mrs Pankhurst and the Suffragettes lent their support to the war effort, though Sylvia Pankhurst dissociated herself from the rest and became a militant opponent of the War. The War settled the issue. Over three million men served in the Armed Forces between 1914 and 1918, some 700,000 of whom were killed in action and many more were wounded. A considerable proportion of them did not qualify for the vote, even if aged over 21, and the principle of manhood suffrage was finally conceded without dissent, removing one potential difficulty over the grant of women's suffrage. At the same time, the contribution made by women to the war effort in general led to a broad acceptance of women's suffrage in addition, although the Representation of the People Act 1918 gave the vote only to women over 30. The extension of the vote to women over 21 had to wait until 1928.[2]

At the same time, women of voting age became entitled to sit in the Commons. The first to do so was Nancy Astor, returned in a by-election early in 1919.[3] One loophole remained in the law, in that women who held peerages in their own right were barred from the Lords, and this was not closed until the Peerage Act 1963.

24.2   A NEW UPPER HOUSE

Though its recommendations of 1918 were never acted upon, the Bryce Commission's statement of the proper functions of a second chamber remains a model:

---

2   The age of majority, and thus the voting age for both sexes, was lowered to 18 by the Family Law Reform Act 1969.

3   The first woman elected to Parliament was Countess Markewicz, formerly Constance Gore-Booth, in December 1918. As a Sinn Feiner, she was among those who refused to swear allegiance to the Crown and so never took her seat.

(a) examining and revising Commons Bills;

(b) initiating Bills on non party-political matters;

(c) providing a forum for untrammelled debate on major issues;

(d) delaying Bills for a sufficient time for public sentiment to be made clear.[4]

The future of the House of Lords is currently under consideration.[5] By the House of Lords Act 1999, which came into force at the end of the 1998–99 parliamentary session, all rights to speak and vote in the Upper House were removed from hereditary peers, other than the Earl Marshal and Lord Great Chamberlain, as Great Officers of State, and 90 others were elected by their fellows under transitional provisions.[6] Since then, a Royal Commission has reported and a White Paper has been produced, provoking much debate within Parliament and elsewhere. It is at present unclear what new legislation will be introduced, and when and in what form such legislation will take effect.

24.2.1 The problem

It became increasingly accepted during the 20th century that it was not appropriate for membership of a legislative house of a modern democracy to be based on birth, and that the House of Lords in its existing form lacked legitimacy. On that basis, it could not continue in its existing form. That is where consensus begins and ends. The issue of re-structuring the House of Lords is one of peculiar difficulty, bedevilled not only by conflict over matters of principle, in particular the proper functions of a future Upper House and how its membership should be made up in order to enable it to fulfil that function, but also by petty class antagonisms and elements of national, regional and party-political myth.

As to function, there is a polarisation between those advocating an Upper House which acts as an effective restraint on the potential abuse of power by the Executive, at a time when the House of Commons has ceased in practice to perform this role, and those who argue that no body should be in a position to limit the legislative power of a government which commands a majority in the Commons. Inevitably, there are many shades of opinion between these extremes, though there is a reasonable degree of consensus, at least outside the party-political sphere, around the Bryce formulation.

These functions seem to point to a future Upper House as a body separated at least in part from party politics, able to give reasoned and objective consideration to legislation and policy, and to employ its powers vis à vis the government of the day in a principled manner, while remaining sensitive to the government's possession of a popular mandate. This in turn suggests a body whose members, or at least a majority

---

4   I Loveland, *Constitutional Law: A Critical Introduction*, 1996, Butterworths, p 204.

5   This section concentrates on the House of Lords as a legislative body. There is also discussion, though as yet no formal proposals, on reconstituting the Lords of Appeal in Ordinary as a Supreme Court and making fundamental changes to the role of the Lord Chancellor. It is suggested in particular that the Lord Chancellor should cease to sit as a judge, though the present Lord Chancellor is reportedly opposed to the idea.

6   Section 2(2) of the House of Lords Act 1999. This provision results from an amendment inserted during the passage of the Bill by Viscount Cranborne, then Conservative leader in the Lords. It has been made clear by the government that this will not survive further re-structuring of the membership of the House. As a *quid pro quo*, those hereditary peers who do not sit in the Lords are now permitted to sit in the Commons and vote in elections by virtue of s 3(1).

of them, should not owe their position to party influence but to their personal stature and qualities, in particular, independence of mind and expertise in matters of public importance. However, no government is likely to relish the existence of an Upper House with sufficient power and legitimacy to be able to exercise its functions in a way which is effective in restraining executive excess. There have been numerous examples over the past 30 years in which a government whose Commons majority might be very small (and based on a minority of votes actually cast) proceeded with policies which aroused deep hostilities among substantial elements in the population and deep concern over issues of principle even among government MPs. The Poll Tax introduced by the Thatcher government is a particularly good example.[7] It is no accident that the relevant legislation in such cases was the subject of major amendment in the House of Lords, that governments of both the main political persuasions then claimed that the unelected Upper House was seeking to subvert democracy by attempting to frustrate the actions of an elected government and threatened to alter the powers or the composition of the Lords in order to prevent the House from acting in a similar fashion in the future – that is, acting as a check on the executive.

In consequence, all the proposals for changes in composition emanating from the major political parties, whether at the time in government or in opposition, have included a majority party-political element. There is then controversy over the means by which the members of a reconstituted House of Lords should obtain their positions. Should they be elected, either by the 'first past the post system' used in respect of the House of Commons, or by proportional representation, or appointed and, if so, by whom and on what basis? Should there be a combination of methods and, if so, which methods and in which proportions?

24.2.2 Early proposals for change

The Bryce Commission reported in 1918, proposing that the future Upper House should consist of 246 members elected by MPs, together with a further 81 elected by a joint standing committee of both Houses. This was rejected by a Cabinet committee. Government proposals followed in 1922 for a House of 350 members, the majority directly or indirectly elected from outside the existing House, the remainder drawn from hereditary peers elected by their fellows and others nominated by the Crown. No action was taken.

In consequence of the acceptance that the House of Lords in its unreconstituted form lacked the legitimacy of the Commons, there was from 1945 also an acceptance – at least among peers active in the House – that its powers, restricted as a consequence of the Parliament Acts to those of delay, scrutiny and amendment, ought to be employed in a responsible manner. In particular, it was accepted that when the Conservatives were out of office, they should not use their permanent majority in the Lords merely as an instrument of party politics.

In 1945, following the election of a Labour government under Clement Attlee with a very large majority and plans for radical social legislation and nationalisation of basic industries, the Conservative leader in the Lords, the 5th Marquess of Salisbury, proposed the convention that Opposition peers should not seek to delay Bills for

---

7   See below, pp 431–32.

which the government had obtained a popular mandate through their inclusion in the party's election manifesto. The Salisbury Convention dealt only with complete Bills, but 20 years later, in a debate on the War Damages Bill 1965, a highly controversial piece of legislation since it was retrospective in its effect and had been introduced in order to save the government from paying large sums in compensation,[8] Lord Salisbury made further proposals concerning amendments.

Under normal parliamentary procedures, the House of Lords is entitled to amend Bills during their passage. Following amendment, a Bill returns to the Commons to repeat its stages in the amended form. The Commons may accept the amendments or reject them, and in either case, the Bill then returns to the Lords. During the passage of the War Damages Bill, the Lords inserted an amendment in order to remove its retrospective effect, and thus its utility in the eyes of the government. The Commons then reversed that amendment. What, Lord Salisbury considered, was the proper approach to be taken by the Lords when the Commons rejected amendments made by the Lords for reasons of principle, and considered by them to be essential for the avoidance of injustice? He suggested that the Lords should only insist on their amendments, and so re-insert them, where:

(a) the question raised issues important enough to justify such drastic action; and

(b) the issue was one which could readily be understood by the people and on which the Lords could expect their support.

The Bill had cross-party support, if only because of concern to limit the cost to the government, and hence to the taxpayer, of a loophole in the law. However, the Lords were gravely concerned at its retrospective nature and the potential abuse of parliamentary supremacy. On the facts, and in the face of Labour threats to seek further reductions in the powers of the Lords if they were returned to power in the forthcoming election, Lord Salisbury considered that the amendment in question was not one on which the Lords should insist, and he persuaded his fellow Conservative peers not to continue to oppose the government. However, underlying his formulation is a sense that the power to insist on amendments ought to be used sparingly and as a means of preventing a government from abusing the power to legislate conferred by a majority in the Commons. Given that the government had power via the Parliament Acts to override the House of Lords, insistence on amendments was essentially an instrument of persuasion, to be used to encourage the government to reconsider and to open their minds to the views of the public at large. Salisbury's successor as Conservative leader in the Lords, Lord Carrington, suggested during the Labour government of 1974–79 that the Lords should not oppose a government Bill for which there is a mandate, but may use their power to delay where:

(a) the constitution is at risk; or

(b) public opinion is so clearly against the government that the electorate should be consulted before the law is enacted.

---

8   The Bill was designed to reverse the decision in *Burmah Oil v Lord Advocate* [1965] AC 75, a test case with massive financial implications, in which the House of Lords ruled that the plaintiff company was entitled to be recompensed for the full value of oil installations in Rangoon which had been destroyed by British troops in order to prevent them from falling into Japanese hands in 1942, rather than only to receive limited compensation under a statutory scheme.

From the late 1940s, re-structuring of the House of Lords emerged again as a political issue, albeit not one of great urgency. Cross-party discussions in 1949 produced a broad acceptance of the Bryce formulation on functions and a consensus that in a re-structured House, there should not, so far as possible, be a permanent majority for any one party.

Two lesser but important developments occurred during the Conservative government of 1951–64. The first was the introduction of life peers under the Life Peerages Act 1958,[9] which can be said to mark the beginning of a chain of events by which the future membership and role of the House of Lords became an avowedly party-political and controversial issue. This change came about because the increasing volume and complexity of legislation after 1945 – resulting from a much enlarged role for government as the result of the Welfare State – meant that the Commons increasingly lacked time and resources for the detailed scrutiny of Bills. In order that the Lords could take on some of this burden, the government sought to augment its traditional membership with persons who had made a distinguished contribution to public life and who could claim expertise in one or more fields of endeavour. Such persons could then make an informed and reasoned contribution to the legislative process. This was the original philosophy behind the advent of life peerages, which are granted by the sovereign on the advice of the Prime Minister. Being granted for the lifetime of the recipient only, the link with expertise and merit was made explicit, and the doubts of traditionalists who feared the wholesale grant of peerages to parvenus were to some extent assuaged. However, to a great extent, the power to create life peers, in practice exercised by the Prime Minister, has become a tool of party politics, a high proportion of peerages being granted for openly partisan reasons, particularly since 1979.[10]

In 1963, a Peerage Act was passed in order to enable heirs to hereditary peerages to continue to sit in the House of Commons. The immediate impetus came from the case of Anthony Wedgwood Benn, a sitting Labour MP at the time when he succeeded his father as the 2nd Viscount Stansgate in 1960. This triggered a by-election in his constituency, at which Wedgwood Benn, following the example of Charles Bradlaugh in the 1880s and in the hope of publicising what he regarded as the injustice of his position, stood. Like Bradlaugh, he won the seat but was prevented from taking it up.[11] A joint committee of both Houses reported in 1962 and the ensuing Act allowed any existing hereditary peer not of the first creation[12] to renounce his peerage within one year from the Act's commencement. Any person inheriting a peerage thereafter might disclaim it within one year of his predecessor's death or on attaining his majority. In either case, the rights of his own heirs were unaltered but were postponed

---

9   Prior to 1958, peerages were occasionally granted for life to specific individuals, the earliest known example in England dating from 1377, but the Life Peerages Act made provision for this to be done on a regular basis for the first time.

10   Any writer on this subject can produce a multitude of examples where the power has been abused and the honour thoroughly debased, their precise identity depending on his own prejudices.

11   See *Re Parliamentary Election for Bristol South East* [1961] 3 WLR 577.

12   Ie, not a peer whose peerage has been created for him. It was considered, and rightly so, that a person who accepted a peerage of his own volition was in quite a different position from one whose peerage came by accident of birth.

until his death.[13] The 1963 Act made other changes affecting the composition of the House of Lords by allowing peeresses in their own right to sit, along with all holders of Scottish peerages.[14]

Shortly before the 1964 election, the Labour leader, Harold Wilson, warned the House of Lords that if it delayed government Bills, his party would seek a mandate to amend the Parliament Acts so as to put an end to the Lords' power to block legislation. Initially, the Wilson government (1964–70) did not give the matter particular priority, though the controversy over the War Damages Bill provided an opportunity to create an all-party committee to consider change. This Committee recommended removing voting rights from hereditary peers, limiting their participation to speaking in debates only, although the sovereign could bestow life peerages on individual hereditary peers.

A major area of controversy under the Wilson government was policy towards Rhodesia, now Zimbabwe. This had been a British colony since the 1890s with a legislative assembly and, latterly, a considerable degree of internal autonomy. In 1965, the Rhodesian Prime Minister, Ian Smith, made a unilateral declaration of independence, whereupon Parliament, at the instigation of the Wilson government, passed the Southern Rhodesia Act 1965 which declared the Smith regime illegal and re-imposed full direct rule from Westminster. This had no practical effect whatsoever and the government attempted to bring the Rhodesians to heel by means of economic sanctions. In June 1967, the House of Lords used their powers relating to delegated legislation, unaffected by the Parliament Acts, to veto an Order in Council under the prerogative authorising such sanctions, and this led the Wilson government to give effect to its earlier threats.[15]

The White Paper *House of Lords Reform*, produced in November 1967, largely re-stated the proposals of the all-party committee, in particular the division between voting and non-voting peers. There should be 230 voting peers, each subject to a minimum attendance requirement, the hereditary peers being non-voting peers. The government of the day should have a small majority of voting peers but not an overall majority. It was also recommended that the Lords' power to delay Bills should be reduced to six months. The White Paper was approved by the Lords with a substantial majority, but was rejected by the Commons as a result of an alliance between right-wing Conservatives who considered that the plan went too far and left-wing Labour MPs who believed it did not go far enough. A subsequent Bill based on the White Paper was withdrawn by the government after it ran out of time.

---

13 Two other immediate beneficiaries were the leading Conservatives, the 14th Earl of Home, an MP and minister before his father's death under his courtesy title of Lord Dunglass, and known after his renunciation as Sir Alec Douglas-Home, and Quentin Hogg, 2nd Viscount Hailsham. On the former's death, his heir duly succeeded as 15th Earl of Home, while the latter's son, also a Conservative MP, followed paternal example in disclaiming the viscountcy.

14 The Act of Union with Ireland provided for the election of Irish representative peers in the same fashion as those of Scotland. Under the transitional provisions in the Government of Ireland Act 1920, those already serving remained in the Lords for life, but other Irish peers remained outside.

15 The economic sanctions were given effect by a second Order in Council shortly afterwards.

24.2.3 The Thatcher years and after

During the Labour government of 1974–79 and, in particular, during the Thatcher government of 1979–90, the House of Lords was increasingly drawn into matters of controversy, and its constitutional role, hitherto the subject of relative consensus, became a political issue once more. This was in the main because of an increased incidence of government defeats in the Lords, in both absolute and percentage terms. During the period 1974–79, there were 445 divisions in the Lords, in 355 of which the government was defeated (80%). This contrasts very sharply with a 'defeat rate' of 3.7% under the Conservative government of 1959–64. Loveland notes that in the later period, the Lords rarely opposed a government Bill a second time, but that, nevertheless, their actions were obstructive of a tight legislative programme and caused delays which on occasions led to Bills being dropped.[16] That this level of opposition to government policy cannot simplistically be attributed to the Conservatives using their permanent majority in the Lords against a Labour government is made clear by the fact that a high incidence of government defeats continued under Margaret Thatcher, particularly as her government's policies became increasingly right-wing in the latter half of the 1980s. Rather, there seems to have been a continuing level of concern at government's attempts to force through highly controversial pieces of legislation which raised significant issues of principle.

In this surge of anti-government activity, however principled, the pre-1999 House of Lords was sowing the seeds of its own destruction. Although it had no power of veto over Bills and, in the final analysis, a determined government could usually force the Lords to give way over amendments, nevertheless, a refusal by the Lords to pass government legislation unamended was capable of causing severe disruption to the legislative programme, as well as more general embarrassment to the government.

Further, although the Conservatives themselves met with considerable resistance in the Lords when in government, they gave ammunition to elements hostile to the hereditary element by cynical whipping of the 'backwoodsmen' in crucial debates both in government and in opposition. Although there was a relatively equal balance between the parties among regular attenders in the 1980s and 1990s, whether hereditary or life peers, together with a small but influential group of 'cross-benchers' independent of party ties, there was a large Conservative majority among those peers – a sizeable majority of hereditary peers – who attended infrequently. In the Thatcher years in particular, the backwoodsmen were deployed on a number of occasions in order to give the government a majority in crucial votes. This inevitably detracted from whatever appearance of legitimacy their more principled brethren among the hereditary peers could gain by their actions, either in making a regular and constructive contribution to the work of the Lords[17] or by absenting themselves from the House entirely.

In consequence, the Blair government came to power in 1997 with a manifesto commitment to remove the hereditary peers from the House of Lords and to undertake a considerably more vague 'reform' of the second chamber. It is a matter of concern that the House of Lords Act 1999 took effect before the government had

---

16 Loveland, *op cit*, p 214.
17 Perhaps the most obvious example to come to an academic mind is the Liberal Democrat peer Earl Russell, a distinguished scholar as the historian Conrad Russell.

produced any substantive plans for long term re-structuring of membership, and no clear timescale for implementing that re-structuring. Since then, a Royal Commission under the former Conservative minister, Lord Wakeham, has reported, and a White Paper has been produced, whose contents have aroused enormous controversy, which continues at the time of writing.[18]

24.2.4 The current position

Briefly, the White Paper proposes a membership of 750, reducing to 600 over 10 years. The current 587 life peers will remain, although a scheme will be created for their voluntary retirement. In the longer term, the membership will be 80% appointed, with levels of membership set for specific groups, including 16 Church of England bishops,[19] and specific representation for women and ethnic minorities. 20% of members will be elected on a party list basis. Recent debates in both Houses on the White Paper, as well as extensive coverage in national newspapers, have shown very high levels of concern over specific elements of the proposals as well as the broad terms, and reflect fears that an Upper House re-structured in this way would lack both legitimacy and independence.

It is argued, for example, that a 20% elected element is too small to give legitimacy, yet large enough to be a weapon for an unscrupulous government, the more so if elected under a party list system. A membership consisting entirely of appointees, it is argued on the one hand, would enable the Lords to become an 'assembly of notables', owing their position to their personal standing. On the other hand, an appointed House would lack the legitimacy which comes from election by the will of the people, and the power to appoint can too easily become the tool of government. If appointments are to be based to some extent on giving representation to groups currently under-represented in the political system, which groups should be accorded such special status, and in what proportions both *inter se* and in the re-structured House as a whole? Should steps be made to ensure the independence of the new House from the government of the day? If so, what should they be? Should there be a non party-political element? If so, what proportion of the House should it be, and how should its individual members be selected? How should the independence of such members be preserved during their term of membership? Should the appointed element be appointed for life, for the duration of a Parliament, or for longer terms designed to foster their independence from party ties (15 years has been suggested)?

---

18 *The House of Lords: Completing the Reform* (Cm 5291, 2001).
19 Reduced from the current 26.

CHAPTER 25

THE EMERGENCE OF MODERN MONARCHY: THE 20TH CENTURY

25.1   THE FIRST WORLD WAR

25.1.1 Image building

Although George V and the royal family committed themselves to the war effort from August 1914 onwards, the public standing of the monarchy for much of the conflict was compromised by the close ties of blood between the British royal family and Germany. All British monarchs from George I onwards except George V himself, whose mother was Danish, had had German mothers or, in the case of Edward VII, a German father. Kaiser Wilhelm II, the leading 'hate figure' of the day, was George V's first cousin, as were two reigning German princes. The king's consort, Queen Mary, was descended, through a morganatic marriage, from the southern German ruling house of Wurttemburg. Both had numerous relations serving in the German army.

The outbreak of war was accompanied by a vicious outburst of anti-German sentiment and it was not long before aspersions were cast on the royal family's patriotism.[1] Attention was also drawn to the apparent anomaly that the Kaiser and the Austrian Emperor Franz Josef were Colonels-in-Chief of British regiments, and they and six German princes were Knights of the Garter. The Kaiser was also a British Field Marshal and Admiral of the Fleet. Several German princes, all closely related to George V, held British titles. At the same time, several holders of German titles, closely related to the king by blood or marriage, were resident in Britain and serving in the British Armed Forces.[2]

Material in the Public Record Office and in the Royal Archives demonstrates clearly that Asquith's government hoped the issue would go away and that the king and Lord Stamfordham, who dealt with the government on his behalf, believed that taking action against the king's German relations to rectify these anomalies was small-minded and dishonourable, and would anyway contribute nothing to the war effort.[3] Those concerned were quietly left out of all new editions of the Army and Navy Lists from the end of August 1914 and the banners of the 'enemy' Knights of the Garter were taken down from St George's Chapel, Windsor, when extremists threatened to storm the chapel after the sinking of the *Lusitania* in April 1915, but no more was done until the latter half of 1916. At this stage, apparently prompted by the refusal of clemency to Roger Casement – having allowed one British renegade to hang for treason, how could the government refuse action against other high-profile

---

1   The Kaiser and his family were at the same time under suspicion of less than wholehearted commitment to the German war effort because of their British connections. The Kaiser's American dentist even records a surreptitious visit to his surgery by the Kaiser's son-in-law, the Duke of Brunswick, who had been ordered by the Kaiser not to show his face in Berlin after an angry crowd assembled outside his palace demanding his immediate return to the front (AN Davis, *The Kaiser I Knew*, 1918, Hodder & Stoughton, pp 202–03).

2   The best known was Prince Louis of Battenberg, father of Earl Mountbatten of Burma, and First Sea Lord until his resignation on 30 October 1914 after a vicious press campaign.

3   These matters are dealt with in detail in A Lyon, 'A reaction to popular hysteria: the Titles Deprivation Act 1917' (2001) Liverpool Law Review 173–203.

individuals merely because they were the king's relations? – Asquith announced that there would be legislation to remove British titles from persons serving in the Armed Forces of enemy powers. This resulted in the passing of the Titles Deprivation Act 1917, a measure framed in very unusual terms so as to avoid any further embarrassment to the monarch and to minimise the possibility of publicity when its provisions came to be used.[4]

As the Titles Deprivation Bill went through Parliament in 1917, the king acted to dissociate the British monarchy from its German connections. By a Royal Warrant under the prerogative on 25 June, he renounced for himself and the other persons affected the German titles which they held, and adopted the surname of Windsor for the royal family.[5]

25.1.2 Wartime government

In the interim, a political crisis occurred in which George V's personal intervention was an important element in securing a peaceful resolution. Not only did the king demonstrate his own abilities as a statesman, the affair shows that the sovereign's role remained crucial in the appointment of a Prime Minister in any circumstances in which the position was less than clear-cut and, through his choice of Prime Minister, in the appointment of a government.

The Liberal government elected in 1910 was converted into a three-party coalition in May 1915 by the introduction of Conservative and Labour ministers. This increasingly ran into difficulties through failure to achieve a quick end to the war. At the same time, Conservative successes in a number of by-elections made them the largest single party in the Commons.

By December 1916, it was clear that Asquith could not continue in office. George V summoned Bonar Law, the Conservative leader, and asked him to form a government. Bonar Law, however, considered it unlikely that he could attract sufficient support. A dissolution of Parliament was the obvious solution, or would have been in peacetime. However, the king felt an election would be unduly disruptive to the war effort and would not necessarily guarantee an effective government. Much as he had refused the guarantees Asquith had sought over the Parliament Bill, he was not prepared to guarantee a dissolution. Having consulted colleagues, Bonar Law then confirmed that he was not in a position to form a government. In this uncertain situation, how was a

---

4   It was accepted that the titles involved were held by virtue of the prerogative and that what had been granted by the prerogative could be removed by the prerogative. However, with the exception of a few very ambiguous medieval cases, no person had ever been deprived of a peerage other than for treason via attainder. A Bill of Attainder required some form of trial, and there was serious doubt as to whether the individuals concerned could actually be liable for treason in all the circumstances. As finally passed, the Act gave power to a Committee of the Privy Council to declare that any peer or British prince came within the purview of the Act and that an Order in Council giving effect to deprivation would be made after the Committee's report had been laid before both Houses of Parliament for a period of one month. Such an Order was made on 28 March 1919, affecting three royal persons and one non-royal peer.

5   Up to this date, there had been doubt as to whether the royal family had a surname at all and, if they had, what it was. 'Windsor' was chosen by George V himself as being quintessentially English and because Windsor had been the site of a royal residence since the 1070s.

Prime Minister to be appointed who would have the necessary legitimacy to govern effectively at a time of continuing crisis?[6]

At the suggestion of AJ Balfour and Arthur Henderson, a Labour member of the coalition, the king set out to find a workable formula by negotiation. He convened a conference at Buckingham Palace with the intention of creating a broad-based government which could command all-party support with the minimum of upheaval. The conference comprised Asquith, Bonar Law and Henderson as leaders of the three main parties, together with Balfour and Lloyd George, now the leading member of Asquith's government. Initially, it was proposed that Bonar Law be Prime Minister, with Asquith in a senior position, but the latter refused to serve under Bonar Law, so that, ultimately, Lloyd George emerged as the preferred candidate.[7]

25.2   GEORGE V AND HIS PRIME MINISTERS

George V played a pivotal role in the choice of a Prime Minister on two more occasions, due in no small measure to the reputation for fair dealing which he had already earned. Initially, he seems to have acted very much in the role of arbitrator, encouraging the politicians to produce a workable solution which would command political legitimacy. On the second occasion, the solution was in principle his own.

In 1923, Bonar Law, who had headed a Conservative majority government since the general election the previous year, resigned after being diagnosed with terminal cancer of the throat. In the analogous circumstances of Campbell-Bannerman's resignation in 1908 and Lord Salisbury's retirement, the outgoing Prime Minister had recommended a successor, and Edward VII followed that recommendation. Now, the situation was unprecedented in that Bonar Law felt unable to recommend a successor and was too ill to be consulted.

In 1990, Margaret Thatcher, having lost the confidence of her Cabinet, resigned as Conservative leader and, after the party elected John Major in her place, resigned as Prime Minister. The queen then invited Major to form a government, so that it was effectively the party machine which selected the Prime Minister. In 1923, however, there was no system of electing party leaders. The two leading members of the Conservative Cabinet were the Foreign Secretary, Lord Curzon, and Stanley Baldwin, the Chancellor of the Exchequer. Unable to consult the outgoing Prime Minister, the king consulted a number of senior Conservatives, but they were divided as to which candidate was the most suitable. There were concerns on the one hand about Curzon's

---

6   The Battle of the Somme, the largest British offensive yet on the Western Front, ground to a halt in November 1916 after 450,000 casualties. The campaign in Mesopotamia, designed to safeguard oil supplies needed by the Armed Forces, had proved a costly and ignominious failure, following closely on the failure of the Gallipoli campaign the previous year. The Battle of Jutland, on 31 May–1 June 1916, gave the Royal Navy a strategic victory but at the cost of 6,000 men and 11 ships. Earlier in 1916, the Germans had launched an offensive around Verdun designed not to gain ground but to 'bleed France white', and French casualties there approached one million. On the Eastern Front, the Russians were in serious difficulties and would within a few months be effectively removed from the War by the revolution of March 1917.

7   V Bogdanor, *The Monarchy and the Constitution*, 1995, Clarendon, pp 99–101.

arrogant personality,[8] and the potential difficulty of working under him, and on the other about Baldwin's relative inexperience.

Eventually, the king sent for Baldwin. Lord Stamfordham later told AJ Balfour, who had favoured Baldwin on the basis that a Prime Minister ought to sit in the Commons, that the latter's advice had confirmed the king in his own preference for Baldwin. However, there are suggestions that the peerage issue may have been stressed in order to cloak a rejection of Curzon on grounds of suitability. Bogdanor notes that suggestions had been made during the First World War that legislation be passed to enable peers to speak in the Commons, and that this could have been pursued had there been the necessary will in favour of Curzon. Further, the king made it clear when he sent for Baldwin that he did not seek to establish a new constitutional doctrine that the Prime Minister should always be a member of the Commons, and later spoke in similar terms to Curzon. Other indications suggest that the king made his choice primarily on pragmatic grounds; that Baldwin was much more likely to enjoy the confidence of his own party. Finally, a letter from Stamfordham to the editor of The Times in 1928 suggests that the king, as on other occasions in his reign, was influenced by concern for the public standing of the monarchy; that if he appointed a Prime Minister from the Lords and this 'experiment' proved a failure, he would be considered out of touch with public opinion.[9]

25.2.1 The National Government

The position in 1931 was much more complex, involving, as in 1916, the creation of a workable government in a time of national crisis rather than a simple choice between two opposing candidates for Prime Minister.

A Labour government was in power under Ramsay MacDonald, but not only was this a minority administration, it was also deeply divided over economic policy at a time of world depression. The Cabinet split in August on the issue of cuts in unemployment benefit and other public spending in order to keep Britain on the gold standard,[10] then considered essential to the country's economic well being and to the financial standing required to obtain credit from abroad. After a period in which MacDonald endeavoured to keep his Cabinet together and to attract support from other parties in order to give effect to the cuts, it became clear that this would prove impossible.

Amid an atmosphere moving towards panic, the king, who had been following events from Balmoral, returned to London on Saturday 22 August, apparently on his own initiative. On the Sunday morning, MacDonald offered his resignation, informing him that he was not prepared to recommend Arthur Henderson, his main Cabinet opponent, as his successor. The king was reluctant to accept MacDonald's resignation,

---

8　The subject, when he was still an undergraduate, of the following doggerel:
　　My name is George Nathaniel Curzon,
　　I am a most superior person.
　　My face is clean, my head is sleek,
　　I dine at Blenheim once a week.

9　For a narrative of events and full discussion, see Bogdanor, op cit, pp 90–93.

10　The gold standard meant that paper currency was backed by gold reserves of equivalent value. At this time, Britain had a public expenditure deficit of some £120 million, mainly because of a fall in tax revenues resulting from the worldwide economic depression. The proposed cuts were calculated as saving £100 million.

having a very high regard for MacDonald's capabilities and also concerned to ensure continuity in government. Once more, the obvious solution was a dissolution, but, as in 1916, this was considered too disruptive, not least because the public spending issue was gravely pressing and the delay necessitated by an election would certainly leave Britain unable to continue on the gold standard.

Over the previous year, the principle that a coalition 'National Government' should be formed to deal with the worsening economic crisis had been much discussed. Acting on MacDonald's advice, the king consulted the other party leaders in the course of 23 August. Sir Herbert Samuel, the acting Liberal leader, also considered a National Government the best solution to the crisis, provided that MacDonald could bring in a strong body of the existing ministers. For the Conservatives, Stanley Baldwin indicated, apparently against his personal inclinations, that he would be prepared to serve in a National Government headed by MacDonald.

After a stormy Cabinet meeting on the Sunday evening, MacDonald went to Buckingham Palace and tendered his resignation a second time. Again, the king was reluctant to accept, telling MacDonald that he was in his view the only man capable of leading the country through the crisis, and that both the Conservatives and Liberals were prepared to serve in a National Government under his leadership. After MacDonald advised further discussions with Samuel and Baldwin, a conference between the three was hastily convened and took place at Buckingham Palace on the following morning.

A memorandum subsequently prepared by Sir Clive Wigram, Stamfordham's successor as the king's private secretary,[11] demonstrates that the primary role in the discussions was taken by George V, who impressed on MacDonald, Samuel and Baldwin the need to agree a solution that day. The king declared his full confidence in MacDonald and stressed the need for the three party leaders to work together in the national interest. In the course of that morning (24 August), agreement was reached on the basis that the National Government would hold office until the necessary measures had been taken to ensure Britain's overseas credit. Parliament would then be dissolved and a general election fought along party lines in the normal way. The three party leaders agreed specifically that the National Government would not fight the election as an entity. Further, the National Government was to be a 'co-operation of individuals' rather than a grouping of parties as was the normal nature of coalitions – the nearest parallel was the Ministry of All the Talents of 1807. The National Government, with a Cabinet of four Labour members, four Conservatives and two Liberals, took office the following day.

George V had played a pivotal role in resolving the immediate crisis, but any improvement was only temporary. Public spending reductions affecting the Royal Navy included a cut of 25% in the pay of most junior ratings, and the attempt to implement this triggered a serious mutiny (the Invergordon Mutiny). Though this was settled without violence when the government agreed after four days to reverse the pay cut, the fiscal measures required forced Britain off the gold standard. At the same time, MacDonald's opponents in the Labour Party expelled him from the party, along with those of his colleagues who had joined the National Government, condemning them as 'class traitors'.

11 Cited in Bogdanor, *op cit*, p 107.

At this point, the National Government lost its emergency and temporary nature. Contrary to the earlier commitment that it would not seek election, it sought to give itself legitimacy by appealing to the electorate against the 'unpatriotic' stance of its Labour opponents. The king, considering that its continuing in office was in the best interests of the country, refused once again to accept MacDonald's resignation and did not seek to enforce the earlier commitment. Instead, he granted a dissolution without conditions and, after a campaign which the Conservatives and Liberals, together with the Labour ministers, fought under a National Government umbrella, the government was endorsed with a majority of 554 seats to 52, and 67% of the vote.

25.3 THE ABDICATION

25.3.1 Background

Monarchy in the 20th century was faced, and continues to be faced, with a basic dilemma. The sovereign reigns, and each new sovereign succeeds, essentially by consent, by the will of the people rather than the will of God. The monarchy exists because the British people, or at least the majority, wish it to continue to exist or, in a negative sense, they allow it to continue to exist because they have no reason to replace it with any alternative institution. The sovereign, in both public and private life, ought therefore to be a living manifestation of the values expected by the people of their monarch.

This raises two difficulties. First, should the monarchy attempt to conform to the values of its age? If so, what are they? Or should it be essentially unchanging, a manifestation of 'timeless' values? If so, what are they? Second, in modern times as much as in earlier eras when monarchs ruled directly, what are the consequences if a sovereign is not prepared to conform to public expectations?

By the mid-1930s, 250 years had passed since the throneworthiness of an individual, his capacity to reign in accordance with prevailing philosophies of kingship, had been a major political issue. Apart from George III, who inspired considerable affection as a benevolent paternal figure, none of the Hanoverian kings had been popular. This did not create any particular threat to the monarchy as an institution, not least because in the 18th and early 19th centuries, the king was and was expected to be a remote figure, set quite apart from the mass of his subjects. The republicanism of the 1860s and 1870s seems largely to have been a reaction to Queen Victoria's invisibility following the death of Prince Albert, at a time when the monarch was expected to take an increasing public role.

However, with the advent of a 'public service' monarchy, which particularly occurred under George V, and the development of a popular mass media which occurred during the late 19th century and after, it became necessary for the monarch and the royal family to conform, and to be seen to conform, to a particular image and ideal.

George V's philosophy focused very strongly on the responsibilities of the monarch. In his view, he was in a very real sense the servant of his people. His paramount responsibilities were to the British nation and British Empire, and to the monarchy as an institution. Much as medieval monarchs were expected to conform to a warrior stereotype, so the new philosophy of monarchy required subordination at all times of self to duty.

A difficulty for the monarchy which emerged during the 20th century was the dichotomy that developed in the attitudes of the British people to 'their' monarch and the members of the royal family as people. Royal persons are no longer surrounded by a mystique arising from semi-sacred status; their position is no more than an accident of birth and they are 'people like us'. At the same time, the public have greater expectations of members of the royal family in relation to behaviour in public and in private than they do of non-royal persons – the royal family are in a position of privilege and that privilege must be earned.

In part, this dichotomy has emerged because the monarchy has itself endeavoured to present a particular image to its subjects. Just as Queen Victoria's public image before 1861 laid stress on her happy family life, so that of George V emphasised domesticity and simple tastes. The consequences when a monarch failed to conform to the expectations of his subjects and the philosophy of the public service monarchy emerged with full force in the year after his death. Not only did his successor's refusal to accept the restrictions imposed on him by his position as sovereign lead to his abdication and exile, for the first time in a century, there was a very real and immediate danger of a direct confrontation between a sovereign and his ministers and, unprecedentedly, over an issue of a sovereign's personal life.

25.3.2 Edward VIII and Mrs Simpson

George V's eldest son, who succeeded him as Edward VIII on 20 January 1936, seemed at first sight to conform admirably to the public service philosophy. Born in 1894, he was a cadet and midshipman in the Royal Navy, then a junior officer in the Grenadier Guards throughout the First World War. There is much evidence that he was impatient with official policy which prevented him from serving in the front line, particularly as that policy did not prevent Prince Albert, the only other among George V's sons who was of military age, from serving at sea with the Royal Navy.[12] The Prince of Wales made several tours of the British Empire during the 1920s, in which he established an image of dash and glamour very much in keeping with the post-war world. Not only did he have enormous personal charm and charisma – *I danced with a man, who danced with a girl, who danced with the Prince of Wales* ran a popular song of the day – he seems also to have had a genuine concern and affection for the less fortunate elements in the British populace, and he was in a very real sense the Diana, Princess of Wales of his day.

But even before the heir apparent succeeded to the throne, there were concerns, voiced only in private, about his suitability, especially as George V grew older and his health deteriorated sharply after a serious illness in the late 1920s. There were indications that the Prince of Wales was all too inclined to put his personal inclinations above his responsibilities and did not have the devotion to duty exemplified by his father, and increasingly by Prince Albert, now Duke of York. There was particular concern over the Prince's private life. Where the Duke of York followed the new ideal, enjoying an unpretentious lifestyle with his Duchess and two young daughters, the

---

12   He also took part in the Battle of Jutland, making him the only monarch since George II with personal experience of front-line military action.

Prince of Wales remained a bachelor, frequented nightclubs and conducted a series of affairs with married women.

Why should the marital intentions of King Edward VIII have caused such controversy? In 1936, the matrimonial practices of the royal family were in a period of transition. Prior to 1914, intermarriage, by arrangement, with continental dynasties had been the norm, to such an extent that the most recent male member of the British royal family to contract a valid marriage[13] elsewhere was James II, when he married Anne Hyde as Duke of York. The demise of most of the continental dynasties in 1918 made this practice impossible; George V therefore encouraged his children to seek marriages among the British aristocracy. The first to do so was his only daughter, Princess Mary, who married the 6th Earl of Harewood in 1922, the second the Duke of York in the following year. The new policy proved popular. Nevertheless, royal consorts in the inter-war period came from a narrow social stratum, and the mores of the time, when divorce was uncommon and extra-marital relationships were frowned upon, demanded their unimpeachable public probity.

It was a direct assault on the ideas of the day and the form now assumed by the monarchy when Edward VIII in the autumn of 1936 informed Stanley Baldwin, now Prime Minister, of his intention to marry Wallis Simpson. That Mrs Simpson was an American commoner was not in itself a particular problem. The British aristocracy had intermarried extensively with American heiresses since the 1870s;[14] an American counterpart to the Duchess of York would probably have been entirely acceptable. However, she had already divorced one husband and was in the process of divorcing a second. Once the second divorce had been made absolute, there would be no legal bar to the marriage, but there were serious difficulties in reality, linked intimately to popular expectations concerning the monarchy. Specifically, would the British public be prepared to accept Mrs Simpson as queen, as she would become if the couple married, under the well-established principle that a royal bride acquired through marriage the same status as her husband?

Ultimately, the issue was not put to the test, and controversy over Mrs Simpson's public acceptability has raged ever since. Baldwin advised the monarch that the public would not accept her as queen, or even as the king's wife via a morganatic marriage, though the views of the public were never canvassed and the British press maintained a self-imposed silence on the king's liaison until the crisis reached its final stages.[15] In strict constitutional terms, there was the further difficulty that the king was Supreme Governor of a church that did not recognise divorce, or remarriage after divorce, a matter which would shortly become of enormous symbolic importance in the coronation ceremonies scheduled for 12 Mary 1937. Finally, if the king chose to follow his personal inclinations and marry Mrs Simpson in the face of the presumed hostility of his subjects, he would act in a manner entirely contrary to the concept of public

---

13 Ie, a marriage not rendered void by the provisions of the Royal Marriages Act 1772.

14 The marriage of Winston Churchill's father, Lord Randolph Churchill, and Jennie Jerome, daughter of a New York newspaper magnate, is the best known.

15 One contemporary observer suggests that the outcome of the crisis might have been different had the press not adopted a policy of self-censorship and 'public opinion had been allowed gradually to form a favourable opinion of Mrs Simpson, and her excellent influence on the king', who was, he claims, much happier in himself as a result of their liaison and would therefore make a better king. See J Gunther, *Inside Europe*, 1940, Hamish Hamilton, pp 306–07.

service monarchy, and the faith of the populace in the monarchy as an institution could only be damaged.

The mythology of the Abdication Crisis of 1936 is that as the matter came to a head in November and early December 1936, Baldwin informed the king that his subjects would not accept Mrs Simpson as queen, that he pressed the king to renounce her and that, in the final analysis, he forced the king to choose between Mrs Simpson and the throne. Bogdanor sees Baldwin's role as a good deal more subtle,[16] though there is an element of truth in the myth in that Baldwin first informed the king that the public would not accept Mrs Simpson as queen, then that the compromise of a morganatic marriage was also unacceptable, leaving the king in the position that, unless he wished to trigger a yet more serious crisis by refusing to accept the advice of his ministers, he was left with two alternatives. These were to renounce Mrs Simpson[17] or to abdicate. He chose the latter.

In Baldwin's eyes, the paramount issue was the well being of the monarchy. As the king reigned by the consent of the people, his wife, who reigned with him as queen consort, must be acceptable to the people. The Prime Minister, as head of a government which also represented the will of the people, was entitled to advise the king in relation to the nation's opinion; indeed, he was under a duty to do so.[18]

Although Baldwin was of the view, as were the Labour Opposition, that the British public would not accept Mrs Simpson as queen, he shrank from being seen to advise Edward VIII as to any course of action. He was concerned to ensure that whatever decision the king made should be seen as reflecting his own free will. For that reason, he resisted pressure from within his Cabinet and from senior civil servants formally to advise the king to renounce Mrs Simpson.

Initially, it seems that Baldwin explored the possibility of preventing the issue of marriage from emerging into a concrete form. Was it possible, he asked the king on 20 October 1936, when he apparently feared that the matter would become public at any moment, that Mrs Simpson could be persuaded to discontinue her divorce action? While she remained married to another, there could be no question of her marriage to the king. The king declared himself unwilling to attempt such persuasion and Mrs Simpson duly obtained a *decree nisi* on 27 October which, under the law pertaining at that time, would be made absolute after six months. She would then be free to remarry.

On 16 November, Baldwin made it known to the king informally that marriage to Mrs Simpson was not acceptable to the government, although there had been no specific discussion on the point and, at the time, the possibility of the king's marriage was known only to four other Cabinet members. Here, it would seem, Baldwin was giving advice while at the same time proclaiming that he was not giving advice. The king informed him that he was prepared to 'go' in order to marry Mrs Simpson.

---

16   See Bogdanor, *op cit*, pp 135–44, from which the narrative of events is taken, although my analysis and conclusions differ. I have also made use of the near-contemporary account of the crisis in Gunther, *ibid*, pp 297–309.

17   There seems to have been no question of her remaining the king's mistress.

18   Quoted in Gunther, *op cit*, p 302. In the same way, the separation and ultimate divorce of the present Prince of Wales in the period 1992–96 was regarded by the then government as a matter in which it had some role, on the basis of the Prince's position as future monarch, and was the subject of a number of statements to the House of Commons by the Prime Minister, John Major. By contrast, the contemporaneous breakdown in the Duke of York's marriage was treated as a private matter affecting only the parties.

The possibility of a morganatic marriage was then raised by the king, who asked on 25 November for formal advice on the issue. A morganatic marriage represented a compromise solution, under which the couple could contract a valid marriage but Mrs Simpson would not acquire any royal status. Presumably, she would also not perform any public role. Any children of the marriage would be legitimate, but would not have royal status and would be excluded from the succession. Such marriages were not uncommon among continental dynasties, but, Baldwin declared, were contrary to the British tradition. Such a marriage would also require specific legislation.

At this point, the government showed its hand. Baldwin informed the king that the Cabinet would not support such legislation, citing the opposition of the governments of all the dominions except the Irish Free State, which, having been consulted along with the rest, had for its own reasons declared its lack of interest in the matter. Baldwin also expressed the government's opposition to the king's suggestion that he make a radio broadcast to appeal to the public for support in his desire to marry Mrs Simpson.

Here was the nub of the crisis. Marriage to Mrs Simpson would represent a rejection of ministerial advice that the marriage was not acceptable to the public, in Britain or the dominions. If the king insisted on broadcasting to the nation, he would be appealing to the public over the heads of his ministers, which was also constitutionally improper, as it was now well-established that the sovereign did not deal directly with his subjects in matters where the government had competence. If the king continued in his refusal to renounce Mrs Simpson, there were three possibilities:

(a) he could abdicate; or, if he were not prepared to abdicate,

(b) the Prime Minister and Cabinet could resign; or

(c) the king could dismiss the Prime Minister, if, indeed, that prerogative remained intact after a century of disuse.

A period of uncertainty lasting more than a fortnight followed, during which the affair exploded into the public domain. It was reported at an emergency Cabinet meeting on 27 November that the king believed a large proportion of the population would accept a morganatic marriage, and there are indications that he was prepared to defy the government to the extent of insisting on such a marriage and to demand the necessary legislation, though he conceded that the public would not accept Mrs Simpson as queen. The Marquess of Zetland, Secretary of State for India, informed the Viceroy of India that day that if the king maintained this position in the face of governmental advice that this was impossible, the government, in direct conflict with the king, was likely to resign.[19]

In a further letter of 5 December, Zetland took a still more pessimistic view, stating that a body of unofficial advisors was seeking to stiffen the king's resolve to resist the advice of his ministers, and setting out with admirable clarity the potential consequences of his remaining obdurate:

> ... Supposing that the King refuses to give a decision on either of the only two options which are open to him so long as the present Government remains in office ... what will happen? The Government may be forced to resign. The Labour Party would almost certainly refuse to form a Government; but the King has almost certainly been led to

19   Cited in Bogdanor, *op cit*, p 142.

believe that Winston [Churchill] would. Winston could not survive in the present House of Commons, but it would be open to him to demand a dissolution. And therein lies the supreme danger, for the country would be divided into two opposing camps on the question whether or not the King should be permitted to marry … without making her Queen. The Dominion Prime Ministers are strongly opposed to a morganatic marriage, and legislation would be needed not only here, but in every Dominion as well, and it would not, so far as I can judge, be forthcoming. On this issue it might well be that the Empire would disintegrate, since the throne is the magnet which at present keeps it together, while there might arise a situation in this country which would not be far from civil strife.[20]

No British monarch had ever voluntarily abdicated. Not only was abdication unprecedented, it amounted to a challenge, for the first time since 1714, to the hereditary nature of monarchy. That the person of the monarch was separate from the institution of the monarchy and that the heir apparent or immediate heir presumptive succeeded on his predecessor's death irrespective of apparent suitability or lack of it gave certainty and was one of the strengths of hereditary monarchy. Further, would the people see abdication as, effectively, the deposition by the government of a king whose personal popularity remained immense?

If Edward VIII were to abdicate, there was then the question of his successor. His heir presumptive, the Duke of York, was seen as a worthy but rather dull figure. Like his brother, he had served in the Royal Navy, and latterly in the newly-formed Royal Air Force, though he had spent much of the war medically unfit for active service. He was particularly known for his interest in industry and social work, having developed the Duke of York's Camps, in which young men from public schools and from the shop floor were encouraged to mix on an equal basis in a programme of outdoor activities. All the evidence suggests that he was reluctant to become king, not only because he did not relish supplanting a brother of whom he was very fond, but because he did not feel himself fitted to meet the responsibilities of kingship. Not only was there doubt in his own mind about his suitability, there was doubt in the minds of others, since he had a strong distaste for large-scale public events and a severe stammer.[21] If he were to be passed over, his elder daughter, the present queen, was only 10 years old, so that the issue of a regency would arise. The possibility that the third brother, the Duke of Gloucester, should succeed was apparently mooted at high level, though not pursued.

On 10 December, Edward VIII decided that he would not renounce Mrs Simpson, but that he would not marry her against the advice of his ministers. This left no alternative but abdication. A Declaration was executed on the same day, by which he abdicated and renounced all rights of succession in the future for himself and any heirs of his body, and the throne was vested in the Duke of York, who had by now indicated his willingness to accept the crown. This was given legal effect by His Majesty's Declaration of Abdication Act, which went through all its parliamentary stages on 11 December, and was required because the succession remains governed by the Act of Settlement which, under the ordinary principles of parliamentary supremacy, can only be amended by Act of Parliament.

---

20 Cited in Bogdanor, *op cit*, pp 142–43.
21 This had been largely overcome through speech therapy in the 1920s, but was apt to re-emerge under stress.

25.3.3 Aftermath

The immediate crisis passed and the Duke of York, as George VI (1936–52), proved a far more popular and successful king than anyone anticipated. There was still a current of popular sympathy for Edward VIII, created Duke of Windsor shortly after the abdication, and a backlash against Baldwin, who was accused of driving him from the throne.

However, there was also a strong popular sense that Edward VIII had abandoned his duty for purely selfish reasons, and the obvious contrast between him and his brother, who had accepted the throne much against his own wishes, served only to benefit the latter. The new king also seems, along with the government, to have sought to encourage a sense of continuity between his own reign and his father's. His choosing to reign as George VI rather than in his baptismal name of Albert is an obvious manifestation of this. There seems also to have been a policy of keeping the Duke of Windsor out of Britain and out of the public consciousness, which endured until the Duke's death in 1972, at least in the first years on the basis that his presence in Britain was likely to prove divisive.[22]

Though the immediate crisis was short-lived, its effects on the monarchy have been profound. In the medium term, the removal of the 'unreliable' Edward VIII and his replacement by a ruler fully prepared to embody the public service ethic strengthened the monarchy. George VI's unassuming nature, his commitment to his duty as monarch and his doggedness in the face of difficulties such as his stammer held a natural and very strong appeal for his subjects during the Second World War, which broke out less than three years after his accession. The crisis also served to confirm the monarchy in the pre-eminence of the public service ethic and the desirability of unchanging values. For this reason, the monarchy has frequently since then, and increasingly since the early 1980s, been accused of being old-fashioned at best, of existing in a time-warp and of failing to adapt itself to changed circumstances and changed ideas. Controversy on the subject now rages and may well continue to do so.

There are also indications that the Abdication continues to have profound effects on the internal dynamics of the royal family. Certainly, the attitudes of the present queen to her role as monarch and to the duty-versus-self issue seem to have been shaped by the Abdication and its aftermath, by the 'good examples' of her father and grandfather, as against the 'bad example' of her uncle Edward VIII. It may also not stretch credibility too far to see the Abdication as an important element in the melodrama of Diana Princess of Wales and its consequences for the monarchy in recent years. As the present Prince of Wales approached and then passed the age of 30 without marrying, there seems to have been a rising sense, in the context of the lingering spectre of Edward VIII and Mrs Simpson, that he must marry and, further, that the woman he married must not have even the suspicion of a 'past'. Lady Diana

---

22 Following his marriage, the Duke of Windsor lived in and around Paris until the German occupation of France in 1940. There was concern in this period about his meetings with Hitler and other Nazi leaders, and the possibility that he was being cultivated by them for their own purposes. He and his wife then returned to Britain and an official post was found for him as Governor of the Bahamas, a backwater in which he was regarded as safely out of the way. In 1945, the couple returned to Paris, remaining there until both their deaths and visiting Britain only rarely. Full details may be found in Philip Ziegler's magisterial *King Edward VIII: The Official Biography*, 1990, HarperCollins.

Spencer, an 'English rose' of good family, and only 19 years old at the time of the engagement, seemed to fit the bill admirably.

25.4   MONARCH AND PRIME MINISTER SINCE 1940

Constitutionally speaking, the first decades after the Abdication were calm. Though in political matters, the position was anything but tranquil, with the Second World War and the slide into Cold War between the western powers and the communist bloc, the established framework continued to function in an orderly and relatively non-controversial fashion. Long term trends continued: the scope of governmental activity expanded greatly as the result of the creation of the Welfare State under the Labour government of 1945–51, the establishment of a benefit system intended to cover the British subject 'from the cradle to the grave' and financed by a combination of social insurance and general taxation, rather than the earlier piecemeal system, nationalisation of the coal and steel industries and the establishment of a state-run National Health Service.

There was continued development by evolution in other spheres, notably in relation to the appointment of a Prime Minister, which became by the 1970s a matter for the political parties rather than the monarch. A strong hint of this was seen in May 1940. The situation has similarities with those of both 1916 and 1923. Though Britain declared war on Germany on 3 September 1939 in response to the German invasion of Poland, there was no attempt to send military aid to Poland – a combination of geography and the rapid collapse of Polish resistance made this impossible. There followed an uneasy autumn and winter in which there was a strong body of British opinion in favour of a negotiated peace. The only warlike action occurred at sea, where German U-boats quickly established an effective blockade. Everything changed with the German invasion of Denmark and Norway in April 1940. Norway, unlike Poland, was sufficiently close to Britain for its occupation to pose a danger, and so an expeditionary force was hastily despatched. This and elements of the Royal Navy also sent to Norway were heavily mauled for little benefit. In consequence, the Conservative government's war strategy was heavily criticised and its majority was reduced from around 240 to 81 in an adjournment debate on 8 May.

At this point, the Prime Minister, Neville Chamberlain, concluded that the government could no longer function effectively in its existing form and that a coalition must be created. However, whereas in 1915, Asquith had enjoyed sufficient personal prestige and the confidence of the Commons to be able to re-structure his government as a coalition under his continued leadership, Chamberlain considered that there was no prospect of Labour and the Liberals being willing to serve under him; a replacement must be found. As in 1916, the disruption of an election was to be avoided and the new government was to be created with the minimum of upheaval. The alternative candidates were therefore the two leading figures in the Conservative Cabinet: Lord Halifax, the Foreign Secretary, and Winston Churchill.

In 1916, King George V had persuaded the interested parties to enter into a conference to settle the matter. In 1923, with Bonar Law unable to recommend a successor, he took soundings from the leading Conservatives in order to make a decision between two rival candidates. Now, however, it was Chamberlain who took the crucial steps, convening a meeting with Halifax, Churchill and the Conservative

Chief Whip, which took place on 9 May 1940. The consensus among politicians of all parties seems to have been in favour of Halifax, but he declined the office, being apparently of the view that it should not be held by a peer in time of war, and that by remaining as Foreign Secretary, he would be in a position to 'rein in' Churchill in his more unreliable incarnations. Interestingly, and contrary to a constitutional myth that held sway for a period,[23] there seems to have been no objection to Halifax on the ground of his peerage, and George VI apparently believed that it would have been possible for legislation to be passed to place the peerage 'in abeyance' for the duration of his term. That left only Churchill. On the following day, 10 May, Chamberlain went to Buckingham Palace and offered his resignation, recommending Churchill as his successor. Though the king distrusted Churchill as a former partisan of the Duke of Windsor, he accepted that recommendation.

Of course, the events of 8–10 May can be seen not as a new departure, but no more than an example of the established practice whereby an outgoing Prime Minister could recommend his successor. Certainly, in 1955, when he retired after a second term as Prime Minister, Churchill recommended Anthony Eden as his successor. The position in 1957, when Eden resigned on grounds of ill-health, seems to have combined two forms of earlier practice. Unlike Bonar Law, Eden was in a position to be consulted, and stated his preference for RA Butler, who had acted as Prime Minister during his absences through illness. Eden also encouraged Queen Elizabeth II to consult the Cabinet. The two leading Conservative peers, Lord Kilmuir, the Lord Chancellor, and Lord Salisbury, then took soundings among the Cabinet, most of whom favoured Harold Macmillan, the Chancellor of the Exchequer, as did Winston Churchill, the only living former Prime Minister among the Conservatives. The queen's Private Secretary also took soundings among Conservative MPs with similar results. The queen sent for Macmillan.

The situation in October 1963, when Harold Macmillan unexpectedly announced his intention to resign, again on health grounds, was vastly more complex than any other during the 20th century. Instead of two candidates, there were four, all with similar degrees of capability and ministerial experience. They were RA Butler for a second time, Reginald Maudling, the Chancellor of the Exchequer, and two ministers sitting in the Lords, the 14th Earl of Home, the Foreign Secretary, and Viscount Hailsham, Lord President of the Council and Minister for Science. That the two last were peers was not of itself a difficulty, since the Peerage Act now allowed them to renounce their peerages in order to return to the Commons, in which they had both sat before the deaths of their fathers.[24]

As in 1940, it was the outgoing Prime Minister who took charge of the procedure within the Conservative Party by which his successor was chosen. Much ink has been expended on the propriety of this procedure and on Macmillan's eventual advice to the queen that it was Home who enjoyed the confidence of the party and could thus command the support of a majority of the Commons. No formal election took place, but there was a detailed canvass of Conservative peers and MPs, and some non-parliamentary activists, along with the Cabinet, in the course of the party conference which, by coincidence, was in progress at the time. This seems to have produced a

---

23   Until the publication of the standard biography of Halifax: A Roberts, *The Holy Fox: A Biography of Lord Halifax*, 1991, Weidenfeld & Nicolson.

24   See above, pp 392–93.

majority in favour of Home as the first choice of those canvassed, though not necessarily of the Cabinet. Macmillan was sufficiently concerned about the potential response of the defeated candidates that in advising the queen to appoint Home, he suggested she lose no time in summoning him to the Palace, in case of a revolt by them. For what presumably were the same reasons, Home himself did not accept office immediately, but first sought to establish that he could persuade his three rivals to accept office and so form an effective administration. This he did and, after renouncing his peerage, took office as Sir Alec Douglas-Home.

Against a background of the Conservative defeat in the 1964 election, and a sense that informal soundings were no longer an appropriate way to select a party leader or, indeed, a Prime Minister, the Conservatives in 1965 followed the other main parties in creating a procedure for a formal leadership election. Thus, the appointment of a Prime Minister became effectively a matter for the party machine of the party gaining a majority in the general election, rather than an exercise of the royal prerogative. However, none of the leadership election procedures of the main parties is designed to produce a speedy result. In 1990, a one week interregnum followed Mrs Thatcher's announcement that she would not stand in the second ballot for the Conservative leadership, having failed to achieve an outright victory in the first ballot. In 1976, when Harold Wilson resigned as Labour Party leader, the party election process dragged on for six weeks before James Callaghan became leader, Wilson resigned as Prime Minister and informed the queen that Callaghan was the choice of the party.[25] What if a Prime Minister were, without warning, to suffer a fatal heart attack while in office? *Prima facie*, one of the Cabinet would act as Prime Minister until the party election had been completed.

However, there is no formal provision for the appointment of an acting Prime Minister and of the main parties, only the Labour Party appoints a deputy leader who automatically becomes leader in the event of the leader's death or incapacity.[26] The appointment of an acting Prime Minister may therefore very easily become a cause of division within the government, and the situation might best be resolved by the monarch acting in a similar manner to George V in 1916 and 1923, establishing, either by a conference of interested parties or by 'soundings' to discover which of the possible candidates could command the support of his Cabinet colleagues and, more widely, of the party's MPs. If the death of the Prime Minister occurred at a time of national crisis, it is possible that a monarch might choose not to wait for the party election procedure to run its course before making a permanent appointment, but it seems likely that this route would only be followed if there was only one clear candidate for the party leadership, so that the party election was in effect a rubber stamping exercise, and it was clear that the party was prepared to unite behind the monarch's decision.

---

25 Bogdanor, *op cit*, p 85.
26 Bogdanor, *op cit*, pp 86–87.

CHAPTER 26

BRITAIN AND EUROPE:
THE EUROPEAN COMMUNITY[1]

26.1   INTRODUCTION

A consequence of the Second World War and its aftermath was greatly increased British involvement with continental Europe. The United Kingdom had never sought to divorce itself entirely from European affairs; nevertheless, in the 19th century and the first half of the 20th century, there was a strong sense of separateness, and a greater concern and identification with its overseas possessions, particularly the old dominions where, except in South Africa, the populations were still largely of British origin. Each of the dominions lent Britain valuable support in both World Wars, providing bodies of troops which were large in proportion to their populations and raised entirely by voluntary enlistment. In the First World War, Australians, Canadians, New Zealanders and South Africans fought under British command on the Western Front and in the Middle East, and Canadian and Australian formations in particular were among the elite of the British forces. In the Second World War, the dominions similarly provided large military contingents – the first units of the Canadian Army arrived in Britain before the end of October 1939. As well as land forces, the dominions provided a significant proportion of RAF aircrew and the Royal Canadian Navy played a major role in the Atlantic convoy war. From 1941, virtually all RAF pilot and navigator training was carried out in Canada, South Africa and Rhodesia, using facilities put at British disposal by the relevant governments. Though India was affected from 1942 by a large-scale campaign for independence and terrorist activity by extremists, the Indian Army made in terms of manpower the largest contribution to the war in Burma. Volunteers from elsewhere in the Empire also served under British command in significant numbers.

After 1945, not only did a significant part of Britain's overseas trade continue to be with the Commonwealth, there was a sense of responsibility towards the Commonwealth, whose non-white nations, beginning in 1947 with India and Pakistan, were starting to become independent entities. There was also a sense of a 'special relationship' between Britain and the United States, based on wartime co-operation, ties of language and sentiment. The war served to strengthen a sense of separateness from continental Europe. Alone of the European belligerents, Britain had escaped enemy occupation. From the fall of France in the summer of 1940 to the German invasion of the Soviet Union in June 1941, Britain had stood alone, supported only by its dominions. When Allies came, they came from outside western Europe, and it was the Americans who were much the more immediate and visible.

26.2   BEGINNINGS

From the late 1940s, this traditional philosophy conflicted increasingly with a new political sense that Britain was a European nation and ought to play a much greater

---

1   Except where indicated, material in this section is taken from I Loveland, *Constitutional Law: A Critical Introduction*, 1996, Butterworths, pp 475–558.

role in European affairs. This first emerged in the military sphere. Unprecedentedly, Britain maintained a large army in continental Europe in time of peace as a party to the four-power occupation of Germany and Austria. This presence was initially intended only to endure for the immediate post-war period, until the process of de-Nazification was complete and democratic governments were established. However, there was a rapid breakdown in relations between the three western parties to the occupation – Britain, the United States and France – and the Soviet Union, so that a substantial portion of the British Army, together with elements of the RAF, remained in Germany through Britain's role in the North Atlantic Treaty Organisation (NATO), of which Britain was a founder member in 1949.

At the same time, a change began in the balance of Britain's overseas trade. Although the tariff system in force since before the Second World War favoured the 'sterling area' – the countries of the British Commonwealth – there was a slow but definite shift in favour of trade with continental Europe as post-war reconstruction created new export markets. The post-war atmosphere also created a mood among the continental states for a greater degree of co-operation as a means of fostering economic recovery and to prevent such a war from happening again.

The first substantial manifestation of the new mood was the European Coal and Steel Community, created in 1951 between France, Germany and Italy. Coal and steel were among the most important elements of any nation's war-making capacity, and integration of these industries would, it was considered, make war between the member states impossible. Co-ordinated rebuilding of these basic industries, which in Germany's case had been devastated by the war, would hasten the re-development of their economies. Britain held aloof from this development, but in the next few years, Holland, Belgium and Luxembourg also joined the ECSC.

A Conservative government was returned in 1951 under Winston Churchill, now 76 years old. Though much concerned with developments in Europe, its main emphasis was with preventing Soviet expansion. The 'Iron Curtain', a description Churchill himself had coined, now lay across Europe from the Baltic to the Adriatic, dividing the Communist states of eastern Europe, dominated by Soviet Russia, from the democratic west. Churchill, himself half-American, and the leading figures in his Cabinet, Anthony Eden and Harold Macmillan, the latter also half-American, were firm believers in the 'special relationship' between Britain and the United States. This, along with the United States' continued role in continental Europe through its membership of NATO, was the main source of protection against further Communist expansion.

Another concern was the development of closer ties between Britain and the newly independent Commonwealth countries, and between those countries themselves and the older dominions. Quite apart from ties of tradition and sentiment, the Commonwealth enabled Britain to benefit from sources of cheap food which Europe could not match. There were other sources of concern. One was Egypt, formerly a British protectorate, but now an independent state with whose new government Britain maintained an uneasy relationship. The Suez Canal was vital to Britain's trade with the Far East; Britain was the majority shareholder in the Anglo-French Suez Canal Company, and a large garrison was maintained in the Canal Zone to protect British interests. Others were Kenya and Malaya, where armed insurrections were in progress. War in Korea, where British troops were deployed under the auspices of the United Nations, lasted from 1950 to 1953.

In the circumstances, co-operation between the countries of western Europe was of little interest to this government. In any event, European integration constituted a threat to British sovereignty. Consequently, Britain refused to join a western European military alliance mooted in 1954 that would have created a unified European Defence Force. Given that Britain was the strongest military power in western Europe, this killed off the scheme. Britain did, however, agree to maintain a permanent military presence in mainland Europe.

26.3   THE COMMON MARKET

In this context, it was to be expected that Britain would show little enthusiasm when in 1955, the six ECSC members held talks in Brussels on greater European integration and invited Britain to join them. Indeed, the British government was actively hostile. A vague commitment by the ECSC members to 'an ever-closer union' centred on a 'Common Market' in which there would be no barriers to trade between member states or to movement of labour and capital, and a common external tariff. The Conservative government, in which Eden replaced Churchill as Prime Minister in April 1955, saw this as a first step towards political federalism and a threat to Britain's trading relationships with the Commonwealth. The six states continued with the negotiations, which culminated in the execution in March 1957 of the Treaty of Rome, which created a European Economic Community (EEC) and a European Atomic Energy Community (Euratom) to stand alongside the existing ECSC.

The European Community was thus originally an organisation for free trade and economic co-operation, though it went considerably further than any earlier body. The Treaty of Rome made provision for the phased dismantling of tariffs between the member states, the establishment of free movement of workers, goods, services and capital across national boundaries, and a common agricultural policy, common tariffs on imports from non-member states, and uniform competition laws. Policy was formulated by a European Commission, composed of Commissioners who would put aside national loyalties and work for the good of the organisation as a whole. Decision-making was entrusted to a Council of Ministers representing each member state. Each state was allowed a number of votes in the Council of Ministers proportionate to its population. Certain matters, such as the admission of new members, required unanimity; other matters were dealt with by qualified majority voting, structured so that no single state or combination of states could dominate the others; the remainder were dealt with by simple majority. What level of integration beyond this was envisaged by those who framed the original Treaty is a matter for speculation and considerable controversy.

What is certain is that the Treaty of Rome created institutions with powers to make laws in order to give effect to these policies, in particular to promote economic harmonisation so that all member states would operate on an equal footing, and these laws would form part of the domestic law of those states, something which had not occurred in any previous organisation dedicated to economic co-operation.

What is also certain is that the British government began to regret a lost opportunity. Though the mid to late 1950s were a time of unprecedented national prosperity, with low unemployment, the development of consumer industries and earnings rising faster than prices – 'You've never had it so good', claimed Harold Macmillan in the summer of 1957 – the economies of the EEC member states were growing faster than Britain's. With the balance of British trade continuing to swing towards continental Europe and away from the Commonwealth and the Americas, Britain created an organisation which both complemented the EEC and was intended as a rival, if more limited in its scope. This was the European Free Trade Association (EFTA), comprising Britain, Denmark, Norway, Sweden, Austria, Switzerland and Portugal, and providing for free trade in goods between these seven.

As events proved, the creation of EFTA did not bring Britain any particular benefits, since its members did not include any other major industrial power and the organisation merely created a free trade zone among Britain's leading European markets. However, EFTA did not, unlike the EEC, give rise to any issues of incompatibility with Britain's continued preferential tariff structure in the sterling area. Increasingly, there was to be a conflict between loyalty to the Commonwealth and the desire of successive governments to share in the faster-growing prosperity of those states which had joined together in the EEC.

By 1961, Harold Macmillan, more orientated towards Europe than either of his predecessors, decided to seek admission to the EEC on the basis that Britain needed to compete with the major industrial nations of western Europe – the six EEC members – on equal terms, and the Commonwealth countries were themselves loosening their ties with Britain. Britain was also gradually losing her former place as one of the major world powers, for reasons which had much to do with her relatively small population base and prospects for industrial expansion by comparison with the emerging superpowers. There was a sense that increasing collaboration with Europe might be the most realistic way of maintaining British influence on the world stage.

Given the continuing strong sense of loyalty towards the Commonwealth among the British public, the issue was extremely sensitive. The Labour leader, Hugh Gaitskell, condemned the move, and by no means all Conservatives shared Macmillan's philosophy. It was therefore handled very cautiously. Macmillan, publicly at least, though it was the ardently Europhile Edward Heath whom he appointed to head the negotiating team, made a request to know the terms on which Britain would be admitted if an application were to be made. In view of this caution, France in particular seems to have concluded that Britain was not prepared to commit itself wholeheartedly to the EEC. President de Gaulle nurtured a personal animosity towards Britain arising from his wartime dealings with the British government[2] and became implacably opposed to British membership when Britain rejected a suggestion of greater military co-operation with France in favour of joining with the Americans in the possession and deployment of Polaris missiles. This put an end to the negotiations, since the Treaty of Rome required unanimity among member states for the admission of new members.

---

2   De Gaulle was a comparatively junior officer when entirely on his own initiative, he declared himself head of the Free French forces in Britain in the summer of 1940, after the French government accepted German peace terms. He was in a different position entirely from the governments of other occupied countries, such as Poland and Norway, which had chosen exile rather than seek accommodation with Hitler and had a legitimacy which he lacked. The Free French were divided among themselves as to whether to accept de Gaulle's self-appointment. The British government was therefore cautious in its handling of de Gaulle, who was in any case a difficult man.

The 1964 election returned the first Labour government for 13 years, under Harold Wilson, who was markedly more pro-European than Gaitskell. Like Heath, he saw both political and economic advantages to EEC membership, and made a formal application to join in 1967. This was vetoed by de Gaulle.

26.4 BRITISH ENTRY INTO THE EEC

Events of the late 1960s created a context in which a future membership application stood a greater chance of success. De Gaulle resigned as French President in 1969 and his successor, Georges Pompidou, increasingly concerned about the growing economic power of West Germany, saw Britain as a useful counter-balance to prevent German domination of the EEC. At the same time, British trade with Europe was becoming more important as compared with the Commonwealth, where only Canada remained among Britain's half-dozen leading trading partners. The 1970 election then brought Edward Heath to power. There was considerable hostility towards his pro-EEC policy, both within his own party and among the public, who remained to be convinced of the economic advantages of membership as against the loss of cheap access to produce such as New Zealand lamb and Caribbean sugar, quite apart from concerns over the restrictions membership would place on the independent exercise of sovereignty. However, Heath went ahead with an application in the second half of 1970.

Acceptance of the British application was considerably more likely than it had been previously, but at the same time, the advantages of membership were less clear-cut. Had Britain chosen to join the EEC at its inception, it would have been in a strong position to dictate the form of the organisation and the detailed terms of the Treaty of Rome, and to deal expressly with issues relating to sovereignty which have caused so much difficulty since. Even in the early 1960s, the EEC had yet to establish itself fully. In 1970, by contrast, Britain was seeking to join an organisation which had acquired a position of strength and would be accepted as a member only on terms which were advantageous to the organisation and its founder members. Britain had little room for manoeuvre.

Once the terms of Britain's entry had been negotiated over the closing months of 1970 and the first half of 1971, it remained to convince the British Parliament and people of the advantages of accession to the EEC. Though accession to a multi-national organisation dedicated to greater European integration, whose law would form part of the domestic law of the UK, was a major constitutional change, the Heath government refused to countenance a referendum on the issue. To the government, the electorate had given a mandate for membership by electing a party whose manifesto committed it to seeking EEC membership. A sense of grievance was only increased when the Norwegian government withdrew its own application for membership following a hostile referendum. Controversy on this issue has raged throughout the 30 years since.

In its pronouncements to the public, the government stressed the economic aspects of the organisation, then referred to as 'the Common Market'; the term 'European Economic Community' did not come into general parlance until later, and 'European Community' later still. Membership would bring higher standards of living, though it was admitted that food prices would rise because of the ending of cheap imports from the Commonwealth under preferential tariffs, and Britain would be required to make large contributions to the central EEC budget. Little prominence was given to the implications of a series of decisions of the European Court of Justice (ECJ) which had already established that provisions of EEC law overruled inconsistent provisions of a member state's domestic law,[3] even provisions forming part of the constitution of a member state.[4] Earlier still, in the Dutch case of *Van Gend en Loos v Administratie de Belastingen*,[5] the ECJ had declared that the EEC did not simply create mutual obligations between the member states, it was:

A new legal order of international law for the benefit of which the states have limited their sovereign rights, and the subjects of which comprise not only the member states but also their nationals.

Though a strong element in the population remained unconvinced, there was sufficient acceptance among politicians of the government's arguments for the House of Commons to approve the terms negotiated and for the government to be given the necessary authority to enter into a Treaty of Accession by 356 votes to 244 in October 1971. The Conservatives gained 330 seats at the 1970 election, Labour 287 and the other parties a total of 13. The vote represented a rebellion by 69 Labour MPs who defied a three-line whip instructing them to oppose the measure, and the abstention of a further 20. Heath had permitted the Conservatives a free vote; 43 of them voted against the accession terms; had the Labour rebels obeyed the whip, the government would have been defeated.

The Treaty of Accession was duly signed on 22 January 1972, but formal entry into the EEC required its ratification by Act of Parliament and creation of the necessary mechanisms to incorporate EEC law into domestic law. This was achieved by the European Communities Act, a piece of legislation which in the years since has caused enormous controversy and exercised a great many judicial and academic minds.

The significant provisions are ss 1–4. Section 1 provided that the Act applied to the Treaty of Rome, together with the Treaty of Accession, and that it might be made applicable to any EEC Treaties made subsequently by means of an Order in Council. This in effect gave a government power to use prerogative powers to incorporate new Treaties into domestic law, which would then have paramountcy over domestic law, without any need for parliamentary approval.

Section 2 then provided for the incorporation of EEC law into domestic law. This section was framed in a particularly ambiguous and opaque fashion, creating extreme difficulties in its interpretation.[6] Crucially, it was necessary to give paramountcy, as

---

3   *Costa v ENEL* [1964] ECR 585.

4   *Internationale Handelsgesellschaft mbH v Einfuhr- und Vorratsstelle fur Getreide und Futtermittel* [1972] CMLR 255. Though the final decision in that case was not made until after the UK Treaty of Accession was concluded, nevertheless, the ECJ had declared earlier ([1970] ECR 1125, para 3) following an Art 177 (now Art 234) reference by the West German courts that:

The validity of a Community measure or its effect within a Member State cannot be affected by allegations that it runs counter to either fundamental rights as formulated by the Constitution of that State or the principle of a national constitutional structure.

5   [1963] ECR 1.

6   As a student, I was informed by a lecturer in this subject that she had been present when the Parliamentary Counsel responsible admitted orally that his instructions had been to 'Fudge it'!

required by EEC law, not only to such EEC law as was already in existence at the time the Act took effect, but also to such EEC law as might be enacted in the future, contrary to the doctrine of implied repeal, the constitutional principle that even in the absence of express provision for repeal, any term in a later Act which is inconsistent with a term in an earlier Act repeals that earlier term to the extent of the inconsistency.[7] *Prima facie*, any provision of a future Act of Parliament which was inconsistent with a provision of EEC law would impliedly repeal the portions of the 1972 Act providing that EEC law should have supremacy since, by passing the later Act, Parliament demonstrated that it no longer intended EEC law to have supremacy.

Section 2(1) appears to provide that all directly effective and directly applicable EC law,[8] 'from time to time arising by or under the Treaties' shall be enforceable in the UK domestic courts. Section 2(2) then makes provision for the implementation into national law of EC law which is not directly applicable – principally directives – by means of statutory instrument or Order in Council.[9] Section 2(4) then provides that 'any enactment passed or to be passed ... shall be construed and have effect subject to the foregoing provisions of this section', apparently giving any directly applicable or directly effective EC legislation passed after the Act's coming into force paramountcy over inconsistent provisions of domestic law.

This was unprecedented and it is not an over-statement to term it revolutionary. In particular, if all directly applicable and directly effective EEC law, whatever its date of enactment, was to have paramountcy over inconsistent provisions of UK law, could the UK ever lawfully withdraw from the EEC?

Under the normal principles of parliamentary sovereignty, the UK Parliament has power to do anything except bind itself. Any Act of Parliament is capable of repeal or amendment, express or implied, by a subsequent Act of Parliament. This is as true of constitutional legislation as any other – it is moral and political pressures which limit the possibility of repeal. However, the terms of s 2(4) appear to preclude its own repeal, even expressly.

Since 1972, where the issue has been addressed by the courts, notably in the *Factortame* litigation, the British judiciary has held to the view that a withdrawal from the EC is possible. According to Lord Bridge of Harwich,[10] EC law has paramountcy over national law because Parliament in passing the 1972 Act intended this. However, if a future Parliament were to provide otherwise, the UK courts would be obliged to give effect to national law.

---

7   See, eg, *Ellen Street Estates v Minister of Health* [1934] 1 KB 590.

8   EC law which is directly applicable automatically becomes part of the domestic law of member states without any requirement for implication by national authorities. EC law which is directly effective gives rights to individuals which are enforceable in the national courts of member states. The two concepts are separate, so that a provision may be directly applicable without being directly effective, and vice versa.

9   Statutory instruments emerged during the 19th century as a means of dealing with non-controversial matters without the need for full parliamentary scrutiny. Essentially, a specified minister or body is given power by an 'enabling Act' to make legislation within set limits. Opportunities for scrutiny by Parliament are limited. During the 20th century, the use of statutory instruments became much more widespread, many Acts being passed as 'skeletons' to create powers to make statutory instruments. This is particularly the case with legislation on social security benefits; a Social Security Act creates administrative mechanisms, while levels of benefit and criteria for eligibility are set by statutory instruments.

10   *R v Secretary of State for the Environment ex p Factortame (No 2)* [1991] 1 AC 603, pp 658–89.

When asked the direct question as to whether it would be lawful to withdraw, however, an earlier court evaded the issue. In *Blackburn v Attorney General*,[11] the courts were asked to rule on whether the Conservative government in negotiating a Treaty of Accession, and Parliament in legislating to ratify that Treaty, would be acting lawfully. On the first point, it was held that the government's Treaty-making powers arose from the prerogative, that the exercise of a prerogative power was not justiciable, and so was not capable of scrutiny by the courts.[12] Dealing with the latter issue, it was argued on behalf of the applicant that the one thing a Parliament was not competent to do was to compromise its own sovereignty by passing legislation which limited its future powers and was incapable of repeal. Lord Denning, who gave the leading judgment, fudged:

> We have all been brought up to believe that, in legal theory, one Parliament cannot bind another and that no act is irreversible. But legal theory does not march alongside political reality … Take the Acts which have granted independence to the Dominions and territories overseas. Can anyone imagine that Parliament could or would reverse those laws and take away their independence? Most clearly not. Freedom once given cannot be taken away. Legal theory must give way to practical politics …

> What are the realities here? If Her Majesty's Ministers sign this treaty and Parliament enacts provisions to implement it, I do not envisage that Parliament would afterwards go back on it and try to withdraw from it. but if Parliament should do so, then I say we will consider that event when it happens. We will then say whether Parliament can lawfully do it or not …

The European Communities Act came into force on 1 January 1973.

26.5   THE REFERENDUM

The early years of Britain's membership of the EEC were not prosperous. Inflation had already reached unprecedented levels before entry – at times 25% per annum for sustained periods – and there were high levels of unemployment, at least in comparison with the boom years of the 1960s. Rather than leaving matters to market forces as was traditional Conservative practice, the government attempted in two ways to deal with the excessive wage demands which, in the ministers' view, were the main trigger of inflation.

First, in 1971, the government introduced the Industrial Relations Act, which attempted to prevent trade unions from forcing through excessive wage demands and damaging British industry's competitiveness abroad. The Act required all unions to register on an official register and to conduct secret ballots among their members and then allow a 60 day cooling-off period before proceeding with a strike. Failure to do so rendered a union liable to the employer concerned for economic losses caused by a strike. This legislation was greeted by a wave of union militancy which made it completely ineffective.

---

11   [1971] 2 All ER 1380.
12   It was only later, in *Council of Civil Service Unions v Minister for the Civil Service* [1985] AC 374, that the House of Lords accepted, by a majority, that the exercise of some prerogative powers was susceptible to judicial review. This, however, did not include the power to enter into treaties.

In the winter of 1972, the National Union of Mineworkers rejected a pay offer and went on strike. Britain was far more dependent on coal as a source of power than today; in particular, power stations were very largely coal-fired. A system of 'flying pickets' was organised not only to prevent rebel miners from working but to prevent the movement of stockpiled coal around the country. Before long, there were power cuts. Nevertheless, the miners commanded considerable support from a public who were by no means convinced of the need for rigid control of wages, and demanded an end to the power cuts and the difficulties they caused. The government appointed a commission to recommend an appropriate pay increase for the miners. This recommended a 21% rise, but even this was not accepted by the NUM, and the strike continued until February 1973.

By this time, the government had imposed a strict wages and prices policy. This was on a voluntary basis as far as private employers were concerned, since the government had no direct means of controlling them, but was compulsory in relation to public sector workers who, in an era where the coal, steel, gas, electricity and water industries were all nationalised, were far more numerous than today and included many manual workers with a tradition of militancy. Further high wage demands followed and, by December 1973, the miners had imposed an overtime ban. At the same time, the Arab-Israeli war of October 1973 (the 'Yom Kippur War') was followed by a huge increase in the world price of oil. With severe shortages of both coal and oil, the government declared a state of emergency under the Emergency Powers Act 1920, imposing a three day week on British industry to conserve fuel. Still the miners threatened an all-out strike, and with the press and public demanding to know whether it was the Cabinet or the miners that governed Britain, Edward Heath called a general election for 28 February 1974.

That the country was deeply divided is demonstrated by the election result. The Conservatives actually polled more votes than Labour, but gained fewer seats: 296 to 301. The remaining parliamentary seats were spread among the smaller parties, resulting in a Labour minority government led by Harold Wilson. The immediate crisis was defused by a 'Social Contract' with the unions, agreed before the election, but the government's position was precarious. A second election therefore followed in October 1974, which gave Labour an overall majority of three.[13]

In its manifesto before the October election, Labour pledged to re-negotiate the terms of Britain's membership of the EEC and, having done so, to hold a referendum on continued membership. A White Paper was produced in March 1975 which listed four areas for re-negotiation: the Common Agricultural Policy, Britain's contributions to the EEC budget, relations with the Commonwealth and Britain's right to pursue independent regional and industrial policies. Some concessions were made and the package was passed by the House of Commons by 396 to 170. However, the Labour Cabinet was split, no fewer than seven ministers rejecting the re-negotiated terms and seeing continued EEC membership not only as economically disadvantageous, but as damaging to national sovereignty. Fewer than half the Labour MPs voted in favour.

The referendum took place in an atmosphere which strongly suggested that in the public mind, it had come too late. Membership had not brought the economic advantages claimed, but there was a sense that there was no going back to the

---

13 This summary of events is taken mainly from M Pugh, *State and Society: British Political and Social History 1870–1992*, 1994, Arnold, pp 288–91.

pre-1973 position – too many markets had been lost and relations with the Commonwealth were irreparably damaged. The turnout was low (64.5%) and of those who voted, two-thirds were in favour, for whatever reason, of continued membership on the re-negotiated terms.[14] Since then, the referendum result has been used as a justification for the failure of successive governments to put the ever-increasing scope of EC power to further referenda.

26.6   THE THATCHER YEARS

The Labour government of 1974, like its Conservative predecessor, was ultimately brought down by trade union militancy. The economy continued in difficulties, with rising unemployment and a serious balance of payments deficit, representing a large surplus of imports over exports. Attempts by the government to improve matters by measures that included a 5% ceiling on pay increases triggered another wave of union militancy. There was a series of strikes in 1978–79, particularly in public services such as railways and refuse collection, bringing about a so called 'winter of discontent' that caused James Callaghan, who had earlier replaced Wilson as Prime Minister, to call an election in May 1979 after losing a vote of confidence in the Commons. This election brought the Conservatives under Margaret Thatcher to power.

Though Mrs Thatcher and certain of her ministers inveighed intermittently about the relentless advance of the EC and the restrictions it placed on their own pursuit of a free market economy as a cure for all domestic evils, the EC tide continued to flood in during the 11 years of Thatcherism through amendment of the Treaty of Rome to increase the powers of the EC institutions.

26.6.1 The Single European Act

By the early 1980s, the original members of the EC, who remained more committed to economic integration than Britain, concluded that the pace of harmonisation in the fundamental fields of movement of goods, capital, persons and services was much too slow. The Treaty of Rome envisaged that the process would be complete by 1970, but this was far from achieved even 14 years later, when the European Commission concluded that the national laws of member states still contained too many effective barriers to free movement, despite the huge volume of EC legislation designed to break down these barriers. By no means all the members believed that 'harmony' necessarily meant 'uniformity', and there were difficulties in gaining sufficient agreement for further legislation, particularly in more controversial areas such as employment protection. Something, the European Commission decided, had to be done.

In consequence, a Commission White Paper of 1985 proposed a move away from the pursuit of uniformity alone, and the amendment of the Treaty of Rome in order to make it easier for the Commission to gain agreement from the Council of Ministers to new legislation. This latter was, constitutionally speaking, the more fundamental element of the Single European Act (SEA). Further, the SEA considerably extended the

---

14 See D Childs, *Britain since 1945*, 2nd edn, 1986, Routledge, pp 78–80.

scope of the EC's harmonising activities to include environmental protection, regional development, technical research and innovation, and some aspects of social policy. The scope of qualified majority voting was much extended, reducing the ability of individual member states to oppose the advance of integrationist EC legislation.

A European Parliament had existed for many years. Its membership was made subject to direct election in 1980 and, at the same time, each member state's allocation of members was made proportionate to population. The name 'Parliament' is a misnomer, as its powers are very largely consultative rather than legislative. The European Parliament is, however, strongly perceived as a force for European integration, as a focus for the development of a 'European' spirit among citizens of member states. Steps were therefore taken in the SEA to strengthen the powers of the Parliament.

26.6.2 The Maastricht Treaty

The idea of political union through federalism emerged much more strongly in the late 1980s. A major difficulty and source of controversy was – and remains – a lack of a common conception in Europe on the meaning of 'federalism'. To the British, the term is redolent of the constitutional systems found in the United States of America, Canada and Australia. A hostile speech made by Mrs Thatcher in Bruges on 20 September 1988 had the effect of bringing issues relating to sovereignty very much to the fore and strengthening the increasing polarisation of the Conservative Party into Europhile and Eurosceptic elements.

At the same time, the ECJ was taking an increasingly interventionist approach towards national legislation, requiring national courts to interpret it in a manner which gave effect to EC objectives even if, in the case of Britain, the relevant EC legislation was neither directly applicable nor directly effective and therefore outside the scope of s 2(4).[15] Though in *Marleasing*, the ECJ included the caveat 'so far as is possible', a case such as *Webb v EMO Air Cargo*[16] demonstrates clearly the lengths to which the UK courts were now prepared to go to achieve the conformity with EC objectives now demanded.

Again in the late 1980s, the issue of the development of common financial policies and, in particular, a single currency began to emerge strongly, with obvious implications for the future sovereignty of members. As originally executed, the Treaty of Rome required member states to maintain the stability of their currencies and approximate equilibrium in balance of payments, and gave the Commission powers to intervene in the event of a member state suffering a serious crisis in these spheres. This was seen in some quarters as an initial stage towards 'monetary union', which would require a common currency to remove the problems caused by varying exchange rates, and the formation of an EC Central Bank to control internal money supply and interest rates. As controversy over the introduction of the Euro has shown, the possession by a country of its own individual currency is of huge symbolic importance and also gives national governments an important tool of financial and economic control.

---

15 Cf *Von Colson v Land Nordrhein-Westfalen* [1984] ECR 1891; *Marleasing SA v La Commercial Internacional de Alimentacion SA* [1990] ECR I-4135.
16 [1992] 2 All ER 929; *Webb v EMO Air Cargo (No 2)* [1995] 4 All ER 557.

A European Monetary System (EMS) emerged in the late 1970s, becoming fully effective in 1979. Its main element was an Exchange Rate Mechanism (ERM), with narrow limits on permitted fluctuations in exchange rates. Membership was not compulsory, and the matter attracted little interest in Britain until 1989 when, on the instructions of the Council of Ministers, Jacques Delors produced a plan for achieving complete economic and monetary union between member states. First, there should be a gradual 'convergence' of economies in fundamental matters such as inflation rates, the balance of payments and economic growth. This was to be followed by compulsory membership of a much more restrictive ERM, and finally by the creation of a single currency.

This proposal received a hostile reception in Britain, as a very significant step towards the creation of a federal Europe. However, it was generally welcomed on the continent and it was agreed at a summit to set the process in train in 1990. This included amendments to the Treaty of Rome in order to give the necessary legislative authority, and the process began which brought about the Maastricht Treaty of 1993, though this went considerably beyond the monetary sphere.

In October 1990, Britain joined the ERM and, at a summit which took place in Rome shortly afterwards, the 11 other member states expressed their willingness to accelerate plans for further monetary integration. Mrs Thatcher reacted angrily to this, and Sir Geoffrey Howe, a senior minister and leading Europhile, then resigned. In his resignation speech on 13 November, he attributed most of Britain's current economic ills to the failure to join the ERM earlier. He then claimed that it was mistaken to regard greater European integration as involving the inevitable surrender of national sovereignty and national identity, that a more constructive approach for the British government was to take a central role in the policy-making processes of the EC. Britain would then be better placed to move EC development in a direction which reflected British interests. Michael Heseltine, another Europhile, then challenged Mrs Thatcher for the Conservative leadership, a move which led ultimately to her resignation as Prime Minister.

The Maastricht Treaty, or Treaty on European Union, was negotiated in 1993 and imposed a timetable for the implementation of the Delors scheme for monetary union. It contained other far-reaching provisions in relation to political integration. Although at Britain's insistence the final text contained no mention of a 'federal' Europe, this omission was to a considerable extent cosmetic. The EEC, now formally the 'European Community' or 'EC', was to be only one of three 'pillars' of a more wide-ranging European Union, whose other pillars were defined as a Common Foreign and Security Policy, and a Common Justice and Home Affairs Policy. This could be seen as an extension of the encouragement of political 'co-operation' introduced by the SEA, were it not that under the Treaty, they would be serviced by the existing EC institutions. Events since then, particularly in relation to the former Yugoslavia, have shown clear attempts to formulate a foreign and defence policy for all EC member states, though with somewhat mixed results. The Treaty sought further to develop a sense of 'European identity' among citizens of EC member states and to blur the traditional bonds of nationality by creating a new EU citizenship and enabling citizens of any member state to stand and vote in national and local elections in any other member state.

Finally, the 11 member states other than Britain agreed to incorporate the EC Social Charter into their domestic legal systems. This was devised in 1989 following the SEA and constituted the EC's first significant action in the social policy sphere, covering matters such as remuneration and protection against unfair dismissal, redundancy and unsafe working conditions. The Thatcher government saw this as an unjustified encroachment on national autonomy and damaging to the competitiveness not only of British industry but, through causing an increase in labour costs, to the interests of the employees it was intended to protect.

Under Art 236 of the Treaty of Rome,[17] the Maastricht Treaty could not take effect without ratification by all the member states under the procedures of their national constitutions. Unlike the SEA, the Treaty proved highly controversial in several member states. In Britain, the major difficulty came over the Social Charter, since the commitment to the Common Foreign and Security Policy and common policy in Justice and Home Affairs did not affect domestic law directly and could be dealt with by exercise of the prerogative. The extensions to the powers of the European Parliament included in the Treaty did require ratification, and a proportion of MPs of all parties also demanded that Parliament ratify the Social Charter. The whole matter was made more explosive still by the breakdown of the ERM since the negotiation of the Treaty, and the recent decision of the ECJ in *Francovich v Italian Republic*,[18] which established a principle by which a person might recover damages to reflect losses arising from the failure of a national government to implement provisions of EC law.

The Conservative government sought to ratify the Treaty via a two-clause Bill, which stated that the relevant parts of the Maastricht Treaty, including both the Social Charter and the British 'opt-out' from it, were added to the list of Treaties incorporated by the 1972 Act. However, the opposition groups tabled two amendments, both of which were supported by different groupings for different reasons. The more far-reaching would remove the Social Charter from the list of measures to be ratified. If this were passed, then the Treaty as a whole would not be ratified under UK law for the purposes of Art 236. By this means, those who opposed the 'opt-out' hoped to force the government to opt in rather than lose the Treaty entirely. By contrast, the Conservative Eurosceptics hoped that the Treaty would fall in its entirety, so that the EC could not pursue integration beyond the stages covered by the SEA. However, in the final analysis, few Conservative rebels were prepared to take the step of voting against the government and the outcome was the extremely unusual one of a tie. In accordance with established practice, the Speaker used her casting vote and, according to convention, used it in favour of the government, so that the amendment was defeated.

The second amendment, designed to prevent the ratification of the Treaty until the Commons had voted on the opt-out, was passed by eight votes. John Major thereupon announced that the vote on the opt-out would be considered as an issue of confidence, with the implication that the defeat of the government would lead to a dissolution and general election. Faced with this possibility, the Eurosceptics backed down and voted with the government, with the consequence that the Treaty as a whole was ratified, the UK having opted out of the Social Charter.

---

17 Now Art 48 of the Treaty on European Union.
18 [1993] 2 CMLR 66.

26.7   THE CURRENT POSITION

There at the time of writing the position remains, though 10 new members are expected to join the EU in 2004, and deliberations at the summit held in Biarritz on 13 October 2000 indicate the directions that developments are likely to take over the next few years. Among changes discussed are:

(a) the agreement of a Statement of Principles to define the limits of the responsibilities of the Commission, and national and regional governments;

(b) the creation of a second chamber of the European Parliament, to be composed of representatives of national parliaments, to provide democratic oversight of the Common Foreign and Security Policy;

(c) a reduction in the size of the Commission, currently made up of two members from the UK, France, Germany Italy and Spain, and one each from the remaining member states, since the current structure is likely to become increasingly unworkable as further states join;

(d) an extension of qualified majority voting from matters currently requiring unanimity.

Those provisions which were agreed are contained in the Treaty of Nice of December 2000, currently subject to ratification by the parliaments of member states. From 2005, the largest states will lose their additional Commissioners and as new member states join, a rotation system may be introduced to keep the size of the Commission below 27 members. Qualified majority voting is extended to an additional 39 areas, excluding taxation, immigration policy and social security. Votes have been re-allocated to reflect the admission of new member states, with the effect that the three largest states will be able to veto decisions by acting in combination.

The power of the EC and EU vis à vis national governments has been expanded enormously since Britain's entry into the then EEC in 1973, through the decisions of the ECJ which have consistently given paramountcy to EC law in an ever-widening range of circumstances, the sheer quantity of EC law and because the powers of the EC institutions have been extended into additional spheres. The single currency came into effect in all member states except the UK on 1 January 2002. The British government has announced that this country will join the single currency when and if five conditions are met, and if a national referendum produces a majority in favour. Plans are afoot for the creation of a 60,000 strong European army, a proposal to which Britain is opposed. It remains to be seen what will happen.

CHAPTER 27

DEVOLUTION

27.1 INTRODUCTION

Given the intensity of debate on Scottish and Welsh devolution in recent years, the creation of a Scottish Parliament and Welsh Assembly, the emergence in Scotland and Wales of a strong sense of separate identity, and demands from some quarters for regional autonomy for parts of England, it seems surprising that Scottish and Welsh nationalism only emerged as significant political issues from the late 1960s.

27.2 BACKGROUND

27.2.1 Scotland

Under the Acts of Union, Scotland retained its separate legal and educational systems, which acted as significant foci for national pride in the 18th and 19th centuries. This was particularly true of Scottish education, which established a tradition of excellence and relative openness to talent early. Although the Highlands were treated virtually as a conquered land after the 1745 Rising, Scotland benefited from the closer ties with England created by the Union. Large numbers of Scots took advantage of their superior education to move south and take up posts in government service and the professions. In the 19th century, expatriate Scots were in many ways the backbone of the British Empire.

Within Scotland, however, there were considerable regional divisions. There was a linguistic divide between the Gaelic-speaking north and west, and the Lowlands, where the common tongue was Scots, which belongs to a completely different language group and has no greater affinity with Gaelic than English with Russian.[1] This division was in part broken down by the imposition of Standard English from the early 19th century, but a strong sense of differing identities remains even today.

Economically and politically, there were further divisions. From early medieval times, wealth, power and influence were almost entirely confined to the Lowland areas, and a Highland-Lowland dichotomy has continued into modern times. The Highlands did not share in the advantages which accrued from commercial and industrial development, and only the great landowners acquired much in the way of political influence. By contrast, the central belt around Edinburgh and Glasgow was among the major industrial areas of Great Britain from the early 10th century, and Aberdeen and Dundee also emerged as important commercial centres. These four cities and the Glasgow industrial hinterland formed the main centres of population. The remaining Lowland areas – south of the Forth and Clyde and the east coast plain – were dominated by agriculture. The Highlands were traditionally an area of

---

1   Scots Gaelic is a Q-Celtic or Goidelic tongue, cognate with Irish Gaelic and Manx. The precise status of Scots, whether it is a language as such or a dialect of English, is a matter of controversy, but its affinities lie with English and the Germanic languages.

subsistence agriculture – crofting – but from 1745 onwards, they were increasingly dominated first by sheep raising, then in the later 19th century by sporting estates, and recently by tourism.

Scotland in the 19th century was generally well-integrated into national politics. Pugh notes that Scotland provided no fewer than four of the seven Prime Ministers between 1894 and 1922 (Rosebery, Balfour, Campbell-Bannerman and Bonar Law) and that Gladstone sat for most of his career as MP for Midlothian.[2] Liberalism in Scotland developed a particular concern with land tenure and the problems of crofters in a context where, on 1878 figures, half the land was owned by only 68 individuals, many senior peers and most absentees outside the grouse season. There was sufficient acceptance of a specifically Scottish dimension to government for the office of Secretary of State for Scotland to be created in 1885, with Cabinet status from 1892 and, in 1907, a Scottish Grand Committee in Parliament to deliberate on legislation of special significance to Scotland. Administrative responsibility in a number of spheres, including agriculture, fisheries, health, education and prisons, was given to local boards operating under the supervision of the Secretary of State, and further responsibilities, including highways, road transport, ancient monuments and appointment of magistrates, were added after a Royal Commission on Scottish Affairs in 1952. The Scottish Office, based in Edinburgh, was created in 1945.

Until the late 1960s, Scottish nationalism largely took a cultural form, most obvious in the romantic 'tradition' that was to a considerable extent invented in the 1820s and after, with clan tartans, bagpipe music and a sentimentalising of the Jacobite past. Given the linguistic divide, attempts to promote the Gaelic language failed to have much unifying effect. Although the example of Irish nationalism led to the creation of a Scottish Home Rule Association in 1885 and the introduction of a number of Bills for the creation of a Scottish Parliament before 1914, political nationalism made no serious headway.

27.2.2 Wales

Welsh government and administration was fully integrated with that of England from the 16th century, and Wales was considerably less affected than Scotland by regional divisions. Apart from the industrial south, where a boom based on coal and steel occurred in the 19th century, and the slate-mining districts of the north, the country was mainly agricultural and the population was relatively homogenous. A sense of a single and unequivocal national identity was therefore able to develop to a much greater extent than in Scotland.

More than 80% of the Welsh population belonged to non-conformist congregations, so that there was particular support for the anti-tithe movement of the 1830s, and later for the disestablishment of the Anglican church in Wales. The religious influence also brought about the first specifically Welsh statute of modern times, the Welsh Sunday Closing Act of 1881, which prohibited pubs from opening on Sundays. From the 1850s, a romantic nationalism emerged but, unlike that of Scotland, it was linked directly with the Welsh language and poetic and musical tradition.

Politically, Wales remained within the mainstream, although a distinctive Welsh Liberalism emerged after 1867. Politicians such as Lloyd George cut their teeth on the

2   M Pugh, *State and Society: British Political and Social History 1870–1992*, 1994, Arnold, p 74.

grievances of Welsh tenant farmers against their landlords and a campaign for fair rents and security of tenure. Disestablishment became a political issue in the 1880s,[3] along with education. Gladstone gave some encouragement to Welsh educational aspirations; in 1872, his government granted a subsidy to the new university college at Aberystwyth, which in 1893 joined with later foundations at Cardiff and Bangor to form the University of Wales. Some radicals followed the Irish example by forming the *Cymru Fydd* to seek Home Rule. Under Lloyd George, its members briefly took control of the North Wales Liberal Federation, but its nationalist agenda was firmly opposed in the south, and Cymru Fydd never became a serious political force.

A specific executive authority for Wales came much later than in Scotland, the post of Secretary of State for Wales only being created in 1964, along with a Welsh Office based in Cardiff.

27.3   THE EMERGENCE OF A NATIONALIST AGENDA

Although a nationalist party *Plaid Cymru* ('Party of Wales') was founded in Wales in 1925 and the Scottish Nationalist Party in 1934, these remained well outside the political mainstream. However, after the Second World War, there emerged a sense that Scotland and Wales were being neglected by successive governments, in a context where their economies were declining and unemployment was increasing, with pockets of severe urban deprivation in Scotland in particular. This underpins first a resurgence of Liberal support in the Scottish Highlands, and then by-election victories for the nationalist parties at Carmarthen in 1966 and Hamilton in 1967. From 1968, the Scottish Nationalists also began to gain seats from Labour in local elections in the Glasgow-Edinburgh industrial region.

At this time, nationalism became a literally explosive issue in Northern Ireland. The 1921 settlement created a two-chamber Parliament and governmental structure with a considerable degree of autonomy in matters such as education. Both were entirely dominated by the Protestant elements in the population, and Catholics were heavily disadvantaged and frequently actively discriminated against in spheres such as employment and housing. A Catholic civil rights movement emerged in the later 1960s, inspired in part by the example of black Americans, but this, along with the attempts of moderate Unionists in the government to legislate to rectify the most pressing grievances, produced a backlash. Clashes between civil rights demonstrators and police, and concern over abuses by the latter, led the Home Secretary to send British troops to restore order in the summer of 1969.

Initially, these were welcomed by Catholics as a neutral force, but the situation rapidly deteriorated. This only encouraged sympathy among Catholics for the cause of a united Ireland, which had not been a major political issue since the 1920s. From 1972, a full-scale terrorist war was in progress between extremists on both sides of the political and religious divide, with the army and police as targets of both and an apparently ineradicable sense of alienation from the politics and government of the British mainland. The Northern Ireland (Temporary Provisions) Act 1972 gave extensive powers to the Secretary of State for Northern Ireland, and the dominant position vis à vis the Northern Ireland government.

---

3   This was finally achieved by the Welsh Disestablishment Act 1914.

In 1973, the Conservative government, concluding that the Northern Ireland administration was incapable of restoring order within the foreseeable future, abolished the Parliament and imposed full direct rule on the province. Despite various attempts to produce a solution which would bring about an end to the violence, satisfy the aspirations of the moderate majority and encourage the population as a whole to co-operate in their shared interests, there the position remained until the late 1990s.

In 1968, apparently as a sop to the Scottish and Welsh nationalists rather than with any urge towards concrete change, the Wilson government appointed a Royal Commission under Lord Kilbrandon to examine the possibility of devolution of power from Westminster. This reported in 1973 and recommended an elected Parliament in Scotland and a Welsh assembly, with powers in purely domestic matters. By now, nationalist activity had considerably increased.

From the late 1960s, the use of the Welsh language emerged as a political issue in Wales, particularly in the educational context. Though the great majority of campaigners sought to persuade by appeals to reason, militants mounted a campaign of uprooting English-language road signs and in 1969 threatened to disrupt the investiture of the Prince of Wales at Carnarvon Castle. A small extremist group, motivated more by anti-Englishness than concern for the Welsh language, went so far as to mount arson attacks on English-owned holiday cottages.

In the early 1970s, the discovery of North Sea oil and emergence of an oil industry based on Aberdeen and Shetland provided an ideal opportunity for the Scottish Nationalists who, under the slogan 'It's Scotland's oil', called for an independent economic policy to capitalise on the new resource and reverse the effect of decades of Anglocentric government. At the same time, Britain's membership of the EEC gave further impetus to Scottish Nationalists by inviting unfavourable comparisons between Scotland's position and those of the smaller EEC member states. Though only the most extreme believed that with the aid of North Sea oil Scotland could 'go it alone', nevertheless, a degree of internal autonomy within the UK seemed a realistic goal.

The election of October 1974 returned 11 Scottish Nationalist and three Plaid Cymru members to Parliament. These figures were significant for a Labour government whose overall majority was three, and where the nationalists had 30% of the Scottish vote and 11% of the Welsh vote, the more so as Labour governments had historically been disproportionately reliant on Scotland and Wales for their majorities.

In this context, and apparently in the hope of wooing the Scottish and Welsh electorate back to the Labour fold, the Callaghan government produced plans based on the Kilbrandon Report. The Scotland and Wales Bill which went before Parliament in the 1976–77 session provided for the creation of a Scottish assembly, but without revenue-raising authority or powers in the vital spheres of agriculture and industry. All funding would come from a block grant from the UK Parliament; an effective power of veto was left in the hands of the Secretary of State for Scotland. There were other significant limitations on its powers; for example, the powers in education excluded all matters relating to the universities. The Welsh proposals were still more limited, envisaging a Senate of 100 members elected by proportional representation with legislative powers in specified areas. The Bill was also seriously flawed in that it failed to address what has since become known as the 'West Lothian question' – the position of Scottish and Welsh MPs in debates on exclusively English legislation.

Despite the very limited degree of devolution proposed, the Bill proved highly controversial and was eventually passed in a much amended form. Crucially, referenda were to take place in Scotland and Wales before the new assemblies could be created, and not only must a majority of persons voting be in favour of the changes, but that majority had to represent at least 40% of the total electorate in Scotland and Wales respectively.

In the event, the Labour government's plans were in part the victim of surrounding circumstances. When the referenda were held, in March 1979, the Callaghan government was in serious difficulties and suffering extreme unpopularity as a result of the 'winter of discontent', so that support for a Labour-sponsored measure was compromised. In both referenda, the turnout was low, which proved critical in Scotland, where there was a narrow majority – 51.6% – in favour, but a failure to reach the 40% threshold. In Wales, the change was comprehensively defeated, with only 20% of votes in favour.

The Thatcher government was firmly opposed to devolution, but nationalist sentiment hardened during the 1980s as a result of the centralising policies which were pursued and economic changes which created or severely exacerbated differences in prosperity between south-eastern England and other areas.

27.3.1 Scotland and the Poll Tax

There was particular anger over the Poll Tax which was introduced in the late 1980s to replace domestic rates. The system of rates had a number of serious flaws. Since it was based on property values, it was linked only indirectly with a ratepayer's ability to pay, and there was also no direct connection between the amount payable and the level of services actually provided. Second, since rates were levied only on householders, a substantial proportion of the population was not liable, limiting public accountability.

One of the major priorities of the Thatcher government was to lessen the power and influence of local authorities in the large urban conurbations, which were largely Labour-controlled and pursued policies which Thatcherites regarded as wasteful and ideologically unsound. There was general political acceptance that the rating system must go. However, there was no consensus on what should replace it. The government sought to convey to voters the true cost of electing a council that followed expensive policies by creating a tax which would be levied at a flat rate on all adults resident in the area administered by that council.

A flat rate tax is necessarily regressive in its effect. Not only is no account taken of ability to pay, but the tax bears disproportionately on the less well-off. The requirement for all adults to be included in a register maintained by councils was opposed by civil libertarians. More generally, there was concern that, among some local authorities at least, high levels of spending resulted from high levels of need rather then profligacy. Forecasts that there would be extensive non-payment were met by enforcement provisions which included the ultimate penalty of imprisonment for non-payment. Overall, the Poll Tax introduced under the Local Government Finance Act 1988 was deeply unpopular. As far as the Scots were concerned, it only added insult to injury that under the 1988 Act, the Poll Tax came into effect in Scotland one year earlier than in England.

In the event, the Poll Tax was the subject of a widespread campaign of deliberate non-payment and reliance on technical legal points to frustrate attempts by local authorities to enforce payment via the courts. Violent demonstrations also occurred and the government eventually conceded defeat, replacing the Poll Tax with a Council Tax payable only by householders and linked to property values. However, as far as Scotland was concerned, the damage was done, and opposition parties took full advantage of this during the remaining years of Conservative government. There was anyway a sense of 'democratic deficit' in Scotland and Wales, where the proportion of Conservative seats had historically been lower than in England, and this became much more marked during the Thatcher years. Parliamentary boundary changes were also seen as an attack on Scottish representation in Scotland, although Scotland in terms of population is actually somewhat over-represented by comparison with England.

In the 1995 local elections, the Conservatives failed to achieve a majority on any local council in Scotland, and in the 1997 general election, quite unprecedentedly, they did not win a single Scottish seat. Though anti-Conservative sentiments in Wales were less extreme, still in 1997 Labour obtained all but a handful of seats, and most of that handful went to Plaid Cymru or the Liberal Democrats, both also committed to some form of devolution.

27.4   THE 1997 REFERENDA

On coming to power in 1997, Labour lost no time in holding referenda in Scotland and Wales on the principle of whether a Scottish Parliament and a Welsh Assembly should be established, and whether a Scottish Parliament should have powers to raise revenue. Although no detailed proposals were issued beforehand and there were no clear indications of the extent of the powers that might be devolved, the referenda took place in September 1997. In Scotland, 74.3% of persons who voted were in favour of a parliament, 63.5% in favour of its having powers of taxation, on a 60% turnout. In Wales, the position was much more equivocal: only some 50% of the electorate voted, and of these a bare 50.3% were in favour. White Papers containing detailed proposals duly followed, and the necessary legislation was passed in the 1997–98 parliamentary session.

27.5   DEVOLVED GOVERNMENT

27.5.1 Scotland

The Scotland Act 1998 was much more far-reaching than its Welsh counterpart, since the new Scottish Parliament was given power to make primary legislation in all areas except those specifically reserved to Westminster, and to raise revenue by means of an additional income tax of up to 3 p in the pound. Given that power was given to the Scottish Parliament in areas not reserved to Westminster, the structure created is reminiscent of the United States, although Westminster retains full powers to legislate for Scotland,[4] whereas the United States Congress has no powers in areas reserved to

---

4   Section 28(7) of the Scotland Act 1998.

the states. The Blair government has insisted at all stages that the Scotland Act is not intended as the first step towards a federal system and that devolution will strengthen the UK rather than the reverse.[5] Whether these assertions will prove accurate remains to be seen.

The Scottish Parliament, which sat for the first time in May 1999, meets for fixed terms of four years, although there is provision under the Act for extraordinary dissolution and election if a two-thirds majority of members vote for dissolution, but the Parliament elected under this provision may sit only for the balance of the current four year term.[6] There are 129 members, 73 elected by proportional representation from the constituencies of the UK Parliament. Much more controversially, the remaining 56 members are selected on a party list basis from the eight European Parliament constituencies in Scotland, and the seven seats for each constituency are allocated in proportion to the votes cast for each party. Each voter has two votes.

The Scotland Act creates a Scottish Executive consisting of a First Minister appointed by the queen after being chosen by members of the Scottish Parliament from among their number, and holding office at pleasure, and such other ministers as the First Minister may appoint, together with the two Law Officers (the Lord Advocate and Solicitor General for Scotland). Members of the Executive are responsible to the Scottish Parliament in the exercise of their powers.[7] Their appointment must be approved by the Scottish Parliament, but the Act does not specify any mechanism for approval, nor does it specify the mechanism by which the First Minister is to be chosen. An election was held in May 1999 when the first appointments were made. The European Convention on Human Rights is also incorporated into the domestic law of Scotland.

The Scottish Parliament has power in all areas not specifically excluded from its competence, which are listed in Sched 5 and embrace the constitution, foreign affairs and defence, the Civil Service and the law relating to treason, as listed in Part I. Part II then contains a lengthy list of specific reservations and their exceptions.[8]

Section 29 provides that an Act of the Scottish Parliament is void if it is outside the legislative competence of the Parliament and there are detailed procedures to minimise the risk of this occurring. Under s 31(1), the member of the Scottish Executive responsible for a Bill must certify before its introduction that it is within the Parliament's competence,[9] and the Presiding Officer (broadly equivalent to the Speaker) must additionally consider this at the time of introduction.[10] Within four weeks of the passing of any Bill, the Advocate General, Lord Advocate or Attorney General may refer the Bill to the Judicial Committee of the Privy Council for a ruling on competence, and such a reference prevents the Bill being submitted for the royal assent pending that ruling.[11] A ruling on compatibility with EC law may be sought

---

5   Cf *Scotland's Parliament*, Cm 3658, 1997, HMSO, para 3.1.
6   Section 2(1) of the Scotland Act 1998.
7   *Ibid*, ss 44–45.
8   A convenient list of the areas in which the Scottish Parliament has competence is contained in H Barnett, *Constitutional and Administrative Law*, 3rd edn, 2000, Cavendish Publishing, pp 472–74.
9   Section 31(1) of the Scotland Act 1998.
10 *Ibid*, s 31(2).
11 *Ibid*, ss 32–33.

from the European Court of Justice.[12] As yet, no references have been made under either provision.

Certain areas remain unclear. In particular, there is no certainty on the consequences should the Scottish Parliament and UK Parliament pass incompatible legislation in an area where both are competent. Presumably, a constitutional convention will be applied whereby Westminster will not normally seek to legislate in areas in which Edinburgh has competence, but such a convention cannot, of course, be legally binding. Second, the West Lothian question has not been addressed, so that MPs sitting at Westminster for Scottish constituencies have full power to speak and vote on matters which affect England alone, although under s 86, amending the Parliamentary Constituencies Act 1986, constituencies are to be allocated in Scotland on the same basis as in England, so that Scotland's historic over-representation at Westminster will disappear. Third, the limits of the powers of the Scottish Executive remain undefined.[13] The relationship between the Executive and the Secretary of State for Scotland is also undefined, though it was envisaged in the White Paper that the latter would represent Scotland's interests in relation to matters reserved to Westminster, and it may be presumed that he will adopt a liaison role between the Scottish Executive and the government. Finally, there is nothing in law to prevent an individual from sitting as a member of both the Edinburgh and Westminster Parliaments, as has occurred in the first session of the Scottish Parliament, with the obvious consequence that by attempting to meet the responsibilities of both, they will succeed in neither.[14]

The Scotland Act places no upper limit on the size of the Scottish Executive. The original First Minister, Donald Dewar, created five posts, dealing with education; industry; agriculture, environment and fisheries; home affairs and devolution; and health and culture. In addition, he created a Cabinet consisting of the Lord Advocate (also a member of the Scottish Executive), chief whip and seven ministers. Each of the seven ministers was given a junior minister. This gives a total of 19 ministers, excluding the Law Officers, a vastly larger executive body than before devolution, when one Cabinet minister and his junior minister were held sufficient.[15]

27.5.2 Wales

The Government of Wales Act provides for a much more limited degree of devolution Essentially, the Welsh Assembly has powers in areas where the Secretary of State for Wales previously had executive responsibility, although as those came from a mass of primary and secondary legislation, the limits of the Assembly's power have yet to be established. In general terms, the Assembly has power in the following areas:

---

12   *Ibid*, s 34.

13   *Ibid*, ss 53–54.

14   See (1999) *Daily Telegraph*, 22 February.

15   There has been much concern since May 1999 over the cost of the new system and whether the additional expense over the pre-devolution system can be justified. Particular criticism has been levelled at the escalating cost of the new Parliament building, claimed to be currently well over £50 million.

(a) agriculture, farming, fisheries and food;

(b) ancient monuments and historic buildings;

(c) culture, including museums, galleries and libraries;

(d) economic development and industry;

(e) education and training;

(f) the environment;

(g) health;

(h) highways and transport;

(i) housing;

(j) local government and social services;

(k) housing and town and country planning;

(l) sport and tourism;

(m) water and flood defence;

(n) the Welsh language.

In these areas, the Assembly has power to make delegated legislation on the basis of various enabling Acts. Unlike the Scottish Parliament, it has no power to make primary legislation, nor can it raise revenue. Funding for the Assembly's work comes from a central government grant. The Secretary of State for Wales allocates this grant between the Welsh Office and Assembly, though the Assembly determines its own spending priorities. There is also an expectation that the Assembly will act as an advisory body to Parliament in matters relating to Wales. Under a Protocol adopted between the Assembly and the Secretary of State in January 2000, the Secretary of State is under a duty to consult the Assembly on the government's legislative programme and to ensure that the interests of Wales are considered in the formulation and drafting of primary legislation.[16]

The Assembly sits for fixed four year terms, but it has no power to dissolve itself. It consists of a single chamber of 60 members, of whom 40 are elected from single-member constituencies on a simple majority basis. The remaining 20 are chosen from party lists, in proportions reflecting the total vote for each party. As in Scotland, each voter has two votes. The 1998 Act provides for a Leader of the Assembly, elected by the members, and an Executive Committee comprising the heads of the various subject committees which may be created within the Assembly, together with the First Minister and Assembly Ministers.[17]

As to the Executive Committee, there is nothing to prevent all its members from belonging to the same party. The Secretary of State for Wales is expected to liaise with the Executive Committee, but continues to represent the interests of Wales at Cabinet level. He may attend Assembly meetings and participate in proceedings (though not the proceedings of the committees), but has no vote.

It is the Assembly to which the executive functions of the Secretary of State and Under-Secretary of Wales have been transferred, not ministers, and *prima facie*, the

---

16 See N Burrows, *Devolution,* Sweet & Maxwell Modern Legal Studies, 2000, Sweet & Maxwell, p 81.

17 The Act creates a Subordinate Legislation Committee, an Audit Committee and a Committee for North Wales and provides for the establishment of further committees.

Assembly exercises those functions collectively, all assembly members being members of the executive as well as the legislative branch of government. However, the Assembly then delegates the day to day exercise of executive functions to a Welsh Cabinet consisting of the First Minister, elected by the Assembly,[18] and Assembly Ministers appointed by the First Minister.[19]

Whereas in Scotland, ministers are accountable to the Scottish Parliament in a fashion modelled on that of Westminster, the Government of Wales Act creates a considerably more complex structure, reflecting the fact that it is the Assembly itself which has overall executive responsibility. Accountability is defined in the Act in terms of a linkage between a member of the Executive Committee and a field in which the Assembly has executive authority. By s 56(3), the First Minister must either make one of the Assembly Ministers accountable in each of those fields, or remain accountable himself. Each member of the Assembly has, by standing orders made under s 56(7)(a), authority to submit written or oral questions to the member of the Executive Committee who is accountable in relation to particular field or fields. Once an Assembly Minister has been appointed to be accountable in any field, a subject committee is set up to formulate policy in that field.[20] Interestingly, although an Assembly Minister is *ex officio* a member of such a subject committee and must participate in its work and provide it with information as to Welsh Cabinet policy in the relevant field, he is prevented by s 57(4) from chairing the committee. Neither is he accountable to the committee, but to the Assembly as a whole. It appears that the intention is to create a collegiate government and encourage collective formulation of policy and decision-making. It remains to be seen whether this objective is actually achieved. Currently, there are seven Ministers in addition to the First Minister, and 19 committees, including four regional committees.

Both the relevant Acts make provision for circumstances where one or other body, the Scottish Parliament or Executive, or Welsh Assembly, is alleged in the course of civil or criminal proceedings to have acted outside its legislative or executive powers.[21] As yet, there has been no case law in this sphere and it remains to be seen how frequently and in what circumstances issues of this nature will arise.

27.6 NORTHERN IRELAND

In recent years, there has also been some attempt to create a structure of devolved authority in Northern Ireland, but in the peculiarly difficult political circumstances of that province, it is not yet clear whether that currently in place is capable of functioning effectively. Indeed, at the time of writing (November 2002), devolved government has been suspended for an indefinite period. Crucially, any structure has to be acceptable to the various terrorist organisations and their political allies, at least to a degree which will induce them to renounce their unlawful activities on a

---

18   Section 53(1) of the Government of Wales Act 1998
19   *Ibid*, s 53(2).
20   *Ibid*, s 57.
21   Schedule 6 and s 98 of the Scotland Act 1998; Sched 7 and s 109 of the Government of Wales Act 1998.

permanent basis.[22] The events of the past 30 years, and since the main terrorist organisations declared official ceasefires in 1994, are not such as to inspire confidence. An atmosphere of mutual suspicion and recrimination remains and seriously hampers attempts to secure government by consensus.

It has been accepted by successive British governments since 1972 that any workable solution to the sectarian problems of Northern Ireland requires the acceptance of all political and religious groups, and the co-operation of the government of the Irish Republic. Ideologically, if not practically, a consistent sticking point has been Art 2 of the 1937 Irish constitution, which provides:

> The national territory consists of the whole island of Ireland, its islands and the territorial seas.

Although the Northern Ireland (Constitution) Act 1973 provides that the province shall not cease to be part of the UK save with the consent of a majority of its population in a referendum held for that purpose, nevertheless, any form of co-operation with the Dublin government has been seen by more extreme Unionists as a first step towards incorporation into the Republic by the back door, and by even the more moderate as something to be approached with extreme caution. In a similar fashion, the Republican and Nationalist portions of the population have been reluctant to accept any structure which does not include the government of the Republic as a means of protecting their interests. Mutual suspicion between the British and Irish governments, with on the British side a concern that the Republic has over many years provided a safe haven for terrorists, has not made a difficult task any easier. In addition, the various terrorist groups, while in recent years professing commitment to a permanent ceasefire, have procrastinated to an extreme degree over giving up their very large stocks of weapons and explosives.

The deliberations of a Northern Ireland Forum created in 1983, and on which all the major political parties in the North and South were represented, resulted in an Anglo-Irish Agreement (the Sunningdale Agreement) in 1985 that accepted the principle that no constitutional change concerning the relationship between Northern Ireland and the Republic could come about except by the consent of the majority of the population of Northern Ireland. In 1993, on the initiative of John Major, a Downing Street Declaration was negotiated between the British and Irish governments and involved the major Northern Ireland political parties, by which it was again agreed that there would be no change in the status of the province without the consent of its population, though the British government would not oppose union with the Republic if that was the will of the majority. The British government thereby professed neutrality over the future status of Northern Ireland. In September 1994, the IRA declared a ceasefire, followed by the major Loyalist groups.

---

22 In dealing with issues relating to Northern Ireland, the writer is bedevilled by problems with nomenclature. 'Protestant' and 'Catholic' carry strong political as well as religious overtones. In the strictly political sphere, 'Republican' denotes those seeking a united Ireland by peaceful and democratic means. Their main political representatives are the Social Democratic and Labour Party (SDLP). Those seeking a united Ireland by any means are generally referred to as 'Nationalists'. The main Nationalist party is Sinn Fein, which has associations with the Provisional IRA. Those committed to keeping Northern Ireland within the UK via the normal democratic process are 'Unionists', though there are many shades of Unionism. Protestant terrorist groups are inaccurately known as 'Loyalists'. Geographically, there are also difficulties in nomenclature, all the terms in use carrying a degree of political loading.

There followed a period of hope that a workable framework for peace in Northern Ireland might emerge after a quarter of a century of violence, the deaths of 3,000 people and serious injury to many more. In February 1995, the two governments agreed a set of Frameworks for the Future which included principles of 'equality of opportunity, equity of treatment and parity of esteem' and explicitly stated that any future settlement must be operated by and have the allegiance of all elements in the population. This necessarily involved the rejection of the 1921 model of devolution. Instead, there was to be a negotiated settlement based on dialogue between the political representatives of all elements within the population, concerning the relationships between those elements, between the two parts of Ireland and between the UK and the Republic.

These Frameworks aroused some opposition in the Unionist camp, not least because the IRA, represented in negotiations by Sinn Fein, showed a very marked reluctance to demonstrate their good faith and commitment to a lasting peace by giving up their arsenals. In February 1996, the ceasefire ended when the IRA bombed Canary Wharf in London and engaged in renewed terrorist activity on the British mainland, though not initially in Northern Ireland. For the rest of the year, negotiations remained at an impasse.

After the May 1997 election, the Blair government made further overtures to Sinn Fein, which in September called another ceasefire and announced a renunciation of violence. All-party talks then began, with the American Senator George Mitchell as a neutral chairman, but were interrupted in February 1998 when the IRA once more broke the ceasefire, leading to Sinn Fein's expulsion from the talks. A tense period then followed, with frenzied negotiation leading to the terms embodied in the Good Friday Agreement of 10 April 1998.

The Good Friday Agreement is prefaced by a Declaration of Support which states that past events have left a 'deep and profoundly regrettable legacy of suffering', and that the future must be based on reconciliation, tolerance, mutual trust, and respect for human rights. The underlying relationships recognised by the Frameworks, those between the different elements within the population, the two governments and the two parts of Ireland, must be conducted on the basis of partnership, equality and mutual respect. All the parties agreed to renounce violence and to commit themselves exclusively to peaceful and democratic means, and accepted that the people of Northern Ireland might legitimately and by majority choose the future status of the province. Following this statement, the Agreement contained five main elements:

(a) Northern Ireland was to remain part of the UK, and the Republic would amend its constitution to remove its claim over the province;

(b) a Northern Ireland Assembly of 108 members elected under proportional representation would be created, to be operated by an Executive of 12 members;

(c) a North-South ministerial council would be created to co-ordinate relations between Northern Ireland and the Republic;

(d) a Council of the [British] Isles was to be established, its membership drawn from the Parliaments of the UK, the Irish Republic, Scotland and the Welsh Assembly;

(e) all participants in the Agreement committed themselves to the disarming of terrorist organisations.

This Agreement was then followed by an agreement between the two governments on its implementation. This recognised the principle of majority choice over the status of Northern Ireland, with a commitment to pass the necessary legislation to bring about a united Ireland should that be the wish of the majority. The UK agreed to repeal the Government of Ireland Act 1920 and to hold a referendum on whether Northern Ireland should remain within the UK, at such a time as the Secretary of State determines that a majority of the population would be likely to vote in favour of change. The Irish government agreed to amend the Republic's constitution to recognise that a united Ireland could 'only be brought about by peaceful means with the consent of a majority of the people, democratically expressed, in both jurisdictions in the island'.

Referenda were held on 10 May 1998 in both Northern Ireland and the Republic before the Good Friday Agreement could be put into effect. In Northern Ireland, the vote was 71.12% in favour, on a turnout of 80.98%; in the Republic 94.40% were in favour, though the turnout was markedly lower. The Northern Ireland Act 1998 was passed to embody the Agreement into the domestic law of the UK, providing that the transfer of power to the Assembly would take effect by Order when the Secretary of State determined that 'sufficient progress' had been made in implementing the Agreement. Elections followed in June for the Northern Ireland Assembly, which, like the Executive, would initially sit in shadow mode, power not being devolved until the terrorists had decommissioned their weapons.

Under the provisions of the 1998 Act, the Assembly sits for fixed four year terms, though provision is made for dissolution and extraordinary elections on the basis of a majority vote of members.[23] The Westminster constituencies are used, each returning six members elected under proportional representation.[24] Unlike elections to the Scottish Parliament and Welsh Assembly, all members are elected on a named candidate basis, reflecting the particular need for candidates to inspire the trust of voters. The first election produced an Assembly with a broad balance of representation between the two main political traditions, which met for the first time on 15 July 1998.

The Northern Ireland Act allows the UK Parliament to continue to legislate for Northern Ireland, but gives the Assembly power to amend the provisions of Acts of Parliament insofar as they form part of the law of Northern Ireland.[25] The Assembly does not have power to raise revenue, but, like the Welsh Assembly, it does have power relating to the allocation of a central government grant. The devolved structure reflects elements of those in Scotland and Wales, since the Assembly has power to make primary legislation, but executive power is devolved to the Assembly itself, rather than to the Executive. That executive power essentially embraces matters devolved to the pre-1972 Northern Ireland government and in the interim period dealt with by the Secretary of State and the Northern Ireland Office:

(a) agriculture;

(b) economic development;

(c) education;

(d) the environment;

---

23 Sections 31–32 of the Northern Ireland Act 1998.
24 *Ibid*, ss 33–34.
25 *Ibid*, s 5.

(e) finance;

(f) health and Social Services.

Schedules 2 and 3 set out matters reserved to the UK Parliament. It is further provided that the Assembly may not make legislation which is incompatible with the European Convention on Human Rights or EC law, or which discriminates against any person or class of person on the basis of religious belief or political opinion. As does the Scotland Act, the Act requires the Presiding Officer of the Assembly to consider whether any Bill is within the Assembly's legislative competence before its introduction and again when it has completed its stages; if he considers a Bill not to be within competence, he must refer it to the Secretary of State. Again in a similar fashion to Scotland, the Attorney General for Northern Ireland may refer a Bill to the Judicial Committee of the Privy Council for a ruling on competence, and the Judicial Committee may seek a ruling on compatibility with EC law from the ECJ.[26] A Bill may not be presented for the royal assent when a ruling is pending. Further, if the Secretary of State considers that a Bill contains provisions which are incompatible with international obligations, the interests of national security or defence, or the protection of public safety or public order, he may decide not to submit the Bill for the royal assent.[27] Security matters, and those relating to policing and prisons, remain the responsibility of the Secretary of State, along with foreign policy and taxation.

The highly charged political situation in Northern Ireland led to the inclusion in the Act of provisions intended to enable the Assembly and Executive to operate effectively in an atmosphere of entrenched suspicion and recrimination. These endeavour to walk a very narrow line between enabling former terrorists who have sincerely renounced violence to participate in the democratic process, while making possible the exclusion, in the wider interests of the population of Northern Ireland as a whole and the promotion of permanent peace, of those whose commitment is less than wholehearted. There is also provision in the legislation for the suspension of the powers of the Assembly and Executive and temporary re-imposition of direct rule.

The Executive is headed by a First Minister and Deputy First Minister, between them representing the two main political traditions. Candidates for the two posts must stand jointly, and in order to be elected, a pairing must not only gain a majority of all the votes cast by Assembly members, but a majority of designated Unionist and Nationalist votes. Once elected, if either ceases to hold office, the other falls with him.[28]

The First Minister and Deputy First Minister jointly chair the Northern Ireland Executive, which consists of themselves together with the ministers. The number of ministerial offices is determined by the First Minister and Deputy First Minister acting jointly, but may not exceed 10, or such higher figure as is specified by the Secretary of State.[29] Allocation between parties is determined by the 'd'Hondt system', named after an 18th century political scientist, whereby each party receives ministerial offices under the formula of the number of seats that party gained in the last Assembly election divided by the total number of ministerial offices, plus one. Where that formula produces the same total number of ministerial offices for two or more parties,

---

26   *Ibid*, s 12.

27   *Ibid*, s 14.

28   *Ibid*, s 16.

29   *Ibid*, s 17.

the party with the greatest number of first preference votes in the Assembly election has first choice of offices.[30] Use of this formula after the 1998 election gave the Ulster Unionists and SDLP three seats each, and Sinn Fein and the Democratic Unionists two each. The Assembly elected David Trimble, leader of the Ulster Unionists, as First Minister, and Seamus Mallon of the SDLP as Deputy First Minister. Power was formally devolved to the Assembly by the Secretary of State's Order on 2 December 1999.

Ministers and their Departments may make subordinate legislation in matters in which they have competence under the relevant legislation, but their powers to do so are circumscribed by provisions analogous to those restricting the powers of the Assembly to make primary legislation. Ministers may not make, confirm or approve any subordinate legislation, or do any act, insofar as that legislation or Act is incompatible with EC law or rights under the European Convention on Human Rights, or which discriminates, or aids or incites another person to discriminate, against a person or class of person on the basis of religious belief or political opinion.[31] Where subordinate legislation contains provisions dealing with matters exempted or reserved from the Assembly's competence under Scheds 2 and 3, the Secretary of State has a power, not accorded to his counterparts in Scotland and Wales, to revoke that legislation.[32] More generally, he may prohibit any action proposed by a minister or department which would be incompatible with international obligations, the interests of defence or national security or the protection of public safety or public order,[33] and when on any of those grounds he considers that action should be taken, he may by order direct that such action be taken.[34] The Secretary of State for Northern Ireland is thus given considerably more power than his counterparts.

As yet, none of these powers and safeguards have been tested.

Uniquely, under s 30, the Assembly has power to exclude a minister or a political party from the Assembly on the basis of a resolution that the minister or party no longer enjoys its confidence because of a lack of commitment to non-violence and to exclusively democratic processes, or because of a failure to observe the terms of the pledge of office (analogous to the Oath of Allegiance taken by MPs, but without references to the British Crown). If such a resolution is passed, then for a renewable period of 12 months, the Assembly may exclude that person or party entirely or prohibit members of that party from holding ministerial office. The section seeks to ensure that this power will be used rarely and on a non-sectarian basis, since a motion for such a resolution may only brought by at least 30 members of the Assembly, by the First Minister and Deputy First Minister acting jointly, or by the Presiding Officer. The Secretary of State may also serve a notice requiring the Presiding Officer to move such a motion. At the time of writing, no such motions have been moved.

Attempts to bring about a peaceful transition to devolved government in Northern Ireland have been dogged by difficulty, predominantly because of procrastination by the terrorist organisations on the decommissioning of weapons. Following the Good Friday Agreement, an international commission was created to

---

30   *Ibid*, s 18.
31   *Ibid*, s 24.
32   *Ibid*, s 25.
33   *Ibid*, s 26.
34   *Ibid*, s 26.

deal with this matter, under the leadership of General John de Chastelain, a Canadian, but despite the commission's efforts, little concrete progress has been made and serious doubts must remain as to the commitment of the terrorists and their political allies to a permanent and stable peace. This is despite very extensive concessions designed to create an atmosphere of goodwill, including the accelerated release of most terrorist prisoners and the re-structuring of the Royal Ulster Constabulary. A generally suspicious and hostile atmosphere has not been improved by continued terrorist activity, whether by 'punishment beatings' by particular groups in areas which they control, of which 331 were reported during 2001,[35] or by splinter groups, most notoriously the Real IRA, who were responsible for the bomb which exploded in a shopping area in Omagh, close to the border with the Republic but until then relatively free from sectarian violence, on 15 August 1998, killing 29 people and injuring some 250.

---

35 (2002) *The Times*, 21 January.

CHAPTER 28

THE EUROPEAN CONVENTION ON HUMAN RIGHTS AND THE HUMAN RIGHTS ACT

28.1 INTRODUCTION

The European Convention on Human Rights, incorporated into the law of Scotland and Northern Ireland by their respective devolution Acts, and that of the UK as a whole under the terms of the Human Rights Act 1998, is in its origins and provisions very much a product of the world as it was in the immediate aftermath of the Second World War.

In 1945 and after, full details emerged of the actions of the Nazi regime which held power in Germany from 1933 and occupied much of Europe in 1939–45. There was a deeply held sense that such abuses must never be allowed to happen again. In addition to a policy of genocide which resulted in the systematic liquidation of some six million Jews, the Nazis disposed of smaller but significant numbers of gypsies, disabled and mentally handicapped persons and homosexuals as part of a policy of purging the population of its 'undesirable' elements, as well as executing or imprisoning large numbers of ideological opponents and seeking to repress all opposition. Since the 1930s, the Soviet regime had pursued active policies of repression towards political enemies. A large-scale 'purge' of the Communist Party and national institutions took place in the years 1937–40 and a system of labour camps falling outside the normal criminal justice system was created, for which the writer Alexander Solzhenitsyn – who himself spent eight years in a labour camp after criticising the dictator Stalin – coined the name 'Gulag Archipelago'. Although the Nazi government had been destroyed, in the late 1940s, the Soviet regime was extending its power over much of eastern Europe.

In this period, several international organisations were formed in Europe and elsewhere with the intention of establishing and maintaining democratic government and institutions, and encouraging member states to resolve their differences by peaceful means. Among these was the Council of Europe, formed by the governments of 25 states with the broad aim of fostering democratic government within western Europe. There was a particular sense of revulsion that the Nazi regime had been able to achieve power entirely through the democratic process and then to consolidate its position by manipulating a democratic constitution through its own mechanisms for amendment. In the eyes of the Council of Europe, in the particular political and intellectual milieu of 1949–50, there was a fundamental need for the individual citizen to be protected against potential abuses by his own state, and a sense that the state should not be able to justify repressive action against its citizens by arguments of necessity and of the interests of the majority, as totalitarian governments had frequently sought to do. The Council of Europe therefore agreed to create a framework of basic rights applicable to all individuals, and a structure by which these could be enforced against governments.

This is the philosophy behind the European Convention on Human Rights, drawn up in 1950 and ratified by the UK along with other member states of the Council of Europe in 1951. Its terms were based on the principles set out in the United Nations Universal Declaration on Human Rights of 1948, and embodied the particular concerns of the time in its emphasis on the importance of the physical security of the individual and on freedom to hold and propound ideas. The Convention therefore contains provisions to protect freedom of thought, conscience, religious belief and the expression of all these, as well as a more general right to respect for private and family life, home and correspondence. Although the Convention also sets out 'permitted derogations' – grounds on and circumstances in which these basic rights may be limited or even abrogated altogether – the basic philosophy is that a government must demonstrate strong and objectively justified reasons for doing so, and cannot simply rely on arguments of 'state necessity'. The Convention then provided an enforcement mechanism in the form of a multi-national European Court of Human Rights and European Commission on Human Rights.

28.2   THE TERMS OF THE CONVENTION

It is convenient to make a broad distinction between those Convention rights which are 'rigid' – where there are no exceptions or the permitted exceptions are defined in narrow and specific terms – and those which are 'flexible', in that the Convention allows cognisance to be taken of wider public interests. An example of a completely rigid provision is Art 3, which prohibits torture or 'inhuman or degrading treatment or punishment' in absolute terms, with no permitted derogations whatsoever. It is therefore necessary for a person petitioning the Court to establish only that the act complained of constitutes torture or inhuman or degrading treatment. Article 2, the right to life, is couched in terms which permits limited exceptions, including, as originally drafted, the imposition of the death penalty, which was accepted as a proper element in criminal justice systems at that time. Article 2(2) provides:

> Deprivation of life shall not be regarded as inflicted in contravention of this Article when it results from the use of force which is no more than *absolutely necessary*:[1]
>
> (a) in defence of any person from unlawful violence;
>
> (b) in order to effect a lawful arrest or to prevent the escape of a person lawfully detained;
>
> (c) in action lawfully taken for the purpose of quelling a riot or insurrection.

These exceptions were considered in a UK context in the case of *McGann, Farrell and Savage v United Kingdom*, where, notoriously, the Court concluded that the force used had been 'more than absolutely necessary' in the defence of persons from unlawful violence, when the SAS shot three IRA terrorists who were carrying out a reconnaissance for the purpose of planting and detonating a large bomb in Gibraltar in March 1988.[2]

Article 8, guaranteeing a person's right to 'respect' for his private and family life, home and correspondence, is an example of a flexible right, the exceptions being set out in broad terms. Article 8(2) provides:

> There shall be no interference by a public authority with the exercise of this right except such as is in accordance with the law and is necessary in a democratic society in the

---

1   My emphasis.

2   It should be noted that the Court, unusually, departed from the conclusions of the Commission, which had held the use of force to be within the bounds of what was necessary, and that the Court reached its decision by a majority of one.

interests of national security, public safety or the economic well being of the country, for the prevention of disorder or crime, for the protection of health or morals, or for the protection of the rights and freedoms of others.

Permitted derogations from Art 9 (freedom of thought, conscience and religion), Art 10 (freedom of expression) and Art 11 (freedom of assembly) are couched in similar though not identical terms.

28.3 ENFORCEMENT

Article 19 of the Convention provides for the creation of a European Court of Human Rights, to adjudicate on allegations of breach of Convention rights, and a European Commission on Human Rights, to decide first on the admissibility of applications made to the Court and to investigate the allegations and report on them in detail. Judges of the Court are appointed for renewable nine year terms, on the basis of nomination by a member state and election by the Consultative Assembly of the Council of Europe. The number of judges is equal to the number of member states. The judges sit in an individual capacity and are required to be independent of national interests.

Application to the Court and Commission may be made either by member states on the basis that another member state is in breach of the requirements of the Convention, though this is extremely rare, or by an individual alleging that a member state has breached his own Convention rights, where the right of 'individual petition' has been granted by a national government. Article 26 requires an individual petitioner to have exhausted all domestic remedies before making an application and under Art 25, he must establish that the alleged breach has affected him directly. For example, in *Magee v United Kingdom*, the petitioner could not allege that the requirement for a person appointed as a QC to swear allegiance to the British Crown breached his right to freedom of thought and conscience. He had not been invited to become a QC, so the requirement had not prevented him from becoming a QC.[3] The Commission may also reject applications brought for improper motives, such as seeking a political advantage or solely for publicity,[4] or where the substance of the complaint has already been adjudicated upon in an earlier case.[5]

If the Commission considers the application admissible, it will seek to negotiate a 'friendly settlement' between the parties. Where no settlement is achieved, the Commission produces an opinion setting out its view of the breach, which is considered by a Committee of Ministers comprising the foreign ministers of the member states. The Committee has the power to produce its own judgment by a two-thirds majority, operating in closed session, or may refer the application to the Court. In practice, the Court hears the great majority of cases which are ruled admissible.

A judgment of the Court binds the member states and compliance normally requires a state to change the provision of domestic law which has been found to

---

3   (1993) 19 EHRR CD 91.
4   Article 35(3) of the Convention.
5   Article 35(2)(b) of the Convention.

offend against a Convention right. For example, in *Malone v United Kingdom*,[6] the Court held that the tapping of Mr Malone's telephone under a warrant issued by the Home Secretary violated Art 8, as the domestic law which governed the Home Secretary's power to issue such warrants was vague. Previously, a domestic court had found the tapping to be entirely lawful. There was no domestic law giving Mr Malone any enforceable right of privacy in relation to his telephone calls and on the facts, there was no trespass to his property, for which positive authority was required under *Entick v Carrington*, since the physical interference with the telephone had taken place at the exchange and not on his land.[7] Following the Court's decision, the government took steps to obtain the passage of the Interception of Communications Act 1985, which regulates the exercise of the prerogative in this sphere and creates a mechanism for redress of grievance.

28.4   THE UK AND THE CONVENTION

28.4.1 The European Court

The Convention binds signatory states only at international level. At its inception, the signatories were not required to incorporate it into domestic law as the philosophy was that it ought to be enforced by extra-national institutions created for that purpose. The individual citizen needing protection against his own state could not rely on domestic institutions, as they themselves might be subverted. However, it became increasingly the norm for member states to incorporate the Convention into domestic law or to include analogous provisions in their constitutions. Although the UK was closely involved in the drafting of the Convention, and several provisions of the Convention are modelled on freedoms developed under the common law, the approach of successive governments towards the Convention was extremely cautious. It was not until 1965 that a British government permitted individual petition to the Court, and it was only in 1998 that legislation was passed to render Convention rights directly enforceable under domestic law.

This delay was the subject of much criticism by the growing body of human rights protagonists, but a proportion of the criticism appears misconceived. In particular, the statistic is often quoted that between 1966, when individual petition first become possible, and 1997, a total of 50 applications were made which were upheld by the Court,[8] more than in the case of any other signatory state except Turkey. However, when individual cases are considered in detail, it becomes apparent that a considerable proportion of applications were upheld on the basis not that there had been a clear breach of a Convention right, but rather that domestic law failed to provide the positive protection for Convention rights which the Court's jurisprudence required. This is a reflection the British constitutional tradition of freedom under the law rather than the granting of positive rights, and ought to be seen as such.

---

6   (1984) 7 EHRR 14.
7   *Malone v Metropolitan Police Commissioner* [1979] Ch D 344.
8   See H Barnett, *Constitutional and Administrative Law*, 3rd edn, 2000, Cavendish Publishing, pp 883–84.

Malone v United Kingdom makes a good example. The interception had been initiated because of police suspicions, apparently justified on the facts, of Mr Malone's involvement in the large-scale handling of stolen goods, and a wish to obtain evidence against him for use at trial. The Court held that this purpose fell within the permitted derogations under Art 8, but found a violation of Art 8 on the basis that interference with the right is permitted only insofar as it is 'in accordance with the law'. Under UK law, interception of telephone calls is permitted where a warrant is issued by the Home Secretary under prerogative powers deriving from the sovereign's traditional responsibility to protect his or her people. These powers were ill-defined and there was no mechanism by which the Home Secretary's decision could be made the subject of independent scrutiny or by which the person affected could challenge the issue of the warrant. National law was therefore defective, in that it did not provide positive protection against potential abuse by the Home Secretary.

In a similar fashion, a number of applications have been brought, and upheld by the Court, under Art 6, which sets out a right to a fair and public trial in detailed terms, including a requirement that the case be heard by an 'independent and impartial tribunal established by law'. A particular focus of case law has been on whether a particular body with judicial or quasi-judicial powers constitutes an independent and impartial tribunal for this purpose. Case law suggests that the Commission and Court are very much influenced by appearances as distinct from realities, and are prepared to find a violation of Art 6(1) on the basis of a possibility that a system might be abused, even though there may be no evidence that an abuse has actually occurred or is likely to occur.

For example, there may be a finding of a violation on the basis that a decision-maker might be influenced, consciously or unconsciously, as a consequence of a link with a particular body or office-holder, and the tests applied under Convention jurisprudence are less stringent than the 'real danger of bias' test formulated by the House of Lords in *R v Gough*.[9] The Court looks for the provision of positive safeguards against the possibility of abuse, which are frequently absent from a system which has evolved over a lengthy period and in which there has been little incidence of actions which might trigger a review and re-structuring of that system. A good example is the much-publicised case of *Findlay v United Kingdom*.[10]

On 29 July 1990, following a drinking bout, Alexander Findlay, then a Lance Sergeant in the Scots Guards, held members of his unit hostage with a loaded service pistol, threatening to kill himself and some of them, but surrendered after firing two shots into a television set. He subsequently pleaded guilty to seven offences at a General Court-Martial on 11 November 1991 and was sentenced to a combination of penalties which reflected the serious nature of the offences and were consistent with those which a civilian court might have imposed in analogous circumstances.[11] However, Mr Findlay and his legal advisors appear to have considered the sentence unjust on the basis that the offences were allegedly the consequence of undiagnosed post-traumatic stress syndrome brought on by service in the Falklands campaign of

---

9   [1993] AC 646.

10   (1997) 24 EHRR 221. For detailed consideration of this case, see AE Lyon, 'After *Findlay*: a consideration of some aspects of the military justice system' [1998] Crim LR 109–22 and references therein.

11   Two years' imprisonment, together with reduction to the ranks and dismissal from the service.

1982. At that time, there was no provision for appeal against sentence alone in cases dealt with by court-martial, and so no means of appeal following a guilty plea. Having exhausted the procedure for review of sentence available under the Army Act and applied unsuccessfully for leave to seek judicial review of the court-martial findings, Mr Findlay made application under Art 6, alleging that a court-martial did not constitute an independent and impartial tribunal for its purposes.

The Court found in his favour on the basis that the role of the Convening Officer, who at the material time occupied a pivotal position in court-martial procedures, being responsible for the decision to prosecute, the framing of the charges and the administration of the court-martial, was not sufficiently separated from the military chain of command to prevent an appearance of the possibility of bias in the proceedings as a whole. Further, since the Convening Officer, not himself legally qualified, was required to scrutinise the record of the proceedings and had power to quash a verdict of guilty and/or a sentence, there was an appearance that the final decision as to both guilt and innocence was made by a non-judicial body, which was also contrary to Art 6(1).[12]

Detailed scrutiny of the decision and examination of the background establishes very clearly that the Court based their views on appearances and did not consider the way in which the system was operated in practice. Specifically, there were mechanisms in place to ensure that both the Convening Officer and the president and members of the court-martial were not influenced by their superiors in the military chain of command in reaching their decision, and the Convening Officer invariably made his decisions on the basis of legal advice. It is important to note that the Court did not suggest – and in Art 6(1) cases is at pains to stress that it does not – that the appearances of lack of independence and impartiality which it found had had any effect on the outcome of the proceedings. What was important was that the system did not contain mechanisms to prevent the possibility that the system might be abused. The Armed Forces Act 1997, passed after the Commission's opinion in 1995, therefore sought to create those mechanisms, in the main by giving formal effect to what was already established practice. In fact, the only truly innovatory provision in the 1996 Act was that appeal against sentence alone became possible.

It is important to note that the court-martial system, which has its origins in the early 18th century, originally developed under active service conditions in areas far removed from the British Isles, where lawyers were not available and obtaining advice from trained lawyers would lead to unrealistic delays. It therefore evolved procedures which operated within the local chain of command and did not require lawyers. Though lawyers played an increasing role during the 20th century, they were formally incorporated into the system only to a limited extent.

Similarly, in *Starrs v Ruxton*,[13] the Scottish High Court, applying Art 6(1) following the incorporation of the Convention into Scottish law under the Scotland Act 1998, concluded that temporary sheriffs appointed to try criminal cases in Scotland lacked sufficient appearance of independence. This was on the basis that they did not have security of tenure but were appointed for periods of 12 months at a time by the Lord

---

12 It is important to note that the Convening Officer had neither the power to reverse an acquittal nor to increase any sentence. His discretion post-trial could be exercised only in favour of the offender.

13 2000 JC 208.

Advocate, a member of the Executive.[14] Since the Lord Advocate was responsible for appointing temporary sheriffs and might then either appoint an individual to be a permanent sheriff, or renew his appointment as a temporary sheriff, there was an appearance that a temporary sheriff might be influenced in his judicial decision-making by a desire not to lose the favour of the Lord Advocate. As in *Findlay*, there was no suggestion that the independence of any temporary sheriff was actually compromised. However (the crucial point in relation to the Convention), there was no objective guarantee that something of that kind could never happen.

A third area which gave rise to findings of violations of Convention rights was the approach taken by the UK courts in dealing with areas where there was a conflict between a freedom traditionally available and the public interest, as in *Sunday Times v United Kingdom*.[15] In the late 1950s and early 1960s, the drug thalidomide was extensively prescribed to treat morning sickness in pregnancy, resulting in the birth of a number of children with severe deformities. Their parents later sought to bring an action in negligence against the manufacturers, Distillers Ltd, and were encouraged to do so by articles in the *Sunday Times*. Distillers obtained an injunction under the common law of contempt of court to prevent the publication of further articles, on the basis that publication was likely to cause prejudice to future legal proceedings. The House of Lords eventually ruled that the public interest in ensuring the integrity of judicial proceedings outweighed the public interest in freedom of expression on a matter of major importance.[16] Following an application under the Convention, the Court ruled that the traditional English approach of seeking to find the proper balance in the individual case between two conflicting forms of public interest violated Convention rights. It was not a matter of making:

> ... a choice between two conflicting principles, but ... a principle of freedom of expression that is subject to a number of exceptions which must be narrowly interpreted ... It is not sufficient that the interference belongs to that class of exceptions listed in Article 10(2); neither is it sufficient that the interference was imposed because its subject matter fell within a particular category or was caught by a legal rule formulated in general or absolute terms: the Court has to be satisfied that the interference was necessary having regard to the facts and circumstances prevailing in the particular case before it ...[17]

28.4.2 The UK courts

During the 20th century, the UK courts developed principles of judicial review of executive action. Administrative law deals with the operation of government, the actions and decisions of the executive at both central and local level, and is pre-eminently concerned with the powers and responsibilities of government in relation to the individual. Historically, the higher courts have exercised control over public bodies to ensure that they act within their powers and exercise those powers in accordance with the law.

---

14   Under s 11 of the Sheriff Courts (Scotland) Act 1971.
15   (1979) 2 EHRR 245.
16   *Attorney General v Times Newspapers* [1974] AC 273.
17   As in *Malone v United Kingdom*, an element in the Court's reasoning was the lack of precision in the common law governing contempt, leading to the passing of the Contempt of Court Act 1981.

Initially, the courts concerned themselves with the existence of power in a particular sphere and the scope of that power. Examples can be seen in the *Ship Money Case* and in *Entick v Carrington*, as well as the very large number of cases turning on the interpretation of powers granted to executive bodies by statute. Gradually, the courts came to adjudicate not only on the issue of whether the action of the body concerned fell within the scope of the power available to that body, but also, in the case of powers granted by statute or by delegated legislation, whether that power had been exercised in lawful manner, under principles enumerated by Lord Greene MR in *Associated Provincial Picture Houses Ltd v Wednesbury Corporation*.[18] The *Wednesbury* principles required that a decision or action must not be unreasonable in the sense of being 'so outrageous in its defiance of logic or accepted moral standards that no reasonable decision-maker ... could have come to it',[19] that the decision-maker must take account of all relevant considerations and erase from his mind all irrelevant considerations, and must follow any procedural requirements laid down in the legislation concerned. In addition, a power must be used only for a proper purpose, not, for, example, solely in order to give political advantage.[20]

Further, where a decision may affect a person's existing rights or he has a legitimate expectation of being granted a right, the decision-making procedure must comply with the principles of natural justice embodied in two Latin maxims: *audi alteram partem* – 'Hear the other side', meaning that the person affected by the decision must be given a proper opportunity to put his case before the decision is made; and *nemo judex in sua causa potest* – 'No man may be judge in his own cause', meaning that there must be an absence not only of actual bias but of an appearance of bias on the part of the decision-maker.

Since the 1960s, judicial review has evolved as a highly flexible instrument by which the courts can scrutinise the actions of public bodies – a broad concept which embraces bodies whose powers are public in nature as well as those which derive power from statute or the prerogative[21] – and quash a decision already taken or, in limited circumstances, prohibit a particular action in the future or require an act to be done. This is on the basis of the doctrines of the separation of powers and of parliamentary sovereignty.

However, judicial review is subject to the limitation that the courts cannot consider issues involving the merits of any action, but only the lawfulness of that action. A court reviewing an administrative action will not normally substitute its own view for that of the decision-making body, considering that to do so would amount to poaching on the preserves of the executive and so offend against the separation of powers. Instead, it will quash the original decision and so require the decision-maker to consider the matter afresh. Generally, there is nothing to prevent the decision-maker

---

18 [1948] 1 KB 223.

19 *Per* Lord Diplock in *Council of Civil Service Unions v Minister for the Civil Service* [1985] AC 374.

20 For a recent example, see *Porter v Magill, Weeks v Magill* (2001) *The Times*, 14 December, where the House of Lords held the use of a council's powers to sell council houses for the sole purpose of encouraging individuals to vote for the party in power was a gross abuse, and entitled the District Auditor to impose a surcharge under s 20 of the Local Government Finance Act 1982 on the leader and deputy leader of the council concerned, making them personally liable for the entire loss caused to the council, estimated at £26 million.

21 See *Council of Civil Service Unions v Minister for the Civil Service* [1985] AC 374; *R v Panel on Takeovers and Mergers ex p Datafin plc* [1987] QB 815.

from coming to the same decision a second time, provided that the original defects are not repeated.

There is a fundamental difference in approach between that of the UK courts in dealing with allegations of unlawful action by public bodies and that under the Convention. Where the facts disclose interference with a positive right, the executive must, under the principle in *Entick v Carrington*, demonstrate positive authority for that interference. However, when, as in *Malone*, there is no interference with any such right, the executive is presumed to have acted lawfully. The approach taken under Convention jurisprudence is diametrically opposed. In deciding whether there has been an actionable breach of the Convention, a court must first consider whether the subject matter of the applicant's claim falls within a right or freedom guaranteed by the Convention, then whether there has been a contravention of that right or freedom and, if so, whether that contravention falls within the permitted derogations. Further, in deciding whether an action falls within a permitted derogation, a court must consider the issue of proportionality; it must be satisfied not only that interference with a Convention right is 'necessary in a democratic society', but in addition that it goes no further than is strictly necessary to achieve the desired end.[22] Repeatedly, the UK courts refused to accept 'proportionality' arguments on the basis that to do so would inevitably involve them in issues of merit, though it was suggested in *R v Secretary of State for the Home Department ex p Brind* that the action of a public body might be so wanting in proportionality as to bring it within the scope of *Wednesbury* unreasonableness.[23]

As part of the development of judicial review, during the 1980s and 1990s, the domestic courts were prepared to make use of the Convention as a tool of statutory interpretation, applying a presumption that Parliament did not intend to legislate in a manner incompatible with Convention rights other than by express and unambiguous words. Therefore, when a provision was capable of two meanings, only one consistent with the Convention, the courts became prepared to presume that Parliament intended to legislate in conformity with the Convention (*In Re M and H (Minors)*).[24]

However, they were not prepared to employ this approach when the terms of the instrument at issue were unambiguous. This was demonstrated in *Brind*, involving the Home Secretary's exercise of his powers under s 29(3) of the Broadcasting Act 1981 to prohibit broadcasting by representatives of organisations proscribed under anti-terrorist legislation, notably Sinn Fein. It was alleged, *inter alia*, that this involved a violation of the right to freedom of expression contained in Art 10. The court could not give effect to Convention rights without the authority of Parliament, and Parliament had not chosen to incorporate Convention rights into domestic law. The statutory power was unambiguous; there was thus no scope for employing Art 10 as a tool of interpretation. Applying the *Wednesbury* principles, the House of Lords held that the Home Secretary had not acted unlawfully and there is a strong suggestion in Lord Bridge's speech that his action would have fallen within the permitted derogations under Art 10 in any event.[25]

---

22 Cf *Dudgeon v United Kingdom* (1982) 4 EHRR 149.
23 [1991] 1 All ER 720, *per* Lord Ackner.
24 [1988] 3 WLR 485, *per* Lord Brandon of Oakwood, p 498.
25 There was no bar on publication of the words used by representatives of terrorist organisations, simply on their being spoken by the representatives themselves.

Similarly, the courts were prepared to rule in conformity with Convention rights in areas where the common law was uncertain, unclear or incomplete, as in *Attorney General v Guardian Newspapers (No 1)*,[26] where the government sought to obtain an injunction to prevent the publication in the UK of Peter Wright's book, Spycatcher, which included a great deal of highly sensitive material about the inner workings of the British Security Services.

28.5   THE HUMAN RIGHTS ACT

The Labour government elected in 1997 had made incorporation of the Convention into the domestic law of the UK a major manifesto commitment. Their reasons for doing so were to a considerable extent cosmetic. There was no suggestion that there was any substantive failure to give effect to Convention rights. Instead, it was argued that as a result of non-incorporation, the rights set out in the Convention, originally drafted with major input from British lawyers, were no longer seen as British rights.[27] There is also a sense of a certain degree of embarrassment at the relative frequency with which applications made to the Court had been successful, and an underlying suggestion that British judges might be more robust in their approach.

In framing the legislation, the government sought to create an instrument which would give effect to the Convention without detracting from the traditional principle of parliamentary supremacy. The Act therefore provides as follows:

(1) In all cases where Convention rights are in question, the Act gives 'further effect' to the Convention, whether the litigants are private persons or public authorities, by:

(a) obliging UK courts to decide all cases before them in compatibility with Convention rights unless prevented from doing so by primary legislation which cannot be read compatibly with the Convention, or by delegated legislation made under such primary legislation;

(b) introducing a new obligation on courts to interpret existing and future legislation in compatibility with the Convention where possible;

(c) requiring courts to take ECtHR case law into account in all cases, insofar as they consider it relevant to proceedings before them.

(2) The Act does not make Convention rights directly enforceable in proceedings brought against a private litigant, nor against a quasi-public body acting in its private capacity. However, the Convention will have an indirect effect in such cases, through the court's obligation to construe the law, where possible, in compliance with the Convention.

(3) Section 7 creates directly enforceable rights against public bodies, and against quasi-public bodies when exercising their public functions, by:

(a) creating a new ground for judicial review;

(b) creating a new cause of action against public bodies which fail to act in compliance with the Convention;

(c) making Convention rights available as a defence in cases brought by public bodies against private individuals or bodies.

---

26 [1987] 1 WLR 1248.
27 *Rights Brought Home: The Human Rights Bill*, October 1997, Cm 3782, paras 1.11–1.17.

The Act will not permit the Convention to be used so as to override primary legislation. If a statute is clear in its terms and clearly incompatible with the Convention, the courts must give it effect. This is also true of delegated legislation made under incompatible primary legislation. This preserves the concept of parliamentary supremacy. However, in such circumstances, the higher courts have power to issue a 'declaration of incompatibility' and the government may make use of a special fast-track procedure to amend the legislation so as to remove the incompatibility.

It should be noted that courts are only required to interpret UK legislation into conformity with the Convention 'so far as is possible'. Further, the courts have no power to set aside UK legislation on the grounds of incompatibility with the Convention. This preserves parliamentary supremacy and would seem to be the true reason for the Act's failure to incorporate Art 13 (the requirement to provide effective remedies for breach of Convention rights). As a court cannot set aside UK legislation, and a declaration of incompatibility under s 4 does not affect the parties to the case in respect of which it is made, the Act does not go far enough to satisfy Art 13.

Section 10 has been much criticised as a 'Henry VIII clause', in that it creates a fast-track procedure by which ministers may amend Acts of Parliament by means of delegated legislation, in order to deal with instances of incompatibility with Convention rights. The section provides that the power applies if:

(1) a declaration of incompatibility has been made under s 4 and all rights of appeal have come to an end; or

(2) if it appears to a Minister of the Crown or Her Majesty in Council that, having regard to a finding of the European Court of Human Rights made in proceedings against the UK after this section came into force, a legislative provision is incompatible with a UK obligation arising from the Convention;

(3) if a Minister of the Crown considers that there are *compelling reasons* for proceeding under this section, he may by order and following the procedure set out in Sched 2 make such amendments to the legislation *as he considers necessary to remove the incompatibility*.[28]

An obvious concern is that 'compelling reason' is not defined, and the remarks of the responsible Ministers during the Committee Stage of the Bill in the Commons suggest that this phrase was introduced in order to assuage the fears of the House that these powers would be used routinely to amend primary legislation, so bypassing Parliament. However, they suggest that 'compelling' is less stringent than 'exceptional' and that the phrase 'compelling reason' is intended to be applied in a broad and flexible manner.[29] As yet, the power under s 10 has not been used, so the issue remains to be tested.

Special provisions relating to Arts 9 and 10 were inserted during the passage of the Bill through Parliament, in response to concerns expressed by the churches and the media lobby respectively.

Section 12 applies where a court is considering whether to grant any relief which, if granted, might affect the exercise of the Convention right to freedom of expression and provides that interim injunctions to restrain publication of material prior to the

---

28 My emphasis.
29 See *Hansard*, HC, 24 June 1998, col 1140 and 21 October 1998, cols 1300–58.

trial of the substantive issues between parties are not routinely to be granted *ex parte* in order to preserve the status quo between the parties, and only if the court is satisfied that the applicant is likely to establish at trial that publication should not be allowed. When application is made for such an injunction, the court is required to have particular regard to the importance of the Convention right to freedom of expression and, where the proceedings relate to material which the respondent claims (or which appears to the court) to be journalistic, literary or artistic material, to the extent to which the material has, or is about to become, available to the public, and whether it is in the public interest for the material to be published. The existence of this provision must be a matter of concern, since earlier case law, notably *Attorney General v Guardian Newspapers (No 2)*,[30] makes it clear that even in cases where there are very strong grounds for restraining publication, the courts will not exercise their powers when the information at issue is already within the public domain. In cases such as those arising from *Spycatcher*, the only realistic remedy for the applicant is a permanent injunction to prevent publication, so that refusal to grant an injunction to restrain publication prior to trial of the substantive issues means that one party is denied any prospect of effective remedy.[31]

Section 13 provides that if a court's determination of any question under the Act might affect the exercise by a religious organisation of the Convention right to freedom of thought, conscience and religion, it must have particular regard to the importance of that right. During the Bill's passage through Parliament, the churches were concerned that in their public role they could be regarded as breaching the Convention if, for example they refused on grounds of doctrine to carry out marriage ceremonies for homosexual couples. 'Religious organisation' is not defined, but, according to statements in the Commons, it is intended to be construed broadly enough to cover religious charities.

Under s 6, a 'public authority' will act unlawfully if it acts in a way which contravenes a Convention right, unless domestic legislation makes it impossible to act in accordance with the Convention. Effectively, this creates an additional ground for judicial review, with the additional element that the courts are permitted to apply the doctrine of proportionality and so to consider issues of merit as well as legality. 'Public authority' is not defined in the Act, and is capable of being construed to include any body which has some functions which are public in nature, when exercising one of those functions. According to the Lord Chancellor, Lord Irvine of Lairg, in introducing the Human Rights Bill into the House of Lords, the term was intended to include not only 'obvious' public authorities such as government departments and the police, but bodies which have a mixture of public and private functions, though he gave no examples.[32] At the Committee Stage, the Lord Chancellor gave the Press Complaints Commission as an example of a body whose functions which might well be held to be entirely public, and Railtrack as a body which had public functions in relation to rail

---

30 [1990] 1 AC 109.

31 In the *Spycatcher* litigation, it was not possible to prosecute Wright under the Official Secrets Act 1911 as he was resident in Tasmania and so outside the jurisdiction of the UK courts. Attempts to obtain injunctions in the Australian courts to prevent publication in Australia proved unsuccessful. Case law since then suggests that it might have been possible to obtain an order to require Wright to account to the British authorities for his profits from the book, but this remedy would have been of limited practical value.

32 *Hansard*, HL, 16 November 1997, col 123.

safety, in the exercise of which it would be likely to fall within the scope of s 6, and private functions as a property developer, in which it would not.[33]

The significance of the Human Rights Act has been enormously debated in both the philosophical and practical sphere. Constitutionally speaking, it contains none of the mechanisms which, in the case of the European Communities Act 1972, give rise to argument that it is incapable of repeal. The Human Rights Act, like the Act of Settlement, is an Act drafted in normal form, and in the strict legal sense is as capable of repeal or amendment as any other. The Act came into force on 1 October 2000 and, at the time of writing, it is difficult to assess its practical impact on the jurisprudence of the UK courts, and the extent to which national law will be found incompatible with Convention rights as incorporated.

Official statistics published by the Lord Chancellor's Department and available on their website show that arguments based on the Human Rights Act were raised in the following numbers of cases received between 1 January and 31 March 2001:

	Total cases	HRA issues
Court of Appeal:		
Criminal Division	1,872	161 (8.6%)
Civil Division	1,178	110 (9.34%)
High Court:		
Administrative Court	1,264	261 (21%)
Queen's Bench Division		56
Chancery Division		24
Family Division		2
Crown Court[34]		214 (<0.5%)

According to the Lord Chancellor's Department, the percentages of cases raising human rights points do not differ greatly from those pertaining before the Act's commencement date, and the number of cases based wholly on the Act is very small indeed. An analysis by the Lord Chancellor's Department of 255 cases heard in the first year of the Act's operation showed that 48 claims based on the Act were upheld, three-quarters of them (36) under s 6, 10 under s 3 and two under s 4, though in an additional 128, the claim had some impact on the court's reasoning or procedure. The remedies granted were as follows:

Declaration, injunction or order	19
Quashing of order or decision	21
Retrial	4
Administrative action	2
Declaration of incompatibility	2
Damages	1
Other	8
Total	49

---

33 *Hansard*, HL, 24 November 1998, col 784.

34 No figure are given for total cases in the Crown Court, or in the High Court outside the Administrative Court.

Early case law suggests that the courts may be prepared to go to considerable interpretative lengths in order to find national legislation to be compatible with Convention rights and so avoid making a declaration of incompatibility. It has been suggested that in *R v A*, dealing with the general prohibition in trials for rape on admission of evidence relating to a complainant's previous sexual experience,[35] the House of Lords effectively rewrote the relevant provision so as to broaden the scope of permitted questioning in a way which brought compatibility with Art 6 but went against the clearly expressed intention of Parliament in framing that section.[36]

A further issue is that of retrospectivity. A declaration of incompatibility, since quashed on appeal, was made by Keith J in *Matthews v Ministry of Defence* on 22 January 2002.[37] One element of the traditional prerogatives of the sovereign was the legal principle that 'the king can do no wrong' which, prior to the Crown Proceedings Act 1947, prevented, *inter alia*, any person from bringing an action in contract or tort against an emanation of the Crown. The 1947 Act removed this immunity, but s 10 created an exception applicable to members of the Armed Forces who were killed or injured while on duty. If the Secretary of State certified that the death or injury would be treated as attributable to military service for the purpose of entitlement to a war pension, the serviceman or his estate was precluded from bringing any action in negligence, in order that servicemen carrying out their duties were not distracted by the prospect of legal action against them. Section 10 was repealed in 1987, but acted to prevent legal action by any person injured prior to that date. Alan Matthews became aware in 1999 that he was suffering from an asbestos-related illness which was potentially attributable to his service in the Royal Navy between 1955 and 1968. On a preliminary point, and on the basis that the courts were now required to give effect to the Convention and Convention jurisprudence, it was held that s 10 breached Art 6. The effect of the decision was to make the Human Rights Act retrospective in practice, and potentially as far back as 1951, although there will be no substantive effect unless the government chooses to pursue further legislation in respect of s 10.

In the case of *R v Director of Public Prosecutions ex p Kebilene*,[38] the Court of Appeal appeared to give the Act some scope for retrospective effect, based on s 22(4) (which, unlike the bulk of the Act, came into force at the time of royal assent on 9 November 1998) and s 7(1)(b). According to their ruling, once the main provisions of the Act came into force on 1 October 2000, a person against whom proceedings were brought by a public authority and which were heard wholly or partly after the commencement date was entitled to rely on the Convention as a defence in those proceedings, whether or not the matters alleged against him occurred before or after the commencement date. On that basis, the Court of Appeal upheld the contention of the applicant in that case that the provisions of ss 16A–B of the Prevention of Terrorism (Temporary Provisions) Act 1989 were incompatible with the presumption of innocence guaranteed by Art 6(2). The area of retrospective effect introduced by *Kebilene* is potentially very wide, as it is applicable to all criminal cases brought between 9 November 1998 and 30 September 2000, unless all proceedings have been exhausted by the latter date.

35 Section 41 of the Youth, Justice and Criminal Evidence Act 1999.
36 M Beloff (2001) *The Times*, 2 October.
37 See (2002) *The Times*, 23 January.
38 (1999) *The Times*, 3 March.

FURTHER READING

Constitutional history is but one aspect of broader British history, and the absence of accessible specialist texts is both a cause of difficulty and an opportunity when recommending further reading. A great many works have already been noted in the text, but I take the opportunity here to make more general suggestions, some on matters tangential to the main theme of this book.

My first 'adult' historical reading, at the age of nine, was two volumes by Sir Arthur Bryant, both (I have since become aware) hopelessly over-romantic, but enough to stimulate still further my precocious appetite for all things historical. In recent years, teachers and others seeking to make history more 'relevant' and 'accessible' to the present-day student have too often succeeded in depriving the subject of all its excitement and interest. I have therefore concentrated here on books which manage to convey that excitement whilst giving a more accurate representation of history *wie es wirklich war* (as it really was) than Bryant managed.

Students seeking an overview of British history are well served by Norman Davies and Simon Schama with *The Isles: A History* (1999, OUP) and *A History of Britain* (2000, Hyperion) respectively. The former has also produced a fascinating if individualistic *Europe: A History* (1996, OUP), which is highly recommended. Books on specific periods and individuals are available in abundance, but of very variable quality. I confine myself here to those I have found particularly valuable, a choice which, being a personal one, is bound to be idiosyncratic. For the pre-Conquest era, the best single book is perhaps PH Sawyer, *From Roman Britain to Norman England* (2nd edn, 1998, Routledge). Those interested in art and literature as well as 'straight' history will find much to enjoy in P Hunter Blair, *The World of Bede* (2nd edn, 1990, CUP), and readers interested in continental Europe and the Near East will appreciate Peter Brown's *The World of Late Antiquity: From Marcus Aurelius to Muhammed* (1971, Thames & Hudson). Frank Barlow's *The Feudal Kingdom of England 1042–1216* (5th edn, 1999, Longman) is excellent on the Norman Conquest and the 150 years after.

Readers interested in particular rulers need look no further than what is now the Yale English Monarchs Series. All the published volumes in the series are of high quality and it would almost be churlish to single any out, but I have particularly enjoyed Frank Barlow's *Edward the Confessor* and *William Rufus*, CW Hollister's *Henry I*, WL Warren's *King John* and Michael Prestwich's *Edward I*. The short-lived Edward VI has a splendid memorial in the volume by Jennifer Loach, edited by two of her colleagues after her untimely death from cancer. Biographies of non-royal persons not only provide information on their subjects, but also act as a microcosm of the age in which the subject lived. There are a number of writers who are not professional academics but who have produced a succession of lucid and scholarly biographies and other works, not least Christopher Hibbert (*The Marlboroughs, John and Sarah Churchill 1650–1744*, 2001, Viking; *Nelson: A Personal History*, 1994, Viking, and numerous others); Elizabeth Longford (*Byron*, 1976, Weidenfeld & Nicolson; and *Wellington*, 2 vols, 1969, Weidenfeld & Nicolson); and Philip Ziegler (*King Edward VIII: The Official Biography*, 1990, HarperCollins; and *Melbourne: A Life of William Lamb, 2nd Viscount Melbourne*, 1978, Fontana).

War looms large in this volume, and for the 14th and 15th centuries, Jonathan Sumption is at work on a study of the Hundred Years War of which two volumes were published in 1999 (*Trial by Battle* and *Trial by Fire*, both published by Faber & Faber). Barbara W Tuchman's *A Distant Mirror: The Calamitous 14th Century* (1979, Penguin) is a magnificent portrait of an age, viewed through the microcosm of the life of

Enguerrand de Coucy (1340–97), a leading French nobleman who was also son-in-law to Edward III. AJ Pollard's *Late Medieval England 1399–1509* (2000, Longman) is a useful overview. The plague which hit western Europe in the late 1340s is the subject of Philip Ziegler's *The Black Death* (1998, Penguin).

The 'giant' figures of the 16th century have all been written about extensively by historians. John Guy's *Tudor England* (1990, OUP) is a good general text on the Tudors. SB Chrimes's volume on Henry VII in the Yale English Monarchs Series is also well worth seeking out. Antonia Fraser's *Mary Queen of Scots* (1969, Weidenfeld & Nicolson) has stood the test of time as a thoroughly researched and readable book, though by no means all will agree with her assessment of Mary's character and capabilities. David Starkey's *Elizabeth: Apprenticeship* (2000, Chatto & Windus) is the first of two volumes.

The upheavals of the 17th century are the subject of a plethora of volumes. Readers seeking primarily a narrative of events are recommended to read Maurice Ashley, *England in the Seventeenth Century* (1961, Penguin), *The English Civil War* (1974, Thames & Hudson) and *The Glorious Revolution of 1688* (1966, Hodder & Stoughton). Antonia Fraser has contributed biographies of Oliver Cromwell (*Cromwell, Our Chief of Men*, 1973, Weidenfeld & Nicolson) and Charles II (*King Charles II*, 1979, Weidenfeld & Nicolson).

For the 18th and early 19th centuries, I must warmly recommend *Redcoat: The British Soldier in the Age of Horse and Musket* by Richard Holmes (2002, HarperCollins). This covers the British Army from Monmouth's rising to the Crimean War, but is a portrait of British society in that time as much as military history. Again, there are many books dealing with aspects of the period. Readers interested in the American Revolution may turn to Barbara W Tuchman, *The First Salute* (1989, Michael Joseph) and Christopher Hibbert, *Redcoats and Rebels: The War for America 1770–1781* (1990, Grafton), the first by an American, the second by an Englishman.

The 19th and 20th centuries have again spawned a vast number of volumes, many of them highly specialist. Two useful 'leads-in' to the politics of the time are the biographies by Andrew Roberts (*Salisbury, Victorian Titan*, 1999, Weidenfeld & Nicolson; and *The Holy Fox; A Biography of Lord Halifax*, 1991, Weidenfeld & Nicolson). Much of interest on the political crises of the period can be found in Vernon Bogdanor's *The Monarchy and the Constitution* (1995, Clarendon) and Ian Loveland's *Constitutional Law: A Critical Introduction*, 1996, Butterworths). Martin Pugh has written *The Making of Modern British Politics 1867–1945* (3rd edn, 2002, Blackwell), *The March of the Women; A Revisionist Analysis of the Campaign for Women's Suffrage, 1866–1914* (2000, OUP) and *The Pankhursts* (2001, Allan Lane). For those interested in European politics on the eve of the Second World War, I can do no better than to recommend John Gunther's *Inside Europe* (Hamish Hamilton), originally published in 1936, though now difficult to find (my copy was originally a school prize given to an uncle in 1940).

On the central issues of the present day, the question of the re-structuring of the House of Lords remains in the air, and the best sources of information must be the quality newspapers. A useful introduction to the European Union can be found in Karen Davies, *Understanding European Union Law* (2000, Cavendish Publishing); S Douglas-Scott's *Constitutional Law of the European Union* (2002, Longman) is rather more specific. On the subject of human rights in general, there is Richard Stone, *Civil Liberties and Human Rights* (4th edn, 2002, OUP).

INDEX